CORPORATE INFORMATION SYSTEMS MANAGEMENT
Text and Cases

CORPORATE INFORMATION SYSTEMS MANAGEMENT
Text and Cases

F i f t h   E d i t i o n

Lynda M. Applegate

F. Warren McFarlan

James L. McKenney

All of the Graduate School of Business Administration
Harvard University

Boston   Burr Ridge, IL   Dubuque, IA   Madison, WI   New York   San Francisco   St. Louis
Bangkok   Bogotá   Caracas   Lisbon   London   Madrid
Mexico City   Milan   New Delhi   Seoul   Singapore   Sydney   Taipei   Toronto

Irwin/McGraw-Hill

*A Division of The **McGraw-Hill** Companies*

This book is printed on acid-free paper.

1 2 3 4 5 6 7 8 9 0 DOC/DOC 9 4 3 2 1 0 9

ISBN 0-07-290283-3

Vice president/Editor-in-chief: *Michael W. Junior*
Senior sponsoring editor: *Rick Williamson*
Developmental editor: *Christine Wright*
Marketing manager: *Jodi McPherson*
Project manager: *Karen J. Nelson*
Production supervisor: *Michael R. McCormick*
Freelance design coordinator: *JoAnne Schopler*
Supplement coordinator: *Rose M. Range*
Compositor: *GAC Indianapolis*
Typeface: *10/12 Century Schoolbook*
Printer: *R. R. Donnelley & Sons Company*

Library of Congress Cataloging-in-Publication Data

Applegate, Lynda M.
    Corporate information systems management : text and cases / Lynda
M. Applegate, F. Warren McFarlan, James L. McKenney. — 5th ed.
        p.   cm.
    Includes bibliographical references and index.
    ISBN 0-07-290283-3
    1. Information technology—Management. 2. Management information
systems. 3. Information resources management. 4. Information
technology—Management—Case studies. I. McFarlan, F. Warren
(Franklin Warren) II. McKenney, James L. III. Title.
HD30.2.A65 1999
658.4'038'011—dc21   98-54098

http://www.mhhe.com

To Karen, Mary, Paul, and Christopher

Preface

Corporate Information Systems Management, Text and Cases, Fifth Edition, is written for students and managers who desire an overview of contemporary information technology (IT)—computing, communications, business solutions, and services—management. It explains the relevant issues of effective management of information services activities and highlights the areas of greatest potential application of the technology. No assumptions are made concerning the reader's experience with IT, but it is assumed that the reader has had some course work or work experience in business management.

Our purpose is to provide perspective on the management implications of the information explosion—as evidenced by the doubling of the number of volumes in the Library of Congress between 1933 and 1966, another doubling between 1967 and 1979, and yet another doubling by 1987. Huge leaps in the growth of scientific knowledge have stimulated a dramatic increase in the number of new products based on new information technologies that range from the sophisticated supercomputer to the humble, ubiquitous facsimile machine to the exploding presence of the Internet. These products have influenced the very heart of a corporation's strategy and operations, and they will continue to do so. In many cases, the firm's competitiveness and its very survival are at stake. The radical changes in IT are coupled with the increasingly global nature of business; this puts an enormous burden on individual managers to keep abreast of events and to make intelligent decisions and plans. The broad objective of this book is to help managers harness the power of new technologies to enable them to make better decisions and more effectively manage their firms, thereby enabling them to compete more effectively.

Since the first edition of this book appeared in 1983, IT and its applications have continued to evolve dramatically. This fifth edition addresses this evolution by emphasizing issues related to the development of an IT-enabled strategy and organization design that permit a firm to simultaneously achieve the scale, scope, and efficiency that come from being large and the flexibility, speed, and responsiveness of being small. We highlight the special challenges related to electronic commerce within and between organizations and pay particular attention to the key enabling technologies (e.g., client-server architecture, the Internet) required to implement the information infrastructure required for the 21st century. Finally, we focus on a variety of options for managing the information resource—from "insourcing" to "outsourcing." This book will help present and future managers identify, implement, and deliver effective information services.

Corporate Information Systems Management, Fifth Edition, is organized around a management audit of the information services activity. This management audit details the questions that should be asked in identifying whether a firm is appropriately using and managing its IT assets. The book's text, examples, tables, and figures convey and illustrate key conceptual frameworks. Chapter 1 presents an overview of key questions to ask in assessing the effectiveness of an IT activity. Chapter 2 presents frameworks we have found useful for analyzing and structuring problems in the field. Subsequent chapters show how IT can best be applied and how the IT activity can best be organized, planned, and managed.

The material in this book is the outgrowth of directed field-based research we have conducted at the Harvard Business School since the early 1970s. We thank Deans John McArthur and Kim Clark for making the time and resources available for this work.

We are particularly indebted to the many firms and government organizations that provided us with so much time and insight during the course of our research. All of the examples and concepts in this book are based on observation of actual practice. Without the cooperation of these organizations, it would have been impossible to prepare this Fifth Edition.

We are especially grateful for the many valuable suggestions and insights provided us by our Harvard Business School colleagues Bill Bruns, Jim Cash, Richard Nolan, Donna Stoddard, John Sviokla, and Shoshana Zuboff as well as Professors Eric Clemons of the Wharton School, Janis Gogan of Babson College, and Keri Pearlson and Sirkka Jarvenpaa of the University of Texas/Austin. In addition, we acknowledge the valuable work of our doctoral students and research assistants Karen Barone, Melinda Conrad, Carin Knoop, Kirk Goldman, and Katherine Seger-Weber. Lynn Salerno and Bernard Avishai, in their editorial capacity at the *Harvard Business Review,* and editors Barbara Feinberg and Paul McDonald provided valuable assistance. We would also like to express our appreciation to Heather Darcy and Maureen Donovan, who typed and edited numerous versions of the work.

Lynda M. Applegate
F. Warren McFarlan
James L. McKenney

Contents

Module
1

The Challenges of Managing in an Information Age

We are at the dawn of an age of networked intelligence—an age that is giving birth to a new economy, a new politics, and a new society. Businesses will be transformed, governments will be renewed, and individuals will be able to reinvent themselves—all with the help of information technology.

Tapscott, 1996[1]

The 1990s have been a time of dramatic change. The decade dawned as a time of retrenchment as large, established firms struggled to shed the rigid structures and static processes that remained as a legacy of the industrial era. As the decade draws to a close, we find ourselves in a time of unparalleled business innovation led by bold entrepreneurs with a vision of a global networked economy.

Module 1 provides an overview of the challenges that managers face as they chart these new waters. Chapter 1, "The Information Technology Challenge," identifies, from a managerial viewpoint, the key forces shaping the information technology (IT) environment and senior management's most frequent questions in assessing their firm's IT activities. Chapter 2, "Manageable Trends," discusses the key trends that are defining the potential of IT to enable new business opportunities. Two cases—"Verifone (1997)" and "A Tale of Two Airlines in the Information Age"—are included that highlight both the power and the peril of managing in an information age.

---

[1]Don Tapscott, *Digital Economy: Promise and Peril in the Age of Networked Intelligence* (NY: McGraw-Hill, 1996).

Chapter

1

The Information Technology Challenge

The rapid evolution and spread of information systems technology (IT)[1] during the last 40 years is challenging both business and IT management to rethink the very nature of the business. New industry players are emerging (e.g., cable operators, systems integrators). New internal organizational structures are being defined, and responsibilities are being reallocated among players in many industry value chains. Major investments in computer hardware and software are often required to capture the benefits of powerful new technologies. Systems are being developed that profoundly affect how firms operate and compete; not only large corporations, but also mid-size and very small firms (that is, under $1 million in sales) are feeling the impact. New company formation is exploding to take advantage of new application opportunities. IT's influence in large corporations is pervasive, affecting the smallest departments and managerial decision-making processes to an extent not even visualized 10 years ago.

Because many senior managers received their educations and early work experiences before the wide-scale introduction of computer technology, or in environments where the capabilities of IT were very different from those of today, they often fail to understand technology and its potential applications. They lack sufficient grasp of the issues to provide appropriate managerial direction. In addition, many IT managers, given their early experiences with technologies so different from those of the 1990s, are also finding themselves unprepared to deal with current issues. (For example,

---

[1]In this book, IT refers to the technologies of computers and telecommunications (including data, voice, graphics, and full motion video).

understanding the programming challenges of mainframe-based COBOL—
a systems development language that is still in common use within many
organizations in the 1990s and lies at the root of the Year 2000 problem—
does not prepare a person to deal with the challenge of implementing
systems based on client-server architectures, object-oriented programming
languages, the Intranet, and other key technologies for the 21st century.)

Over the past two decades, virtually all of the frameworks that guide
IT management practice have been challenged. IT managers must continually struggle to address day-to-day operating problems, while assimilating
new technologies and managerial approaches. IT managers who are not
committed to continuing personal development quickly become obsolete;
those who cannot similarly develop their employees find their businesses
obsolete.

This book is aimed at two different audiences. The first is the general
manager who is responsible for providing direction for all business activities. For this group we offer frameworks for evaluating and guiding IT activity in the firm. The book defines policies that must be executed and provides
insights into the specific challenges of execution. Methods for integrating IT
management with the overall activities of the firm are suggested.

For its second audience, senior IT management, this book provides an
integrated view of IT management issues for the early 21st century. Key
frameworks for organizing and understanding a bewildering cluster of operational details are identified. The focus for IT senior managers is to move
from analysis of the "bark composition of individual trees" to an overall perspective of the IT "forest" and its management challenge. The book thus
integrates the needs of two quite different—though operationally interdependent—audiences and provides a common perspective and language for
communication.

It would be a serious mistake to think of the problems of IT management
as totally different from those found in other business areas. The issues of
IT organization, for example, can be approached using general organization
design theory.[2] Issues of IT strategy formulation are heavily influenced by
theories of industry analysis[3] and business planning.[4] Notions of budgeting,
performance measurement, transfer pricing, profit center management, and
so forth, from the general field of management control are also relevant

---

[2]For example, see P. Lawrence and J. Lorsch, *Organizations* (Boston, MA: Harvard Business
School Press, 1986).

[3]For example, see M. Porter, *Competitive Advantage* (NY: Free Press, 1985) and A. Chandler,
Scale and Scope: The Dynamics of Industrial Capitalism (Cambridge, MA: The Belknap Press
of Harvard University Press, 1990).

[4]For example, see J. Bower, *Managing the Resource Allocation Process: A Study of Corporate
Planning and Investment* (Boston, MA: Division of Research, Harvard Business School Classics,
1986), and J. B. Quinn, H. Mintzberg, and R. James, *The Strategy Process* (Englewood Cliffs,
NJ: Prentice Hall, 1988).

here.[5] In addition, the fields of operations and technology management have aided our understanding of the management of IT operations (e.g., networks and data centers).[6] Insights from all of these disciplines are relevant for our understanding of IT management issues.

IT MANAGEMENT CONCEPTS

Integrating the IT "business" into the rest of the firm poses many organizational design and strategy formulation challenges. The following four concepts are essential for an understanding of the successful management of IT.

Strategic Relevance

The strategic impact of the IT activity varies among industries and firms and, over time, within an individual firm. Like the telephone, IT can be used in all firms to enhance operations; but, in a growing number of firms in the 1990s, it is also a core differentiator and strategy enabler. In some cases, such as encyclopedias, the entire product and way of accessing it may be totally transformed with little or no market remaining for the previous product or distribution formulation. Further, IT may be more significant to some operating units and functions within a firm than to others. This notion of a variation in strategic relevance is critical for understanding the diversity of potential IT management and operational approaches.

Corporate Culture

The corporate culture—embodied by the organization's shared values and operationalized in its processes (e.g., the approach to corporate planning, philosophy of control, and speed of core product/technological change)—influences how the IT business should be managed. In addition, there are also generic tools that define the "state-of-the-art"; client-server IT architectures, browsers, and graphical user interfaces are examples of generic IT tools for the mid-1990s. Combining these generic tools with the values, culture, and processes of a particular firm is the art of management. A combination that works in one corporate environment can fail abysmally in another.

---

[5]For example, see R. Anthony, *The Management Control Function* (Boston, MA: Harvard Business School Press, 1988) and K. Arrow, "Control in Large Organizations," in *Behavioral Aspects of Accounting,* edited by M. Schiff and A. Lewin (Englewood Cliffs, NJ: Prentice Hall, 1974).

[6]For example, see K. Clark and T. Fujimoto, *Product Development Performance* (Boston, MA: Harvard Business School Press, 1991) and J. Heskett, *Managing in the Service Economy* (Boston, MA: Harvard Business School Press, 1986).

Contingency

IT management is also influenced by the notion of contingency. Because IT-enabled management systems were often introduced during the 1960s and early 1970s to simplify information-intensive transaction processing, structured and mechanistic approaches resulted in great improvement in the likelihood of system success. But as these new approaches and tools were assimilated into the firm, the initial surge of value from their introduction often gave way to frustration because of a perceived strait jacket effort. In many cases, because of their inherent rigidity, these approaches answered some types of challenges very well and others not at all. For example, the emergence of personal computers (PCs) in the 1980s enabled relatively free-form end-user approaches to information processing, which, in turn, posed challenges to prior mainframe-based systems and applications. More complex and flexible IT management approaches and tools were required to fit with the needs of a complex, changing business environment. As we face the challenge of managing the complex organizational designs of the 1990s, which are enabled by complex, distributed IT architectures, the notion of contingency will become even more important. Similarly, Internet, Intranet, and Extranet technologies have a remarkably different impact on the performance of different organizations (very important for some firms and not important at all for others).

Technology Transfer

The dramatic rate of IT evolution demands careful management attention. Failure to successfully manage the introduction and assimilation of emerging technologies results in a costly and ineffective collection of disjointed "islands of technology." Since changes in the IT infrastructure often directly affect organizational performance, implementation problems can also be catastrophic. Success can only come if people are able to change the way they act and the way they think. As a result, IT must be considered a tool to expand the "intelligence" of the people within the organization. Without a concomitant change at the individual level, technical success is likely to be accompanied by administrative failure.

CHALLENGES IN MANAGING IT

An understanding of the following factors that make the assimilation of IT a particularly challenging task is essential if a sensible IT management strategy is to be developed.

A Young Technology

At least in its modern form (with high-speed and high-performance computers and networks), IT has had a very short life.[7] As a result, the theory of IT management is still in its infancy; in contrast, management disciplines such as accounting, finance, and production have had thriving bodies of theory and practice in place since the turn of the century. Throughout the 1900s, significant changes in knowledge and theory have occurred in these established disciplines and have been assimilated into an organized field of thought. Evolution, not revolution, has been the challenge in these fields.

The challenge in IT, conversely, has been that of harnessing an exploding body of knowledge within a very short time frame. Not surprisingly, the half-life of administrative knowledge in this environment has been quite short. While building on past knowledge, most of the theories and frameworks discussed in this book have been developed within the past two decades. Indeed, this Fifth Edition differs markedly from its predecessor, which was published only three years earlier (before the widespread explosion of the Internet). We expect that this knowledge explosion will continue (and anticipate the need to significantly revise this book within the next few years).

Technological Growth

Another source of administrative challenge is the fact that the field has undergone sustained and dramatic growth in the cost performance of its technologies. Over a billion-fold improvement in processing and storage capacity has occurred since 1953, and the rate of change is expected to continue through the early 21st century. (As with all technologies, a point of maturity will be reached, but we are not yet there.) Further complicating this, some core technologies—such as central processing unit (CPU) size and speed—have grown explosively, while others, such as software development tools, have grown more slowly. Others, such as the emerging availability of cheap, high-capacity bandwidth, deeply constrain the viability of emerging end-consumer products.

The technology explosion has enabled the development of new value-added applications, as well as improvements in old ones. One painful aspect of this has been that yesterday's strategic coup may be today's high-overhead, inefficient liability—outperformed by those "fast followers" that improved on the original design and took advantage of the latest technologies. The natural tendency to resist change has been exacerbated by the prevailing accounting practice of writing off software expense as it is incurred,

---

[7]The computer was introduced in most large firms during the late 1950s and 1960s.

rather than capitalizing it and amortizing it over a period of years. These practices conceal two facts: (1) that the organization has an information asset and (2) that it is aging and often very inefficient.

IT End-User Coordination

The complexities of developing systems have created IT departments filled with specialists. These specialist departments with specialized vocabularies inherently have had a difficult time developing and maintaining close relationships with the users of their services; this has been a significant problem for IT and business management for many years. While the proliferation of new technologies has changed the nature of the dialogue, the technocrat-versus-generalist problem remains.

Specialization is required to develop expertise and competence within a given discipline, but, in the process, specialists often develop their own language systems. To communicate with each other, they use words such as *bits, bytes, DOS, CICS, HTML,* and so on, none of which have any meaning to general managers. At the same time, general managers have a quite different language that includes such terms as *liquidity, margin,* and *asset valuation*—terms that may not have meaning to IT specialists. While it is clear that the continued penetration of IT to all parts of the organization has helped communication between IT specialists and end users, substantial problems remain. New approaches to integrating IT and business are still required to address this long-standing problem.

For numerous reasons, education only partially addresses this technical versus generalist gap. For many college and high school students, a course on IT literacy involves developing a homepage, engaging in widespread browsing on the Internet, and learning to use PC-based word-processing and spreadsheet packages. While these experiences may help to demystify the technology and expand confidence, they do not help develop the skills necessary to actively participate in managing the information resource of a firm (which must run reliably in a bulletproof fashion year after year). Similarly, experience within the business environment in preparing spreadsheet programs as a staff analyst or working with a word-processing package does not provide the necessary perspective on the issues involved in defining and managing large-scale database management systems and global telecommunications that are vital to the firm's success. More importantly, these educational and work experiences can provide a false sense of confidence—a little knowledge can be very dangerous.

In the past, some general managers were better able to deal with IT issues than others. One of our colleagues describes the world as being divided equally into two classes of people—"poets" and "engineers." This split, of course, is also evident in the ranks of general management. Recently, however, graphical user interfaces (for example, the interface found on the Apple Macintosh and on computers running Microsoft Windows) and massive interconnectivity via the Internet have made technology easily accessible to virtually everyone. Both the poets and the engineers can now gain firsthand experience with using IT. (Again, this is different from building IT.)

Specialization

The increased complexity of contemporary technology has created a number of IT subspecialties in increasingly narrow areas of expertise. This explosion of new knowledge and skills poses a new managerial challenge. As IT evolved, the number of experts required to manage the wide range of application development languages, data management approaches, telecommunications methodologies, and operating environments proliferated, which in turn increased the complexity of coordination and control. Today most organizations have given up attempting to build and maintain all of this specialized expertise inside the firm and are turning to the outside. For many this involves outsourcing portions, or in some cases, all of the IT activities. This, of course, challenges the firm to shift from internal to external approaches to coordination and control. For example, hardly anyone, in urban areas, finds it cost-effective to do in-house PC maintenance in their firm.

Shift in Focus

A fifth challenge is the significant shift in the types of applications being developed. Early applications that automated clerical and operational control functions (e.g., inventory management, airline seat reservations, and credit extension) were heavily focused on highly structured problems, such as transaction processing for payroll and order processing. In these instances, the efficiency benefits of the automation could be precisely specified. (Note: In some cases [for example, the airline reservation systems of the late 1970s and early 1980s], automation also led to improved decision making and radical change in the basis of competition within the industry that could not be fully specified in advance.)

Increasingly, today's uses of IT are targeted toward less structured types of problems (for example, decision support and some nontransactional aspects of electronic commerce). As a result, structured, objective analysis of the advantages is extraordinarily difficult. Often, investment and decisions are based on management judgment that, while exceedingly important, is difficult to quantify in a meaningful way. Although these applications offer the potential to dramatically transform organizations and industries, the lack of clear specification makes precise justification very difficult. The need to simultaneously manage organizational and technological change within this environment of uncertainty has resulted in failure rates that still exceed 50 percent.

The design and implementation of applications that transform work, processes, organizations, and industries require a very different approach than would be used to design and implement systems that automate existing business systems and structures. The detailed systems study, with its documentation and controls prior to programming, is often too rigid and fails to build the end-user commitment necessary for success. Interactive "joint application design" and "rapid prototyping" are proving to be the best approach when the goal is to transform organizational processes. These approaches also appear to be required when building systems to support end-user decision making and intelligence. These new applications and application development methodologies are also forcing a shift in the way projects are evaluated. This is not an argument for a more permissive approach to system design and evaluation, but rather a cry to be more involved and creative while maintaining discipline.

In combination, these factors create a very complex and challenging managerial environment. They form the backdrop for the discussions of specific managerial approaches in the succeeding chapters.

QUESTIONS FROM SENIOR MANAGEMENT

In viewing the health of an organization's IT activity, our research has indicated that senior managers often ask questions in six critical areas. Four of these areas are essentially diagnostic in nature, whereas the remaining two are clearly action oriented.

1. Is the firm being affected competitively either by failing to implement required IT applications or by faulty implementation of strategic applications? Is the firm missing opportunities that, if properly executed, would give it a competitive edge or, more pessimistically, enable it to survive? How important is IT to success in the industry? Failure to do well in a competitively important area is a significant problem; failure to perform well in a nonstrategic area is often less critical to the overall health of the firm.

2. Is the firm targeting its IT application development efforts effectively? Is it spending the right amount of money, and is it focusing on the appropriate applications? At times, management asks this question for the wrong reasons. We are sure that many are familiar with the following scenario. An industry survey that compares IT expenditures for a firm's leading competitors is circulated among the senior management team. Immediately, attention is focused on those dimensions in which the firm is distinctly different from its competitors—most often attention is

focused on those areas where the firm is spending a significant amount more than the competitors. This causes great excitement. After much investigation, it is often discovered that either the company uses a different accounting system for IT than its competitors and therefore the numbers are not directly comparable (e.g., they have excluded telecommunications expenses from their figures while the firm has included them), or the company has a different strategy, geographical location, and/or mix of management strengths and weaknesses than its competitors, and, therefore, what competitors are or are not doing with IT is not directly comparable.

Raising the question of effectiveness is appropriate, but attempting to answer it solely with industry surveys of competitors' expenditures is not. The IT management challenge is much too complex. Similarly, the rules of thumb on expenditure levels have become much less useful as the range of technologies and opportunities has increased. For example, a major catalog company that worked tirelessly to translate its catalog onto CD/ROM less than three years ago now has the catalog fully available electronically via the Internet and believes that within the decade up to a third of its products will be sold that way.

3. Is the IT asset of a firm being managed efficiently? Sometimes a firm is spending appropriately, but is not getting the appropriate productivity out of its hardware and staff resources. This is a particularly relevant issue in the late 1990s, given the extreme shortages in qualified IT professionals and intensified international competition. On the one hand, the global telecommunications highway allows the firm to access competent development staff around the world (for example, in India and the Philippines) at a fraction of European and U.S. costs. On the other hand, unless standards are rigorously enforced, the new distributed IT architectures can lead to an explosion of support costs.

4. Is the firm's IT activity sufficiently insulated against the risks of a major operational disaster? The appropriate level of protection varies by organization, relative to the level of strategic and operational dependence on IT. In most instances, business managers underestimate the degree to which their firms are dependent on IT. Even small interruptions in service can cause massive customer defections or significant—and costly— operational disruption. For example, a 2-minute interruption of the air traffic control system over La Guardia airport resulted in a 40-minute delay to landing aircraft. An 8-hour downtime for Amazon.com caused such problems that its stock price dropped.

5. Are IT and business leaders capable of dealing with the IT-related management challenges? Historically, senior business leaders have been quick to replace the IT senior management team for performance problems. While often the quickest and most apparent solution to the problem, the high turnover can exacerbate the underlying cause of the problems. Failure to identify and address the underlying problems can

spell disaster for the new team that is brought in to "clean up the mess;" the effort ultimately fails, with the cycle of poor performance continuing. This same cycle of failure can also be seen in outsourcing arrangements; business management often erroneously believes that it can solve IT performance problems by "throwing the problem over the wall" to be fixed by an IT vendor. Without commitment to actively participate in problem definition and solution, the outsourcing relationship may also be doomed to failure. Clearly, the skills and expertise required to manage the information resources of a firm have sharply changed over time with the evolution of the technology and its potential uses within the firm; the leadership skills and perspectives appropriate today may not have worked in the past and may not work in the future. In many situations, the problem is also compounded by a lack of suitable explicit performance-measurement standards (metrics) and objective data for assessing performance. As will be discussed in subsequent chapters, we believe the development and installation of these metrics are absolutely vital.

6. Are the IT resources appropriately placed in the firm? Organizational issues such as where the IT resource should report, how development and hardware resources should be distributed within the company, what activities, if any, should be outsourced, and the existence and potential role of an executive steering committee are examples of topics of intense interest to senior management.

These questions are intuitive from the viewpoint of general management and flow naturally from its perspective and experience in dealing with other areas of the firm. We have not found them as stated to be easily researchable or answerable in specific situations and have consequently neither selected them as the basic framework of the book nor attempted to describe specifically how each can be answered. Rather, we have selected a complementary set of questions that not only form the outline of the book but whose answers will give solutions to the earlier questions.

CONCLUSION

This chapter has identified, from a managerial viewpoint, the key forces shaping the IT environment and senior management's most frequent questions in assessing the activity. In this final section, we would like to leave you with some questions we believe both IT management and general management should ask on a periodic basis—every six months or so. They are a distillation of the previous analysis and, we believe, a useful managerial shorthand.

1. Do the perspective and skills of the IT team, IT users, and general management team fit the firm's changing strategy and organization and the

IT applications, operating environment, and management processes? There are no absolute final solutions—only transitional ones.

2. Is the firm organized to identify, evaluate, and assimilate new information technologies on a timely basis? In this fast-moving field, an internally focused, low-quality staff can generate severe problems. Unprofitable, unwitting obsolescence (from which it is hard to recover) is terribly easy here. There is no need for a firm to adopt leading-edge technology (indeed, many are ill equipped to do so), but it is inexcusable not to be aware of its possibilities.

3. Are the strategic planning, the management control, and the project management systems—the three main management systems for integrating the IT environment with the firm—defined and appropriately implemented and managed?

4. Are the security, priority-setting, and control systems for IT operations appropriate for the role IT plays in the firm?

5. Are appropriate organizational structures and coordinating mechanisms in place to ensure IT is appropriately aligned to the needs of the firm?

To help answer these questions, this book presents a framework for analysis that encompasses four organizing concepts: *strategic relevance, corporate culture, contingent action planning,* and *managed IT technology transfer.* In each of the areas of IT—organization, strategic planning, management control, project management, and operations—we will examine the implications of these concepts. We realize that today's world is diverse—people with varied ideas, goals, skills, and backgrounds work within organizations with different strategies, organization designs, processes, and cultures; and they are supported by an ever-expanding set of increasingly powerful technologies. We have attempted to identify a sequence of frameworks that allows better analysis of the problems and issues facing organizations in relation to IT. In order to formulate realistic action plans, readers must apply this discussion to their own business situations.

Chapter

2

Manageable Trends

The preceding chapter identified key issues that make the assimilation of information technology (IT) challenging and discussed the implications of these issues for management practice. This book is designed to provide a comprehensive treatment of these key issues[1] by focusing on six themes that reflect current insight into management practice and guidance for administrative action. This chapter discusses the nature and implications of each theme. Because they represent what we believe to be the most useful ways to think about the forces driving how IT is being used and managed within firms as we enter the 21st century, these themes also provide the organizational basis for the chapters that follow. Our expectation, as mentioned in Chapter 1, is that additional experience and research with existing technologies and the emergence of new technologies will inevitably produce new—as yet unimagined—uses of IT in subsequent years.

Six manageable trends will be discussed in this chapter:

1. *IT influences different industries, and the firms within them, in different ways.* The type of impact strongly influences which IT management tools and approaches are appropriate for a firm.
2. *Telecommunications, computing, and software technologies are evolving rapidly and will continue to evolve.* This evolution will continue to destabilize the economic viability of existing IT-based systems and offer new types of IT application opportunities.
3. *The time required for successful organizational learning about IT limits the practical speed of change.* As the organization gains familiarity with

---

[1]An analysis of these areas for a firm, complete with appropriate recommendations, is referred to as an IT management audit.

a new technology, management's approach to assimilating that new technology must change.

4. *External industry, internal organizational, and technological changes are pressuring firms to "buy" rather than "make" IT software and services.* This shift in the nature of the IT make-or-buy decision creates major IT management challenges.

5. *While all elements of the IT system life cycle remain, new technologies both enable and require dramatically different approaches to execution.* This significantly increases the complexity of the IT management challenge.

6. *Managing the long-term evolution of the partnership between general management, IT management, and user management is crucial for capturing the value of new IT-enabled business opportunities.*

THEME 1: STRATEGIC IMPACT

It is increasingly clear that different industries are affected in fundamentally different ways by IT. In many industries, IT has enabled massive transformation of the strategy of the firm and the "value chain" of activities through which it is executed, and the roles of different players; in fact, some players may be left without a role. Technology is now a core component of many of the products that we use every day. For example, today's car now includes more computing capacity than was available in the country in 1960, and over 800 programmers at a major defense contractor are required to develop software for the control panels of airplanes and submarines. IT has also revolutionized our notion of service. Supported by IT, retailers like L.L. Bean now distribute catalogs of their products—previously available only in standard paper format, now in interactive, multimedia CD-ROM and over the Internet—directly to customers who can order products by telephone (or the Internet) and pay for them using secure financial credit networks. A whole new category of Internet service and information providers have emerged to fill these sorts of needs. Within the firm, computer-aided design and manufacturing (CAD/CAM); factory automation and control systems; and IT-enabled purchasing, distribution, sales, and marketing systems have enabled firms to simultaneously compete on quality, speed, and cost. The ability to create new IT-based products and services and to streamline, integrate, and time-synchronize internal operating and management processes is transforming industries and the firms within them. As industry leaders "raise the bar," many firms are finding that IT innovation has become a strategic necessity.

Table 2–1 presents a series of questions for managers as they contemplate IT marketing (customer focus) opportunities. If the answer to most of the questions is no, IT probably will play a rather limited role in transforming marketing. Conversely, if the answer is yes, technology has played or will

---

TABLE 2–1   Marketing (Customer Focus) Questions for Managers

- Does the business require a large number of routine interactions each day with vendors for ordering or requesting information?
- Is product choice complex?
- Do customers need to compare competitors' product/service/price configurations simultaneously?
- Is a quick customer decision necessary?
- Is accurate, quick customer confirmation essential?
- Would an increase in multiple ordering or service sites provide value to the customer?
- Are consumer tastes potentially volatile?
- Do significant possibilities exist for product customization?
- Is pricing volatile (can/should an individual salesperson set price at point of sale)?
- Is the business heavily regulated?
- Can the product be surrounded by value-added information to the customer?
- Is the real customer two or more levels removed from the manufacturer?

---

play a major role. Table 2–2 provides a similar set of questions for managers contemplating IT opportunities in operations.

The complexity of answering those questions for an individual firm is shown in the following example. In the airline industry, the reservation system, heavily used by travel agencies, has given its leading developers, American Airlines and United Airlines, major marketing (customer focus) and operational advantages. It has also enabled better aircraft utilization, new services such as "frequent flyer" programs, and the development of joint incentive programs with hotels and car rental agencies. In addition, the ongoing operations of seat allocation, crew scheduling, maintenance, and so on, have been profoundly influenced by IT. When an IT system fails, airline operations suffer immediately. Additionally, in some cases the technology has created substantial stock-market value. For example, American Airlines created substantial additional value when the SABRE reservation system was spun off as a separate company, whose stock is now traded. Conversely, some airlines invested less heavily in IT; some of them have paid a significant penalty in terms of their ability to differentiate their services in the eyes of the buying public and coordinate and cost-effectively deliver their services; in fact, failure to invest in IT has been cited as a leading cause for several airline failures (e.g., People's Express).[2]

In the banking industry, several banks (e.g., Providian Financial Corp., Citibank, and Chase Manhattan) have moved aggressively to distinguish

---

[2]D. Copeland and J. McKenney, "Airline Reservations Systems: Lessons from History," *Management Information Systems Quarterly* 12, no. 2 (1988), p. 352.

TABLE 2–2   Operations Questions for Managers

- Is there large geographic dispersion in sourcing?
- Is sophisticated technology embedded in the product?
- Does the product require a long, complex design process?
- Is the process of administering quality control standards complex?
- Is the design integration between customer and supplier across company boundaries complex?
- Are there large buffer inventory buffers in the manufacturing process?
- Does the product require complex manufacturing schedule integration?
- Are time and cost savings possible?
- Are direct and indirect labor levels high?

---

their products and services through effective use of information technology. Other banks, however, have used it primarily to transform the back office (e.g., check processing). The prime reason Tom Theobold, CEO of Continental Bank (subsequently merged out of existence), gave for outsourcing the IT function in 1991 was that over the past 20 years, he had been unable to find a bank that had developed and maintained sustainable competitive advantage through use of IT.[3] The problem of defining the competitive potential of IT is further complicated by the fact that while some firms fail to reap competitive benefits from their IT investments, others dramatically change the basis of competition.

The impact between industries varies significantly. Defense, for example, with CAD/CAM, robotics, and embedded technology, has been primarily affected on the operations side. The marketing impact on defense has been considerably less significant, not only because of the much lower transaction rate but also because the much higher transaction value introduces a different set of marketing forces that are less sensitive to technology's impact.

Conversely, retailing has been heavily impacted both operationally and from a marketing perspective. Retailing operations have been dramatically altered by bar coding and point-of-sale scanning technology that have enabled just-in-time ordering, massive cost-reduction programs, and major reductions in inventory levels. Quick response systems in retailing and efficient consumer response systems in grocery stores have placed pressure on suppliers, distributors, and brokers to adapt their processes to survive, and some have not survived. Similarly, display management, database marketing, and point-of-sale terminals that capture customer information at the time of a sale have made important marketing contributions, enabling micromarketing and other tailored marketing approaches. As mentioned earlier, the late 1990s have seen the explosion of electronic-based catalogs

---

[3]R. Huber, "How Continental Bank Outsourced Its 'Crown Jewels,'" *Harvard Business Review,* January–February 1993, pp. 121–29.

through the Internet that have dramatically altered the concept of shopping for certain categories and customers. No longer must the customer go to a fixed location with fixed hours; today, shopping is done any time and any place.

Interestingly enough, as one player in an industry incorporates IT into its products and/or value chain, others within the industry are also forced to respond. For example, retailers like Wal-Mart—which uses IT extensively to coordinate and control operations—have put pressure on their suppliers to implement IT-based operations to continue to be able to sell products in Wal-Mart. The ability to ensure one-day inventory turnaround and computer-to-computer information sharing has become the price for staying as a supplier.

A Contingency Approach to IT Use

Figure 2–1 identifies the different competitive investment strategies facing industry players as they consider their relative position versus industry leaders. Some firms have already used IT to transform marketing and production and the organization design and management processes required to support IT-enabled operations. Under the guidance of strong leadership, they have developed a defensible position relative to the competition. Within these firms, senior business leaders assume responsibility for planning and executing IT strategy for the firm. For example, the Chief Executive Officer (CEO) of Springs Industry has the Chief Information Officer (CIO) reporting to her and considers herself ultimately responsible for IT direction and implementation; at Southwire, the CIO sits on the company's executive committee. For these firms, IT has been defined as a core capability of the firm.

FIGURE 2–1   Targeting IT-Based Investment

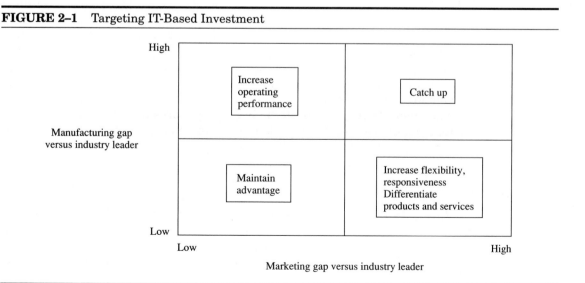

Other firms find themselves in a position where the opportunities for IT-enabled marketing are minimal, but significant opportunities exist to use IT to support manufacturing and logistics. For these firms, IT investments are often targeted towards streamlining, integrating, and coordinating production and distribution while controlling costs and improving product quality. Since these IT-enabled operating processes cut across many internal organizational boundaries, they require centralized oversight and an interfunctional, team-based approach to implementation and management. Strong relationships between IT and senior management must be in place to support the requirements for interfunctional integration.

A third group of firms face the primary challenge of catching up with industry leaders by better differentiating their products and services to meet the needs of ever more-focused markets. Many of these firms now face the need for IT investments in research and development as well as in the development of the marketing support systems and infrastructures needed to track industry trends and manage marketing strategy and execution. For these firms, the ability to capture detailed data on individual buyer preferences, competitor prices, and product moves is critical. Similarly, the capacity to leverage information and communication technologies to decentralize authority for product/market decisions, while simultaneously ensuring organizationwide integration and control, can dramatically increase customer satisfaction and speed of response. For example, one firm implemented handheld computers that fed store delivery information to a corporate data warehouse where it was integrated with competitor intelligence data, manufacturing/logistics data, and financial data, thereby enabling a much better understanding of market and business dynamics and enabling a 15 percent increase in sales per square foot in their customers' stores. By coupling this capability with sophisticated management and decision support systems, it was able to decentralize decision authority for product/market strategy and execution to 22 area business teams. As mentioned above, strong IT and general management links were needed to assure success.

Finally, some firms find themselves in a deep catch-up situation, having been outmaneuvered on both dimensions by strong industry leaders. Comprehensive, coordinated efforts are needed by both the CEO and IT management to enable the organization to achieve a defensible competitive position. The combination of being outmaneuvered by competitors, the long lead times required to develop a competitive response, and the high capital investment costs often create a situation so serious that the survival of the corporation is at stake. This is the situation in which People's Express and Frontier Airlines found themselves during the mid-1980s, as American and United Airlines used IT to redefine the basis of competition within the industry. The massive level of IT investment needed to maintain competitive position within the industry served to "weed out" competitors that had failed to recognize early the opportunities that IT would provide for integrating operations, identifying and meeting customer expectations, and differenti-

FIGURE 2–2   Categories of Strategic Relevance and Impact

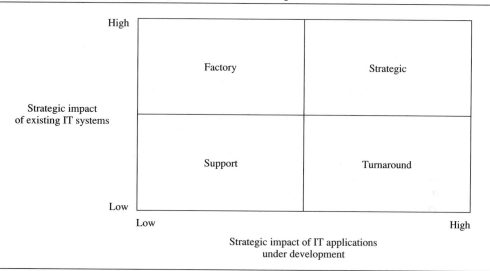

ating products and services. By the late 1980s, both firms were out of business. A more recent example is the beleaguered Encyclopedia Britannica, which failed to respond as the Internet and CD-ROM technology changed their business from paper to on-line.

A Contingency Approach to IT Management

Embedded in the previous discussion are two criteria that have profound importance to the management of IT in an individual firm. The first is that for some firms, the second-by-second, utterly reliable zero-defect quality of IT operations is crucial to the survival of the firm. Even small interruptions in service or disruptions in quality may have a profound impact. In other firms, it would take significant disturbances in IT operations over an extended period to have a major impact on the firm's overall operations.

The second factor is that whereas new IT development initiatives are of great strategic importance for some firms, for other firms, the new IT applications under development are useful but not strategic.[4] Understanding an organization's position on these two dimensions is critical for developing an appropriate IT management strategy. Four categories are identified (see Figure 2–2).

---

[4]In the late 1990s, few firms can be found for which IT is not strategic; however, the relative degree of strategic importance does continue to influence IT investment and management strategies.

Strategic.   For a growing number of firms, IT is essential for executing current strategies and operations and the new IT applications in development are crucial to future competitive success. IT strategy, the backbone of such firms' competitive success, receives considerable attention. Banks, insurance companies, and major retail chains frequently fall into this category. Appropriately managed, these firms require considerable IT planning, and the organizational relationship between IT and senior management must be very close; in fact, in some of these firms the head of the IT function, broadly defined, sits on the board of directors.

Turnaround.   Some firms receive considerable IT support for operations, but are not absolutely dependent on the totally uninterrupted, fast-response-time, cost-effective functioning of IT to achieve operating objectives. Their new IT applications, however, are absolutely necessary to enable the firm to achieve its strategic objectives. A good example of this was a rapidly growing manufacturing firm. The IT used in its factories and marketing and accounting processes in the mid-1990s, though important, was not absolutely vital to its effectiveness. Nevertheless, the rapid growth in the number of products, number of sites, number of staff, and so forth, of the firm's domestic and international installations severely strained its operations, management control, and new-product-development processes. New IT applications were being developed to enable the company to centralize key customer relations and transfer production scheduling from 63 plants into two national customer centers; this would enable the firm to dramatically improve service, sharply lower administrative costs, and significantly decrease the cost of operations. These new products required new IT reporting structures and substantially more involvement from the firm's executive committee than had previously existed. Once implemented, the new IT-enabled operations would become strategic to the firm's future success.

Another firm entered the turnaround category by systematically underinvesting in IT development over a period of years until its existing systems were filled with Year 2000 problems. Its highest priority in early 1998 is implementation of an IT system that will integrate operations and replace the 15 million lines of code that would have stopped working on January 1, 2000. Missing the project deadline is not optional. This critical project will replace nonessential systems with a system that will embed IT in the very fabric of day-to-day operations. Whether the company shifts from the turnaround category to the factory or strategic category depends on whether they continue to roll out new strategic uses of IT or simply maintain the new systems.

Factory.   Some firms are heavily dependent on cost-effective, totally reliable IT operational support to enable internal operations to run smoothly. System downtime causes major organizational disruption that can generate customer defections or significant loss of money. The CEO of an investment bank became fully aware of the operational dependence of his firm on IT when a flood above the data center brought all securities trading to a halt. Failure to ensure an off-site redundant data center crippled the bank's trading operations and caused massive financial losses. Needless to say, the CEO has a new appreciation for the importance of IT in running critical areas of business operations; a redundant data center was implemented shortly after the incident.

Firms in the factory quadrant of Figure 2–2 are using IT, like the investment bank, to enable critical, time-dependent operations to function smoothly; but the IT applications under development, although profitable and important in their own right, are not fundamental to the firm's ability to compete. For the firms in this category, even a one-hour disruption in service or deterioration in response times has severe operational, competitive, and financial consequences. In the late 1990s, mid-sized firms in this quadrant often turn to outsourcing to gain access to specialized expertise and costly security systems to help manage their risks.

Support. For some firms, the strategic impact of IT on operations and future strategy is low. For example, a large professional services firm spends nearly $30 million per year on IT activities that support more than 2,000 employees; all agree that the firm could continue to operate, albeit unevenly, in the event of major IT operational failure. And the strategic impact of the IT applications in development, viewed realistically, is quite limited.[5] IT had a significantly lower organizational position in this firm than in those in other industries, and the commitment to linking IT to business planning activities, particularly at the senior-management level, was essentially nonexistent. Within the past two years, however, the firm spent a significant amount of money equipping 15,000 of its consulting professionals and field representatives with laptop computers, electronic mail, and a variety of specialized applications that allowed them to access and share information. Since the key to the firm's success lay in recruiting, developing, and retaining highly competent professionals with a broad range of skills and deep expertise within targeted areas, and in managing client relationships, this new IT initiative would shift the firm's focus toward the upper turnaround quadrant.

To diagnose how strategically important IT is for a firm or business unit, careful analysis of its impact on each part of the value chain is essential. A more in-depth discussion of this analysis is provided in Chapter 3. In addition, competitors' use of IT and new IT developments must be monitored on a regular basis to ensure that major opportunities have not been missed. For example, 15 years ago most firms in the retailing industry were

---

[5]In 1998, Internet-based e-mail and knowledge management systems are being implemented by many professional services firms. These systems are expected to change the basis of competition for all firms in the industry.

appropriately positioned within the support category. Within several years, the technology became available to allow a then-small player, Wal-Mart, to change the basis of competition by driving service and cost to new levels; the past 15 years have been spent by retailers trying to catch up in an industry in which IT rapidly moved from support to strategic.

THEME 2: INTEGRATING CHANGING TECHNOLOGY PLATFORMS

At the heart of the IT challenge lies the dramatic, sustained, long-term evolution of IT cost/performance and the merging of a variety of technology platforms. IT applications that were nonexistent in 1992 were state-of-the art by 1995 and by 1997 were routine; obsolescence has been just a few years down the road.

The 1980s and 1990s saw the development of increasing communication and information storage capacities, which, in turn, supported an explosion of new types of software and IT applications. For example, in 1998, many consider the useful life of a personal computer to be three years or less (the three-year-old machine still runs but cannot support the new state-of-the-art applications). The tremendous improvement in price/performance has enabled integration of video, voice, data, and graphics and facilitated the explosion of new multimedia technology. This has radically changed the capabilities and potential uses of IT. For example, in 1998, full-motion digital video and voice annotations, and Internet hotlinks can routinely be attached to documents, information reports, and spreadsheets.

The new technologies have forced the integrated management of computing, telecommunications, office support, and broadcast technologies in firms. The ability to capitalize on the real business opportunities afforded by the integration of these technologies can only come through combined standards and policies. In this book, when we refer to IT departments, activities, or policies, we include all of these technologies. At present, most firms have begun the difficult process of coordinating these technologies; many have now successfully integrated all of them.

There are two major reasons why these technologies are managed as an integrated whole: (1) today's most important IT applications require an extensive network of physical interconnections (e.g., Groupware on-line desktop information retrieval systems, electronic mail groupware, and end-user programming); and (2) execution of IT application development projects utilizing technologies that are managed independently would be exceedingly difficult and cost-ineffective.[6]

---

[6]Projects that involve integration across technology platforms are usually large, high-risk, and costly; in addition, success often depends on substantial organizational and work-related changes.

The rapid evolution of technology has also necessitated a very different approach to IT management. Figure 2–3 highlights the changing nature of IT management.

Era I

From the 1950s to the early 1970s, the manager of data processing was the single source for providing information processing services and for managing technology expertise. To use an industrial analogy, IT operated as a "regulated monopoly." If someone wanted access to computing capabilities and technology expertise, there was no alternative but to go to the data processing manager. The primary focus of applications was organization wide (payroll, accounting, production scheduling, and order entry). New applications were justified on either a cost-elimination or a cost-displacement basis.

Era II

Era II began with the introduction of minicomputers and time-sharing in the early 1970s. It was dramatically accelerated in the early 1980s by the personal computer, which introduced a wide range of new channels for users to acquire technology expertise and information processing capabilities. This led to a relatively "free market" for IT services—users no longer had to go to the IT manager to gain access to computer and communications technology. In Era II's free-market arena, the rigid top-down controls, developed and implemented in Era I, were no longer applicable. Individuals were the primary decision makers, and with sufficient discretionary resources to reinforce that independence, they could purchase computers that had 50 times the capability of earlier computers, at less than 1 percent of the price.

FIGURE 2–3 The IT Environment

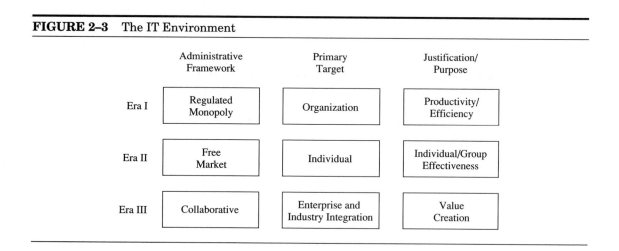

	Administrative Framework	Primary Target	Justification/ Purpose
Era I	Regulated Monopoly	Organization	Productivity/ Efficiency
Era II	Free Market	Individual	Individual/Group Effectiveness
Era III	Collaborative	Enterprise and Industry Integration	Value Creation

During this period, individual and work unit effectiveness became the key justification measure for project justification; but Era I applications and their administrative systems could not and did not disappear. Rather, the IT management environment was made more complex with the additional challenge of managing easily accessible, individually exploited technology concurrently with Era I technology.

Era III

In the 1990s, a new era is emerging in which the power of widely distributed, flexible information management systems and communication networks enables virtually instantaneous delivery of information and knowledge to the desktop, laptop, and home of individuals located all over the globe. When combined with the seamless integration of data, voice, video, and graphics, managers will be able to communicate and share knowledge "any time, any place, and in any form." Today's explosive growth of the Internet technologies suggests this is no longer a dream but reality.

THEME 3: ASSIMILATING EMERGING TECHNOLOGIES

The task of implementing a portfolio of IT systems projects that are built around continually evolving technologies is an extraordinarily complex endeavor. Early involvement of end users whose daily activities will be influenced by the adoption of the technology has been shown to be a critical success factor. New IT innovations, however, are often complicated by the fact that user jobs may be eliminated by the new technologies that employers are working so hard to help implement. Successful implementation of IT also often requires that users adopt dramatically new ways of performing intellectual tasks. To accomplish this, old procedures and attitudes must be abandoned, and new patterns must emerge and be accepted by individuals and work groups.

Since IT was introduced in organizations, there has been an ongoing effort to understand the managerial issues associated with the evolution of IT and organization. Early work by Thomas Whisler and Harold Leavitt[7] on IT and the demise of middle management, by Dick Nolan on the evolution of IT and organization as a process of organizational learning,[8] and by Chris Argyris[9] on double-loop learning discusses approaches for dealing

---

[7]Thomas L. Whisler and Harold J. Leavitt, "Management in the 1980s," Harvard Business Review, November–December 1958, pp. 41–48.

[8]Richard L. Nolan, "Managing the Crisis in Data Processing," Harvard Business Review, March–April 1979, pp. 115–26.

[9]Chris Argyris, "Double-Loop Learning on Organizations," Harvard Business Review, September–October 1977, p. 115.

with individual acceptance and use of IT. Field research by Jim Cash and Poppy McLeod frames the issues within the context of the diffusion of technology innovation.[10] Successful implementation of a technology often requires that individuals learn radically new ways of performing intellectual tasks, causing changes in information flows as well as in individual roles. Frequently, this requires more extensive organizational changes involving structures, operating processes, management processes, human resource management systems, culture, and incentives. We describe the technology innovation and diffusion process within four phases.

Phase 1. Technology Identification and Investment

The first phase involves identifying a technology of potential interest to the company and funding a pilot project. An alternative approach is to use the business-planning process to identify promising IT applications that require technology innovation and fund investigation of their potential as part of the budgeting process. The first approach involves a "grass roots" effort that can be used to define potential benefits and risks and system implementation difficulties early in the process and to garner support by demonstrating the potential payoff. The latter approach requires the commitment of senior management to serve as product champions for systems innovations early in the process. Because it is inappropriate to demand objective payoffs at the pilot project stage, top-level management commitment is often difficult to secure.

Phase 2. Technological Learning and Adaptation

The objective during the second phase is to encourage user-oriented experimentation with the newly identified technology through a series of user-defined pilot projects. The primary purpose of the experimentation is to develop a broad base of user-oriented insights into how the new technology might be used to add value in the business and to make users aware of the existence of the technology. Frequently, the outcome of phase 2 provides a much different perspective on the technology than the one held by IT experts at the end of their phase 1 pilot.

The length of this phase varies with the type of technology, the characteristics of the users, the tasks for which the technology is used, and the organizational and environmental context.[11] For example, at one firm, a

---

[10]J. Cash and P. McLeod, "Managing the Introduction of Information Technology in Strategically Dependent Companies," *Journal of Management and Information Systems* 1 (1985), pp. 5–23.

[11]L. Applegate, "Technology Support for Cooperative Work: A Framework for Introduction and Assimilation in Organizations," *Journal of Organizational Computing* 1, No. 1 (1991), pp. 11–39.

pilot project designed to test the use of laptop computers by the sales force was so successful that it progressed through phase 2 within several months and was fully deployed within 18 months (6 months ahead of schedule) to all 10,000 sales representatives. The technology, while new to the company, was not "new to the world"; the task that the technology would support was well defined, as was the influence of the technology on the task; careful attention was paid to involving and training both the users (and their bosses) from the start of the process, and incentives, compensation, and performance management systems were realigned to "fit" the new IT-enabled work process.

Phase 3. Rationalization/Management Control

By the time a technology has reached phase 3, it is reasonably well understood by both IT personnel and key users. The basic challenge in this phase is to develop appropriate systems and controls to ensure that the technologies are utilized efficiently as they diffuse throughout the organization. In earlier phases, basic concerns revolve around stimulating awareness and experimentation; in this phase, they center on developing standards and controls to ensure that the applications are done economically and can be maintained over a long period of time. Formal standards for development and documentation, change control, cost-benefit studies, and user charge-out mechanisms are all appropriate for technologies in this phase. Failure to develop and maintain these standards can be extraordinarily expensive.

Phase 4. Maturity/Widespread Technology Transfer

By the time a technology enters the fourth phase, the required skills have been developed, users are aware of the benefits, and management controls are in place. A common pitfall in this phase is that enthusiasm for the technology dies while there is still opportunity to use it to add value. Lacking sufficient attention and resources, maintenance of existing applications may suffer and new value-creating uses may not be explored. Careful vigilance is also required in this phase to ensure that out-of-date technologies and applications are not extended beyond their useful life.

The four phases (innovation, learning, rationalization, and maturity), which are now clearly understood within most well-managed firms, provide a useful base around which to develop a strategic view of the diffusion of technology throughout the firm. As experiments with a specific technology spread, new innovations should be encouraged. Knowledgeable business managers have usually proven to be better sources of new application ideas than either technology experts or single-minded champions. As noted earlier, different technologies may pass through the phases in radically different ways. In addition, few firms progress through these phases in the orderly sequence of events that we describe here. Expect a certain amount of cycling back and leaping forward.

There are no hard and fast guidelines for deciding how much to allocate to exploiting technologies at different phases of evolution. Clearly, firms in the strategic category in Figure 2–2 can expect to spend more on phase 1 and phase 2 technology investments than those firmly positioned in the *support* category. But no matter what quadrant a firm is in at any point in time, it is important to remember that a new technology may offer a new business opportunity that can trigger a move from one quadrant to another.

In most firms, technologies in all four phases exist simultaneously in an organization at any point in time. The art of management in the late 1990s is to simultaneously bring the appropriate management perspectives to bear on each technology. This calls for IT management and general management to be both subtle and flexible, qualities they often neither possess nor see as necessary. A "one-size-fits-all" approach to IT management simply will not work.

THEME 4: SOURCING POLICIES FOR THE IT VALUE CHAIN

A significant issue in repositioning IT over the past decade has been an acceleration of the pressures that are pushing firms toward greater reliance on external sources for software, help desk, networking, and other computing support. This is called outsourcing, but, as we discuss in future chapters, there is a wide variation in the definition of that word within the industry. Escalating costs of large-scale system development projects, limited staff, availability of industry-standard databases and networks, the availability of software packages, and a dramatic increase in the number of potential applications have been some of the factors driving the trend to use outside sources—a trend that we believe will continue to accelerate into the early 21st century. The realization that they do not develop their own word-processing or spreadsheet software leads managers to ask: "Do I need to develop my order-processing system? If I can specify the process, can I hire someone to write the code, or are there packages that can be adapted?" Facing significant pressure to focus on core competencies and the rapidly increasing complexity of technology management, many have expanded their thinking: "Do I really need to run my large computing centers, corporate networks, help desks, personal computer (PC) maintenance, etc.? Can I safely delegate the operation of the infrastructure to enable me to focus my energy and resources on creating value-added IT applications?"

Factors to consider as firms struggle with the answers to these questions are summarized in Table 2–3. The preference to buy rather than make has significantly influenced IT management practice as dissatisfaction with internally supplied services grows. The proliferation of end-user computing packages has resulted in the fact that in many firms in the mid-1990s less

TABLE 2–3 IT Sourcing: Pressures to "Make/Own" versus "Buy"

Decision Criteria	Pressure to "Make/Own"	Pressure to "Buy"
Business strategy	IT application or infrastructure provides proprietary competitive advantage.	IT application or infrastructure supports strategy or operations, but is not considered strategic in its own right.
Core competencies	Business or IT knowledge/expertise required to develop or maintain an application is considered a core competency of the firm.	Business or IT knowledge/expertise required to build or maintain an IT application or infrastructure is not critical to the firm's success.
Information/process security and confidentiality	The information or processes contained within IT systems or databases are considered to be highly confidential.	Failure of routine security measures, while problematic, would not cause serious organizational dysfunction.
Availability of suitable partners	There are no reliable, competent, and/or motivated partners that could assume responsibility for the IT application or infrastructure. (Included are the financial viability of the partner, perceptions of quality of the partner's products and services, and perceptions of the ability to form a compatible working relationship over the life of the contract.)	Reliable, competent, and appropriately motivated vendors (or other partners) are available.
Availability of packaged software or solutions	The IT application or infrastructure required by the firm is unique.	Packaged software or solutions are available that would meet the majority of business requirements.
Cost/benefit analysis	The cost of purchasing the product or service and/or coordinating and controlling interorganizational relationships and operations is greater than the cost of performing the service in-house.	The cost of purchasing and managing the service is significantly less than the cost of performing the service in-house.
Time frame for implementation	There is sufficient time available to develop internal resources and skills to implement the IT application and/or to develop the IT infrastructure required by the firm.	The time required to develop internal resources and expertise and/or to implement the IT application or infrastructure project exceeds the organization's demand for the product or services.
Evolution and complexity of the technology	The firm is able to attract, retain, and develop the range of IT experts needed to implement IT applications and infrastructures at a reasonable cost.	The firm is unable to keep pace with the rapidly changing and increasingly complex technologies required by the firm.
Ease of implementation	Software development tools that provide rapid IT application development are available.	Tools to support rapid application development are not available or are viewed to be insufficient or ineffective.

than 1 percent of all software has been developed by the IT group. The IT organization has increasingly turned into an in-house systems integration function, and new management processes have had to be defined to deal with this reality. For example, internal management control systems must be checked to ensure that they do not motivate inappropriate "make" versus "buy" decisions. When software development is being outsourced, clear interorganizational project management systems and audit procedures must be in place to ensure that both the vendor and the customer are able to deliver on their commitments. Firm implementation risk on a fixed-price contract can be strongly related to vendor viability. A "good" price is not good if the supplier goes under before completing the project. Provisions for "death" and "divorce" become critical in situations where a firm is outsourcing operational IT components (e.g., data centers, networks) since the normal length of these contracts can be as much as 10 years (although contracting horizons are dramatically shrinking).

THEME 5: APPLICATIONS DEVELOPMENT PROCESS

Traditionally, the activities necessary to produce and deliver information systems have been characterized as a series of steps:[12]

1. Design—definition of the functions and relevant technologies, followed by detailed system design
2. Construct—test and code the system (or buy)
3. Implement—train users and motivate use, redesign processes, reorganize
4. Operate—day-to-day running of IT-enabled business processes
5. Maintain—upgrade technology and adapt system to changing requirements

Since the First Edition of this book was published, very different types of technologies and projects have dramatically influenced the system development process. At one extreme are the traditional projects that were once the mainstay of the industry. These projects are noted for being large, requiring extensive development periods (often well in excess of 18 months), and significantly influencing the nature of work and organization across multiple areas of the business. These projects are inherently very complex. Often, the information required, how it will be processed, and the end results of the project are not clearly specified at the outset. In the late 1990s, the traditional system life cycle continues to be appropriate for these projects, but the steps in the process are not performed in a highly structured and sequential

---

[12]It is worth noting that this list of responsibilities remains with the firm irrespective of whether all or a portion of the system development process and IT operations/management is outsourced. The job of IT and business management is to ensure that those tasks are performed in the most effective and efficient manner, irrespective of where or by whom they are performed.

fashion as in the past. There is a significant increase in the levels of inter-action among a wide variety of IT and business professionals, each of whom brings different areas of expertise and management responsibilities; even vendors get in the act. This results in a much more interactive and iterative process; in addition, to manage complexity, these large projects are often subdivided into a number of smaller projects that may be managed in very different ways. For example, one team may use joint application develop-ment and rapid prototyping[13] to build the user interface for the system, while a second team conducts a pilot project of a portion of the system that will use a state-of-the-art technology that is new to the firm.

At the other extreme are more focused projects that may involve the con-struction of a decision support system (DSS) for a group of end users. This type of project may use rapid prototyping and joint application development methods from the outset. Alternatively, a team may be working on the intro-duction and assimilation of a new technology using the phased approach to organization learning discussed earlier in this chapter. Finally, some projects may involve the use of computer-aided software engineering (CASE) tools.[14] The key to understanding the complexity of the applications development challenge in the late 1990s is to appropriately select and implement a system development methodology based on the nature of the project and the experience and expertise of both business and IT profession-als. In addition, it is critical to remember that all projects require careful management by both business and IT professionals throughout all phases of the project.

The remainder of this section defines the components of the traditional system development life cycle and also identifies those aspects most likely to be mismanaged in the late 1990s. While changing technology and improved managerial insights on the use of technology have significantly altered the way each of these steps can be implemented, they continue to provide a use-ful framework with which to consider the range of system development activities; in fact, the increasing shift toward purchasing IT application development services increases the need for careful attention to IT project

---

[13]Joint application development is a system development methodology that involves both business users and IT professionals in all parts of the system design, development, and imple-mentation process. Rapid prototyping refers to the process of building a smaller version of the system that has limited functionality; this allows IT professionals and business users to better define requirements and test key areas of functionality prior to full-scale system development.

[14]CASE tools are software programs that help system developers design and code business software. Some of the tools support designers in developing system specifications. Once those specifications are defined in the computer, the CASE tools automatically generate computer code—the instructions that tell a computer what to do—and then check the code for inconsis-tencies and redundancy. Others help developers, or even end users, design and implement information reporting or decision support systems. CASE tools often embody a specific approach to system development, which makes them more appropriate for some types of pro-jects than for others.

management. This is especially true in firms where the role of the IT manager is beginning to resemble that of an information broker.

Design

The objective of the design step is to produce a definition of the information service desired. This includes identification of the users, the initial tasks to be implemented, and the long-run service and support to be provided. Traditionally, the process is initiated by either a user request or a joint IT department-user proposal based on the IT plan. The design step is a critical activity that demands careful attention to short- and long-term information service requirements as well as reliable service delivery. Management of the design phase was traditionally done by the IT staff; in many organizations in the late 1990s, the user is taking the lead.

Design normally begins with a feasibility analysis that provides a high-level picture of the potential costs and benefits of the proposed system and the technical/organizational feasibility of the project. If the results of the analysis are favorable, an explicit decision is made to proceed. This is followed by substantive collaborative work by a team of users, IT professionals, and experts to develop a working approach to, and set of specifications for, the system design. The design team should include key internal and external stakeholders who could either influence or be influenced by the new system. As a result, the team required to design interorganizational systems—those that enable on-line communication, information sharing, or management/execution of core operating processes between different firms—may require membership of key customers, suppliers, distributors, or other business partners. In other cases, vendors or consultants with specialized expertise may be included on the system design team. Depending on the system's scope, these design efforts may range from formal systematic analysis to informal discussion followed by rapid prototyping. The end product of design is a definition of the desired service accompanied by an identification of the means (including in-house or purchased services) for providing it.

Construction

A highly specialized activity that combines both art and logic, system construction involves selecting appropriate computer equipment and creating/or buying the specific computer programs that are needed to meet system requirements. Professional judgment is needed in the following areas:

1. Selection of computer equipment, networking routers, software programming languages or packages, etc. If the decision is made to outsource

development, independent contractors or a specialized software development firm can be hired. Particular attention must be paid to long-term maintainability to avoid getting stranded in a "technological dead end."

2. Documentation of both the technical program structure and end-user operating instructions must be created. The importance of comprehensive, understandable documentation is often overlooked. Inadequate technical documentation can lead to excessive cost; inadequate user documentation can result in poor acceptance of the system.

3. Appropriate testing must be performed to ensure system robustness.

While this set of activities is primarily technical in nature, intense coordination and control are required to ensure that the project remains on track, within budget, and focused on user requirements. Even the best designs require numerous interdependent decisions. Large project teams must coordinate closely to ensure that the system components will work together flawlessly. Frequent interaction with end users is also required to ensure that the system requirements do not change. The decision to outsource portions of the project, or the entire project, markedly increases the coordination and control costs, and the technical decisions listed above must still be managed inside the firm.

Implementation

Implementation involves extensive user-IT coordination as the transition is made from the predominantly technical, IT-driven task of construction to user-driven management of the completed system. Whether the system is bought or made, the implementation phase is very much a joint effort. Extensive testing, which disrupts normal business operations, must be performed; training is required; work procedures and communication patterns are disrupted. Often, achievement of the benefits of the system is dependent on the ability of individuals and groups to learn to use the information from the system to make better decisions and add value to the business. It is essential to shape the organization's operational and management structure, processes, and incentives to exploit the potential of an IT system. In this world of electronic commerce, the impact of the system extends to groups and individuals outside the organization, which further complicates implementation. Perhaps most critical is the need to carefully define the activities that are required to ensure that the benefits of the project are achieved and documented.

Operation

In many settings, system operation receives little attention, as IT staff members focus their efforts on the enormous backlog of projects still waiting to be done. This can lead to intense frustration and conflict because of cumbersome, inefficient operating procedures. Further, as significant portions of systems have migrated from the mainframe to the desktop, users become the system "operators" and are becoming all too aware of the complexity of the task and the damage of errors in previous phases of system development. Much of this difficulty can be traced to the faulty identification and communication of the system operating requirements at the design phase. As systems become more complex, and as goals for the system become less certain, the difficulty of clearly specifying requirements up front becomes a major factor that complicates both implementation and operation.

In complex systems that will be operated by IT professionals, formal procedures are often in place that specify that operating personnel must "sign off" on a new system. The specific criteria for testing and approval are defined as part of the system design phase. This control mechanism distributes responsibility and authority for system development and serves as an important quality-control mechanism on operational excellence. This role separation is particularly important when the same department is responsible for both constructing and operating a system.

After the system is built and installed, measures must be developed to assess actual service delivery and its cost-effectiveness and quality. While many believe that "postimplementation audits" are unnecessary for all system projects, increasing attention has been focused on the lack of control over end-user-developed systems. For example, a financial services organization received a great deal of attention recently when Year 2000 problems forced them to stop providing forecasts that went more than two years in the future. They suffered loss of both reputation and revenues.

Maintenance

System maintenance refers to enhancements or changes in a system that has passed into the operation phase. It requires cycling back through the design, construction, and implementation activities. The need for system maintenance often arises from changes in the business or technical environment (e.g., changes in tax laws, organization changes such as new offices or mergers, business changes such as new product lines and acquisition of new technology).[15] It can be as simple as changing a number in a database of depreciation rates or as complex as rewriting the tax portion of the payroll. Effective maintenance faces two serious problems:

1. Most professionals consider it dull and unchallenging because it involves working on systems created by someone else. Consequently, the work is

---

[15]The word *maintenance* is a complete misnomer because it implies an element of deferability that does not exist in many situations. *Modernization* is a better term.

often delegated to inexperienced employees or those who have shown less system development aptitude.

2. Maintenance can be very complex, particularly for older systems. It requires highly competent professionals to safely perform necessary changes in a way that does not bring the system (and the firm) to a crashing halt.

Several IT departments are developing IT quality procedures to help focus attention on "continuous improvement." Quality teams search out opportunities for enhancement, and continuous improvement becomes everyone's job. This change in mind-set must be accompanied by a shift in emphasis from operating efficiency to customer satisfaction that is reflected in goals, performance measurement, and incentives. Newer IT system development tools provide support for continuous improvement by enabling end users to customize the system to meet the changing business need while effectively isolating the internal processing instructions from changes that could harm overall system operation. Managing the operations and enhancement of end-user-developed systems remains an area of particular concern for organizations that are becoming more dependent on locally developed information. The move to client-server computing is helping companies gain control of these applications.[16]

In summary, the complexity of the system's life cycle is evident from the above description. At any time, an organization may have hundreds of systems, each at a different position, within this life cycle. Traditionally, the IT department has been organized to support a phase of the system development life cycle (e.g., system analysis, programming, operations, etc.), rather than a specific application system. This inevitably creates friction because it forces the passing of responsibility for an application system from one IT unit to another as it passes through these steps. Until recently, the user was responsible for coordination of the system development process as responsibility was rotated among IT specialists.

THEME 6: PARTNERSHIP OF THREE CONSTITUENCIES

Much of the complexity of IT management stems from managing the conflicting pressures of three different and vitally concerned constituencies: IT management, user management, and general management of the organization. The relationships between these groups vary over time as the organi-

---

[16]Client-server computing allows end-user-developed systems to be transferred to a separate computer—designed as a "server"—for ongoing operation. The server, while it may be housed locally, is often controlled by a central computer/network operations center. With client-server computing, the operating responsibility can be shared between end users and IT professionals, and formal quality procedures can be implemented.

zation's familiarity with different technologies evolves, as the strategic impact of IT shifts, and as the company's overall IT management skills grow.

IT Management

A number of forces have driven the creation of an IT department and ensured its continued existence. The IT department provides a pool of technical skills that can be developed and deployed to resolve complex problems facing the firm. An important part of its mission is to scan leading-edge technologies and to ensure that potential users are both aware of their existence and aware of how they could be used to solve business problems. Because many systems are designed to interconnect different parts of the business, IT professionals have become key integrators who can help identify areas of potential interconnection between the needs of different user groups and thus facilitate the development of integrated business solutions. From their earliest roots, IT has involved process analysis and redesign. As a result, in many firms, IT professionals are becoming the "business process reengineering" specialists—a role of increasing importance within firms in the 1990s. In a world of changing technologies and changing business opportunities, this unit is under continuous pressure to remain relevant. As end users become more involved in system development activities, a new relationship must be forged to ensure that the unique skills and expertise of both groups are utilized to their fullest to solve business problems.

User Management

Specialization of the IT function has taken place at a cost. System design, construction, operation, and maintenance tasks have become the responsibility of the IT department, yet the user continues to assume responsibility for the business activities that the systems support. This is an obvious point of friction. Additionally, in the past, the "mysterious" requirements of the technology alienated users from the system development and operations process, increasing the barriers to effective collaboration.

At times, vendors and consultants capitalize on this conflict by aggressively marketing their services directly to the users, who are then faced with the additional pressure of choosing among alternatives without fully understanding the criteria upon which to base their decision. Increasing user IT sophistication and experience, when coupled with the increasing availability of packaged, user-friendly software, has dramatically altered the conditions that initially led to IT specialization. In many firms, the boundaries are blurring as "hybrid" professionals with both business and technical expertise become more prevalent at both the user and IT specialist levels.

But new state-of-the-art technologies continue to require specialized exper-tise (whether located internally or externally to the firm). Appropriately, the relationship and apportionment of responsibilities between the IT specialist and the user are being reappraised continuously. The management of these complex transitions is clearly general management's responsibility.

General Management

The broad task of general management is to ensure that appropriate struc-tures, systems, and management processes are in place for ensuring that the overall needs of the organization are met. As IT assumes an increasingly visible role within an organization, executives' ability and interest in play-ing this role are a function of both their comfort with IT and their perception of its strategic importance to the firm as a whole. Since many have reached their positions with little exposure to IT issues or with exposure to radically different types of IT issues, they are often ill-equipped to assume this responsibility. It is important to note that much of this book is aimed at helping general managers assume a more active role in managing the infor-mation resource of the firm. As a new generation of managers with more experience and higher comfort levels with IT take on increasing responsibil-ity, we expect more general managers will take a more active role.

In summary, as each group's perspective and attitudes evolve, some prob-lems are solved while new ones arise. Managing the changing roles and rela-tionships is one of the most complex issues facing all three groups as they attempt to harness the power of IT in the 1990s.

SUMMARY

In this chapter, we have identified the manageable trends that are relevant to all aspects of managing information services in the 1990s. Table 2–4 maps the remaining chapters and identifies each chapter's emphasis in relation to our six organizing themes.

TABLE 2–4   Map of Chapters and Themes

	Strategic Impact	Technology Integration	Managing Rapidly Evolving Technologies	IT Sourcing Policies	Application Development Process	Partnerships among Constituencies
Chapter 3 Effects of IT on Strategy and Competition	•	•				•
Chapter 4 Electronic Commerce: Trends and Opportunities	•	•	•			•
Chapter 5 Information, Organization, and Control	•					•
Chapter 6 IT Architecture: Evoluation and Alternatives		•	•			•
Chapter 7 Organizing and Leading the Information Technology Function	•		•	•		•
Chapter 8 Managing IT Outsourcing	•			•		•
Chapter 9 IT Operations		•		•	•	•
Chapter 10 IT Management Processes			•	•		•
Chapter 11 A Portfolio Approach to Information Technology Development	•		•		•	•
Chapter 12 Global Issues	•	•				•
Chapter 13 The IT Business	•		•	•		•

Case 1–1

VERIFONE (1997)[1]

In the 1996 VeriFone Annual Report, Hatim Tyabji, chairman, president, and chief executive officer, wrote the following in the "Letter to Our Shareholders":[2]

> When I talk about VeriFone—to our customers, stockholders or employees—I often like to begin by underscoring what it is we do, and in our view do better than anyone else. VeriFone develops, markets, and supports the hardware and software systems that enable electronic payment, on a global scale, among consumers, merchants, and financial institutions. To describe our business in a phrase—*WE MOVE MONEY.*
>
> These are very exciting times for the Company. The nature of electronic payments is expanding rapidly, with emerging technologies creating new opportunities in markets like Internet and consumer systems. As the global leader in electronic payment systems, we are in a unique position to leverage our competencies, our customer and technology partner relationships, and our resources in pursuit of these opportunities
>
> . . . Just as we made "Slide and Go" credit and debit card transactions fast, secure, and easy, we are aiming to make "Click and Go" secure Internet transactions a standard payment solution.

This case was prepared by Professors Donna B. Stoddard and Anne Donnellon of Babson College and Professor Richard L. Nolan.

[1]Copyright © 1998 by the President and Fellows of Harvard College.

Harvard Business School case 398-030.

[2]The 1996 VeriFone Annual Report Letter to Our Shareholders appeared in seven languages: English, Chinese, French, German, Japanese, Portuguese, and Spanish.

In July 1997, VeriFone was in transition. The Hewlett Packard (HP) acquisition of VeriFone and the various Internet strategic alliances positioned VeriFone for the future. However, the changing nature of its products introduced management challenges. One employee notes, "Historically, VeriFone sold gray boxes. Today, we are selling client/server Java-based systems and a myriad of peripheral devices. The skills that a sales person needs to be successful are fundamentally different." As Tyabji looked to the future, he needed to ensure that VeriFone had the appropriate sales force and resources to develop and sell VeriFone's future products and services.

Payment Systems

VeriFone coined the term *Transaction Automation (TA)* shortly after introducing its first generation of software-driven products in the mid-1980s. The term was adopted by most of the competitors and analysts in the industry and initially referred to electronic point-of-sale payment systems.

Until the early 1980s, most credit card transactions were processed manually and depended upon paper-based systems. At an average cost of $0.60 per transaction, authorizations were time-consuming and typically involved looking up long, illegible lists of customer names or telephoning representatives from "bank card member associations" (e.g., VISA or MasterCard) to validate account numbers. The actual settlement stage (which took seven to ten days) required a retailer to physically provide paper drafts to an associated bank before collections from the cardholder's bank could be initiated (see Exhibit 1).

Deregulation of the banking industry (in the mid- to late 1970s) and the telecommunications industry (in the early 1980s) paved the way for electronic computer-based point-of-sale systems by providing enhanced services at lower costs to users. These systems automated a large variety of transactions, from credit card authorization and draft capture and settlement to collection and transmittal of election results. They gained popularity for the convenience afforded to

EXHIBIT 1   Automation of Credit and Settlement

Credit Authorization

Voice

Electronic

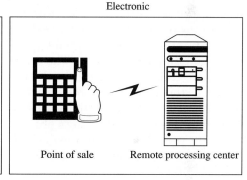

Point of sale   Remote processing center

Point of sale   Remote processing center

60 seconds, 60¢

5–15 seconds, 5¢–15¢
Reduces time, cost, and fraud.

Settlement

Manual

Electronic

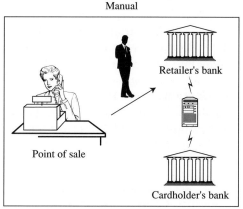
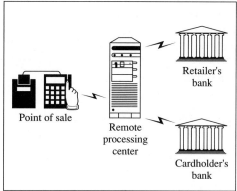

Retailer's bank

Point of sale

Cardholder's bank

Point of sale

Remote processing center

Retailer's bank

Cardholder's bank

customers and for reduced processing costs, decreased incidence of fraud, and gathering accurate customer information. An automated authorization process required only the cardholder's account number (captured by swiping the card), took only a few seconds, and cost $0.05–0.15. The settlement stage (now accomplished within 24 hours) was processed electronically between the point of sale and the retailer's bank and the cardholder's bank.

Company Overview

From its beginning, VeriFone Corporation specialized in the automation and delivery of secure payment and payment-related transactions to a wide range of markets. The company's mission, "To create and lead the transaction automation industry worldwide," set the boundaries for the business the company pursued. The company's philosophy statement provided the guiding system of values under which business was conducted (see Exhibit 2).

Founded in 1981 by William Melton, an entrepreneur with a habitual distaste for structure and bureaucracy, VeriFone initially provided simple electronic check verification systems. Soon thereafter, the company expanded its scope to include

---

EXHIBIT 2   VeriFone Philosophy Statement

We are committed to:

Building an Excellent Company

Meeting the Needs of Our Customers

Recognizing the Importance of Each Individual

Promoting Team Spirit

Focusing Accountability in Everything We Do

Fostering Open Communication

Strengthening International Ties

Living and Working Ethically

---

low-cost, terminal systems for the retail end of credit card and check authorization.[3] In 1997, VeriFone's product offerings included smart card technology for merchants, Internet payments solutions for merchants, banks, and consumers, client/server payment processing solutions for financial institutions, and products to enable the emerging consumer home banking marketplace. Exhibit 3 highlights VeriFone management's view of the payment marketplace in 1997. By the end of 1996, VeriFone had shipped more than five million transaction automation systems, which had been installed, in over 100 countries. The company's 1996 revenue and profit exceeded $470 million and $39 million, respectively (see Exhibit 4).

VeriFone's traditional terminal and printer products competed with products from vendors such as Hypercom. In the smart card arena, VeriFone's competitors included companies such as Diebold and Schlumberger. In the virtual world, there were a number of start-up and traditional companies who sought to define that marketplace. The Internet portion of the electronics commerce market alone was expected to reach $95 billion in the United States by the year 2000 according to a research report from the International Data Corp., a Massachusetts-based research firm. VeriFone's Omnihost software, which was marketed to banks, provided a client/server solution that tied all of these components together.

VeriFone's leadership position in secure payment solutions was recognized by many, including Hewlett Packard, which acquired VeriFone on June 25, 1997, for $1.29 billion. According to a VeriFone press release,[4]

---

[3]From Hossam Galal, Donna Stoddard, Richard Nolan, and John Kao, "VeriFone: The Transaction Automation Company (A)," HBS case No. 195-088, Harvard Business School Publishing, 1994, p. 1.

[4]Http://www.verifone.com/corporate_info/html/hp_merger.html. "HP Completes $1.29 Billion Merger with VeriFone."

HP and VeriFone share a joint vision for the expanding opportunities of electronic commerce over the Internet. The capabilities and technologies of the two companies complement each other, with HP's focus on Internet security technologies, enterprise-computing solutions, and professional services and support; VeriFone's expertise in the movement of money; and both companies' focus on the financial-services industry, businesses, governments and consumers worldwide. The companies' relationship also includes providing end-to-end solutions based on the VISA/MasterCard Secure Electronic Transaction (SET) protocol, the emerging standard for secure credit-card payments over the Internet.

Some in the financial community were surprised by the one-for-one stock swap that HP arranged with VeriFone. One employee noted, "HP purchased us for our Internet products and strategy. However, today those products generate less than 10% of our revenue." Analysts familiar with the payment industry and VeriFone believed that HP made a very shrewd decision to invest in a small, entrepreneurial company with global leadership in high growth markets.

Organization Structure

In 1997, VeriFone had approximately 3,000 employees working in more than 30 facilities, including regional offices, development centers, manufacturing, and distribution centers located throughout North and South America, Europe, Asia, Africa, Australia,

---

EXHIBIT 3   VeriFone's Vision of the Payment Market

Total Solution

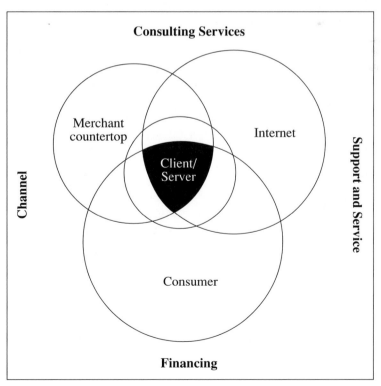

EXHIBIT 4   Verifone—Financial Statements (in thousands)

	12/31/96	12/31/95
Income statement		
Net sales	$472,460	$387,016
Cost of goods sold	256,250	202,356
Gross profit	216,210	184,660
R&D expenditures	53,434	45,036
Selling, general and administrative expense	109,259	97,887
Income from operations	53,517	41,737
Interest and other income	2,875	4,993
Interest expense	1,090	948
Income before tax	55,302	45,782
Provision for income taxes	16,038	13,277
Net income	$ 39,264	$ 32,505
Balance sheet		
Assets		
Cash	$ 47,395[a]	$ 72,882
Marketable securities	515	9,939
Receivables	131,192	96,419
Inventories	59,524	76,611
Other current assets	33,692	34,472
Total current assets	$272,318	$290,323
Net property and equipment	64,722	50,942
Investment and advance to subsidiaries	19,329	15,360
Deposits and other assets	48,611	22,891
Total assets	$404,980	$379,516
Liabilities		
Accounts payable	31,641	20,693
Other current liabilities	95,438	58,631
Total current liabilities	$127,079	$ 79,324
Deferred income taxes	37,818	33,602
Noncurrent capital leases	517	2,205
Total liabilities	$165,414	$115,131
Shareholder equity	239,566	264,385
Total liabilities and net worth	$404,980	$379,516
Global employees	2,850	2,471

[a]Note: In fiscal 1996, VeriFone repurchased 2.5 million shares of common stock for an aggregate cost of $100 million.

and the Pacific (see Exhibit 5). VeriFone management chose its geographic sites to enable close contact with customers and physical proximity to emerging markets and "centers of excellence"—areas known for their intellectual or capital resources.

EXHIBIT 5   Worldwide Facilities

Manufacturing and Distribution

Beijing
Kaohsiung, Taiwan
Kunshun, China
Costa Mesa

Systems Development

Atlanta
Dallas
Paris
Hawaii
Bangalore
Palo Alto
Santa Clara
Singapore
Taiwan
Tampa
Uxbridge, U.K.

Sales

Barcelona
Boston
Buenos Aires
Chicago
Frankfurt
Johannesburg
London
Madrid
Mexico City
Milan
Montreal
New York
Sao Paulo
Seattle
Sydney
Tokyo
Toronto

Tyabji described VeriFone's corporate model as a decentralized network of locations. He liked to refer to this as the "blueberry pancake" where "all berries are the same size, all locations are created equal." One of Tyabji's least favorite terms was *corporate headquarters*. Indeed, many corporate functions, such as Human Resource Management and Management Information Systems, were run decentrally out of multiple global locations, including Dallas (Texas), Bangalore (India), Taipei (Taiwan), and Honolulu (Hawaii), rather than out of Redwood City (California), the nominal corporate headquarters for the company.

Because of its geographic dispersion and heavy reliance on information technology to enable coordination and communications, VeriFone was frequently described as a "virtual company." For example, in 1994, an *InformationWeek* article noted, "VeriFone, the world's largest supplier of credit card verification equipment does have a base in Redwood City, California—if only to comply with Securities and Exchange Commission requirements. According to Tyabji, however, the workplace is where the employee is."[5] The article continued,

> The anywhere/anytime culture works only because VeriFone's 34 locations in nine countries are hooked to the company's Digital VAXmail systems over private leased lines. Employees also exchange mail and documents over the Internet. Nearly all of VeriFone's employees are equipped with a laptop. New employees get a laptop before they get a desk. There are no executive secretaries. Paper memos are verboten.

Although electronic communication and email were used extensively, VeriFone executives acknowledged the importance of face

---

[5]Clinton Wilder, "Who Needs an Office," *InformationWeek,* June 6, 1994, pp. 60–62.

to face communication. Roughly a third of the staff traveled more than half of the time. Tyabji himself logged over 500,000 miles per year as he visited VeriFone locations and customers. Also, once every six weeks, Tyabji's direct reports (see Exhibit 6) met for five days at a different location around the globe. These meetings allowed this dispersed group of executives to address important issues face to face. It also allowed them to meet and work with employees at the various VeriFone locations. Further, each VeriFone location had video-conferencing capability, which was used extensively.

In 1997, there were three geographically based sales organizations. In the United States, VeriFone marketed its secure payment systems products directly to major multi-lane retailers, petroleum companies, convenience stores, banks and transaction processors, and indirectly to retail merchants, healthcare providers and government agencies through a variety of distribution channels—including financial institutions, processors, value-added resellers and systems integrators (Exhibit 7). In Africa, Asia, Canada, Europe, Latin America, and the Middle East, VeriFone systems solutions were sold directly to merchant service providers and through a network of distributors called VeriFone International Partners. VeriFone client/server and network management software products, as well as its systems integration services for the Internet, were marketed directly to financial institutions, processors, and retail establishments.

In recognition of the increasing importance of software and services, the company added two new business groups. The Centum Consulting Group was formed in 1996 to provide advisory services to customers on

EXHIBIT 6   VeriFone Corporate Organization

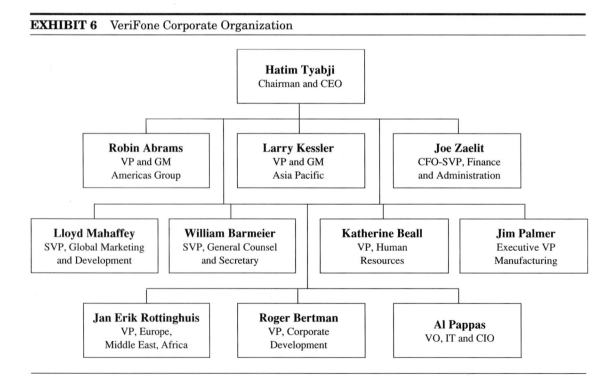

electronic payment strategies and alternatives. Additionally, the Professional Services group helped design, build, support and manage electronic payment solutions for VeriFone's customers.

VeriFone Culture[6]

Many of the core values that characterized VeriFone's culture in 1997 (commitment to excellence, dedication to customer needs,

―――

[6]Selected paragraphs in this section were excerpted from Galal et al., 1994, p. 7.

promotion of teamwork, recognition of the individual, a global mindset, and ethical conduct) were instilled by Melton and the other founders. Soon after Tyabji assumed the leadership of the company in 1986, he took deliberate steps to inculcate these values, so that they would remain at the heart of the company's internal and external activities. He personally wrote a corporate philosophy manual and tirelessly evangelized about it to his employees. He pushed management to develop other novel approaches for communicating the corporate values and providing guidance to the far-flung work force.

EXHIBIT 7   Distribution Channels

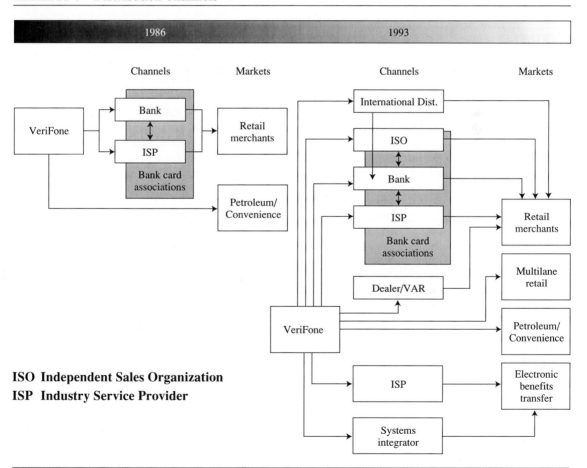

ISO Independent Sales Organization
ISP Industry Service Provider

One result was a constant stream of communiqués to all "VeriFoners" via the company's email system. Another was a series of notes and anecdotes that were collected and shared as "Excellence in Thought" and "Excellence in Action" (see Exhibit 8). By 1997, employees could also access VeriFone Virtual University (VVU) using a web browser. VVU provided up-to-date product and market information, VeriFone policies and procedures information, and training on a host of topics.

Since its founding in 1981, VeriFone management recognized individualism as a source of creativity. This tradition was formalized in 1987 with the publication of the philosophy document, which explicitly stated, "The people who know best how the job should be done are the ones doing it. We involve employees directly in the management of their own areas of responsibility." When describing what is was like to work at VeriFone, employees typically made comments that provided evidence that the company was really committed to this ideal. For example, when asked what was special about VeriFone, one employee noted, "the people, its culture of urgency and the autonomy to do your own thing." When asked why they joined VeriFone, the typical executive answered, "Hatim, and the opportunity to make a difference." Lloyd Mahaffey, senior

---

EXHIBIT 8   Sample of "Excellence in Thought" Note Sent to Staff

---

1-MAR-1989	08:35:43.66
From:	HATIM_T
To:	1_STAFF
Subject:	Innovation

Two of the basic tenets of our company are "We do not merely compete, we set new industry ground rules" and "We constantly challenge traditional methods of conducting business." In a word, if we are to be true to our credo, we must constantly innovate in all disciplines.

Another major characteristic of our company is we listen and act on ideas, as appropriate, wherever they emanate from. I feel very strongly that we must create an environment where our people are motivated to bring forth fresh exciting initiatives, so that we can evaluate them and do what is right for the overall company.

In that context, I am attaching (below) an e-mail from Dick Cowan, which I have read and reflected on many times. Let us take Dick's statement to heart, and most importantly, put them into practice. Intelligent execution of the principles Dick puts forth will make us a much stronger company.

Hatim

10-APR-1988	08:42
From:	HATIM_T
To:	1_EXEC
Subject:	Innovation

All: Thought you would find Dick Cowan's ideas refreshing and helpful, as each of you embark on making this important initiative a reality in your respective groups. Hatim.

4-APR-1988	18:11
From:	JIM_P
To:	HATIM_T, JIM_P
Subject:	Innovation . . . Thought You'd

Find Dick's Ideas Fresh and Instructive

4-APR-1988	14:46
From:	RICHARD_C
To:	JIM_P, LANCE_N, MIKE_C, KHAN_M, DOUG_E, DAVID_CO, RICHARD_C
Subject:	Innovation Management Mindset

My Action Item:

"Develop a management mindset and management techniques for fostering innovation at the individual and department levels."

After looking at all the books on innovation I realized that nowhere is there to be found a

EXHIBIT 8   Sample of "Excellence in Thought" Note Sent to Staff *(Concluded)*

simple set of techniques that management should follow to produce innovation. We should be very happy about this for were such a set available our competition could immediately kill us! A technique that worked in one situation may be a disaster in another.

What I would like to come up with is an ever-changing set of techniques which we become aware of and follow. The techniques themselves are always changing as what works today may not apply tomorrow. Innovative techniques are themselves an S curve! With regard to product, we should always perceive ourselves to be at the top of an existing curve; hence the immediate need.

This will be an ongoing activity and I would greatly appreciate feedback from any of you so that I can groom our list of techniques.

Here is a list of what most of the people smart about innovation offer:

1. Challenge assumptions.
2. Understand the fundamental limits of your products.
3. Never pass judgment on an idea as to its being right or wrong without really under standing it and its origin.
4. Have "outsiders" investigate existing camps. We tend to polarize job assignments. Ex: Joe has been working on interpreters for year. The problem here is that Joe will continue to do things as he knows how for years to come using techniques of years gone by. Stir the pot when possible!
5. Understand the competition. Look at their products, not just their success stories but their failures. Often in their failures may be a potential opportunity which they perceived but moved in the wrong direction.
6. Recognize that during a period of transition, as we move between S curves, there will be a period of discontinuity or "chaos." We need to learn to be effective managers during this time of hard sailing.

7. Have frequent visits with the ultimate users of our products. This cuts through the many layers of interface and puts the person who can make a change happen in immediate contact with those requesting that a change take place. Don't kid yourself for a moment that you know what the customer really wants.
8. Look at existing products if currently existing limits vanished. For example, what if the time for a host computer to authorize a transaction went to zero? What would that do to the user's view of our product? Would our product be more or less attractive? Would we then do things differently?
9. Simplify. If you have a hard time understanding or using something, the customer will only have a harder time. For example, and this is not meant against any of our platforms, but have you ever watched the number of keystrokes required to pull a download? Could this not be done using a special card swipe?
10. Make bureaucracy-busting a habit throughout your organization.
11. Look for differences in what your department is doing and what the company says it's doing.
12. Investigate interfaces. Interfaces are weak areas and weak areas cause problems. Studying interfaces often produces the insight we need to be innovative.
13. Foster competition for different solutions to problems. Reward the best. Make certain that the worst solution is rejected by its author as a true endorsement of the best solution. Understand all proposals because even if they appear to miss the target, they may offer something which can further improve the best.

vice president and general manager, Global Marketing and Software Systems Division who had been with the company for 18 months noted, "VeriFone is the biggest start-up that I have ever seen. There are pockets of innovation everywhere."

A senior executive noted, "The VeriFone environment can be best described as entrepreneurial. Executives who succeed here are typically those who are driven to succeed and who derive self-esteem from their work. We have a workaholic culture." Another manager continued, "Managers at VeriFone are not told what to do. They are held accountable for their actions/performance but this is an environment where people are rewarded for taking risks and trying new things."

This corporate culture both respected and transcended the national boundaries its work activities crossed. The corporate philosophy manual was translated into a number of languages, including English, Chinese, French, German, Japanese, Portuguese, and Spanish. When VeriFoners signed on to their email system, a list of holidays and the local times at VeriFone's various locations around the world automatically appeared on the screen. When corporate programs were being rolled out around the world, corporate managers traveled to the various facilities to get local reaction and to offer advice on how to tailor the programs to local needs, interests and constraints.

A manager, located at a VeriFone location a few thousand miles from Redwood City considered the cultural issue as he prepared to interview a prospective candidate. He noted,

> During an interview, we emphasize certain aspects of the VeriFone culture: the sense of urgency, the open communication, the empowerment. Empowerment is real. I am not driving my staff. They have objectives that they create and submit to me. It's not easy to work here. You are left alone to create your own way of adding value to the corporation. But you have to

produce. This is different from the way other companies in this area work, many of which are more structured and hierarchical, and do not allow creativity to be given much of a chance.

VeriFone's cultural zeal to identify and meet customer needs was reflected and created in numerous ways. Executives were constantly asking two questions, "where is the customer's pain?" and "can VeriFone make money by alleviating this pain?" Facilities were placed near emerging markets and even technical employees were urged to travel to become well acquainted with clients, examples of the practice the company called "forward deployment." The driving principles in product design at VeriFone were low cost, high value, high reliability, and high volume.

When combined with VeriFone's IT capability, this culture of customer responsiveness often had amazing outcomes. For example, when a new sales rep in Greece was told by a large customer that a competitor had raised concerns about VeriFone's expertise in debit cards, he sent out to the whole company an email request for information on debit installations and any references that could help him make the sale. Within 24 hours, he had 16 responses and 10 references, including the names and phone numbers of established customers with debit card installations. The next day, able to say that VeriFone had 400,000 installations worldwide, the rep closed a very big deal with the Greek bank.

Another notable feature of VeriFone's day-to-day functioning was the speed of action and decision making. Experimentation was encouraged at every level of the organization. As Tyabji maintained:

> We can try 10 different approaches to solving a problem. We may fail at eight of them, but we will still have succeeded at two of them. We don't know if something will work ... we can analyze it to death and go into paralysis or we can try it out in a controlled fashion.

The 1995 decision to acquire Internet capability by buying a small Internet consulting company exemplified this propensity to take calculated risks. Within two months, the acquisition was considered and finalized. The decision to be acquired by HP was similarly made within a very short time frame. Likewise, senior personnel were hired without the elaborate assessment that many companies conduct. "I don't read resumes," explained Tyabji when he discussed his hiring of Robin Abrams, Vice President and General Manager, Americas Group. "After several intensive hours together, it was clear that we shared strong mutual respect and commonality of views, and we agreed to work together."

Another executive described a similar approach to hiring, "I interview people intensely, then I make a decision based on my feeling about whether this person will fit our culture. If I make the decision on purely logical data, it takes too long. My intuition is a lot more reliable."

VeriFone, despite Tyabji's commitment to creating a self-sustaining culture, was largely a reflection of the leader himself. Roger Bertman, vice president of Corporate Development noted, "The company, like the man, is intensely operationally focused." Bertman continued,

> In a virtual company, there is a much greater requirement for coordination and leadership than in most companies. Virtuality puts a much greater burden for communication on the CEO and the executive management team. Hatim knows what's going on. You can make mistakes but you have to be committed to the plan.

A long-term employee expressed a similar sentiment. He noted,

> Hatim leads by example. He generally cares about people and spends a lot of time with employees and customers as he travels the globe. He has an incredible memory and seems to be on a first name basis with every employee in the company.

> In a nutshell, Hatim works hard. He is open to new ideas and is willing to take risks. If you have an idea and can justify why it should be implemented, he will support you. However, just as he is accountable to the board of directors, he holds employees accountable for their actions.

In spite of its culture of urgency, VeriFone management wanted the company to be perceived as a "human company." Hence, VeriLife, an umbrella for a number of human resources programs, had been implemented to help employees and their families deal with the demands that VeriFone placed on their lives (see Exhibit 9).

The company introduced a profit sharing plan in 1995 whereby employees received a payout equal to approximately five working days of base salary earnings if the company achieved its target net income after taxes equal to 9% of revenues. That plan was enhanced in 1996 and again in 1997. The incentive plan for executives was different. As one executive described it, "The profit-sharing plan encourages innovation and risk-taking . . . the benefits of succeeding are very great and the penalties for failing are not so great as to discourage you." For executives with significant business unit responsibilities, the VeriFone plan provides bonuses on a steeply ascending sliding scale from 10% up to 100% of salary for exceeding financial objectives for net income and EVA.[7] There were no financial consequences for not meeting objectives, but everyone knew Tyabji noted and remembered such performance disappointments.

---

[7]Economic value added (EVA) principles of financial measurement focused on the efficient management of capital. For example, managers were measured on how well they managed three elements of the balance sheet, namely, accounts receivable, inventory, and fixed assets.

Financial Management and Control

When asked to describe the control process at VeriFone Joseph Zaelit, senior vice president of Finance and Administration noted, "The control process starts with the vision. A shared understanding of where we are going makes it easier to get buy-in for the resource allocations that ultimately have to be made." Zaelit continued,

> For example, we had a planning session in 1994 that involved the top 50 people in the company. We considered internal factors and external factors including our competition, emerging technologies and the market place.

EXHIBIT 9   VeriLife Overview

An essential ingredient in VeriFone's philosophy is that each individual is important. We stand behind that belief by continually introducing opportunities for personal growth. Our VeriLife Programs include initiatives that encourage you to balance work and family needs.*

VeriLife Programs

Employee Assistance Program—a confidential resource and referral service for employees and their families to seek help with a wide range of personal and work-related problems including marital/relationship issues, family/child issues, emotional issues, alcohol/drugs.

VeriGift—a program that enables VeriFoners to assist fellow employees who, because of a catastrophic personal or family situation, are facing time off from work without pay. Through VeriGift, a U.S.-based employee may donate earned, unused vacation hours to help provide additional paid leave to an employee who urgently needs it.

VeriHealth—health fairs that are periodically offered to promote wellness and a higher quality of life.

VeriKid—a cultural exchange program designed to introduce VeriFone families to the lifestyles and customs of other VeriFoners around the world. VeriKid offers employees' children ages 15–18 the chance to experience life in another country for a summer, a semester or an academic year. The program encourages VeriFone families to participate as "host families" for visiting students. To encourage VeriFoners to pursue this incredible opportunity, the Company will help subsidize the cost of participating in VeriKid as an exchange student.

VeriPal—connects children of VeriFone employees through the Company's email system. Children, ages 8–18, are encouraged to exchange messages about their interests and daily activities. Parents can help their children log on to the VAX at home, or they can send and receive the VeriPals' letter through email at the office, after hours.

VeriShare—provides VeriFoners the opportunity to get more involved with their communities and the organizations that need capable, helping hands of people who care. With VeriShare, the Company sponsors up to 80 volunteer hours each year per VeriFone location with 20 or more employees. Volunteers are paid for time spent working on community activities.

*From the *Roads to Total Compensation Guidebook,* a VeriFone Human Resources publication, 1997.

We agreed that the core competency that we wanted to exploit was our understanding of payments. Hence, we narrowed our focus. Whereas we had previously viewed ourselves as "The Transaction Automation Company," we concluded that our niche was payments, and we vowed to dominate the payment-processing niche. At the time we understood payments, but our knowledge of the Internet was sketchy.

In September 1994, we decided that within one year we would be able to demonstrate, with a working prototype, how we would provide secure payments on the Internet. Hatim asked Roger [Bertman] to lead this initiative. We knew we could not make our target without acquiring some Internet talent. Roger established an alliance with EIT.[8] Within six months, the companies decided to merge.

Because financial commitments had been made without this acquisition being planned, funds to make it had to come from other budget items and/or generated through increased revenues. "But having participated in creating the vision, everyone understood its importance and willingly did what was necessary to contribute needed funding," said Zaelit.

The company had what Zaelit characterized as "an MBO[9] environment." The annual planning process began with the senior management team establishing the three-year plan. Financial targets for EVA, revenue, and gross margin were then proposed for, and negotiated with, each business unit. Performance was tracked weekly by operating controllers and shared electronically with the top 250 people in the company.

---

[8]Electronic Information Technology.

[9]MBO stands for "management by objective," a performance management approach which starts with the establishment of performance objectives for the upcoming period, usually in collaboration with the employee. It concludes with the measurement of performance against those objectives.

The EVA measure had only recently been introduced as a measure of executive performance. It included accounts receivable, inventory management and fixed asset measures, and constituted 50% of an executive's bonus. The other 50% was based on revenues and contribution margins.

Zaelit characterized VeriFone's controls in general as "fluid and relevant." Lloyd Mahaffey indicated that business metrics, while very important, were not necessarily the best measures of effectiveness in the market and then went on to describe a set of marketing activities he called "constantly tuning into the market." This tuning was accomplished through email, face-to-face communication with customers, conference calls with field reps, reading on customers, competitors, channels, and technology. His direct reports provided weekly forecasts of revenue, contribution margin, and new business prospects, target dates for closing.

Jim Palmer, executive vice president, Manufacturing and Distribution, characterized his control measures this way, "My organization is expected to meet costs and dates and exceed quality." Palmer continued, "More explicitly, manufacturing is expected to systematically reduce cost of goods sold and development is expected to release products for production when we said we would. Additionally, it is understood that managers and employees at all levels are expected to meet their commitments and improve. When I review the performance of managers in my organization, 20% of the review is focused on how well we are meeting operating goals, and 80% is focused on what we are doing to improve. We must prevent atrophy."

VeriFone's Future

Smart cards and the 1996 Olympics
Smart cards, which are the same size as conventional credit cards, contain an embedded

microprocessor chip, sometimes in addition to the magnetic strip, which appears on most payment cards. The chip holds far more information and is capable of making independent computations needed to increase security and perform application functions, such as calculating the remaining stored value following a purchase. With advanced security levels, smart cards can protect existing credit and debit card systems from fraud. A single card could also offer numerous applications to consumers, integrating debit, credit, stored value and loyalty programs, in addition to health care and government benefits. Some industry experts predicted that, in time, smart card readers would be incorporated into computers and TV set-top boxes to facilitate anonymous electronic transactions.

A recognized core competency of VeriFone was its ability to quickly mobilize forces in support to exploit new opportunities. For example, as of February 1996, VeriFone was not scheduled to participate in the VISA Cash smart card experiment at the 1996 Atlanta Olympics. A sales executive noted, "Hatim said, "Get us into the Olympics!" The executive continued,

> As of February, we did not have announced products that we could show the customer, but we had prototypes in R&D and we committed to have our products ready by May. Initially First Union, one of the banks that had partnered with VISA, was unwilling to let us get involved. But we persevered and they agreed to let us install a few hundred terminals at the Olympics. Our competitors had a number of problems but our technology worked well. The VISA cash pilot continued until December 1996.

Given the success at the Olympics, the senior management team wanted VeriFone to continue to focus on smart cards but acknowledged that most sales managers and reps had their hands full with the traditional product line. They also acknowledged

that there was a lot of expertise that one needed to have to be effective in that ever-changing market. In late 1996, Hatim asked Bob Wilson, a sales vice president, to lead the smart card initiative. Bob agreed but asked for a team and a sales quota. In July 1997, there was a team of five focused on the smart card marketplace. That team had 67 active projects and had closed deals with over a dozen customers.

The Citibank Consumer Banking Pilot
In April 1997, Citibank and VeriFone announced an agreement under which Citibank would implement VeriFone's VeriSmart system and distribute its Personal ATM™ devices that would allow customers to download electronic cash to smart cards securely and conveniently in the privacy of their own home. The pilot, scheduled to take place in late 1997, would involve several thousand customers and merchants in a New York "neighborhood." Selected Citibank customers would receive a VeriFone Personal ATM device, a hand-held smart card reader that would let them connect, via any telephone line, directly to their bank account and download electronic cash onto their stored-value card.

VeriFone's VeriSmart client/server system would provide the direct connection between the Personal ATM device and Citibank's centralized customer computer server. The VeriSmart system would allow consumers to use a range of devices such as the Personal ATM to download "cash" from their bank accounts. The digital money could then be spent at any establishment in the "neighborhood" that had a smart card reader, a device similar to the credit and debit card readers found in most stores and businesses today.

Secure Payments on the Internet
In 1997, VeriFone's Internet Commerce Division offered Internet payment solutions for all of the parties in an Internet transac-

tion, the consumer, merchant, and financial institution. In addition to the hardware products that it offered, such as PIN pads and smart card reader/writers, VeriFone offered a suite of software products. vWallet, a software application marketed to financial institutions and credit card processors, allowed the consumer to store data, such as credit card numbers, in a virtual wallet so there would be no need to re-enter them for each purchase. It also managed the consumer's digital credentials. vGate and vPOS software allowed the use of the MasterCard/VISA Secure Electronic Transaction (SET) protocol between the merchant and the financial institution.[10] vGate, VeriFone's Internet gateway, accepted Internet payments and allowed the processing institution to accept Internet transactions without altering their current host systems. vPOS, merchant software, captured order and payment information and provided capabilities to help the Internet merchant manage the virtual store. Additionally, VeriFone had also established alliances with

a number of technology vendors including Microsoft, Netscape, Oracle, VeriSign, and GTE Cybertrust.[11]

Moving Forward

With the agreement that it would continue to operate autonomously as a wholly-owned subsidiary of HP, VeriFone seemed destined for continued success. Similarly, the strategic alliances with Microsoft, Netscape and the other technology vendors suggested that VeriFone was well positioned. As Tyabji and his senior management looked to the future, they were intent on focusing their attention to ensure that VeriFone maintained its leadership position in the payments marketplace. Organizational and operational issues were in the forefront of their minds. Aligning human resource capabilities within the organization to the company's ambitious new strategy would clearly be one of the most pressing priorities in the immediate future.

---

[10]SET was expected to become the industry standard for handling secure Internet credit card transactions.

[11]See http://www.verifone.com/products/software/icommerce/html/technology.html for details on these alliances.

Case 1-2

A TALE OF TWO AIRLINES IN THE INFORMATION AGE: OR WHY THE SPIRIT OF KING GEORGE III IS ALIVE AND WELL![1]

At 5:30 PM on February 15, 1995, 200 feet off the ground, Professor Roger McPherson gazed anxiously through the fog as his airplane moved to touch down at Hartsfield Airport in Atlanta, more than 1 hour and 15 minutes late. He had 30 minutes to catch his 6:00 PM flight to London, where he would be meeting with the executive leadership of a major British power company on their information strategy issues.

He felt fortunate, however, to be flying this carrier, which had a reputation for outstanding service and was even more comfortable because he had a full-fare first-class ticket and was a Gold Card member. Professor McPherson was always uneasy about the large premium charged for full, first-class tickets, but knew in a crunch that it often meant the difference between a made connection and a missed one. He well remembered a decade ago, flying this airline from Milan to London to connect to a flight to New York. Bad weather then had also reduced his 1-hour and 30-minute connect time to 10 minutes. A discussion of the problem with the first-class cabin attendant had resulted in a phone call from the pilot to London (the airline's hub city), a car to

This case was prepared by Professor F. Warren McFarlan.
[1]Copyright © 1995 by the President and Fellows of Harvard College.
Harvard Business School case 195-240.

whisk him and one other passenger to the New York flight which took off only one minute late. That extraordinary service had made Professor McPherson a 10-year devotee of the airline.

In the information age, he knew it would be different and he was secure. The airline flying to London would have identified him off their computer as a close-connecting passenger. It would have noted he checked no bags through, and they would be anxious to capture his $2,500 fare, about 10 times that of the average passenger, on an only moderately loaded flight.

As his plane pulled into the gate at 5:40 PM, he knew it would be tight but probably doable, particularly given the fact that all planes were coming in late. Moving his 57-year-old frame into a dim recollection of a high school 400-meter specialist, he set off. Two escalator rides and one train ride later, the gate hove into sight and he braked to a halt at 5:53 PM. It was close but he had done it.

Looking through the airport window, however, he was stunned to see the air bridge detached from the plane with splendid teutonic efficiency 7 minutes early. The door to the bridge was closed, no agent in sight, and he was reduced to waving his bags through the window to the pilot, 20 yards away (it had, after all, worked once in a similar situation on Continental Airlines).

Alas, by 5:58 PM the plane was pushed back, the agents emerged and quite cheerfully (and unregretfully; they had no clue who he was) endorsed him onto another airline that would leave 1 hour and 45 minutes later. He would be 30 minutes late for his meeting in London, but that was doable. Distinctly irritated as he straggled off to the new airline's (Atlanta-based) first class lounge to begin a frantic series of phone calls and faxes to the United Kingdom, McPherson began to see the beginning of a lecture on service in the information economy and that technology is only a small enabling piece of a total service concept.

At 7:50 PM, comfortably seated in the first-class cabin of his new carrier, McPherson jerked to attention as the captain came on to announce that because of a leak in the hydraulic system, there would be an aircraft change and a 2½-hour delay. Sprinting off the plane, McPherson realized that the 3-month planned meeting with the power company executives would be over before he got there. The following day he was due in Frankfurt to give the keynote address at a major information systems conference. Flying to the United Kingdom to connect to Frankfurt would be a hassle and tiring since the purpose of stopping in the United Kingdom was now totally negated. Glancing up on the departure board, McPherson was surprised to see his new airline flashing a 7:55 PM boarding departure for a plane to Frankfurt, nine gates away. Pulling into the gate at 8:02 PM, he discovered several things:

1. The plane was at the gate and with commendable dispatch, the gate agent relieved him of his London boarding pass and his London-to-Frankfurt ticket and hustled him onto the plane minutes before the door closed.
2. The cabin attendant, giving him his favorite drink, explained that because of favorable tail winds across the Atlantic and the fact that eight passengers (plus now McPherson and one other) had very tight connections, they had decided to hold the plane for 15 minutes to get the extra passengers and still arrive on schedule. The note of pride in the cabin attendant's voice was evident.

Approximately one-and-a-half hours later, wined and dined, McPherson drifted off to sleep, reflecting on what a remarkable case study in administration had played out in front of him in the previous two hours. Information technology, operations strategy, management control, an empowered (also unempowered) work force and service management had all interwoven themselves into a tableau. A revised format for his speech in Frankfurt began to emerge. Best of all, he would not have to go through a case release process because it had all happened to him.

Information Technology and Strategy

The shifting base of competitive advantage is a natural byproduct of the shift from the industrial economy, where effective deployment of capital was the key to success, to the information economy, where information is the key. Yet few executives have shifted their thinking to focus directly on the information they must dominate to compete in the 21st century.

McGee and Prusac, 1993[1]

The coevolution of technology, work, and the workforce over the past 30 years has dramatically influenced our concept of organizations and the industries within which they compete. No longer simply a tool to support "back-office" transactions, IT has become a strategic part of most businesses, enabling the redefinition of markets and industries and the strategies and designs of firms competing within them. As functionality and performance have rapidly improved, the "IT bar" has been reset at ever higher levels. But while all firms use IT, many managers have grown increasingly frustrated by their inability to fully exploit the business value of their IT investments and assets.

Module 2 examines the impact of IT on industries, markets, and the strategies of the firms that compete within them. Chapter 3, "Effects of IT on Strategy and Competition," provides frameworks for assessing the impact of IT on strategy. Chapter 4, "Electronic Commerce: Trends and Opportunities," examines the evolution of electronic commerce from the pioneering efforts of American Airlines and American Hospital Supply to the actions of today's Internet pioneers. The module ends with three cases— Canadian Airlines, H.E. Butt Grocery, and Internet Securities—that examine how general managers are using IT to change the basis of competition in their industries and create value for all constituents.

---

[1]J. McGee and L. Prusac, *Managing Information Strategically* (NY: John Wiley and Sons, 1993).

Effects of IT on Strategy and Competition

To solve customer service problems, a major distributor developed an on-line order processing system and made it available for direct access by its key customers. The system was intended to cut order/entry costs, to speed processing time, and to provide more flexibility to customers. Although, initially, the company's expectations were modest, the system gave them significant competitive advantage; customer satisfaction increased, and the distributor also noted that revenues increased and market share improved. These benefits continued as long as the company continued to innovate. But five years later, in an attempt to control internal costs, the firm turned away from its commitment to customer service. Despite improved operating efficiency, profits and market share rapidly declined.

Elsewhere, a regional airline testifying before Congress claimed that the automated reservation system of a national carrier was "anticompetitive" and was forcing small airlines out of business. By locking in the travel agents to a common electronic distribution channel, the large firm was "locking out" competition. In addition, by providing access to information on the price of all flights on all carriers, the system allowed the large airline to systematically underprice the smaller firm. The airline ultimately went bankrupt.

Finally, a large aerospace company required major suppliers to acquire compatible computer-aided design (CAD) equipment to link directly to its design workstation or face being dropped as a supplier. The aerospace firm claimed that access to these direct computer-to-computer links dramatically reduced the total cost of, and time for, design changes and parts acquisition, while simultaneously improving quality. In addition, these on-line linkages enabled the firm to significantly reduce inventory levels, which further enhanced process efficiency; without these improvements in cost, quality, and cycle time, the aerospace firm would not have been able to respond to the demands of its customers.

These examples capture the changing nature of the role of information technology (IT) within organizations and industries. Dramatic improvements in the price/performance of IT over the past three decades, when coupled with the increased penetration of IT within the firm and the learning that accompanies experimentation and use, have allowed computer systems to move out of the back office and to create significant competitive advantage. Particularly important are systems that electronically link customers and suppliers. For many firms the evolution of IT-enabled strategy and organization design has been extraordinarily expensive and has extended over a number of years. Airline reservations systems, for example, evolved over 30 years and continue to evolve.[1]

Although such IT initiatives offer an opportunity for a competitive advantage, they also increase strategic vulnerability. In the case of the aerospace manufacturer, competitive position improved dramatically, but at the cost of independence. Once electronic linkages were in place and processes were redesigned to tightly integrate across organizational boundaries, it was much harder to change suppliers.

In some cases IT supported new business strategies that, if successfully executed, produced dramatic gains in market share. But, like any strategy, those gains were fleeting. As was the case for the distributor discussed at the beginning of the chapter, failure to continue to innovate resulted in loss of advantage. Opportunities for IT-enabled competitive advantage vary widely from one company to another, just as the intensity and the rules of competition vary widely from one industry to another. Similarly, a company's location, size, and basic product technology shape potential IT applications. These opportunities are not restricted to the large firms; they affect even the smallest companies as well as creating opportunities for new entrepreneurial ventures. In different situations, a company may appropriately attempt to be either a leader or an alert follower.

A strategic advantage for a first mover can become a strategic necessity for other firms in the industry as the rules of competition shift. Over the past decade, the stakes have become so high in many firms that attention to IT strategy has become a major responsibility of senior management.

The complexity of the IT management challenge increases considerably when IT penetrates to the heart of a firm's (or industry's) strategy. To facilitate planning, general managers need a comprehensive framework that

---

[1]James L. McKenney, *Waves of Change: Business Evolution through Information Technology* (Cambridge, MA: Harvard Business School Press, January 1995), pp. 16–38.

FIGURE 3–1 Impact of Competitive Forces

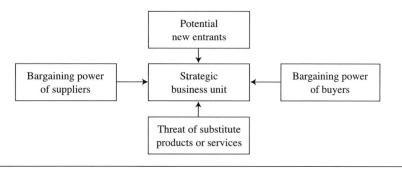

views the use of IT from a strategic rather than a tactical perspective. Michael Porter's industry and competitive analysis (ICA) framework has proven very effective in this respect.[2]

FORCES THAT SHAPE STRATEGY

Porter's work, directed at both strategic business planners and general managers, argues that many of the contemporary strategic planning frameworks view competition too narrowly and pessimistically because they were primarily based on projections of market share and market growth. He explains that the economic and competitive forces in an industry segment are the result of five basic forces: (1) bargaining power of suppliers, (2) bargaining power of buyers, (3) threat of new entrants into the industry segment, (4) threat of substitute products or services, and (5) positioning of traditional intraindustry rivals. Figure 3–1 presents these five competitive forces, and Figure 3–2 provides a detailed description of the factors that determine the relative strength of each force.

Although Porter's initial work did not include IT as a component of the framework, it has proven extremely useful in this regard. Table 3–1 describes the impact of IT on the five competitive forces.

Column 1 lists the key competitive forces that shape competition in a given industry segment. In a specific industry, not all forces are of equal importance. Some industries are dominated by suppliers (for example, OPEC in the petroleum industry in the 1970s), while other industries are preoccupied with the threat of new entrants and/or substitute products (such as the banking and insurance industries).

---

[2]Michael E. Porter, *Competitive Strategy: Techniques for Analyzing Industries and Competitors* (NY: The Free Press, 1980).

FIGURE 3–2   Elements of Industry Structure

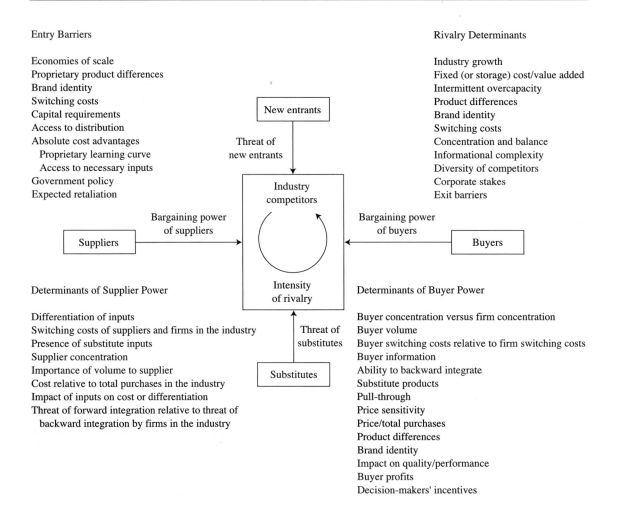

Entry Barriers

Economies of scale
Proprietary product differences
Brand identity
Switching costs
Capital requirements
Access to distribution
Absolute cost advantages
   Proprietary learning curve
   Access to necessary inputs
Government policy
Expected retaliation

Rivalry Determinants

Industry growth
Fixed (or storage) cost/value added
Intermittent overcapacity
Product differences
Brand identity
Switching costs
Concentration and balance
Informational complexity
Diversity of competitors
Corporate stakes
Exit barriers

Threat of
new entrants

New entrants

Industry
competitors

Bargaining power
of suppliers

Suppliers

Bargaining power
of buyers

Buyers

Intensity
of rivalry

Threat of
substitutes

Substitutes

Determinants of Supplier Power

Differentiation of inputs
Switching costs of suppliers and firms in the industry
Presence of substitute inputs
Supplier concentration
Importance of volume to supplier
Cost relative to total purchases in the industry
Impact of inputs on cost or differentiation
Threat of forward integration relative to threat of
   backward integration by firms in the industry

Determinants of Buyer Power

Buyer concentration versus firm concentration
Buyer volume
Buyer switching costs relative to firm switching costs
Buyer information
Ability to backward integrate
Substitute products
Pull-through
Price sensitivity
Price/total purchases
Product differences
Brand identity
Impact on quality/performance
Buyer profits
Decision-makers' incentives

Column 2 of Table 3–1 lists key implications of each competitive force. For example, when new entrants move into an established industry segment, they generally introduce significant additional capacity because they frequently have allocated substantial resources to gain a foothold in the industry. Typically, new entrants cause a reduction in prices or an increase in costs.

Column 3 lists some examples of how IT can be used to change the balance of power among these five forces. For example, IT can raise barriers to entry by increasing economies of scale, increasing switching costs,

TABLE 3–1   Impact of Competitive Forces

Force	*Implication*	*Potential Uses of IT to Combat Force*
Threat of new entrants	New capacity Substantial resources Reduced prices or inflation of incumbents' costs	Provide entry barriers Economies of scale Switching costs Product differentiation Access to distribution channels
Buyers' bargaining power	Prices forced down High quality More services Competition encouraged	Buyer selection Switching costs Differentiation Entry barriers
Suppliers' bargaining power	Prices raised Reduced quality and services (labor)	Selection Threat of backward integration

Traditional intraindustry rivals	Competition
	  Price
	  Product
	  Distribution and service
		Cost-effectiveness
		Market access
		Differentiation
		  Product
		  Services
		  Firm

differentiating a product or service, or limiting access to key markets or distribution channels.

Porter describes three *generic strategies* for achieving proprietary advantage within an industry: cost leadership, differentiation, and focus (see Figure 3–3). The latter strategy—focus—has two variants: cost and differentiation.

Each generic strategy involves two key choices: (1) the competitive mechanism—a firm can lower its cost or differentiate its products and services; and (2) the competitive scope—a firm can target a broad market or a narrow one. Cost leadership and differentiation strategies are targeted toward a broad market, while focused strategies seek to lower costs (cost focus) or differentiate products and services (differentiation focus) in a narrow industry segment. The specific actions required to implement each generic strategy vary widely from industry to industry, as do feasible generic strategies in a particular industry. Selecting and implementing the appropriate generic strategy are thought to be central to achieving long-term competitive advantage in an industry.

At the core of the concept of generic strategies are two basic principles. First, competitive advantage is believed to be the goal of any strategy. Second, it is believed that a firm must define the type of competitive advantage

---

FIGURE 3–3   Three Generic Strategies Related to Competitive Advantage and Scope

Competitive Advantage

	Lower Cost	*Differentiation*
Broad Target	Cost leadership	Differentiation
Narrow Target	Cost focus	Differentiation focus

Competitive Scope

---

it seeks to attain and the scope within which it will be attained. Porter believes that the decision to be "all things to all people" is a recipe for strategic mediocrity and below-average performance. More recently, attention has shifted from a focus on the specific strategy of a firm to a focus on core competencies.[3] This shifts the focus of attention from a specific strategy to the underlying organizational competencies that will enable (or prevent) a firm from reaching that strategy. Chapter 6 addresses this important issue in greater depth.

SEARCH FOR OPPORTUNITY

Five key questions can be used to guide an assessment of the impact of IT on strategy.

Can IT Build Barriers to Entry?

A successful entry barrier offers not only a new product or service that appeals to customers but also features that keep the customers "hooked." The harder the service is to emulate, the higher the barrier to entry. A large financial service firm sought to build an effective barrier to entry when it

---

[3]G. Hamel and C.K. Prahalad, "Strategic Intent," *Harvard Business Review,* May–June, 1989.

launched a unique and highly attractive financial product that depended on sophisticated software that was both costly and difficult to implement. The complexity of the IT-enabled product caught competitors off guard; it took several years for them to develop a similar product, which gave the initiating firm valuable time to establish a significant market position. During this time, the firm continued to innovate, enhancing the original product and adding value to the services. Competitors not only had to catch up, but had to catch a moving target.

The payoff from value-added features that increase both sales and market share is particularly strong in industries within which there are great economies of scale and where customers are extremely price sensitive. By being the first to move onto the learning curve, a company can gain a cost advantage that enables it to put great pressure on its competitors.

Systems that increase the effectiveness of the sales force represent another kind of entry barrier—a knowledge barrier. For example, several large insurance companies have implemented sophisticated, customer-oriented financial-planning support packages that have greatly expanded the ability of their agents to deal with the rapidly changing and increasingly complex knowledge requirements within the industry. By increasing the capabilities of the sales force (a key strategic resource of the firm), these insurance companies have created significant barriers to entry that are exceedingly difficult to emulate. With the advent of the Internet in the late 1990s, many companies are finding that knowledge barriers are among the most potent of competitive forces.

Can IT Build in Switching Costs?

Are there ways to encourage reliance on IT-enabled products and services? Can industry participants be encouraged to embed these products and services into their operations in such a manner that the notion of switching to a competitor is extremely unattractive? Ideally, an IT system should be simple for the customer to adopt at the outset, but then, through a series of increasingly complex—yet very valuable—enhancements, the IT system becomes tightly intertwined with the customer's daily routine. Proponents of electronic home banking hope to capitalize on the potential of increasing switching costs. Indeed, in France, a $3 billion "virtual" bank exists that has no branches; customers, who have tightly integrated their financial records into the bank's IT systems, conduct all transactions electronically.[4]

A manufacturer of heavy machines provides another example of how IT can add value to and support a company's basic product line while also

---

[4]Tawfik Jelassi, *European Casebook on Competing through Information Technology* (Englewood Cliffs, NJ: Prentice Hall, 1994).

increasing switching costs. The firm embedded into its product software that enables remote monitoring and, in some cases, correction of problems. In case of mechanical failure, the diagnostic device calls a computer at corporate headquarters, where software analyzes and, if possible, solves the problem. If the problem cannot be solved remotely, the computer pages a mechanic and provides a complete record of the current problem and the maintenance history of the product. Availability of parts required to fix the problem is also noted, and technical documentation is provided. Now installed around the globe, the system has dramatically improved service quality and response time, significantly enhanced customer loyalty, and decreased the tendency of customers to buy service contracts elsewhere.

The joint marketing program of MCI, Citibank, and American Airlines, through which customers can earn American Airlines frequent flyer miles whenever they use the telephone or their credit cards, is another example of how IT can support value-added services that enhance customer loyalty and increase switching costs.

Can IT Change the Basis of Competition?

In some industries IT has enabled a firm to fundamentally alter the basis of competition within the industry. This occurs when a firm uses IT to radically change either its cost structure (cost advantage) or its product/service offerings (differentiation advantage).

For example, in the mid-1970s, a major distributor of magazines, a very cost-competitive industry segment, used IT to significantly lower its cost structure by developing cheaper methods of sorting and distributing magazines. By radically reducing both headcount and inventory, it was able to become the low-cost producer in the industry. Because buyers were extremely price sensitive, the distributor was able to quickly increase market share, but it didn't stop there. Having attained significant cost advantage, the distributor then differentiated its products and services. Recognizing that its customers were small, unsophisticated, and unaware of their profit structures, the distributor used its internal records of weekly shipments and returns to create a new value-added product—a customized report that calculated profit per square foot for every magazine sold and then compared these data with aggregate information from comparable customers operating in similar neighborhoods. The distributor could thus tell each customer how it could improve its product mix. In addition to distributing magazines, the company used IT and the information it generated to offer a valuable inventory-management service. In this example, the distributor initially used IT to change its competitive position within an industry; it then used IT to fundamentally change the basis of competition.

Dramatic cost reduction can significantly alter the old ground rules of competition, enabling companies to find strategic opportunity in the new cost-competitive environment. For example, there may be an opportunity for sharp cost reduction through staff reduction or the ability to grow without hiring staff, improved material use, increased machine efficiency through better scheduling or more cost-effective maintenance, or inventory reduction. In the drug wholesale industry, for example, from 1971 to 1996, the average operating cost/sales ratio of the major players dropped from 16 percent to 2 percent mostly through the use of IT, and a fragmented industry of 1,000 firms was consolidated to approximately 100, with the top five players controlling 80 percent of the market.

Understanding when to take advantage of these competitive opportunities can be particularly difficult and troublesome. For example, in 1998, few people doubt that home banking is becoming important to financial services. The importance was less clear in the mid-1980s, when pioneering banks launched home banking services that failed miserably. The situation confronting libraries is another excellent example of the uncertain nature of competitive decisions. Drawing on over 1,000 years of tradition in storing books made of parchment and paper, today's libraries are at a crossroads. Soaring materials costs, expansion of computer databases, networking, the Internet, and electronic links between libraries have made the research facility of 1998 utterly unrecognizable from that of 1990. In many cases, the period of transition is relatively short, the investments high, and the discontinuity with the past dramatic.

As managers consider opportunities to use IT to radically alter the basis of competition, it is often difficult, especially in the early stages, to distinguish the intriguing (but ephemeral) from the pathbreaking innovations. The consequences of action (or inaction) can be devastating if managers misread the cues.

Can IT Change the Balance of Power in Supplier Relationships?

The development of IT systems that link manufacturers and suppliers has been a powerful role for IT within the firm. For example, just-in-time inventory systems have dramatically reduced inventory costs and warehouse expenses, while also improving order fulfillment time. Traditionally, companies have used inventory to buffer uncertainty in their production processes. Large safety stocks of raw materials and supplies are kept on hand to allow operations to run smoothly. But inventory costs money; it ties up capital, it requires costly physical facilities for storage, and it must be managed by people. Increasingly, companies are using IT to link suppliers and manufacturers; by improving information flow, they are able to decrease uncertainty, and, in the process, reduce inventory, cut the number of warehouses, and decrease headcount while also streamlining the production process. In some cases, they have been able to pass inventory responsibility and its associated responsibilities from one player in an industry value chain to another.

A large retailer capitalized on these advantages by electronically linking its materials-ordering system to its suppliers' order-fulfillment systems.

Now, when 100 sofas are needed for a particular region, the retailer's computer automatically checks the inventory status of its primary sofa suppliers; the one with the fastest availability and lowest cost gets the order.

Equally important, the retailer's computer continually monitors its suppliers' finished-goods inventories, factory scheduling, and commitments against its schedule to make sure enough inventory will be available to meet unexpected demand. If a supplier's inventories are inadequate, the retailer alerts the supplier; if a supplier is unwilling to go along with this system, it may find its share of business dropping until it is replaced by others. As a purely defensive investment, a major textile manufacturer recently undertook an $8 million IT project to build a new order-entry-and-fulfillment system; failure to do so would have meant the loss of its top three customers.

A major manufacturer proposed CAD-to-CAD links with a $100-million-a-year-in-sales pressed-powder metal parts manufacturer. Within 18 months, this system shortened the product design cycle from eight months to three.

Such interorganizational systems can redistribute power between buyer and supplier. In the case of the aerospace manufacturer identified at the beginning of the chapter, the CAD to CAD systems increased dependence on an individual supplier, making it hard for the company to replace the supplier and leaving it vulnerable to major price increases. The retailer, on the other hand, was in a much stronger position to dictate the terms of its relationship with its suppliers.

Can IT Generate New Products?

As described earlier, IT can lead to products with higher quality, faster delivery, or less cost. Similarly, at little extra expense, existing products can be tailored to meet a customer's special needs. Some companies may be able to combine one or more of these advantages. In addition, at little additional cost, as in the case of the on-line diagnostic system for machine failure described earlier, electronic support services can increase the value of the total package in the consumer's eyes.

Indeed, mergers are currently being planned around those capabilities. For example, a catalog company and a credit card company recently examined the possibility of combining their customer data files to facilitate cross-marketing and offer a new set of services.

In another example, credit card companies have become voracious consumers of delinquent accounts receivable data from other firms; indeed, there is a whole industry dedicated to the collection and organization of these data. Similarly, nonproprietary research data files often have significant value to third parties.

In some cases, a whole new industry has emerged. For example, a number of market research firms now purchase data from large supermarket chains, analyze it, and then sell it back to the supermarkets in scrubbed and easily analyzable form. The market research firm organizes these data by ZIP code into a research tool for retail chains, food suppliers, and others interested in consumer activity.

Finally, the information content of products has increased markedly. For example, today's upscale cars have more than 100 microcomputers in them controlling everything from braking to temperature. Sewing machines use microcomputers to control everything from stitching pattern to complex thread shifts. Fighter aircraft and submarines have highly sophisticated automated control systems.

ANALYZING THE VALUE CHAIN FOR IT OPPORTUNITIES

An effective way to search for potential IT opportunities is through a systematic analysis of a company's value chain—the series of interdependent activities that bring a product or service to the customer. Figure 3–4 shows a typical value chain[5] and briefly defines the meaning of each component. In different settings, IT can profoundly affect one or more of these value activities, sometimes simply by improving effectiveness, sometimes by fundamentally changing the activity, and sometimes by altering the relationship between activities. In addition, the actions of one firm can significantly affect the value chain of key customers and suppliers.

Inbound Logistics

As illustrated earlier, in many settings IT has expedited procurement of materials. One major distribution company, for example, installed hundreds of personal computers on supplier premises to enable just-in-time, on-line ordering. The company required its suppliers to maintain adequate inventory and provide on-line access to stock levels so that they can appropriately plan orders. This system decreased the need for extensive warehousing of incoming materials and reduced disruptions due to inventory shortfalls. The need to maintain inventory safety stocks and the associated holding costs were reduced for both the supplier and the buyer.

A retail chain's direct linkage to its major textile suppliers not only improved delivery and enabled inventory reduction but also provided the flexibility to meet changing demand almost immediately. This, in turn, offset the impact of the lower price offered by foreign suppliers, thus enabling U.S. textile manufacturers to gain share in this cost-sensitive, highly competitive, fast-response environment.

---

[5]Michael E. Porter, *Competitive Strategy* (NY: Free Press, 1980).

FIGURE 3–4   The Value Chain

Support activities	Corporate infrastructure						
	Human resource management						
	Technology development						
	Procurement						
		Inbound logistics	Operations	Outbound logistics	Marketing and sales	Service	
		Primary activities					Margin

Activity	Definition
Inbound logistics	Materials receiving, storing, and distribution to manufacturing premises.
Operations	Transforming inputs into finished products.
Outbound logistics	Storing and distributing products.
Marketing and sales	Promotion and sales force.
Service	Service to maintain or enhance product value.
Corporate infrastructure	Support of entire value chain, such as general management, planning, finance, accounting, legal services, government affairs, and quality management.
Human resource management	Recruiting, hiring, training, and development.
Technology development	Improving product and manufacturing process.
Procurement	Purchasing input.

Source: Michael E. Porter and Victor E. Millar, "How Information Gives You Competitive Advantage," *Harvard Business Review,* July–August 1985, p. 151.

Operations and Product Definition

Information systems technologies can also influence a manufacturer's operations and product offerings. In 1989, a manufacturer of thin transparent film completed a $30 million investment in new computer-controlled manufacturing facilities for one of its major product lines. This change slashed order response time from 10 weeks to two days and improved quality levels significantly.

A financial services firm, having decided to go after more small private investors (with portfolios of about $25,000), introduced a flexible financial instrument that gave its investors immediate on-line ability to move their funds among stocks and other financial products, provided money market rates on idle funds, and offered the same liquidity as a checking account. The company—the first to introduce this service—captured a huge initial market share, which it has maintained over the years by continued product enhancement. In the first two years, the company achieved six times the volume of its nearest competitor. Five years later it still retained a 70 percent share of the market.

A major insurance company that defined its business as a provider of diversified financial services improved its services to policyholders by allowing immediate on-line access to information on the status of claims and claims processing. The company also provided on-line access to new services and products, including modeling packages that enabled corporate benefits officers to tailor various benefit packages, balancing cost and employee service. In response to client demand, it sold either software for claims processing or claims-processing services. The company credits these IT-enabled product initiatives for its ability to maintain its position at the top of its industry despite tremendous competition from other diversified financial services companies.

Outbound Logistics

IT can also influence the way services and products are delivered to customers. As mentioned earlier, the reservation system, provided chiefly by United Airlines and American Airlines, has profoundly affected smaller airlines that do not furnish this service. Indeed, in December 1984, the Civil Aeronautics Board, believing that the systems strongly influenced purchasing behavior, issued a cease-and-desist order that required that all carriers' flights be fairly represented. Automatic teller machines, as well as theater-ticket and airline-ticket machines, allow cash and services to be rapidly and reliably delivered to customers where they work or shop. In 1998, the Internet has become an important retail channel for all types of physical and information-based products and services.

Marketing and Sales

Marketing and sales, functional areas often neglected in the first three decades of IT, are now areas of high impact. In many firms, the sales force has been supplied with a wide array of personal portable technologies that enable firms to collect detailed customer and market data, and then to package and deliver the data back to the sales force—and directly to customers.

A large pharmaceutical company offered on-line order entry for its products and those of its noncompetitors. This service increased its market share and revenues. The companies excluded from the system threatened legal action because of damage to their market position.

In the industrial air conditioning industry, a major corporation built a microcomputer-based modeling system to help architects (its key customers) model the heating and cooling system requirements for commercial properties. The system, which significantly reduced design time for the architects, led many of them to consider the company's products more favorably. The advantage was short-lived, as a competing corporation subsequently made a similar computer model available via a communication network; in addition, it allowed the architects to access detailed information on cost and part availability.

An agricultural chemicals company developed a sophisticated on-line crop-planning service for its major agricultural customers. From a personal computer, using a standard telephone connection, farmers can access agricultural databases containing prices of various crops, necessary growing conditions, and the costs of various chemicals to support different crops. They can then access various models and decision support systems, tailor them to their unique field requirements, and examine the implications of various crop rotations and timing for planting. The model also helps the farmers to select fertilizer and chemical applications and to group their purchases to achieve maximum discounts. Finally, with a few keystrokes, farmers can place orders for future delivery. Similar services have been offered by a major seed company in coordination with a state agricultural extension service. To strengthen its marketing of agricultural loans, a major bank has offered a similar crop-planning service. This example shows how three companies in different industries are now offering the same software to the end consumer.

Over the past decade, a major food company has assembled a national database that keeps track of daily sales of each of its products in each of the 500,000 stores it services. This database is now totally accessible through a wide-area network to market planners in their 22 regional districts. Combined with market and competitor data from market research companies, this information has significantly increased the precision and sophistication of market planning and execution. Similarly, one of the store chains, using a customer loyalty card and the market data, can precisely identify which customers buy which brands of competing merchandise. This information is of extraordinary importance to suppliers as they focus their coupon efforts.

After-Sales Service

IT is also revolutionizing after-sales service; for example, on its new line of elevators, an elevator company has installed on-line diagnostic devices. These devices identify potential problems before the customer notices a difficulty, thus enabling the service representative to fix the elevator before it breaks down, reducing repair costs and increasing customer satisfaction. "The best elevator is an unnoticed elevator" in the words of their CEO.

A large manufacturer of industrial machinery has installed an expert system on its home-office computer to support product maintenance. When a machine failure occurs on a customer's premises, the machine is connected over a telephone line to the manufacturer's computer, which performs an analysis of the problem and issues instructions to the machine operator. Service visits have decreased by 50 percent, while customer satisfaction has significantly improved.

Corporate Infrastructure

A large travel agency has electronically connected via satellite small outlying offices located near big corporate customers to enable access to the full support capabilities of the home office. These network capabilities have transformed the organizational structure from one large central corporate office to many small full-service offices, resulting in a 27 percent growth in sales.

Management Control.   A major financial services firm used to pay a sales commission on each product sold by its sales force; thus, the sales force had maximum incentive to make the initial sale and no incentive to ensure customer satisfaction and retention. Using its new integrated customer database, the company implemented a new commission structure that rewarded both the initial sale and customer retention. This approach, made possible by new technology, aligned the company's strategy and its sales incentive system much more effectively.

In some instances, IT has dramatically enhanced coordination by providing greater access to a more widely connected network using fairly simple but powerful tools such as voice mail, electronic mail, groupware, and videoconferencing. New networked "workflow" systems are also enabling tighter coordination of operations. For example, due to high capital costs and operating expense, every major U.S. air carrier uses a network to monitor the precise location of all its aircraft. It knows each airplane's location, the passengers on-board, their planned connections, and the connection schedules. It can instantaneously make decisions about speeding up late flights or delaying connecting departures. The opportunities for controlling fuel costs and preventing revenue loss amount to tens of millions of dollars a year. Trucking companies and railroads use similar methods to track cargoes and optimize schedules.

Human Resources

Human resources management has also changed. For example, to facilitate important personnel decisions, an oil company has given personal computers to all its corporate management committee members, thus giving full on-line access to the detailed personnel files of the 400 most senior members in the corporation. These files contain data on five-year performance appraisals, photographs, and lists of positions for which each person is a backup candidate. The company believes this capability has facilitated its important personnel decisions. Additionally, special government compliance auditing, which used to take months to complete, can now be done in hours.

Technology Development

To guide its drilling decisions, a large oil company processes vast amounts of data gathered from an overhead satellite. The company uses this information to support oil field bidding and drilling decisions. Similarly, CAD/CAM (computer-aided design and manufacturing) technology has fundamentally changed the quality and speed with which the company can manufacture its drilling platforms.

A seed company considers its single most important technology expenditure to be computer support for research. Modern genetic planning involves managing a global database of millions of pieces of germ plasm. These database planning and molecular simulation models—the keys to their future—are not possible without large-scale computing capacity. Repeatedly, their detailed data files have allowed them to find a germ plasm thousands of miles away in Africa to solve a problem in an Iowa cornfield.

Procurement

Procurement activities are also being transformed. For example, with a series of on-line electronic bulletin boards that make the latest spot prices instantly available around the country, a manufacturing company directs its nationwide purchasing effort. The boards have led to a tremendous improvement in purchasing price effectiveness, both in discovering and in implementing new quantity pricing discount data, as well as ensuring that the lowest prices are being achieved.

A retailer, by virtue of its large size, has succeeded in its demand for on-line access to the inventory files and production schedules of its suppliers. This access has permitted the company to manage its inventories more tightly and to exert pressure on suppliers to lower price and improve product availability.

New market opportunities also abound. For example, an entrepreneurial start-up provides desktop software to allow traders and others with intense needs for fast-breaking information to pull relevant material from over 400 continuous news feeds (e.g., Reuters, Dow Jones),[6] analyze the information,

---

[6]Since the news feeds have different data sources, key items picked up by one might be missed by several others.

and deliver it to end users. The firm's revenues—$40 million in 1997—are growing rapidly.

In summary, a systematic examination of a company's value chain is an effective way to search for profitable IT applications. This analysis requires keen administrative insight, awareness of industry structure, and familiarity with the rules of competition in the particular setting. Companies need to understand their own value chains as well as those of key customers and suppliers in order to uncover potential new service areas. Similarly, understanding competitors' value chains provides insight on potential competitive moves. Careful thought is needed to identify potential new entrants to an industry—those companies whose current business could be enhanced by an IT-enabled product or service.

THE RISKS OF INFORMATION SYSTEMS SUCCESS[7]

Problems and Evaluations

While previous sections of this chapter focus on opportunities, this section discusses the potential problems that can arise when a firm's efforts are "too successful." Management policies and procedures that help ensure that potentially high-risk projects are appropriately evaluated are also discussed.

Systems That Change the Basis of Competition to a Company's Disadvantage.   When information systems are used to gain competitive advantage in a given industry, there is often a requirement for continued enhancement to sustain competitive position. An organization that is not prepared to stay the course with continued investments in information systems may be better off not entering the race in the first place.

This lesson was learned, through experience, by a U.S. commercial appliances manufacturer, whose products were typically purchased and installed by building contractors who worked from a set of technical specifications for size, capacity, and so forth. Historically, the company had offered contractors a mail-in consulting service that could translate specifications into products and instructions for wiring, plumbing, and so forth.

Initially, the company developed mainframe software that captured this consulting expertise. Contractors continued to send specifications by mail; the company would feed the requirements through the mainframe and mail back a neatly printed list of products and instructions. (As would be expected, most of the recommended products were manufactured by the company itself.) Over time, the appliance market evolved and so did the

---

[7]The material in this section has been adapted from Michael R. Vitale, "The Growing Risks of Information Systems Success," *Management Information Systems Quarterly,* December 1986.

microcomputer industry. The system was a huge success; the company significantly increased its market share, but development stopped there. A competitor—larger, older, and equipped with a more progressive information systems staff—developed a similar system. Software was provided to contractors at no charge, as were network connections to the company's mainframe. Analysis could be performed immediately, and the required products, made almost exclusively by that system's owner, could be ordered at the push of a key. Over time, the second company recaptured its lost market share and more. In 1998, the product is easily accessible on the company's Internet homepage. Each of these key changes evolved in a period of one to two years, from interesting idea to dominant concept.

By introducing customers and competitors to the use of information systems but then failing to track or adapt to changes in the technology, the first company turned an initial IT success into a competitive failure.

Systems That Lower Entry Barriers.   As described earlier, IT has been used to raise barriers to entry in many industries. In situations where extensive investment in hardware and software is obligatory for all participants, the investment required for entry is also increased. In other circumstances, information systems have been used to capture distribution channels, again increasing the cost and difficulty of entrance.

On the other hand, by making an industry more attractive, a company may in fact trigger action by other competitors that have greater IT resources to expend. A major seller of health and casualty insurance faced that dilemma. The firm did the majority of its business on a payroll-deduction basis with very small employers who did not offer insurance as a fringe benefit. Because many of its customers did their payrolls by hand, bookkeepers became a major target for the insurer's sales force. The primary competition was not so much from other insurers as from the bookkeepers' lack of time and willingness to handle additional deductions. To help overcome this obstacle, the insurer considered offering a computerized payroll preparation package for small companies. The development of such software was considered to be well within the capabilities of its IT group, and its sales force was already in contact with many potential customers for the new service. Pricing was designed to provide some profit, but the main intent was to create tighter links to small customers.

Before much work had been done on the new payroll system, the vice president for IT recognized a danger. Although it might well be possible to convince customers to do their payrolls by computer, he could see there was a risk that the business would go not to the insurer but to one of the large, experienced firms that dominate the payroll business and could offer a more sophisticated customized package. Any of these organizations could, if they chose, also offer health and casualty insurance to small businesses. The link to customers might be tighter, but it was not clear whether his company would be at the other end! This strategic analysis led the company to drop the idea of offering payroll service because to continue the project would, in the company's opinion, have risked opening its primary line of business to new competitors. (Ultimately, of course, the business did disappear.)

Systems That Bring on Litigation or Regulation.   In the category of things that work too well for their own good are systems that, after achieving their initial objectives, continue to grow in size and effectiveness and eventually give rise to claims of unfair competition and cries for government regulation. Possible outcomes are forced divestiture of the systems or an agreement to share them with competitors.

The airline reservations systems used by travel agents illustrate this danger. The United and American reservation systems control the offices of nearly 80 percent of U.S. travel agents. Some of their competitors have claimed that this level of penetration allows the two big airlines to effectively control the industry's channels of distribution. Examples of such alleged domination include biased display of data, close monitoring and control of travel agents, and inaccurate data on competitors' flights.

After a lengthy investigation of these claims, the Civil Aeronautics Board (CAB) ordered changes in the operation and pricing of computer reservations systems. Nevertheless, United and American were sued by 11 competitors, which demanded that the two carriers spin off their reservations systems into separate subsidiaries. United and American opposed the suit but did agree, along with TWA, to provide unbiased displays.

Although they deny unfair practices, United and American have never denied using their reservations systems to gain competitive advantage. Indeed, the two airlines claim that the systems are not economically viable on the basis of usage fee income alone—they were intended to generate increased sales. (United and American may already have recovered their investments in the reservations systems by making these sales.) The precedent of government intervention suggests, however, that future developers of competitively effective systems may find their returns limited by law or regulation. American ultimately spun its SABRE system off as an independent and separately traded company.

The central theme of this controversy is that there is such a thing as an unfair "information monopoly" and that control of electronic channels of distribution may be unacceptable to the public. The U.S. Justice Department investigation of Microsoft is a contemporary example of these issues.

Systems That Increase Customers' or Suppliers' Power to the Detriment of the Innovator.   Although IT can strengthen a company's relationships with its customers and suppliers, in some circumstances it also provides tools and expertise that enable the customers and suppliers to function on their own; in fact, this change may be an inevitable outcome of evolving IT penetration in an industry.

An overnight delivery company, for example, instituted very fast delivery of electronically transmitted messages between its offices. The original was picked up from the sender and put through a facsimile machine at a nearby office; the transmitted image was received at an office near the recipient and delivered by hand.

As fax technology grew, the delivery company announced that it would place facsimile machines on its customers' premises and act as a switch among the installed machines. Delivery promised to be even quicker, since there would be no need to take the original copy to the sending office or to deliver the received copy; but the value the delivery company was able to add to off-the-shelf facsimile technology was questionable. Little existed to prevent its customers from installing similar equipment directly; indeed, the manufacturer of the facsimile machines advertised its products prominently as the ones supporting the delivery company's system. The firm soon abandoned this line of business but could not disrupt the cannibalization of the traditional business by the new technology.

Interestingly, many firms face the same dilemma as they contemplate the impact of the Internet on their traditional business. American Express and Dow Jones have decided to attack the problem head-on by launching Internet-based new businesses—American Express Interactive and Wall Street Journal Interactive, respectively. Today these new businesses run parallel to, but separate from, their existing businesses. Both firms recognize, however, that a new integrated business that merges the physical and virtual worlds will most likely emerge over time.[8]

Bad Timing.   Determining the time to make a bold move requires a careful balancing of cost and culture. Get there too early with an expensive, clumsy technology in an unreceptive customer environment (e.g., home banking in the 1980s) and you have a real fiasco. Get there too late, as the regional airlines and hundreds of drug wholesalers did, and you also lose. Behind the technology issues lie very real marketing and business policy issues.

Investments That Turn Out to Be Indefensible and Fail to Produce Lasting Advantages.   There are numerous reasons an investment can turn out to be indefensible. In general, interorganizational systems with high potential daily transaction rates are very successful, while those with low daily transaction rates (one to two per day or less) can become strategic liabilities. In addition, features of great value to end users, but easily replicable by the firm's competitors, may provide less proprietary advantage than those that inherently are hard to replicate. Similarly, systems that enable a

---

[8]See L. M. Applegate, *Building Information Age Businesses* (Boston: Harvard Business School Publishing, 1998) HBS No. 399-097.

firm to start simple and continue to add new features and services as technology and industry conditions change are more effective than one-time moves that stand as fixed targets for competitors.

Inadequate Understanding of Buying Dynamics across Market Segments. It is very easy to inappropriately apply a set of concepts that works in one market niche but not in another. For example, airline reservations systems have been widely cited as an example of effective IT use. As noted earlier, however, during the late 1980s, one of the most successful airlines has been Southwest. Aiming at the very price-sensitive market, it carved out a scheduling and service strategy in which reservation systems play a distinctly subordinate role.

Cultural Lag and Perceived Transfer of Power. Some systems require customers to purchase expensive technology that has few other uses. This was the case with the failure of home banking in the United States in the 1980s. A related issue is the concern by one party in an interorganization system that it will be manipulated by the other party. Regrettably, not all IT efforts are win-win situations.

Assessing Competitor Risk

Understanding competitive risks is the first step in managing them. Understanding, in turn, is a two-phase process: (1) predicting in detail the industry-level changes that may be brought about by development and implementation of particular information technologies and (2) assessing the potential impact of these changes on the company.

Increasing use of information systems is often naively viewed as inevitable. Certainly, situations occur where firms must invest in and adapt to IT in order to remain viable, even if the increase in technological intensity causes a complete reevaluation and reformulation of the firm's strategy. But some technological "advances" have remained in an embryonic stage for years. Electronic home banking and home shopping, as noted earlier, are two examples where the concept was there 10 to 15 years ahead of its market. Sometimes these developments are stalled because of cost, IT capability, or consumer acceptance; other times, they are held back by lack of support from established industry participants. Rather than uniformly criticizing "laggards" for technological backwardness, it is more appropriate to entertain the possibility that these laggards may understand the technology completely and are prepared to utilize it when it becomes necessary but are unwilling to precipitate a potentially unfavorable change in their competitive environment.

An appropriate place to start in considering the potential impact of a new strategic use of IT is with the motivation for the new system. As noted earlier, potential justifications include raising entry barriers, increasing switching costs, reducing the power of buyers or suppliers, deterring substitute products, lowering costs, and increasing differentiation.

When a firm considers new investments in strategic IT systems, it must candidly assess whether it will obtain a *sustainable* competitive advantage or whether it will maintain the current competitive situation at an increased level of cost. Additional caveats in this area include recognizing that IT software purchased from a nonexclusive source is unlikely to confer lasting advantage. Also, the movement of skilled IT personnel between firms often results in a rapid proliferation of strategic ideas, which puts the pioneering firm under pressure to keep innovating and building new services. In the absence of strong, first-mover advantages, some investments in information systems, regardless of their short-term glitz and appeal, may simply not pay off competitively over the long run.

As will be discussed later, the long-term commitment of top management is essential in executing these strategic moves; the company must have a clear picture of its long-range strategy, how this move fits into it, and the resources and capabilities of competitors, both current and potential.

A crucial component of the assessment is analysis of the likely long-term consequences of a new system. Initial development cost and short-term benefits may not be an accurate indicator of its potential effects. To help this assessment, some organizations have found it useful to prepare an "impact statement" that lays out the competitive changes expected to result from a new information system, focusing on both the substantial benefits accruing from an improved competitive situation and the risks. Consideration of the positive impacts of the new system on competition forces broad thinking on potential negative impacts as well.

Over time, the key to managing these sorts of strategic risks will be the organization's ability to learn from its experience so that it can continue to roll out strategic IT applications as and when appropriate. There must be a common understanding among general managers and senior IT executives about which pieces of the development effort should be considered "directional"—that is, likely to have a major effect on the organization's future competitive position. A thorough review of the potential impacts should be carried out before such systems are developed and again before they are implemented.

THE CHALLENGE

Achieving the advantages while avoiding the pitfalls requires IT management—and user management—plus imagination. The process is complicated by the fact that, while many IT products are strategic, the potential benefits are subjective and not easily verified. Often a strict return-on-investment (ROI) focus may turn attention towards narrow, well-defined targets rather than to broader, strategic opportunities that are harder to analyze.

A NEW POINT OF VIEW IS REQUIRED

To address the issues raised here, managers need to reevaluate their perspectives and biases.

Planning Issues

The CEO must insist that the end products of IT planning clearly communicate the true competitive impact of the expenditures involved. Figure 3–5 provides a framework that identifies how many firms define their priorities for the allocation of financial and staff resources.

In viewing the framework, business managers should realize that an extraordinarily large amount of the systems development effort is often devoted to the repair and maintenance of worn-out legacy systems and adaptations to the Year 2000 problem[9] that fail to address current business conditions. Also, a vital but often unrecognized need exists for research and development to keep up with the technology and to ensure that the company knows the full range of possibilities. Distinctly separate are the areas where a company spends money to obtain significant competitive advantage or to regain or maintain competitive parity. Finally, projects where the investment is defined for pure measurable ROI can be viewed quite differently.

The aim of the ranking process is to allocate resources to areas with the most growth potential. Each company should have an IT plan that vividly communicates to the CEO the data derived from Figure 3–5, explains why IT expenditures are allocated as they are, and enumerates explicitly the types of competitive benefits the company might expect from its IT expenditures and the impact on resource allocation decisions.

Confidentiality and Competition

Until recently, it has been the industry norm for organizations to readily share data about IT systems and plans on the grounds that, since IT was

---

[9]"Legacy" refers to transaction processing systems that were originally designed to perform a specific task. Over time, these systems may not accurately reflect business needs. In addition, as hardware and software improvements occur in the information systems marketplace, older information systems solutions tie an organization to an out-of-date platform that is unable to deliver value-creating applications and is costly to operate and maintain.

FIGURE 3–5 Identifying Resource Allocation Priorities by Strategic Business Unit

Goal of IT expenditure	Growing, highly competitive industry	Relatively stable industry, known ground rules	Static or declining industry
Rehabilitate and maintain system	1	1	1
Experiment with new technology	2	3	3
Attain competitive advantage	2	2	3*
Maintain or regain competitive parity	2	3	4
Define return on investment†	3	3	4

*Assuming the change is not so dramatic as to revolutionize the industry's overall performance.
†In an intensely cost-competitive environment, defined ROI is the same as gaining competitive advantage.
Note: Numbers indicate relative attractiveness or importance of the investment, with 1 denoting the highest priority.

primarily a tool for back-office support, collaboration would allow all firms to reduce administrative headaches. Managers today, however, must take appropriate steps to ensure the confidentiality of strategic IT plans and thinking. Great care should be taken in determining who will attend industry meetings, what they may talk about, and what information they may share with vendors and competitors. Given that key people can leave, considerable thought must be given to who will participate in the totality of the planning process.

Executives should not permit use of simplistic rules to calculate desirable IT expense levels. For example, the common practice of comparing IT budgets using ratios such as percent of sales can be misleading. We have observed some companies spending 10 percent of their total sales on IT that are clearly underinvesting; we have seen others spending 1 percent that are overspending.

The IT-Management Partnership

To make full use of the opportunities that IT presents, managers must work in close partnership with technical specialists. Bridging the gap between IT specialists, business management, and general management is, however, an enduring problem. Often uncomfortable with technology, many business managers are unaware of the new options IT provides and the ways in which it can support strategy. For their part, IT professionals are often not attuned to the complexities and subtleties of strategy formulation and execution. They are generally not part of the strategy development process.

Partnership is necessary. IT experts understand the economies of the technology and know its limits and can also help move the organization towards the potential of tomorrow's technology. A change that is clumsy and inefficient in today's technology might eliminate the need for architecture redesign in the next generation. For example, very rich, interrelated databases today may be slow to access, presenting serious cost (and possibly response-time) problems. Tomorrow's faster computer and communications technology may eliminate these problems.

General managers and business managers bring insight to corporate and business priorities. They have detailed knowledge of the industry dynamics and the value chains for different areas of the business and can help identify the most appropriate path to follow for implementation. Synthesis of the two worlds is essential.

SUMMARY

Finally, many firms have found it helpful to establish a senior level IT steering committee. The following questions can guide the committee agenda.

1. *What business are we really in?* What value do we provide to our customer? Can today's communications and computer technologies add value? Can IT help us redefine our business to higher value-added segments?

2. *Who are our biggest competitors today and in the future? Who else does, or could, provide the same products or services?*
3. *Can we use technology to integrate our own value chain activities to improve efficiency and effectiveness of operations?* Can we use technology to integrate our value chain with that of our customers, suppliers, distributors, and so forth? Can we introduce significant switching costs?
4. *Can we use IT to create entry and exit barriers?*
5. *Are any big changes in our industry looming on the horizon (e.g., deregulation, trade agreements)? Can technology help us compete in the new setting?*
6. *Will future changes in related industries influence the competitive situation? Can IT help us compete effectively in the new environment?*
7. *What are the risks involved in IT-enabled strategic initiatives? Can these risks be managed?*
8. *Have we appropriately prioritized our IT spending? Should we reevaluate our investment criteria and budget planning process?*

These last two questions may be the most difficult of all. The answers require reevaluation of today's priorities and skills in light of tomorrow's requirements.

Electronic Commerce: Trends and Opportunities[1]

A fundamental shift in the economics of information is underway—a shift that is less about any specific new technology than about the fact that a new behavior is reaching critical mass. Millions of people at home and at work are communicating electronically using universal, open standards. This explosion in connectivity is the latest—and for business strategists, the most important—wave in the information revolution. . . . Over the next decade, a new economics of information will precipitate changes in the structure of entire industries and in the ways companies compete.

P.B. Evans and T.S. Wurster, 1997[2]

Technology can sometimes catch us off guard. When Rutherford B. Hayes, the 19th President of the United States, saw a demonstration of the telephone in the late 1880s, he reportedly commented that while it was a wonderful invention, businessmen would never use it. Hayes believed that people had to meet face-to-face to conduct substantive business affairs, and he was not alone in his assessment. Few of his contemporaries could foresee the profound changes that the telephone and other technologies of the day—including production machinery, transportation, electricity, and the telegraph—would bring. The shift from an agricultural to an industrial

---

[1]Portions of this chapter are adapted from L. Applegate, *Building Information Age Businesses* (Boston: Harvard Business School Publishing, 1998) HBS No. 399-097.

[2]P.B. Evans, and T.S. Wurst, "Strategy and the Economics of Information," *Harvard Business Review,* September–October 1997.

economy; the exodus of people from rural to urban areas; the shift from craft-based work to mass production; and the decline of small, owner-operated firms in favor of large, vertically integrated multinationals—these radical changes evolved incrementally and were most clearly understood when viewed retrospectively.

Many believe we are in a similar period of upheaval as we shift from an industrial to an information economy.[3] Although information technology (IT) has evolved over four decades, we are now experiencing a period of radical change as the *cumulative* impacts of technological, organizational, social, and economic adaptations coalesce, giving rise to new business models. In a world in which information crosses the globe in seconds, profound changes are occurring within and between organizations as firms large and small rewrite the rules of commerce.

One such technology that has galvanized our attention in the late 1990s is the Internet. Many consider the Internet a revolutionary technology that, like the telephone a century before, will radically change the way companies do business in the future. But, like most so-called revolutionary technologies, the Internet really represents the integration of a number of core technological innovations that have evolved gradually over a period of years. Similarly, its impact on business and society will be a product of many evolutionary changes that have transformed organizations and the industries within which they compete. This chapter focuses on the impact of IT on industries and markets. Chapter 5 addresses the impact of IT on organizations.

THE EVOLUTION OF INTERORGANIZATIONAL SYSTEMS

In a 1966 *Harvard Business Review* article, Felix Kaufman implored managers to think beyond their own organizational boundaries to the possibilities of interorganizational systems (IOS)—networked computers that enable companies to share information and conduct business electronically across organizational boundaries.[4] Despite the visionary tone of the article, Kaufman's predictions were already becoming a reality. An entrepreneurial sales manager at American Hospital Supply Corporation (AHSC) had already created a system that allowed the company to exchange order-processing information with its customers across telephone lines. Another enterprising manager—this one at American Airlines—had begun to offer

---

[3]See, for example, C. Hecksher and A. Donnellon, *The Post-Bureaucratic Organization* (Palo Alto, CA: Sage Publications, 1994); Handy, C., T. Allen, and M.S. Morton, *Information Technology and the Corporation of the 1990s* (New York: Oxford University Press, 1994); and *The Age of Unreason* (Boston: Harvard Business School Publishing, 1990), among others.

[4]F. Kaufman, "Data Systems That Cross Company Boundaries," *Harvard Business Review,* January–February 1966.

large travel agencies computerized reservation terminals to simplify the air-line reservation process for key accounts. From these entrepreneurial actions grew two legendary IT systems that changed the face of their respective industries. In doing so, they helped change the role of IT so that it became a tool to support commerce—the organizational strategies, structures, and systems through which an organization conducts business with buyers, sellers, and other industry participants.

Today, many of the most dramatic and potentially powerful uses of IT involve networks that transcend company boundaries. These IOS enable firms to incorporate buyers, suppliers, and partners in the redesign of their key business processes, thereby enhancing productivity, quality, speed, and flexibility. New distribution channels can be created, and new information-based products and services can be delivered. In addition, many IOS radically alter the balance of power in buyer-supplier relationships, raise barriers to entry and exit, and, in many instances, shift the competitive position of industry participants.

When one thinks of success stories in the history of electronic commerce, the American Hospital Supply and American Airlines (AA) stories immediately come to mind. Both systems were conceived as modifications of internal IT systems to enable simple electronic data interchange (EDI) and grew into legendary strategic systems.

IOS Evolution at American Hospital Supply and American Airlines[5]

When they first launched their systems, neither AHSC nor AA viewed their efforts as a launch pad for electronic commerce. AHSC initially installed its punch-card system to enable better coordination and management of its internal order entry, inventory control, and accounts payable activities. Having learned the benefits of the system firsthand, an enterprising sales-person then convinced a customer who was having trouble with their inventory to install a card reader in their storeroom. A simple extension of the internal AHSC system allowed the hospital purchasing clerk to order supplies over standard telephone lines.

This simple system for monitoring the status of supplies and for ordering electronically allowed AHSC to offload a major portion of the work required to process orders and manage inventory, while dramatically improving the efficiency and quality of the order fulfillment and inventory management processes for both AHSC and the hospital. Accuracy improved, delivery times decreased, and both AHSC and the hospital were able to reduce their inventory without fear of stockouts. Within the first year it was introduced, more than 200 customers begged to use the new on-line order system. AHSC

---

[5]See J. McKenney, *Waves of Change* (Boston: Harvard Business School Press, 1995) for a detailed discussion of the history of the evolution of these and other strategic IT systems.

willingly gave away the punch-card readers and cards to the hospitals for free and trained them on the new electronic order process; within months, the internal savings were more than enough to offset the cost of the technology and the training.

Over the years, the AHSC system, which became known as ASAP, was continuously improved to take advantage of emerging new technologies. By 1985, many hospitals ordered their supplies through personal computers (PCs) or mainframes linked directly to AHSC's mainframes. In addition, AHSC had also convinced its suppliers—hospital supply manufacturers—to distribute their products through ASAP, thus creating an electronic marketplace that became a dominant distribution channel within the industry. By the mid-1980s, ASAP generated over $11 million per year in order-processing productivity benefits and an additional $4 million to $5 million in incremental revenues for AHSC.

Like the AHSC story, AA's initial system efforts were targeted toward improving the efficiency of a key operating activity—the reservation process—and their initial electronic commerce forays were based on a marketing manager's firsthand understanding of the potential benefits for AA's customers. In the late 1960s, the manager gave a computer terminal to several large travel agencies to enable them to directly connect to AA's internal reservation system and thus simplify the process of booking a flight. Both AA and the travel agents discovered that the new IT-enabled reservation process greatly increased efficiency and quality. But in the regulated airline industry, with its simple, stable pricing and route structure, most customers booked their flights directly. Since travel agents played a minor role as intermediaries in the distribution channel, the need for on-line linkages between travel agents and AA was minimal.

This picture changed when the U.S. airline industry was deregulated in 1978. Airlines now had the freedom to change prices to respond to—and drive—market demand, and they could change routes in weeks rather than years. This greatly increased the complexity, uncertainty, and rate of change of market information, pushing customers to rely more heavily on travel agents.

AA, capitalizing on lessons learned during its earlier experiments with connecting travel agents to its internal computer reservation system, was able to begin installing an updated version of its on-line reservation system, which it called SABRE, within travel agencies more than six months earlier than its main competitor, United Airlines. The lead proved invaluable; it enabled American to lock in many key travel agencies before United was able to respond. To achieve maximum penetration quickly, AA, like AHSC, did not charge travel agents for the computer terminals. But, unlike the stable hospital supplies industry of the 1970s, AA recognized that in the highly competitive, postderegulation-era airline industry, its competitors (especially United) could quickly neutralize AA's lead by installing their own terminals for free. Thus, AA created contracts with stiff penalties for any travel agent that used a competing system. The travel agents, struggling to adjust to much more complex and rapidly changing pricing and route structure as they served a rapidly increasing volume of clients, gladly accepted both the terminals and the contracts. In addition, since other airlines did not have the expertise, money, or time to develop their own reservation systems, AA was able to induce other airlines into participating in SABRE, thereby creating an electronic distribution channel for conducting airline reservation transactions and for accessing reservation information—which AA controlled.

United responded quickly with a similar system and similar contracts. As the implications of participation in captive electronic channels became evident, other airlines filed Department of Justice (DOJ) complaints against AA and United, charging that the use of electronic networks had destroyed industry competitiveness.

Despite DOJ intervention, the channel power afforded to the owners of the airline industry electronic markets afforded significant advantage, and, by the mid-1980s, AA's SABRE and United's APOLLO reservation systems had become the dominant platforms for booking airplane, hotel, and other travel reservations.

Pioneers in the history of electronic commerce, like AHSC and AA, blazed new trails. Software to exchange information with outside parties needed to be developed, network standards needed to be created, and new legal and governance rules and frameworks needed to be defined. The systems were costly to develop, but, once in place, they provided tremendous barriers to entry and significant proprietary advantage. Ownership of the systems used to support electronic commerce enabled firms to gain control over both the flow of business transactions and the information about those transactions, enabling network owners to assume the powerful role of channel manager.

The path to becoming a channel manager was remarkably similar.[6] Each firm began by building internal capabilities and learning of the benefits from using technology to automate internal processes. In both cases, the newly automated activities were at the boundaries of the organization, and thus their benefits were felt by sales and marketing managers who interfaced with customers. It did not take long for an enterprising employee to recognize the value of having their customers link into these systems directly.

The evolution of electronic commerce also began modestly. Initially, simple EDI systems were installed, which required little to no integration of processes or direct access to corporate databases and business information.[7] Since the systems used simple public telephone networks, neither AHSC nor AA controlled the networks. Finally, the systems only involved the customer half of the market (see Figures 4–1 and 4–2).

---

[6]While this chapter focuses on two legendary examples, the lessons discussed here have been validated within a broad range of industries.

[7]Simple EDI systems involve only the automation of data transactions. Neither the sender nor the receiver gains access to the other party's databases or business information systems.

FIGURE 4–1   Evolution of American Hospital Supply's (AHSC) ASAP System

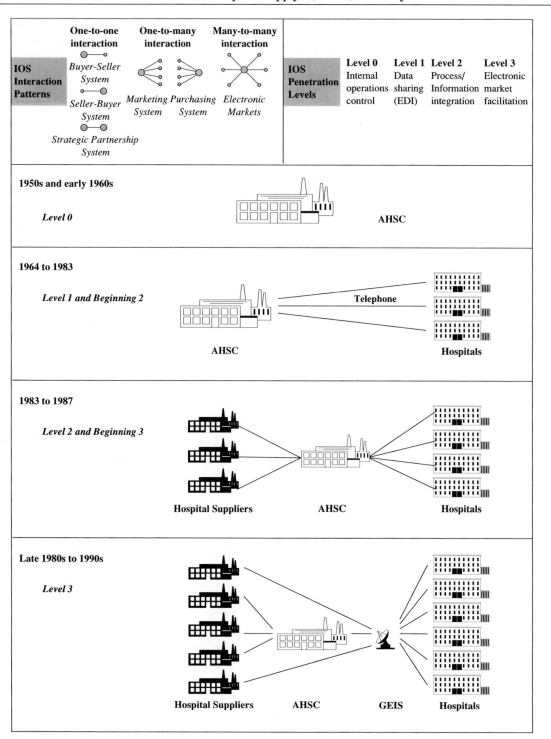

FIGURE 4–2 Evolution of American Airlines' (AA) SABRE System

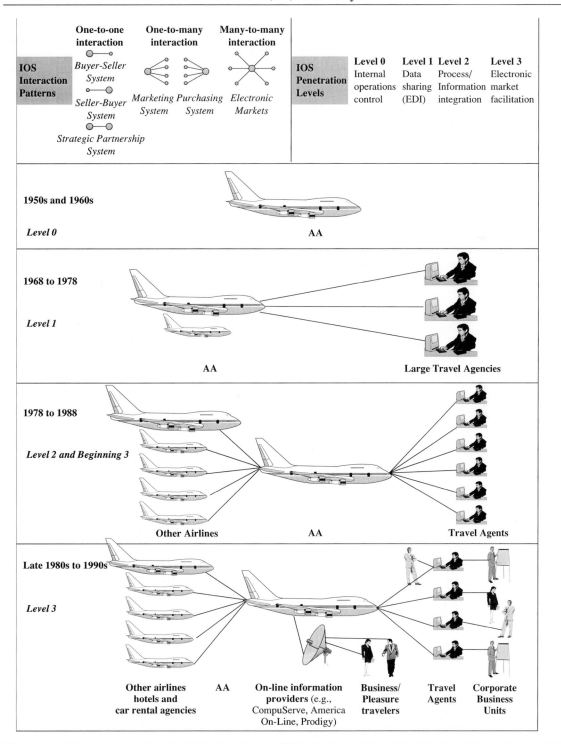

By the mid-1980s, electronic commerce activities had progressed significantly. The simple electronic distribution channels had evolved to include suppliers, thus creating an electronic marketplace, and the levels of proprietary ownership had increased to include control of processes, information, and networks.

Even before the emergence of the Internet, however, the power of these channel managers had begun to erode. As technology penetrated markets and industries, the cost and expertise required to implement interorganizational systems decreased markedly, enabling broader participation and a wider range of opportunities. Reliable, low-cost, third-party on-line information providers and network facilitators, like America Online and Prodigy, had emerged as viable alternatives to proprietary networks. By the early 1990s, both AHSC and AA (in the consumer travel area) had shifted from owning the network to the use of third-party information service providers. In 1994, Max Hopper, who was then head of information technology at AA, emphatically stated that on-line travel reservations systems had become a commodity.[8]

In 1998, many believe that the Internet has further eroded the opportunity for firms to gain proprietary advantage through electronic commerce as consumers, suppliers, and other industry participants tap into this powerful, nonproprietary, low-cost global platform for doing business. Despite competitive, economic, and security concerns, the "gold rush" was on as new entrants and established players rushed to create the Internet electronic markets upon which business would be conducted in the future. As they did they also sought to shape the future role of the channel "captain" within these new marketplaces.

Evolution and Revolution: Introduction of the Internet

While many believe that the Internet burst on the scene in the mid-1990s, technology insiders know that, having been conceived and developed over 30 years ago, its core technology was well established by the time it was opened for commercial use[9] (see Figure 4–3).

Until recently, the use of the Internet was restricted to government, research, and educational purposes. While the ban on public use was lifted in 1993, it was the commercialization of the World Wide Web (WWW) and user-friendly browsers in 1993 and 1994 that fueled the rapid penetration of the Internet into homes and businesses worldwide. In 1994, 3 million people, most of them in the United States, used the Internet. By 1997,

---

[8]M. Hopper, "Rattling SABRE: New Ways to Compete on Information," *Harvard Business Review,* 1990 no. 90307.

[9]See L.M. Applegate, "Paving the Information Superhighway: Introduction to the Internet," *Building Information Age Businesses* (Boston: Harvard Business School Publishing, 1998).

FIGURE 4–3   Evolution of the Internet, 1969–1995

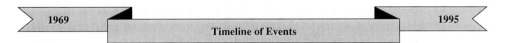

1969 — Timeline of Events — 1995

1969: The Defense Department commissions ARPANET to research computer networking. Later in the year, the first nodes of the system go on-line at UCLA, Stanford Research Institute (SRI) and the University of Utah.

1971: Fifteen individual nodes of ARPANET go on-line, joining 23 host computers.

1972: Operators create the first e-mail program to send and receive messages across the network. Norway and England become the first international connections to ARPANET.

1975: Usenet newsgroups are established between Duke University and the University of North Carolina.

1982: The Transmission Control Protocol and Internet Protocol (TCP/IP) is approved as the communications standard for ARPANET. This leads to the first definition of an Internet as a connected set of networks using TCP/IP.

1983: Desktop workstations come into being.

1984: The number of computers on ARPANET breaks 1,000.

1986: The National Science Foundation creates the NSFNet backbone on ARPANET (56 KB), and establishes five supercomputing centers to provide high-speed computing power for all users. Cleveland FreeNet comes on-line and offers free public Internet access.

1987: The number of computers on ARPANET breaks 10,000.

1988: The first businesses begin to connect to the system for research purposes.

1989: The number of computers on ARPANET breaks 100,000. The first e-mail relay begins between a commercial on-line service (CompuServe) and the ARPANET through Ohio State University.

1990: ARPANET ceases to exist. The network is now officially referred to as the Internet.

1991: WAIS and Gopher, Internet search and navigation tools, are released by Thinking Machines Corporation and the University of Minnesota, respectively.

1992: World Wide Web (WWW), a hyperlinked interface to the Internet, is released by a Swiss research network. The number of computers on the Internet breaks one million. NSFNet relaxes its restriction on commercial Internet traffic. By the end of the year, half of all Internet traffic is commercial in nature. First audio multicast (March) and video multicast (November) — real-time broadcasts of video and audio via computers connected to the Internet — take place.

1993: The White House goes on-line after the National Information Infrastructure (NII) Act is passed in September. Stephen King becomes the first author to publish a short story on the Internet. First books about using the Internet for business appear. Businesses and media take an interest in the Internet as the number of users climbs above 14 million. Mosaic, graphical WWW browsing software, is released. The use of the Web proliferates by more than 30,000 percent.

1994: The U.S. Congress brings its Internet server on-line. Shopping malls, advertising, and mass marketing surface on-line.

1995: IBM, Microsoft and Oracle join Sun in proclaiming their "grand strategy" for network computing.

Adapted from *Internet Business Advantage,* 1995.

40 million people around the world were connected;[10] by early 1998, the number of people using the Internet had soared to 100 million.[11] One expert predicted that 1 billion people would be connected to the Internet by 2005[12] (see Figure 4–4).

This expansion of use coincided with dramatic increases in computer, software, services, and communications investments that were, in turn, making the vision of Internet-based electronic commerce a reality. While businesses began using the Internet for commercial transactions with customers, suppliers, and business partners in early 1995, it was not until 1997 that Internet-based electronic commerce really began to catch on. By July 1997, approximately 1.7 million Internet business sites had been registered, up from approximately 600,000 one year earlier.[13] Consider this:[14]

- In 1996, Amazon.com, the largest Internet bookstore, recorded sales of less than $16 million. In 1997, revenues increased to $148 million.
- Auto-by-Tel, a Web-based automotive marketplace, processed a total of 345,000 purchase requests for autos through its Web site in 1996, generating $1.8 billion in auto sales. As of the end of November 1997, the Web site was generating $500 million a month in auto sales ($6 billion annualized) and was processing over 100,000 purchase requests each month.
- Cisco Systems closed 1996 having booked just over $100 million in sales on the Internet. By the end of 1997, its Internet sales were running at a $3.2 billion annual rate.
- In January 1997, Dell Computers was selling less than $1 million of computers per day on the Internet. The company reported reaching daily sales of $6 million several times during the December 1997 holiday period.
- In 1997, Egghead Software announced that it would close all of its retail outlets and begin selling all of its software from its Internet Web site.

While the above are primarily examples of consumer electronic commerce, business-to-business Internet commerce was also on the rise (see Table 4–1). In 1998, businesses that used the Internet to buy, sell, distribute, and maintain products and services had begun to realize significant cost savings and increased sales opportunities. And these benefits increased as the network of businesses conducting electronic commerce grew.

Not surprisingly given the sophistication of industry participants, Internet-based travel was predicted to be one of the fastest growing areas of

---

[10]Mary Meeker and Sharon Pearson, *Morgan Stanley U.S. Investment Research: Internet Retail* (Morgan Stanley, May 28, 1997).

[11]U.S. Department of Commerce, *The Emerging Digital Economy,* April 15, 1998, National Technical Information Service (www.ntis.gov/yellowbk/1nty800.htm), order no. PB98-137029.

[12]Nicholas Negroponte, "The Third Shall Be First: The Net Leverages Latecomers in the Developing World," *Wired,* January 1998.

[13]www.netsol.com (March 21, 1998).

[14]U.S. Department of Commerce, op. cit.

FIGURE 4–4   Penetration of the Internet, 1998

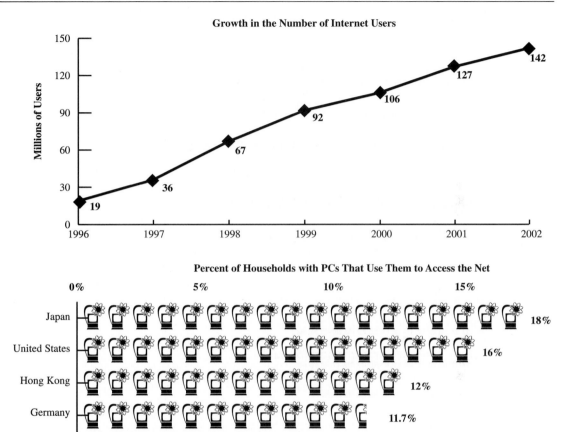

Growth in the Number of Internet Users

Percent of Households with PCs That Use Them to Access the Net

(Continued)

electronic commerce, with sales estimates of over $8 billion by the year 2001.[15] By 1998, consumer-oriented Internet travel sites, such as Microsoft's Expedia, the Internet Travel Network, and Travelocity, had become established brands, and new competitive battles were being fought by established players (for example, AA and American Express) and new entrants (for

---

[15]Forrester Research Report, 1998.

FIGURE 4–4   Penetration of the Internet, 1998 *(concluded)*

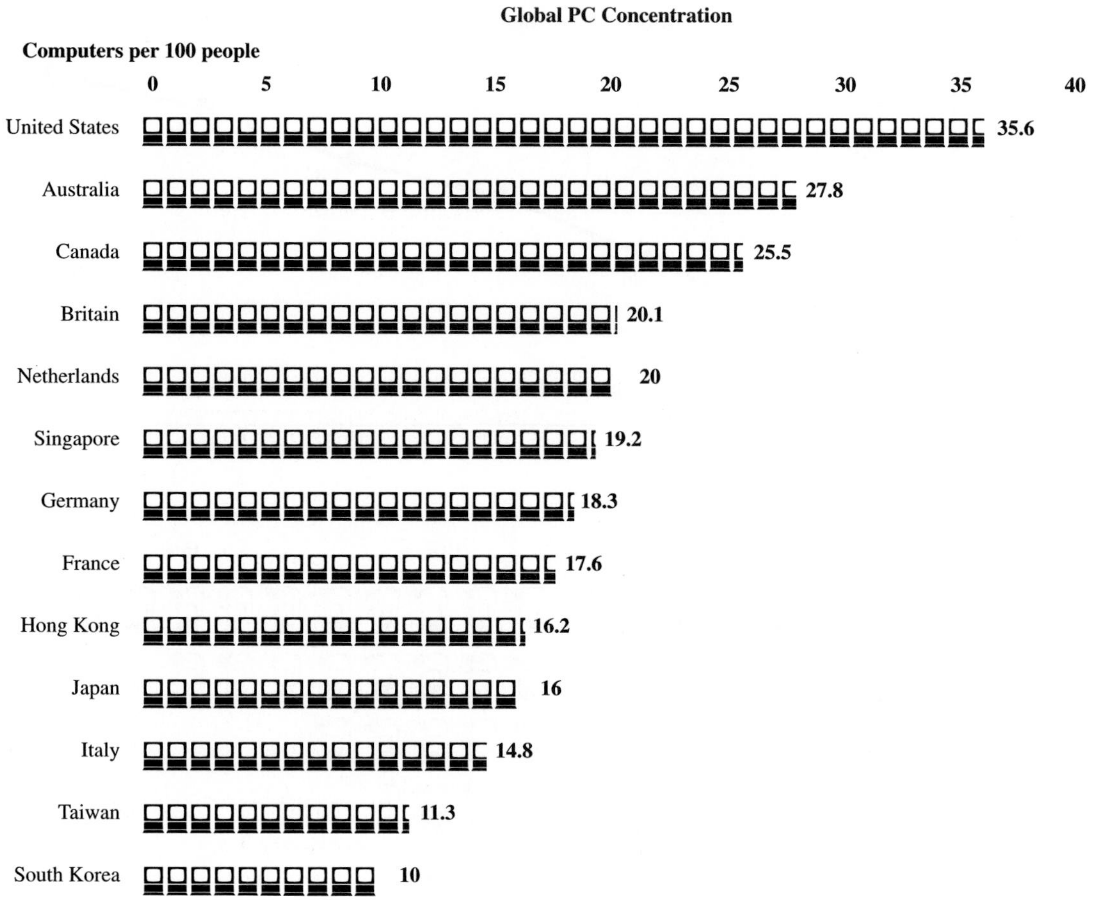

Global PC Concentration

Computers per 100 people

	0	5	10	15	20	25	30	35	40

United States   35.6

Australia   27.8

Canada   25.5

Britain   20.1

Netherlands   20

Singapore   19.2

Germany   18.3

France   17.6

Hong Kong   16.2

Japan   16

Italy   14.8

Taiwan   11.3

South Korea   10

Source: *eStats,* March 23, 1998.

example, Anderson Consulting) to gain control of the corporate market-place.[16]

Cumulatively, the technologies that make up the Internet have resulted in four key features that are enabling some revolutionary changes in the ways firms do business (see Table 4–2). First, it is a truly global, open information

---

[16]L. Applegate, "AXI Travel–American Express Interactive," Harvard Business School HBS Case No. 399-014.

TABLE 4–1   Comparison of Projections on the Growth of Internet-Based Electronic Commerce

	Consumer Revenues ($M)				*Business-to-Business Revenues ($M)*	
	1996	*1997*	*1998*		*1996*	*2000*
e-land	$750	$1,500	$3,700	eStats	$500	$140,000
Forrester	518	1,138	2,371	IDC	210	153,000
Multi-Media Research	520	850	N/A	Yankee Group	125	134,000
Jupiter	575	1,250		Forrester	600	66,430

Source: *eStats* via eMarketer, March 23, 1998.

TABLE 4–2   Comparison of Traditional and Internet Commerce

Traditional Electronic-Commerce Networks	*Internet Electronic-Commerce Networks*
Closed standards limit participation to individuals and/or companies that have access to proprietary software and networks.	Open standards enable global connectivity; anyone with a browser and Internet access can participate.
Proprietary ownership of the network enables owner to set commerce standards and policies.	Shared ownership of the network; collaboration is required to define and manage commerce standards and policies.
Rigid software limits functionality and flexibility.	Modular, flexible software enables business flexibility.
The high cost, long time frame, and specialized expertise required to develop commerce solutions provide powerful barriers to entry.	Lower cost and expertise and shorter time frames to develop business solutions increase the ease of developing a competing system, which, in turn, lowers barriers to entry.

and communication platform for storing, displaying, and communicating information. Any company or individual, using any type of computer and network equipment, can connect to the Internet and gain access to information and markets around the world. Second, no single organization, company, or government agency "owns" the thousands of interconnected yet independently owned and managed networks that make up the Internet. Third, the Internet is a flexible and powerful platform for communicating and interactively sharing information in all of its many forms (for example, data, text, voice, video, and graphics). Finally, the cost, time, and expertise required to connect to this vast network of information are very low—a fraction of what it would cost and the time and expertise that would be required to develop and maintain a proprietary, global network.

These features of the Internet both extend what we already know and enable exciting new opportunities. They also create new challenges and risks.

LEARNING FROM THE PAST AS WE CREATE THE FUTURE

The low cost, flexibility, shared ownership, and global connectivity of the Internet dramatically expand opportunities for electronic commerce. Yet proprietary advantages from business ventures on the Internet can be fleeting. The old model for evaluating electronic commerce opportunities no longer applies, and new rules are yet to be written. As managers venture forward, the lessons from the history of electronic commerce can help guide the way. Three key lessons are discussed below:

Lesson 1: Build internal capabilities

Lesson 2: Penetrate quickly and leverage the community

Lesson 3: Exploit the economic value of information

Lesson 1: Build Internal Capabilities

Both AHSC and AA were successful in their electronic commerce ventures because they built their linkages to outside suppliers, distributors, and customers as extensions of systems that coordinated and managed activities inside their companies. The same technologies that were used to lower the cost and improve the ability to integrate, coordinate, and control operations inside the firm were expanded to enable integration, coordination, and control of activities across firm boundaries. This enabled AHSC and AA to outsource—and effectively manage—increasingly more complex activities and processes.

This same fundamental principle also holds true when considering electronic commerce on the Internet. While the economic benefits from marketing and selling on the Internet remain elusive, there are sizable opportunities to be gained by using the power of the Internet to streamline, coordinate, and manage internal operations. By targeting these Intranet[17]

---

[17]Over the past few years, new terminology has been developed to define certain classes of Internet network systems. *Intranets* are secure corporate networks that use the Internet communication protocol. *Extranets* are secure interorganizational networks that use the Internet communication protocol to link a company to customers, suppliers, and business partners. The public *Internet* refers to publicly available network systems that use the Internet protocol.

projects to improve "high leverage–high leakage" information-intensive processes and to support key decisions at the interface with customers, suppliers, and business partners, managers can position their company for electronic commerce in the future.

General Electric (GE) is an excellent example of an Internet pioneer that laid the foundation for electronic commerce by building internal capabilities.[18] GE began exploring the potential of the Internet as a platform for electronic commerce in 1994. At that time the Internet and the World Wide Web were in their infancy. Despite the fact that the technology could be used for little more than publishing and e-mail, managers at GE could already see its promise as both an open platform for global communications and a powerful tool to manage and communicate information in its many forms (data, text, audio, video, pictures, and graphics). Mark Mastriani, who at that time was manager of technology for GE and a key champion of the company's early Internet efforts, said,

> We knew that GE could exploit the Internet's features to achieve our vision of becoming number one or number two in all of our businesses and a truly global company. But, we also knew that it would be several years before the Internet lived up to its potential and that there was also a chance that the technology would never catch on. Rather than wait, we decided to get started while carefully managing the risk.

In 1994, one of GE's key corporatewide strategic initiatives was to streamline processes to improve productivity and better serve customers and business partners. "As we thought about how to start learning more about the Internet," Mastriani remarked, "we decided to tie into important business initiatives that were already in process." Mastriani continued:

> One of those initiatives involved the redesign of the sourcing process. In 1994, GE purchased $25 billion worth of products and services per year. We knew that our current way of doing business could be inefficient for GE and its sourcing partners. As we looked at processes to target for improvement, "high leverage–high leakage" ones, such as sourcing, rose to the top of our priority list.

The sourcing initiative involved the centralization of sourcing information and the processes through which GE dealt with external suppliers, contractors, and vendors. As one team worked to redesign the sourcing process and build the necessary databases, a second team began the process of transitioning GE's global network from a variety of incompatible local and wide-area networks to an integrated global network using the Internet protocol and common e-mail and Web browser tools. The new sourcing databases and systems were then linked to the company's internal Intranet.

---

[18]L.M. Applegate, *TPN Register: The Trading Process Network,* Harvard Business School Publishing, No. 399-015.

Four GE business units were recruited to pilot test the new Internet-based sourcing process.[19] The four prototypes delivered tangible business benefits to the business unit sponsors and enabled further refinement of the organizational and technology infrastructure required to transform sourcing within all of GE (see Table 4–3).

Between 1994 and 1995, the sourcing initiative was managed and funded at GE corporate headquarters; the solution became known as the Trading Process Network (TPN). In early 1996, sponsorship and management of TPN were transferred from GE's corporate headquarters to GE Information Services (GEIS), and in June 1996, TPN was launched as an Internet-based service commercially available to all GE suppliers through GEIS.

Throughout 1996, the benefits that GE and its suppliers achieved through the use of TPN continued to grow. By 1997, a decision was made to partner with Thomas Publishing's Thomas Register subsidiary[20] to launch TPN as an independent limited liability corporation. The new company was called TPN Register. Orville Bailey, president of TPN Register and an original member of the TPN project team at GE, commented:

> TPN Register combines GEIS' supply chain management technology and services with the supplier products and services of Thomas Publishing's Thomas Register business unit. Through the combined efforts of these two industrial age powerhouses, this new information age company and its partners offer a full range of electronic commerce products and services, including Internet-based supply chain management solutions, business process consulting, and back-end system integration. The marketplace is in its infancy and is growing exponentially.

By June 1998, TPN Register procurement solutions were being implemented at 14 companies, 3 of which were implementing full enterprise roll-outs. Once fully implemented, these three companies would trade in excess of $1.5 billion per year. (In 1996–1997, GE businesses traded in excess of $1 billion using the TPN service.) Procurement cost savings for customers were in excess of $20 million per year.

GE followed a path similar to the one we saw used by successful electronic commerce pioneers of the past; they began by using IT to streamline, integrate, and coordinate internal activities; extended the technology to a key external constituent; and then created an electronic marketplace. Yet, as we

---

[19]GE Lighting (a pioneer in the use of EDI among GE business units), GE Aircraft Engines (a business unit that was actively working with government and defense industry partners in the development and deployment of computer-aided logistics systems through the CALS initiative), GE Medical Systems (a leader in the use of IT within GE businesses), and GE Capital volunteered to take part in the pilot test.

[20]Thomas Register (www.thomasregister.com) was an industrial catalog publisher; at the time of the joint venture, Thomas Register's industrial catalogs were used by over 90 percent of the Fortune 500, providing up-to-date information on over 55,000 products and services from over 155,000 industrial suppliers.

TABLE 4–3   Summary of GE Activities and Benefits

Key Activities	*Sample Benefits*
1994–1995: Build internal capabilities	**Auction Prototype** Savings: 20–25% reduction in the cost of sourced components **GE Lighting Prototype** Speed: 7–14 days to 1 day Savings: 100% savings on printing and mail costs; 50% headcount reduction; 20% reduction in the price of sourced components **GE Medical Prototype** Speed: 20 days to 5 days Savings: 100% savings on printing and mail costs; 11% reduction in the price of sourced components
1996: Launch TPN as a platform for electronic commerce for GE business units	**GE Benefits** Volume: $1 billion in contracted transactions managed through TPN Speed: 50–80% cycle time reductions Savings: 10–20% savings in procurement and order-fulfillment costs **Sample Supplier Benefits** Speed: 55% cycle time reduction Savings: 54% reduction in cost of request for quote (RFQ) process Quality: 100% data accuracy
1997: Launch TPN Register as a 50/50 joint venture between GE and Thomas Publishing	**TPN Register Benefits (June 1998)** Number of customers: 14 Customer retention: 100% Customer savings: up to 20% of procurement cost Revenues: N/A Profits: N/A Market share: N/A

look at some of the high-profile Internet electronic commerce success stories, we see some who have not followed this same evolutionary path. Instead, firms like Amazon.com (www.amazon.com) launch their Internet market-place before building the foundational systems and infrastructure. They penetrate quickly and then work diligently to put in place the required infrastructure.

Clearly, there are times when the benefits of moving quickly to establish a central position within a new market outweigh the benefits of following the much less risky and "safe" path. But despite their success in capturing the minds and hearts of consumers—and the capital markets—Amazon.com has found that rapid growth demands flawless execution. Examination of their annual report confirms the significant investments required to develop the infrastructure and systems to coordinate and manage the flow of physical goods.[21]

Lesson 2: Penetrate Quickly and Leverage the Community

AHSC and AA achieved a dominant position within their industries through a strategy of rapid penetration and value creation for all members of the community. By giving away the terminals and software required to do business electronically, AHSC and AA created strong linkages to customers in the industry. They trained customers to use the technology and even helped them redesign their processes to ensure that all parties achieved maximum value. Once hospital customers were using AHSC systems, hospital suppliers sought to join the community. The same pattern was evident in the travel industry. (Note: In the travel industry large airlines—for example, United—and coalitions of airlines—for example, Galileo and Amadeus—formed competing market platforms.) As new electronic markets evolved, membership in the community expanded and the value to all participants increased. The strategic necessity of belonging to the community also increased.

Once more, we see history repeating itself on the Internet. Recall how Netscape and Microsoft gave away their browser software, thus sparking the "browser wars" of 1995 and 1996.[22] Today, we see a number of companies—from traditional software suppliers,[23] communications suppliers,[24] and network services providers[25] to broadcasting companies,[26] content providers, and entertainment companies[27]—jockeying to set the standards for both the flow of information within Internet-based electronic markets and the software that will be used to conduct business over it. New entrants are also lining up, and some (e.g., RealNetworks and Yahoo!) have achieved a dominant position by capitalizing on an early mover advantage.[28]

---

[21]See P. Ghemawat, *Amazon.com and BarnesandNoble.com*, Harvard Business School Publishing, HBS Case No. 798-063, 1998, for a more in-depth analysis of Amazon.com's strategic positioning and execution.

[22]D. Yoffie, *Browser Wars*, Harvard Business School Publishing, no. 798-094.

[23]For example, IBM, Hewlett-Packard, Microsoft, Oracle, and SAP.

[24]For example, Cisco and Lucent Technologies.

[25]For example, AT&T, MCI, and U.S. West.

[26]For example, NBC and BBC.

[27]For example, Time Warner, Disney, and Nintendo.

[28]Learn more about these companies by visiting their Web sites at www.realnetworks.com and www.yahoo.com.

These players hope to be in a position to define the standards and rules that will govern Internet-based electronic commerce. If successful, they could exert significant control over global electronic markets, which, in turn, could result in consolidation of power within the hands of several large players. Of special concern to many are those companies which are in a position to exert control over both the technology standards governing Internet-based market channels and the content that flows over those channels (for example, large software companies such as Microsoft, IBM/Lotus, and Intuit, or communications companies such as AT&T and MCI/WorldCom). Reminiscent of airline complaints to the Department of Justice in the mid-1980s, Microsoft has been particularly vulnerable as a recent target for DOJ action.

As a common global intraindustry platform, the Internet represents an important new channel for doing business that enables customers to gain access to the "total product and service solutions" required to complete complex business transactions. Companies that have taken advantage of this new channel include a new breed of "solution aggregator" called a "portal player." These aggressive competitors are establishing themselves in a central position within Internet market channels, assuming control of those value chain activities that directly touch the customer. At a minimum, these activities include marketing and sales. For information-based products and services (e.g., financial services, publishing, entertainment), portal players can also assume distribution and even product design roles. In the latter case, these aggregators can piece together customized solutions from a wide range of product/service offerings to meet unique customer requirements. (Figure 4–5 compares the Internet portal approach with the traditional approach to accessing financial services products. In this figure, we assume that current channels of distribution will coexist—at least for a short period—with Internet channels.)

Intuit is an excellent example of a company that is aggressively positioning itself as a portal player within the financial services industry. Its Quicken.com (www.quicken.com) Internet service provides consumers and small business owners with access to a wide range of financial services products, including home banking, insurance, investment management, and financial information and advice. Today, Quicken.com serves as an alternative channel for customers to access integrated financial services and for financial services providers to market and distribute their products and services to a greatly expanded customer base. In the future, Intuit hopes to become a dominant channel for the financial services industry.

Other industry players are also vying for this coveted position. Microsoft, for example, has visions of playing a similar role—not just within financial services, but across a wide range of industries. (Visit www.msn.com to explore the range of services available on the Microsoft Network.) While their Investor.com service (www.investor.com) competes directly with Intuit's Quicken.com, Microsoft has launched several new services that use an alternative approach. These new services provide access to a wide range

FIGURE 4–5 Channels of Distribution in the Financial Services Industry

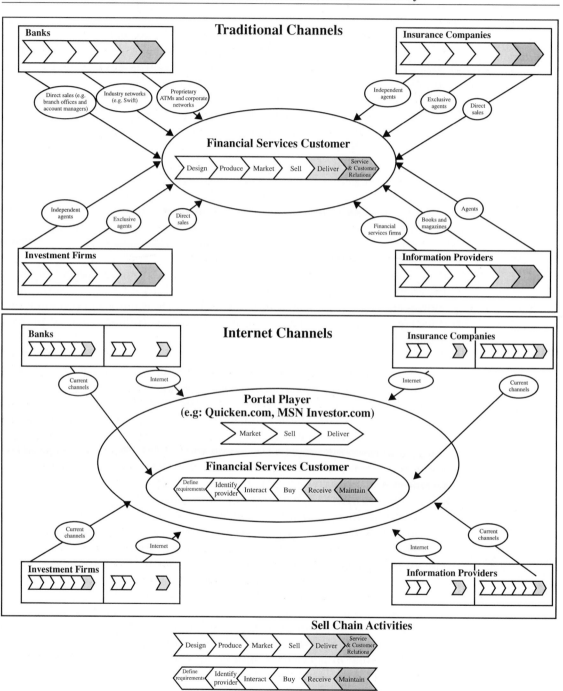

FIGURE 4–6   Life Event Internet Portals

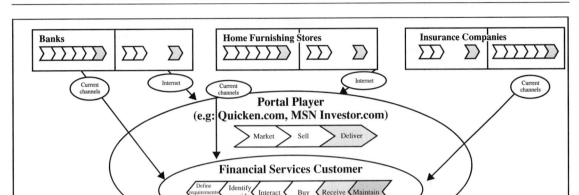

of information, products, and services that customers may need as they embark on a "life event"—buying a home, planning a trip, and so on.

Utilizing the life event approach, in July 1998, Microsoft launched the Microsoft Home Advisor (www.homeadvisor.msn.com), which simplifies the process of purchasing a home. Among the many features of the service, consumers can access information on homes available in different areas of the country, information on mortgage rates, and software to analyze the amount they can afford to spend. Home Advisor then enables the consumer to shop for the best mortgage price and, once the home is purchased, to shop for furniture and homeowners insurance (see Figure 4–6).

Using strategic relationships and intelligent marketing, solutions aggregators like Intuit and Microsoft sit at the center of an intraindustry electronic marketplace—without a doubt an enviable position. RealNetworks— a Seattle-based firm that, in summer 1998, controlled approximately 96 percent of the streaming media[29] software market on the Internet—has

---

[29]RealNetworks developed the technology that would allow people to start listening to sound and watching video the moment that the information began to download into the local computer. By playing "streaming" media, the network speed and capacity requirements were dramatically reduced, thus allowing a wide variety of media types to be delivered over the Internet. See K. Goldman and L. Applegate, *RealNetworks: Converging Technologies/Colliding Worlds,* Harvard Business School Publishing, HBS Case No. 399-052.

demonstrated the power of community loyalty in success in Internet electronic markets.

Founded in 1994, RealNetworks introduced the Internet community to the idea of streaming media in April 1995 when it launched its first product—RealAudio. Even at the time of the founding, Rob Glaser, CEO and founder, had a larger vision; he saw a time when everyone, no matter whether they were at home or at work, would use the Internet to receive information in all its many forms, including audio, video, and animation: "You talk about the 15 hours a week that people spend listening to the radio, or the 20 hours they spend watching TV—four or five years from now we'll talk about the 10 or 15 hours a week that people spend experiencing audio-visual information over the Internet. It'll be just a standard part of the media fabric of people's lives."[30]

When they launched their first product, management took several actions that would prove crucial to the company's immediate success in establishing itself at the center of an electronic marketplace for streaming audio and video on the Internet. First, they decided to have major content players, including both ABC and National Public Radio, signed on at the time of the launch as anchor content suppliers. Second, as we have seen throughout history, they decided to give away a basic model of both the consumer side of the software that sits on a user's PC and the server side of the software that content providers use to develop streaming media content. Finally, two days after the first product release, RealNetworks announced that its basic consumer product—the RealPlayer—would be bundled with the most popular Internet browsers of the day, including Netscape Navigator and Microsoft Explorer.

These actions, along with a strong commitment to creating a quality product that delivered a unique experience on the technologies of the day, led to lightning-fast penetration. In the first six weeks after the release, over 250,000 people all over the world downloaded the player; within seven months, over 1 million people were using the RealPlayer to view content from hundreds of media suppliers, including ESPN Sports, Fox, NBC, MSNBC, BBC, CBS, and C-Span, which had built their content to run on RealNetwork servers.

Three years later, interest had not waned; in spring 1998, over 400,000 people visited the RealNetworks Web site every day—placing it among the top 20 Web sites in terms of daily traffic—and visitors downloaded over 100,000 copies per day of the company's free software. In addition, over 23 million people had filled out an information profile and had given the company permission to inform them of new products, interesting programs, and content provider promotions—and that number continued to grow by 450,000 per week.

---

[30]Robert Reid, "Real Revolution," *Wired*, October 1997.

How does community loyalty like this add tangible business value to RealNetworks? To understand the economics of a community model, it is critical to understand how revenues are generated on the Internet.

The most popular revenue model on the Internet is advertising. While it has still not been perfected, the emerging metric for Internet advertising is called "effective CPM"—the site's ability to turn page views into revenues—measured by:

$$\text{Revenues} = (\text{number of visitors/day}) \times$$
$$(\text{number of pages viewed/visit}) \times (365 \text{ days/year}) \times \text{CPM}[31]$$

In fall 1997, the average CPM price was \$15 to \$75[32] depending on the reach of the site.[33] Tables 4–4 and 4–5 list the top 10 and 15 Internet sites in terms of reach.

The importance of reach was summarized in a recent quote by Robert Reid:[34] "Giving away service over the Web has a real first-mover advantage

---

TABLE 4–4   Top Web Sites in Terms of Reach*

Web Domains				Shopping			
From Work		*From Home*		*From Work*		*From Home*	
yahoo.com	50.6	aol.com	44.9	amazon.com	11.5	bluemountainarts.com	8.2
netscape.com	38.2	yahoo.com	41.8	bluemountainarts.com	6.8	amazon.com	8.1
aol.com	35.3	geocities.com	25.5	barnesandnoble.com	5.0	CNET Software Download Services	5.2
microsoft.com	32.2	netscape.com	24.5	CNET Software Download Services	5.0	columbiahouse.com	4.4
excite.com	28.4	microsoft.com	23.8	hotfiles.com	3.9	barnesandnoble.com	4.4
geocities.com	23.0	excite.com	22.9	columbiahouse.com	3.6	ebay.com	3.7
infoseek.com	22.7	infoseek.com	14.9	cdnow.com	3.3	hotfiles.com	2.5
lycos.com	19.8	tripod.com	13.7	ebay.com	3.0	cdnow.com	2.4
altavista.com	17.1	angelfire.com	12.4	onsale.com	2.8	bmgmusicservice.com	2.3
msn.com	13.0	lycos.com	11.8	bmgmusicservice.com	2.8	musicblvd.com	2.3

*Reach is a measure of the unduplicated audience, measured as a percentage of all Web users, that accessed a given Web site at least once during the month in which it was reported. (Source: www.mediatrix.com.) The statistical margin of error is reported as ± 3 percentage points.

Source: www.mediametrix.com (March 1998).

---

[31]J. Kiggen, *Cowen Internet Observer,* September 25, 1997.

[32]Ibid.

[33]Reach is a measure of the unduplicated audience, measured as a percentage of all Web users, that accessed a given Web site at least once during the month in which it was reported. (Source: www.mediatrix.com.) The statistical margin of error is reported as ± 3 percentage points.

[34]R. Reid, *Architects of the Web: 1000 Days That Built the Future of Business* (NY: John Wiley and Sons, 1997), p. 260.

TABLE 4–5   Top 15 Internet Domains* in January 1998

Domain	Type	Reach†
Geocities.com	Community	23.9
Tripod.com	Community	10.1
ZDNet.com	Computer information	8.7
Sony.com	Entertainment	8.5
Real.com	Video and audio	7.2
Disney.com	Entertainment	6.8
Amazon.com	Bookseller	6.8
Pathfinder.com	Entertainment	6.5
Weather.com	Weather forecasts	5.9
CNet.com	Computer information	5.5
Bluemountainarts.com	On-line greeting cards	5.1
MSNBC.com	News	4.8
Ustreas.gov	Government	4.7
ESPN.com	Sports	4.1
CNN.com	News	3.9

*Excludes search engines, browsers, directories, Internet service providers, and commercial on-line and host services.

†Reach is a measure of the unduplicated audience, measured as a percentage of all Web users, that accessed a given Web site at least once during the month in which it was reported. (Source: www.mediatrix.com.) The statistical margin of error is reported as ± 3 percentage points.

Source: www.mediametrix.com, January 1998

to it. This is because success in this model is measured in traffic and traffic on the Web begets more traffic on the Web."

Advertising, while important, is not the only source of revenue available to firms conducting business on the Internet. Revenues from product sales, transaction fees, subscription or membership fees, and commissions and consulting/service fees are also critical.[35] (See Table 4–6 for a summary of revenue sources on the Internet and how RealNetworks adds to its revenue stream.)

A RealNetworks marketing executive summarized how the company's position at the center of a loyal community of streaming media customers and industry participants translated into tangible business value. "We are at the center of a nexus of relationships," he explained. "We have detailed information on every market transaction—what content people buy and how often they use their subscriptions. We get instant feedback on the results of our marketing, advertising and promotions and, because everything is deliv-

[35]D. Cohen, L. Skeete Tatum, and D. West, "Defining Success in E-Commerce," Harvard Business School Field Study Report, May 1998.

TABLE 4–6   Internet Revenue Models

Revenue Type	Description	RealNetworks Example
Product sales	Sell or license physical or information-based product	Sell and license streaming media software
Advertising	Market other companies' products or promotions	Sell advertising space on Web site; inform customers of special promotions and programming content
Subscription fee	Charge for regular receipt of product or information	Customers can purchase yearly upgrade subscription
Membership fee	Charge to belong to a private group or service	None
Commission or transaction fee	Agent, broker, or intermediary charges for service provided; can be a set fee or a percentage of the cost of a product or service	Customers who contract with RealNetworks to host their audio/video programming pay a transaction fee based on number of viewers
Service/consulting fee	Charge for services provided; either set or variable fee—the latter is often based on time, materials, and expenses incurred while working on a project	Customers can contract with RealNetworks consultants to design and develop streaming media content to be delivered over the Internet

ered in digital form over the Internet, we can react instantly based on the market feedback we get. This costs a fraction of what it would for traditional [business channels]. We are just beginning to understand how to fully exploit the value of all that market information."

Lesson 3: Exploit the Economic Value of Information

The word *information* comes from the Latin word *infomare,* which means "to put into form." Thus, at its most basic level, information can be used to structure and simplify what was previously complex. Both AHSC and AA recognized and capitalized on this inherent property of information to create tremendous value inside their organizations and in the way they did business with customers, suppliers, and business partners. Within both the airlines and the hospital supply industries, AHSC and AA began by using IT to automate and integrate value chain activities, but once they had automated the processes, they also gained control of valuable information about each and every transaction that flowed down the information value chain—information that had tremendous economic value in its own right.

Since AHSC and AA owned the networks and the software that controlled the transactions, they also controlled the information. They used the information captured through direct links to their customers to improve the efficiency and effectiveness of internal operations, to develop a more detailed and timely understanding of market dynamics, and to fine-tune both their product line and their price to continually drive customer expectations to higher and higher levels that competitors could not match. The information was also used to create new information-based products and services, such as frequent flyer programs, that further enhanced customer loyalty. By the late 1980s, both AHSC and AA had spun off new divisions charged with developing, marketing, and distributing information-based products and services.

As managers consider Internet-based electronic commerce opportunities, it is critical to design electronic commerce businesses to capture digital information on internal and external market dynamics and, with careful attention to safeguarding the privacy of all participants, to exploit the economic value of digital information.[36] As was demonstrated by RealNetworks, once information is available in digital form, it can be packaged and delivered to increase organizational intelligence, to create new products and services, and to add value to existing ones. These information-based products and services possess some very interesting properties (see Table 4–7). First, they are reusable. Unlike physical products, information can be "sold" without transferring ownership and "used" without being consumed. As Shikar Ghosh, CEO of Open Market, observed: "I sell information to you, and now you own it. Yet I still own it, and we both can use it." Second, information-based products are easily customized. The same information can be presented in different forms (e.g., text, graphics, video, audio) and in varying levels of detail. It can be combined with information from other sources to communicate different messages and to create new products and services. Third, information-based products and services possess an inherent "time value." As the speed of business accelerates, the time value of information increases.

Internet Securities, Inc., is one of a growing number of Internet entrepreneurs that are building their companies on a carefully designed strategy to exploit the economic value of information delivered on the Internet. Founded in June 1994 by two brothers, Gary and George Mueller, Internet Securities provides hard-to-find financial, business, and political information to business professionals on a subscription basis.[37]

The company grew quickly despite the presence of large competitors—for example, Dow Jones and Reuters—pursuing their own Internet strategies. By

---

[36]This statement raises significant ethical and privacy concerns that must be addressed. In 1998, there are no clear guidelines and the laws concerning information sharing and use differ in different countries. Thus it is critical that managers err on the side of caution and follow a practice of informed consent similar to that followed at RealNetworks.

[37]L. Applegate, *Internet Securities, Inc.: Building an Organization in Internet Time,* Harvard Business School Publishing, no. 398-007.

TABLE 4–7	Properties of Digital Information That Influence Its Economic Value
Reusable	Can be sold without transferring ownership Can be consumed without being depleted
Customizable	Can be presented in different forms (e.g., video, audio, text) Can be broken up and reconfigured
Time-valued	The inherent time value of information can be exploited Value can degrade (or increase) over time
Productized	Can be used to create new products and services or enhance the value of existing ones

June 1998, Internet Securities was providing information on 25 countries—including China, Russia, India, Poland, Brazil, Argentina, Turkey, and Hungary, among others. They employed 175 people in offices located in 18 countries around the world. Their service linked over 600 information suppliers[38] to approximately 650 institutional customers, including JP Morgan, Merrill Lynch, GE Capital, Deutsche Morgan Grenfell, KPMG, Federal Express, Sun Microsystems, Lucent Technologies, Motorola, and Ing Barrings.

What differentiated Internet Securities from the myriad entrepreneurial ventures launched on the Internet during the past few years? For starters, the founders identified a market opportunity in which there were a number of very large, price-insensitive customers that had significant need for information that was difficult and costly to obtain through traditional channels—local newspapers, word of mouth, company reports. In addition, a fair amount of local expertise was required to make sense of the information and to ensure its validity and reliability, which added to the complexity and cost of linking buyers and sellers.

The information suppliers, on the other hand, were small and eager to find a low-cost channel to distribute their information to global markets. They had few resources for reaching global customers on their own, and Internet Securities' potential competitors (current on-line information providers like Dow Jones and Reuters) recognized that it would be costly and risky to attempt to develop these emerging markets.

The above scenario represents an ideal Internet-based information brokering opportunity. There was significant value to be gained by all parties in the relationship; but the cost, complexity, and expertise required to package and distribute the information made it extremely difficult for information suppliers, customers, or a third-party information provider to create a viable

---

[38]Suppliers include the Business World Update, Citibank, Duff & Phelps, The Economist, Financial & Economic Research International, Infotrade, PlanEcon, and a wide range of local information providers.

business. Finally, the Internet's low cost, shared ownership, global scope, and powerful tools for packaging and distributing information made it feasible to unite buyers and sellers where it had not been feasible before.

But despite the going-in advantages, Internet Securities recognized that the window of opportunity would not last long. As a result, they needed to move very quickly to penetrate available markets and lock in suppliers. Experienced country managers were needed in every new market to establish relationships and negotiate contracts with local information suppliers, and to supply the expertise required to interpret, analyze, validate, and make sense of the information. Sophisticated database technologies and transaction systems were needed to manage the large volumes of information to enable efficient and flexible storage, packaging, and retrieval of the large quantities of information.

By early 1996, experienced managers were being hired to oversee the rapidly growing firm, formal management systems were being implemented, and regional headquarters offices were being established in Europe and Asia. This all occurred within months of launching the product in June 1995. But despite the rapid pace at which Internet Securities moved to seize the opportunity, competitors—including large information providers like Reuters—prepared themselves to respond.

As the time frame for capturing value from Internet-related business opportunities decreases, information brokering activities like we see at Internet Securities begin to resemble arbitrage activities in the financial community. Like financial arbitrage, there is money to be made for those who are able to identify a short-term window of opportunity, respond to it quickly and effectively, and then exit the market or move on to a related opportunity just as quickly when buyers and sellers have the tools and know-how to link directly. This type of *information arbitrage* requires that Internet entrepreneurs—be they the founders of start-up firms or managers within an established organization—become expert at accessing, analyzing, packaging, and delivering information to increase its economic value. Like financial arbitrageurs, they must line up all of the parties and resources required to do the deal before they set the process in motion. There must be value to be gained by all parties in the deal, and managers must learn to use the Internet and related information technologies and capabilities to facilitate market transactions and, more importantly, to harness the economic value of the information generated by those transactions.

The evolution of Internet Securities provides an excellent example of a firm that has fashioned its business model to exploit an information arbitrage opportunity on the Internet (see Table 4–8). Initially, the company served simply as an information broker, uniting buyers who had a great need for emerging market information with sellers who had the required information and were highly motivated to sell it but had no efficient means of getting it to buyers. Once they had created the electronic market and established themselves in the center of it, Internet Securities hired local content specialists to provide increasingly sophisticated analyses of oppor-

TABLE 4–8 From Information Broker to Electronic Market Facilitator: Evolution of an Information Arbitrage Strategy

Evolutionary Stages	Key Activities
Information broker	• Identify an unfilled need for high-value information content that is difficult to access through available channels • Build a community of interest between suppliers and customers • Penetrate quickly through "giveaway" strategies, contracts, and partnership arrangements • Deliver value to all parties initially through linkages, information collection and categorization, and transaction coordination
Content specialist	• While paying careful attention to privacy rights, collect information on market transactions • Create organizational capabilities to make sense of information and use it to add value to products and services • Distribute value to all members of the community
Electronic market facilitator	• Build a web of alliances to extend scale and scope of the community • Develop interactive tools to establish closer links with community members and to facilitate linkages among community members • Develop intelligent agents and filters to customize the experience of all members of the community • Build organizational capabilities to deepen commitment and loyalty of all community members

tunities and risks within each local area, and as the company grew, regional specialists evaluated opportunities and risks within world regions (e.g., eastern Europe, the Middle East and Africa, Asia, and South America). It was not until the company solidified its position as a content specialist that the firm began to build a base of "information assets" that added to the internal value of the firm and set the stage for the company to enter phase 3, during which it would exploit these information assets.

Key to capturing the full value of a firm's information assets is the ability to capture detailed information on all business transactions between buyers, suppliers, and channel intermediaries. Internet Securities found a way to do just that. Internet Securities used information on market transactions to motivate its information suppliers to deliver the information that its customers found most useful; they pay their information suppliers 15 percent of customer revenues directly attributable to their specific content.

To make this payment scheme work, Internet Securities' internal systems must track each and every time that a specific user within one of their customer organizations views a specific piece of information from one of their suppliers. These transactions are stored in a database that not only feeds their accounting systems but is also available for use by management and field sales to better understand what information their customers want and where to get it. Gary Mueller, CEO and founder, explained the value of this detailed information to their growing company:

> We use the information generated by our transaction and billing systems to feed a management database, which allows us to report sales on a weekly basis. I can review our online sales charts and know exactly which of our information products is selling to individual information users within each customer site. We know who is using our service and how they are using it. We also have the same detailed information on all of our information providers. We know exactly what information each provides and how well, and where, it is selling.
>
> This information is also available on our company-wide Intranet and all employees have access to it. So a country manager and local sales people can tell exactly how well information is selling and can work with information providers to help them target and deliver the most valuable information. They can also see what local customers are viewing and can use this information to help increase subscription revenues. For example, if information on China or India is not selling well in Poland, the local sales people will know immediately and can talk to customers to find out why. Access to this detailed, timely operating data benefits local employees since their bonuses are tied to increasing revenues related to both customers and information providers in their market.

Amazon.com has used a similar approach to differentiate their on-line bookstore. Those who have used the service often remark that they appreciate being notified of other books that may be of interest. For example, by drawing information from their accounting and transaction systems, Amazon.com can provide a shopper with a list of the top three books that other customers bought who also bought the one being evaluated.

The value of this type of information asset is enormous; but, like other internal assets, it takes time to evolve. The faster the penetration within a market, the faster a company can build internal information assets. Building the systems that capture this valuable transaction information must be done when the business is launched or valuable information will be lost forever. In addition, there must be a strong commitment to learning how to use these information assets and to enable that learning to take place very quickly. In rapidly changing Internet markets, the value of information assets degrades rapidly.

As can be seen from the above examples, sustainable advantage in electronic commerce—whether it is on the Internet or over traditional channels—is built on internal capabilities and assets. Failure to develop and fully exploit these assets and capabilities leaves the most successful

Internet entrepreneurs—be they entrenched players or new entrants—vulnerable. In the past, assets and capabilities were built slowly; in 1998, they must be built in "Internet time." Netscape learned their lesson the hard way.[39] Amazon.com, RealNetworks, and Internet Securities hope they can successfully lay the foundation, penetrate quickly, and exploit the economic value of their information assets before their competitors.

CONCLUSION

> In turbulent times, an enterprise has to be managed to withstand sudden blows and avail itself of sudden, unexpected opportunities. This means that in turbulent times, the fundamentals have to be managed, and managed well.[40]

The pioneers in electronic commerce blazed new trails. They spent hundreds of millions of dollars over several decades to develop and deploy the electronic commerce software and networks that would become the platforms for doing business within their industries. But, once in place, these systems and the skills and capabilities that were developed in building and deploying them provided tremendous barriers to entry and significant proprietary advantage. Ownership of the systems used to support electronic commerce enabled firms like AHSC and AA to gain control over data, processes, information, and the network of business relationships and, thus, to assume the powerful role of channel manager.

The evolution of technology, our understanding of how to use it, and our comfort with doing business on electronic channels have changed the rules for business success developed by the early pioneers. The cost and expertise required to implement interorganizational systems have decreased markedly, enabling broader participation and a wider range of opportunities. And, even before the Internet, reliable, low-cost, third-party on-line information providers and network facilitators had emerged as viable alternatives to proprietary networks.

In 1998, the Internet and its associated technologies have provided a new business platform and the business rules for success have become even more uncertain. Companies and consumers can now tap into global, nonproprietary Internet business channels at a fraction of the cost. This new business environment is remarkably simple to use and enables access to information in all of its many forms—data, text, voice, video. The scope and reach of the Internet have led to massive convergence across industries and markets worldwide. Clearly, it is a time of opportunity and risk.

Reflecting on the advice of Drucker and the lessons learned by the Internet pioneers of today, managers should approach electronic commerce

---

[39]With the launch of Microsoft's Internet Explorer browser, Netscape's share of the browser market dropped precipitously from 87 percent in April 1996 to less than 60 percent in 1997.

[40]P. Drucker, *Managing in Turbulent Times* (NY: Harper & Row, 1980).

on the Internet by starting with the basics—a deep understanding of their business and its market and industry dynamics. They must also have a deep understanding of the *capabilities* of the new technologies and the potential ways that they can be used to change the way their company and the industry does business. They must accurately define their own capabilities for doing business in this new environment and then work aggressively to build the competencies required.

The lessons from the history of electronic commerce help frame the questions to be asked and the solutions to be sought:

- Is your company capitalizing on the potential benefits of electronic commerce? Could actions by competitors or new entrants leave you vulnerable? Are there actions you should take to preempt competitive actions by others?
- Are you developing and fully exploiting your internal information assets? Are you harnessing the power of the information embedded within your products and services to add value to customers, suppliers, and business partners? Are there potential new information-enabled products and services that could substitute for, or enhance, your current offerings?
- Are you capturing the potential benefits of electronic channel integration? Can IT and the information it delivers be used to eliminate product and market complexity, thereby allowing you to simplify, streamline, and better manage supply and distribution channels, and dramatically decrease costs?
- Are you building the electronic communities that will be required to do business in the future? Are you delivering value to each member of the community to build community loyalty?
- Have you selected your partners wisely? Do you have a shared vision and common purpose? Do you bring equal, and complementary, power and resources to the relationship? Are you and your partners financially viable, and is the relationship financially and competitively sustainable? Have you defined shared systems of authority and accountability to ensure that all members work together to deliver value?
- Is the technical infrastructure you have in place the right one to enable the types of electronic commerce you are considering? Are you maintaining the appropriate balance between experimentation and control as you move to Internet-based business platforms? Have you instituted appropriate levels of privacy, security, and control?

Like President Hayes when he assessed the potential of the telephone for conducting "substantive business affairs," many managers underestimate the Internet's far-reaching potential to rewrite the rules of business. Don't let your firm be caught off guard.

Case 2–1

CANADIAN AIRLINES (A): RESERVATIONS ABOUT ITS FUTURE[1]

Computerized Reservation Systems (CRS or "res systems") have evolved from their inception as a means to track the inventory of seats available on flights to becoming, according to some airlines at least, "anticompetitive weapons" used "unlawfully" to obtain and exercise monopoly power. While American Airlines' SABRE and United Airlines' APOLLO dominate the domestic U.S. market, in other countries the national carriers fought desperate rearguard actions to limit the CRSs' intrusion and control of the airlines' distribution channel. But the huge costs of developing res systems effectively forced most into co-host agreements with the two industry leaders. In Canada, an effective response to the encroachment of SABRE into local markets was further complicated by the bitter and fractious rivalry between the two leading Canadian carriers, Air Canada and Canadian Airlines.

The Canadian Market for Air Travel

Most nations' air carriers are not only businesses, but also symbols of national pride and longtime beneficiaries of extensive government subsidies. By contrast, the U.S. market for air travel is fiercely competitive

---

This case was prepared by Research Associate Chris Marshall under the supervision of Professor Warren McFarlan.

[1]Copyright © 1994 by the President and Fellows of Harvard College.

Harvard Business School case 195-101.

and has no single dominant carrier. The Canadian market is caught somewhere between these two extremes. Unlike the United States, Canadian air routes are quite regulated, with its many unprofitable rural routes supported by subsidies from the federal government in Ottawa, Ontario. Like the United States, there is fierce competition between the two dominant carriers, in this case Canadian Airlines (CND) and Air Canada (AC).

Canadian airlines only carried 2 percent of the world's passengers in 1993, compared with about 40 percent by U.S. carriers. The Canadian market is strung out on an east-west axis close to the southern border and comprises perhaps a dozen profitable city markets. By contrast, the U.S. market is made up of hundreds of profitable cities, comprising nearly half the total world domestic market; U.S. airlines also leverage this huge domestic market into dominance of the transborder routes. By 1989, the Canadian-U.S. market had become the largest bilateral air relationship in the world, its 13 million passengers generating approximately $2.3 billion in revenue. While the Canadian airlines provide a more complete coverage of Canadian markets beyond the key cities, they cannot provide the same competitive coverage of the U.S. airlines. In those situations in which the transborder traffic was local, between Canadian and U.S. gateways only, such as Toronto–LA, the Canadian airlines are competitive. Their big problem, however, is the lack of so-called cabotage rights in the United States—the right to carry domestic traffic within a foreign country; for instance, Canadian airlines flying to Chicago and on to Los Angeles cannot pick up U.S. passengers in Chicago. Most U.S.-bound Canadian passengers seek transport beyond the U.S. gateway hub, and since they wish to avoid troublesome transfers, they often opt for the more convenient U.S. carrier.

The late 1980s saw the rise of the airline megacarrier and significant consolidation in the industry worldwide. The seven major Canadian carriers of 1985: Air Canada, Canadian Pacific, Pacific Western, Nordair, Quebecair, EPA, and Wardair and a few mostly independent connector airlines had been reduced by 1990 to two prime carriers, Air Canada and Pacific Western Airlines (PWA) and its primary subsidiary Canadian Airlines International Ltd. The reasons for this consolidation were twofold: firstly, deregulation in the U.S. market in the late 1970s had been followed by a shakeout of the powerful American carriers, and secondly, global expansion required increasingly close alliances with domestic airlines to obtain various access privileges with foreign governments. With such a small captive domestic market (about 25 billion passenger miles), Canadian and Air Canada were ranked only 23rd and 20th in world revenues and 40th and 13th in profits respectively amongst the world's airlines (1990 rankings). Eager to avoid too much direct competition between the two airlines, the federal government's traditional policy on international routes has been to "divide the skies," favoring Air Canada on US, Atlantic and Caribbean routes while preferring Canadian Airlines on the Pacific and South American routes.

Based in French-speaking Quebec, the nation's largest carrier, Air Canada, is a former Crown corporation that went public in 1988 (see Exhibit 1). In return for flying to many parts of the vast and remote areas of the North West Territories and the Yukon, it had control of the most profitable routes between Canada's few major cities such as Toronto, Montreal, Edmonton, Vancouver and Calgary, as well as most routes to the United States.

By contrast, Canadian Airlines, the country's other major carrier, based in English-speaking Calgary, Alberta, is very much a creature of the market (see Exhibit 2). Formed in 1987, Canadian is a conglomeration of CP Air, several regional charters, and one international charter. Eighteen years of sustained growth by Canadian's parent company, PWA, made it confident of its abilities to compete with Air Canada and weather any storms presaged by deregulation south of the border. Canadian's routes included Asia east of Burma, notably Australia, but excluded Singapore, Malaysia, Korea and the Philippines which were assigned to Air Canada. Canadian also had access to most of the Latin American market except for the Caribbean, but the carrier had limited access to Europe in the form of a few flights to the United Kingdom and Germany.

The Threat of Strategic Reservation Systems

Typically, reservation systems are placed in the travel agents' offices and their terminals used by the agent to access seat availability for airlines displaying seats on the system. By the late 1980s, the dominant systems in the U.S. market were SABRE from American Airlines and APOLLO from United Airlines (see Exhibit 3). SABRE supports more than 109,000 terminals in more than 25,000 locations in fifty countries, providing fares and schedules for 665 airlines, 20,000 hotels, and 52 car rental companies, handling more

EXHIBIT 1   Profile of Air Canada

Performance Data (C$millions)	1993	1992	1991	1990	1989
Operating revenue	3,598	3,501	3,485	3,899	3,618
Operating income	1	(197)	(200)	(11)	103
Net income	(326)	(454)	(218)	(74)	149
Current assets	1,373	925	978	N/A	N/A
Total assets	5,039	4,810	4,921	4,579	4,121
Current liabilities	1,007	851	850	N/A	N/A
Long-term debt	3,435	3,330	2,970	N/A	N/A
Operating cash flow	23	(193)	(141)	49	149
Cash flow	(427)	(290)	308	N/A	N/A
Avg. number of employees	18,200	19,400	20,600	23,100	23,200
RPM (millions)	13,768	14,391	13,658	16,577	16,278
Yield per RPM (cents)	17.1	16.3	17.4	16.8	16.3
Load factor (%)	65.1	66.5	68.4	71.4	69.7

Air Canada's primary hubs are Toronto, Montreal, and Vancouver.

Source: Air Canada Annual Report.

EXHIBIT 2   Profile of PWA[1] (taken from annual reports)

Performance Data (C$millions)	1993	1992	1991	1990	1989
Operating revenue	2,973.1	2,877.0	2,871.5	2,745.6	2,648.7
Operating income	(64.9)	(108.7)	(112.1)	(11.7)	(10.4)
Net income	(291.8)	(543.3)	(161.7)	(14.6)	(56.0)
Current assets	501.5	510.6	N/A	N/A	N/A
Total assets	2,265.4	2,461.9	2,811.1	2,964.4	2,911.6
Current liabilities	780.6	938.2	783.1	913.6	N/A
Long-term debt	1,406.4	1,476.6	1,445.2	1,394.6	N/A
Operating cash flow	117.1	(106.4)	N/A	N/A	N/A
Cash flow	(104.1)	(189.8)	(124.0)	(43.0)	(71.2)
Avg. number of employees	15,200	14,850	N/A	N/A	N/A
RPM (millions)[2]	13,417	13,324	12,673	13,851	14,732
Yield per RPM (cents)	16.6	16.2	16.9	16.0	14.6
Load factor (%)[3]	69.2	66.9	64.1	64.8	67.2

[1]Canadian Airlines' primary hubs are Toronto, Calgary, and Vancouver.
[2]Revenue passenger miles (RPM) is a measure of passenger traffic. It is the number of revenue passengers multiplied by the total distance flown.
[3]Load factor is a measure of the total capacity utilization, calculated as the available seat miles divided by revenue passenger miles.

Source: PWA Annual Report.

than 60 million transactions a day. American Airlines has not disclosed its profits from SABRE, but it is estimated that in 1990, SABRE attained a 30 percent pretax margin on nearly $500 million of revenues for American.

The growth and development of CRS is a story of technological innovation and opportunism combined with strategic insight on the part of both United and American. In the late 1970s, few people in the industry appreciated their importance, with many airlines (such as Frontier Airlines described in the appendix) making the decision to outsource much of their systems capabilities. Unfortunately, as these airlines began to recognize in the early 1980s, res systems allowed airlines to lock in travel agents (over 80 percent of U.S. tickets are sold through travel agents), and enabled greater control and understanding of the changing market for seats. Many airlines seriously underestimated the power of res systems, resulting in the premature demise of some firms, such as Frontier Airlines in the late 1980s (see the appendix for Frontier's case against United's "anticompetitive" use of reservation systems). The early entrants, American Airlines and United Airlines, deflected some of this criticism by allowing co-hosting arrangements whereby other airlines could display their seat availability on their systems for a fee. But as noted in the appendix, subtle and important differences remained in how American and United displayed other airlines' seats on their systems.

Canadian SABRE Rattling

Just two years after its introduction into Canada in 1986, American's SABRE system had captured a fifth of the market in Toronto, and quickly swallowed up 20 percent of all the reservations made by Canadian passengers. Both Canadian and Air Canada watched nervously the utiliza-

tion of SABRE in the Canadian market. While it was clear that neither airline could afford the huge start-up costs involved in developing a complete reservations systems to compete with SABRE, neither could they be passive observers to the increasing foreign control of their primary distribution channel. By 1987, the Canadian national carriers acknowledged that they needed access to major reservations systems to remain viable.

The Gemini Partnership

From the mid 1980s onwards, American and United followed very different CRS strategies in their efforts to have their systems penetrate the international market. American kept adding functionality to the SABRE system, trying to improve its appeal with foreign travel agents. By contrast, United distanced itself from its APOLLO system, forming the Covia partnership to manage its reservations. Recognizing an opportunity to jump-start the development of their own res systems, Canadian Airlines and Air Canada put aside their traditional rivalry and agreed with Covia in 1988 to take equal stakes in Gemini Group Automated Distributed Systems Ltd, a partnership to build a reservation system to serve the bilingual Canadian market.

Observing the U.S. experience with the competitive implications of reservation systems, several consumer groups brought a case against the partnership suggesting that domestic competition would be reduced as a result. The competitive implications of developing the Gemini system were considered by the Federal Competition Tribunal in Ottawa; after much deliberation, it was decided that domestic competition would be diminished still further if the airlines failed to remain competitive by not joining this partnership. In the words of the Tribunal:

The determination of whether or not a given situation will result in a substantial lessening of competition is a speculative decision. . . . An order (such as this) is a web of interrelated provisions. . . . It is of significance that there has been little evidence that the merger will lead or will likely lead to a substantial lessening of competition. In addition, the tribunal notes the general trend is toward the formation of large, jointly-owned CRSs. [However] it is clear that the implementation of some of the terms [of the merger] will require the diligent and continual surveillance of the Director [of the Competition Tribunal].

From these complex beginnings, by 1993 Gemini had become the largest private communications network in Canada. This C$100 million investment consisted of an enormous computer center in Winnipeg, and leased fiber optic communications lines that ran from the system's backbone between Toronto, Montreal, and Winnipeg to 10,500 Gemini terminals at travel agents across the entire country. Gemini employed 700 people, most of whom were technicians at the Winnipeg center. The Winnipeg operation was responsible for all aspects of the system except the network, which was controlled from Gemini's HQ and technical center in Toronto. These Canadian systems provided airline seat allocations only. Hotel and car rental reservations were handled by Covia from their operations center in Denver, Colorado.

During this same period, SABRE was able to maintain its market share in Canada. Its major position was in Toronto where it reached about 50 percent market share and had quite limited presence in Montreal because of its lack of a French interface.

Canadian's Mounting Difficulties

In 1988, PWA, the holding company of Canadian Airlines, had had 18 consecutive years of profits. The following three years,

however, saw a dramatic turnaround in their fortunes. Rhys Eyton, the CEO of PWA noted several general reasons for the steadily worsening fiscal performance of the carrier: a worldwide recession coinciding with the Persian Gulf War, all in the context of overcapacity in the airline business. Analysts suggested two other reasons for PWA's weak performance, their (1989) acquisition of Wardair, an international charter operator just short of bankruptcy, and customer aversion to PWA's aging Terminal 1 in Toronto, in the middle of a refit.

Since 1990, all the world's airlines had lost a total of $15 billion. During the same period, PWA had lost more than C$1 billion (see Exhibit 2). With more than C$3 billion in debt in 1993 and a current ratio (current assets/current liabilities) of about 0.65, PWA's future was clearly in doubt. Air Canada too was hurting, but severe cutbacks had allowed it to improve its current ratio from 1.09 in 1992 to 1.36 in 1993 (refer back to Exhibits 1 and 2).

Attempts to Save Canadian Airlines

Financially weakened, PWA desperately sought to cut costs and find cash injections. Its deep distrust of Air Canada made it look for potential alliances with partners south of the border. By spring 1992, AMR, the parent company of American Airlines, was close to making a life-saving deal with PWA in return for Canadian's replacement of Gemini with the SABRE system. The AMR deal was within days of being signed in July 1992 when a nervous AMR added a fatal new condition, demanding that PWA's balance sheet be bolstered by C$195 million in new equity. Suddenly the deal was dead.

Within the month, PWA and Air Canada were talking about a possible merger. But by August 17, Air Canada's initial offer, believed to involve extensive cutbacks at PWA, was rejected. Soon after, a group representing most of Canadian's employees proposed that the employees make an equity investment in PWA through a wage give back plan and indicated that financial support from certain provincial governments might allow PWA to complete a deal with AMR Corporation. To secure this equity, the company had the difficult political task of wringing loan guarantees out of the governments of Ottawa, Alberta, and British Columbia, their major stakeholders. Canadian did convince the federal government in Ottawa to buy three Airbus A310 aircraft for C$150 million. An even bigger obstacle was securing PWA's release from their contractual obligations to Gemini. Publicly desperate, PWA sought to get the partnership declared insolvent by withholding their own contributions. On a chilly September morning in Toronto, at the Gemini headquarters, the then president of Gemini, Mr. Paul

---

EXHIBIT 3   Regional Presence of Selected Major CRSs (June 1993)

CRS	Region	Locations	Terminals	Owners
Gemini	Canada	3,500	10,500	Covia, Air Canada, and Canadian
Galileo Intl	Africa/	1,900	5,677	United Airlines 38%, British Airways
(includes	Middle East			14.7%, Gemini (Canada), Southern Cross
Galileo,	Asia Pacific	3,133	9,200	(Australia), Swissair 13.2%, KLM 12.1%,
Covia, and	Europe	8,445	27,000	USAir 11%, Alitalia 8.7%, Olympic
Gemini)	Latin America	240	500	Airways 1%, Air Canada 1%, Aer Lingus
	North America	15,500	57,000	0.1%, Austrian Airlines 0.1%, TAP Air
	Total	29,218	99,377	Portugal 0.1%
SABRE	Africa/	526	1,299	AMR Corp 100%
	Middle East			
	Asia Pacific	1,476	5,325	
	Europe	3,032	7,685	
	Latin America	980	2,289	
	North America	19,099	92,645	
	Total	25,113	109,243	
All CRS	Total	94,806	331,830	

Adapted from *Airline Business,* August 1993, p. 34.

EXHIBIT 4   A Comparison of Various Canadian and U.S. Airlines

1993	Canadian	Air Canada	American	United
Passengers (millions)	7.63	9.5	82.6	69.8
RPMs (millions)	13,417	13,768	97,706	101,846
Fleet size	82	121	667	544
Employees	15,200	18,200	91,973	81,500
Operating revenues (millions US$)	2,229	2,726	14,785	14,511

Adapted from *Air Transport World,* June 1994.

Nelson, found himself facing what he later described as a "well-orchestrated plan" by PWA's representatives on the Gemini board to declare Gemini bankrupt. The attempt failed by just one vote. "It was a total surprise," Nelson said at the time. Not surprisingly, observers noted little love lost between PWA and Nelson after that. The partnership countered fiercely. Nelson explained, "We're just not going to be put to sleep like an old dog. We've really stuck to our guns since Gemini represents an important and significant technology for Canada."

That resistance made many senior PWA managers doubtful of any deal with AMR. So on September 2, 1992, there was much relief at Canadian when Air Canada proposed a new offer. This offer had several important elements: Canadian Airlines would continue to he managed from Calgary while Air Canada would continue to be managed from Montreal; each company would have a separate president/COO; there would be equal representation from both companies on the board of directors; duplication of international services would be eliminated; and there would be "adjustment of excess capacity in Canada to permit the continuance of separate operations." The merger was expected to result in the elimination of 6,000 jobs, spread evenly between the two airlines as well as the elimination of the many duplicate services. Shareholders of both companies would receive one common share of the new holding company for each existing share. Canadian shareholders would hold a 40 percent interest in the new company, with Air Canada owning the remaining 60 percent. The proposal was subject to regulatory approval and would expire on September 9, 1992. PWA agreed to the deal and signed a pre-merger agreement on October 8, 1992.

But just one month later, Air Canada scuttled the talks saying that its bankers would not let it near a deal because of PWA's financial condition. The Canadian employees revised their rescue plan; their new offer would inject about C$650 million into the company. Their plan would provide $125 million in salary reductions over three years, a further C$125 million from a public stock issue, and C$150 million in loan guarantees from the Alberta, British Columbia and federal governments, and a C$246 million investment from AMR Corporation. But to secure AMR involvement, Canadian's relationship with Gemini would need to be terminated.

In November of 1992, the Gemini partnership countered against PWA with a C$1 billion lawsuit on the grounds that their negotiations with AMR involved a breach of fiduciary duty. Simultaneously, Gemini sued AMR for C$0.5 billion, alleging unlawful interference with Gemini's business activities.

Within days, PWA started a counter suit against Air Canada for C$1 billion, charging it with predatory pricing aimed at driving PWA out of business. On December 1, 1992, Covia entered the fray, filing a C$1.2 billion suit against PWA and AMR, alleging unlawful interference with Gemini's business activities. Throughout the legal process Canadian's reservations continued to be handled by the Gemini system.

But time was running out for Canadian; on November 29, 1992, PWA unilaterally stopped all nonoperational payments to creditors and began seeking additional voluntary concessions. Shortly afterwards, the Canadian Transport Minister announced that the federal government would provide up to C$50 million in interim loans to keep the company afloat while its options were being evaluated. The following day, the firm suspended all interest payments to its lenders and major lessors as a first step to restructuring its C$3.2 billion debt. The firm continued to pay trade creditors.

At the end of May, the Canadian National Transportation Agency (NTA), after weighing weeks of testimony at public hearings and volumes of written submissions, approved the AMR deal, arguing that it was necessary for Canadian's survival and Canadian's demise would have a more deleterious affect on the domestic market than would the proposed deal with AMR. Air Canada appealed. On June 23, 1993, the cabinet of former conservative Prime Minister Brian Mulroney rejected Air Canada's appeal of the NTA ruling.

The AMR deal was still conditional on PWA being released from its obligations to Gemini. The legal battle continued throughout the summer and into the fall of 1993. The issue faced by the court was whether Canadian could survive without the AMR deal (a question largely resolved in the earlier hearings), and more awkwardly, what would be the effect on Gemini and its other partners if PWA were allowed to leave the partnership. The arguments were based on choosing the lesser of two evils; if Gemini would be allowed to continue intact, the

---

EXHIBIT 5   Critical Events in the Efforts to Save Canadian Airlines

Jul. 27, 1992	AMR Talks Terminated.
Aug. 17, 1992	Air Canada Offer Rejected.
Sep. 1, 1992	PWA Proposes Gemini Dissolution: The motion was defeated by four of the six board members in attendance.
Sep. 2, 1992	Air Canada Merger Proposal.
Sep. 3, 1992	Aircraft Sale Completed: Proceeds from the sale amounted to $150,000,000, approximately two-thirds of which represents debt that will be repaid by the company.
Early Sep. 1992	PWA rejects a proposal from an employee group because of a lack of support by the union and the provincial governments.
Sep. 9, 1992	Air Canada Proposal Accepted.
Oct. 8, 1992	Agreement Signed: The company has signed a pre-merger agreement with Air Canada, setting out the terms and conditions that will govern the proposed merger.
Oct. 29, 1992	Revised Employee Rescue Bid.
Nov. 3, 1992	Air Canada Terminates Pre-Merger Agreement.
Nov. 12, 1992	Gemini Files $1B Suit against Canadian and AMR.
Nov. 13, 1992	PWA and Union Agree to Worker Investment.
Nov. 25, 1992	Federal Assistance to Canadian.
Nov. 30, 1992	Suspension of Interest Payments.
Dec. 2, 1992	Covia Files $1.2B Suit against Canadian and AMR.
Dec. 30, 1992	Provisional AMR Agreement Signed.
Apr. 3, 1993	Insolvency of Gemini Denied.
Apr. 30, 1993	PWA Resumes Interest Payments.
May 27, 1993	NTA Approval of Canadian/AMR Alliance.
Nov. 25, 1993	Tribunal Decision: The Competition Tribunal has ruled that Canadian Airlines is free to leave its Gemini Group hosting contract. The decision allows Canadian Airlines to transfer the hosting of its internal reservation system from the Gemini Group to American Airlines' SABRE system.
Dec. 1993	Settlement between PWA and Gemini Partners.

AMR deal would not go through and Canadian would surely fail, whereas the effects of PWA's exit from Gemini were not considered so injurious to Air Canada or Covia.

Frustrated with the time-consuming legal process, AMR set a deadline of December 31, 1993, to close any deal with PWA. Knowing that time was running out for PWA, that August, Air Canada offered to buy Canadian's international routes for C$200 million in cash and C$800 million in assumed liabilities. PWA rejected the AC offer, arguing that it would not survive as a purely domestic carrier. Without the deal, many thought Canadian was doomed, and

its arch rival was eager to prevent closure of the deal by forcing PWA to abide by its commitment to Gemini.

In November 1993, an Ottawa court decided that to preserve airline competition, the AMR deal had to proceed and if Air Canada would not release Canadian from its obligations to Gemini through a negotiated settlement by December 3, 1993, then Gemini would be dissolved effective November 5, 1994. In what many believed to be the last act of this drama, PWA settled its lawsuit against the other Gemini partners, for an amount that some analysts estimated to be around C$500,000 (see Exhibit 5).

Appendix

REPORT TO CONGRESS ON COMPUTER RESERVATIONS SYSTEMS: COMMENTS OF FRONTIER AIRLINES, INC.

Normal market forces have not disciplined the travel agency computer reservation systems market. Normally, competition between United's Apollo system, American's SABRE system, TWA's PARS system and other lesser competitors for placement of computer reservation systems at travel agencies would discipline this market. However, this has not been the case as demonstrated by abuses which have occurred. Set forth below are examples of past practices, as well as future prospects, of the anticompetitive impact of United's control of the Apollo system.

United uses Apollo in an unfair and uncompetitive manner.

(a). United has discriminatorily excluded carriers from Apollo. For over two years United refused to allow Frontier to become an Apollo co-host for "competitive" reasons. Although Frontier was finally allowed to become a co-host in July of 1982, our prior efforts to join Apollo were stalled by United's claim that its Apollo system did not have the capacity to handle Frontier. However, during the same time period at least three other major carriers were granted co-host status. After repeated inquiries, Frontier was finally told in August of 1981 by a United Vice President that it was to he excluded for "competitive" reasons. Further entreaties by Frontier were similarly rebuffed, until soon after the Department of Justice and the CAB began their investigative efforts into anticompetitive aspects of automated reservation systems.

Frontier also understands that Midway Airlines' complete schedules—direct and connecting—were expunged from Apollo for a period of time. (During the period Frontier was denied co-host status, its direct flights remained in the Apollo system.) United therefore has the power to completely eliminate smaller carriers' schedules from Apollo unless a fee is paid, regardless of the impact on the carrier, the public or travel agents. Air California now pays such a fee for inclusion of its direct flights, and had Frontier not become a co-host, United threatened complete expulsion of all our flights from Apollo unless a fee were paid.

(b). "Tying" arrangements under Apollo. In order to become a co-host under United's Apollo system, Frontier was forced to also agree on a "net ticketing arrangement" with United. Under the "net ticketing arrangement," Frontier pays United a dollar amount for tickets written by United on Frontier, and United pays Frontier a dollar amount for tickets written by Frontier on United. However, Frontier did not want this agreement, since United writes more tickets on Frontier, and we asked that separate negotiations be held on this subject. United refused, saying it was a package deal. Frontier estimates that the ticketing "tying" arrangement will cost the company about $350,000 in 1983. Thus, United used its power in the "tying" product—co-host status in the Apollo system—to impose its will with respect to a separate agreement ticketing. Interestingly, in Frontier's negotiations with TWA, a similar package deal was presented to Frontier, i.e., membership in PARS coupled with net ticketing, but TWA agreed to sever the two products and negotiate each separately.

(c). Bias problems continue even after achieving co-host status. Even after Frontier achieved co-host status under Apollo, and during Frontier's long-standing co-host status under SABRE, bias problems continue to exist which give host carriers such as United and American an unfair competitive advantage

Host carriers continue to maintain a super-bias which displays their schedules in a superior manner to that afforded co-host carriers. For example, when a travel agent requests flight information from Apollo, the system will display schedules of co-hosts from the desired time *forward,* while United alone will display backwards in time (about two hours) in addition to displaying schedules after the desired time. More comprehensive and complicated rules are employed to display connecting schedules—always designed to give United a leg up on its co-hosts.

In addition to the super-bias enjoyed by United as a host carrier, some co-hosts are more equal than other co-hosts in the tradition of Orwell's *Animal Farm.* Thus, Delta is accorded a special display on Apollo. Host carriers also retain the right to create new categories of co-hosts such as that United has accorded to Delta and thereby create new echelons of bias among co-hosts for which differentiated (and higher) rates can be charged.

(d). Host carriers have an unfair advantage—their computerized access to confidential information of the competitors. United and American have *exclusive* and *immediate* access on their respective Apollo and SABRE systems to highly sensitive sales data which they can use to their competitive advantage. United, for example, generates reports for each Apollo travel agency identifying by market the total number of passengers carried in the period, and the amount and percentage of traffic carried by each competitive carrier in the market. This information is not available to co-hosts such as Frontier. The only information United will give Frontier is the total number of passengers carried by Frontier, and currently even this limited information (which does not indicate Frontier's share of the total market, or other carriers' shares) is available about one month in arrears.

Access to this information gives United/American a tremendous and unfair competitive advantage. United sales representatives have immediate knowledge whether United and its competitors are losing/gaining market share, and United can promptly take measures (e.g., bonus incentives, lower fares, more schedules) to rectify the developing situation. The *immediate* access of United sales representatives to this data allows United sales representatives to contact travel agents long before Frontier knows of market changes. At several travel agencies where Frontier has made inroads into United market shares, the agents have mentioned "pressure" from United sales representatives to increase United market shares, as reflected in a recent article appearing in *Travel Agent*:

> Agents are also becoming accustomed to receiving printouts of their reservation histories with little comments, sometimes nasty at that, asking why some other carrier was used instead of them. (October 11, 1982, p. 19.)

(e). United coerces agents into exclusive use of Apollo. While Frontier has finally attained co-host status in Apollo, United still maintains its schedule bias over Frontier in the system, and Frontier's schedules enjoy a superior display vis-à-vis United in American's SABRE system. Therefore, United's efforts to maintain exclusivity with travel agents using Apollo—particularly in the crucial Denver market—harms Frontier (not to mention travel agencies and the public). United uses several means to preclude competition by SABRE and other automated systems.

> *The 95% Rule.* Over the last year, United has added a clause to its Apollo contract requiring the travel agent to ". . . process 95 percent of its tickets containing at least one United segment through the Apollo equipment." To assure compliance, United has the right to audit the agency's books and records without notice. The admitted purpose of this provision, according to United's Senior Vice President in charge of marketing (John Zeeman), is to prevent agencies from maintaining two systems:
>
> He agreed that this section would have the effect of forcing agents to make a choice between two or more systems, but he said the written document is only a manifestation of a continuing policy of pushing agents to make such choices. It is clear that any agency with two airline systems could not possibly satisfy the 95 percent rule, but Zeeman said United would not let such an agency have the option of signing the contract anyway. The agency would be asked to choose between Apollo and the second system. (*Travel Weekly,* November 15, 1982.)

The December issue of *Frequent Flyer* speaks of the same subject:

> But to American and United, second automated res systems are pure anathema. Reportedly, both carriers have threatened to pull their computer terminals out of agencies that install a competitor's hardware.
>
> United admits that it discourages Apollo users from using another system, particularly SABRE: "We feel than it is not an effective way to do business," says Zeeman. ("New Reservations about Airlines Computers," pp. 45 and 49.)

Other Coercive Efforts. The September 13, 1982, issue of the *Aviation Daily* contains another example of United pressure to preclude a Colorado Springs travel agency from using two systems:

> Myers originally wanted two systems in order to get boarding passes and last-seat availability for both carriers. He said a succession of meetings between Ambassador Travel and each airline made it clear that United prefers an exclusive arrangement so that it can look at any agency's business and determine if it is delivering to United a share of business that reflects the carrier's market share in the area.

(f). The pending "Boarding Pass" enhancement to Apollo. United is currently seeking to add a new feature to Apollo which would allow travel agencies to automatically issue boarding to United passengers. This feature, we understand, will not be allowed for Frontier passengers, nor will United permit SABRE users to issue United boarding passes, whether manually or otherwise. This seems to be yet another means to be used by United to enhance its airline market position, by way of its control over the Apollo system.

(g). Host carriers can also control the content of data reaching travel agents. Host carriers have the ability to control the content of information reaching travel agencies. This control has adverse competitive implications to Frontier and other outsiders. For example. Frontier recently instituted a $99 one-way fare in many markets on its system. While United did insert the Frontier fare information into Apollo, United used the same system to undermine Frontier in the eyes of the travel agents using Apollo. Thus, United inserted a "sales message" to agents informing them that it was matching Frontier fares, but gratuitously added that "Because these fares are *non-generative,* we have planned a 3/3/83 travel expiration date *to try to minimize dilution of commission.*" (Wednesday, January 12, 1983, message to Apollo users.)

The clear message by United to the travel agents was that Frontier's new fares would not produce any new passengers, and that all they would do was reduce travel agents' commissions. Standing alone, this may not seem earthshaking, but how many other messages have been sent which Frontier has not seen?

Other examples of potential anticompetitive effects of hosts' control of information in their automated systems include:

- The host carrier alone knows the intricate details of the bias system program. The host also controls when changes are made, as well as variations to bias that are implemented from time to time in "special" markets, where a host may perceive a lower usage of its service or an opportunity to improve market penetration. Despite continuous efforts. Frontier has not been able to effectively monitor its schedules in the Apollo and SABRE systems.
- At times, Frontier schedules are "dropped" from Apollo/SABRE, or fares are delayed in their entry. Frontier's monitoring catches some of these problems, but not all of them. The host always explains these problems as attributable to a computer mistake or other vagary of the system, and Frontier is in no position to contest these explanations. However, with a prime competitor controlling the system, a co-host's doubts are never really satisfied.
- From time to time, Frontier receives reports from travel agents that Apollo/SABRE seats reflect Frontier flights as being fully booked, whereas, in fact, seats remain to be sold. Again, these occurrences may be unintentional breakdowns, but a co-host never really knows.

(h). Other means host carriers use to maintain exclusivity or to proselytize travel agents.

- According to the October 1982 *Michigan Travel Bulletin,* a tour wholesaler in the Detroit area was told by United that its Winter Hawaii Program was in jeopardy, ostensibly because of unavailability of aircraft.
- United discriminates against non-Apollo agencies by withholding information. For example, we understand United has informed travel agents that only Apollo users will be able to sell special "last-minute" fares based on seat availability, and that

these fares will be denied to SABRE travel agencies. In a similar vein, United has threatened to steer commercial accounts to/from travel agencies depending upon their usage of the Apollo system.
- Large bonuses paid to travel agencies to switch automated systems (e.g., "New Reservations about Airline Computers," *Frequent Flyer,* December 1982. pp. 45, 46.)
- *Business Week* of August 23, 1982, confirms these practices:

> To compete, United this spring began offering what one agent calls "convenience money" as well as bonuses on increases in United sales, contract buyouts, and free installation to tempt agencies and not just SABRE users to take Apollo, (p. 68).
>
> Some agents resent United's pressure tactics, says one: Using power and money to buy market share may be a wise move for United from an airline point of view. But its insistence on getting rid of other airline systems, and *the thinly veiled threat that it will give us rotten service if we don't,* has dire implications for an agent's independence, (supra, p. 69).

(i). Concerns about charges Exclusion from either Apollo or SABRE can have devastating results because of the number of agencies they serve, and this is particularly true with respect to hub-and-spoke carriers who rely heavily on a favorable display of connecting flights. In this context, a host carrier can charge just about all it pleases. Since Frontier initially negotiated to become an Apollo co-host, segment charges imposed by United have increased 5 to 10 times the originally quoted rates. Frontier is very concerned that United's leverage on the Apollo system will enable it to extract excessive fees in the future.

FRONTIER AIRLINES, INC.

David N. Brictson (Vice President-General Counsel)

Case 2–2

H. E. BUTT GROCERY COMPANY: A LEADER IN ECR IMPLEMENTATION (ABRIDGED)[1]

Fully Clingman, COO of the H. E. Butt Grocery Company (HEB), was pleased with the progress the company had made in implementing category management (CM) and continuous replenishment (CRP). These programs had enabled the company to reduce prices to strengthen customer loyalty and increase sales while maintaining or improving profit margins. Despite the success of these programs, Clingman was concerned about the planned expansion of several mass-merchandise chains into the south Texas market with superstores that combined grocery and general merchandise

---

This case is an abridged version of a case prepared by Theodore H. Clark and David C. Croson under the supervision of Professors James L. McKenney and Richard L. Nolan.

[1]Copyright © 1995 by the President and Fellows of Harvard College.

Harvard Business School case 196-061.

formats. HEB's market position was strong, but these low-cost nationwide chains represented a serious threat.

The Efficient Consumer Response (ECR) vision for improving grocery channel performance was developed by a joint industry project team that included manufacturers, retailers (including HEB), and wholesalers. The ECR vision suggested multiple new programs, including CRP and CM, that would improve total channel efficiency and allow grocery retailers to compete more effectively with mass merchandisers (e.g., Wal-Mart) and club stores (e.g., Sam's Club) for sales of

traditional supermarket products. HEB was a leader in CM and CRP implementation, but Clingman wondered whether all the ECR ideas made sense for HEB. In addition, how should HEB respond to the introduction of mass-merchandise chain superstores?

Company and Industry Background

H. E. Butt Grocery Company was the thirteenth largest grocery retailer in the United States, with 1992 sales of approximately $3.2 billion (see Exhibit 1). U.S. retail grocery sales in 1992 totaled $376 billion, with

EXHIBIT 1   Leading U.S. Retail Grocery Chains—Comparison of Total Sales and Number of Stores

Sales Rank	Company Name	Number of Stores	1992 Sales ($ millions)
1	Kroger Co.	2,215	22,145
2	American Stores Company	925	19,051
3	Safeway Inc.	1,105	15,152
4	Great Atlantic & Pacific Tea Co.	1,202	10,499
5	Winn-Dixie Stores, Inc.	1,166	10,337
6	Albertson's, Inc.	651	10,174
7	Food Lion, Inc.	1,012	7,196
8	Publix Super Markets, Inc.	416	6,305
9	Vons Companies, Inc.	346	5,596
10	Pathmark Stores, Inc.	147	4,340
11	Giant Food, Inc.	156	3,473
12	Stop & Shop Supermarket Co.	120	3,352
13	H. E. Butt Grocery Company	213	3,204
14	Fred Meyer, Inc.	72	2,854
15	Ralphs Grocery Company	160	2,841
16	Grand Union Company	252	2,800
17	Bruno's, Inc.	256	2,658
18	Smith's Food & Drug Centers, Inc.	121	2,650
19	Food 4 Less Supermarkets, Inc.	249	2,475
20	Meijer, Inc.	80	2,300
21	Hy-Vee Food Stores, Inc.	160	2,250
22	Hannaford Bros. Co.	95	2,066
23	Giant Eagle, Inc.	134	2,060
24	Dominick's Finer Foods, Inc.	101	2,000
25	Stater Bros. Markets	108	1,821

Source: *Progressive Grocer Marketing Guidebook,* 1993.

the top five national retailers representing about 21 percent of total sales. The grocery channel consisted of companies in three major subcategories: retailers,[2] distributors, and manufacturers (see Exhibit 2). Retail grocery competition was regional in scope, with the largest chains operating in multiple regions but without any truly national competitors.

Distributors supplied retailers with goods in case quantities and could be (1) independent, (2) owned by a group of retailers called a *cooperative,* or (3) owned by a retail chain (a *captive distributor*). Most retail chains used captive distributors, vertically integrating to combine retail stores and distribution. Vertical integration was not limited to retailer/distributor combinations; some manufacturers also vertically integrated into distribution by providing direct store delivery (DSD) for their products. Manu-

---

[2]Retailers with 10 or more stores were generally described as *chains,* and smaller retailers were called *independents;* chains provided more than 70 percent of total U.S. retail grocery sales.

facturer DSD was common for (1) branded products where freshness was critical (e.g., dairy products, snack foods, and breads), (2) branded products with large movement volumes (e.g., soda and beer), and (3) products that required extensive in-store inventory management (e.g., greeting cards and panty hose).

Manufacturing and retailing were each highly concentrated in horizontally differentiated segments of the overall grocery channel. Retailers were highly *geographically* focused, with the top three retail chains in a geographic market (e.g., city) generally controlling 70 percent or more of sales. Manufacturers were focused on *product categories,* with a single manufacturer often controlling 40 percent or more of a single branded product category (such as salty snacks or soap). Both methods of dominance offered significant scale economies, leading to structural concentration and focused strategies.

Channel pricing policies encouraged retailers and distributors alike to purchase significant quantities of goods far in advance

---

EXHIBIT 2 Simplified Grocery Industry Functional Value Chain

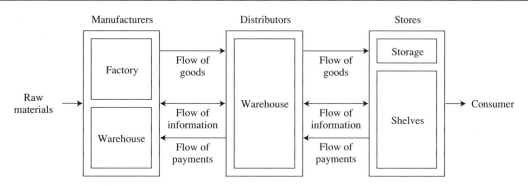

Flow of goods is frequent and high volume and may be provided by trucks owned by one of the channel members or by a third party.

Flow of information was minimal for most channel members in the early 1990s, mostly conducted via voice telephone, paper mail, and face-to-face communications.

of demand at reduced promotional prices, to be offered later to customers at the standard retail price—a practice known as "forward buying." Manufacturers typically offered retailers a wide variety of promotional allowances and rebates, whose complexity, combined with forward buying, made it difficult to determine the actual net cost of a product on the shelf.

Periodic price promotions to consumers were useful in increasing total product consumption but caused systematic forward buying as an unintended consequence. In addition to the incentive to make arbitrage profits on merchandise, forward buying on promotions also gave retailers an incentive to push the over-inventoried product through to consumers in the place of products not promoted, purchased, or warehoused in large quantities. Large purchases at the tail end of promotions also allowed manufacturers to sell product in advance of consumer demand, resulting in higher short-term accounting profits. Thus, the practice of forward buying provided manufacturers with some long-term product push, and changes in the level of forward buying affected short-term profits.

By 1990, large inefficiencies across the channel motivated retailers and manufacturers to begin investigating alternative channel-supply approaches that eliminated or discouraged forward buying and dramatically reduced inventory levels across the channel. The *Efficient Consumer Response* (ECR) report, published in 1993 by Kurt Salmon Associates under the auspices of the Food Marketing Institute (FMI), proposed a number of technological and managerial changes that promised total annual savings of approximately $30 billion if implemented completely.

An important driver of the ECR project and other efforts to improve efficiency and change channel policies was the growth of alternative store formats competing with supermarkets for consumer dollars. Discount drugstores (e.g., Walgreens), discount department stores (e.g., Wal-Mart), and wholesale-club stores (e.g., Sam's Club) had all gained market share in products frequently purchased in supermarkets.

The combination of technological and managerial innovations, developed and refined in cooperation with vendors, enabled Wal-Mart to sell products profitably at prices lower than most grocery retailers could maintain. The new channel design pioneered by Wal-Mart was copied by other discount retailers and, by 1993, had become the dominant channel design for discount merchandisers and warehouse-club stores. The ECR proposal recommended that similar changes be pursued in the retail grocery channel. Changing channel policies and behavior, as suggested by the ECR proposal, required the emergence of a new attitude of trust and cooperation between retailers and manufacturers. Such trust was difficult for many managers, who had learned to negotiate in a "win-lose" environment and had problems believing the ECR "win-win" promise.

Retail Store Operations

HEB operated over 200 full-service supermarkets throughout central and south Texas, with average sales per store of approximately $300,000 per week. Information technology had long been an important part of the company's strategy to control costs and keep prices low. A compulsive focus on improving efficiency, supported by technology and systems, enabled HEB to offer very low prices while still achieving attractive profits for the chain. In 1989, the drive to reduce costs and prices led HEB to adopt an Every Day Low Price (EDLP) strategy. Charles Butt, chairman and CEO of

HEB, was active in the chain's management and strongly believed that maintaining low prices was critical for the company's long-term strength.

Technology and Systems to Support Retailing

A leader in POS (point-of-sale) scanning adoption in the 1970s, HEB had implemented scanner systems in all of its stores during the 1980s. Store operation was supported by other systems, including automated time and attendance reporting, direct stock delivery receiving and invoicing, and electronic mail (e-mail) [which, by 1990, accounted for as much traffic as all other on-line data systems combined]. With the introduction of POS scanners and the data they provided, the use of information systems had become integral to store operations. Equipment reliability was of major concern because scanner malfunctions caused customer delay and lost sales. Dedicated minicomputer systems, designed specifically for POS scanning, provided acceptable reliability but limited flexibility for integrating the systems with other applications.

HEB had installed UNIX-based minicomputers in all stores during the early 1990s. These in-store processors were linked to the headquarters (HQ) mainframe and to all other systems within the stores, including the POS scanners. Much of the dialogue between the stores and headquarters used this computer-to-computer link in an ongoing exchange of information on sales, orders, and personnel.

To strengthen this network, HEB installed a VSAT communications system[3] linking all stores to the HQ computers during the early 1990s. This system enabled a major increase

---

[3]A VSAT communication system is a *"very small aperture terminal"* (VSAT) satellite.

in the flow of internal communications at minimal cost and facilitated the development of software applications linking stores and HQ systems tightly together.

Communication infrastructure was an important element of retail store operations. For example, one store manager at one of HEB's larger stores used his e-mail system extensively both from home and at the office. He also relied heavily on the Motorola hand-held radios carried by all managers and assistant managers in the store. During a one-hour interview, the store manager handled five requests for information or advice without significantly interrupting the interview.

Store managers relied heavily on technology support since the volume of sales had increased dramatically during the previous decade with no increase in management staff or selling floor space. Shifting store-to-HQ communications to the e-mail link enabled HEB to "keep managers on the floor, not in the office." Since a store manager's typical schedule required him to work 60 hours or more per week, the ability to handle many e-mail communications from home in the evenings was helpful. E-mail links to all stores allowed store managers to communicate useful ideas and innovations to other store managers directly. HEB's culture limited most communications to a hierarchical store-to-HQ or HQ-to-store flow, but lateral communication was possible and occasionally helpful.

Retail Pricing and Merchandising Strategy

Bob Chapman, VP of procurement, carefully examined successful retail strategies and future trends in the industry during the late 1980s. Wal-Mart and Food Lion were shifting to EDLP and away from traditional promotion-oriented pricing. HEB in the 1980s was departmentally organized, with the grocery department responsible for procuring all grocery products.

Beginning in 1989, HEB shifted to a mixed EDLP and promotional-pricing strategy. This combination of EDLP and limited promotions had been very effective in stimulating sales. EDLP was the primary pricing policy for the chain but was supplemented with specials that focused on perishables and snack-food items. The move to EDLP reduced average prices to customers, requiring HEB to find cost savings in order to maintain company profitability.

One challenge for retail managers at HEB was improving pricing accuracy. Each store's scanning system operated independently; consequently, the centrally generated price changes were not always updated correctly at the store level. Also, some stores failed to update shelf pricing labels on time due to lack of staff, time, or attention, resulting in customer complaints that items were not scanned correctly even when the scanned price was correct. The failure to implement pricing changes at the store level was a serious concern for HEB management.

Store Ordering and Inventory

Each HEB store had a limited storage space for inventory. This storage area, located in the rear of the store, was primarily used for bulky items sold in large quantities (e.g., soft drinks and diapers) and for promotional items experiencing a temporary surge in demand. On-shelf inventory for most items was sufficient to cover sales for several days. This inventory buffer enabled the store to miss a product shipment if the store made a mistake in ordering or if the warehouse was out of stock without running out of stock on the shelf.

Ordering was still largely a manual process of inspecting shelf stock and back-room inventory levels to determine what product order quantities were needed. A store employee entered orders into a hand-held computer terminal while walking up and down the aisles looking for items requiring replenishment. The employee scanned the store shelf tag of an item to be ordered and manually entered the quantity requested. After verifying that these items were not in the store's back room, the employee transmitted the order to the HQ mainframe using the satellite network. The mainframe computer then routed the order to one or more of the seven HEB product warehouses for selection, loading, and delivery to the store.

Some managers at HEB believed that POS data could be used to automate this ordering process. However, scanning accuracy was not yet sufficient to support computer-assisted ordering (CAO). Accuracy was only about 90–95 percent for scanning items, and at least 97 percent accuracy would be needed to make a CAO system cost-effective. Increasing store POS accuracy to take this step in improving operating efficiency had thus become a critical issue for store managers during 1993.

Warehouse Operations and Logistics

HEB operated an extensive warehousing and transportation system to service its more than 200 retail stores. Information technology, an important element of its distribution system, had enabled HEB to dramatically reduce logistics costs over a 10-year period.

Over 1,300 vendors supplied products to the chain, but the top 100 represented 65 percent of HEB's total volume. If these larger vendors converted to an ECR approach, the performance of the entire logistics and warehousing system could dramatically improve. The ECR report suggested retailers and manufacturers could reduce total channel inventory levels from

104 days to 61 days for dry-grocery products by combining information technology innovations with organizational and process changes. Distribution warehouses were projected to experience the greatest reduction in inventory levels, from 40 days under traditional processes to 12 days using ECR, and most of these warehouse inventory savings resulted from the effective use of CRP.

Category Management Background and Strategy

The conversion from buyers (who related to the total line of a vendor) to category[4] managers required new skills and capabilities, resulting in the need to replace many of HEB's experienced buyers. Before the change to CM, four buyers and four assistant buyers handled all grocery product procurement at HEB; only one grocery buyer made the transition to category manager. By 1993, there were 15 category managers for grocery products, including three handling only DSD products. Each of these category managers had much greater total responsibility, but managed a narrower set of products than the buyers they replaced, and were rewarded by an aggressive compensation system for reaching bonus.

CM had proven effective for HEB. Clingman noted that the company's operating profits increased significantly with each category manager added. These profit improvements helped fund the shelf-level price reductions of the EDLP strategy, which was implemented at the same time as the shift to CM.

CM evolved as new responsibilities were added over time, with the category manager effectively acting as a general manager for

---

[4]Categories were products from multiple vendors with similar characteristics (e.g., pickles, candy, or soups). Prior to CM, procurement was often structured around vendors rather than product categories.

the categories under his or her responsibility. Tim Flannigan, director of category planning and analysis, described CM as more than a program or initiative at HEB; it had become the philosophy around which the company operated by 1993. Category managers were HEB's primary profit centers, with almost complete responsibility and authority for all decisions affecting their categories.

A Commitment Not to Divert

Diverting referred to the practice of a wholesaler or retailer buying products using manufacturers' promotional or volume discounts only to resell the product to another retailer or wholesaler at a price below list but above the promotional price. From the manufacturers' perspective, this activity offered quick profits to wholesalers and retailers at the manufacturers' expense. Manufacturers who suffered from diverting spent significant amounts of time and money verifying orders to protect the integrity of their complex pricing structures. HEB had not practiced diverting to other retailers since starting CM in 1989, and Clingman viewed this commitment not to divert as part of an overall commitment to improving channel cooperation.

Continuous Replenishment and Electronic Data Interchange

HEB was one of the first companies to team up with Procter & Gamble in a CRP relationship. In November 1989, Chapman introduced the concept of CRP in an HEB operating committee meeting based on news that P&G had formed an alliance with Wal-Mart to reduce inventory and product supply cost for both partners. Fully Clingman asked HEB senior managers to set up a similar arrangement with P&G before the first of the year. Chapman observed:

Fully's concern was that he didn't want to be at a competitive disadvantage to Wal-Mart. I was tickled to death that Fully made that demand. The deadline itself was silly, but it threw down the gauntlet to the rest of the executive team that this was something to pay attention to.

The underlying logic of CRP was that P&G would supply HEB with products based directly upon warehouse shipment and inventory data rather than upon receipt of HEB-generated purchase orders. Using HEB-provided warehouse and inventory data, P&G would determine the order quantity needed, assemble the delivery, and notify HEB electronically that the shipment was coming. The information on retail store demand for products on CRP was electronically transmitted to the manufacturer daily (based on scanner readings of cases leaving the warehouse to the stores).

Although HEB was the second grocery retailer to adopt the new CRP system with P&G, the time between the introduction of the first and the second grocery-chain CRP linkages with P&G was so short that the two retailers were essentially both first movers in the adoption of CRP and developing the systems and processes needed to support it. Together, P&G and HEB worked to develop the policies and process changes needed to implement CRP in a grocery channel context, and both companies learned from each other. The relationship the two companies established through CRP also extended into other areas of channel cooperation as the "channel partners" worked together to eliminate nonvalue-added costs throughout the channel.

By directly coupling their information systems, HEB and P&G eliminated six to ten days from the previous order cycle. In addition, P&G agreed to give HEB the average deal price paid during the prior year for *all* products, recognizing that HEB purchased almost the entire annual requirements for all P&G products at deal prices by forward buying. This long-term, net-price deal eliminated the incentive to forward buy and facilitated adoption of the CRP innovation.

The major benefits of CRP for HEB were a dramatic reduction in inventory levels and reduced ordering and logistics costs in routinely supplying its warehouses. The benefits for P&G included more predictable demand and commensurately smoother manufacturing processes, as well as reduced logistics costs. The success of the CRP trial with P&G encouraged HEB to expand the relationship to other vendors. In early 1991, Clingman and Chapman visited top executives at General Mills, Quaker, Pillsbury, Campbell Soup, and other large food manufacturers among HEB's major suppliers.

EDI was essential for CRP since the volume of data transmitted and the frequency of transmission both increased dramatically in comparison with the traditional ordering process. Traditional ordering systems involve the transmission of purchase orders for a limited subset of a vendor's product line. CRP required daily transmission of data on store orders and warehouse inventory levels for all of the vendor's SKUs; it increased the total data transmission volume between companies by a factor of 100 over the traditional ordering system. In addition, data quality and timeliness became more important with the lower inventory levels since any errors could lead to retail-store stockouts.

Using a PC for EDI transmission enabled HEB to implement the new ordering process quickly without relying on expensive, time-consuming mainframe software development. This allowed HEB to gain experience in implementing the new process and to begin adapting the organization to take advantage of CRP capabilities quickly.

Expanding the CRP Program

By the end of 1991, HEB had implemented CRP with four vendors and was working with others to begin using the new process. None of the vendors cared whether HEB used mainframe- or PC-based EDI. Although using a PC minimized initial cost, the processes within HEB for using PC-based EDI links were manually very intensive and would clearly limit the expansion of CRP. Therefore, in late 1991, HEB began developing a mainframe system to replace the PC system used for the pilot CRP implementations.

The transition to the mainframe opened a new era of expansion for HEB in the development of electronic trading relationships. By the end of 1992 there were 10 active CRP vendors and a large pent-up supply of vendors interested in joining the program. During 1993, 26 new vendors were added to the CRP program, and CRP represented 31 percent of volume. Additionally, CRP vendors' assumption of responsibility for ordering reduced the time category managers required for buying administration, freeing more time for real CM.

CRP and Improved Channel Coordination

In contrast to the image of two computers talking with one another via EDI and eliminating the need for human interaction, CRP implementation encouraged extensive interpersonal contact between HEB and its CRP partners. Essentially, the use of CRP provided a parallel channel for communication of detailed information about product demand and replenishment needs, allowing the existing communications channel to be used more effectively for discussing new opportunities to improve product merchandising and further improve total channel logistics.

HEB was not concerned about the prospect of other retailers investing in CRP to erode its first-mover advantage, but rather was concerned that other retailers were not investing in CRP quickly enough to encourage manufacturers to take the plunge. Vendors incurred initial investments to start CRP and needed a sufficiently broad core of retail partners to make the investment pay off.

Because CRP implementation was a process facilitated by cumulative learning, vendors that had CRP implementation experience with grocery stores were able to move quickly with HEB once the initial negotiations were completed.

Negotiating and establishing CRP relationships with new vendors required as long as one year for vendors without prior CRP experience and less than two months for vendors with prior CRP experience. Vendors would run CRP in parallel with the traditional paper-based purchase-order-driven system for several weeks to test the all-electronic program before making a final commitment to CRP.

HEB's relationship management approach implemented by category managers helped overcome resistance from those vendors still skeptical about CRP's benefits, shifting their perspective from a short-term "win-lose" view to a long-term potential "win-win" view. The requirement of a nonantagonistic mindset was one reason few buyers were able to make the shift to the new category manager role.

The creation of stronger interorganizational relationships was one of the most important benefits of CRP implementation and provided a model for developing more effective relationships with non-CRP vendors as well. Ideas developed with CRP partners to improve channel operations could often be expanded to all vendors to reduce HEB's and vendors' total costs.

By the end of 1993, 34 vendors were on CRP and over 30 percent of HEB's grocery product purchases (in dollars) used CRP for replenishment orders. Overall warehouse inventory turns for grocery products went from 11.3 to 23.4 between 1991 and 1993.

This increase in inventory turns was due to the increased numbers of CRP relationships, the new purchasing system, and increased shifting from promotional pricing and forward buying to long-term pricing agreements (e.g., EDLP) with vendors. With CRP vendors, overall inventory turns had increased even more dramatically. Part of this improvement in inventory turns with CRP was caused by the adoption of long-term pricing agreements required to implement CRP. The logistics efficiencies enabled by implementing CRP provided further inventory reductions beyond the benefits of EDLP pricing.

During the first half of 1994, HEB increased the number of vendors on CRP to more than 60 and significantly expanded the use of CRP with existing vendors. By August 1994, HEB had reached almost 60 percent of all grocery replenishment volume using CRP. CRP had become the standard in the organization, with category managers encouraging non-CRP vendors to get on the program.

In spite of this rapid expansion of vendors using CRP, HEB intentionally limited CRP use to only those customers willing to cooperate with it to reduce total channel costs. An example of HEB's intentionally limiting CRP adoption was its decision not to allow a vendor to become a CRP partner until problems with damaged products through improper pallet loading were resolved. Although HEB deducted for all damaged products, the handling of the damaged goods and the paperwork required for deductions increased total costs in the channel.

Improved Operating Performance through CRP Relationships

Warehouse stockout levels for non-CRP products averaged about 6 percent overall in 1991, and stockout levels with CRP were less than 1 percent. A target service level of 97 percent (or 3 percent stockout level)

seemed to be about the right level since the retail stores had enough inventory on the shelf for most products to be able to miss a distribution-center shipment without experiencing product stockouts on the retail shelf. HEB worked with vendors to increase stockouts to the target level, and by 1994 CRP and non-CRP services levels were both almost exactly at 97 percent, with category managers and vendors both targeting and meeting the same overall performance standards.

Better logistics management through CRP also enabled optimizing both cube and weight loading of trucks, resulting in substantial savings in transportation cost. Some vendors were more aggressive than others in managing inventory, and not all products benefited equally from the shift to CRP. Large bulk products that were relatively stable in demand, such as pet food, were extremely well suited for CRP.

The dramatic improvements realized for some products surprised some HEB managers who had not realized that such service levels and inventory turns were possible. For example, one beverage product had inventory turns of over 25 per year before CRP, which was respectable for even CRP products. After several months of CRP operation, the vendor was able to increase product turns to more than 100 per year!

Efficient Consumer Response

Efficient Consumer Response (ECR) was introduced by David Jenkins, former chairman of Shaw's Supermarkets, at the Food Marketing Institute convention during January 1993. ECR was a broad term covering multiple technological and managerial innovations and was described as a new channel paradigm that would transform retailers, distributors, and manufacturers into more efficient and interlinked organizations (see Exhibit 3).

EXHIBIT 3 The ECR Vision—A Continuous Channel Process

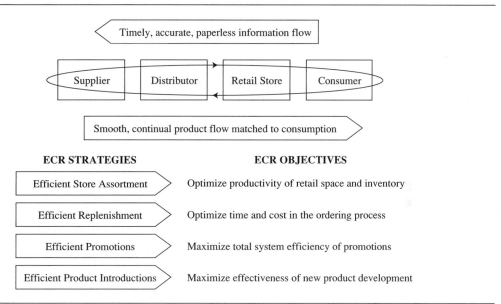

Source: Adapted from Kurt Salmon Associates, Inc., *Efficient Consumer Response: Enhancing Consumer Value in the Grocery Industry* (Food Marketing Institute, Washington, D.C.: 1993).

A long-term aspect of ECR at HEB was computerized store ordering (CSO). This was an implementation of CRP principles *within* the firm for automated ordering, based on POS data, from the store to the warehouse. Combining CSO with CRP would enable the development of a fully linked channel, with vendor shipments driven by individual stores' POS data. Wal-Mart had shifted to this completely integrated approach to channel inventory management, and HEB management believed that automated ordering using POS data would eventually become a requirement to remain competitive in the grocery channel.

Unfortunately, scanning integrity in 1993 was inadequate to support a CSO process. Dick Silvers, vice president of MIS, believed that HEB needed to improve scanning accuracy from 95 percent to 98 percent to sup-

port CSO, making scanning accuracy a major priority of the retail store operations group over the next year. HEB also needed to develop the ability to forecast store demand more accurately to facilitate CSO development once scanning accuracy was adequate to support such a system. Little historical data had been saved on daily item movements by store, making preliminary analysis of demand patterns difficult without a history upon which to base initial predictions. Improving the capability to forecast store demand using daily scanner movement would significantly reduce uncertainty in ordering. This movement toward a more sophisticated planning and tracking system for store ordering could enable HEB to increase product variety in the stores without increasing the risk of stockouts.

Using POS data in an integrated channel, the CSO and CRP process could also enable

HEB to cross-dock product shipments from vendors directly to stores. Wal-Mart's distribution cost for most products was about 2.6 percent of sales, similar to HEB's cost. But for cross-dock shipments, Wal-Mart's distribution cost was only 1.3 percent, representing an enormous advantage. J. C. Penney had experienced similar savings using cross-docking. HEB experimented with cross-docking for some fast-moving products during 1993 and 1994 (e.g., private-label sodas). However, the point of ordering needed to shift from the store to the warehouse (via CSO) or to the manufacturer (via POS-driven CRP) for cross-docking to be practical for more than a few product categories.

The Evolution of Information Technology at HEB

The potential of CSO, cross-docking, and other elements of the ECR program suggested that information technology was becoming an even more important component of the future infrastructure of the company. Electronic shelf tags were one technology that Silvers was considering as having a potentially major impact on store operations and capabilities. Such tags could increase price credibility with consumers when the store promised immediate matching of any lower price in the market, providing the customer with a real low-price guarantee. (An HEB store would require 20,000 to 28,000 electronic shelf tags which would display prices and be updated by radio frequency signals from a store computer.) [A tag cost roughly $8.00, so the investment was considerable.]

HEB clearly recognized that POS data were important to improve the store ordering process and move from a reactionary mode of operations to a forecasting and planning model. Some vendors valued grocery retailers' POS data sufficiently to provide partial funding for a new start-up firm called Efficient Marketing Service (EMS), which offered free expert "data scrubbing" services to supermarket chains, providing cleaned-up data that were more useful for planning and analysis. HEB did not have the capability to "scrub" its own POS data and was pleased to have EMS provide the service for them. EMS not only provided these services for free to retailers, they also paid the supermarkets for the right to sell the data to vendors.

The logistics and warehouse operations area viewed information technology as critical for operations and a substitute for inventory in the channel. As information replaced inventory, it also replaced skills required under the old inventory-based processes with new information-based skill requirements. As an unpleasant side effect, however, almost half of the skilled managers in the warehouse were replaced because they were unable to adapt to the new systems.

Future Issues and Challenges

Clark was concerned about CRP's effectiveness during times of high inflation, when HEB could profit from purchasing more inventory than is required to satisfy immediate customer demand. Forward buying provided a good inflation hedge during the 1970s and cost the company little compared to the gains on the short-term investment.

Silvers wanted to see HEB move more quickly in expanding EDI capabilities such as invoicing, receiving, and payment. He was also interested in exploring other ways that HEB could use technology to improve operations, such as electronic shelf tags. He was interested in the potential for joint ventures, partnerships, and alliances with other firms to improve HEB efficiency or operations, such as with a trucking firm.

Case 2–3

INTERNET SECURITIES, INC.: BUILDING AN ORGANIZATION IN INTERNET TIME[1]

Global finance, more than any other industry, is being fueled by the free flow of information. . . . [In the 1990s,] information about money is probably worth more than the money. What separates the winners from losers in this community is nothing more than the milliseconds it takes to get access to this precious information.

Nicholas Negroponte[2]

Founded in June 1994 by two brothers, Gary and George Mueller, Internet Securities, Inc., provides hard-to-find financial, business, and political information to business professionals on a subscription basis. What differentiates Internet Securities from a myriad of other information providers is that the company concentrates solely on information from emerging markets and the information is primarily available on the Internet's World Wide Web. (Exhibits 1, 2, and 3 summarize the ISI Emerging Markets service. Visit the company home page at http://www.securities.com.) The founders described the situation they faced in January 1998.

Internet Securities has grown quickly since we launched our service in June 1995. We are now providing information on more than 25 emerging market countries including China, Russia, India, Poland, Brazil, Argentina, Turkey, Hungary, and many others. We have 18 offices in 18 different countries around the world. We provide information from more than 600 information providers and have approximately 650 institutional customers including JP Morgan, Deutsche Morgan Grenfell, KPMG, and ING Barings.

In less than four years, we built this company from a few people doing all the work out of a third floor walk-up apartment to over 175 people performing specialized roles in offices around the world. Our employees accepted lower wages because we gave them an equity stake in the business. We owe it to them, to our investors, and to ourselves to ensure that we build and safeguard the value of this firm.

In the first year after the launch we believed that rapid growth and expansion of services were critical to the company's success. But growth also strained our informal organizational structure and management systems. Our previous motto had been to grow fast. Over the past year it was to grow strong, yet still keep pace in an environment that demands that companies manage in "Internet time." As we entered 1998, we were a much stronger organization. It's now time to pick up the pace. As we do so, we need to be sure that we have the

---

This case was prepared by Professor Lynda M. Applegate with assistance by Research Associate Kirk Goldman.

[1]Copyright © 1998 by the President and Fellows of Harvard College.

Harvard Business School case 398-007.

[2]Nicholas Negroponte was the director of the MIT Media Center and author of the book *Being Digital*. He was also a partner in Applied Technology, Inc., which had invested in Internet Securities.

EXHIBIT 1 The ISI Emerging Markets Service

Categories of Information include:

- **News.** Internet Securities signs agreements with the newswire services as well as the leading news periodicals in its local markets. Stories are incorporated into the ISI Emerging Markets service database on an immediate, daily or weekly basis. With some publications, articles appear on the service the evening before they are published.
- **Company Financial Information.** ISI Emerging Markets provides basic financial statements (income statement, balance sheet, ratios, etc.) for public companies from both public and private sources. The service also provides data for unlisted companies and select private companies. Much of this information is made available to the user in spreadsheet format.
- **Industry and Analyst Reports.** The company also signs agreements with leading brokerages in emerging markets. These brokerages include their company, market and other reports on the ISI Emerging Markets service.
- **Equity and Fixed-Income.** ISI Emerging Markets also covers daily updates of the equity and debt markets. Sources include local stock exchanges, and top domestic and international banks.
- **Macroeconomic Data.** The service includes spreadsheet or tabular formatted basic economic statistics, cross-sectional and historical, acquired from government and private sources.
- **Surveys, General Reports and Other Useful Resources.** General reports on countries and industries from major financial information sources such as the Financial Times are made available.

Differentiating Features

- **Comprehensive Information.** ISI Emerging Markets provides comprehensive online information that consolidates business, financial and other information for emerging markets.
- **Exclusive Online Source.** Many of the information providers are only available online via ISI Emerging Markets.
- **Presentation.** The ISI Emerging Markets service uses the Web's easy-to-use, graphical interface which is Windows, Mac, or UNIX compatible and offers "Point and Click" navigation. The service is very easy to learn and use, even for first-time users.
- **Information Retrieval.** The service features automatic downloading of data into spreadsheets and word processing programs on the user's computer.
- **Searchability.** The company's proprietary search engine enables users to search entire databases of text, spreadsheets, graphs, and other files to locate information of interest. This feature provides users with an easy-to-use means of full-text searching, printing and saving articles from the service.
- **Local Language Support.** ISI Emerging Markets supports multiple languages and allows users to access a variety of information, including information from local sources not available in English. It is even possible to search and display the results in the local language.
- **Flexible Access.** Because the ISI Emerging Markets service does not require dedicated terminals, leased lines, or special equipment, the customer can access the service from any computer, modem, and telephone line. Clients may even dial in to the service from their portable laptop computers when traveling, which presents a significant cost and flexibility advantage over fixed-terminal services. This feature also keeps distribution costs low and allows Internet Securities to invest more resources in providing the information and features the customers want.

(continued)

EXHIBIT 1 (continued)   The ISI Emerging Markets Service

- **Access to Archived Data.** ISI Emerging Markets information service includes archived records so that historic searches of information in original format are possible.
- **Relatively Inexpensive.** The ISI Emerging Markets information service is relatively inexpensive in comparison to traditional data sources (periodicals, fax services, primary data-gathering) and in comparison to other online information services.

Internet Securities' information providers include news organizations, banks and financial institutions, government bodies, private companies, and research organizations which supply the types of data described above. Internet Securities signs contracts with these information providers from both the geographic focus areas ("in-country") and in the developed financial markets. In addition, Internet Securities includes developed market information providers to add summary analysis and "brand name" credibility to the ISI Emerging Markets service.

Sample of Branded Information Providers (June 1998)

Alliance Friday News Dispatch; ASIDA; Business Central Europe; Business World Update; CASE Research; CASH; CBnet; Citibank; Chip News; Duff & Phelps; Economic Daily; Economist Intelligence Unit; Financial & Economic Research International; First Investment Trust Research; Futures Market provided by UFIE Co. Ltd.; Horizon; Informed Business Services; Infotrade; PlanEcon; WEFA Group.

Sample of In-Country Information Providers (June 1998)

Brazil:

Agencia Estado; Agroanalysis; Advanstar Editora; Banco Hoje Magazine; BM&F; BNDES; Bovespa; Carta Capital; Central Bank of Brazil; CVM; Economist Intelligence Unit; EFC Consultores; Enfoque Sistemas; Folha de Sao Paulo; Gazeta Mercantil; Jornal do Brazil; LCA Consultores; Macrometrica; Ministry of Finance; O Estada de Sao Paulo; O GLOBO; Previsa; Trend Consultores.

Poland:

Gazeta Bankowa; Gdansk Institute for Market Economics; GUS (State Statistical Office); KSH; Ministry of Finance; National Bank of Poland; NFI; Notoria; PAIZ; Parkiet; Pekao S.A.; Penetrator Brokerage House S.A.; Pentor; Pioneer Polish Securities Co.; Polish News Bulletin; Polish Press Agency; Pretor; Raiffeisen; Warsaw Voice.

China:

Bank of China; Business Beijing; CCPIT; China Chemical Week; China Contact Information (DCCB); China Daily; China Electric Power Information Center (CEPIC); China Law Information Service; China Petroleum Newsletter; China Watch; IDG China; Investment Institute of State Planning Commission; P&T Market; Shanghai Stock Exchange; Shenzhen Stock Exchange; SinoScan; US Embassy, Beijing Daily Commercial Briefs; Xinhua News Agency (China Economic Information Service).

(continued)

EXHIBIT 1 (concluded)   Representative Client List (June 1998)

International Investment Management Companies	*Commercial and Investment Banks*	*Local ("In Country") Banks and Corporations*	*Multinational Corporations*
AIG	Banque Indosuez	Bank Gdanski	Boeing
Brunswick Capital Management	Bear, Stearns & Co.	Bank Handlowy	Eli Lilly
Creditanstalt	Citibank	Banque Paribas	Federal Express
Credit Suisse Asset Management	European Bank for Reconstruction Development	Brunswick	Lockheed Martin
Fidelity Management and Research	OFC	Lukoil	Lucent Technologies
Foreign and Colonial	ING Barings	Matav	Mitsubishi
GE Capital	JP Morgan	Menatep	Motorola
Putnam Investment Management	Merrill Lynch	Moscow Narodny Bank	Novell
The Pioneer Group	Morgan Stanley & Co.	Polski Bank	Polaroid
Wellington Management	World Bank	Raiffeisen	Price Waterhouse
Societe General		Wood and Company	Siemens
			Sun Microsystems
			United Technologies

organizational and business infrastructure in place that will be needed as the company grows. In our business, we aren't capital constrained like Amazon.com; we are people constrained. That means we need to be sure that we are hiring and developing the management talent that we will need for the business as it will look 6 to 12 months from now.

Today we are profitable in many of our markets and, by the end of 1998, we plan to be cash flow positive. Once we achieve these business goals, we will consider going public. We should have $15 to $20 million in subscription revenues by then. We have been very successful at growing our customer base and over 90 percent of our customers have renewed their subscriptions. Our established customers have been upgrading the level of services that they buy from us by about 20 percent per year. This subscription model provides tremendous business stability. I don't believe in "concept IPOs." We don't need the capital for expansion, and as a high-end, business-to-business information service, we don't need to build a consumer brand. Why should we subject ourselves to the risk of going public too soon?

Industry Background

During the late 1990s, the market for business information was undergoing significant change and had become highly competitive. Traditionally dominated by large, well-capitalized companies such as Reuters, Dow Jones, Dun & Bradstreet, and Bloomberg, technological changes over the past decade—especially the commercialization of the Internet—had resulted in the entry of many small competitors (see Appendix A). In 1994, as Gary and George Mueller developed

EXHIBIT 2   Internet Securities Business Development Model

Emerging Country Rollout Plans

Stage	Estimated Length	Estimated Cost	Key Activities
1	3 months	$10,000/month	Establish a presence in the country
			Learn about the local information market
			Establish relationships
			Create business and information infrastructure
2	3 months	$10,000/month	Begin marketing Internet Securities services to developed countries
3	6 months	$10,000/month	Sell Internet Securities services in developed countries
			Gather and format information for sale locally
			Begin marketing Internet Securities services locally
			Sell Internet Securities services locally
Total Time/$ to Open an Office	12 months	$120,000	

Internet Securities Offices

Number	Location	Employees	Office Type
1	Boston MA, USA	42	World headquarters
2	London, England	17	Europe headquarters
3	Budapest, Hungary	8	Sales and product development
4	Istanbul, Turkey	8	Sales and product development
5	Prague, Czech Republic	11	Sales and product development
6	Sofia, Bulgaria	6	Sales and product development
7	Warsaw, Poland	8	Sales and product development
8	Kiev, Ukraine	4	Sales and product development
9	Moscow, Russia	14	Sales and product development
10	Bombay, India	12	Sales and product development
11	Beijing, China	8	Sales and product development
12	Santiago, Chile	19	Sales and product development
13	São Paulo, Brazil	10	Sales and product development
14	Buenos Aires, Argentina	5	Sales and product development
15	Bucharest, Romania	2	Sales and product development
16	Mexico City, Mexico	6	Sales and product development
17	Brussels, Belgium	1	Sales
18	Hamburg, Germany	1	Sales

EXHIBIT 3   Internet Securities Business Model

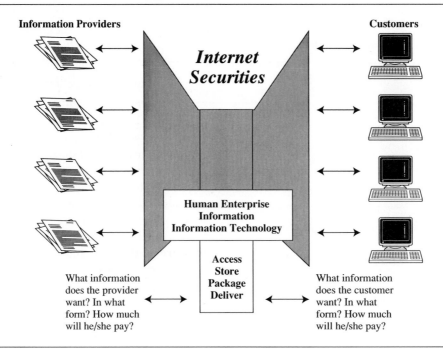

Information Providers

Internet Securities

Customers

Human Enterprise
Information
Information Technology

Access
Store
Package
Deliver

What information
does the provider
want? In what
form? How much
will he/she pay?

What information
does the customer
want? In what
form? How much
will he/she pay?

the Internet Securities business plan, the largest online information providers each had revenues over $1 billion, yet it was also estimated that there were over 3,000 online financial information companies in the United States alone.

New entry into the market was common; Desktop Data, Individual Inc., and M.A.I.D. were examples of successful new entrants during the 1990s. Small and large acquisitions and partnerships were also commonplace: for example, GALT Technologies was acquired by Intuit in November 1995 for $9 million; Thomson International acquired Westlaw in February 1996 for over $3 billion; and in late 1995, Microsoft launched the Microsoft Network, MSN, and partnered with General Electric to form MSNBC. Internet-related acquisitions and initial public offerings (IPOs) were fueling the indus-

try's dynamic growth. Reuters' CEO, Peter Job, emphasized his company's interest in acquiring small firms with high growth potential (see Appendix B).

Internet Securities believed that the market for online information on emerging markets was large and growing. Not only were business professionals from developed markets eager to gain access to accurate, reliable, and up-to-the-minute information, so too were business professionals in the emerging markets. In many emerging markets, Internet Securities reported, there were in excess of 10,000 expatriates who worked locally under the sponsorship of a large firm headquartered in a developed market. Most of these professionals had the technological tools and the funds, motivation, and expertise to access and use local information if it was available. Local business professionals also constituted a sizable and growing group of potential users. In Poland, Internet Securities reported, there were more than 1,000 Polish business professionals in Big Six accounting firms. The penetration of the Internet in these emerging economies fueled the growth of both the supply of, and the demand for, information.

Creating the Business Concept

Internet Securities was founded in June 1994 by Gary and George Mueller. After spending several years in Germany on a Fulbright Scholarship, Gary had worked as a consultant, specializing in Eastern Europe privatization. "I was in Germany when the Berlin wall came down in November 1989," Gary recalled. "That was an incredibly moving experience. I knew then that I definitely wanted to be involved in helping to transform emerging economic markets."

George graduated from Carnegie Mellon University in 1993 with a B.S. degree in both electrical and computer engineering. Prior to joining Internet Securities full time, George won the Enterprise Award in Entrepreneurship in 1994.

Both Gary and George also drew on a background of working with entrepreneurs and a family legacy of entrepreneurial spirit. "Throughout our childhood, our entire family was involved in building new businesses," the two brothers explained:

> Our grandfather built a successful manufacturing business, and our grandmother built a successful antique business. Our father owns two manufacturing firms, and our mother launched and ran a vintage clothing business. Finally, our uncle was founder or owner of seven different companies.

With their combined interests and knowledge, Gary and George decided to start Internet Securities. They chose Poland as the first emerging market to enter.

Developing the Technical Infrastructure

The development of the technical infrastructure for Internet Securities' information service began in early 1994. (See Exhibit 4 for a summary of the technical architecture.) Jae Chang and Mike Hayward, both graduates of Carnegie Mellon University, developed the initial software that would be used to prototype the service using free software—"freeware"—available on the public Internet. Internet Securities then contracted with Bell Atlantic for a high speed, secure data line ($2500 per quarter) and paid an Internet service provider $605 per quarter for Internet access. While this bootstrap effort worked reasonably well for developing the software in the United States, the company soon found that more sophisticated solutions would be needed as they attempted to access information in developing countries. Hayward and Mikhail Ruttman, also a graduate of Carnegie Mellon University, set up the technological platform in Poland and Russia respectively. Hayward explained, "In Poland our providers and customers waited months if not years for a data line, and, even if a line was secured, they were plagued by problems. You get countless busy signals and can't connect and, if you do get in, you get disconnected partway through a session."

To overcome these problems, Internet Securities partnered with a Polish banker to form an Internet access company, Internet Technologies. Reliable phone lines were obtained by leasing office space for both Internet Securities' local office and Internet Technologies in the Warsaw Marriott, which had excellent proprietary network services. The $2,400 per month rent was deemed to be well worth the money. "We get great telephone lines and the most prestigious address in Warsaw. It has really helped our image and credibility with both information providers and customers," Gary explained.

EXHIBIT 4   ISI Emerging Markets Service Minimum Information Technology Requirements and Costs (June 1998)

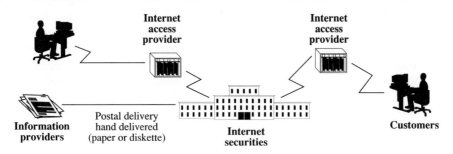

Provider IT Requirements	Est. Cost[a]	ISI IT Requirements[b]	Est. Cost	Customer IT Requirements	Est. Cost
Personal Computer workstation	$1,500-$2,000	Personal Computers (130)	$390,000	Personal Computer	$1,500-$2,000
Modem (14.4 or higher)	$60-$100	Web/network Servers (40)	$600,000	Modem (14.4KB or higher)	$60-$100
Internet Access (dial-up)	$20-$50/month	Routers/Security (15)	$45,000	Internet Access (dial-up)	$20-$50/month
Internet Software	$0-$20/month	Development Workstations (30)	$45,000	Internet Software	$0-$20/month
		Software	$500,000		

[a]For comparison purposes the estimated costs are in US$. Internet Securities states that these costs are representative of those incurred by their information providers and customers in many different countries.
[b]Numbers in parentheses represent the number of computers of each type.

Solving the technical problems was only the first step in providing access to the information. Many of the Polish information providers had little experience with IT and most had never heard of the Internet. "What's this Web?" was a frequent question.

Hayward explained, "We've gotten the service to work on equipment that amazes me. But many managers need help learning how to work with computers. Sometimes they blame us for their mistakes. For example, a Polish information provider, who accessed the system through an international call from Poland to Pittsburgh, once forgot to disconnect from the service when he was done. He left his computer connected to the Pittsburgh office for eight hours at the equivalent of US $3 per minute. You can imagine his phone bill. Another information provider stored all of his back-up data on disks that were stored on a windowsill beside the coffeepot."

Contracting with Providers and Developing the Information Content

As the technical team worked on the IT infrastructure, Melissa Burch worked to sign on information providers. Whenever possible, contracts contained exclusivity clauses that prevented the information provider from selling the same information to other online information providers. But these contracts were difficult to obtain. "Often the information providers will only agree to wording that states that Internet Securities will be the exclusive provider on the Internet or the World Wide Web," explained Melissa Burch and Rafael Sokol, who were hired to develop the information service for Poland—the first emerging market Internet Securities entered. The length of the formal agreement also limited the opportunity for exclusive distribution rights. For example, neither the publisher of the *Warsaw Business Journal* (Thompson Barnhardt) from the United States nor the publisher of *Nowa Europa* (John Gates) from Britain was willing to sign a long-term contract in spring 1995. "In this business, three years is a lifetime," Barnhardt said.[3] "Six months is the best that I can do right now." Gates agreed. "I'm not ready to commit to a long term relationship at this time," he stated.[4] Burch commented that her overriding objective was to "get good information as quickly as possible and present it in a format that people want. Without that we don't have a business."

Information providers were typically paid 15 percent of subscriber revenues attributable to that supplier's content. Burch and the local team had the freedom to offer more for "unique information that customers really want." Some information providers agreed to a multi-tier pricing structure, with a higher percentage of revenues for more valuable information. In 1996, information value was defined informally by Internet Securities local country managers who were responsible for developing an emerging market. "I would offer more for real time information, such as same-day stock prices and today's news," Burch explained. "I would also offer more for hard-to-find information that our customers told us they desperately needed, especially if I can certify the information as highly reliable and accurate. If I had any questions about the price I should offer to a supplier, I sent an e-mail to Gary and George." Using this approach, Burch was able to sign agreements with over 30 information providers in Poland by the time the service was launched in June 1995.

Selling the Service to Customers

The Internet Securities business plan stated that the company would market and sell its services in both developed and emerging markets. Initially, Gary Mueller assumed responsibility for signing up customers within developed markets. He chose London, New York, Boston, and Washington D.C. as the initial sites for local offices in developed countries. Rafael Sokol assumed responsibility for developing the local customer base in Poland. He found local business professionals wary of making a long-term commitment. Sokol stated: "They are eager to participate in a free trial, but are more reluctant to pay for the service. They need time to get comfortable in using the technology and are unsure of the value of the information we provide. We have to be patient."

Gary said, "Initially, we looked at the marketplace and noted that the high-end information companies charged over $1000 per month for each 'terminal'—access device—or for each user. At the same time, smaller niche players priced their products around $250 per month per user. For example, Technical Data Corp. priced its products at $250 per month. Each of these companies had a long history on which to base their pricing. Next, we surveyed potential customers."

[3]Interview in Warsaw, Poland, on August 3, 1995.
[4]Interview in Warsaw, Poland, on August 4, 1995.

Despite the intensive research, determining the right price to charge was complex. In early 1998, Internet Securities had a fixed-rate pricing structure. Some information was offered on the Internet for free to help introduce potential customers to the service. The standard subscription price was $250 per country per user per month, with a sliding scale to encourage volume purchases. Each subscription was one year in length with the fee paid up front. By January 1998, Internet Securities had approximately 650 institutional clients. In June 1998, the company had a 90 percent customer retention rate.

Building an Organization in Internet Time

Launching the Service

The informal organization and ad hoc systems and communications, which worked well while the company was small, began to break down as Internet Securities transitioned from "building the business concept" to "going to market." In 1995, Gary and George hired functional experts in sales, marketing, operations and control.

Andy Hannah, a certified public accountant with eight years' experience at Deloitte & Touche, was hired in summer 1995 as vice president of finance. Hannah remarked, "Internet Securities is very similar to other start-ups I've seen. There were no systems to reconcile accounts, segregate duties, or ensure accurate financial statements. It was certainly not a crisis since there were accounting and billing systems that enabled Gary and George to keep close tabs on cash flows. However, once we received our second round of financing [$1.5 million] in early 1996, the company needed to get serious about accounting."

During early 1996, Hannah instituted basic financial and accounting controls and a formal budgeting process. As he explained to employees, "A well-designed budgeting system is the most basic form of control in companies; it's the blueprint outlining the strategy and business plan, and it gives management a way to measure progress toward business goals."

In mid-1995, Jack Phillips and James Fant were hired to develop a formal sales and marketing organization in the United States and Europe, respectively. Phillips, who had graduated with Gary from the Harvard Business School, assumed the role of worldwide Sales Manager. He established his office in New York and oversaw Fant's, located in London. At the same time, Jason Green was hired to manage IT in the London office. By June 1997, Internet Securities sold its services in three ways: direct sales, telesales, and direct mail.

Phillips recalled, "Gary and the team in Europe had proven that the product could sell both in London and the local markets. The next step was to scale up to deliver a successful service around the world. To do that, we created a global sales organization: we promoted salespeople in London and the local Eastern European markets; hired new people; and opened low-budget sales offices in New York, Boston, and Washington. Mostly, though, this meant setting local sales targets, hiring the players, and training the team in the most effective ways to sell the product."

Fant said, "The key was to get the sales force's skill set consistent with the company's mission. In many former socialist countries, salespeople were viewed with disdain. We needed to cut through this stereotype and develop credibility—good people, good products, and complete openness. In emerging markets in Europe, we found that it was easier, faster, and cheaper to develop local people into top-quality sales people. There is a lot of talent out there, waiting to be trained and pointed in the right direction. But the biggest challenge we have faced has been to convince our sales force that the targets we are aiming for are eminently achievable. People's negative beliefs about what is possible have to be continually broken down and recast. If there is any one idea that I would say has applied throughout, it is that you cannot get where you want to be tomorrow by doing the same things you did yesterday. Constant evolution, improvement, and open-mindedness have been the order of the day."

Jason Green stated, "In the early stages of the company the information formatting group worked alongside the technical development group in Philadelphia. They were a tightly knit community working toward a common goal. But as we started to grow and brought more and more countries online, we found we needed to change the way we worked. The centralized groups could no longer meet all of our needs. We needed local groups that could be proactive but we still needed to ensure that the service had a consistent 'look and feel' and quality level. Introducing Information Specialists and a Technical Manager in each country enabled us to add the local support, while preserving the tightly-focused operating community feel. The central editorial, sales and technology groups ensured the consistency and quality control."

Dealing with Business and Organizational Complexity

The company grew from fewer than 20 people in February 1996, to approximately 30 by June, and to 120 by September of the same year, and from one location in Poland to over 175 people located in 18 offices around the world by June 1998. As the business became more complex and operations became more dispersed, coordination difficulties increased. Melissa Burch described her frustration as she attempted to open the Ukraine office in early 1996. Always an enthusiastic user of e-mail, she initially believed it was an excellent way for a virtual organization to coordinate work. But as the number of locations and people increased, the limits of e-mail became obvious. Burch complained:

> People in Pittsburgh weren't reading my e-mail. I repeated myself over and over. At times it seemed like I was sending messages into a black hole. Information providers were willing to pay to get their data on our service. They were excited about working with us. But we couldn't get them signed on because I couldn't talk to Pittsburgh.

The rapid pace of geographic expansion also began to cause problems. At first, Burch attempted to serve as the unofficial advisor to new country managers. But as the number increased, she found it more and more difficult to provide the guidance they needed. In late fall 1995, Navin Nagiah, who graduated with a master's degree in electrical engineering from the University of Kansas, and Charles Chang, a postdoctoral fellow at MIT working on the "China Relations" project, were hired as country managers for India and China respectively. Nagiah recalled his orientation:

> Jae Chang dropped me off at the airport, and from then on I was on my own. There was so much that needed to be done—find a place to live, establish a bank account, look for an office, obtain a business license for operation, get to know the business climate, solicit information providers, get reliable phone lines, get marketing material, buy a computer, printers and fax machine, and get information flowing.

Ellen Holman, country manager for the Czech Republic, voiced her concerns:

> I didn't know what I was getting into. Melissa filled me in on a lot of the details of what I needed to do to get started, and someone else showed me how to use e-mail and the file transfer software. But sometimes I didn't know who to call to answer a question. Everyone was overloaded.

Neil Shepherd, country manager in Budapest, raised a different concern: "Private matters are difficult to discuss over e-mail. Sometimes I just have to pick up the phone. But finding people available on the other end is tough."

In January 1996, Burch organized the "Pioneers List"—an electronic bulletin board where country managers could discuss common concerns. Shepherd was enthusiastic: "The Pioneers List really improved things. We could discuss things and help one another. For example, I was having trouble getting information providers to sign our long contracts. I learned that, in Russia. Melissa used shorter contracts, rather than bicker with the providers. Now I'm changing my strategy." Ellen Holman added that the Pioneers List addressed "a need for communication among country managers." She recommended that Gary and George hire a "manager of the country managers. We needed more training, and needed someone we could call on for day-to-day answers and help." In fall 1995, Yolanda Lozano, a graduate of Carnegie Mellon's Graduate School of Public Policy, was hired to serve as regional leader of Latin America: and, in June 1996, Susan Pratt joined Internet Securities immediately after graduation from the Harvard Business School to serve as regional leader for Central and Eastern Europe. The regional leaders assumed responsibility for training and coaching country managers and served as a coordinating link between the country managers in the field and the corporate headquarters in Boston.

Creating a Formal Organization

By summer 1996, it became clear that a more experienced senior management team was needed in sales/marketing and operations. (See Exhibits 5 and 6 for an overview of the organization chart in January 1998 and for short biographies of the management team.) "Early on, a start-up needs— and can only afford—young managers," Jack Phillips explained. "But by 1996, the business had become too complex. It was time to hire a seasoned marketing and sales manager. In effect, I hired my own boss." Cameron Lochhead, who had 16 years' experience in electronic publishing, most recently as senior vice president and general manager of Technical Data Corporation—a subsidiary of Thomson Financial Services— joined the firm as senior vice president for worldwide sales, marketing, and product development. Phillips now reported to Lochhead along with Randy O'Neil and Richard Garnier who were brought in by Lochhead to head North American and Western European Sales, respectively. Phillips explained:

> I transitioned to more of a product manager role. I'm like the editor-in-chief of Business Week. There is an acute need for tighter editorial control—for someone to work with our information specialists and technical people to refine our service to provide more valuable information, and to ensure consistency and a professional and appealing look. In our role as information intermediaries, we need to ensure that products and services add value to both our customers and our suppliers. I will be spending more time ensuring that we maximize the value that we deliver to both.

Michael Fix, who had over 11 years of experience working in general management and sales in the online information services industry, joined the company in May 1996 as managing director for European Operations. The regional leaders reported to him. Country managers reported to each regional leader. Reporting to them were one or more information specialists and editors who understood the local business market, a small sales force appropriate to the size of the market in that area, and the required

EXHIBIT 5   Internet Securities Organization Structure (June 1998)

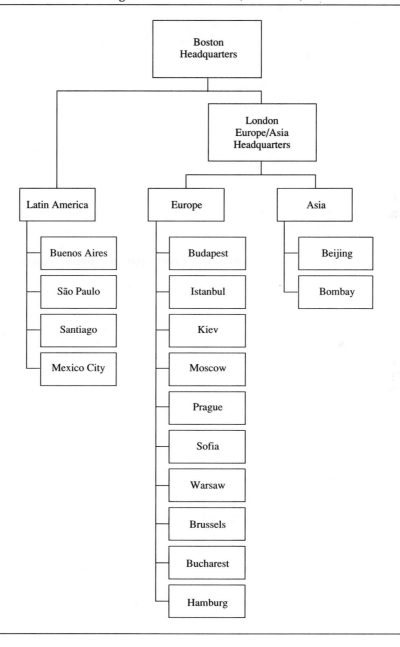

EXHIBIT 6   Internet Securities Senior Management Team (June 1998)

Gary Mueller   President and CEO, Internet Securities. Over four years experience in privatization transactions and private enterprise in Poland and Russia. Received both a BA and an MBA, Harvard University.

Andrew Hannah   CFO, Internet Securities. Eight years of experience with Deloitte & Touche in accounting and finance. University of Pittsburgh, MBA.

Michael Fix   Chief Operating Officer, Internet Securities. Eleven years of general management, sales management, and sales experience in the online information industry.

Chito Jovellanos   Senior Vice President of Product Development and Technology, Internet Securities. Fifteen year veteran of the financial services industry.

EXHIBIT 7   Internet Securities Country Office Structure (June 1998)

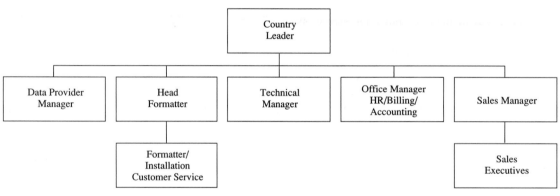

---

technical expertise (see Exhibit 7). As the number of country offices in a region grew, regional headquarters offices were created and the informal regional leader role was replaced by a director of regional operations. By June 1998, the company had restructured into three regional divisions (Europe, Latin America, and Asia) and Michael Fix had been promoted to Chief Operating Officer. "When Michael joined the company," Gary explained, "he had sales experience, general management experience, and international experience. His skills really matched what we needed and his personal-

ity and management style fit well with the company culture."

As they restructured the company and brought in top management talent, Internet Securities also turned attention to the task of creating the financial controls required by the rapidly-growing company. Andy Hannah stated, "The accounting and finance function has grown significantly since we launched our product in 1995. We've raised more capital and leveraged our venture capital to obtain lines of credit at Silicon Valley Bank. During the past few months we developed a very sophisticated financial information system that will be implemented worldwide by mid-1998. We hired an accountant to work in each region and developed one to two month operating budgets for each office. The quality of our internal reporting has been raised by 1000 percent. We now have formal planning and budgeting processes in place and issue quarterly reports that are comparable to those available in public companies." Andy explained:

We roll up the entire company's books within ten days of month-end and formally close the books. Considering that we are in 18 different emerging markets, each of which has their own currency, this requires a significant amount of staff time as well as accurate systems. Most entrepreneurial firms do not have strong systems and processes until much later in their development. We put these systems in ahead of the curve. We believe that it provides a tremendous level of discipline in the firm and also enables us to better understand our business. We catch problems much earlier and can take actions to solve them before they escalate. We can also spot opportunities much faster.

We also report sales on a weekly basis. As a result, we can review our online sales charts and know exactly which of our information products is selling to individual users within each customer site. We know who is using our service and how they are using it. We also have very detailed information on all of our information providers. We know exactly what type of information they provide and how well, and where, it is selling. This information is critical to driving the business.

This information is available on our company-wide Intranet to enable all employees to have access to information that helps them do their jobs better. A country manager and local sales people can tell exactly how well our information products are selling and can work with information providers to help them target and deliver the most valuable information. They can also see what local customers are viewing and can use this information to help increase subscription revenues. For example, if informa-

tion on Russia or Brazil is not selling well in Poland, the local sales people will know immediately and can talk to customers to find out why. Access to this detailed, timely operating data benefits local employees since their bonuses are tied to increasing revenues related to both customers and information providers in their market.

"As we worked to achieve information control," Hannah continued, "we also focused attention on ensuring that we had control of our operations." Fix, working with the regional directors, reviewed operating processes in the field and at corporate headquarters. Based on the review, Internet Securities redesigned their worldwide operating processes and, in late 1997, published their first Worldwide Policy and Procedures manual. The policies and procedures clearly delineated those processes and activities that would be standardized across the company and those that were at the discretion of the country manager. Regional and corporate management met monthly to review operating performance.

To further support coordination and control of operations, the company created a corporate headquarters office in Boston, Massachusetts. The Pittsburgh office closed during the first quarter of 1997, and all personnel and activities were transferred to Boston. In addition, many of the product development, marketing. and sales activities that had been dispersed in offices around the world also moved to Boston. Lochhead was thrilled: "The product development, operations, and sales people must work together face-to-face if we want to deliver real value to customers."

Carol Linburn, who joined Internet Securities following her graduation from Harvard Business School in 1996, said, "When I started last August, Internet Securities headquarters was a one-room apartment with fewer phone lines than people. The company was basically a group of very young, very enthusiastic people who were willing to parachute into new markets and establish offices with less than ample resources. The energy, enthusiasm and youth are still here, as are the budget constraints, but now we have a much more experienced management team, a formal organization structure, and a more clearly-defined way of working. Many people think that if you add formal structures and controls to an entrepreneurial company, you kill the entrepreneurial spirit. We have found just the opposite. People find it much easier to get their work done without the chaos." No new country offices were opened between Fall 1996 and Spring 1997 so that resources could be directed toward increasing the effectiveness and efficiency of product development, sales, marketing, and operations. With controls in place, Internet Securities resumed geographic expansion in Fall 1997.

Current Issues

As they reviewed their notes in preparation for a meeting of the Board of Directors, Gary and the senior management team reflected on the progress that had been made over the past year as they attempted to shift from a strategy of "growing fast" to "growing strong." They were pleased with their progress and felt that the structures and systems that had been put in place would be sufficient to carry them through the next phase of growth. But even as he looked back with pride, Gary knew that he must also look ahead. As he did, two issues captured his attention. The first was related to the company's next phase of aggressive growth.

> If there is one lesson that I have learned over the years, it's that, as the head of an Internet start-up, I need to be managing in two time-frames simultaneously. I need to be actively

involved in what's happening today while I simultaneously work to create the future. In doing so, I must begin building the business today that I think we will need 6 to 12 months from now. I need to ask myself what could go wrong and then develop contingency plans to deal with and prevent these risks. But more importantly, I need to ask myself what could go right and to plan for success. The latter is really more challenging for an Internet firm. If I don't build the organizational and business infrastructure that will be needed to manage the volume of business ahead of time, I will need to rush to put it in place when the company is in operating crisis. That's when mistakes happen; especially, when trying to hire and develop people. So, our big challenge today [spring 1998] is to ensure that we develop the organization required for success in late fall and early 1999.

Another concern that occupied senior management attention in June 1998, was the potential of an aggressive new competitor entering the market. Until recently, Internet Securities had been small enough to operate below the radar of most established competitors. As the company grew and became successful, it was emerging from the clouds. Gary Mueller explained:

> The large players are now Internet savvy and, thanks to our efforts, so are the information providers and customers in our profitable markets. Yet the competition still seems to be responding in much the same way. We are still up against large players like Bloomberg and Reuters. The companies that buy our service are also buying the services of our competitors, yet our customers continue to expand the level of business they do with us. Today, our top 10 customers pay 4 times as much for our service as a year ago. To continue to maintain this position, we need to ensure that we continue to provide value to our customers and information providers. That value depends on our ability to know exactly what information they want to see, how they would like it presented and analyzed, and what customized information and

tools they would like to have. We need to continue to refine the information that we provide to our employees and we need to attract and develop the most talented people in the industry. To this end, we recently hired Michael Schires who came to us from Reuters where he was a senior marketing executive involved in emerging markets. Prior to Reuters he had worked in investment banking so he has first hand knowledge of both the information side of the business and the customer requirements. Why did Schires leave Reuters to join us? Before, his #1 priority [emerging markets] was Reuters' 500th; his #2 was their 2000th. At Internet Securities, Schires' #1 priority is our #1 priority. We believe that our focus is the key to our success.

Appendix A

GROWTH IN NUMBER OF SUBSCRIBERS TO ONLINE INFORMATION SERVICES

Consumer

Company	Service	Number of Individual Passwords/Subscriptions				Percent Change in Number of Individual Passwords		
(Parent)		30-Sep-97	31-Dec-96	31-Dec-95	31-Dec-94	30-Sep-97	31-Dec-96	31-Dec-95
America Online	America Online	9,400,000	7,500,000	4,500,000	1,500,000	25.3%	66.7%	200.0%
Compuserve, Inc. (H&R Block)	CIS, Nifty-Serve, Sprynet	5,341,000	5,314,000	4,025,000	2,660,000	0.5%	32.0%	51.3%
Microsoft Corp.	Microsoft Network	2,300,000	1,700,000	600,000		35.3%	183.3%	
Prodigy Services	Prodigy	1,065,000	900,000	1,400,000	1,200,000	18.3%	-35.7%	16.7%
AT&T WorldNet	WorldNet	970,000						
CUC International	NetMarket, Traveler's Advantage, Auto-Vantage, Privacy Guard	355,000						
Telescan Inc.	TIP, Billboard, CSN, AIA, Schwab, Fidelity, Wall Street City, American Express Financial Direct, Netcom	345,000	234,000	180,000	143,000	47.4%	30.0%	25.9%
Reality Online Inc. (Reuters)	Reuters Money Network, Moneynet.com	201,100	103,000	42,000	31,000	95.2%	145.2%	35.5%

Consumer (continued)

Company	Service	Number of Individual Passwords / Subscriptions				Percent Change in Number of Individual Passwords		
		30-Sep-97	31-Dec-96	31-Dec-95	31-Dec-94	30-Sep-97	31-Dec-96	31-Dec-95
Dow Jones Interactive Publishing	Wall Street Journal Interactive	150,000	70,000			114.3%		
Peapod	Peapod	56,300	33,007			70.6%		
Delphi Internet Services Corp.	Delphi	20,000	50,000	65,000	100,000	−60.0%	−23.1%	−35.0%
IDT Corp.	Genie	20,000	20,000	55,000	100,000	0.0%	−63.6%	−45.0%
Ft. Worth Star-Telegram	Star Textnet, Arlington Online, Ft. Worth Online, Northeast Town Online	7,000	8,011	4,300	4,300	−12.6%	86.3%	0.0%
Others (4)		132,000	439,500	430,300			−70.0%	2.1%
Subtotal		20,230,400	16,064,018	11,310,800	6,168,600	25.9%	42.0%	83.4%

Business / Professional

Company (Parent)	Service	Number of Individual Passwords / Subscriptions				Percent Change in Number of Individual Passwords		
		30-Sep-97	31-Dec-96	31-Dec-95	31-Dec-94	30-Sep-97	31-Dec-96	31-Dec-95
Reed Elsevier	LEXIS-NEXIS	839,000	788,300	744,345	707,000	6.4%	5.9%	5.3%
Individual Inc.	First!, Heads Up, News-Page, Hoover Company Link	680,000	462,000	90,000	35,000	47.2%	413.3%	157.1%
Multex Systems Inc.	MultexNET, Multex Publisher, Multex-EXPRESS	325,000						
Dow Jones Interactive Publishing	Dow Jones News/Retrieval	284,000	253,600	233,000	220,000	11.9%	8.8%	5.9%
Hoover's Inc.	Hoovers	209,198						

Business/Professional (continued)

Company	Service	Number of Individual Passwords/Subscriptions				Percent Change in Number of Individual Passwords		
(Parent)		30-Sep-97	31-Dec-96	31-Dec-95	31-Dec-94	30-Sep-97	31-Dec-96	31-Dec-95
Desktop Data	NewsEDGE	169,438	123,061	80,613	42,516	37.7%	52.7%	89.6%
Knight-Ridder Information	Dialog, Datastar	176,000	200,000	200,000	158,000	−12.0%	0.0%	26.6%
Physician's Online Inc.	Physician's Online	159,256	138,480	69,456		15.0%	99.4%	
Wavephore	Newscast	158,000	45,090			251.1%		
Data Transmission Network Corp.	DTN Agricultural and Financial Services, DTN Energy, DTN Auto, DTN Weather Center	156,000	145,900	95,900	81,999	6.9%	52.1%	16.9%
Dow Jones Interactive Publishing	DowVision	151,000	118,000	110,000		27.9%	7.3%	
Experian Information Solutions	Experian Information Services	140,000	139,000	103,000		0.7%	34.9%	
Dun & Bradstreet	Direct Access, Desktop Solutions	90,000	105,000	77,400	120,000	−14.3%	35.7%	−35.5%
ClariNet Communications	ClariNet Business Edition	68,107	57,794			17.8%		
CDB Infotek (Choicepoint)	CDB Infotek	36,500	36,100	33,000	18,000	1.1%	9.4%	83.3%
Thomson Corp.	Information America	35,100	33,600	28,000	23,000	4.5%	20.0%	21.7%
Official Airline Guides (Reed)	OAG Electronic Edition	30,000	49,000	52,000	50,000	−38.8%	−5.8%	4.0%
Reuters	Business Briefing	30,000						
Questel Orbit (France Telecom)	ORBIT Search Services, Questel	28,080	24,400	23,000	21,000	15.1%	6.1%	9.5%

Business / Professional (continued)

Company		Number of Individual Passwords / Subscriptions				Percent Change in Number of Individual Passwords		
OneSource	Business Browser	25,500						
American Lawyer Media	Counsel Connect	25,311	46,600	35,000	17,000	−45.7%	33.1%	105.9%
OCLC Online Computer Library Center	FirstSearch	20,472	13,214	9,635	8,214	54.9%	37.1%	17.3%
Ovid Technologies	Ovid Online	5,600	5,000	4,000	14,000	12.0%	25.0%	−71.4%
NewsWare	NewsWatch	5,300						
OCLC Online Computer Library Center	EPIC	5,081	4,295	4,525	4,739	18.3%	−5.1%	−4.5%
M.A.I.D.	Profound	5,000	3,800	1,200	4,000	31.6%	216.7%	−70.0%
Southam Electronic Publishing	Informart Online	4,980	4,500	4,000	3,500	10.7%	12.5%	14.3%
Legi-Tech	Legi-Tech	600	508	1,000		18.1%	−49.2%	
CenStats (U.S. Census Bureau)	Censtats	229						
Others (4)			138,108	207,401	466,817	31.6%	−33.4%	−55.6%
Subtotal		3,862,752	2,935,350	2,206,475	1,994,785	31.6%	33.0%	10.6%

Sources: Compiled from the Electronic Information Report's Online Subscriber Surveys, (First Quarter, 1998; FYE 1996; First Quarter 1996), by Cowles/Simba Information Inc. Produced by Business Information Analyst George Jenkins.

Financial (Continued)

Company (Parent)	Service	Number of Individual Passwords/Subscriptions				Percent Change in Number of Individual Passwords		
		30-Sep-97	31-Dec-96	31-Dec-95	31-Dec-94	30-Sep-97	31-Dec-96	31-Dec-95
Reuters Holdings PLC	Reuters' Real-Time Data Services	396,400	362,000	327,100	296,700	9.5%	10.7%	10.2%
Dow Jones Information Services	DJ News Service (Broadtape)	215,000	207,900	200,000	140,000	3.4%	4.0%	42.9%
Automatic Data Processing	Power Partner, Shark	97,500	96,968	98,000	97,900	0.5%	−1.1%	0.1%
Dow Jones Financial Services	Dow Jones Markets	90,000	93,500	98,500	90,000	3.7%	−5.1%	9.4%
Bloomberg Financial Markets LP	The Bloomberg	84,390	70,561	55,000	43,000	19.6%	28.3%	27.9%
McGraw-Hill/ Standard & Poor's	S&P MarketScope	77,545	76,100	74,000	70,000	1.9%	2.8%	5.7%
Thomson Financial Services	ILX	73,500	65,000	50,000	42,000	13.1%	30.0%	19.0%
Bridge Information Systems	Bridge	70,000	36,000	43,000	9,972	94.4%	−16.3%	331.2%
Data Broadcasting Corp.	MarketWatch, Signal, QuoTrek, BMI, Sports Products, BondVU, Agcast	38,060	40,400	33,000	28,000	−5.7%	22.4%	17.9%
Track Data	Track OnLine, Dial/Data, InfoVest, MXNT	30,500	25,000	18,500	16,486	22.0%	35.1%	12.2%
PC Quote Inc.	PC Quote	10,300	4,000	3,000	4,700	157.5%	33.3%	−36.2%

Financial (Concluded)

Company		Number of Individual Passwords/Subscriptions				Percent Change in Number of Individual Passwords		
	Service	30-Sep-97	31-Dec-96	31-Dec-95	31-Dec-94	30-Sep-97	31-Dec-96	31-Dec-95
(Parent)								
Other Companies and Services				10,500	70,000		–85.0%	
Subtotal		1,183,195	1,077,429	1,010,600	908,758	9.8%	6.6%	11.2%

Total

	Number of Individual Passwords/Subscriptions			
	30-Sep-97	31-Dec-96	31-Dec-95	31-Dec-94
Total	25,276,347	20,976,797	14,527,875	9,072,143

Appendix B

INTERNET IPO DEALS, 1994–1998

1998

Company Name	Ticker	Category	Deal Date	Amount (Millions)	IPO Price	Stock Price 31-May-98	% Change Since IPO
Advanced Communications Group	ADG	ISP	12-Feb-98	$112.0	$14.00	$11.25	−19.6%
Brio Technology, Inc.	BRYO	Search engine	01-May-98	$ 31.9	$11.00	$15.50	40.9%
Caliber Learning Network, Inc.	CLBR	Content provider	05-May-98	$ 79.8	$14.00	$17.00	21.4%
Cdnow, Inc.	CDNW	Content provider	10-Feb-98	$ 65.6	$16.00	$21.94	37.1%
Command Systems	CMND	Other Services	13-Mar-98	$ 32.4	$12.00	$ 5.13	−57.3%
CyberShop International, Inc.	CYSP	E-commerce	23-Mar-98	$ 18.2	$ 6.50	$10.94	68.3%
DoubleClick, Inc.	DCLK	Content provider	20-Feb-98	$ 59.5	$17.00	$34.75	104.4%
Exodus Communications, Inc.	EXDS	E-commerce	19-Mar-98	$ 67.5	$15.00	$34.72	131.5%
IBS Interactive, Inc.	IBSX	E-commerce	15-May-98	$ 7.2	$ 6.00	$ 8.75	45.8%
Icon CMT Corp.	ICMT	Infrastructure	12-Feb-98	$ 38.5	$10.00	$17.56	75.6%
ISS Group, Inc.	ISSX	Infrastructure	24-Mar-98	$ 66.0	$22.00	$40.25	83.0%
VeriSign, Inc.	VRSN	E-commerce	30-Jan-98	$ 42.0	$14.00	$36.25	158.9%
Verio Inc.	VRIO	ISP	12-May-98	$126.5	$23.00	$24.00	4.3%
Via Grafix Corporation	VIAX	Content provider	04-Mar-98	$ 28.6	$13.00	$ 6.81	−47.6%
Visual Networks, Inc.	VNWK	Other services	06-Feb-98	$ 43.8	$12.50	$35.31	182.5%

Company Name	Ticker	Category	Deal Date	Amount (Millions)	IPO Price	Stock Price 31-May-98	% Change Since IPO
Amazon Books	AMZN	Content provider	14-May-97	$ 54.0	$18.00	$88.63	392.4%
At Home Corporation	ATHM	Infrastructure	11-Jul-97	$ 94.5	$10.50	$41.00	290.5%
Audio Book Club	KLB	E-commerce	22-Oct-97	$ 23.0	$10.00	$ 5.00	−50.0%
Concentric Network Corporation	CNCX	ISP	01-Aug-97	$ 51.6	$12.00	$22.63	88.6%
EarthLink Network	ELNX	ISP	22-Jan-97	$ 26.0	$13.00	$55.38	326.0%
Fine.com International Corporation	FDOT	E-commerce	12-Aug-97	$ 7.2	$ 6.50	$ 5.00	−23.1%
FreePages Group PLC	FREEY	Content provider	09-Apr-97	$ 77.0	$15.39	$11.00	−28.5%
Genesys Telecom. Laboratories	GCTI	Infrastructure	17-Jun-97	$ 45.0	$18.00	$30.91	71.7%
Go2net, Inc.	GNET	Search engine	23-Apr-97	$ 12.8	$ 8.00	$26.00	225.0%
HomeCom Communications, Inc.	HCOM	E-commerce	07-May-97	$ 6.0	$ 6.00	$ 5.00	−16.7%
InterVU Inc.	ITVU	Infrastructure	20-Nov-97	$ 19.0	$ 9.50	$18.38	93.5%
Navidec Inc.	NVDC	ISP	11-Feb-97	$ 6.0	$ 6.00	$ 6.75	12.5%
Net.B@nk, Inc.	NTBK	Content provider	29-Jul-97	$ 42.0	$12.00	$24.25	102.1%
NetSpeak Corporation	NSPK	Content provider	29-May-97	$ 21.0	$ 8.75	$20.38	132.9%
Network Solutions, Inc.	NSOL	Infrastructure	26-Sep-97	$ 59.4	$18.00	$41.06	128.1%
New Era of Networks, Inc.	NEON	E-commerce	18-Jun-97	$ 33.1	$12.00	$28.50	137.5%
NewCom, Inc.	NWCM	Infrastructure	16-Sep-97	$ 19.0	$ 9.50	$15.13	59.3%
N2K, Inc.	NTKI	Content provider	17-Oct-97	$ 63.3	$19.00	$18.31	−3.6%
ONSALE, Inc.	ONSL	Content provider	17-Apr-97	$ 15.0	$ 6.00	$29.50	391.7%
PC411, Inc.	PCFR	Content provider	16-May-97	$ 6.6	$ 5.00	$ 1.19	−76.2%
Peapod, Inc.	PPOD	Content provider	11-Jun-97	$ 64.0	$16.00	$ 7.13	−55.4%
Pegasus Systems, Inc.	PEGS	E-commerce	07-Aug-97	$ 46.4	$13.00	$26.25	101.9%
PowerTrader, Inc.	PWTD	Content provider	03-Nov-97	$ 5.1	$ 3.00	$ 0.22	−92.7%
Preview Travel, Inc.	PTVL	Content provider	20-Nov-97	$ 27.5	$11.00	$28.88	162.5%

1997 (Continued)

Company Name	Ticker	Category	Deal Date	Amount (Millions)	IPO Price	Stock Price 31-May-98	% Change Since IPO
RealNetworks, Inc.	RNWK	Infrastructure	21-Nov-97	$ 37.5	$12.50	$24.78	98.2%
Shopping.com	IBUY	Content provider	25-Nov-97	$ 11.7	$ 9.00	$24.00	166.7%
Software AG Systems, Inc.	AGS	Infrastructure	18-Nov-97	$100.1	$10.00	$23.38	133.8%
Scoop Inc.	SCPI	Content provider	16-Apr-97	$ 6.5	$ 4.50	$ 1.48	−67.1%
SportsLine USA, Inc.	SPLN	Content provider	13-Nov-97	$ 2.08	$ 8.00	$26.63	232.9%
2Connect Express, Inc.	CNTCU	Other services	12-May-97	$ 6.5	$12.50	$ .063	−95.0%
USWeb Corporation	USWB	Other services	05-Dec-97	$ 37.5	$ 7.50	$20.75	176.7%
Visual Data Corporation	VDAT	E-commerce	30-Jul-97	$ 6.0	$ 6.00	$ 3.88	−35.3%

1996

Company Name	Ticker	Category	Deal Date	Amount (Millions)	IPO Price	Stock Price 31-May-98	% Change Since IPO
Abacus Direct	ABDR	Other services	27-Sep-96	$ 71.0	$14.00	$52.38	274.1%
Advanced Radio Telecom	ARTT	Infrastructure	06-Nov-96	$ 33.8	$15.00	$10.69	−28.7%
Brilliant Digital Entertainment, Inc	BDE	Content provider	21-Nov-96	$ 10.0	$ 5.00	$ 2.75	−45.0%
CCC Information Services	CCCG	Other services	16-Aug-96	$ 79.0	$11.50	$22.00	91.3%
CheckPoint Software Technologies Ltd.	CHKPR	Other services	28-Jun-96	$ 58.8	$14.00	$26.88	92.0%
C/NET Inc.	CNWK	Content provider	02-Jul-96	$ 32.0	$16.00	$38.50	140.6%
CompuServe (H+R Block)	CSRV	Online services	19-Apr-96	$552.0	$30.00	N/A	N/A
Connect Inc.	CNKT	E-commerce	16-Aug-96	$ 12.1	$ 6.00	$ 2.56	−57.3%
Cybercash Inc.	CYCH	E-commerce	15-Feb-96	$ 40.8	$17.00	$17.69	4.1%
Cylink Corporation	CYLK	Infrastructure	16-Feb-96	$ 87.0	$15.00	$11.38	−24.1%
Digex Inc.	DIGX	Other services	17-Oct-96	$ 45.5	$10.13	N/A	N/A
Excite Inc.	XCIT	Search engine	03-Apr-96	$ 34.0	$17.00	$60.19	254.1%
E*TRADE Group Inc.	EGRP	E-commerce	16-Aug-96	$ 59.5	$10.50	$22.13	110.8%

1996 *(continued)*

Company Name	Ticker	Category	Deal Date	Amount (Millions)	IPO Price	Stock Price 31-May-98	% Change Since IPO
Farallon Communications Inc.	FRLN	Infrastructure	13-Jun-96	$ 36.0	$16.00	$ 9.69	−39.4%
First Virtual Holdings Inc.	FVHI	E-commerce	13-Dec-96	$ 18.0	$ 9.00	$ 1.75	−80.6%
IDT Corp.	IDTC	ISP	15-Mar-96	$ 46.0	$10.00	$ 32.94	229.4%
Individual Inc.	INDV	Content provider	15-Mar-96	$ 35.0	$14.00	N/A	N/A
Infoseek Inc.	SEEK	Search engine	11-Jun-96	$ 41.4	$12.00	$ 29.25	143.8%
Lycos Inc.	LCOS	Search engine	02-Apr-96	N/A	$16.00	$ 61.06	281.6%
Metromail Corp. (R.R. Donnelley & Sons)	ML	Content provider	13-Jun-96	$246.0	$20.50	N/A	N/A
Mindspring Enterprises, Inc.	MSPG	ISP	14-Mar-96	$ 15.6	$ 8.00	$ 60.66	658.3%
Netlive Communications Inc.	NETL	Other services	14-Aug-96	$ 5.2	$ 5.50	$ 1.63	−70.4%
Online System Services Inc.	WEBB	ISP	23-May-96	$ 7.4	$ 6.75	$ 14.13	109.3%
Open Market Inc.	OMKT	E-commerce	22-May-96	$ 72.0	$18.00	$ 14.41	−19.9%
Open Text Corp.	OTEXF	Search engine	23-Jan-96	$ 60.0	$15.00	$ 15.88	5.9%
OzEmail Limited	OZEMY	ISP	28-May-96	$ 44.8	$14.00	$ 23.00	64.3%
Raptor Systems Inc.	RAPT	Infrastructure	16-Jan-96	$ 27.5	$11.00	N/A	N/A
Security First Network Bank	SFNB	E-commerce	23-May-96	$ 48.8	$20.00	$ 10.25	−48.8%
SmartServ Online, Inc.	SSOL	E-commerce	21-Mar-96	$ 8.6	$ 5.00	$ 2.19	−56.2%
THINK New Ideas, Inc.	THNK	E-commerce	26-Nov-96	$ 15.1	$ 7.00	$ 30.88	341.1%
UOL Publishing, Inc.	UOLP	Content provider	26-Nov-96	$ 18.6	$13.00	$ 8.50	−34.6%
V-One Corp	VONE	E-commerce	25-Oct-96	$ 15.0	$ 5.00	$ 3.31	−33.8%
Websecure, Inc.	WEBS	ISP	10-Dec-96	$ 8.0	$ 8.00	N/A	N/A
Yahoo!	YHOO	Search engine	12-Apr-96	$ 38.9	$13.00	$116.88	799.1%

1995

Company Name	Ticker	Category	Deal Date	Amount (Millions)	IPO Price	Stock Price 31-May-98	% Change Since IPO
Secure Computing Corp.	SCUR	E-commerce	17-Nov-95	N/A	$16.00	$ 10.88	–32.0%
Netscape Communications Corp.	NSCP	Browser	09-Aug-95	N/A	$28.00	$ 27.38	–2.2%
Spyglass, Inc.	SPYG	Browser	27-Jun-95	$ 34.0	$17.00	$ 10.88	–36.0%
UUNet Technologies	UUNT	ISP	25-May-95	$ 76.1	$14.00	N/A	N/A
Checkfree Corp.	CKFR	E-commerce	27-Sep-95	$108.0	$18.00	$ 22.48	24.9%

1994

Company Name	Ticker	Category	Deal Date	Amount (Millions)	IPO Price	Stock Price 31-May-98	% Change Since IPO
Ascend Comunications	ASND	Infrastructure	12-May-94	$ 26.0	$13.00	$ 47.06	262.0%
Cascade Communications Corp.	CSCC	Infrastructure	29-Jul-94	$ 30.0	$15.00	N/A	N/A
Netcom	NETC	ISP	15-Dec-94	$ 24.1	$13.00	N/A	N/A
Security Dynamics	SDTI	Infrastructure	14-Dec-94	$ 35.2	$16.00	$ 24.84	55.3%

Notes:
- Metromail was acquired on 4/10/98 by Great Universal Stores PLC.
- In 9/97, Compuserve was acquired by WorldCom for $1.2 billion.
- Digex was acquired by Intermedia Communications in 7/97 for $153 million or $13/share.
- On 11/17/97, Farallon Communications changed the company name to Netopia, Inc., ticker NTPA.
- In 2/98, Individual, Inc. merged with Desktop Data, Inc. to form NewsEdge Corporation.
- On 2/5/98, Raptor Systems merged with AXTENT Technologies.
- Websecure was delisted by NASDAQ in 6/97. It is no longer in business.
- MFS Communications purchased UUNet Technologies in 8/96 for $2 billion.
- In 7/97, Ascend Communications acquired Cascade Communications in a $3.7 billion stock deal.
- On 1/21/98, ICG Communications acquired Netcom.

Sources: IPO Central, Lexis-Nexis, Datastream.

Information Technology and Organization

From many quarters we hear that the hierarchical organization must wither away. In this view of the future, middle managers have the life expectancy of fruit flies. Those who survive will not be straw bosses but Dutch uncles dispensing resources and wisdom to an empowered labor force that designs its own jobs. Enabled, to use a trendy term, by information technology and propelled by the need to gain speed and shed unnecessary work, this flat, information-based organization won't look like the pharaonic pyramid of yore, but like—well, like what?

Stewart, 1992[1]

Designing and implementing the structures and systems that enable an organization to accomplish its goals and execute its strategies constitute one of the most formidable tasks of the general manager. While many believe that the key to competitive advantage lies in defining a blockbuster strategy, in fact, this is only a portion of the task. In the 1990s, most managers have come to recognize that flawlessly *executing* strategy day after day and year after year is what really counts. Until recently, the business rules governing how to design an organization to execute strategy were fairly straightforward. Large firms were designed as hierarchies, small firms were designed as entrepreneurial organizations, and professional services firms (for example, multinational consulting companies and large law firms) were designed as adhocracies. At times, complex organization designs, such as the matrix, were used to enable a firm to focus attention on two or more separate areas

---

[1]T. Stewart, "The Search for the Organization of Tomorrow," *Fortune*, May 18, 1992.

(for example, geography and products). But in the 1990s, these familiar business rules do not always apply. Hybrid organizational models that take advantage of the power of digital information have proliferated.

Module 3 provides an opportunity to analyze the components of the information age organization and the IT architecture required to support it. Two chapters are included. Chapter 5, "Information, Organization, and Control," provides an overview of traditional organization design models and discusses how emerging information age organization models are building on the past as they define new models for the 21st century. Chapter 6, "IT Architecture: Evolution and Alternatives," provides an overview of traditional IT architecture models (including the mainframe and PC eras) as the foundations for a new networked computing model required by the information age organization. The module ends with four cases—Taco Bell (1983–1994), Frito-Lay, Inc. (1980–1986 and 1987–1992), and MicroAge, Inc.—that enable a longitudinal examination of the intersection of IT and organization design. A key insight that emerges from the cases in this module is that the ability to harness the value of IT requires a fundamental shift in thinking concerning the design of the organization and the IT architecture and the ways in which both are implemented and managed.

Chapter

5

Information, Organization, and Control[1]

Managers and academics spent the majority of this century building and perfecting the hierarchical organization. If we are to believe the press, however, they are now busily destroying it, proposing in its stead networked, process-oriented, shamrock, learning, team-based, and fast-cycle organizational models (to name but a few).[2] While the details of these visions vary, common themes can be found. The 1990s organization, it is argued, is flat, fast, flexible, and focused on areas of core competency. Inside, empowered, interfunctional teams of knowledge workers are reengineering and continuously improving core business processes. Managers—the few who are left, that is—are acting as "coaches." They are getting their companies to "think globally and act locally." They are forming strategic alliances and partnerships that will enable them to focus on core competencies while expanding organizational capabilities, scale, and scope. Some are attempting to create virtual corporations, managing a vast network of independent firms that

[1]This chapter is adapted from L.M. Applegate, "In Search of a New Organizational Model: Lessons from the Field," Shaping Organization Form: Communication, Connection & Community (eds. G. DeSanctis and J. Fulk) Newbury Park, Ca: Sage, 1998.

[2]W. Powell, "Neither Market nor Hierarchy: Network Forms of Organization," *Research on Organizational Behavior,* 12:295–336, 1990; R. Reich, *The Work of Nations* (NY: Vintage Books, 1991); J. Rockart and J. Short, "The Networked Organization and the Management of Interdependence," *The Corporation of the 1990s* (NY: Oxford University Press, 1991); C. Perrow, "Small Firm Networks," *Networks and Organizations* (edited by N. Nohria and R. Eccles) (Boston: Harvard Business School Press, 1992); F. Ostroff, and D. Smith, "The Horizontal Organization," *McKinsey Quarterly,* 1:148–68, 1992; P. Drucker, "The Coming of the New Organization," *Harvard Business Review,* January–February 1988; P. Senge, *The Fifth Discipline* (NY: Doubleday, 1990); J. Quinn, *The Intelligent Enterprise* (NY: Free Press, 1992).

must all work together to deliver products and services to customers. This is definitely not the "pharaonic pyramid of yore"!

But how many managers have actually succeeded in designing a firm that resembles this vision? Take a walk around most large, established organizations and you will find that many vestiges of the hierarchy remain. Standardized jobs, rigid procedures and policies, and the hierarchical chain of command continue to define how much of the work is performed. While many organizations have downsized and delayered,[3] authority and accountability for decisions continue to depend on hierarchical level. And although employees find themselves working in teams and spending a significant portion of their time at meetings, except in small firms (under $250 million), work and compensation continue to support individual performance and achievement.

Clearly, the hierarchy is not dead. Yet, when asked what their firms should look like within the next five years, many managers express strong support for the visions of a new organization that captured our attention in the literature.[4] In focus groups, many state that their firms are in the middle of—or are embarking on—change initiatives designed to create a more flexible and adaptive organization. These managers' dilemma, however, is that they cannot sacrifice efficiency for speed. They cannot abandon formal control systems as they empower employees to make decisions addressing real-time customer needs.

CEO Jack Welch summed up this dilemma as he discussed the challenges that General Electric faced as it entered the 1990s (see Figure 5–1). "At the beginning of the decade," he wrote, "we saw two challenges ahead of us, one external and one internal. Externally, we faced a world economy that would be characterized by slower growth, with stronger global competitors going after a smaller piece of the pie. Internally, our challenge was even bigger. We had to find a way to combine the power, resources, and reach of a large company with the hunger, agility, spirit, and fire of a small one."[5] Percy Barnevik, CEO of Asea Brown Boveri (ABB), echoed these comments: "ABB is an organization with three internal contradictions. We want to be global and local, big and small, and radically decentralized with centralized reporting and control. If we resolve those contradictions, we create real organizational advantage."[6]

---

[3]In a survey of over 500 managers conducted by one of the authors, on average, two layers had been removed from their firms and the number of direct reports to each manager had increased from five to eight between 1987 and 1993. (See *Business Transformation Self Assessment: Summary of Findings, 1992–1993,* Harvard Business School No. 194 013, for a summary of the survey's key findings.

[4]In viewing managers' support for the features of the new organization designs we cannot ignore the potential effects of "salesmanship" on the part of management consultants and academics.

[5]J. Welch, "Managing in the 90s," GE Report to Shareholders, 1988.

[6]R. Simons, and C. Bartlett, *Asea Brown Boveri,* Harvard Business School No. 192-139.

FIGURE 5–1   The Organization and Information Technology Design Challenge of the 1990s

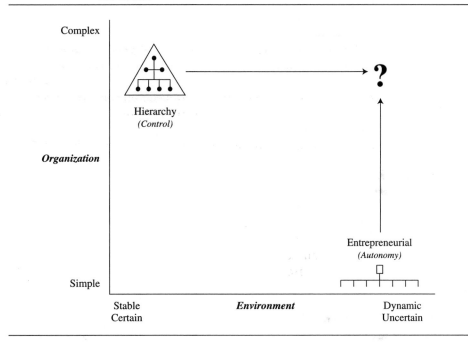

Curiously, as dramatic as it seems, this organization design dilemma is not new; early descriptions of similar "hybrid" organization models (for example, the matrix) emerged in the 1950s and 1960s.[7] The matrix was originally billed as the "obvious organizational solution" to the need for control and efficiency, while simultaneously enabling flexibility and speed of response. Decades ago, proponents of the matrix argued for an organization design remarkably similar to the one that is being called for today. For example, they stressed the need for "adaptive, information-intensive, team-based, collaborative, and empowered" organizations. But firms that adopted the hybrid designs of the 1960s and 1970s soon learned that the new structures and systems bred conflict, confusion, information overload, and costly duplication of resources. Bartlett and Ghoshal[8] described why many firms

---

[7]T. Burns and G.M. Stalker, *The Management of Innovation* (London: Tavistock, 1961); J. Woodward, *Industrial Organization, Theory and Practice* (London: Oxford University Press, 1965); J.D. Thompson, *Organizations in Action* (NY: McGraw-Hill, 1967; P. Lawrence and J. Lorsch, *Organization and Environment* (Boston: Harvard Business School Press, 1967, 1986); L. Greiner, "Evolution and Revolution as Organizations Grow," *Harvard Business Review,* 50(4):37–46, 1972; J. Galbraith, *Designing Complex Organization* (Reading, MA: Addison Wesley, 1973).

[8]G. Bartlett, and S. Ghoshal, *Managing Across Borders* (Boston: Harvard Business School Press, 1989).

adopted the matrix, only to abandon it several years later: "Top-level . . . managers . . . are losing control of their companies. The problem is not that they have misjudged the demands created by an increasingly complex environment and an accelerating rate of environmental change, nor that they have failed to develop strategies appropriate to the new challenges. The problem is that their companies are organizationally incapable of carrying out the sophisticated strategies they have developed. Over the past 20 years, strategic thinking has outdistanced organizational capabilities."

Given such problems, we might legitimately ask, "If the matrix failed in the past, why are we trying this again?" Interestingly, one of the major sources of difficulty with the matrix was the dramatic increase in the need for timely information to successfully manage it.[9] While the hierarchy managed complexity by minimizing it, the matrix organization demanded that managers *deal with complexity directly*. Product managers had to coordinate their plans and operations with functional managers. Senior management teams at corporate headquarters, attempting to reconcile overall organization performance and plan corporatewide strategy, were faced with a dizzying array of conflicting information from functional and business managers.

In the 1960s and 1970s, information moved slowly and channels of communication were limited. The mainframe computer systems of the day were designed to support centralized information processing and hierarchical communication channels (see Figure 5–2). The microcomputer revolution of the 1980s provided tools to decentralize information processing, which helped improve local decision making, but the technology to support both local and enterprisewide information sharing and communication was not adequate to meet the information processing and communication demands of the matrix. Only recently has information technology (IT) become capable of meeting that challenge. The "networked IT revolution" of the 1990s—reflected in the emergence of distributed client-server systems, electronic commerce, and the growing interest in the Internet—provides an information processing and communication infrastructure that matches the information and communication requirements of a firm that wishes to operate as if it were both big and small.

In theory, if a firm could harness the power of these new technologies, it could gain access to a vast store of real-time information, and to a variety of communication channels through which to debate the meaning of that information and to coordinate work. Managers once stymied by the incomplete and inaccurate flow of information from the workforce could access relevant and timely information on operations and business conditions all over the world. Employees, who traditionally had limited understanding of the firm's

---

[9]Research in the mid-1960s suggested that successful firms operating in uncertain and complex environments developed systems to improve vertical and lateral information processing in the firm. See J. Galbraith, *Designing Complex Organizations,* op. cit., and P. Lawrence and J. Lorsch, *Organization and Environment,* op. cit.

FIGURE 5–2   The IT Design Challenge Parallels the Organization Design Challenge

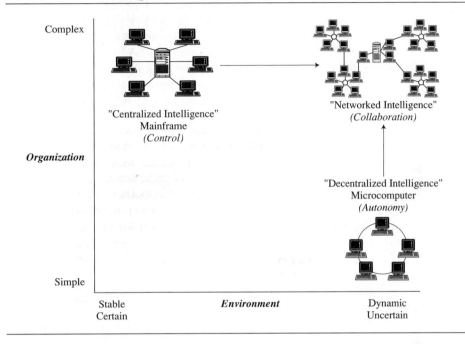

strategy and direction, could gain a deeper understanding of the impact of their local decisions and actions on corporate performance. Communication systems could permit a variety of choices—from real-time videoconferencing to text-based electronic mail—to speed the transfer of ideas across the organization and around the world.

Can firms take advantage of the information management and communication tools this revolution provides to create an "information age organization" that simultaneously manages speed and complexity? Although the networked IT infrastructure can provide important *tools,* it can define neither the information that needs to be in the systems nor the meaning of the information and how to use it to coordinate and manage the business. Nor can the networked IT infrastructure define the organizational structures, processes, and culture required to enable people to use the information to make decisions and take actions. Finally, these tools cannot provide incentives that would motivate people to use the information to meet both organizational and personal objectives. Rather, to accomplish their overarching goals, *firms must change the way they are organized, and employees at all levels must become "information literate"*—not just computer literate. Implementing networked information and communication systems in a traditional, hierarchically structured organization simply won't work. A much more comprehensive approach to organization change is required. And, for most managers, implementing the technology is the least complicated part; redesigning the organization and defining the information to manage it constitute major constraints on their attempts to meet the challenges of the 1990s.

Clearly, managers in the 1990s are caught in a profound dilemma. The organizational designs for executing their complex strategies depend upon a much more dynamic, networked approach to managing and communicating information, yet effective deployment of a networked information infrastructure means that managers must adopt a more flexible and adaptive organization design.

This chapter summarizes the insights gained from managers around the world as they attempt to redefine their organizations to meet the challenges of managing in an information age. All have directly confronted the conflicting pressures of managing speed and complexity—of creating organizations that simultaneously capture the benefits of being big and small. This has forced them to confront the fact that control must be maintained even as flexibility and speed are sought, that authority systems must be redefined to ensure that empowerment does not become anarchy. They have had to recognize that rhetoric cannot camouflage the fact that organizations do not change unless the behavior and personal values of the employees within them change. And they have had to solve the fundamental problems of simultaneously evolving both the organization and the information infrastructure required to manage in the 1990s.

Their insights suggest that these managers are indeed defining a hybrid organizational model—which we have labeled the *information age organization.* The information age organization does not abandon traditional organization design principles, but instead builds upon and redefines them, as it harnesses the power of information age technologies for an information age workforce. As such, the characteristics of the information age organizational model represent an interesting blend of tradition and transformation. (See Appendix A for a summary of the characteristics of traditional organizational models.)

LEARNING FROM MISTAKES

There is much to be learned from careful examination of a failure. Consider the disaster that befell Barings Bank.[10] A February 28, 1995, article in the *Wall Street Journal* proclaimed: "The warning lights should have been blinking. The collapse of 233-year-old Barings PLC due to a staggering $1.2

---

[10]R. Stevenson, "Markets Shaken as a British Bank Takes a Big Loss," *New York Times,* February 27, 1995; G. Millman, "Barings Collapses: Financial System Bears Up Well," *Wall Street Journal,* February 28, 1995.

billion loss from unauthorized derivatives trading raises an important question: How many other Barings are out there?"[11]

The huge losses were traced to the actions of a 27-year-old trader in Singapore who had been given authority to trade financial derivatives on behalf of the firm on the futures market. While most securities firms grant similar authority to traders, press reports implied that the potential for abuse of power appeared to be greater at Barings because the bank also delegated to the same individual authority for the back-office transaction systems that reported on trades. In addition to granting broad authority for a highly volatile activity to someone halfway around the world, Barings' risk management systems were also said to be ineffective. Over a few months' time, the trader wiped out the entire capital reserves of the bank.

While no firm can totally insulate itself against such disasters, the hierarchy specifies a number of structures and systems that help to safeguard a large firm.[12] Authority systems limit decision making and actions by *strict segregation of responsibility and duties, standardization of jobs, direct supervision,* and *restricted access to information and assets everywhere but the very top of the firm.* In theory, the hierarchy is designed so that, short of sabotage, no single employee or work unit can make a decision or take an action which could immediately threaten the entire organization. Even at the top of a firm, the CEO is responsible to a board of directors that includes external members representing shareholder interests.

Similarly, hierarchical control systems are designed to ensure "tight control" of operating processes through multiple intersecting checks and balances. At lower levels, control systems are based on *action controls*—employees are told exactly what they are supposed to do and supervisors watch to see that they do it.[13] As one moves up in the hierarchy, managers are evaluated and compensated based on their ability to meet predefined performance criteria; these *results controls* help focus managerial attention and actions on organizational priorities and ensure coordination of actions and decisions across functional boundaries. *Personnel controls* ensure that the right people with the right skills are recruited, hired, developed, motivated, and retained. Finally, *transaction controls*—accurate and complete documentation of financial and legal transactions with regular review by senior management, the board of directors, and external auditors—ensure risk and asset management.

Current "new age organization" buzzwords exhort managers to "empower" their people and expand their areas of responsibility, to wipe out middle

---

[11]S. Lypin and G. B. Krecht, "How Many Other Barings Are There?" *Wall Street Journal,* February 28, 1995.

[12]In small, privately held firms, authority for most decisions is retained by the CEO/founder, and controls are based on direct oversight and supervision.

[13]K. Merchant, *Rewarding Results* (Boston: Harvard Business School Press, 1989); R. N. Anthony, *The Management Control Function* (Boston: Harvard Business School Press, 1988).

management ranks and create "self-managing" teams. *But they do not specify how control and authority are to be maintained once the traditional systems have been disrupted.* Managers often learn important lessons about the complexity of organizational control and authority systems as they embark upon these change initiatives. Unfortunately, some—like Barings—learn their lesson too late. But others use the insights gained from their "brushes with disaster" to reevaluate their strategy, the organization design, and their change implementation process.

A consumer products firm (revenues of $5 billion) learned the hard way about the dangers of altering hierarchical control and authority systems as it attempted to implement a new micromarketing strategy. The firm survived and was able to use these painful lessons to help define a new approach to authority and control for the information age firm. Its story provides an important lesson for managers in the 1990s.

Founded in 1961 via the merger of two entrepreneurial organizations, the firm was subsequently reorganized as a centralized, functional hierarchy to achieve economies of scale. "We were very successful during the 1970s," the then-CEO explained. "Our centralized structure provided us with economies of scale and efficiencies that our small, regional competitors could not match." A senior manager added, "Our strategy was to create a quality product and offer it at a very low price. We relied on geographic expansion to fuel growth."

Senior management managed a single budget and assumed responsibility for all profit and loss decisions. Each year, functional operating plans and the budgets to accomplish them were set in the corporate office, and the major responsibility of managers in the field was to "meet plan." "We leveraged our size by simplifying the business to a national pattern and by focusing our efforts on a minimum number of national, high-leverage, well-executed marketing and product initiatives," one senior manager explained. "This led us to practice . . . 'black box management'—we put money, programs, and people in one end and got sales, share, and profitability out the other."

Employees were carefully selected to fit within specified job descriptions and then "indoctrinated" through extensive orientation programs so they understood policies and procedures; each year direct supervisors evaluated most employees using a standardized evaluation form supplied by the corporate human resources department. Bonuses were tied to "meeting plan." Because the highly paid sales force (which received commissions based on sales dollar volume) was on the road a great deal and could not be monitored very closely, salespeople were given a detailed procedure book—which they called "The Bible"—describing the exact approach for selling every product to every type of customer.

No deviations from these standard operating procedures were permitted because agreement from other parts of the organization could not be guaranteed. If a salesperson recognized an opportunity to increase sales significantly, she or he—unlike the trader at Barings—could not unilaterally make the changes to implement the new quota; purchasing, manufacturing, and logistics would all need to be involved to meet the increased demand. Instead, consistent with the design principles of the hierarchy, the salesperson's idea had to be "sold" to the boss and then passed up the ladder until it reached the senior vice president in corporate headquarters. There, the purchasing, manufacturing, marketing, sales, and distribution managers would need to meet together to evaluate and approve the idea. Since this firm planned production during its yearly planning cycle, the opportunity was often long gone by the time the senior management team could decide to act upon it.

These hierarchical authority and control structures and systems were extremely effective as long as the company could grow through geographic expansion and competition was minimal. But as it entered the 1980s, the picture changed. "As we moved into the 1980s, our competitors began to get stronger," recalled one manager. "They started buying up small regional competitors and became more aggressive in their pricing and promotions. At the same time, we had saturated our traditional markets. There was little new territory to conquer unless we could identify every niche of market opportunity through sophisticated micromarketing. We also needed to dramatically increase the rate of new product development."

Another senior manager continued: "When we saw that sales growth had slowed, we were surprised. The machine that had churned out 18 percent growth year after year had hiccuped. We were doing the 'right' things but they weren't working. The aircraft carrier that we had built needed to be refitted as a PT boat."

Responding to these pressures, senior management set out to redesign their organization to address industry changes. Reflecting their functional orientation, they initially attempted a functional redesign. The sales force was "empowered" to make product/market decisions for their individual customers. The research and development (R&D) unit was asked to speed up the new-product development process. Quality teams were formed in manufacturing to squeeze out costs while improving quality. Functional senior vice presidents were responsible for implementing the changes within their respective units.

Problems stemming from these changes surfaced immediately, but, lacking access to timely information on business performance, the senior management team was not aware of the chaos occurring at the operating level until significant damage had been done. "When we attempted to decentralize decision making and increase the rate of new product development," a manager explained, "we lost control. Paper-based processes and hierarchical management control systems simply were not timely and flexible enough to permit us to react to the rapidly changing market conditions. New products went stale in warehouses. At times, the sales force received news of local promotions long after the increased inventory had been shipped to the warehouses, and other times inventory did not arrive until after a promotion had taken place. New products were being introduced into factories focusing on decreasing costs. Finally, senior management reporting systems were not timely enough, nor did they contain detailed enough information to recognize that a problem was developing." Profits declined by 14 percent that year—the first time in the history of the firm that profits had not risen—and the CEO resigned.

CREATING THE INFORMATION AGE ORGANIZATION

Analysis of both failure and success has clarified several important lessons for the design of the information age organization.

- *Speed counts, but not at the expense of control.* In the turbulent 1990s, speed counts. New products must be introduced ever more quickly, order fulfillment cycles must be cut dramatically, and managers are exhorted to create organizations that can turn on a dime. But we know that taking one's time has its advantages. A driver racing along the freeway at 55 miles per hour is much more vulnerable to serious injury than he or she would be if meandering along at 5 miles per hour.[14] The right decisions must be made quickly; there is no margin for error. Skill and expertise— especially in dealing with unforeseen circumstances—are critical. Constant vigilance is necessary. The rules of the road must be clear and followed without question. We must trust that the actions of other drivers will not put us at risk. Safety nets (for example, seat belts, air bags) become much more important to minimize damage in the event of a crash. In short, the faster we go, the more important it is—and the harder it is— to keep control of our car. Managers of fast-cycle organizations face the same dilemma. The faster the pace, the greater the need to monitor business operations and clearly define and enforce the "rules of the road."

- *Empowerment is not anarchy.* When asked to define the term *empowerment,* some managers describe vague efforts to "push decision making down the line." Others equate empowerment with "getting rid of (or bypassing) middle management." Most have a hard time describing exactly who will make what decisions and fail to recognize that decision authority is tightly linked to a more complex set of organization design features, including structure (e.g., how people are grouped into units and how those units coordinate activities to develop and deliver products and services to customers) and incentives (e.g., performance evaluation methods, compensation). Many learn the hard way that isolated efforts to "empower" a particular employee or employee group can lead to disaster

---

[14]It is important to note that freeways have a minimum as well as a maximum speed limit. Going too slowly can also be very dangerous in this fast-paced world.

when not accompanied by a more comprehensive redefinition of authority and control throughout the organization. For example, in an empowered organization, senior management must be *more* involved, not less; and organizational boundaries and value systems must be more clearly communicated, closely monitored, and consistently enforced.

- *Transforming an organization requires more than just changing the structure.* It is not enough to simply take out layers or redraw boxes on an organization chart. The resulting organizational confusion can help to shake up an entrenched organization and create the "conditions" for change early in the change process, but it cannot harness the energy of the workforce to recreate an organization with a common purpose and direction. True change occurs deep within the organization as individuals and work teams redefine the way they work and the values that guide decision making and action.

These lessons from the field suggest that building and sustaining an information age organization require that managers adopt a comprehensive approach to organization change that addresses the need to rethink the nature of control and authority (see Figure 5–3). "Smashing together" features of the hierarchy with features of an entrepreneurial firm will not

---

FIGURE 5–3   The Emerging Information Age Organization

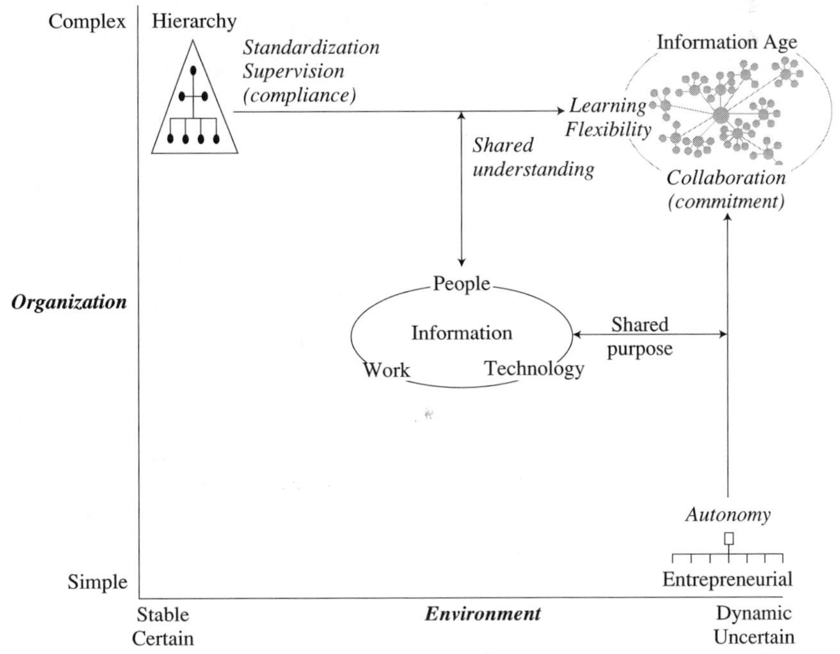

work. Neither will simply "layering" collaborative structures (e.g., team-based units and incentives) over a traditionally structured organization. In addition, change must not stop at the doors of corporate headquarters but must be infused throughout every part of the organization. Work must change and people must change. New knowledge and skills are needed, and the personal values and frameworks that people use to make decisions and take actions must be realigned with new organizational priorities and goals. Finally, the demand for information will increase dramatically as employees and managers at all levels attempt to cope with the greater complexity, uncertainty, and speed of change. Transforming the firm's information infrastructure is a critical component that both supports and enables the organizational transformation.

Maximizing Flexibility, Innovation, and Control

Most managers agree that the pace of change and the intensity of competition in business have accelerated over the past decade to a point where our current ways of doing business are no longer effective. Some firms, like the consumer products firm described earlier, attempt to speed up the rate of new-product development and shift to a customer-focused, "micromarketing" approach without considering the impact on operations in all parts of the firm. They make changes within their functional boundaries that cause devastating problems in other parts of the firm. They fail to view their organizations as a set of integrated, horizontal operating processes (e.g., order fulfillment, new product development) that must be redesigned in concert.[15]

Other firms recognize the integrated nature of their operations by implementing "business process reengineering" efforts. But as they squeeze all excess time and cost out of product development, order fulfillment, and customer service processes, they fail to change the way these new integrated, "fast-cycled" processes are managed. Either approach invites disaster.

In the 1990s, managers must recognize that organizational control is determined by two tightly integrated sets of processes. Operating processes are the series of activities that define how a firm designs, produces, distributes, markets, sells, and supports its products and services. Management processes are those activities through which a firm defines strategic direction and coordinates and controls the operating processes that execute strategy. Thus, to maintain organizational control, both operating and management processes must be not only streamlined but also *integrated and time-synchronized* (see Figure 5–4).

---

[15]It is important to note that the consumer products firm did make changes to isolated functional activities, but no attempt was made at end-to-end process redesign.

FIGURE 5–4   Streamlining the Business Cycle

1.   The business cycle is composed of two types of related processes.

Operating Processes: The activities through which an organization designs, produces, markets, delivers, and supports its products and services.

Management Processes: The activities through which an organization *manages* the design, production, marketing, delivery, and support of its products or services.

How

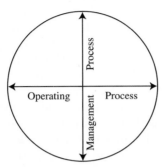

2.   Many companies attempt to streamline the business cycle by streamlining operating processes without a corresponding streamlining of management processes.

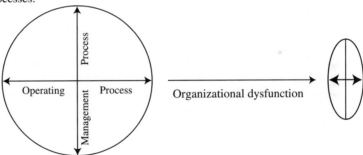

3.   The key is to streamline, integrate, and "time-synchronize" both operating and management processes.

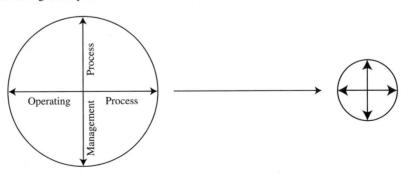

Recall how the consumer product firm, in attempting to implement a micromarketing strategy, significantly increased the number of products and product variations, the rate of new-product development, and the number of special promotions. These actions dramatically increased operating complexity and required a more responsive order-fulfillment cycle. The business calendar, heretofore planned and controlled in corporate headquarters one year in advance, was now being revised daily by field sales employees attempting to respond to local competitive actions and meet the unique needs of their customers. Field sales' decision to offer a new promotion within their local region had significant implications for manufacturing and logistics—both of which were neither in on the decision nor informed in a timely enough manner to adjust supply and production schedules.

This firm learned several important lessons from the problems they encountered. After confirming that they had accurately assessed the environmental conditions and that the strategy itself was indeed correct, they identified problems with both the organization redesign and its implementation. "I don't think any of us fully appreciated how highly leveraged and integrated our business truly was until the abortive attempt at implementing the micromarketing strategy in 1986," the new CEO said. "The problems were so abrupt and severe that it made a lasting impression on all of us. Three major lessons came from this situation. First, it became very clear that we needed to recast our vision for change as a corporatewide initiative rather than just a [functional] initiative. Despite our functional organization, our operations were highly integrated, and our standardized processes and procedures were highly effective and efficient at controlling and coordinating them. We couldn't make a change in one area without causing problems somewhere else. Where before we believed we were transferring decision-making authority on isolated decisions to individual line employees, we now recognized that we would need to create interfunctional management teams—composed of managers from all of the functional areas of the business—that would manage profitability and operations as we had in corporate headquarters, but would now do so in the field. Second, we became aware that we could not give up the efficiency and control benefits that we achieved through our centralized structure to gain the flexibility and speed that we wished to achieve by decentralizing decision making. It became clear that the organization we needed to create was really a hybrid organization that would allow us to achieve the benefits of centralization and decentralization simultaneously. Finally, the need to provide the information to support both decentralized decision making and centralized control was essential and, we believed, would need to precede organizational restructuring."

As noted in Figure 5–4, the ability to design a firm that optimizes flexibility and innovation while maintaining control requires a fundamental shift in the nature of control from standardization and supervision, which are based on compliance, to a learning model that preserves flexibility and fosters commitment.[16] Systems thinking—the ability to see a situation or problem in its totality—is at the heart of learning; it demands an understanding of the causal relationships between individual components of a system and the whole.[17] This would imply that a learning model of control requires the development of a shared purpose (or direction) and a shared understanding of the individual actions needed to achieve that purpose. Causal relationships between organizational goals and business dynamics (the interrelationships among internal operating processes and the external environment) must be fully understood, and the understanding must be translated into effective action.

Figure 5–5 illustrates the features of a control system rooted in organizational learning rather than in compliance. It is founded on a deep understanding of core operating processes. Reminiscent of Frederick Taylor's compulsion to define the most efficient means of turning out a product of 100 percent consistency, it begins with streamlining and time-synchronizing operating processes.[18] But there the similarity ends. Rather than segregate and structure those processes, managers in an information age organization seek to *integrate and continuously improve* them. To do that, detailed and timely information is essential—information to coordinate the flow of activities and to provide decision makers with a thorough understanding of process dynamics.

Processes must be managed by interfunctional teams that are "close to the action" and in direct contact with the information. These teams must have ample opportunity to debate the meaning of the information and to adjust tactical strategies and actions based on a timely review of business performance.[19] They must be able to relate local business outcomes to the decisions and actions that they have taken and to organizational priorities and "system" performance. Management processes must be streamlined, integrated, and time-synchronized with operating processes and the inherent cycle of change in the business environment.

The "rules of the road," which ensure safety and the smooth flow of operations—yet do not define the route to be traveled or how to get there—must

---

[16]R. Walton, *Up and Running* (Boston: Harvard Business School Press, 1988).

[17]P. Shrivastava, "A Typology of Organizational Learning Systems," *Journal of Management Studies,* 20:7–28, 1983; H. Simon, "Bounded Rationality and Organizational Learning," *Organization Science,* 1:133, 1991; P. Senge, *The Fifth Discipline: The Art and Practice of the Learning Organization* (NY: Doubleday, 1990); D. Garvin, "Building a learning organization," *Harvard Business Review,* July–August 1993.

[18]The principles of scientific management, which specified the careful analysis and design of operations to achieve maximum efficiency and consistency, were an important foundation for the design of hierarchical organizations. F. Taylor, *The Principles of Scientific Management* (NY: Harper & Row, 1911).

[19]While IT can support the more intense nature of communication and information sharing, face-to-face dialog remains at the heart of an interactive, fast-cycled learning model of control. See R. Simon, *Levers of Control* (Boston: Harvard Business School Press, 1995) for an excellent description of the design and implementation of "interactive" control systems.

FIGURE 5-5 Redefining Control

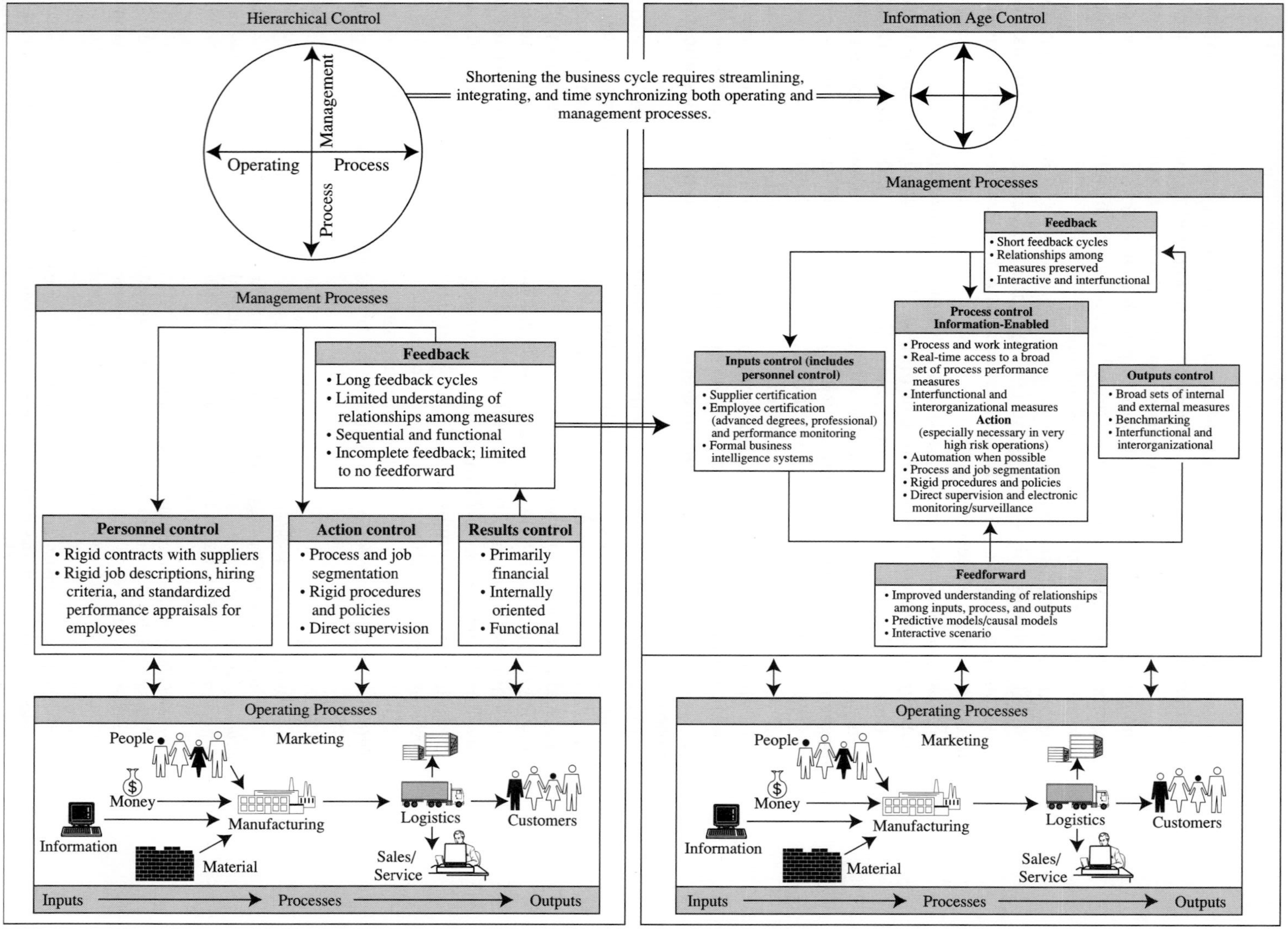

188

Hierarchical Control

(circle diagram: Management — Process / Operating — Process)

Management Processes

Feedback
- Long feedback cycles
- Limited understanding of relationships among measures
- Sequential and functional
- Incomplete feedback; limited to no feedforward

Results control
- Primarily financial
- Internally oriented
- Functional

Action control
- Process and job segmentation
- Rigid procedures and policies
- Direct supervision

Personnel control
- Rigid contracts with suppliers
- Rigid job descriptions, hiring criteria, and standardized performance appraisals for employees

Operating Processes

Inputs — Processes — Outputs

Information, Material, Money, People → Manufacturing → Marketing, Logistics, Sales/Service → Customers

---

Shortening the business cycle requires streamlining, integrating, and time synchronizing both operating and management processes.

Information Age Control

Management Processes

Feedback
- Short feedback cycles
- Relationships among measures preserved
- Interactive and interfunctional

Outputs control
- Broad sets of internal and external measures
- Benchmarking
- Interfunctional and interorganizational

Process control Information-Enabled
- Process and work integration
- Real-time access to a broad set of process performance measures
- Interfunctional and interorganizational measures
  Action (especially necessary in very high risk operations)
- Automation when possible
- Process and job segmentation
- Rigid procedures and policies
- Direct supervision and electronic monitoring/surveillance

Inputs control (includes personnel control)
- Supplier certification
- Employee certification (advanced degrees, professional) and performance monitoring
- Formal business intelligence systems

Feedforward
- Improved understanding of relationships among inputs, process, and outputs
- Predictive models/causal models
- Interactive scenario

Operating Processes

Inputs — Processes — Outputs

Information, Material, Money, People → Manufacturing → Marketing, Logistics, Sales/Service → Customers be clearly communicated, closely monitored, and consistently enforced. "Safety nets" that guard the organization against catastrophic injury must be in place, well maintained, and effective. Core values that stress integrity, honesty, and commitment to a shared purpose serve as the glue that binds the organization together. Finally, a learning model of control demands that timely and detailed information be available to enable a deep understanding of process performance and the causal relationships among actions, decisions, and outcomes. The information must be widely shared and fact-based. Managers and decision makers at all levels of the firm must be able to access the information directly and must possess the skills and experience to extract meaning that guides effective action and decisions.

Taken together, these features of information age control fit well with our definition of organizational learning. They mandate an active approach to problem finding and a deep understanding of the dynamics of the business—how it works today and how it could work more effectively and efficiently in the future. They demand a commitment to shared goals and a shared understanding of how to achieve those goals. They are information-intensive and require that managers become "information literate." They require that people and technology unite to acquire, analyze, and store information as a source of future organizational memory and experience. Finally, they require that people have the motivation, skills, and knowledge to turn information into action. Above all, an information age learning model of control must ensure that we resolve the paradox between tight control and flexibility, between efficiency and innovation, and between stability and speed. Managers in the information age cannot afford to give up any one of these goals. (Table 5–1 summarizes the features of information age control.)

Maximizing Independence and Interdependence: Collaboration, the Missing Organization Design Criterion

Empowerment, teams, networked and collaborative organizations—all of these 1990s buzzwords describe different facets of organizational authority structures and systems: the formal and informal structures, coordinating mechanisms, responsibilities, and incentives that define the distribution of power and accountability within a firm.

Traditionally, the formal distribution of authority within an organization has been viewed as a trade-off between centralization and decentralization (see Figure 5–6). Organizations were considered networks of relationships among principals (owners and senior management) and self-interested "agents."[20] In hierarchical organizations, the cost and risk of coordinating

---

[20]M. Jensen and W. Meckling, "Theory of the Firm: Managerial Behavior, Agency Costs, and Ownership Structure," *Journal of Financial Economics* (1973), pp. 305–60; E. Fama, "Agency Problems and the Theory of the Firm," *Journal of Political Economics* (1980), pp. 288–307.

TABLE 5–1   Characteristics of Information Age Control

Operating Processes

- Integrated, streamlined, and time-synchronized product/service delivery and new-product development processes (includes customers, suppliers, channel distributors, strategic partners, etc.).
- Cycle time of operating processes matches cycle time in the environment.
- Increased complexity of operating processes matches the inherent complexity in the environment.
- Efficient, yet flexible, operations.
- Interfunctional and interorganizational.
- Focus on continuous improvement and innovation.

Management Processes

- Integrated, streamlined, and time-synchronized management processes (e.g., planning, resource allocation, performance management).
- Cycle time of management processes matches cycle time of operating processes.
- Efficient, yet flexible, management.
- Interfunctional and interorganizational.
- Increased vertical and lateral interaction.
- Tight control achieved through information versus structure and supervision.

Beliefs and Boundaries

- Clearly defined and widely communicated core values.
- Values are integrated into how people work and make decisions at all levels.
- Clearly defined and widely communicated boundary systems reflect both values and key risks that must be managed.
- Boundary systems are closely monitored and consistently enforced.
- Safety nets ensure that risks are identified and managed.

local operations and aligning individual interests were minimized by centralizing decision making, structuring operations, and developing a deep hierarchy so that operations were executed efficiently and according to clearly defined procedures. This approach implied that decision makers at the top had access to the information they needed to understand local business dynamics, and that they had the time and expertise to analyze that information to ensure that they made the right decisions.

In the face of increased organizational complexity, uncertainty, and speed of change, these critical assumptions could not be met. The solution was to decentralize decision making to the point at which individuals possessed the information they needed to make decisions. But decentralization increased the cost of coordination and control. Senior management attempted to balance these costs and benefits by decentralizing decision authority to middle

FIGURE 5–6   Redefining Authority

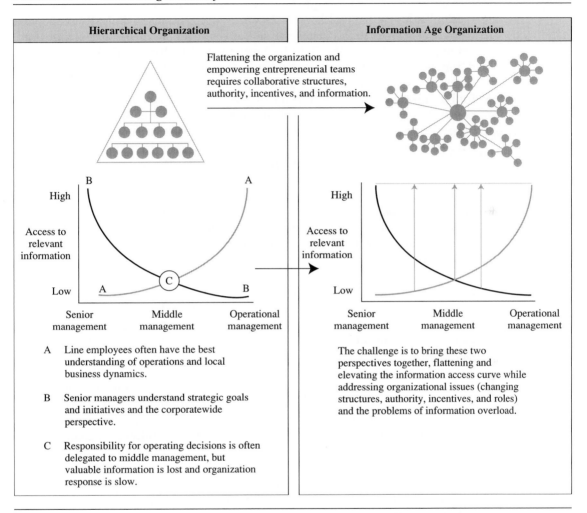

management within autonomous profit centers. But as one president explained, these divisional structures often resulted in layer upon layer of middle managers and large corporate staff units that collected, synthesized, interpreted, and distilled information. One senior manager called this the "tyranny of control." "When we attempted to decentralize our organization," he continued, "we added controllers in all of the newly formed business units. Over time, the number of controllers in corporate headquarters also increased. We had *checkers checking the checkers!*"

As the business environment grew more complex, these slow-to-respond and costly authority structures and systems were no longer acceptable.

Business dynamics and organizational priorities became more fluid, and the amount of information required for effective decision making increased dramatically. Many firms, like the consumer products firm, initially responded to the need to establish a closer link between the perspective of senior management and that of the field by "cutting out" or bypassing the middle. In doing so, they mistakenly maintained some of the principles of hierarchical authority distribution (e.g., functional segregation of duties and authority, individual accountability, and incentives), while abandoning others (hierarchical chain of command and a limited span of control to enable direct supervision). Further, employees were not given the information they needed in a timely enough manner to understand the impact of their local decisions on end-to-end operations and enterprisewide performance.

The transition toward an information age organization demands that we rethink the nature of authority. No longer can it be viewed as a simple, linear trade-off between autonomy and control—centralization and decentralization. Instead, managers must successfully marry autonomy, control, and collaboration. How is this reflected in changes in organization design? In the information age firm, authority is no longer vested in a single individual. Instead, teams of employees representing the range of expertise and accountability required to make decisions and take actions share responsibility for the performance of their unit. Not only must teams ensure that effective decisions can be made and executed, they also represent the important "checks and balances" that help guard against the problems Barings Bank encountered when it "empowered" a single manager with broad authority and responsibility. Shared incentives (e.g., team-based incentives and employee stock ownership plans) augment and reinforce the shared authority and help align individual, team, and organizational priorities. But since personal accountability must still be maintained, performance evaluations and incentives recognize performance against individual goals in addition to team and organizational goals. At the organizational level, stretch targets help intensify effort, clarify priorities, focus attention, and, with supportive structures, systems, processes, and management values, support a commitment to collaborate among independent divisions.[21]

While it no longer accurately reflects how the organization operates, the hierarchical chain of command—albeit flatter—still remains in the information age organization. And in many firms, functional units are still in place, but are becoming centers of functional excellence and career development. Downsizing of middle management, staff, and corporate headquarters has left the organization flatter (often two or more layers are removed) and

---

[21]"Stretch" targets are performance goals that exceed the level of output that can be predicted based on historical data. The degree of "stretch" and policies for how to manage the failure to achieve performance targets are discussed in more detail in *Designing and Managing the Information Age Organization,* Harvard Business School No. 196-003.

leaner, with approximately 50 percent of all U.S. firms reporting workforce reductions (on average approximately 10 percent) in 1994.[22] This trend, which started in the 1980s, has continued unabated throughout the 1990s.

In general, authority for operating strategy development and its execution is moving from corporate headquarters to the field. Interfunctional (and at times interorganizational) operating teams are being inserted into the middle of the firm, where they are granted broad authority for defining operating strategy and the processes, systems, and organizational arrangements to carry out and manage it. They are being held accountable for profitability, stakeholder satisfaction, operating process design, and continuous improvement. They coordinate their businesses (both inside and outside their organizational boundaries) using face-to-face and IT-enabled information sharing, networked communication, and ad hoc adjustment. Work teams are being formed at the line, and broader authority for defining work and the specific activities to carry it out are being pushed down from the middle to the line.

Yet all of these organizational design features cannot work unless each employee develops a new set of management and decision-making skills (e.g., leadership, negotiation, consensus decision making) and gains experience with using those skills to make decisions and take actions. While formal training programs may help, ongoing mentorship is critical. Actions must change and values must change—and this takes time.

As they wait for change to take effect, many senior managers discover that formal boundary and value systems for collaboration—defined, implemented, and enforced by senior management—are crucial. The value systems provide an "unambiguous" statement of the need for collaboration and consensus decision making while maintaining a performance-based culture. Boundary systems make clear the penalties for failure to collaborate. No clearer example of a boundary system addressing collaboration can be found than the one in place at Asea Brown Boveri.[23] "You may have heard the working rule around here," one regional manager explained. "If two managers cannot agree, escalate the issue up to your bosses for a decision. If you cannot agree a second time, go to your bosses again for a decision. But if you cannot agree a third time, both managers will be replaced!" While other firms often take a less strict approach to establishing boundary systems to foster collaboration, the message and consequences are still clearly communicated and unambiguous. (Table 5–2 summarizes the characteristics of information age authority.)

[22]*AMA Research Report* (NY.: AMA, 1994). The survey found that, while middle managers made up only 5 to 8 percent of the U.S. workforce, they were targeted for 18.6 percent of the 430,000 jobs eliminated since 1988.

[23]R. Simons and C. Bartlett, *Asea Brown Bovary: Accountability Times Two, (A) and (B),* Harvard Business School Nos. 192-141 and 192-142.

TABLE 5–2   Characteristics of Information Age Authority

Power Structure

- Flat hierarchy with broader spans of control.
- Downsized corporate headquarters; staff reassigned to the field.
- Strategic partnerships and alliances enable focus on core competencies.
- Networked coordinating mechanisms (e.g., interfunctional teams and matrixed reporting structures) layered over hierarchical reporting structures.
- Functional units remain as center of expertise and career development.

Authority and Decision Making

- Shared authority and decision making replace clearly defined hierarchical authority.
- Senior management more involved in monitoring and understanding operations; responsible for defining, communicating, and consistently enforcing boundary and value systems.
- Interfunctional middle management operating units responsible for operating strategy development, strategy execution, network coordination, and innovation.
- Self-managing work teams responsible for defining and managing local operations and product quality.

Incentives and Rewards

- Shared incentive systems (e.g., team-based incentives) augment and enforce shared authority structures.
- Personal accountability and commitment maintained.
- "Stretch" targets motivate commitment to collaborate, maintain focus on organizational priorities, and intensify efforts to achieve organizational goals.

Roles / Skills and Expertise

- Roles evolve as individuals and teams struggle to redefine work within the new structure and incentive systems.
- Increased analytical/intellectual content of the work.
- People expected to have a broader skill base.
- Information competency at all levels.
- Increase emphasis on the development of leadership and change management skills.

Career Development

- Fewer opportunities for advancement available within the hierarchical reporting structure.
- Expanded jobs and increased lateral movement instead of hierarchical movement.

SUMMARY

Companies spent significant effort during the 1980s reorganizing to meet the challenges of operating in a more dynamic, hypercompetitive world. But as the 1980s drew to a close, many were forced to face the grim reality that the 1990s would demand even more radical change. For most, it became clear that despite their efforts to restructure, they were still being asked to respond even more quickly, to deliver even higher-quality products and services, and to cut costs even more deeply. Technology and changes in the workforce were continuing to demand new organizational initiatives. They had cut layers of management and increased spans of control to the point where many worried that "control" had been lost. They had pushed the hierarchy to the limit, violating many of the major tenets upon which it was based.

Thomas Kuhn's in-depth analysis of scientific revolutions suggests that crisis is a necessary precondition to the emergence of a new theory or model.[24] But when presented with crisis, most people do not immediately reject existing models. Instead, they attempt incremental adjustments that, over time, begin to blur the fundamental structure and assumptions upon which the old models were based. Practitioners are often the first to lose sight of old models as the familiar rules for solving problems become ineffective. At some point, total reconstruction is required. During the transition, however, there is frequently an overlap between the problems that can be solved by the old and new models. But no matter which is used, there is a decisive difference in the modes of solution.

This appears to be the point at which managers find themselves as we enter the 21st century. A crisis, largely driven by a fundamental mismatch between environmental demands and organizational capabilities, has called into question many of the fundamental assumptions of traditional organizational models. Academic thinking in this area is being led by practice. The lessons from managers in the field suggest that a new organizational model is emerging that harnesses the power of today's technologies in the hands of today's workforce to offer fundamentally new approaches to organizing and managing in the information age.

Appendix A:

OVERVIEW OF TRADITIONAL ORGANIZATION DESIGN MODELS

Our attention has been captured by the intensity and pervasiveness of the change initiatives undertaken by companies during the 1980s and 1990s. But these organizational design challenges are not new. The bureaucratic hierarchy and entrepreneurial organizational forms were defined at the beginning of the 20th century,[25] and

---

[24]T. Kuhn, *The Structure of Scientific Revolution* (Chicago: University of Chicago Press, 1970).

[25]F. Taylor, *The Principles of Scientific Management*, op. cit.; M. Weber, *The Theory of Social and Economic Organization* (NY: The Free Press, 1947); H. Fayol, *General and Industrial Management* (London: Pitman, 1949).

the difficulty of balancing the flexibility and responsiveness of the entrepreneurial organization and the efficiency, scope, and control of the bureaucracy was debated extensively during the 1950s and 1960s.[26] The matrix organization, popularized in the 1960s and 1970s, was born of these struggles.[27] During this same period, the adhocracy was defined to meet the special challenge of organizing to support teams of experts (knowledge workers) working together on projects designed to produce complex, radical innovations (the NASA space program, for example).[28] These four traditional organizational models provide a useful perspective on the fundamental principles of organization design that serve as a theoretical foundation for analyzing the organizational design challenges that face companies in the 1990s

THE BUREAUCRATIC HIERARCHY

The traditional bureaucratic hierarchy, first defined at the turn of the century by Frederick Taylor,[29] Max Weber,[30] Henry Fayol,[31] and others, provided a set of detailed guidelines for designing large organizations that could cope efficiently with the complexity of doing business on a broad scale. The organization was broken down into distinct units of specialization, each responsible for one major task associated with designing, developing, manufacturing, marketing, selling, and servicing a product. These units were further subdivided into smaller and smaller units until the job of each individual in the organization was specified in detail.

Founded on the concepts of simplification, routinization, and control, the bureaucratic hierarchy required the ruthless elimination of uncertainty to operate smoothly. The operating core needed to be "sealed off" from all nonroutine events and conditions. Behavior was codified in detailed policies, procedures, and job descriptions that facilitated tight control through direct supervision. Hierarchical chains of authority were developed to deal with situations that fell outside the routine. On average, spans of control of no more than five to seven individuals were required to enable direct supervision,[32] but with highly structured work (e.g., assembly-line production), standardization of tasks and detailed procedures often enabled an increased span of control.[33] When precise specification of actions was not possible,

---

[26]T. Burns, and G.M. Stalker, *The Management of Innovation* (London: Tavistock, 1961); J. Woodward, *Industrial Organization, Theory and Practice* (London: Oxford University Press, 1965); P. Lawrence and J. Lorsch, *Organization and Environment* (Boston: Harvard Business School Press, 1967, 1986).

[27]L. Fouraker and J. Stopford, "Organizational Structure and Multinational Strategy," *Administrative Science Quarterly,* 13:47–64, 1968; S. Davis and P. Lawrence, *Matrix* (Reading, MA: Addison Wesley, 1977).

[28]H. Mintzberg, "Dealing with Structure and Systems," *The Strategy Process* (edited by Quinn, Mintzberg, and James) (Englewood Cliffs, NJ: Prentice-Hall, 1988).

[29]F. Taylor, op. cit.

[30]M. Weber, op. cit.

[31]H. Fayol, op. cit.

[32]L.F. Urwick, "The Manager's Span of Control," *Harvard Business Review,* May–June 1956, pp. 39–47.

[33]H. Mintzberg, op. cit.

planning and control systems defined predetermined performance targets, which again served to minimize uncertainty and define "boundaries" for management actions and decisions. Rewards and incentives were designed to motivate behavior consistent with achieving these targets.

Chandler,[34] in describing the development of the modern industrial corporation, describes the two principal hierarchical models: the *functional* and *divisional* forms. "The initial step in the creation of the modern industrial enterprise," Chandler stated, "was the investment in production facilities large enough to achieve the cost advantages of scale and scope. The second step, which often occurred simultaneously, was the investment in product-specific marketing, distributing, and purchasing networks. The third and final step was the recruiting and organizing of the manager. . . . The resulting managerial hierarchies were established along functional lines." Chandler goes on to describe how, in the early 1900s, large functional departments were formed for production, marketing, sales, and finance, with smaller departments formed for purchasing, R&D, engineering, personnel, and legal.

Once production scale and scope were achieved and the managerial hierarchy was in place, organizations grew through four basic mechanisms: acquiring or merging with firms that made the same basic product for the same basic market (horizontal integration); acquiring or merging with firms that performed tasks upstream (e.g., suppliers) or downstream (e.g., distributors) in the production process (vertical integration); geographical expansion; and product expansion.

The first two growth strategies were often accomplished by absorbing newly acquired units into the existing functional hierarchy. The latter strategies, which greatly increased organizational complexity, gave rise to the divisional organizational model that remains the most common configuration among large, private corporations. The divisionalized form reduced complexity by breaking the organization up into separate units structured around common products, markets, or geographical locations. This necessitated adding a separate administrative layer, the divisional headquarters office. Each division office was headed by a general manager who was held accountable for performance and profitability. Below the general manager level, the organization was often structured as a functional hierarchy.

The strengths of the bureaucracy were rooted in its view of the organization as a machine—a view that reflected the technology and environment of the early 1900s, when the model was defined.[35] But many have argued that such mechanistic approaches to organization work best under conditions in which machines work well:

- When there exists a readily understood and highly structured set of tasks for converting inputs to outputs.
- When the same product is to be produced, or service rendered, over and over.
- When the environment is stable enough to ensure that the needed technology will remain relatively constant, the products and services will continue to meet customers' needs, and the flow of raw materials (including people and capital) will continue uninterrupted.
- When the human "machine" is "compliant" and behaves as "programmed."

---

[34]A. Chandler, *Scale and Scope* (Cambridge, MA: Belknap Press, 1990).
[35]G. Morgan, *Images of Organization* (Beverly Hills, CA: Sage, 1986).

These conditions no longer applied during the turbulent 1980s and 1990s. In their search for a structure better suited for dealing with a rapidly changing, dynamic environment, many large firms turned to the entrepreneurial organization.

THE ENTREPRENEURIAL ORGANIZATION

Entrepreneurial organizations are able to be fast, focused, and flexible because their small size and relatively simple context permit important decisions to be centralized, yet still reflect real-time understanding of the business environment and allow immediate feedback. A single individual (typically the founder), alone or in concert with a small cohort of trusted companions, defines corporate strategy and the organizational design needed to implement that strategy.

"Strategy making in this context," observed Mintzberg,[36] "revolves around a single brain, unconstrained by the forces of bureaucratic momentum." This cohesive center, being in direct contact with operations and markets, can learn quickly and modify its actions as events unfold. Strategy making is often highly intuitive and nonanalytical, thriving on uncertainty and oriented towards a search for new opportunities. Most important decisions are made by the CEO/founder and communicated immediately and directly to the entire organization. Coordination and control are exercised primarily through direct supervision and mutual adaptation; the small size of entrepreneurial firms enables such direct methods, and the changing nature of strategy affords little opportunity for standardization.

The key to success in entrepreneurial organizations is intensive, real-time, organizationwide information sharing and a spirit of collaboration and trust that is founded on a comprehensive understanding of the business overall. But the large number of failed entrepreneurial ventures suggests that these conditions are necessary, but not sufficient, for success. Lack of access to capital and specialized expertise can limit opportunities to pursue new business opportunities, develop new products, and enter new markets; lack of power can render an entrepreneurial firm vulnerable to preemptive, often fatal, actions by larger, more powerful competitors, buyers, or suppliers; and the concentration of knowledge, power, and authority in one or a few individuals limits the ability to deal with the complexity associated with growth.

At the point at which systems must be introduced to enable a firm to manage complexity, an entrepreneur must decide whether to adopt a different management style and philosophy or sell the firm and launch a new venture. Many choose the latter option. The problems faced by Apple Computer founder Steve Jobs and his departure from Apple in the late 1980s, and by Debbi and Randy Fields as they struggled to control their "crumbling" cookie empire in 1992, highlight the difficulty of managing the evolution of an entrepreneurial firm.

As they grow in size and complexity, successful entrepreneurial organizations frequently evolve towards "mature" bureaucratic hierarchies. But, during the late 1960s and 1970s, the limitations of the hierarchy for enabling firms to manage the increasing competitive intensity, uncertainty, and speed of change in the environment led to the development of two new organizational models—the matrix and the adhocracy.

---

[36]H. Mintzberg, *Structure in Fives* (Englewood Cliffs, NJ: Prentice-Hall, 1983).

The Matrix Organization

Bartlett and Ghoshal[37] described the matrix organization as the "obvious organization solution" to the need to directly manage, rather than minimize, environmental complexity. In focusing attention on multiple areas simultaneously (e.g., products and functions, functions and geography, or functions and markets/customers), matrix structures violated important assumptions of the bureaucratic model by incorporating dual reporting, authority, decision-making, and communication channels.[38] The parallel authority and reporting structures of the matrix organization provided a formal mechanism for understanding and managing the diverse, conflicting needs for functional, product, and geographic expertise, knowledge, and focus that matched the complexity of the environment.

Davis and Lawrence[39] identified three conditions they believed justified the increased cost and effort associated with managing and controlling the matrix: (1) significant pressure from the environment to organize around more than one area of focus and expertise; (2) sufficient environmental uncertainty, complexity, and/or interdependency that necessitate implementation of "wide-band" information processing systems; and (3) excessive pressure to share physical or human (e.g., knowledge or skill) resources. Matrix structures became popular in the 1960s and 1970s within "project-oriented" (e.g., aerospace) and multinational firms.

In theory, the matrix was designed to acknowledge and resolve the conflicts that arose among multiple management groups that brought unique, but interdependent, sets of knowledge, skills, and resources to decision making and operations. Its multiple information channels were designed to model the complexity of the business environment, and overlapping authority and accountability were designed to "combat parochialism" and encourage collaboration. In practice, however, the matrix did not live up to its theoretical promise. Power struggles and turf battles led to confusion, conflict, and indecision; dual reporting and authority levels made accountability problematic; lack of tools for managing and communicating information hampered understanding of the business and created information overload; and duplication of resources engendered excessive overhead and cost.[40] Many companies adopted the matrix form during the 1970s only to abandon it in the 1980s.

The adhocracy, an organizational model developed about the same time as the matrix to address similar environmental conditions, exhibited many of the same problems.

The Adhocracy

Mintzberg[41] describes the adhocracy as the organizational configuration most appropriate for "sophisticated innovation." Sophisticated innovation requires that experts unite in interdisciplinary teams to work on complex projects with long time horizons.

---

[37]C. Bartlett and S. Ghoshal, op. cit.

[38]W.G. Englehoff, *Organizing the Multinational Corporation: An Information Processing Perspective* (Cambridge, MA: Ballinger Publishing, 1988).

[39]S. Davis and P. Lawrence, op. cit.

[40]Ibid.

[41]H. Mintzberg, 1983, op. cit.

Examples of organizations commonly structured as adhocracies include professional consulting, investment banking, R&D, biotechnology, and law firms.

How do experts engaged in interdisciplinary project work continue to refine and update their professional skills and knowledge? Most large adhocracies adopt a modified matrix structure, with professionals grouped into functional or market-based units that serve as their "organizational homes," but deployed within project teams to carry out the work of the organization. Liaison units or individuals constitute the primary coordinating mechanism between teams that may be assigned to work on different parts of a project, and between functional/market units and project teams. Coordination within teams is achieved primarily by professional negotiation and leadership, which rely on intensive communication and collaboration. Traditionally, such communication was possible only when team members were colocated, but advanced electronic media such as video and computer conferencing and electronic mail have recently emerged to support coordination among dispersed project teams.[42]

The adhocracy is ideally suited to a simultaneously dynamic and complex environment. But, over time, the uncertainty, inefficiency, and outright "chaos" inherent in the structure often give rise to difficulties. Many employees cannot tolerate the ambiguity and fluidity of the adhocracy; as observed by Burns and Stalker,[43] "[all individuals] some of the time, and many [individuals] all of the time, yearn for more definition and structure." Burnout and high turnover fuel instability and can impair quality and delay project completion, resulting in customer dissatisfaction. The adhocracy's inherent ambiguity, when combined with the high degree of interdependence and autonomy, renders the structure fertile ground for conflict and ruthless competition among team members. Those best able to maneuver within its political system garner the rewards; those unable to comprehend the politics or "fit in" are weeded out.

A final limitation of the adhocracy is that it is ideally suited to finding one-of-a-kind solutions to complex problems; it is not well suited to routine activities. In its pure form, it lacks a repository from which knowledge and skills gained in one project can be captured and routinized for use in similar projects, and efforts to create mechanisms to capture organizational learning are frequently thwarted by professional experts intent on protecting their power domains. (In the 1990s, Internet-based knowledge management systems are being deployed by consulting and professional services firms around the world to enable sharing of best practices, thus significantly decreasing the importance of this final limitation.)

Given these inherent sources of instability and the growth that attends success and age, the adhocracy frequently evolves into a *professional bureaucracy* concentrated on a specific market or focused on a standardized set of services.[44] The latter structure is common in universities, hospitals, and large, established public accounting firms that operate in stable environments. (It is the routinization of products and services that distinguishes the professional bureaucracy from the adhocracy.) Both the professional bureaucracy and the adhocracy rely on standardization of expert skills and knowledge to ensure coordination and control. Such knowledge and skills

---

[42]R. Johansen, *Groupware* (NY: Free Press, 1988); R. Bostrom, R. Watson, and S. Kinney, *Computer Augmented Teamwork* (NY: Van Nostrand Reinhold, 1992).

[43]T. Burns and G.M. Stalker, op. cit.

[44]H. Mintzberg, 1988, op. cit.

are frequently imparted through extensive, often university-based, training that is certified by external accrediting boards. This type of "professional indoctrination" is external for some; physicians, for example, are subjected to an extensive period of internship and residency before being permitted to practice independently with full decision-making authority and accountability. For others, "indoctrination" is internal and must be completed before one can be voted in ("tenured") as a permanent member of the organization. This period is often characterized by direct supervision by a tenured member of the organization who must then support the "junior member's" bid for tenure (examples include associate ranks in law and consulting firms and the assistant professor rank in many universities.)

A FRAMEWORK FOR ORGANIZATION DESIGN

The design and implementation of the structures and systems that enable an organization to accomplish its goals and execute its strategies are among the most challenging tasks facing managers. While many erroneously believe that the key to competitive advantage lies in defining a blockbuster strategy, the most successful managers recognize that the ability to flawlessly execute strategy—day after day and year after year—is the real key to success. (Figure A–1 provides a framework for organization design, and Exhibit A–1 compares the features of the four traditional models using the design framework.)

Flawless execution requires that strategy development and organization design be thought of as a process of learning and continuous improvement that is driven by the need to create value for all stakeholders. Managers must continuously monitor

---

FIGURE A–1   A Framework for Assessing Organization Effectiveness

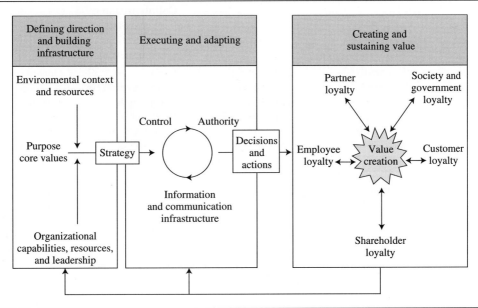

EXHIBIT A–1   Comparison of Traditional Organizational Models

	Bureaucratic Hierarchy	Entrepreneurial	Matrix	Adhocracy
Environmental context	Stable Certain Moderately complex—focus on routine	Dynamic Uncertain Simple—focus on innovation	Dynamic Uncertain Complex—focus on routine	Dynamic Uncertain Complex—focus on innovation
Organizational context	Mature Large	Young Small	Mature Large (often widely dispersed)	Young Medium to large

Authority

Power Structure

	Bureaucratic Hierarchy	Entrepreneurial	Matrix	Adhocracy
Unit groupings	Usually functional Span of control wider at the bottom, narrow in the middle	Usually functional Span of control may be wide	Combination of functional, market, product, and geography	Core expertise
Coordination	Standardization of work Hierarchical supervision	Direct supervision	Standardization of work Hierarchical supervision Collaboration at areas of matrix intersection	Collaboration Professional negotiation Leadership
Power/authority systems	Centralized—senior management team and technical staff Manager assumes responsibility for subordinates' actions and decisions	Centralized—owner/founder Founder assumes responsibility for most decisions	Distributed among matrix managers Hierarchical below matrix manager	Decentralized among individual knowledge workers External accrediting bodies Professionals maintain responsibility for actions and decisions

EXHIBIT A–1 *(continued)*   Comparison of Traditional Organizational Models

	Bureaucratic Hierarchy	Entrepreneurial	Matrix	Adhocracy
Authority (cont.) *People*				
Roles	Formally defined and well understood at top, middle, and bottom	Little formalization Organic Often vague and open to misinterpretation	Like the hierarchy except for the middle, where role is often vague and poorly understood	Like the entrepreneurial organization but more open to informal political manipulation
Skills and expertise	Functional	Primarily functional but may involve cross-training	Functional, market, geography, technology, and/or product	Often highly specialized around product and/or technology
Career development	On-the-job Informal indoctrination Functional and hierarchical progression	Like the hierarchy, but career progression is less hierarchical May be limited potential for advancement	Like the hierarchy, but opportunities for cross-functional development exist	Little formal "in-house" training Heavily dependent on external professional development May be lengthy period of indoctrination before permanent membership is granted
Education	Informal, ad hoc	Informal, ad hoc	Increased formal training for midlevel managers	Highly valued but often external

(continued)

EXHIBIT A–1 *(continued)*   Comparison of Traditional Organizational Models

	Bureaucratic Hierarchy	Entrepreneurial	Matrix	Adhocracy
Control				
Management Processes				
Planning and control	Routine cycle time to fiscal calendar Involvement is usually limited to senior management and technical analysts Action control at bottom and middle Performance control at top	Informal Ad hoc Limited involvement of organization members	Like the hierarchy but greater involvement of matrix managers in planning/control Performance control extends to upper middle management	Project planning and control predominate Business planning is often ad hoc Resource allocation and project approval heavily determined by prestige and influence of project manager
Incentives and rewards	Based on seniority and level in the company at all but senior management level	Determined by owner/founder May be based on organization performance and include stock May be influenced by unique nature of expertise in the company and industry	Like the hierarchy, but performance-based incentives extend to matrix management level	Based on unique nature of expertise in the company and industry
Culture	Command and control Distrust of authority Risk-averse Low commitment	Innovation Risk taking encouraged Often high commitment to organization goals	Like the hierarchy but increased conflict	Chaotic Risk taking encouraged Lots of conflict Strongly influenced by those in power

EXHIBIT A–1 *(concluded)*   Comparison of Traditional Organizational Models

	Bureaucratic Hierarchy	Entrepreneurial	Matrix	Adhocracy
Control (cont.) *Operating Processes*				
Core processes (e.g., product/service delivery and new product development)	Defined and managed by technical analysts located in corporate headquarters	Defined and managed by owner/founder Often ad hoc	Defined and managed by matrix managers Often conflict exists among managers with dual responsibility	Defined and managed by project managers Often ad hoc
Tasks/job design	High degree of standardization Narrowly defined Functional	Little standardization Often broadly defined May be interfunctional	Like the hierarchy, but middle is less standardized and jobs are more broadly defined Liaison units coordinate across functions	Little standardization Defined around core expertise Many liaison mechanisms but may be informal

the environment and the organization's capabilities and performance to quickly recognize when the strategy no longer meets the changing demands of the environment or the changing nature of the organization itself. They must be able to quickly respond by defining and implementing new strategies, structures, and systems that are more appropriate. In this sense, strategic planning and organization design become an ongoing management process—components of an integrated system of strategic control. Flawless execution also requires that managers recognize that the skills, expertise, and 100 percent commitment of every member of the "extended" organization are necessary. While this commitment cannot be mandated through traditional command and control systems, the need to ensure that commitment and capabilities are present—that every member understands and participates in the ongoing process of defining and implementing strategy and that each member is making decisions and taking actions that enable the organization to accomplish its goals—is critical for survival.

Chapter

6

IT Architecture: Evolution and Alternatives[1]

As we enter the 21st century, excitement concerning the potential of information technology (IT) to create a new business environment has never been higher. Nowhere has this excitement been more evident than in the venture community. Consider this: Between January 1 and September 30, 1997, over 1,000 companies received approximately US$5.3 billion in venture capital funding for IT-related entrepreneurial ventures. This represented approximately 49 percent of the total U.S. new venture money spent during 1997, and a fraction of the money spent on IT-related business strategies by entrenched players in the United States and entrenched players around the globe.[2]

But this fascination with IT-enabled business innovation comes at a time of significant uncertainty and change in the industry as both entrenched players and new entrants struggle to position themselves for success in the emerging global "networked" economy. While most agree that Internet-based technologies have progressed at lightning speed since they were first introduced to the business world in the early to mid-1990s, developing common standards and robust commercial technologies takes time.

The challenges of integrating these new technologies with the hodgepodge of computers, networks, and systems already in place within companies adds to the problem. These challenges are intensified by concerns about

---

[1]This chapter is adapted from L.M. Applegate, *Building Information Age Businesses* (Boston: Harvard Business School Publishing, 1998) HBS No. 399–097
[2]This information was compiled from industry databases on venture funding.

what will happen to the trillions of lines of computer code in place in companies, government agencies, and homes around the world when the clock hits midnight on January 1, 2000.[3] The "Y2K problem"—as it has become known—is the most visible manifestation of a larger problem that has plagued companies for decades; 30 years of IT evolution have left most established firms with a "legacy" of outdated equipment and software mixed together with newer technologies. To achieve the grand vision of a networked economy, a new approach to designing and deploying IT is needed.

This chapter explores the challenges that managers face as they attempt to create the IT platform required in the information age. It examines the "three eras" of computing that have marked the evolution of IT in organizations, showing how each introduced a new approach to deploying and managing IT. Launching each era was a series of technical innovations that radically changed how IT could be used within the firm and the industry; in the hands of innovative managers who understood both the power of the technology and its potential business implications, new sources of business value were created.

EVOLUTION AND REVOLUTION: 30 YEARS OF IT IMPACT

If [the auto industry] had kept up with technology like the computer industry has, we would all be driving $25 cars that get 1,000 miles per gallon.

CEO, Fortune 1000 software firm, spring 1998

An automaker's response[4]: This is true, but

- Your car would crash twice a day.
- Every time they repainted the lines on the road, you would have to buy a new car.
- The air bag system would say, "Are you sure?" before going off.
- When your car died on the freeway for no reason, you would just accept this, restart, and drive on.
- Executing a maneuver would cause your car to stop, and you would have to reinstall the engine. For some strange reason, you would accept this too.

This humorous exchange captures the "love-hate" relationship that many have with IT. On the one hand, we see its remarkable power; on the other, we recognize its frustrating limitations. Most managers long for the day when the computer is as simple to use as the telephone. A growing number of technology insiders believe that that day is near.

---

[3]The Year 2000—or "Y2K"—problem is a software bug present in much of the computer code around the world. The bug was introduced when computer programmers used dates that assumed that the year would always be within the 1900s.

[4]This response is adapted from a "Top Ten List" circulated by e-mail to one of the authors.

FIGURE 6–1 Estimated Growth of PCs and Network Computers

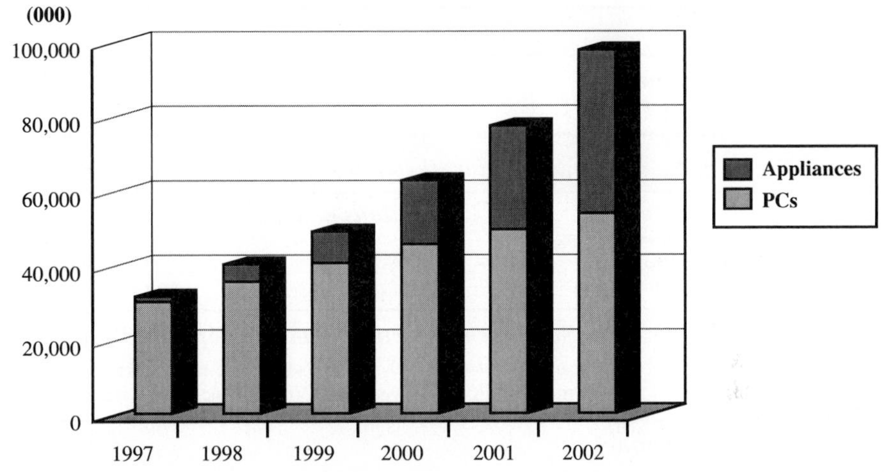

Source: International Data Corporation. "Death of the PC-Centric Era," 1998.

In the late 1990s, the network computer—a simple device that can be plugged into a television set in a home or hotel room, a seat-back monitor on an airplane, or a monitor at work—was introduced into the market. All of the complexity of the user device—in technical terminology this was called the "client"—would now rest in a centrally managed computer called a "server." The server would hold all of the shared data and computer programs; a "smart card" would hold the user's personal information. Management of these powerful servers would be returned to IT professionals in companies and network service utilities (for example, Internet service providers like AT&T, MCI, and IBM). After it was introduced in 1997, sales of this device were expected to skyrocket once network speed and capacity (often called bandwidth) reached sufficient level (see Figure 6–1).

Those who have lived through the three eras of computing believe that, in some ways, we are coming full circle; the new network computing era of the 1990s has many striking similarities to the mainframe computing era of the 1960s and 1970s. As Shakespeare wrote, "What's past is prologue"; an understanding of history is necessary to create the future.

EVOLUTION OF IT ARCHITECTURE

Just as the blueprint of a building's architecture indicates not only the structure's design but how everything—from plumbing and heating systems to the flow of traffic within the building—fits and works together, the blueprint of a firm's IT architecture defines the technical computing, information management, and communications platform (see Figure 6–2). The IT

FIGURE 6–2   Components of an IT Architecture

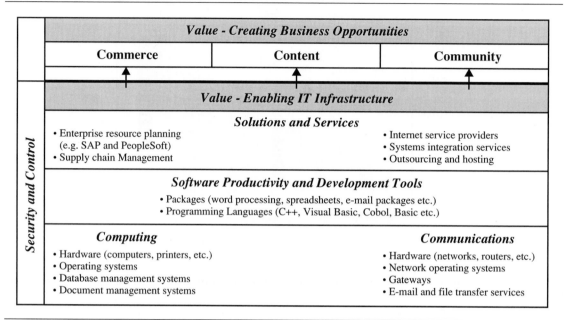

architecture provides an overall picture of the range of technical options available to a firm, and, as such, it also implies the range of business options. Decisions made in building the technical IT architecture must be closely linked to decisions made in designing the IT organization that will manage the architecture, which, in turn, must be linked to the strategy and organization design of the firm itself. Conversely, the organization strategy, structure, incentives, and processes strongly influence how the technology will be designed, deployed, and used within a firm. While this chapter focuses on the technical design, later chapters in this book discuss organization and management of the IT function. (Appendix A provides questions that can be used to assess the IT architecture of a firm.[5])

The IT architecture in place in most organizations in the 1990s represents a mix of old and new technologies that reflect the era in which they were introduced. Three eras have been identified, which, while somewhat overlapping, are nonetheless distinct: the *Mainframe Era,* the *Microcomputer Era,* and the *Network Era.*[6] Each era was ushered in by a series of techno-

---

[5]P. Keen, *Every Manager's Guide to Information Technology* (Boston: Harvard Business School Press, 1991) provides definitions of technical terminology.

[6]R. Nolan and D. Croson, *Creative Destruction* (Boston: Harvard Business School Press, 1995) and J. McKenney, *Waves of Change: Business Evolution through Information Technology* (Boston: Harvard Business School Press, 1995).

logical innovations that enabled a fundamental shift in IT architecture design. Each shift in the technical architecture brought with it new capabilities that added to, and extended, the capabilities of the past. Thus, in most cases, we did not simply replace the old with the new, but added the new technologies to what was already in place. Table 6–1 summarizes the characteristics of the IT architecture during these three eras, each of which is described below. Table 6–2 provides a timeline of key events in the evolution of IT.

Era I: The Mainframe (1950s to 1970s)

In the early days of digital computing, information was processed centrally on mainframe computers. These large, room-sized machines were housed in specialized data centers with raised floors, filtered air, and controlled temperatures. Sophisticated technical expertise was required to program, operate, and maintain these computers, and specialized management information systems (MIS) units were formed. But despite their size, cost, and need for specialized support, the performance of these early computers was only a fraction of what we carry in our briefcases today (see Figure 6–3).

During the 1960s and 1970s, users accessed information from mainframe computers using "dumb terminals"; these terminals were aptly named since they had very limited memory and essentially were unable to perform any local information processing. Given the communications technology available in the 1960s and 1970s, extended work on the mainframe was essentially limited to those residing in the same building that housed the computer; those in remote sites were limited to very brief sessions in which the user would access a single record or piece of data. All other data were "batched" together to be shipped to the mainframe at one time, frequently during evening hours. Business users received most of their information through paper reports, and any change in the report required a change in the program code. These changes could take years to complete and cost hundreds of thousands of dollars.

During the Mainframe Era, IT was viewed as a budgeted expense to be managed on a project-by-project basis within traditional budgeting cycles. This made sense, since a single computer cost hundreds of millions of dollars[7] and business applications were designed as stand-alone projects. During this period, the computer was primarily used to automate existing "back-office" information-intensive activities, and, as a result, it was relatively straightforward to calculate return on investment (ROI) paybacks. Implementing these systems to achieve the desired benefits was also

---

[7]Mainframe computers and associated equipment were justified through capital budgeting procedures.

TABLE 6–1   Three Eras of IT Evolution

	Mainframe Era (1950s to 1970s)	Microcomputer Era (late 1970s to 1980s)	Network Era (late 1980s to present)
IT Paradigm			
Dominant technology	Mainframe: "centralized intelligence"	Microcomputer: "decentralized intelligence"	Client-server and Internet: "distributed intelligence"
Organization metaphor	Hierarchy	Entrepreneurial	Networked/information age
Primary IT role	Automate existing processes	Increase individual/group effectiveness	Create value
Typical user	IT specialists	IT-literate business analysts	Everyone
Location of use	Computer room	Desktop	Everywhere
Justification	Return on investment	Increased productivity and decision quality	Multifaceted business value analysis
Information Management			
Information level	Data	Information	Knowledge
Information storage	Application-specific data files	Hierarchical and relational databases	Hypertext and object-oriented knowledge management systems
Integration level (data, voice, video, graphics, text)	Data only	Beginning support for all information classes but limited integration	Sophisticated integration of voice, video, data, text, graphics
Communication Management			
Connection media	Thick wire coaxial cable, microwave and satellite	Cable, fiber, cellular, satellite; channels remain separate	Cable, fiber, cellular, satellite; beginning channel integration
Transmission protocols	Proprietary (WAN): packet switching, circuit switching	Proprietary (LAN): ethernet, token ring	Merging of LAN/WAN technology: ATM, frame-relay; open standards
Maximum transmission rates	56 Kbps	1 Mbps	10 gbps (and higher)

Source: L. Applegate, *Building Information Age Businesses* (Boston: Harvard Business School Publishing, 1998).

TABLE 6–2   Information Technology Timeline

IT Era	Key Events
The Early Years Before 1960	**1823** Charles Babbage begins work on the first of his machines to mechanize solutions to generate algebra problems. **1890** Herman Hollerith develops the punch card tabulator. **1911** Hollerith's company and others combine; name changed to IBM in 1924. **1930** Claude Shannon's Ph.D. thesis explains how electrical switching circuits can model Boolean logic. **1939** Professor Howard Aiken creates the Harvard Mark I, the first digital computer. **1943** John Mauchley, J. Prespert Eckert, and John von Neumann build ENIAC, the first all-electric digital computer. **1947** The transistor is perfected. **1956** John Barden, Walter Brattain, and William Shockley share the Nobel Prize in physics for the transistor.
Mainframe Era 1960s to 1970s	**1964** IBM announces S/360, the first "family of computers" and the first time that transistors were used. **1964** John Kemeny and Thomas Kurtz of Dartmouth College develop the first BASIC. **1969** Intel begins to build the first microprocessor, the 4004, finished November 15, 1972. **1971** Intel develops the 8008. **1971** IBM has 62 percent of market share for computing. **1972** Gary Kildall writes PL/I, the first programming language for the 4004.
Pre-PC Era 1960s to 1970s	**1962** Tandy Corporation buys Radio Shack electronic stores. **1972** Bill Gates and Paul Allen form Traf-O-Data. **1974** Intel invents the 8080. **1974** Xerox releases the Alto. **1974** Radio Electronics publishes an article calling the Mark 8 "your personal minicomputer." **1975** Microsoft, formerly Traf-O-Data, writes the first BASIC for the Altair.
PC Era Late 1970s and 1980s	**1977** Apple introduces the Apple II, and Commodore introduces the PET computer. **1978** Apple introduces and begins shipping disk drives for the Apple II and initiates the Lisa project. **1979** MicroPro releases WordStar. **1980** The Apple III is announced. **1980** Microsoft signs a consulting agreement with IBM to produce the disk operating system (DOS). **1981** Xerox releases the 8010 Star and 820 computers. **1981** IBM releases its Personal Computer. **1982** Apple announces the Lisa. **1983** IBM announces the PCjr. **1984** Apple announces the Macintosh. **1989** NEC introduced the UltraLite, the first full-featured computer that weighs less than five pounds.

(continued)

TABLE 6–2 (concluded)   Information Technology Timeline

IT Era	Key Events
Network Era 1990s and beyond	**1982** Sun Microsystems is founded on the premise that the "network is the computer" **1992** CERN introduces the World Wide Web. **1993** Intel releases the Pentium chip. **1993** NCSA introduces Mosaic, the first graphical web browser. **1994** Netscape introduces Navigator. **1995** Microsoft releases Windows '95. **1996** Sun Microsystems creates JAVA. **1997** RCA introduces its Network Computer, priced at $295.

Information to build this table was garnered from many sources. We especially want to thank MicroAge Corporation for their assistance.

FIGURE 6–3   Estimated Growth of PCs and Network Computers

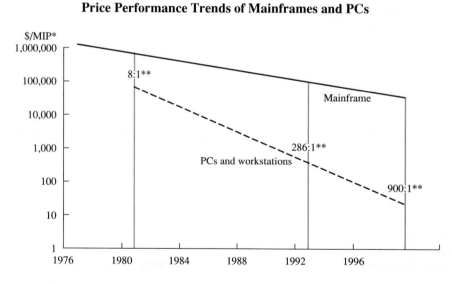

Price Performance Trends of Mainframes and PCs

Consider this:

In 1995, Nintendo introduced a video game computer, priced at $250, that had computing power that would have cost $14 million just a decade earlier.

In 1996, U. S. households spent more on PCs than they did on televisions.

The 1997 Ford Taurus contained more computing power than the first lunar landing module.

* MIP = Millions of Instructions per Second
**Ratio of Dollars per MIP (Mainframes: PCs)

Adapted from: J. McKinney, *Waves of Change: Business Evolution, through Information Technology,* (Boston: Harvard Business School Press, 1995).

relatively straightforward, since IT projects were under the direct control of the IT department and did not require major organizational disruption and change.

Era II: The Personal Computer (Late 1970s to 1980s)

The commercialization of the microprocessor in the 1970s set the stage for the emergence of the personal computing era in the late 1970s and early 1980s. Now computer processing power could sit on the desk of a clerk, business analyst, or manager who had very little specialized computer training. With the introduction of microcomputers and the proliferation of end-user computing and decision support applications in the early to mid-1980s, users began to take back control of their information that had been trapped in mainframe systems. New uses for these locally managed technologies grew rapidly. Personal computers and spreadsheets automated planning, budgeting, and information reporting; personal/portable technologies[8] and associated software to support collaborative work collapsed the geographic and time barriers that defined "workspace" and "worktime"; point-of-sale and automatic credit card scanners automated the sales process; and digital machine control and CAD/CAM (computer-aided design and manufacturing) automated production systems. "Islands of automation" sprang up within factories, in work groups, and on the desks (and in the briefcases) and in the homes of individuals throughout organizations.

As personal computer technology penetrated organizations, measures of organizational efficiency like ROI became less useful. Instead, measures of individual productivity (for example, headcount reduction, sales per employee) and decision quality (for example, customer satisfaction) were needed. With this class of IT application, recovery of the benefits was often tied, not only to the application's successful technical implementation, but also to its use by individuals or groups to make better decisions or change the way they worked. In addition to the change in the type of benefit, there was a significant increase in the level of expenditures related to personal workstations and productivity software (e.g., word processing, spreadsheets)—expenses that were not typically managed through the capital budgeting process. As microcomputers, personal portable technologies, and related software penetrated the workplace and joined the mainframe as a dominant component of the IT infrastructure, it became increasingly difficult to link infrastructure expenses to the business benefits achieved by using the infrastructure.

---

[8]Personal, portable technologies include laptop and notebook computers, personal digital assistants (PDAs), fax machines, and cellular telephones.

The decentralization of computing during the Personal Computer Era greatly increased the information processing power within organizations; for example, between 1982 and 1986 alone, the penetration of personal computing quadrupled information processing capacity in large, U.S.-based companies. The dominance of the central mainframe computer (and the central IT function that managed it) began to erode, but the personal computer did not replace the mainframe. Instead, this new class of computing was added to the existing centralized computing environment, and trade-offs concerning which technologies and applications would be managed centrally by the IT organization and which would be managed locally by end users became a constant source of friction. The problems reached a peak as the strategic value of information for many firms increased in the middle to late 1980s.

Era III: Network Computing (1990s to Present)

Fueled by the increased understanding that stemmed from "hands-on" experience in IT use at the local level, improved networks for sharing information inside and outside the firm, increased complexity and rate of change within the business environment, and the actions of a few visionary managers within information-intensive industries, business managers in a number of industries began to identify strategic opportunities for using IT to shift the balance of power and competitive position of their firms.[9] Senior management took notice—and what they saw both intrigued and concerned them.

While the strategic benefits of IT were becoming increasingly clear, the proliferation of local computing had seriously hampered the ability to share information across the organization. Closing the books at the end of a quarter became more and more difficult, and the ability to compare operations from one unit to another became almost impossible. Struggling to make sense of the rapidly changing business environment, management embraced new approaches to "distributed information processing and management" available through "client-server" computing—a new approach to IT architecture that promised to link mainframe and personal computer (PC) technologies, preserving the benefits of both.

Thus, by the 1990s, we had entered the world of distributed information systems and client-server computing—a world in which users could access and communicate information through a wide variety of powerful workstations and portable technologies (clients) linked to shared information and communication services (servers) through high-performance local and global networks. In the Network Computing Era, the centralized mainframe (often

---

[9]See Module 2 for an overview of the evolution of strategic computing in companies and industries.

called the "enterprise computer") takes its place alongside a wide variety of desktop workstations as merely one more "server" on the network—albeit a powerful one.

Despite the power of the concept, its implementation was initially cumbersome, costly, and difficult to manage. Deployment, maintenance, and operating costs skyrocketed. By the mid-1990s, there was sufficient experience in the use of client-server systems to enable development of detailed cost models. Estimates of $8,000 to $12,000 per workstation per year shocked management, but—as evidenced by the growth of German software computer giant SAP—the pace of evolution to a distributed, networked computing platform did not slow. (See Table 6–3 for a summary of the costs of client-server computing.)

The emergence of the Internet, the World Wide Web, and browser technology in the mid-1990s fueled the transition. Not only were Internet-based client-server systems significantly easier and less costly to deploy and maintain, they were also much more powerful. In 1997, with the commercialization of the network computer and object-oriented approaches to storing multimedia information, the true power of the new network computing model was becoming more evident. As the new network computing model

TABLE 6–3 Comparison of Network Computing Cost for Traditional Client-Server and Emerging Network Computer Devices

Annual Costs by Category	Traditional Client-Server			Network Computer Devices	
	Windows 3.1	Windows '95	Windows NT	NetPC/ZAK-E	NC-C
Desktop capital	$2,076	$2,376	$2,376	$1,465	$1,490
Technical support	1,183	1,089	1,086	877	793
Administration	969	954	954	436	434
End-user operations	4,166	3,453	3,173	1,564	1,561
Desktop annual costs	**8,394**	**7,872**	**7,589**	**4,342**	**4,279**
Network capital	573	585	585	617	686
Network technical support	663	544	671	628	694
Network administration	308	301	315	307	311
Network end user	848	680	708	576	576
Network annual costs	**2,392**	**2,111**	**2,280**	**2,128**	**2,268**
Total costs	**10,786**	**9,983**	**9,869**	**6,469**	**6,547**
Percent change	**7**	**Base**	**−1**	**−35**	**−34**

The Windows 3.1, '95, and NT columns reflect the costs to maintain client-server applications with a personal computer desktop device running the associated operating system. The Net PC/ZAK-E column reflects the cost to maintain a network computer device running the Windows NT 4.0 operating system with the Zero Administration Kit (ZAK). The NC-C column reflects the cost to maintain a network computer device running Java.

Adapted from W. Kerwin, "TCO: New Technologies, New Benchmarks," *Gartner Group Research Note* (#K-TCO-252), December 5, 1997.

penetrated firms and industries, it became evident that new approaches to defining and implementing value-creating opportunities would be required.

VALUE CREATION IN A NETWORKED ENVIRONMENT

It is little wonder that there is confusion concerning the business value of IT in the network era; most managers still struggle as they attempt to assess the value of IT in general. Many continue to view IT as a budgeted expense to be managed on a project-by-project basis within traditional budgeting cycles. As mentioned above, this approach is a throwback to the mainframe era.

As we approach the next millennium, forward-thinking managers have begun to recognize that traditional approaches to valuing IT investments simply won't work. IT can no longer be considered an expense; instead, we must think of IT as a string of value-creating investments that deliver value *today and in the future.* The value of these "future" uses can be thought of as the "options value" of the technology.

Tables 6–4 and 6–5 present a "value-based" approach to framing the business case for IT. The framework separates IT into two broad categories: (1) those reusable, value-enabling technologies that comprise the information and communication infrastructure of a firm, an industry, or a public network and (2) the IT-enabled value-creating business solutions developed and deployed upon that platform. Within each of these broad categories, specific types of benefits have been identified.

The shift to a network computing approach can cut the cost and increase the flexibility and power of a company's information and communication infrastructure. A Fortune 100 global manufacturing company provides an excellent example of the benefits that can be achieved.

The company initiated a project in late 1994 to consolidate their network infrastructure from numerous, incompatible country-based and local networks to a single global Internet-based network. While the cost of the project was over $1 million, the benefits were extensive. The most immediate direct benefit was a 50 percent saving in the cost of network management and operations (Benefit Category I). This cost saving was achieved at the same time that the firm expanded its worldwide network "points of presence" by over 25 percent (Benefit Category II). In addition, the Internet provided an open, global platform that replaced the numerous incompatible networks that had prevented managers, employees, customers, suppliers, and other business partners from sharing information and communicating worldwide (Benefit Category III).

Prior to implementing the integrated, global Internet-based network, the CEO had called the CIO in frustration. "Why can't I send e-mail to Tokyo? I thought we had a global network," he said. While he found the CIO's reply concerning incompatible standards and gateways confusing, the query did

TABLE 6–4   Framing the Business Case for Network Computing

Benefits from Investments in Value-Enabling Infrastructure

Category of Benefit	Organizational Benefits	Market/Industry Benefits
Category I: **Platform improvements**	Improve ability to share information, communicate, coordinate, and control activities inside the organization	Improve ability to share information, communicate, coordinate, and control activities with customers, suppliers, and business partners
Category II: **Options value**	Increase the functionality, flexibility, and "useful life" of the internal IT infrastructure	Increase the functionality, flexibility, and "useful life" of the industry IT infrastructure

Sample Metrics

• Lower operating and maintenance costs –Consolidate data centers –Reduce the cost of operating and maintaining data centers –Streamline and simplify networks (multiprotocol to single protocol) –Decrease headcount for IT professionals • Improve application development process –Reduce cost of IT application development projects –Decrease the time needed to deploy new IT-enabled business solutions	• Increase the useful life of the platform –Decrease upgrade costs for new technologies –Enable flexible, modular ("lego approach") –Streamline and simplify networks (multiprotocol to single protocol) –Decrease headcount for IT professionals	• Increase range of options for new business solutions –Increase the number of value-creating business solutions • Enable new business building opportunities

provide the spark that initiated discussions of a shift to an Internet-based global network. By 1996, the enhanced functionality and savings from the new network, coupled with equally impressive savings and enhanced capabilities due to other infrastructure enhancements—including data center consolidations and new application development methodologies—had enabled the company to reduce the total budget for IT operations and infrastructure maintenance by 50 percent, thus saving the company over *$1 billion* per year (Benefit Category I).

TABLE 6–5   Framing the Business Case for IT: A Value-Based Approach to Identifying Business Opportunities

---

Benefits from Investments in Value-Enabling Infrastructure

Category of Benefit	Organizational Opportunities	Market / Industry Opportunities
Category III Commerce	Improve core operating activities inside the firm (e.g., procurement, sales, customer service)	Improve existing supply/distribution channels that link the firm to customers, suppliers, and business partners or create new ones
Category IV Content	Improve decision making and enhance organizational learning	Exploit the economic value of information by adding value to existing products and services and creating new ones
Category V Community	Enhance collaboration and coordination of work and commitment and loyalty of individuals and teams	Establish a position at the center of an electronic market and maintain that position by ensuring loyalty of all members

---

Sample Metrics

Process Performance Improvements	Increase Shareholder Loyalty	Increase Revenues, Profits, and Value-Added

Savings
• Reduce paper and communications cost
• Reduce headcount
• Reduce cost of supplies, parts, and services
• Reduce transaction and administrative costs
• Reduce inventory costs
• Decrease inventory or work in process
 	
Speed
• Reduce cycle time
• Reduce or remove process bottlenecks
• Eliminate process steps
 	
Quality
• Decrease product defect or service failure rate
• Decrease waste
• Reduce process errors
	• Increased satisfaction and retention
	   Customers
	   Suppliers
	   Partners
	   Employees
		• Increase sales in existing markets
		• Increase revenue from sales in new markets
		• Decrease prices yet sustain margins
		• Increase profitability
		• Improve productivity
		   Revenues per employee
		   Profits per employee
		   Operating margins
		• Increase cash flow
		• Improve competitive position
		• Increase market share
		• Improve analysts' assessments and ratings
		• Increase stock price

Having reaped these immediate benefits, the company is now cashing in on the "options value" of their investment (Benefit Category II). Building upon the new Internet-based global network platform, the company deployed a variety of Internet-based business applications for process and work flow improvement, information sharing, communication, and electronic commerce. For example, the company's key account consulting business unit developed a Web-based system for accessing information available on the public Internet through news services, industry information providers, and corporate Web pages and in internal databases and files located throughout the company. The Web-based system was also used to share consulting methodologies and frameworks, engagement summaries, résumés, and best practices (Benefit Category IV). Using this system, which was implemented at an additional cost of less than $50,000, one key account group decreased engagement time by 40 to 80 percent, thus enabling them to expand services performed with the same number of staff. Revenues increased by 20 percent, and consulting margins improved by 400 percent (Benefit Category III).

Elsewhere in the firm, the internal global network served as the platform for launching a successful new service business, which, in late 1997, contributed a sizable percentage of the company's revenues and profits (Benefit Category IV). Another unit reengineered their manufacturing process, cutting administrative costs by 50 percent, and the U.S. procurement group implemented "buyerless" purchasing, cutting costs by 20 percent and transaction time from 48 hours to 2.5 hours (Benefit Category III).

IMPLEMENTATION ISSUES

The move to develop networked IT platforms is a complex and difficult challenge. Localized "islands of automation" must be merged together, "legacy systems"[10]—many of which are critical for the successful operation of today's business—must be managed, new technologies must be evaluated and successfully introduced, and people must be trained. All this must be accomplished within the context of massive organizational upheaval and change. Many who are considering the task have compared it to changing the tires on a rapidly moving car; those who have been through it believe that they have totally redesigned and built a new car. The remainder of this chapter deals with these management challenges.

---

[10]*Legacy* refers to transaction processing systems that were originally designed to perform a specific task. Over time, these systems may not accurately reflect business needs. In addition, as hardware and software improvements occur in the information systems marketplace, older information systems solutions tie an organization to an out-of-date platform that is unable to deliver value-creating applications and is costly to operate and maintain.

Maintaining a Reliable and Secure Environment for Doing Business

Once upon a time, not so very long ago, business computing was highly centralized and tightly controlled. Most business applications ran on central computer systems managed by information systems departments. This centralized model of organizational computing offered a certain sense of order. Systems managers could readily control the environment from a single point in the system. When business managers asked for a new computer application, they had no knowledge of the level of effort and investment required. If they used the computer at all, they never worried about software updates or system backups.

Then PC and local area network (LAN) technologies took off. Sometime between the late 1980s and the early 1990s (it's hard to pinpoint an exact date) things changed. With high-performance computers on their desktops (or in their briefcases) and network connections readily accessible, people sought to communicate with business colleagues and access information stored in databases located inside and outside the organization. In many companies, mobile workers began to "live on the network."

While the old central systems limited information access and stifled creativity, the decentralized approach was not without its problems. With a major portion of the IT assets sitting on people's desks, the technology could no longer be controlled from afar. Business users were forced to become actively involved in managing an ever-increasing portion of the company's IT assets.

They now had to worry about whether their computers had the latest versions of the word processing, spreadsheet, and e-mail packages used in the firm. When the system broke, they were responsible for getting it fixed. And, to make matters worse, incompatible networks and databases limited the ease with which business users could access information and communicate with distant parts of the organization and with the outside world.

Enter the Internet. The powerful user-friendly approach to accessing and presenting information, coupled with the ease of communicating with people inside and outside the organization, removed many of the limitations of both the centralized and decentralized approaches to computing. But the same features that made the Internet easier to use also made it much more difficult to control. By 1998, security had become the number one concern of both business and IT professionals as they considered moving to an Internet-based network computing infrastructure.

The Internet is a collection of communication and information management technologies that enable a very flexible, yet powerful approach to sharing and communicating information. Two types of networks provide this connectivity—the backbone network, which provides high-speed communication over long distances, and connecting networks, which run at slower speeds and connect an organization's internal network to the backbone. For the most part, the Internet's public backbone networks provide reliable, high-speed communication. In addition, by 1998, firms could establish private, global networks based on Internet communication protocols that were almost as reliable and secure as private global networks based on other communication protocols.

But if you rely on the public Internet, getting a message to the backbone and from the backbone to its destination continues to be plagued by reliability, security, and network performance problems. Because the information that you wish to access or the person with whom you wish to communicate can reside anywhere within the Internet's vast web of networks—and there is no central point of control—you never know whether the message will reach its destination in a reliable and timely manner or whether you will be able to access that critical piece of information. If a segment of the network is down between a firm and its customer, information may not get through—and there is no hotline to call to report the problem or get help. While most of us are accustomed to much higher levels of reliability for conducting business electronically, many companies are willing to put up with the inconvenience to gain access to the global market reach. But managers must consider the unreliable nature of the public Internet as they assess potential uses of the Internet. For some business transactions, total reliability is not required; for others, reliability is paramount. In the latter case, Internet-based virtual private networks may be the best answer.

In addition to reliability and performance issues, many have appropriately expressed concern about the security of the Internet. Maintaining network security across organizational boundaries is always a challenge; on the Internet, however, it is even more difficult. The Internet grew in an uncontrolled manner; anyone anywhere in the world can connect to the Internet with a computer, a modem, a network address, and a connection to an Internet server. Like the problem of figuring out how many locks to put on the door to your house, the level of security you choose to provide depends on how you use the Internet and whether there are any direct links between the Internet and your company's information system.

If a firm uses the Internet only to share information and do business inside the firm—this type of network is often called an Intranet—standard network management and security systems can provide a reliable and safe platform for conducting business. Keep in mind, however, that any time employees are allowed to access internal information systems, e-mail, and networks from their homes or on the road, the firm opens the doors of its network to anyone who has access to public networks. As such, security precautions, similar to those required for conducting business on public networks, must be taken. If a firm is using the Internet to link customers, suppliers, or business partners within a secure interorganizational network—this type of network is often called an Extranet—they will need to set up a virtual private network with special features that enable secure, reliable transmission of information, messages, and business transactions. Conducting business across open, public Internet networks requires that managers assess the potential security risks based on the type of information and the business transactions conducted.

Managers who contemplate conducting business on a public network such as the Internet must assume that anybody in any part of the world might attempt to break into their internal networks, and plan accordingly. They need to secure internal corporate networks from unwanted users by using firewalls—electronic barriers created with dedicated hardware and software systems that screen network traffic and validate the flow of information between internal and external networks. Companies generally designate one or more separate computers as network and Web servers and carefully barricade their internal systems behind the firewall. In some instances, if high levels of security are required, companies install firebreaks—physical barriers with no electronic connections between the Internet server and internal company information systems. (Table 6–6 summarizes the security features necessary for conducting business on public networks.)

In addition to firewalls and firebreaks, passwords can screen prospective users and ensure that only those on an "approved list" can enter the system. Of course, this requires additional administrative overhead and may run counter to the idea behind some types of electronic commerce. The ben-

TABLE 6–6   Internet Security Issues

Problem	*Business Concern*	*Solution*
Authorization	Does a user have permission to access a specific computer or collection of information?	User name and password or other kind of access control mechanisms
Authentication	Is the user truly who he or she purports to be?	Digital certificates and other technologies used to authenticate identity
Integrity	Did the person sending a message actually send it? Can the receiver be sure that the message has not been changed?	Digital signature
Privacy	Is my conversation (or business transaction) private? Is anyone eavesdropping or spying?	Public/private key encryption algorithms
Fraud/theft	Is anyone stealing from me?	Log, audit, systems management policies and procedures
Sabotage	Can someone enter my internal information systems and/or networks and access private information or destroy/alter information?	Firewalls Firebreaks

efits of opening an electronic store, for example, may be reduced if you restrict access to those you already know. Instead, it may be more appropriate to "electronically tag" merchandise so that a warning sounds if someone attempts to leave the "store" with merchandise that has not been purchased or is not for sale. Also, any authorization scheme is open to abuse. While passwords can be encrypted, they may still be easily intercepted in a networked computing environment populated with technologically sophisticated users.

In some situations, a company may wish to require individuals to validate that they are who they say they are. One approach to authenticating users is to issue digital certificates. Another approach combines special hardware and software. Authorized users, able to connect to a specific server (or to pass through a company firewall), receive a special handheld device about the size of a credit card. This device contains an encryption algorithm. When an authorized user tries to connect to another company's computer, he or she receives a five-digit (randomly generated) number as an authentication challenge. The user enters the number into the device, receives another five-digit number, and then replies with this number as the key to the challenge. If the remote system is satisfied with the response, the user can access the server.

Another thorny problem with doing business on public networks is protecting the privacy of personal or confidential information. For example, one company created an internal Web application to enable information sharing among internal employees. Despite the fact that the server was behind a firewall and password entry was required, the company found that an intruder had been able to "break in" and steal highly confidential information. The lesson: Firewalls and passwords are not enough to protect highly confidential data. Authentication challenges, digital signatures, and specially designed encryption algorithms may be needed; others require that confidential information, for example, credit card information, be submitted via telephone, thus creating a firebreak. The search continues for a foolproof form of "electronic currency" so that buyers and sellers can safely do business over the Internet.

The on-line world of electronic publishing also raises many new issues about intellectual property. When we buy a published book, we assume that copyright protections and intellectual property rights have been addressed by the author and publisher. Each book is bound to ensure that all portions of the book are considered and protected as a whole. By contrast, in an on-line world, information is transmitted in small bits and pieces that can be reconstructed by many different users in different forms. Copyright laws have yet to accommodate this, and maintaining intellectual property and privacy rights can become a logistic nightmare.

While digital signatures, firewalls, encryption algorithms, and passwords can help to protect our rights, they are not sufficient. Current security, privacy, and information integrity procedures and practices must be examined, and interorganizational information and communication policies must be established. Government regulations and legal issues must also be addressed.

In summary, as network computing and the Internet penetrate the way we do business both inside and outside the organization, managers must incorporate network and information security and integrity issues into their formal organizational control systems. Security and information integrity are no longer the sole responsibility of IT professionals. Instead, IT audits must be incorporated as part of a company's business audit, and risk management systems must incorporate IT risks.

In addition, the strategic nature of IT and the Internet must be acknowledged and managed. Increasingly, firms that take the Internet seriously are establishing a senior position or management team to evaluate opportunities and risks and guide experimentation with this important new platform for conducting business. The senior manager is often within corporate strategy or public relations, and the team may include representation from line businesses, public relations, marketing, and legal. Some firms "capture" all new Internet applications on a secure computer that limits an employee's ability to launch his or her own Internet site until it is approved. The senior management team evaluates potential applications before they are released on the Internet to ensure that they convey an appropriate image, enhance the company's strategy, and do not put the company at risk. The responsibilities of the team are threefold:

- Identify promising uses for the Internet as a tool for electronic commerce and for communicating and disseminating internal information.
- Stop inappropriate or risky uses of the technology before they can harm the company's competitive, financial, legal, or ethical position.
- Move quickly and decisively, but safely.

Assimilating Emerging Information Technologies

As strategy, organization, and IT become inextricably intertwined, business managers must become active players in ensuring the successful identification and deployment of new technologies, such as the Internet. This process requires an ongoing commitment to managing the IT assimilation process.

The process of assimilating a new technology has often been characterized as a series of tasks or stages through which a new technology is identified, assimilated, and institutionalized.[11] Although some have faulted stage mod-

---

[11] L. Applegate, "Technology Support for Cooperative Work: A Framework for Studying Introduction and Assimilation in Organizations," *Journal of Organizational Computing,* 1:11–39, 1991; R. Walton, *Up and Running: Integrating Information Technology and the Organization* (Boston: Harvard Business School Press, 1989); R. Nolan and C. Gibson, "Managing the Crisis in Data Processing," *Harvard Business Review,* March–April 1979.

FIGURE 6–4   The Organization and Information Technology Design Challenge of
the 1990s

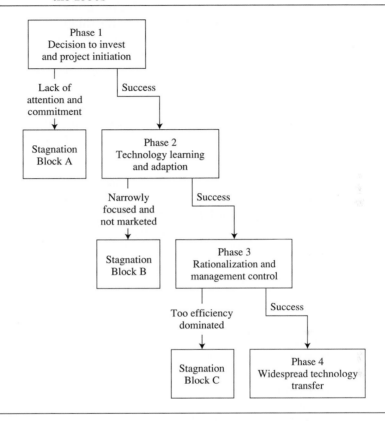

els for failing to depict the "chaotic" nature of true innovation,[12] the models
have proven useful as long as sequential passage from stage to stage is not
assumed. The IT assimilation model presented in Figure 6–4 describes four
stages: technology identification and investment, technological learning and
adaptation, rationalization/management control, and maturity/widespread
technology transfer.[13]

Phase 1: Technology Identification.   The first phase is initiated by a
decision to invest in a new information-processing technology. (Note: This

[12]J. Ettlie, "Organization Strategy and Structural Difference for Radical versus Incremental
Innovation," *Management Science,* 30:682–95, 1984; B. Quinn, "Innovation and Corporate
Strategy: Managed Chaos," *Technology in the Modern Corporation,* edited by M. Horwitch (NY:
Pergamon Press, 1986).

[13]J. Cash and P. McLeod, "Managing the Introduction of Information Technology in
Strategically Dependent Companies," *Journal of Management Information Systems,* 1:5–23,
1985.

technology may be an emerging technology that few firms have implemented, or it may be a more stable technology that is simply new to a given organization.) During the initiation phase, one or more complementary project development efforts are undertaken. These projects are often characterized by uncertainty about the magnitude of the investments required and the benefits to be delivered. Pilot projects are often used to help reduce the uncertainty and to assess the degree of organizational change and skill development that will be required. While these early prototypes often seem quite clumsy, considerable learning takes place. An unsuccessful prototype can cause the firm to "start over" or to abandon the technology. For any number of reasons, a firm may delay future investment in the technology—Stagnation Block A in the figure. The following example describes a firm in which organization learning was blocked in Phase 1.

At the CEO's urging, an insurance company launched a major Executive Information System (EIS) project to put a workstation with access to internal and external information on every senior executive's desk. Eight months into the process, the CEO retired suddenly for health reasons. Without its key sponsor, the project died over the next six months. Two years later the new CEO wanted to revive the project; in the meantime, the technology investment has returned no value to the firm and the technology itself has become hopelessly outdated.

Phase 2: Technological Learning and Adaptation.   The second phase involves learning how to adapt the new technology to particular tasks beyond those identified in the initial projects. As new avenues are explored and learning occurs, the benefits are often quite different from those initially anticipated. Projects in this phase, while not as prone to technical problems, are often still highly uncertain in their costs and benefits, which leads to problems in planning and implementation. Evaluation of 37 different phase 2 technology projects showed that none were implemented as initially planned. In each case, significant learning took place during implementation. Indeed, many of the competitive successes discussed in earlier chapters were phase 2 projects that evolved gradually through a series of successive refinements. Failure to effectively transfer the learning from phases 1 and 2 can lead to Stagnation Block B. An example of this type of block follows.

A large manufacturing company attempted to introduce CAD/CAM into its plants. The initial prototype was successfully tested in one plant. The MIS group then attempted to roll out the technology in several other plants. Prior to the phase 2 rollout, there was no attempt to document the problems faced by the initial plant and the factors that led to the system's eventual success. Nor were users from the first plant involved in subsequent rollouts. Two of the subsequent plants were also successful in implementing the system, but three other plants revolted. The project was halted indefinitely as management attempted to understand the wide discrepancy in results.

Phase 3: Rationalization/Management Control.   This phase typically involves a significant change in the organization's approach to the technology, continued evolution of the uses of technology, and, most importantly, development of management controls for guiding the design and implementation of systems that use these technologies. In this phase, system development methodologies become more structured, the roles and skills required of IT professionals and users become clearer, and the results become more predictable. The most common problem in phase 3 is that in a search for efficiency, control stifles innovation—Stagnation Block C.

For example, a manufacturing company spent three years developing a state-of-the-art distribution center utilizing the most advanced client-server technologies. The technology was pilot tested through implementation of several smaller applications that were highly successful. The skills had been honed throughout the project. Yet when the center opened, rigid control of information access and use was instituted. Because the cost of the new center had overrun the budget, management attempted to minimize additional investments in value-creating applications. In its single-minded effort to gain efficiency, the organization became so focused on standard procedures and cost elimination that enthusiasm for using the system to add value to the business was lost. Further, the rigorous protocols alienated users, who then began to experiment with creating their own system within several branch offices. In this case, rigorous emphasis on control prevented logical growth.

Phase 4: Maturity/Widespread Technology Transfer.   This final phase occurs when the technology is embraced throughout the organization. Efficiency is achieved, but not at the expense of effectiveness. Quite naturally, as time passes, new technologies continue to emerge that offer the firm the opportunity to either move into new application areas or restructure old ones. A firm is thus confronted over time with waves of new technologies and at any one time is managing and assimilating a number of technologies, each in a different phase. In the 1990s, most companies are finding that the rapid pace of technological change is demanding that firms move through these phases in a much more timely manner. This increases the risk and the level of investment in organizational learning. As mentioned earlier, many firms seek partnerships to manage the successful assimilation of new technology.

Managing the IT Legacy

Successful implementation and management of a networked IT infrastructure demand an exceedingly high level of technological sophistication that is frequently unavailable within traditional IT departments. The technologies for successfully creating and delivering integrated systems and distributed information and communications management are only now beginning to emerge in a stable form. Standards remain in flux, and professionals experienced in application development and delivery are in short supply. Such problems are exacerbated when companies grapple with the massive investment that has already been made in legacy systems that must either be abandoned or be adapted to fit within a new distributed IT platform.

Business demands for continued support and maintenance of mission-critical legacy systems exacerbate the problem. There is often a three-year to four-year backlog of value-creating IT applications waiting to be implemented by a seriously overworked IT staff. This often leads to a perception of unsatisfactory support and to dissatisfaction with the IT function. Frustrated users have a tendency towards their own solutions such as individual, stand-alone computers, which further complicates the overall IT management challenge. The following example illustrates the dilemma that many firms face.

In the late 1980s, the senior management of a large insurance company asked one of the authors, "Why does it take us so long to develop our strategic systems?" They went on to describe a strategic IT project believed to be absolutely critical to the success of their core business strategy. The project was three years late, significantly over budget, and a long way from completion. An in-depth analysis of the situation brought the following facts to light. The company had over 20 of IBM's largest mainframe computers—all running at peak capacity to supply the organization with the massive amounts of information needed to run the business. The software generating and managing this information had been developed in the 1960s in an out-of-date computer language that was difficult to maintain and almost impossible to update and change. A large percentage of the IT professionals and the budget was directed toward simply maintaining the status quo and supplying the information needed to keep the organization running. The few staff members who could be spared to work on the strategic systems project encountered numerous obstacles as they attempted to access information tightly embedded within these ancient systems.

In this example, senior management failed to recognize the real source of the problem. As a result, they were looking for the wrong solution. While they expected the consultant to suggest changes in IT leadership, what they really needed was a radical overhaul of their out-of-date and inflexible IT platform.[14]

The insurance company is hardly alone; there are numerous examples of firms facing similar technological challenges as they attempt to develop and deliver IT systems for the 21st century on out-of-date technology platforms.

---

[14]In some cases, existing IT leaderships are not equipped for the task of managing the shift to a networked computing environment and must be replaced. But simply replacing the leader does not address the underlying problem, and the new leader may be just as ill equipped to manage the transition.

Recognition of the true source of the problem and strong support from senior management are needed to break out of this downward spiral.

Given the magnitude and complexity of the task and the pace of technology evolution, many managers have sought partnerships with vendors who will assume responsibility for updating and maintaining the IT platform, thereby freeing up valuable resources so the firm can concentrate on defining and delivering value-added IT applications. The issues facing managers who are considering outsourcing all, or part, of their IT function are discussed in detail in later chapters of this book.

While some turn to outsourcing, other firms address the problem of legacy systems while maintaining control of the IT platform within the firm. Time, expertise, commitment, and leadership are required. Management must firmly believe that the massive investment will provide the company with sustainable proprietary advantages. It must be confident that it will have ample time and skills to implement both the IT platform and the value-creating applications before a competitor can seriously erode those advantages. Many firms spend five years or more and millions of dollars implementing a networked IT architecture. New skills are needed by MIS professionals and end users. Vendors often play an important role in transferring into the firm both the new technologies and the skills needed to implement them; firms can use these vendor partnerships to build internal capabilities. The new architecture often evolves gradually and continues to evolve with changes in the business environment, organization, and technology.

During the late 1990s, many managers were forced to accelerate their efforts to deal with aging legacy systems as they rushed to fix Year 2000 (Y2K) "bugs" that threatened to bring their businesses to a halt at the stroke of midnight on January 1, 2000. Appendix B provides an audit that can be used to assess Y2K readiness and develop appropriate contingency plans.

Merging the Islands of Automation

As firms face the challenge of defining and implementing a networked IT architecture, a variety of system integration obstacles must be overcome. One of the most obvious involves the perennial problem of where to physically locate information and value-creating application systems. In the past, this decision was viewed as a linear trade-off. At one extreme were organizations that created a large, centralized hub connected by telecommunications links to remote computers in the field. At the other extreme were organizations with a small or nonexistent hub at the center, with most—or even all—of their data and hardware decentralized to the field. Between these two extremes lay a rich variety of intermediate alternatives.

Early solutions to this problem were heavily influenced by the technology architecture. The high cost of hardware and the significant economies of scale associated with mainframe computers made it necessary to consolidate processing power into large data centers. In contrast, the low cost and "off-the-shelf" functionality of microcomputers permitted a more decentralized approach. In the 1990s, the availability of technology to implement a distributed architecture enabled processing power and data to be located where it makes the most sense from a business perspective. As firms merge the islands of automation, several trends are noted. (Table 6–7 summarizes decision criteria that can be used as management attempts to balance the distribution of IT resources.)

- Over the past few years, there has been a move to consolidate information processing and network management within a single location. Some large firms are creating a single "mega data center"—backed up by a fully staffed off-site redundant data center—or several large regional mega centers. These centers house powerful servers that manage corporatewide data warehouses and massively parallel information processing. The increasing availability of powerful global networks and Internet global communication standards make this a feasible alternative, although the global telecommunications environment still hampers full realization of the benefits.

- While the information and standards are moving to the center, processing of the information is moving to business operating units. Data replication technologies are the key to making this architecture work. These technologies create and maintain "shadow" databases that contain an up-to-date replica of the data required by local users on local servers. As mentioned earlier, in the late 1990s, network computer devices have been introduced that promise to decrease the complexity, cost, and power of user computing, shifting more responsibility to business unit servers, corporate data centers, and, in many cases, Internet service providers.

- Where is the computer in a client-server architecture? It's not in a single place; it's the network. It has been estimated that up to 40 percent of the cost and effort of implementing a client-server architecture is due to network and distributed information management.[15] Yet most IT professionals do not possess these skills. As a result, these valuable, scarce resources are often managed at the center.

- Successful implementation of a networked computing architecture is most often found in organizations—or portions of an organization—where there is significant pent-up demand for direct access to information. The ability to successfully satisfy this demand requires users who are (or are eager to become) both technically and "informationally" literate. This type of user is predominately found in organizations that are experiencing significant "time-based" competitions and have begun to adopt the

---

[15]H. Ryan, *Preparing to Implement Client / Server Solutions* (Chicago: Auerbach Publications, 1994).

TABLE 6-7 IT Resource Management

Pressure	Toward Centralization	Toward Decentralization	Toward Distribution
Management control	Hierarchical. Standardization. Efficiency. Organizational security, reliability.	Entrepreneurial. Local responsiveness. Effectiveness. Local security, reliability.	Information age. Learning. Efficiency and effectiveness. Global security, reliability
Technology	Efficient use of resources. Specialized, costly equipment that is required by all. Requires specialized expertise to operate and manage.	Effective use of resources. Low-cost "off-the-shelf" equipment that is widely available. Expertise needed to operate and manage is widely available.	Effective and efficient use of resources. Mix of specialized and off-the-shelf. Mix of specialized and general expertise.
Data	Organizational data. Maintain data standards. Level of data sharing can be accommodated by network capacity and budget.	Local data. Maintain data relevance. Desire to optimize network capacity and minimize cost.	Increased need for vertical and lateral information sharing (including interorganizational). Desire to optimize information relevance and standards. High-capacity, low-cost networks are available and manageable.
IT professionals	Scarce resources with specialized knowledge and expertise. Minimize turnover risk/disruption. Richer career paths for IT professionals.	Widely available resources and generalized expertise. Turnover risk/disruption is minimal. Background enables lateral, interfunctional career path.	Mix of scarce and generalized IT professional resources. Optimally manage turnover risk/disruption while providing expanded career paths.
End users	Low level of technical skill Satisfied with routine information reporting. Lack of motivation to manage IT.	Technical sophistication. Desire flexible access to timely information. Motivated to manage IT.	High levels of technical and "information" literacy. High levels of commitment and motivation to become an active player in defining and managing information.
Culture/organizational fit	Organization is structured as a functional hierarchy. "Command and control" culture. IT function has always been centralized.	Organization is structured as decentralized profit centers. "Results" culture. Significant decentralization of IT resources and control.	Organization is structured as a matrix of autonomous, interfunctional teams. "Commitment, collaboration, and results" culture. Both centralized and decentralized IT resources and control.

characteristics of the information age organization that were discussed in Chapter 5. Management at all levels of the firm must be actively committed to transforming the organization; it makes little sense to embark on the difficult and costly task of transforming your IT architecture unless you also plan to transform the business processes it supports.

- The distributed IT architecture of the 1990s incorporates a range of technologies—including data, voice, video, digital production controls, and others—that must all operate in a coordinated and integrated manner. Developing and managing this coordination has not always been easy. In many organizations these technologies evolved through separate streams of technical innovation that were introduced into organizations at different periods of time by different groups. Over the years, incompatible architectures have developed that are often managed by separate organizational units. In the 1990s, many firms continue to manage these technologies in separate units staffed with technology specialists who lack the necessary skills to create an integrated approach to information and communication management. But in the networked computing era, the Internet has begun to break down these walls. The blurring of boundaries among the technologies and the expertise needed to deploy them are also being accompanied by a similar blurring of the boundaries within the industry; consolidation, partnerships, and strategic alliances have radically altered the global information industry.[16] This exerts further pressure on companies to consolidate management of the IT platform and the expertise needed to successfully deploy it.

SUMMARY

The challenge of managing the evolution of the IT architecture of the firm is daunting. While many firms in the 1990s are moving toward a networked IT infrastructure, the choices that are being made and the process through which the evolution takes place are often very different. Managers must consider the influence of legacy systems, organization culture and history, IT and business leadership, the capabilities of IT professionals and end users, and the demands of the business environment.

Continuous reexamination of the IT architecture and its relationship to strategy and organization must be a high priority. Radical change in the price/performance of technology can be expected to continue. The continued merging of core information technologies will alter the possibilities for organizations and players in the information industry. Managers can expect that both the risks and the potential rewards involved in managing technology assimilation will continue to increase.

---

[16]D. Yoffie, *Apple Computer 1992* (Boston: Harvard Business School Publishing, 1992).

Appendix A

GUIDELINES FOR IT ARCHITECTURE ASSESSMENT

Benchmarking Information Technology

- Define the computing platform (e.g., mainframe, minicomputer, microcomputers, and operating systems). Who controls each component? Has the firm adopted industry standard hardware? What is the evolution potential of the computing platform? What is the integration potential of the computing platform? Has the firm adopted a client-server architecture?
- Define the communications platform (e.g., wide-area networks, local area networks, telephone/voice communications, video/teleconferencing, operating systems). Who controls each component? Has the firm adopted industry standard hardware? What is the evolution potential of the communications platform? What is the integration potential of the communications platform?
- What technology is used to manage information (e.g., flat files, hierarchical database management systems, relational database management systems, object-oriented database systems, text management systems, hypertext systems)? What level of technical integration is available for managing data, voice, video, text, and graphics? Is data managed in a centralized or distributed fashion?
- What software "tools" are available for managing and communicating information (e.g., information packaging and delivery tools, information analysis tools, electronic mail, collaborative work tools)? What level of technical integration is available?
- What tools are available to improve the productivity and effectiveness of the software development process (e.g., Computer-Aided Software Engineering tools)?
- What are the key information systems applications? How old are they? Who controls the design and development of the applications? What percentage of the computer applications are "strategic" in nature versus "back-office support"?
- What are the administrative structure and systems for managing information technology? Are necessary backup and security systems in place to manage risk?
- Is the necessary technological expertise available inside the firm or through strategic partnerships? Are education programs in place to ensure that IT professionals develop the necessary understanding of the business and that business professionals develop the necessary understanding of IT? Has business management assumed responsibility for business system development?
- Is there a formal system for tracking new technology developments, experimenting with promising technological innovations, and assimilating new technologies into the organization?
- How does the organization manage IT resource allocation and prioritization of IT projects? What is the current level of IT spending as a percentage of sales? How does this compare to the industry average? Has the pattern of IT spending changed over the past five years? Ten years?
- Who leads the information technology function (e.g., background, reporting level, tenure within the organization, tenure within the position)?

- Is there an IT steering committee in place (e.g., leadership, membership, number of meetings per year, typical agenda)?

Analysis

- What role does IT play within the firm (strategic versus support)? Is this role appropriate given the firm's strategy and its competitive position? Will that role change over the next 5 to 10 years?
- Are the IT architecture and its management appropriate given the strategy and organization design?
- Is IT expertise being developed and managed appropriately?
- Are risks being managed appropriately?
- Are corporatewide resources spent on IT development and management being effectively and efficiently utilized?
- Are opportunities for using IT to add value to the business being identified and exploited?
- What changes are required? Does the firm have the resources and time needed to implement these changes?

Assessing the Information Infrastructure

- Is transaction-level data available that provides a timely, integrated, and detailed understanding of the dynamics of core operating processes (e.g., product/service delivery and new-product development)?
- Is timely and detailed information available on external industry dynamics and on internal financial and market performance?
- Is data stored and managed in a comprehensive, integrated information management system that enables flexible and timely access to common sources of information by decision makers at all levels in the firm and across varying organizational units?
- Has the information management system been designed in a manner that enables its evolution as the business changes and/or organizational members learn more about the dynamics of the current business (e.g., the database has been designed around stable elements of the business and application programs are designed to be independent of database structures)?
- Is an information policy in place that governs organizational and interorganizational access, sharing, privacy, security, and use? Is a communication policy in place that governs organizational and interorganizational communication?
- Are individuals and teams throughout the organization "information literate"? Are they technology literate? What education programs and management systems are in place to ensure information and technology literacy?
- Do all employees actively and effectively participate in defining and managing their personal information requirements?

Analysis

- Is the information infrastructure of the firm appropriately designed and managed given the strategy, structure, authority, people, and processes?
- Are informal and formal information/communication policies coherent and consistent across all organizational levels and units?
- Does the information infrastructure and information/communication policy extend to key external relationships?
- What changes are required? Does the firm have the resources and time needed to implement these changes?

Appendix B

	United States General Accounting Office
GAO	Accounting and Information Management Division

June 1998

Year 2000 Computing Crisis: A Testing Guide

This abbreviated document is reprinted with permission from the U.S. General Accounting Office.
The full report can be obtained from the GAO website (www.gao.gov).

Preface

On January 1, 2000, computer systems worldwide will malfunction or produce inaccurate information simply because the century has changed. Unless corrected, such failures will have a costly, widespread impact on federal, state, and local governments; foreign governments; and private sector organizations. All sectors of the economy, many of which provide goods and services that are vital to the nation's health and well being, are at risk, including telecommunications; public utilities; transportation; banking and finance; commerce and small business; national defense; government revenue collection and benefit payment; and health, safety, and emergency services. Moreover, Year 2000 problems in one sector will cascade to others due to the many interdependencies and linkages among them.

The problem is rooted in how dates are recorded and computed. For the past several decades, systems have typically used two digits to represent the year, such as "98" for 1998, to save electronic storage space and reduce operating costs. In this two digit format, however, 2000 is indistinguishable from 1900. Because of this ambiguity, date dependent software, firmware, and hardware could generate incorrect results or fail to operate altogether when processing years beyond 1999.

Since early 1997 GAO has sought to promote effective national Year 2000 program leadership and management. As part of this effort, GAO published and has since updated a guide that offers a structured, step-by-step approach for reviewing and assessing an organization's state of Year 2000 readiness.)[17] The guide describes five generally sequential Year 2000 program phases and program/project management activities that transcend the phases. The five phases are:

Awareness

Assessment

Renovation

---

[17]*Year 2000 Computing Crisis: An Assessment Guide* (GAO/AIMD 10.1.14, issued as an exposure draft in Feb. 1997; issued final in Sept. 1997).

Validation

Implementation

To supplement this enterprise readiness guide, GAO is publishing more detailed guidance on key Year 2000 phases and transcending activities embedded in its five phase model.[18] One such transcending activity is Year 2000 testing. In fact, although the most concentrated level of testing activity occurs during the renovation and validation phases, important aspects of Year 2000 testings span all five phases of the conversion model.

Complete and thorough year 2000 testing is essential to provide reasonable assurance that new or modified systems process dates correctly and will not jeopardize an organization's ability to perform core business operations after the millennium. Moreover, since the Year 2000 computing problem is so pervasive, potentially affecting an organization's systems software, applications software, databases, hardware, firmware and embedded processors, telecommunications, and external interfaces, the requisite testing is extensive and expensive. Experience is showing that Year 2000 testing is consuming between 50 and 70 percent of a project's time and resources.

To be done effectively, this testing should be planned and conducted in a structured and disciplined fashion. This document describes a step-by-step framework for managing, and a checklist for assessing, all Year 2000 testing activities associated with computer systems or system components (e.g., embedded processors) that are vendor supported. This disciplined approach and the prescribed levels of testing activities are hallmarks of mature software and system development/acquisition and maintenance processes. Organizations that already have mature programs can easily extend them to incorporate effective Year 2000 testing; organizations with immature and undisciplined software development/acquisition and maintenance processes will find effective Year 2000 testing more challenging and demanding, and should therefore ensure that sufficient management attention and resources have been allocated to Year 2000 testing to compensate for the added risk caused by this immaturity. Many organizations are attempting to reduce risk by prioritizing their systems maintenance efforts, limiting or freezing all changes not related to attaining Year 2000 compliance. As is true for all Year 2000 program decisions, the extent to which the testing rigor and discipline defined in this guide is embraced and instituted by each organization should be a business-based, risk-driven decision (i.e., what level of business risk is an organization willing to assume by foregoing the proven tenets of effective testing defined in the guide).

This guide describes five phases of Year 2000 testing activities, beginning first with establishing an organizational testing infrastructure, followed by designing, conducting, and reporting on four incremental levels of system-related testing (software unit testing, software integration testing, system acceptance testing, and end-to-end testing). To support these five phases, the document also describes test oversight and control activities.

An electronic version of this guide is available from GAO's World Wide Web server at the following Internet address: *<http:www.gao.gov>*. If *you* have any

---

[18]In February 1998, GAO issued as an exposure draft *Year 2000 Computing Crisis: Business Continuity and Contingency Planning* (GAO/AIMD 10.1.19).

questions about this guide, please contact me at (202) 512-6412, Keith Rhodes at (202) 512-6412, Randy Hite at (202) 512-6256, Naba Barkakati at (202) 512-4499, or Madhav Panwar at (202) 512-6228. We can also be reached by email at **stillmanr.aimd@gao.gov, rhodesk.aimd@gao.gov, hiter.aimd@gao.gov, barkakatin.anad@gao.gov, and panwarm@gao.gov.**

Rona B Stillman

Dr. Rona B. Stillman
Chief Scientist for Computers
     and Telecommunications

OVERVIEW OF GAO'S MANAGED, FIVE-STEP APPROACH TO YEAR 2000 TESTING

This guide is intended to aid organizations in managing and assessing their Year 2000 testing programs. An effective testing program is an essential component of any Year 2000 program or project. More time is typically spent on testing than any other program or project activity. Because Year 2000 conversions often involve numerous large interconnecting systems with many external interfaces and extensive supporting technology infrastructures, Year 2000 testing should be approached in a structured and disciplined fashion.

This guide presents a Year 2000 test model that provides such an approach. The test model sets forth five levels of test activity supported by continuous management oversight and control activities. The first level establishes the organizational infrastructure key processes needed to guide, support, and manage the next four levels of testing activities, and includes creating institutional structures, identifying and allocating resources, establishing schedules, and formulating policies, plans, standards, etc. for an organization's Year 2000 testing program. The next four levels provide key processes for effectively designing, conducting, and reporting on tests of incrementally larger system components: software unit/module tests, software integration tests, system acceptance tests, and end-to-end tests. The key processes focus on testing of software and system components that the organization is directly responsible for developing, acquiring, or maintaining. Key processes, however, are also defined to address organizational responsibilities relative to testing of vendor-supported and commercial, off-the-shelf (COTS) products and components (e.g., hardware, systems software, embedded processors, telecommunications, COTS applications). (Figure 1 summarizes the model.)

The test model builds upon and complements the five phase conversion model described in GAO's Year 2000 readiness guide.[19] The test model's five levels of test activity span all five phases of GAO's Year 2000 conversion model, with the preponderance of test activity occurring in the conversion model's renovation and validation phases. (Figures 2 and 3 relate the conversion and test models.)

The guide incorporates guidance and recommendations of standards bodies, such as the National Institute of Standards and Technology (NIST) and the Institute of Electrical and Electronic Engineers (IEEE) on Year 2000 testing practices and draws on the work of leading information technology organizations including the Software Engineering Institute, Gartner Group, Software Quality Engineering, Software Productivity Consortium, and the UK Central Computer and Telecommunications Agency.

---

[19]*Year 2000 computing Crisis: An Assessment Guide* (GAO/AIMD-10.1.14, September 1997).

FIGURE 1 Year 2000 Test Model

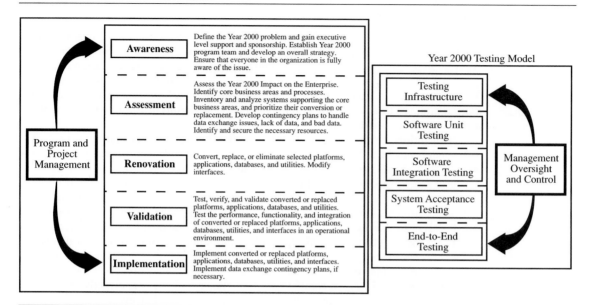

FIGURE 2 Crosswalk Between Conversion Model Phases and Testing Model Levels

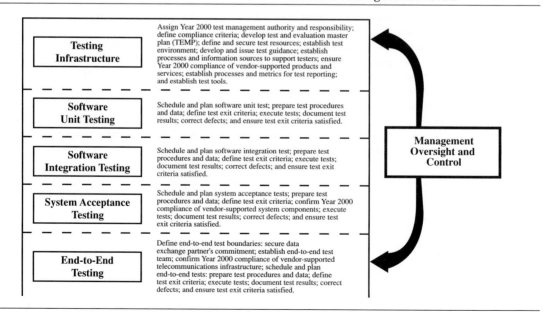

FIGURE 3   Illustrated Approximation of Test Resources Expenditure by Conversion Model Phase

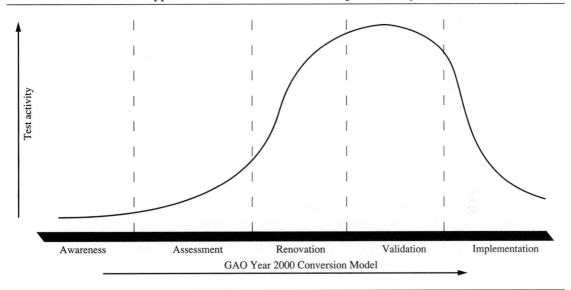

**Year 2000 Computing Crisis:
A Testing Guide Checklist**

❏ Testing Infrastructure
❏ Software Integration Testing
❏ End-to-End Testing

❏ Software Unit Testing
❏ System Acceptance Testing
❏ Management Oversight & Control

Testing Infrastructure

❏ Has Year 2000 test management authority, responsibility, and accountability been assigned?

Has it been assigned at both the program and project levels?
Has it been assigned for each level of testing (unit, integration, acceptance, and end-to-end)?

❏ Has Year 2000 compliance criteria been defined?

Is the compliance criteria documented?
Has the compliance criteria been distributed?
Is the compliance criteria the basis for test plans?

❏ Has an organizational Year 2000 TEMP been developed?

Has the TEMP been distributed?
Is there a process to update the TEMP?
Does the TEMP describe test roles and responsibilities, system/project priorities, test resource needs, individual project test schedules and progress metrics?

❏ Has the organization defined the roles and responsibilities for the quality assurance groups?

Does this quality assurance group have a reporting chain to senior management?

❏ Has the organization estimated test budgets and allocated resources and funding for the test activities?

Are shortfalls in funding assessed for impact and reported to management?

❏ Have the test environments been updated to allow Year 2000 tests?

Have one or more test facilities been established that replicate the operating environment(s)?
Have the facilities infrastructure and logistical capabilities been assessed and augmented?

❏ Has the organization developed and issued organizational Year 2000 test guidance?

Does the guidance define the objectives of Year 2000 testing?
Does the guidance define the types of testing expected?
Does the guidance define the progress metrics that are to be reported?

❏ Has the organization established test management processes and information sources?

Have configuration management processes been defined?
Have quality assurance processes been defined?
Has a change control process been defined?
Has a risk management process been defined?
Has a central library of test information been established?

❏ Has the organization ensured that vendor-supported (COTS) products are compliant?

  Has an inventory of COTS products been established?
  Have vendor certifications of its COTS products compliance been obtained?
  Have steps been taken to validate vendors' claims?

❏ Has the organization defined the test metrics that will be reported?

  Has the report format been defined?
  Has the frequency of reporting been determined?
  Have measures of test progress and results been established?

❏ Has the organization established a library of support tools?

  Have test tools needs been defined?
  Has the adequacy of existing tools been assessed?
  Have new tools been selected?
  Have the tools' acquisition been coordinated across the organization?

Software Unit Testing

❏ Have unit test activities been planned and scheduled, and is the quality assurance group or IV&V agent involved in each phase of unit testing?

  Will peer reviews be used in lieu of unit tests?

❏ Have unit test procedures and data been generated?

  Do the test procedures address relevant date conditions?

❏ Have the exit criteria for unit tests been defined?

❏ Have unit test or peer reviews been conducted?

❏ Have unit test or peer review results been documented?

❏ Have defects identified during unit test or peer reviews been corrected?

❏ Have the unit test exit criteria been satisfied?

Software Integration Testing

❏ Have integration test activities been planned and scheduled, and is the quality assurance group or IV&V agent involved in each phase of integration testing?

❏ Have integration test procedures and data been generated?

  Do the test procedures address relevant date conditions?

❏ Have the exit criteria for integration tests been defined?

❏ Have integration tests been conducted?

❏ Have integration test results been documented?

❏ Have defects identified during integration test been corrected?

❏ Have the integration test exit criteria been satisfied?

System Acceptance Testing

❏ Have acceptance test activities been planned and scheduled, and is the quality assurance group or IV&V agent involved in each phase of system acceptance testing?

  Do acceptance tests include functional, performance, regression, stress, and security testing?

❏ Have acceptance test procedures and data been generated?

❏ Do the test procedures address relevant date conditions?
❏ Have the exit criteria for acceptance tests been defined?
❏ Have compliant vendor-supported systems (COTS) been acquired and installed?
❏ Have acceptance tests been conducted?
❏ Have acceptance test results been documented?
❏ Have defects identified during acceptance tests been corrected?
❏ Have the acceptance test exit criteria been satisfied?

End-to-End Testing

❏ Have the system boundaries for end-to-end testing been determined?
   Have mission-critical business functions been identified?
   Have systems (internal and external) supporting these mission-critical business functions and the systems interrelationships been identified?
   Have the probabilities of the systems in the chain suffering a Year 2000 induced failure been assessed?
❏ Have relevant data exchange partners committed to participating in end-to-end testing?
❏ Has an inter-organization end-to-end test team been established?
❏ Has the telecommunications infrastructure been confirmed as Year 2000 compliant?
❏ Has the end-to-end testing been planned and scheduled?
❏ Have end-to-end test procedures been generated?
❏ Have end-to-end test exit criteria been defined?
❏ Have end-to-end tests been conducted?
❏ Have end-to-end test results been documented?
❏ Have defects identified during end-to-end tests been corrected?
❏ Have the end-to-end test exit criteria been satisfied?

Management Oversight and Control

❏ Has the agency ensured that test activity and progress reporting requirements have been met?
   Are the projects reporting test progress and activity in accordance with defined requirements?
   Are reporting requirements being enforced?
   Are reports from quality assurance, IV&V, and users groups being used?
❏ Has the agency identified deviations from requirements?
❏ Has the agency taken appropriate action to address deviations, problems, and risks?

Case 3–1

TACO BELL INC. (1983–1994)[1]

When John Martin, President and CEO, joined Taco Bell in 1983, he found himself at the helm of a chain of Mexican fast-food restaurants with an appropriate logo—a man sleeping under a sombrero. Having made a career in the fast-food industry as president of La Petite Boulangerie, Hardee's Food Systems and Burger Chef, Martin believed he could wake the man under the sombrero. The question remained, however, as to whether Martin could make him dance to parent PepsiCo's demanding beat. John Martin reflected on those early days:

> Our biggest problem was that we didn't know what we were. We thought maybe we were in the Mexican food business. . . . The reality was, we were in the fast-food business, and by not understanding who we were, who our potential customer was, we were just slightly missing the mark.

Company and Industry Background

The fast-food market, which had grown substantially during the 1960s and 1970s, was showing signs of maturing by the early 1980s. (See Exhibit 1 for statistics on the fast-food industry in the early 1980s.) Com-petition had become more intense as industry participants fought aggressively for every point of market share. In 1982, Taco Bell, a $700 million fast food chain, had 1,489 restaurants, 60% of which were franchised units. The company had 40% of the Mexican fast-food market,[2] but a negligible market share of total fast food. Martin knew that if his company was going to compete with its much larger, more established rivals, he would have to make significant changes.

In the early 1980s, production at Taco Bell was labor-intensive and used low levels of technology. Suppliers delivered fresh, raw food to each restaurant several times a week. Managers and crew members used their time before opening and during lulls in demand to clean and prepare ingredients for menu items. Assembly occurred when customers ordered. Because corporate headquarters stressed food control and customer demand was difficult to predict, there were often shortages for prepared raw ingredients (chopped tomatoes, shredded lettuce, etc.), which resulted in significant delays for customers.

Cooking was also done on-site. Variations in who was cooking and the sometimes frenetic pace often led to inconsistent spicing and stirring. As a result, taste and food quality could vary dramatically even within an individual restaurant. Areas dedicated to food preparation and cooking took up about 70% of the floor plan in a typical Taco Bell

---

This case consolidates two previously published cases: Taco Bell Corp., developed by Professors Len Schlesinger and Roger Hallowell, and Taco Bell 1994, developed by Professor Len Schlesinger. This consolidation was prepared by Professors Dave Delong, Boston University, Lynda Applegate, and Len Schlesinger.

[1]Copyright ©1998 by the President and Fellows of Harvard College.

Harvard Business School case 398-129.

---

[2]Richard Martin: *Nations Restaurant News,* July 16, 1990.

EXHIBIT 1   Early 1980s Fast-Food Industry Statistics

ROI (store level)	18.7%
Operating margin (store level)	15.3%
Sales per dollar of capital cost	$1.14
Hamburger chain, average sales per store	$618,028
Chicken chain, average sales per store	$381,160
Mexican chain, average sales per store	$411,263
Sales growth, 1970–1980 compound annual	16.6%
Labor as a percent of sales (industry average)	21.9%
Food cost as a percent of sales (industry average)	37.2%
McDonald's advertising cost as a percent of sales	5%
Capital necessary to commence operations, McDonald's	$650,000
Capital necessary to commence operations, Kentucky Fried Chicken	$475,000

Source: Robert Emerson, *The New Economics of Fast Food* (NY: Van Nostrand Reinhold, 1990).

restaurant. Even though 50% of some competitors' sales were delivered out of drive-through windows, Taco Bell had none in the early 1980s.

The food assembly line in the kitchen lay parallel to and directly behind the customer service area. As customers waited to place their orders and receive their food, they watched the backsides of crew members as they frenetically assembled each order. One Taco Bell executive referred to this sight as "the good, the bad, and the ugly."

Cashiers took orders and wrote them manually on a plastic board. As the production crew read and filled the orders, cashiers erased existing orders before moving on to the next customer. The system resulted in frequent fulfillment errors.

Within the restaurants, restaurant managers (RMs), assistant restaurant managers (ARMs), and shift supervisors were directly involved with receiving fresh food shipments each week, overseeing food preparation throughout the day, ensuring customer service, overseeing clean-up, and lending a hand when necessary—particularly during meal-time rush hours. RMs also faced the time-consuming task of manually developing work crew schedules in a business with an annual turnover rate of 220%. Taco Bell's manual systems, which were also used for placing orders and performing other administrative tasks, led to significant oversights and errors, provided no data for management analysis, and forced employees to spend a great deal of time in repetitive, paper-intensive, non-value-added tasks.

RMs reported directly to district managers (DMs), who often played the role of policemen, pointing out problems in restaurants and ensuring that corporate standards were maintained. (See Exhibit 2 for a summary of Taco Bell's line organization in 1983.) They regularly performed "white glove" inspections of the physical restaurants and audits of the financial books, often creating antagonistic relationships with their RMs, who they spent almost no time coaching or developing.

1983–1988: Establishing Direction and Implementing Incremental Change

Starting in 1983, John Martin began a series of changes in the Taco Bell organization designed to alter the company's mind-set, as well as its capabilities for pursuing a strategy to compete with the major fast-food chains. The first thing he did was to modernize Taco Bell's physical units. These

EXHIBIT 2 Taco Bell Line Organization, 1983

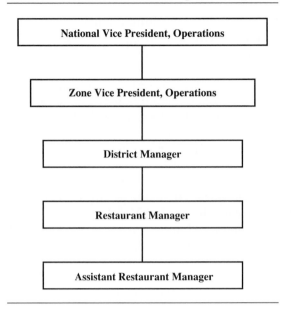

changes included remodeling the restaurants, increasing seating capacity, adding drive-through windows, installing new signs, and outfitting employees in more contemporary uniforms. The company also added new menu items, including Nachos, Taco Salad, Mexican Pizza, Double Beef Burrito Supreme, Seafood Salad, and Soft-Shell Tacos.[3]

In addition, Martin accelerated the company's growth, averaging 249 new stores per year from 1983 to 1988, an increase from less than 100 units per year that had been added in the late 1970s. This expansion also extended Taco Bell's geographic presence into the Midwest, Southeast, and Northeast. In the process, the company replaced its old 1,600-square-foot mission-

---

[3]Dean Takahashi: "Taco Bell . . .", *The Orange County Register,* August 13, 1989. The first four products mentioned are trademarked products of Taco Bell Corp.

style restaurants with more modern 2,000-square-foot units.

During the same period, the parallel food assembly line was replaced by a double assembly line perpendicular to the customer service area. This improved product flow, increased capacity, and made serving easier in the drive-through windows that were being installed. The Plexiglas boards used for writing orders were also replaced by electronic point-of-sale systems (cash registers). These were tied to television monitors over the food assembly line, which indicated what had been ordered. The new electronic system allowed the company to track sales, product mix and inventory much more closely.

Training and development were also improved in the mid-1980s, although training for ARMs and RMs continued to reflect a human resource strategy predicated on very high turnover. Training for district managers, however, was not significantly changed. The head of operations training provided this overview:

> As to training, we were definitely a procedures, policies, and practices organization. We made sure each manager knew how to make every product, knew the appropriate weights for every product—by "knew" I mean had memorized. We were very operationally driven . . . there was a little work on staffing, but only at the crew level, dealing primarily with crew entry and exit.

1988–1991: Transforming the Business

The Mexican segment of upscale restaurants, fast-food, and supermarket food sales grew substantially during the 1980s. In the ongoing battle for market share in the maturing fast-food industry, Taco Bell and its competitors began to introduce new products to attract customers. Some incremental business was generated by this strategy, but the new products also had a negative effect on kitchen efficiency, which influenced both costs and quality of service. The introduction of fajitas, for example, required new grills and exhaust systems costing Taco Bell $30 million. Reflecting on Taco Bell's market position in 1988,[4] Martin said:

> We were really a small player. One of the things that struck us was, perhaps we needed to figure out a different way to go about this—as opposed to trying to compete head-on with the big guys who had well-established, entrenched brands. Maybe instead of directly competing, maybe we ought to try to change the game a little bit. . . . We're really not in the business of making food. We're in the business of feeding people.

Changing the Rules of the Game

Recognizing the industry's margin squeeze, Martin developed a new, more holistic business strategy focused on customer value. As part of the process of determining how to define value, in 1987, Martin commissioned a study to better understand what Taco Bell's best customers wanted from a fast-food restaurant. This was followed by another study in early 1989. The result of these two studies confirmed what Martin suspected from his years in the fast-food industry. Customers said they wanted **FACT:** fast-food **Fast;** fast-food orders **Accurate;**[5] fast food served in a restaurant that was **Clean;** and fast food at the appro-

priate **Temperature.**[6] FACT clarified that, at Taco Bell, a commitment to customer value required a fundamental change in management thinking; the organization needed to stop viewing quality and price as incompatible tradeoffs.

Armed with this information and in an effort to begin "changing the rules of the game," in early 1988, Taco Bell adopted a strategy of value pricing (see Exhibit 3), fully recognizing that, if the company was to dramatically lower prices while preserving quality, it would also have to dramatically reduce costs. To achieve these seemingly incompatible goals, Martin realized that incremental change would not work; a radical redefinition of the business was needed.

K-Minus and SOS

One of the most far-reaching changes implemented at Taco Bell during the late 1980s was an initiative called K-Minus. With "K-Minus" (standing for kitchen minus), the restaurant kitchen became a heating and assembly unit. Virtually all chopping, cooking, and associated clean-up was transferred to corporate headquarters. Ground beef, chicken, and beans all arrived at the restaurant pre-cooked in plastic bags ready to be heated and served. Other food products, such as lettuce, tortillas, and even guacamole, also arrived prepared, packaged and ready for use in assembling menu items. With this bold move, Taco Bell inverted the space configuration of their typical restaurant from a 70% kitchen/30% customer service ratio to 30% kitchen/70% customer service. In addition to enabling dramatic improvements in efficiency and much tighter control of the quality and consistency of its food, K-Minus also greatly expanded seating capacity within the restaurants and

---

[4]During the 1980s, industry labor costs as a percentage of sales grew on average by 18%, but at Taco Bell those costs increased 50%, in part because of the ongoing high costs of turnover. And, with real estate prices and construction costs outstripping the rate of inflation, the industry's average cost to develop a restaurant site increased by almost 8%. Finally, food costs declined by an industry average of 15% during this period, but Taco Bell's costs actually increased slightly from 27% to 30%.

[5]Taco Bell estimated that 60% of orders delivered in the fast-food industry (including at their chain) were delivered incorrectly.

[6]Hot food hot, cold food cold.

EXHIBIT 3 Taco Bell Menu Selections: Price Comparisons

	1983	1988	1991
Taco	$0.67	$0.79	$0.59
Burrito Supreme	1.32	1.65	1.49
Pintos and cheese	0.59	0.79	0.59
Tostada	0.63	0.79	0.59
Pepsi (largest)	0.79	0.99	0.99

Note that the largest Pepsi increased in size during the late 1980s.

provided space to expand drive-through and other non-eat-in sales. A decrease in real estate expenses in proportion to sales and in aggregate labor costs resulted.

To meet customers' demand for speed and quality, Taco Bell also instituted its Speed of Service (SOS) program. This initiative redesigned processes still further and developed specific measures of performance. Recipes were reformulated and heated holding areas were developed. By 1990 Taco Bell restaurants could pre-assemble and hold 60% of their most popular menu items ready for immediate sale for up to 10 minutes. These additional changes increased peak hour transaction capacity by 54%, and reduced customer waiting times by 71%.

The Changing Role of the Restaurant Manager

While it was reconfiguring operations to cut costs and increase speed of delivery, Taco Bell also transformed the roles of its managers. A key point person in implementing the strategy was the restaurant manager; this position was recast as restaurant general manager (RGM). Employees occupying this new role were expected to take on more decision making responsibility and accountability for their restaurant, developing staff and managing P&L. John Martin explained:

The new role of the RGM was born in the notion of self-sufficiency. Restaurants can, in fact, operate by themselves. The bottom line is there's no rocket science in a fast-food restaurant. . . . The difficulty is that you have 1,500 things all going on at once. . . . The typical top-down command and control can't deal with those things under any circumstances.

Taco Bell's senior vice president of human resources offered another view of the role changes:

At the time we designed the new Taco Bell, in late 1989, we realized that we'd need a whole new people system. We were going to be asking people to do new things and we realized that we'd need new training, both in content and delivery. How we paid people would have to be different, and how we managed people would have to change. We'd go to more management by exception, more coaching, broadening spans, taking out layers. Communication would have to improve. The culture would have to change.

There was a two- to three-year timeframe in which we significantly raised the bench on RGM skills. We went through an analysis of the caliber of the original RGMs . . . and we determined that about one-third of our RGMs could grab the spirit of what we were trying to do at the restaurant level. Another third, with development and coaching could achieve the stated standard of performance. We thought that one-third could not make the mark.

To fill the new RGM role, Taco Bell began looking for people with skills and potential different than for the old manager's role. After a brief interview, an RGM candidate took a life-themes indicator test to identify the presence of traits necessary in RGMs. Individuals who were hired began a training program, which under the new strategy focused heavily on leadership and operating management skills. RGMs received training in operational policies and procedures, and five days of leadership training that covered topics such as situational leadership, coaching, managing conflict, restaurant communication systems, creative problem solving and decision making, and implementing change.

Transforming the District Manager's Role

The district manager's role at Taco Bell also changed under the new strategy. With a new title of "marketing manager," by 1990, district managers' spans of control had increased from 6 restaurants to 12. Despite the greatly increased responsibilities some marketing managers tried to retain their traditional "policeman approach" in dealing with RGMs. By 1991, however, the span of control for marketing managers was expanded to 20 restaurants, and they were virtually forced to begin managing by exception and to change from policeman to coach.

Many of the former district managers could not make the transition. To fill the vacancies, Taco Bell took the radical step of looking for talent outside the fast-food industry. They began recruiting sales and product managers with Fortune 500 company experience, and began to hire graduates from the top MBA programs in the country. Convinced they could teach these new general managers about the industry, senior management sought candidates with leadership and management skills who could coach and develop RGMs while also building the business in their area. Ongoing training for marketing managers was also enhanced. By 1990, six days of leadership training included a range of topics such as leadership practices, methods to create a shared vision, coaching, communication, adapting to change, technology/MIS, and finance.

Changing Incentives

Altering compensation and nonmonetary reward systems was also critical to transforming middle management roles at Taco Bell. In 1989, the average base salary for restaurant managers was $28,700 with a

$4,400 annual bonus, which was almost always paid. This compensation was standard in the fast-food industry, and unhappy Taco Bell managers simply "walked across the street" to another fast-food chain. They had no commitment or sense of ownership in the company.

When the skill levels and responsibilities were increased in the new RGM's role, the average base salary was raised to $32,000 (with a range of $26,000 to $40,000). The target incentive bonus was increased to $12,000. Nonmonetary compensation also played a key role in retaining managers, since monetary rewards peaked early in a successful RGM's career. Career paths, which traditionally had been very limited, were redesigned. For example, the RGM was no longer limited to managing a single restaurant. In the new organization, they were able to expand their job and increase their pay by opening new points of distribution[7] and building business through new channels.

Market manager compensation was also redesigned to attract more highly skilled individuals and to create incentives that would keep them challenged. In the late 1980s, the average district manager's salary had been $38,000 with an average bonus of $5,500. By 1991, the average base salary averaged $60,000. The discrepancy was caused by the need to offer a higher base to more experienced managers recruited from outside the industry. Target bonuses for all marketing managers were $1,200 per unit supervised.

---

[7]Points of distribution outside a traditional Taco Bell restaurant were called "pods." Subsequently, they would come to be called Points of Access (POAs). Examples included taco carts in malls and supermarkets, being the vendor for a school lunch program, and operating a Taco Bell Express (miniature, or "sardine") store.

The leaner management organization created special concerns about career advancement for marketing managers. Instead of vertical advancement within the Taco Bell management hierarchy, success needed to be redefined. Potential career moves for market managers included either expanding their current job by growing the Taco Bell business in their area or assuming a new position within the expanding Taco Bell business. New positions included: becoming a manager at one of Taco Bell's larger restaurants (for example, Chevys); assuming a position as an international market manager; or moving into product or business management in Taco Bell's new retail business.[8]

To support the job expansion career approach, Taco Bell created a very broad salary range for marketing managers. Movement through the range was determined by the strength of an individual's performance, the complexity of their market, and job tenure.

Creating Safety Nets
The new, lean Taco Bell had the potential for significant profit and growth if things ran smoothly, but it also had the potential for disaster if company standards were not maintained. With the removal of layers of management and frequent supervision of restaurants, new controls were implemented to ensure adherence to the company policies and value systems. There were three primary "safety nets."

---

[8]During the early 1990s, Taco Bell expanded their business concept beyond the fast-food business. As part of that expansion, they developed a consumer product line to be distributed through supermarkets, convenience stores, and other retail outlets, and they purchased Chevys, a casual dining Mexican restaurant chain. (See Appendix A for summary of the Taco Bell brands in 1994.)

- A toll-free telephone number was installed for customers to comment on Taco Bell's restaurants, food and service. Calls were answered by an external vendor that recorded comments and forwarded them to the relevant operations area.
- Mystery shopping was a second safety net. A mystery shopping service regularly sent individuals to rate restaurants on specific quality issues, and these reports were used in calculating bonuses for restaurant managers.
- Marketing surveys, also known as the customer intercept program, were conducted by teams of Taco Bell employees who would arrive unannounced at a restaurant and spend the day asking customers to fill out brief questionnaires about their Taco Bell experience. The data was used in determining the market manager's bonus and to better understand how the chain was viewed in a particular geographic market.

Developing the Information Infrastructure
Taco Bell's managers needed an information and communication system that would make it possible to perform in their new roles. In 1988, an MIS project was initiated that would provide a personal computer in every store linked to a local POS system, to the marketing managers and to corporate headquarters. Known as TACO (Total Automation of Company Operations), the new system provided the infrastructure, information and analytical tools needed to support new management roles.

TACO reduced operational paperwork for restaurant general managers by at least 10 hours a week. It also provided RGMs with reports on food costs, labor costs, inventory, perishable items, and period-to-date costs, all with variances. TACO also had functions that helped RGMs with labor scheduling and service operations planning; for example, TACO could provide an estimate of the sales volume to anticipate on Friday between 1 and 2 p.m. based on the previous six weeks' volume. The schedule could be adjusted by the RGM to account for holidays or special events, or it could be disregarded entirely at the manager's discretion. Commenting on the value of the computer system, John Martin said:

> The restaurant manager now has more information than the corporation ever gets. He or she has it immediately and has the tools to take care of problems without someone saying, "You've got a problem." Talking empowerment is one thing. Really living it is another.

The information needs of marketing managers were also supported by the system, which provided them with daily, weekly and monthly reports on store operations in their district. TACO also tracked sales for senior management by downloading the information from store registers to a central computer. This eliminated several accounting positions at corporate headquarters.

Finally, TACO had a communications function that was critical for coordinating interactions between marketing managers and store managers. Previously, marketing managers either had to mail information, visit or call store managers. TACO gave marketing managers an electronic mail system that provided another way to communicate with RGMs.

1991–1994: Continuous Transformation—Creating the Learning Organization

From 1988 to 1994 the fast-food industry was mired in a recession and achieved only single-digit growth. But with the changes John Martin had initiated, Taco Bell had grown from $700 million in revenues in 1983 to $1.6 billion in 1988. And at the end of 1993, Taco Bell's total system sales were almost $4 billion. Since the radical changes initiated by Martin in 1988, the company had more than doubled its sales and tripled its profits; in keeping with its value strategy, customer satisfaction had also increased (see Exhibit 4).

But Martin was not satisfied. His strategic vision was no longer limited to the fast-food segment. By late 1991, Martin had reformulated the firm's strategy yet again; to be successful in the future, Taco Bell would create and dominate the convenience food business—a business that reached out to customers any time and any place they were hungry.

John Martin's goal for Taco Bell was to evolve into a $25 billion food retailer with a worldwide distribution system of over 200,000 POAs by the year 2000. To reach this aggressive goal, Taco Bell would have to expand beyond fast foods. The company began a string of acquisitions, and by 1994, Taco Bell had three restaurant brands: Taco Bell, Hot-n-Now, and Chevys Mexican Restaurants. In addition, the company had expanded its signature brand of retail products through Taco Bell New Concepts, Taco Bell Supermarket Retail, and Taco Bell International. (See Appendix A for a summary of the Taco Bell brands in 1994.)

Organizing to Manage Complexity

In anticipation of the expansion of the business, Martin used lessons learned in K-Minus to enable efficient management across multiple brands, channels, and markets. Rather than add multiple layers of infrastructure, the company developed a concept called *shared resources*. Managers were asked to identify the infrastructure requirements for the new lines of business; they then met together to identify how they could capitalize on the strengths of Taco Bell's existing infrastructure or infrastructure that was available elsewhere in

EXHIBIT 4   Company Performance

Financial Highlights ($ billions)

	1993	1992	1991	1990	1989	1988	1987	1986	1985	1984	1983
Total system sales	$3.9	$3.3	$2.8	$2.4	$2.1	$1.6	$1.5	$1.3	$1.1	$0.9	$0.7
Company store sales	2.91	1.95	1.61	1.40	1.17	0.9	0.8	0.7	0.5	0.5	0.4
Average unit sales, total system (in $000)	925	876	814	771	686	589	579	560	550	539	439
Net worldwide operating profit (in $millions)	253	215	181	150	113	76	85	78	68	59	43

Customer Satisfaction (1990-1993)

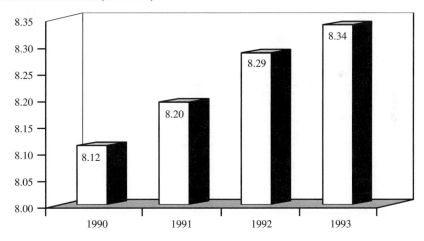

PepsiCo. For example, the Frito-Lay marketing, sales and distribution infrastructure could be used to support the Taco Bell line of retail products.

While the shared resources concept was critical for the success of the new strategy, Martin recognized that the more critical threat to the company's future success was embedded within the very foundation of its current success. That threat was complacency.

Creating a Learning Organization
To ensure future success, Martin realized that Taco Bell would need to move beyond changing its structure, roles and processes; the company would also need to change its culture—the deeply embedded beliefs and values that framed how individuals made decisions and took actions. The new Taco Bell would need to embrace continuous, yet intelligent, change. Survival and success in

the future would depend upon learning faster than the competition. Martin explained:

> [Learning organizations] are able to capture, share and take action on information better and faster than the competitor. A learning organization isn't top-down and it isn't bottom-up. It works side to side. It's an organization that gobbles up information and experiences like a sponge and shares those learnings throughout the enterprise in minutes, hours, and days rather than weeks, months, and years.

Taco Bell believed the benefits of creating such an organization would include: increased individual awareness and collective organizational IQ; greater organizational flexibility and speed of response; institutionalization of employee self-sufficiency and innovation; and increased individual and team productivity. But moving to this self-sufficient learning model involved further refinement of the organizational design. Taco Bell pursued a number of initiatives to create and support a new learning culture.

Pushing Down Decision Making

In the early 1990s, much of Taco Bell's growth was fueled by its greatly expanded use of carts, kiosks, vans, and Taco Bell Express units. Between 1991 and 1993, Points of Access (POAs) increased from 3,670 to 9,707 (see Exhibit 5). Taco Bell's carts and kiosks became a common sight at such varied locations as high school and college cafeterias, airports, malls, convenience stores, gas stations and even the Moscow subway system.

To support such rapid expansion, Taco Bell continued to increase its managers' spans of responsibility. This enabled further movement from the command and control culture of the past, and enabled the company to rapidly increase POAs while simultaneously reducing the traditional field

EXHIBIT 5   Points of Access, 1989–1993

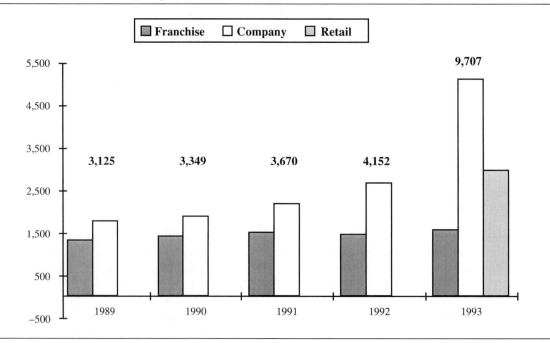

management structure (see Exhibit 6). An integral part of increasing managers' spans of responsibility was the development of team-managed units (TMUs).

TMUs were teams of crew members sufficiently trained to manage a store without a full-time on-site manager. The intent was to create teams of crew members who were capable of performing all of the day-to-day tasks of a general manager (GM).[9] Senior management considered TMUs a natural evolution of Taco Bell's empowerment strategy, and by the end of 1993 there were TMUs in 90% of the company-owned restaurant locations stores. As Taco Bell broadened its business in the early 1990s, TMUs were a critical mechanism that permitted general managers (GMs) to manage multiple POAs. But the teaming concept had several other important impacts. It forced GMs to increas-

ingly become coaches and trainers, working with their crews to help them broaden their jobs and accept new levels of responsibility. Implementing TMUs also helped create a culture of interdependence and information sharing among crews and management that would be essential to creating both self-sufficient crew-run stores and a learning organization in general.

Just as crew members were compensated for assuming additional responsibilities, Taco Bell's compensation system for GMs was changed as well. GMs continued to have a variable pay system, but it was much more highly leveraged. Managers' base pay averaged $30,000, but they were able to earn another $30,000 in bonus pay. GMs were evaluated on three criteria: (1) performance at meeting profit targets, (2) customer service ratings, and (3) actual store sales.[10] To promote information sharing in the new environment, some marketing managers also experimented with a shared incentive

---

[9]In 1992, the titles "Restaurant General Manager" and "Assistant Restaurant General Manager" were changed to "General Manager" and "Assistant General Manager." This change reflected the expansion of their responsibilities beyond the traditional restaurant.

---

[10]Shari Cauldron, "Master the Compensation Maze," *Personnel Journal,* 72, no. 6 (June 1993).

EXHIBIT 6   Span of Responsibility, 1989–1993

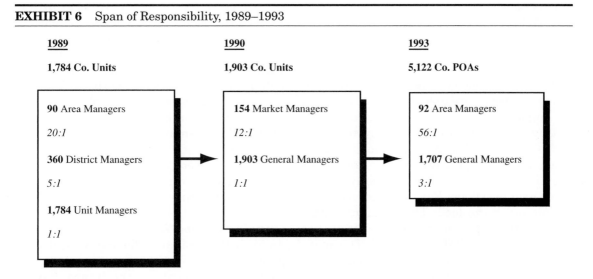

1989	1990	1993
1,784 Co. Units	1,903 Co. Units	5,122 Co. POAs
90 Area Managers	**154** Market Managers	**92** Area Managers
20:1	*12:1*	*56:1*
360 District Managers	**1,903** General Managers	**1,707** General Managers
5:1	*1:1*	*3:1*
1,784 Unit Managers		
1:1		

system by contributing their bonuses to a pool that would be shared equally by all employees in the region. This initiative was designed to promote an environment of greater cooperation and communication among employees.

Expanding Information Access

To support the self-sufficient team-based organization and to facilitate the company's ability to learn and change, access to information changed dramatically at Taco Bell. Initial implementation of the TACO system had provided restaurant managers with information about store operations. But in the new environment, the focus expanded to getting that same information into the hands of crew members actually running the stores. There was wide agreement that the employees closest to the customer and daily operations were in the best position to make full use of this information.

To make information useful to TMUs, Taco Bell introduced TACO II. This new, more user-friendly computer system was designed to provide crew members with the information they needed to make decisions and take action. For example, instead of reporting a ".05% meat variance" yesterday, the system would report that the variance was equal to 300 tacos, which was something crew members could both relate to and act on.

The team-based culture and the new technology system were essential for supporting an empowered organization. Said one marketing manager, "In the old system, the crews were afraid to make decisions because they were afraid they would get reprimanded by the AGM. Now, the crews make their own decisions. For example, our crew people order the food. This is much better because they know more about what we use daily than the AGMs and GMs. The managers don't make tacos and they don't go in back to get boxes of food."

Building an Intellectual Network

The development of an intellectual network was another initiative that Taco Bell saw as critical to its self-sufficiency and organizational learning paradigm. This was intended to be an on-line communications system that allowed every Taco Bell employee to disseminate information, ask questions, get answers and perform their jobs better. Shared data bases would be a key component of the network, incorporating "best practices" information on a wide variety of subjects. The network would also use expert systems such as the company's Contract Authoring System. This PC-based set of real estate contracts had been written and cleared by Taco Bell's legal department, and simple rules were built into the system. Through the use of TACO II, senior management was able to delegate greater authority, while still maintaining necessary control in areas of high risk. In this way, TACO II extended the concept of safety nets from measurement of customer satisfaction to include control of operations.

Taco Bell expected the intellectual network to facilitate knowledge transfer and communication in ways that would allow the company to continue its rapid growth in POAs without a corresponding increase in bureaucracy. The intent was to use the network to maintain a sense of community within the burgeoning organization and to help retain the company's verbal culture. To further support this latter objective and to enhance communications, Taco Bell extended its e-mail systems and installed voice mail and computer conferencing. Managers noted that voice mail quickly became a key component of the communication infrastructure.

Ongoing Innovation

As Taco Bell managed for today, it also organized to ensure that the company would continue to innovate in the future. For example, the company developed a "restaurant of the future" testing site near its corporate headquarters. Here new innovations could be developed and tested. In 1994, there were several innovations being tested at the restaurant of the future. For example, an Automated Taco Assembler capable of making 900 tacos per hour without human assistance was expected to reduce waste, increase consistency and quality, and reduce kitchen labor by 16 hours per day. A Customer Activated Terminal (CAT)—a touch screen ordering system—would enable customers to place their orders from kiosks and roving sales crews to take orders outside the walls of the physical restaurant.

Can Taco Bell Get There From Here?

If you wait until something is broken to fix it . . . there may not be anything left to fix.

John Martin, September 1988

John Martin had long been viewed a futuristic leader in the industry and the company, someone who was constantly willing to think "outside the box" and improve things before they were broken. In his pursuit of value, extraordinary convenience and accessibility, and unparalleled customer satisfaction, John Martin was an acknowledged champion of the consumer, and it appeared that the industry agreed when it awarded Martin the International Foodservice Manufac-

turers Association's 1993 Silver Plate Foodservice Operator of the Year award.

Martin, however, was proud of all that the employees in the company had accomplished (see Exhibit 7). He believed that with a clear vision and the capacity and willingness to change, Taco Bell had only begun to tap into available opportunities. In his words:

> In its more than three decades of operation, Taco Bell has accomplished much. But we know that the best still lies ahead. Today we feed 50 million people each and every week. But our vision is to be broader than just a fast-food restaurant. In the United States, there are one billion feeding occasions every day. That presents us with unlimited opportunities. What's exciting is that our people are on the forefront of the changes we are making in our business. By being empowered to take greater ownership, our people will drive even greater changes. In doing so, not only will we deliver value to our customers, but we will also provide greater value to our people by being an employer of choice. Together we're transforming the careers and jobs that people can have in this industry.

John Martin's vision was certain to bring about dramatic change and progress for Taco Bell and its people . . . and its customers. Yet the year 2000 was only six short years away. Was Taco Bell positioned to be able to achieve its vision of growing to $25 billion in sales and 200,000 POAs? Were the actions to date sufficient to take them there? Only time would tell.

EXHIBIT 7   Summary of Changes at Taco Bell, 1983–1994

	Phase 1: 1983–1988	*Phase 2: 1988–1991*	*Phase 3: 1991–1994*
Context	Fast-food market maturing; New products; Operating costs increase; Mexican segment takes off	Margins squeezed; Battle for market share; Value pricing strategy becomes dominant	Recession in fast-food industry, single-digit growth; Market share falls as competitors respond

(continued)

EXHIBIT 7 (continued)   Summary of Changes at Taco Bell, 1983–1994

	Phase 1: 1983–1988	Phase 2: 1988–1991	Phase 3: 1991–1994
Vision	From regional Mexican restaurant to fast-food restaurant	From making food to feeding people	Dominate convenience food segment
Strategic initiatives	Incremental process redesign; Product/geographical expansion; Infrastructure changes; Build fast-food brand image	Information-enabled business transformation; Customer value orientation	Create an empowered learning organization; Continuous improvement; Extend brand through acquisitions and retail
Process	Modernize facilities; Add drive-through windows; Add new menu items; Accelerate unit growth from 100 to 249 stores per year; Redesign food preparation process	FACT studies; K-Minus and SOS; Increased kitchen capacity enhances non-eat-in sales; Expand into new POAs; Safety nets implemented around customer value	Dramatically extend POAs; Team-based processes replace assembly line; Operational innovations, e.g., robotics, customer-activated terminals, process flow mapping
Power	No change	RGMs take on more decision making within restaurant and assume responsibility for multiple POAs; More management-by-exception; Increase span of responsibility	Continue to increase span of responsibility; Team-managed units replace hierarchical operations at the restaurant level; Extend "empowerment" to crew level
People	Improved operational training and development	Recruit more skilled RGMs; Hire outside industry; New training program for leadership skills; New compensation and nonmonetary rewards; New career paths	Crew members trained to manage stores in teams; Variable pay system; Experiment with shared incentive systems; Career paths extended
Principles	No change in values	Focus on customer value as key principle driving decision making and action; Safety nets implemented to provide necessary boundary checks	Focus is on changing culture and values; Emphasize continuous innovation, empowerment, and learning; Safety nets extended to provide necessary boundary systems

EXHIBIT 7 (concluded)   Summary of Changes at Taco Bell, 1983–1994

	Phase 1: 1983–1988	*Phase 2: 1988–1991*	*Phase 3: 1991–1994*
Information and communication	Install POS system	TACO system provides communication and information infrastructure	TACO II extends access to information and communication infrastructure to TMUs; Intellectual network; Voice mail and computer conferencing complement e-mail
Value created	Total system sales grow from $700 million in 1983 to $1.6 billion in 1988; Net profit grows from $43 million to $76 million	Increased peak hour transaction capacity by over 54%; Reduced customer waiting times by over 71%; Total system sales grow to $2.8 billion; Net profit grows from $76 million to $181 million	Improved customer satisfaction from 8.12 to 8.34; Total system sales grow to almost $4 billion in 1993; Net profit grows to $253 million in 1993.

Appendix A

TACO BELL'S THREE BRANDS

Brand Taco Bell

Brand Taco Bell was the company's core business and it included all of the points of access by which *Taco Bell* reached customers: (1) traditional restaurants, (2) new concepts, (3) international operations, and (4) retail.

Taco Bell Restaurants

Once the company's core distribution outlet, traditional restaurants became just one of many ways to reach new customers.

Taco Bell New Concepts

New concepts included non-traditional points of access such as school lunch programs, carts, Express units, kiosks, and joint ventures with sister companies Pizza Hut and KFC.

Taco Bell International

Taco Bell International operated over 100 non-U.S. POAs in 21 countries at the end of 1993.

Taco Bell Supermarket Retail

After reviewing marketing studies which indicated that Taco Bell had a higher brand awareness among shoppers than Doritos, the company decided to enter the supermarket retail business. The company worked with its sister company Frito Lay, which provided the production and distribution infrastructure for the new Taco Bell products. In 1993, they began test marketing 18 products in 3,000 stores throughout Ohio, Georgia, Chicago, Michigan, and Indiana. The markets were chosen because they offered a diversity of customers, taste preferences, and Taco Bell brand awareness. Taco Bell entered the market with virtually no advertising, except for newspaper inserts and in-restaurant couponing. The success of the tests was immediately evident as Taco Bell quickly became the number one or two food brand in the supermarket Mexican retail food sections. Results were so positive that Taco Bell anticipated expanding to 10,000 supermarkets (POAs) in 1994. Taco Bell executives viewed the 150,000 U.S. supermarkets as 150,000 potential POAs and expected the retail business to be worth several hundred million dollars.

Retail was yet another way for Taco Bell to access a different eating occasion. Executives noted that the people who shopped in grocery stores were often very different from those that frequented Taco Bell restaurants. By entering retail, Taco Bell entered people's homes and went to another place where consumers ate.

Hot-n-Now

Taco Bell's first advance outside Mexican fast food was their acquisition of the double drive-through hamburger chain Hot-n-Now. The Kalamazoo, MI, chain was purchased in 1991 and consisted of 77 stores in 23 markets. The stores sold only hamburgers, French fries, and sodas. They had two drive-through windows and a walk-up window. Operations were designed to provide high-quality fast food in a quick and inexpensive manner.

Taco Bell executives expected Hot-n-Now to become a significant part of their growth for the decade ahead. Industry-wide hamburger drive-through sales reached $25 billion in 1992, making the hamburger drive-through segment larger than the entire chicken and seafood segments.[11] Consistent with Taco Bell's expansionist tendencies, the company planned to increase the chain to 5,000 locations during the next decade.

Chevys

Taco Bell ventured into the casual-dining market with the May 1993 purchase of Chevys Mexican Restaurant. The 37 store chain was a full-service restaurant/bar located primarily in Northern California. Taco Bell's market research indicated

---

[11]Peter Romeo, "Can Lightning Strike Twice?" *Restaurant Business,* August 10, 1993.

that as fast food users aged and had more disposable income, they migrated towards casual dining.

Taco Bell executives saw the Chevys acquisition as a natural step in the creation of a superbrand as well as a natural progression for its broader set of consumers. By capturing an entirely different eating occasion (casual dining) it allowed Taco Bell to access new customers.

Taco Bell planned rapid nationwide expansion for the Chevys chain, taking it to 300 restaurants with $1 billion in sales.

Case 3–2

FRITO-LAY, INC.: A STRATEGIC TRANSITION, 1980–1986[1]

"In the food industry," a senior executive at Frito-Lay explained, "the retailers are slowly becoming more powerful than the manufacturers. As this plays out, it won't be enough just to know our business. We have to know theirs as well. The manufacturers who are important to the store will win. There is no single sustainable competitive advantage in this business. I can't think of a single thing that can't be duplicated. What we try to do is compete with class. We put a good mix of product on the shelves; we out-execute our competition; and we try to be "blue-chip" in every aspect of our business. There's a whole book to be written on the strategic advantage of execution. It's not a few big ideas; it's a whole series of little things that add up to superiority."

Industry and Company Background

Since Herman Lay began store-door delivery of Lay's potato chips and Frito's corn chips in 1932, Frito-Lay, Inc. had grown to be the most powerful competitor in the over $6 billion salty snack industry. By 1986, Frito-Lay claimed 40.6% market share across its product lines and market segments. Acquired by PepsiCo in 1965, the company became its largest profit contributor in 1981. (See Exhibit 1 for a financial summary and Exhibit 2 for a market summary.)

Frito-Lay was a highly respected competitor within the industry. From management of its supplier network to its direct salesforce delivering product in distinctive red and white trucks, Frito-Lay was well known for excellence in execution. But, by the 1980s, the company's goal of paying a minimum of two visits per week to every customer had become a logistical nightmare. In the mid-1960s, 5,000 salespeople sold 30 to 40 products; by 1986, more than 100 products were sold by 10,000 salespeople (see Exhibit 3). Leo Kiely, senior vice president of sales and marketing, explained the dynamics of the business:

We operate in a business that is simple in concept but complex in execution. We deliver our products through our own distribution network to diverse supermarket chains, small groceries, and convenience stores. Once packaged, our products have a 35-day shelf life. At the end of that time, the product was considered stale and

---

This case was prepared by Lynda M. Applegate.

[1]Copyright © 1994 by the President and Fellows of Harvard College. Harvard Business School case 194-107.

EXHIBIT 1 PepsiCo/Frito-Lay: Financial Summary (in millions)

	1970	1975	1980	1981	1982	1983	1984	1985	1986
PepsiCo									
Revenues	$1,122.6	$2,321.2	$5,975.2	$7,023.3	$7,499.0	$7,895.9	$7,699.0	$8,056.7	$9,290.8
Operating profit	100.1	245.7	630.8	708.7	697.8	634.7	798.8	858.9	902.0
Total assets	NA	NA	3,417.5	4,057.1	4,197.5	4,638.3	4,807.0	5,861.2	8,028.6
Net profit	56.0	104.6	291.8	333.5	224.3	284.1	212.5	543.7	457.8
Frito-Lay									
Revenues	325.6	806.7	1,830.7	2,177.9	2,323.8	2,430.0	2,709.2	2,847.0	3,018.4
Operating profit	25.0	89.5	245.8	298.5	326.4	347.7	393.9	401.0	343.0
Total assets	NA	NA	791.9	945.3	949.5	1,110.1	1,254.5	1,487.1	1,603.8
Revenues as a % of the Pepsi total	29.0%	34.8%	30.6%	31.0%	31.0%	30.8%	35.2%	35.3%	32.5%
Operating profit as a % of the Pepsi total	25.0%	37.0%	39.0%	42.1%	46.8%	54.8%	49.3%	46.7%	38.0%
Assets as a % of total	NA	NA	23.2%	23.3%	22.6%	23.9%	26.1%	25.4%	20.0%
Frito-Lay year-to-year revenue growth rate		25.1%	20.6%	19.0%	6.7%	4.6%	11.5%	5.1%	6.0%
Frito-Lay year-to-year operating profit growth rate		101.6%	25.8%	21.4%	9.3%	6.5%	13.3%	1.8%	−14.5%

Particularly significant acquisitions:
Pizza Hut—Acquired in 1977
Taco Bell—Acquired in 1978
Kentucky Fried Chicken (KFC)—Acquired in 1986

EXHIBIT 2   Market Summary (in millions)

	1976[a]	1978	1980	1982[b]	1984	1986
Potato chips	$ 775	$ 909	$1,118	$2,289	$2,514	$2,850
Corn/tortilla chips	367	488	728	1,132	1,246	1,324
Extruded snacks[c]	121	155	242	324	380	467
Pretzels	130	133	175	248	266	293
All others	152	150	167	1,336	1,418	1,836
Total salty snacks	$1,545	$1,835	$2,430	$5,329	$5,824	$6,770

[a]Years 1976–1980 compiled from Bonoma, Thomas, "Frito-Lay, Incorporated (A)," HBS Case No. 582-110.
[b]Years 1986–1986 compiled from *Snack Food Magazine* annual surveys (June issues).
[c]Category primarily consists of cheese curls/balls.

Frito-Lay, Inc.: Market Share (%)

	1976	1978	1980[a,b]
Potato chips	27.3	30.9	36.7
Corn/tortilla chips	85.0	70.3	82.1
Cheese curls/balls	51.6	51.8	57.8

[a]Years 1976–1980 compiled from Bonoma, Thomas, "Frito-Lay, Incorporated (A)," HBS Case No. 582-110.
[b]Years 1982–1986 not available.

Market Summary 1980[a]

Potato Chips		Corn Chips		Tortilla Chips	
Vendor	% Market Share	Vendor	% Market Share	Vendor	% Market Share
Laura Scudder	3.1	RJR Nabisco	3.4	Laura Scudder	1.7
Borden	3.0	Planters	1.7	RJR Nabisco	1.4
Lay's	2.8	Laura Scudder	1.3	Borden	.6
Snyders	2.0	Blue Bell	1.0	Bachman	.5
Seyferts	1.8	Bachman	.8	Granny Goose	.5
Total	12.7	Total	8.2	Total	4.7
Frito-Lay	36.7	Frito-Lay	78.5	Frito-Lay	82.9

Cheese Curls/Balls		Pretzels		Total Salty Snacks	
Vendor	% Market Share	Vendor	% Market Share	Vendor	% Market Share
Planters	5.4	RJR Nabisco	12.4	Borden	5.7
Bachman	4.0	Snyders	6.5	RJR Nabisco	2.5
Borden	2.4	Bachman	6.2	Laura Scudder	2.2
Laura Scudder	2.2	Reisman	5.0	Bachman	2.0
RJR Nabisco	1.9	Keebler	3.9	Snyder	1.7
Total	15.9	Total	34.0	Total	14.1
Frito-Lay	57.8	Frito-Lay	14.2	Frito-Lay	45.8

[a]Based on pound share.

Source: "Frito-Lay Incorporated (A)," Bonoma, T., HBS Publishing Division, 1982.

EXHIBIT 3 Traditional Product/Service Delivery Process

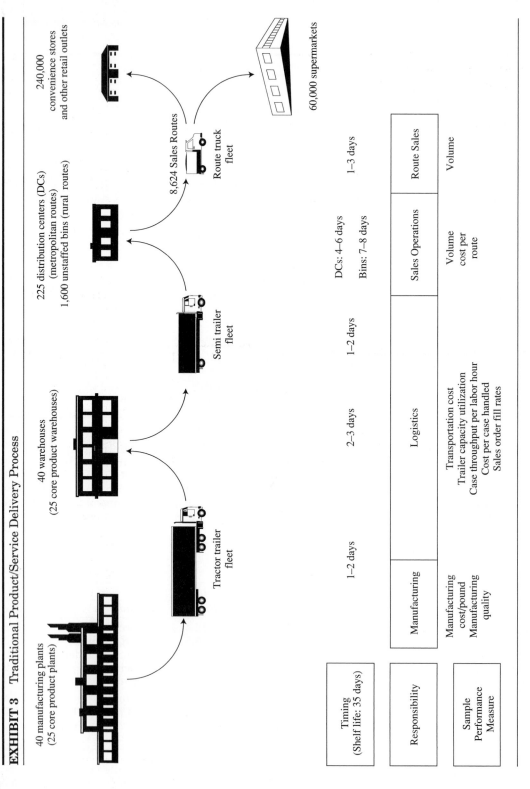

40 manufacturing plants
(25 core product plants)

40 warehouses
(25 core product warehouses)

225 distribution centers (DCs)
(metropolitan routes)
1,600 unstaffed bins (rural routes)

8,624 Sales Routes

240,000
convenience stores
and other retail outlets

60,000 supermarkets

Tractor trailer
fleet

Semi trailer
fleet

Route truck
fleet

Timing (Shelf life: 35 days)	1–2 days	2–3 days	1–2 days	DCs: 4–6 days Bins: 7–8 days	1–3 days
Responsibility	Manufacturing	Logistics		Sales Operations	Route Sales
Sample Performance Measure	Manufacturing cost/pound Manufacturing quality	Transportation cost Trailer capacity utilization Case throughput per labor hour Cost per case handled Sales order fill rates		Volume cost per route	Volume

was discarded. Traditionally it took almost two weeks to move product through our distribution channel. The process of moving product through this pipeline became vastly complicated when you consider that we sell billions of bags of hundreds of products, which may be promoted at various times throughout the year.

Frito-Lay products varied by product category (e.g., corn chips, potato chips), brand, flavor, bag size, and promotional characteristics. Sales volume varied greatly around base volumes according to promotions and time of year. Summer was the high-volume sales season, and it was not uncommon for sales of potato chips to double or triple over the Fourth of July holiday promotion. A Frito-Lay marketing director described the effects of promotions.

Increased sales from promotion lift are one of the major ways we can grow our business. About half of our sales are made to supermarkets, where we promote about 40% of our business. About 80% of our management time is spent trying to understand promotion performance. We know from experience that lift occurs; however, it has historically been very difficult not only to project the magnitude of the lift (so that we can supply the right amount of product), but also to estimate the impact of the promotion on profit, not just sales dollar volume. To complicate the picture even further, we also need to understand the impact of a promotion on our customers. Before they will allow us to run a promotion in their stores, they must be convinced that they too will make a profit.

The U.S. snack market was fragmented with many small, regional competitors when entrepreneurs Herman Lay and Elmer Doolin started separate snack food firms in the early 1900s. By the late 1950s, the two firms owned or distributed more than 18 regional brands, including Fritos corn chips, Lay's and Ruffles potato chips, Rold Gold pretzels, and Cheetos cheese snacks. After expanding their operations separately, they joined forces in 1961, set up headquarters in the Dallas, Texas, area, and stepped up their growth plans. By the time PepsiCo acquired the company, Frito-Lay boasted 46 U.S. plants, more than 150 domestic distribution centers, and a listing on the New York Stock Exchange.

The organization that PepsiCo acquired was highly decentralized. It had grown largely through acquisition of small regional companies, which remained intact after each acquisition. A consulting company, hired in 1968 to help integrate the snack food and beverage divisions, recommended a centralized, functional structure for Frito-Lay to enable it to capitalize on economics of scale in purchasing, manufacturing, distribution, and marketing. The basic structure remained in place until the mid-1980s (see Exhibit 4). D. Wayne Calloway, CEO and president of Frito-Lay, explained:

What we had in the early years was a very decentralized business comprised of many small, regional potato chip companies. Even the manufacturing plants were managed on a regional level. During my first tour of duty at Frito-Lay in the late sixties and early seventies, one of my chief tasks was to help reorganize the company and install centralized planning and control systems.

Calloway pointed out that Frito-Lay was organized into geographic sales centers, or zones:

The zones were financially [and operationally] autonomous in the 1960s. But by 1980, we had here in Dallas seven functional departments, which set policies for the entire company. For instance, our brand management marketing structure assured national consistency across the company.

Frito-Lay was extremely profitable during the 1960s and 1970s, dominating the salty snack market with almost 50% share overall. According to Michael Jordan, who was senior

EXHIBIT 4   Organization Structure (1980)

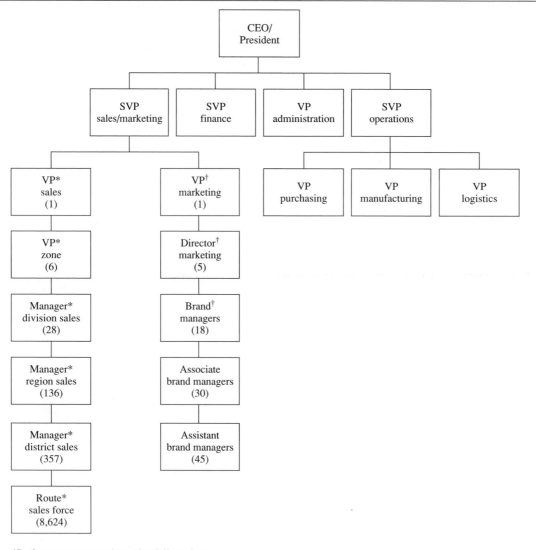

*Performance measured on sales dollar volume
†Performance measured on brand profitability

vice president of operations during the 1970s and was CEO during much of the 1980s:

We were a very successful company during the 1960s and 1970s. Our centralized structure provided us with economies of scale, efficiencies,

and control that our small, regional competitors could not match. Our strategy was to create a quality product and provide excellent customer service through the efforts of our well-trained and well-compensated 10,000-person direct salesforce. We relied on geographic expansion to fuel our growth strategy. Our highly centralized structure also helped us to control costs and manage complexity. Senior management managed a single P&L and assumed responsibility for all profit-and-loss decisions. Functional operating plans and the budgets needed to accomplish them were set in the corporate office, and the major responsibility of managers in the field was to manage to that plan. We leveraged our size by simplifying the business to a national pattern and by focusing our efforts on a minimum number of national, high-leverage, well-executed marketing and product initiatives. This led us to practice what I call "black box management." We put money, programs, and people in one end and got sales, share, and profitability out the other.

But, in the late 1970s, Frito-Lay began to see its traditional growth options evaporating. Its geographic expansion had blanketed the nation, its products were sold in more than 300,000 retail outlets, and there was little new territory to conquer. Attempts to introduce major new national products (brands with $100 million or more in annual sales) had met with marginal success, and established regional and new national competitors, including Anheuser Busch, Borden, and Procter & Gamble, were exerting increasing, competitive pressure. Sales growth slowed from the heady 15–20% of the 1970s to 3–4% in the early 1980s. "When we saw that the sales growth had slowed, we were surprised," explained Charlie Feld, vice president of management information systems (MIS) beginning in 1981. "The machine that had churned out 18% growth year after year had hiccoughed. We were doing the 'right' things but they weren't working. The aircraft carrier that we had built had to be refitted as a PT boat."

As they struggled to make sense of the business downturn, different executives at Frito-Lay presented different views of what had made the company so successful during the 1970s.[2] "The focus of this business is on

execution and marketing control," said Korn. "But if you look around my office, you'll see I have no files of any sort. I run my part of the business with only eight exhibits even though we make almost 170,000 sales calls per day." Calloway countered:

Yes, but formal controls aren't the whole story. The worst sin anyone can commit at Frito-Lay is to fail to communicate. You may have noticed that I have most of the vice presidents within easy reach on this floor—that's no accident.

I think our primary business strengths are distribution and sales. The fact, however, that these areas are subject to rapid change means top management must be involved in the details of the business. That's why we insist on weekly reporting at a minimum. Sales reports are distributed every Friday morning. Manufacturing variance reports arrive each Monday morning. This company is a paper generator, and management has to pick clear, simple measures or it will get buried.[3]

The heart of Frito-Lay is consistency. The Frito-Lay display in Joplin, Missouri, is identical to the one in Waltham, Massachusetts. In fact, the *way* that the display is stocked in Joplin is the same as the way it is stocked in Waltham. (See Exhibit 5 for a summary of Frito-Lay's formal planning and control system in 1980.)

John Cranor, vice president of marketing, continued:

We have to be consistent. We're talking about a business where we served 300,000 outlets last year, each one on an average of two to three times per week. We move almost four billion product units annually.

The Frito-Lay section of a high-volume supermarket exhausts its inventory, or "turns,"

---

[2]The quotes in this section were made in the late 1970s by Frito-Lay managers.

[3]The sales and manufacturers reports were prepared manually by corporate staff who collected handwritten and verbal reports from each plant manager and distribution center manager.

EXHIBIT 5 Summary of Frito-Lay's Formal Planning and Control System in 1980

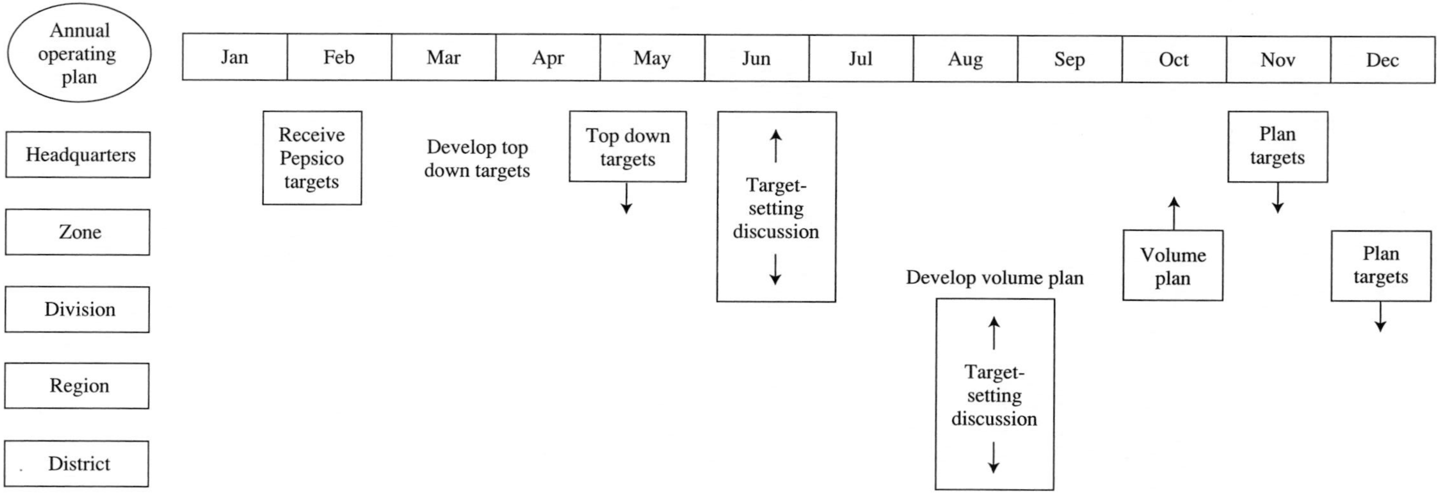

	Jan	Feb	Mar	Apr	May	Jun	Jul	Aug	Sep	Oct	Nov	Dec

Annual operating plan

Headquarters — Receive Pepsico targets | Develop top down targets | Top down targets →

Zone

Division — Target-setting discussion ← →

Region — Develop volume plan | Target-setting discussion ← → | Volume plan ← | Plan targets →

District — Plan targets →

Source: Frito-Lay, Inc.

EXHIBIT 5 (continued) Summary of Frito-Lay's Formal Planning and Control System in 1980

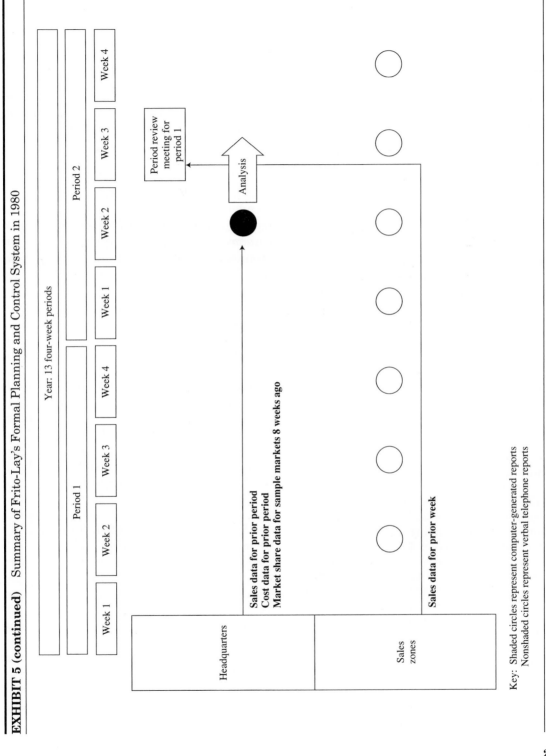

Key: Shaded circles represent computer-generated reports
     Nonshaded circles represent verbal telephone reports

Adapted from: Osborn, C., "Management Support Systems, Interactive Controls, and Strategic Adaptation," unpublished doctoral dissertation, Harvard Business School, 1992.

more than 100 times a year. A particularly well-accepted brand might turn once a day in such a store. We manage all this with a maximum 35-day shelf life on our products and sell half of our volume of goods for cash. You'd better have consistency and control in that kind of an environment, or the whole thing will get away from you in a week.

"No, no, no!" said Jack Demarco, vice president of sales. "All our home office controls and consistency are great. But the real reason this place works so well is that we run our salesforce like an army. They're good, they're disciplined, and they're effective on the street."

Tom Peters and colleagues defined their impression of Frito-Lay's success during the 1970s in their book, *In Search of Excellence.* (See Exhibit 6 for a description of the store-door delivery system commented on in the book and Exhibit 7 for a sample of the detailed procedures in each salesperson's Route Book, which the salesforce called "The Bible.")

> What is striking about Frito is not its brand-management system, which is solid, nor its advertising program, which is well done. What is striking is Frito's nearly 10,000 person salesforce and its 99.5% service level. In practical terms, what does this mean? It means that Frito will do some things that in the short run clearly are uneconomic. It will spend several hundred dollars sending a truck to restock a store with a couple of $30 cartons of potato chips. . . . There are magic and symbolism about the service call that cannot be quantified. . . . The system succeeds because it supports the route salesperson, believes in him [or her] and makes him [or her] feel essential to its success. There are about 25,000 employees in the company. Those who are not selling live by the simple dictum, "Service to Sales."[4]

---

[4]Thomas J. Peters and Robert Waterman, *In Search of Excellence* (NY: Harper & Row, 1982), pp. 164–65.

Strategic Introspection

In the late 1970s, Frito-Lay began to formulate a new strategy that would enable it to meet the challenges of a faster-paced, more competitive environment. The vision started in the sales organization, where Bill Korn, senior vice president of sales and marketing at the time, led a team of sales, marketing, and MIS professionals in defining the "Ideal Sales Organization." The report that came from their efforts provided a series of recommendations which were focused toward redesign of the sales process with decentralization of decision making authority on promotions and product mix to the field salesforce. The centerpiece of their strategy was a micromarketing approach that would require the field salesforce to define "hundreds of local product/market initiatives." Distribution channel options would be expanded to meet the varied requirements of individual customers and new-product development would be markedly increased, enabling the company to focus on smaller share, regional as well as national, brands. "We can't wait for only the $100 million brands to achieve our goals," one manager explained. "Instead, we'll also have to have the $20 million [regional] brands to make it." "In the 1970s, our normal product development cycle was three to four years," another manager commented. "In the future, we need to cut that time in half."

As the Ideal Sales Organization report was circulated throughout the top management team, the operations area also began its own series of studies. Prior to 1980, manufacturing was considered to be a necessary, but not a strategic, component of the business. Marketing was considered the true "powerhouse" where strategy was defined, while sales operations were considered to be a strategic resource for the execution of strategy. One manager com-

---

EXHIBIT 6   Frito-Lay's Store-Door Delivery System (1980)

Frito-Lay's sales and distribution activities revolved around its "store-door" delivery system. In the early hours of the morning, salespeople loaded their trucks with snack food products and began their routes. Their job was to call on existing customers and to line up new accounts. They convinced customers to allocate shelf and end-cap space to Frito-Lay products, and they handled regular account maintenance by restocking shelves and removing stale products. They introduced new products to customers and informed them of promotions.

Most of the salespeople worked from warehouses (that is, a warehouse manager ordered and received product from manufacturing). The salespeople stocked their trucks from the warehouse supply. Approximately 40% of the salespeople, operating from "bin locations," worked in rural areas, where the routes were long and geographically dispersed. Rather than setting up warehouses, Frito-Lay shipped product directly to the salesperson's home or designated storage space.

Customers were divided into two types: supermarkets and "up-and-down-the-street" accounts. The supermarkets were predominantly large chains and up-and-down-the-street accounts were small cash customers. The latter included everything from 7-Eleven franchises to bowling alleys and laundromats. Most of the accounts were serviced twice weekly. Although the time for a sales call varied according to the size of the account, a typical up-and-down-the-street call could be completed in about 45 minutes, not including transportation time. For small customers, the vast majority of the time was devoted to compiling the customer's order from the truck and placing product on the shelves. Supermarkets ordered in case lots; stocking shelves consumed most of the salesperson's time for these customers. For customers with especially strong sales, the salesperson often left "back-stock." The store personnel would then be able to replenish the shelves between sales calls.

To make the stocking activity more routine and to enable substitute drivers to take over routes for vacation and sickness, the "national pattern" was used. It dictated the arrangement of products on the shelves, with a specific place for each product and package size.

---

mented that the approach to manufacturing at that time could be summed up as "Don't screw up." The result was that manufacturing primarily concentrated on ensuring the efficiency of day-to-day operations, rather than defining long-term goals or strategies.

In the early 1980s, as competition and decreased demand eroded pricing freedom, a new emphasis on cost control provided the impetus for manufacturing to begin to rethink how it did business. While the initial focus was on productivity improvement and cost control, in 1982 manufacturing senior management embarked on a strategic planning process to identify the "Ideal Frito-Lay Manufacturing Organization" of the future.

A team composed of the top manufacturing executives—the senior vice president of manufacturing, the five area manufacturing vice presidents, and the vice presidents of quality, industrial engineering, and employee relations—met together to answer the question: "If we built a new Frito-Lay plant within the next few years, what would we want it to look like?"

The group began by developing a mission statement, a charter, and a set of beliefs about the role of manufacturing at Frito-Lay. From these efforts came a general set of strategic goals for manufacturing operations—to operate at the lowest cost, while maintaining the highest quality and being both flexible and innovative. With these

EXHIBIT 7 Sample of the Route Sales Procedure Book—"The Bible"

	Your Route Book
	S-1 To be an effective Frito-Lay salesperson, you must have an organized method of calling on your accounts.
	You also need to know a number of facts about each account.
	• Type of establishment
	• Where is is located
	• How often it is serviced
	• What day(s) you service the account
	Frito-Lay provides a tool to meet the above needs. It is called a Route Book.
	Your District Sales Manager will provide you with a separate route book for each day of the week.
R-1 Route Book	S-2 Each route book contains a number of Route cards.

Source: "Frito Lay, Incorporated (A)," No. 582–110.

EXHIBIT 7 (continued)   Sample of the Route Sales Procedure Book—"The Bible"

			The route cards are placed in the route book in the order of your calls.
			For each call you make on a particular day there is a separate route card.
R-2 **Route Book**		**S-1**	Let's look at a route card and take note of the information which it provides. (See attached.)

R-2
Route Book

S-1

Let's look at a route card and take note of the information which it provides. (See attached.)

Course 5 will go into detail regarding how the information entered on a route card is obtained. For now, just try to become familiar with the layout of the route card.

① It provides information about the account and days of service.
② It is a record of information about the products that an account uses. Note that the products are grouped by price.
③ It contains information about our display, important names, limitations, and where to enter the account.
④ The salesperson uses this section to enter any other necessary information about the account.
⑤ The back of the route card provides a sales history and action plans which need to be taken to build sales.

It's quite clear that a route card is a valuable tool for the salesperson.

R-3
Route Book

S-2

Big/Little Money Maker Route Cards

Each route book will also include special green-colored route cards used to solcit inactive Big/Little accounts. They are called Big/Little Money Maker route cards.

Source: "Frito-Lay, Incorporated (A)," HBS No. 582-110.

EXHIBIT 7 (continued)   Sample of the Route Sales Procedure Book—"The Bible"

ROUTE NO	MN	ACCT NO	SUP	□CASH	□CHG

STORE NAME ①

ADDRESS

STORE NO				SERVICE			
		S	M	T	W	T	F	S

DESCRIPTION				DESCRIPTION			
	DRP	SLTD	CASH	CH PS	PRTZ STIK	PRTZ TWST	PRTZ TT	PRTZ ROD
	TST PS	CH O CH	DPLX	OTML	69¢ CRS	CRS	ON SNK	
	MRSH	FG BRN	PNT STR		79¢ CCG	POT CRSP	PR REG	
	CC REG	CC DC ②	PC EG	PC BBQ	79¢ 8 PK	CC REG	PC REG	TC NHO	CPS CR
25¢	PC SCO	PC DIP	PC DP BBQ	PC NAT	BEEF JERKY	PC REG	PC BBQ	PC SCO
	POT CRSP	TC NA CHO	TC SCO	CPS CR	PC DIP	PC DP BBQ	PC NAT	
	CFS NHO	TC RD TS	TC RD NHO	CRS GO	PRTZ YWST	PRTZ TT		
	CRS ZC	ON SNK	PR REG	PRTZ TWST	89¢ CFS PF	CFS CR	CFS NHO	
	CGC	POP CRN	CHS CRN		CC REG	CC EC	CC BBQ	
29¢	GRN ON	BAC ON	TOST ON		TC REG	TC TACO	TC SCO	TC NHO
30¢	BEEF JKY	HOT SAU	BEEF STK	JAR JKY	TC RD TS	TC RD NHO		
33¢	SM EN DIP	SM EN DIP		99¢	PC REG	PC DIP		
	PC REG	PC DIP	CC REG	CC KS	1.19 C	CC REG	CC KS	
59¢	TC REG	TC TACO	TC NHO	1.29 C	TC NHO			
	CFS PUFF	CFS PUFF		1.39 C	PC REG	PC DIP	VAR PAK	
62¢ 6 PK	CC REG	PC REG	PC DIP	BULK	PC DIP			
	TC NHO	CFS CR		CDY	DRP	CH PB	TOST	CH O CH
63¢	IG BN DIP	IG EN DIP	79¢	TACO DIP	DPLX	OTML	MRSH	FG BRN	PNT BTR

ENTRANCE	DISPLAY TYPE	□FREE STANDING	TOTAL F-L SECTION FT
□FRONT □REAR	□CUSTOMADE □IN-GONDOLA □CLIP RACK	□COUNTER □PSD	

MANAGER

RECEIVING CLERK ③

TIME FACTOR   □DISPLAYABLE ACCOUNT

DRIVING INSTRUCTIONS/REMARKS

④

SALES HISTORY		OPPORTUNITIES
DATE	TOTAL SALES	1
/	$	2
/	$	3
/	$	4
/	$	ACTION TAKEN OR PLANNED
/	$	
/	$	
/	$	
/	$	
/	$	
/	$	
/	$	
/	$	⑤
/	$	
/	$	
/	$	
/	$	
/	$	
/	$	
/	$	
/	$	
/	$	
/	$	
/	$	
/	$	
/	$	
/	$	
/	$	
/	$	
/	$	
/	$	
/	$	
/	$	
/	$	
/	$	
/	$	
/	$	
/	$	
/	$	
/	$	
/	$	
/	$	
/	$	
/	$	
/	$	
/	$	
/	$	

Source: "Frito-Lay, Incorporated (A)," HBS No. 582-110.

goals in mind, the group redefined manufacturing operations using a popular organization development methodology, which included five areas of assessment: (1) define the primary tasks needed to accomplish the goals of the organization; (2) define the product, process, and information technologies needed to perform the tasks; (3) define the human resource expertise and skills needed; (4) establish an organization structure that groups individuals into work units and develop effective communication and management systems for coordinating and controlling operations; and (5) establish a mechanism for evaluation and renewal.

Using this approach, the group defined a set of organization design principles to guide implementation of its new manufacturing strategy. These principles emphasized "people" as the key resource for achieving manufacturing competitiveness in the future. In 1983, the principles were applied at several existing manufacturing locations, and at a new plant built in Casa Grande, Arizona. While there was some evidence of success within isolated manufacturing facilities, most agreed that the most lasting and widespread contribution was the development of a formal program for establishing linkages between manufacturing and the rest of the company. Called the "Point Person" system, each member of the manufacturing strategy team was responsible for regular contacts with an individual in another function, such as marketing, sales, or engineering. The system improved understanding and facilitated communication between manufacturing and the other functions.

The final area of activity that influenced the development of the strategic vision for change at the company concerned the development of the necessary information technology (IT) infrastructure to support the new strategy and emerging organization design. Jordan summarized the thinking of senior management at that time: "We recognized in the late 1970s and early 1980s that we needed to manage in a much more differentiated, focused, and time-sensitive manner to meet the increasing competition in the industry. But to manage the added complexity and speed we would need more accurate, focused, and timely information. During this same time it also became apparent to all of us that access to this type of information was a limiting factor that was preventing us from reacting to the rapidly changing marketplace."

Until the 1980s, the information, perspective, and expertise needed to manage the complexity and speed of the business resided primarily in the heads of Frito-Lay's senior management team, all located in offices next to one another on the same floor in corporate headquarters. The ability to simplify the business to a national pattern and to reduce the pace of decision making to fit within a yearly planning cycle enabled them to make both strategic and operating decisions for the entire organization.

A cornerstone of the "Ideal Sales Organization" report was the need for a handheld computer (HHC) device that would enable the field salesforce to collect data on every sales transaction for every customer (see Exhibit 8). The data would be fed into computers at corporate headquarters over standard telephone lines each evening where they would form the basis for the development of a new corporate information infrastructure, which, when integrated with external market information from supermarket scanners, would be used to enable the new micromarketing strategy. In addition, the HHCs would automate much of the routine paperwork performed by the salespeople and would provide them with up-to-date, detailed information on each customer. By eliminating routine, non-value-added work, the company hoped to free up time so

EXHIBIT 8   On-Truck Equipment for the HHC

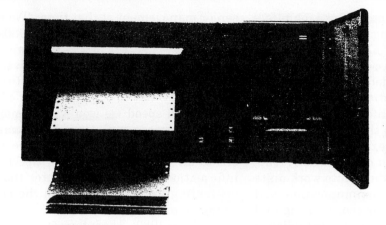

Servicing a Typical Small Account

Without Computer	With Computer

5:00 AM—At the Warehouse:

Without Computer	With Computer
Salesperson checks notebook for standard customer order quantities.	Same.
Picks product and loads truck.	Same.
Fills out consignment order form.	Enters consignment order into computer.

6:00 AM—On the Route—For Each Store:

Without Computer	With Computer
Checks shelves and removes stales.	Same.
Fills out sales ticket.	Enters order quantity in computer.
Enters stales as credits on sales tickets.	Enters stales in computer.
Compiles order from stock on truck.	Printer prints pick list. Salesperson pulls order from stock on truck.
Checks in with store receiver.*	Same.
Puts product on shelves.	Same.
Calculates total order price, applying promotional prices where necessary.	"Confirms" order on the computer. Printer produces sales ticket.
Collects order price, usually in cash, from store manager.	Same.

4:00 PM—At the Warehouse:

Without Computer	With Computer
Turns in sales tickets and fills out "end-of-day" report.	Connects HHC to a modem.†
Paperwork sent to sales administration for scanning.	Sales transaction data sent to corporate computer.
	Price, product, and promotion information sent from corporate computer to HHC.

6:00 PM—At Home:

Without Computer	With Computer
Reviews sales tickets to make sure calculations were correct.	Relax.

*The check-in process involved the salesperson's counting all of the items in the order in front of the store receiver, thus ensuring delivery of exactly what was shown on the order.

†A modem is a computer device that enables data from a computer to be sent to another computer over a telephone line.

that the salesforce would then be able to use the information to implement a customized sales approach with each customer.

Pilot efforts in Mesquite, Texas, and in Minneapolis had documented efficiency improvements of at least one half hour per day for each driver. Furthermore, because each salesperson "bought" the contents of his or her truck each morning, accounting errors were charged directly to take-home pay. In 1985, out-of-balance was $4 million nationwide and growing. This was a source of extreme frustration for salespeople and sales management. It was not uncommon for a salesperson to be disputing up to $500 with the corporate sales service personnel. After implementation of the pilot, a salesperson in Mesquite, Texas, commented.

> The sales calls go faster, the end-of-day process is a snap, and my wife and I don't have to spend an hour every night going over the paperwork to make sure I did all the multiplication right. When we have problems with the handheld computers, no one wants to tell headquarters, for fear they might take them away from us!

Finally, the HHC was seen as a necessary tool to manage the added complexity of the sales process that would result from the micromarketing approach. One of the most compelling benefits of the project was that it replaced the existing sales transaction processing system. Because each of Frito-Lay's retail customers was serviced on an average of twice a week, the sales transaction volume was huge. With the product list growing, transactions were also becoming more and more complex. Each sales transaction for a charge customer now required two tickets reflecting approximately two hundred line items, and these were in addition to end-of-day and ordering paperwork. Further, the complexity increased geometrically when special promotions were applied. To capture

the transactions, Frito-Lay had installed optical scanners in 1974. Feld estimated:

> It would take 1200 or 1300 keypunch operators to handle our current transaction volume. Today we do it with 5 scanners and 40 correction operators. The bad news is that IBM has stopped manufacturing the scanners. By 1988, we won't be able to get them repaired. We knew we needed an alternative, and the handheld computer appeared to be the ideal solution.

The scanners processed 1.7 million documents per four-week period. This transaction volume included sales tickets for all charge customers, salespeople's orders, and daily activity reports. It did not include detailed sales information on up-and-down-the-street customers who typically paid in cash. Each salesperson summarized the cash transactions on one line of his or her daily report, as shown in Exhibit 9.

"We had the idea for the HHC back in the late 1970s," Korn explained,

> but at the time the technology just didn't exist. We approached large computer manufacturers, but they were not interested in helping us with the R&D. We finally found a Japanese firm that was interested in partnering with us on the idea. They offered to develop a prototype for us to test the concept, without requiring us to commit to a large capital investment. We estimated that the cost of a full scale rollout of the HHCs would be approximately $40 million for the hardware.

Monte Jones, director of sales systems development, summarized the project's cost/benefit justification:

> It costs us $12 million per year to run our current system. With the handheld computer, the annual operating costs would increase by only $3 million. The differential is a small price to pay, considering the long-term strategic benefits we expect to achieve. The effective use of the HHC was expected to result in two and a half hours per route per week of time saved pricing the tickets and completing end-of-day paperwork. Sales management was committed

EXHIBIT 9 Sales Ticket Used by the Salesforce (1986)

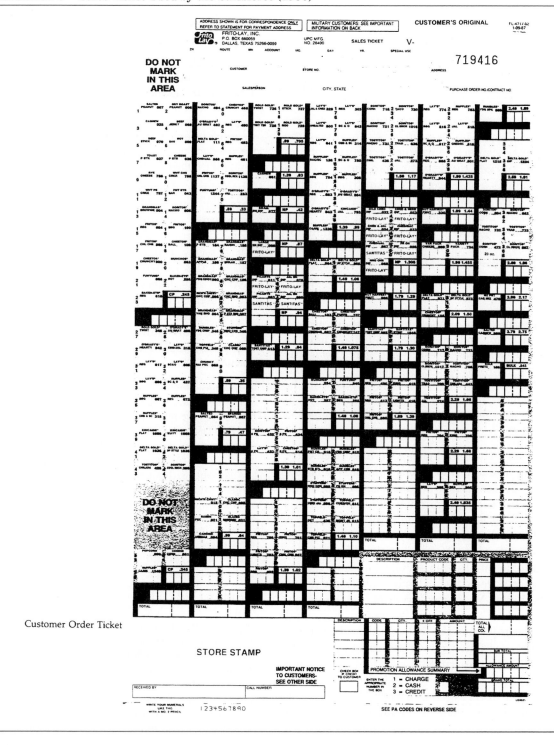

Customer Order Ticket

EXHIBIT 9 (continued)   Sales Ticket Used by the Salesforce (1986)

Frito Lay ® DAILY REPORT

TRUCK MILEAGE CERTIFICATION
DSM SIGNS   AND   ENTERS CERTIFICATION CODE →

SALESPERSON

ZONE	ROUTE	MIN	MO	DAY	YR

810433

SPEEDOMETER READING (ROUNDED TO NEAREST MILES)	END	00
	BEGIN	00
MILES DRIVEN		53

TRUCK ASSET NO.	95	B	
GALS. OF GAS PURCHASED OR OBTAINED FROM COMPANY PUMP (ENTER 10THS OR "0")			51
QUARTS OF OIL ADDED (WHOLE QUARTS)	52		

	TC	AMOUNT	OFFICE USE ONLY
COST OF GAS PURCHASED	50		
COST OF MOTOR OIL PURCHASED	38		
POSTAGE AND MONEY ORDER FEES	42		
TELEPHONE	45		
OPERATING SUPPLIES	41		
NEW STORE OPENING	64		
SCHOOL DISCOUNT	39		
PA ITEM			
ITEM			
ITEM			
OTHER EXPENSE			
PM "A" SERVICE ONLY ENTER ODOMETER READING	55		
TRUCK EXPENSE REPAIRS	46		
TIRES AND TUBES	54		
TRUCK WASHING	56		
SALES TAX COLLECTED INDICATE STATE			
SALES TAX COLLECTED			
OTHER DEBITS			
TOTAL EXPENSES AND ALLOWANCES			
TOTAL SALES (AT STORE DOOR)	98		
LESS CHARGE SALES	32		
EXPENSES AND ALLOWANCES			
CHECKS AND MONEY ORDERS	31		

ATTACH SUPPORTING DOCUMENTS HERE

FL-3930-08

WRITE YOUR NUMERALS LIKE THIS WITH A NO. 2 PENCIL   1 2 3 4 5 6 7 8 9 0

ATTACH SUPPORTING DOCUMENTS AS REQUIRED. DISTRIBUTION: WHITE AND YELLOW: FIELD ACCOUNTING. PINK: SALESPERSON. GOLD: DSM.

to using this time to drive an additional $20 million in annual sales to cover [the increase in] operating costs.

As Korn proceeded with pilot studies to test the feasibility of the new HHC proto-type, it became clear that the MIS organization was not up to the task. During the 1970s, four MIS managers had been hired to "fix information system problems." Between 1978 and 1981, the MIS budget grew from $4 million to $18 million, but management was hard pressed to identify the added value that came from those investments. The HHC project floundered for lack of IT management skills. In April 1981, Charlie Feld was hired by the senior management team to provide the MIS leadership that would be needed to enable implementation of the micromarketing strategy. He inher-ited an organization in crisis—low morale contributed to a turnover among MIS pro-fessionals that exceeded 40% per year and an average seniority that was less than two years, aging software created maintenance nightmares, and a large backlog of system requests resulted in disgruntled users who had begun to develop and run their own stand-alone systems (see Exhibit 10).

Feld spent the early 1980s upgrading the skills and expertise of the MIS professional staff and consolidating and updating the technology and systems within the com-pany's data center. By late 1984, he was ready to turn his attention to the HHC pro-ject, which had progressed very little over the past three years. The strategic impor-tance of the HHC project increased dramati-cally in early 1985, when Korn replaced Jordan as president of Frito-Lay.[5] (See Exhibit 11 for a summary of management succession during the 1980s.)

Implementing the Ideal Sales Organization Vision

Upon assuming control of Frito-Lay, Korn, in a speech to securities analysts, articulated two goals for the company: (1) to sustain at least 6% real sales growth, and (2) to achieve double-digit profit growth. Recogniz-ing that he could not achieve these goals without the micromarketing strategy, Korn began implementation of the key compo-nents of the Ideal Sales Organization report.

Restructuring the Field Sales Organization

Executing the micromarketing strategy required that the field salesforce begin to make promotion and product mix decisions that were formally made by brand market-ing account managers in corporate head-quarters. Recognizing that the current salesforce had neither the expertise and skills nor the access to market information needed to make these decisions,[6] Korn decided to limit the number of people who would be given this responsibility by focus-ing only on key accounts. (In the mid 1980s, large supermarket chains accounted for 75% of the company's profits.) In early 1985, he embarked on one of the first major restruc-turings of the company since the early 1970s—a process the company called "seg-mentation." Before segmentation, each salesperson was responsible for serving all of the snack outlets on his or her route—both grocery stores and "up-and-down-the-street" accounts. The salesforce was compensated with a base salary plus com-mission, which was based on sales dollar vol-ume, regardless of customer type. Because the majority of the commission came from

---

EXHIBIT 10 Frito-Lay, Inc.: Consultant Study Results, 1982

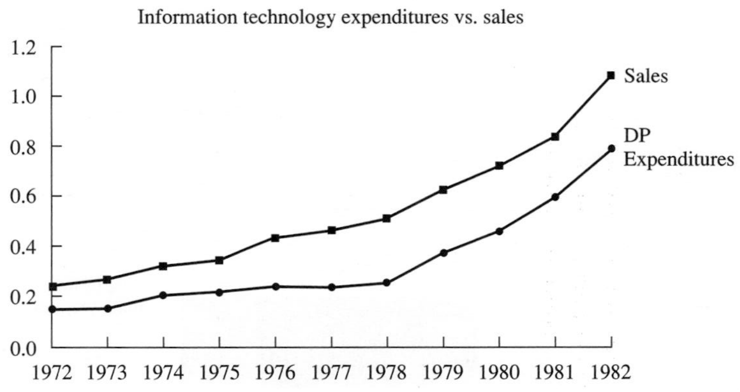

Information technology expenditures as a percentage of sales

Industry average

Frito-Lay

Percentage of sales

0.9 0.8 0.7 0.6 0.5 0.4 0.3 0.2 0.1 0.0

1972 1973 1974 1975 1976 1977 1978 1979 1980 1981 1982

Information technology expenditures vs. sales

Sales

DP Expenditures

1.2 1.0 0.8 0.6 0.4 0.2 0.0

1972 1973 1974 1975 1976 1977 1978 1979 1980 1981 1982

		Compound	
Sales growth	18% → 20%	→ 18%
DP growth	17% → 31%	→ 22%

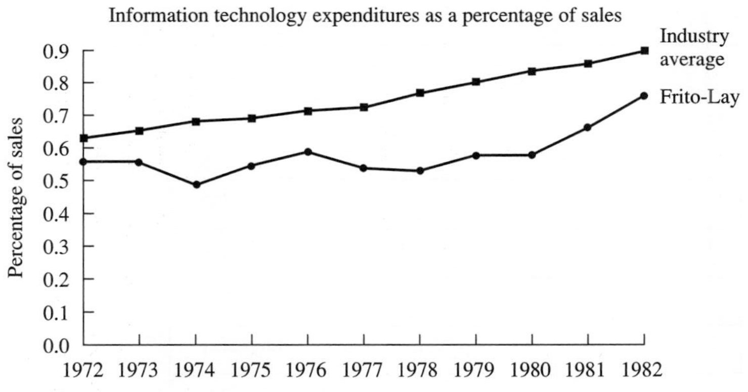

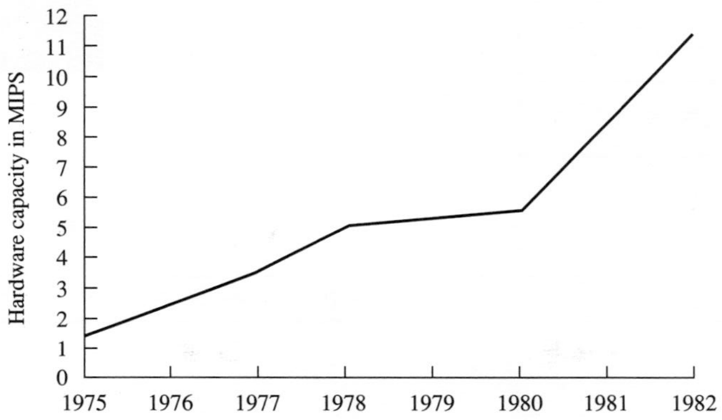

Hardware capacity in MIPS

12 11 10 9 8 7 6 5 4 3 2 1 0

1975 1976 1977 1978 1979 1980 1981 1982

EXHIBIT 10 (continued)   Frito-Lay, Inc.: Consultant Study Results, 1982

Quality assessment of MIS-developed applications

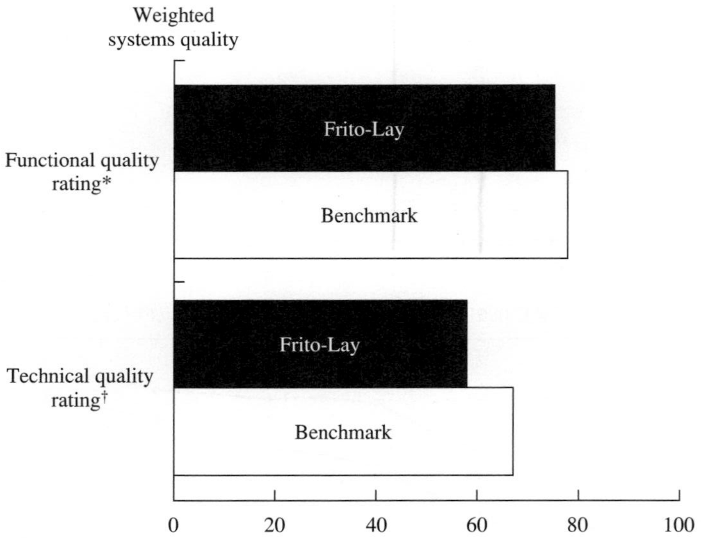

Weighted
systems quality

Functional quality
rating*

| Frito-Lay |
| Benchmark |

Technical quality
rating†

| Frito-Lay |
| Benchmark |

0   20   40   60   80   100

* Rated by end users.
† Rated by MIS staff.

**Percentage of applications developed
outside the centralized MIS area**

Functional area	Percentage of applications developed by functional area
Research and development	100%
Engineering	46%
Manufacturing	30%
Marketing	25%
Employee relations	20%
Distribution	12%
Finance	4%
Sales	1%
Purchasing	0%

EXHIBIT 10 (continued) Frito-Lay, Inc.: Consultant Study Results, 1982

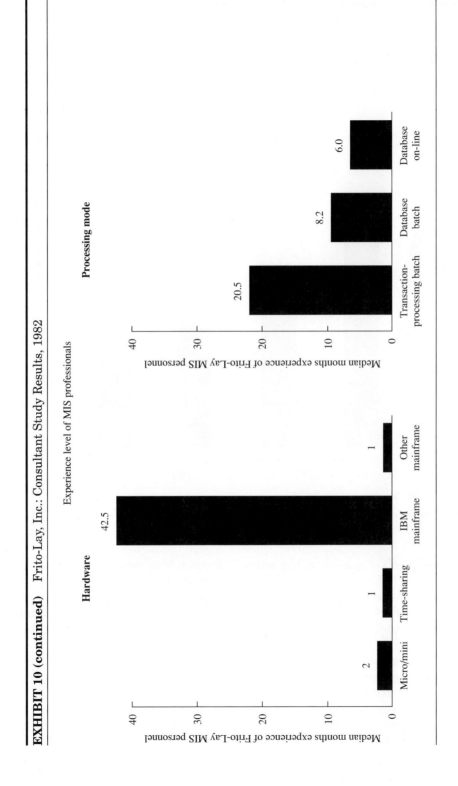

EXHIBIT 10 (continued)   Frito-Lay, Inc.: Consultant Study Results, 1982

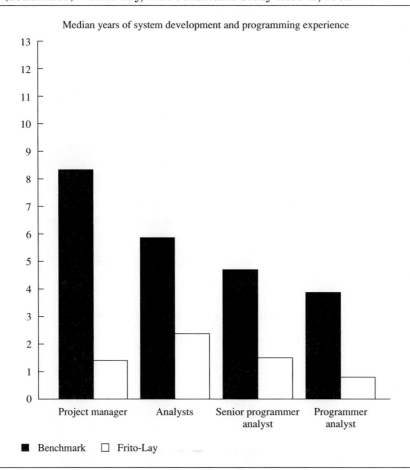

Median years of system development and programming experience

■ Benchmark   □ Frito-Lay

the large supermarket accounts, the salesforce concentrated its attention on them. "Some of the guys were making $40,000 or more in those days," a salesperson remarked. "There was a three-month waiting list to get a job at Frito-Lay."

Under segmentation, the salesforce was divided into two groups: route and supermarket. The route drivers focused attention on the up-and-down-the-street accounts, while the supermarket drivers focused attention on the large supermarket ac-

counts. The work of the route drivers was essentially unchanged. They continued to perform both sales and merchandising activities. (Sales activities included working directly with the store managers to negotiate shelf space and ensure that Frito-Lay products received favorable display within the store. Merchandising activities included restocking the shelves and checking for, and removing, stale product.) But the work of the supermarket drivers changed dramatically. While they continued to perform the

EXHIBIT 10 (continued)   Frito-Lay, Inc.: Consultant Study Results, 1982

MIS resource spending mix

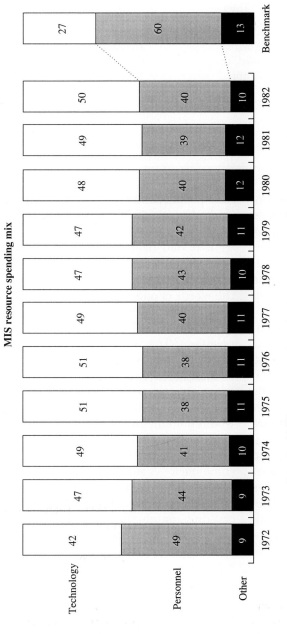

Percent of MIS resources spent on development versus maintenance and enhancement

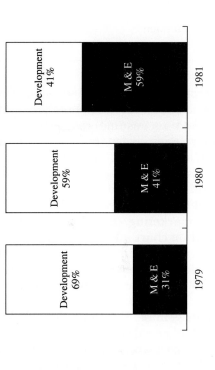

EXHIBIT 11 Management Succession During the 1980s

	1980	1982	1984	1986
CEO/President	Calloway	Calloway	Jordan	Korn
Sales/Marketing	Beeby	Korn	Demarco	Kiely
Operations	Jordan	Jordan	O'Neal	O'Neal
Finance	Anton	Anton	Vacant	Schutzman
Human Resources	Ewing	Ewing	Costello	Messana
Management Information Services	Basso	Feld	Feld	Feld

merchandising activities, a new position, called a key account manager (KAM), was created to assume responsibility for the sales activities for the large accounts. Decision authority on local promotions and product mix was passed down to the KAMs. The KAM position was staffed by high-potential field sales employees and staff from corporate marketing. (See Exhibit 12 for an organization chart after segmentation.)

In addition to the change in their work, segmentation also changed the compensation of both supermarket and route drivers. The route drivers continued to receive 5% of sales dollar volume. But in an attempt to balance the higher sales volumes of large accounts, the supermarket merchandisers were paid $0.05 per bag sold, regardless of the unit price. While the intent of segmentation was to focus attention on the two primary distribution channels while establishing parity in route and supermarket compensation, as implemented, it reduced the take-home pay of most of the salesforce. To soften the impact, the company promised to make up the difference for a year and to make partial payments for two additional years.

The new supermarket routes had different appeal in different parts of the country. In the Southwest, where Frito-Lay held an 80% share of the salty snack market, experienced salespeople asked for the merchandiser positions despite the view by most that the job was much less interesting and challenging than it had been previously. In most other regions, however, drivers with seniority eagerly accepted the convenience routes. In the words of one, "What I liked about this job was the people. Why would I trade my route for a day full of bickering with supermarket receivers? They couldn't pay me enough to do that." Another route salesperson commented, "Segmentation was a disaster. When it first came out, they sent around a human relations guy to talk to us about it. He said he would hold meetings every quarter to help us work out the bugs. He got such an earful of problems at the first meeting that he never came back." A salesperson in another part of the country remarked, "Several guys walked off the job right then. I didn't because I couldn't match the pay anywhere else. If I could, I'd leave tomorrow." A supervisor added, "They talk about 'Service to Sales,' but a program like this tells us what they really think of us."

Despite the implementation difficulties, Korn persevered with the segmentation program. In 1986, he commented:

Segmentation is a critical first step in our strategic repositioning. It allows one segment

EXHIBIT 12   Frito-Lay Organization Chart, 1986 (after segmentation)

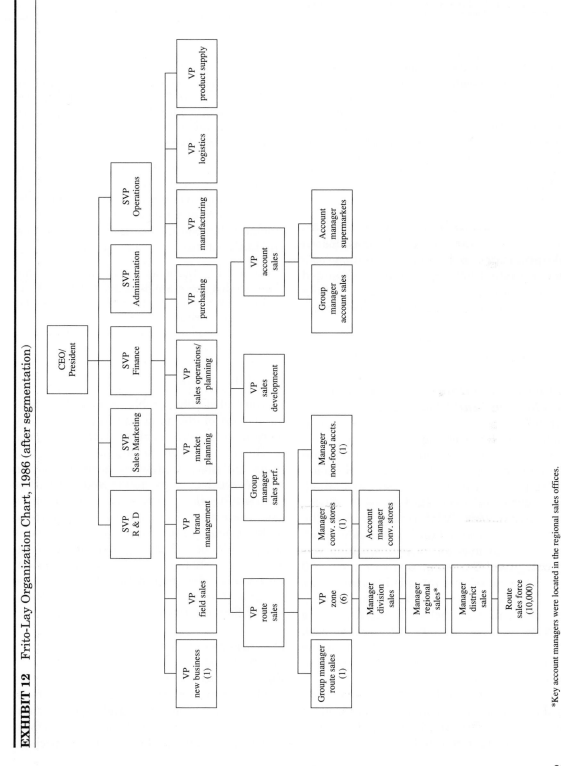

*Key account managers were located in the regional sales offices.

of the Frito-Lay salesforce to focus as never before on supermarkets, the largest and fastest-growing distribution channel. Meanwhile, other members of the route salesforce can concentrate on more complete coverage of the smaller account customer channel. In 1986, we knew that these smaller accounts represented about 80% of our account base but only 25% of our profits. We had very little information on them, and our salesforce had traditionally neglected them in favor of the higher-volume large accounts.

The salesforce turnover was used as an opportunity to hire more college-educated salespeople and to fine-tune the route structure. By late 1986, segmentation extended up to the level of the vice president of field sales, and 6,000 of the 10,000 salespeople were operating under segmentation. The remaining 4,000 worked in rural areas, where segmentation was not feasible.

Increasing the Rate of New-Product Development and Shortening Cycle Times

During the same period, the company also moved ahead with an unprecedented stream of new-product introductions. Dori Reap, director of planning in 1986, explained: "New products were the biggest news for Frito-Lay in 1986. With real growth in the salty snack market of only 3–4%, new products were an avenue toward reaching our growth goals." The company had almost 100 products in 1985 and intended to expand its line to 400 by 1990. The expansion of product development included extensions to existing lines and new snack categories. Some of the extensions were targeted as regional products (e.g., Frito Chili Cheese Corn Chips for the Southwest).

In addition to the larger number of new products, Korn also sought faster product introductions. Bill Elston, vice president of manufacturing, remarked:

Before 1986, a three- to four-year product introduction cycle was normal for us. During 1986, management asked us to turn a "hat trick" by simultaneously introducing Stuffers, Rumbles, and Toppels from R&D to full-scale production in 14 months. We made a significant investment in manufacturing facilities before we had any firm test-market results.

The investment in new manufacturing facilities was consistent with the company's efforts to improve productivity. Of 40 plants, 25 were "core mixing plants," which focused on high-volume brands such as Doritos, Fritos, and Lay's potato chips. Elston continued:

The impact of product proliferation was that we needed more single-focus facilities. Running new products into existing plants was disruptive. Frito-Lay had the volume to build single-focus plants; it's a competitive advantage for us.

Problems Surface

By the end of 1986, problems with the implementation of the micromarketing strategy were beginning to surface. Lacking access to the information to support their decisions, and motivated by an incentive system that rewarded sales dollar volume rather than profitability, the key account managers used their newly granted decision powers to make promotion and product mix decisions that, while beneficial to their accounting, were not beneficial for the organization. Profitability declined in 1986 by 14.5% on a 6% growth in sales. On November 25, 1986, a *Wall Street Journal* headline reported:

President Quits at PepsiCo's Largest Unit

Korn's resignation was announced as part of a major reorganization of PepsiCo's snack food business. Domestic and international snack food divisions were combined to form PepsiCo Worldwide Foods under Michael

Jordan. PepsiCo reported that it had combined the international and domestic snack food businesses to give it "global strike capabilities." Overseas markets were expected to grow faster than domestic markets for several years, and PepsiCo held only about 10% of the $5 billion international snack food market in 1986. As he assumed control of the newly formed PepsiCo Worldwide Foods, Jordan wondered how he could return the domestic business to profitability in the short term, while moving forward with the changes required to ensure long-term viability.

Case 3–3

FRITO-LAY, INC.: A STRATEGIC TRANSITION, 1987–1992 (ABRIDGED)[1]

In early 1987, a manager commented on the events that led Willard Korn to resign from Frito-Lay in December 1986 as profits plummeted:[2]

> When we attempted to change the way we did business, the organization ground to a halt. We did not have the management processes, organization and information systems in place to support the new strategy, and people continued to make decisions as if we were still operating under the old strategy. Paper-based processes and hierarchical management control systems simply were not timely and flexible enough to permit us to react to rapidly changing market conditions. Problems surfaced. New products went stale in warehouses when salespeople found they weren't selling. Information on regional promotions sometimes came long after the increased inventory had been shipped to warehouses, and other times inventory did not arrive until after the promotion had taken place.

Upon assuming the reins of Frito-Lay, Inc. in January 1987, Michael Jordan, CEO of PepsiCo Worldwide Foods, immediately abandoned the micromarketing strategy and returned control of decision making on promotions and product mix to corporate headquarters. He returned to a national pattern and reinstated tight control of strategy execution. Recognizing the need for improved understanding of the needs of key accounts and small customers, he maintained the key account manager position and the segmentation of the salesforce, and then proceeded with the implementation of the handheld computer (HHC) and information systems required to support managerial decision making and operations under the new strategy. He led a re-examination of the vision for change, which reaffirmed the appropriateness of the strategy in general

This case was prepared by Professor Lynda M. Applegate.
[1]Copyright © 1995 by the President and Fellows of Harvard College.
Harvard Business School case 9-195-238.
[2]See *Frito-Lay, Inc.: A Strategic Transition, 1980–1986* (HBS No. 194-107), for a discussion of the events that led up to Jordan's appointment. As CEO of the worldwide snack food business for PepsiCo, Jordan led an aggressive program of global expansion. This case covers only changes to domestic operations.

but clarified and refocused its execution. Jordan explained:

I don't think any of us fully appreciated how highly leveraged and integrated our business truly was until the aborted attempt at implementing the micromarketing strategy in 1986. The problems were so abrupt and severe that it made a lasting impression on all of us. Three major lessons came from this situation. First, it became very clear that we needed to recast our vision for a change as a corporatewide initiative rather than just a field sales initiative. The integrated nature of the business and the absence of time and inventory buffers demanded an interfunctional approach. Where before we believed we were transferring decision-making authority on isolated decisions (e.g., promotions and product mix) to line managers, we now recognized that we would need to create interfunctional business teams who would manage profitably and operations locally. Second, we became aware that we could not give up the efficiency and control benefits that we achieved through our centralized structure, to gain the flexibility and speed that we wished to achieve through our new decentralized structure. It became clear that the organization we needed to create was really a hybrid that would allow us to achieve the benefits of centralization and decentralization simultaneously. Finally, the need to provide the information to support both decentralized decision making and centralized control was essential and, we believed, would need to precede organizational restructuring.

Between 1987 and 1989, Jordan and the senior management team led the company through two interrelated efforts designed to build the organizational and information infrastructure that they believed would enable them to implement the micromarketing strategy without loss of control. The first set of initiatives was focused on improving productivity and gaining control of operating processes. Initial efforts were targeted toward improving understanding of the business, redesigning work, and improving productivity and quality within functional areas. Toward the end of 1989, the emphasis shifted toward integrating, streamlining, and time-synchronizing operating processes across functional areas. The second set of initiatives involved the development of flexible, dynamic, integrated information infrastructure, which would enable line employees and managers throughout the company to obtain access to timely and relevant information to support the micromarketing strategy. (See Exhibits 1 and 2 for a financial and market summary between 1987 and 1992.)

Functional Redesign

Early in 1987, Jordan divided domestic operations into 32 geographic areas, called Frito-Lay Market Areas (FLMAs). "Memo" P&Ls were developed that provided a rough approximation of revenues, costs, and contributions to profit before taxes for each area.[3] The data supplied from these analyses were used to support a new corporatewide quality improvement program. Under the banner of the quality program, management targeted the 10 poorest performing FLMAs for improvement. For the most part, work was redesigned at the local level, but, in some instances, joint efforts from manufacturing, logistics, and sales, and from corporate marketing and product development, were also required. The focus on contribution to profit, rather than just cost, helped functional management develop a better appreciation of the trade-off decisions that needed to be made to balance local and corporatewide objectives. The cumulative impact of the improvements secondary

---

[3]Memo P&Ls provided a general understanding of the business but were not used to formally restructure the company into profit centers, nor were they used to redefine incentive systems.

EXHIBIT 1 Financial Summary

	1987	1988	1989	1990	1991	1992
PepsiCo						
Revenues	$11,485.0	$13,007.0	$15,242.0	$17,803.0	$19,607.9	$21,970.0
Operating profit	1,321.0	1,485.0	1,932.0	2,178.0	2,196.0	2,502.0
Total assets	9,022.7	11,135.3	15,126.7	17,143.4	18,775.1	20,956.2
Net profit	594.8	762.2	901.4	1,076.9	1,080.1	374.3
Frito-Lay						
Revenues	3,202.0	3,514.3	4,215.0	5,054.0	5,565.8	6,132.1
Operating profit	548.0	610.0	774.0	893.0	757.0	985.0
Total assets	1,632.0	1,641.0	3,366.0	3,892.0	4,114.3	4,628.0
Revenues as a % of the Pepsi total	27.9%	27.0%	27.7%	28.4%	28.4%	27.9%
Operating profit as a % of the Pepsi total	41.5%	44.0%	42.0%	41.0%	35.0%	39.0%
Assets as a % of total Pepsi assets	18.1%	14.7%	22.3%	22.7%	21.9%	22.1%
Frito-Lay year-to-year revenue growth rate						
Domestic	4.6%	5.4%	9.5%	19.9%	10.1%	10.2%
International	13.3%	38.6%	72.8%			
Frito-Lay year-to-year operating profit growth rate						
Domestic	31.6%	12.9%	13.8%	15.4%	−15.2%	30.0%
International	20.0%	63.8%	204.0%			

EXHIBIT 2 Market Summary: U.S. Salty Snacks (in millions)

	1987	1988	1989	1990	1991	1992
Potato chips	$2,890	$3,048	$3,275	$3,442	$3,463	$3,480
Corn/tortilla chips	1,421	1,607	1,847	1,950	1,951	1,921
Extruded snacks[a]	535	565	621	676	687	659
Pretzels	303	327	381	422	517	575
All others	2,161	2,353	2,450	2,639	2,884	3,280
Total salty snacks	$7,310	$7,900	$8,574	$9,129	$9,502	$9,915

Frito-Lay, Inc.: U.S. Market Share (%)
Potato Chips

Vendor	1988	1989	1990	1991	1992
Borden	16.4	15.7	15.7	14.9	14.2
Eagle	2.5	5.6	5.8	6.9	8.9
Curtice Burns	NA	NA	2.8	3.5	2.9
Keebler	3.3	NA	NA	NA	NA
Total	22.2	21.3	24.3	25.3	26.0
Frito-Lay	34.9	34.0	34.0	34.4	35.7

Corn / Tortilla Chips

Vendor	1988	1989	1990	1991	1992
Borden	6.7	7.0	6.7	6.4	5.7
Keebler	1.6	1.9	1.3	2.3	1.9**
RJR Nabisco	1.2	NA	1.0	1.3	1.0**
Eagle	1.7	NA	NA	3.0	2.3
Total	11.2	8.9	9.0	13.0	10.9
Frito-Lay	76.9	76.9	66.6	NA	59.5

Cheese Curls / Balls

Vendor	1988	1989	1990	1991	1992
Borden	11.4	11.0	10.5	12.2	12.7**
RJR Nabisco	9.5	8.8	8.0	12.5	11.8**
General Mills	4.7	5.3	5.3	6.7	6.7**
Eagle	NA	3.0	4.8	NA	NA
Total	25.6	28.1	28.6	31.4	31.2**
Frito-Lay	41.7	41.5	54.8	50.0	49.9**

Fabricated Chips

Vendor	1988	1989	1990	1991	1992
Keebler	35.1	47.9	51.8	54.6	52.2
Procter & Gamble	50.9	45.5	37.3	37.0	37.2
Total	86.0	93.4	89.1	91.6	89.4
Frito-Lay	14.0	10.6	10.9	8.3	8.8

[a]Category primarily consists of cheese curls/balls.
**Estimates based on changes in IRI channel.

Source: *Snack Food Magazine* annual surveys.

to the work redesign initiatives within manufacturing and logistics during the mid- to late-1980s added over $500 million to the bottom line.

During this same period, the field sales organization was also concentrating its efforts on redesigning its work processes and improving productivity. These efforts were inextricably linked to the implementation of handheld computers (HHC).

Nationwide rollout of the HHC began on schedule in February 1987 in the Los Angeles region, winner of the 1986 award for best-run sales organization. The L.A. region served as a prototype site. It pilot-tested the use of the HHC, redesigned the sales process to achieve maximum productivity and effectiveness, and defined the information and reports that the salesforce and its supervisors would need from the system to do their jobs. Members of the L.A. field salesforce then joined the rollout team to work with other members of the field salesforce. The pace of the rollout accelerated month to month, with completion in July 1988, six months ahead of schedule.

Recognizing that realization of benefits from the HHC would be dependent on the salesforce's use of the information to improve the decisions it made and how it performed its work, Jordan asked sales management to commit to a 1% reduction in the cost of sales prior to the rollout. Each region was allowed to define how it wanted to achieve this objective. Most employed some combination of decreasing "stales," increasing sales volume, and rationalizing routes. Jordan emphasized the importance of these up-front commitments:

> By setting productivity targets before the rollout, we focused the attention of each field sales area on identifying ways to use the technology to change the way we did business. Sales management felt comfortable accepting these commitments because we had demonstrated in the L.A. region that these productivity improve-

ments were achievable and members of the field sales team from L.A. worked with the field salesforce to help it achieve its targets. I believe it's important to set these kinds of targets and not just give the technology away for free in projects where it is difficult to cost-justify the technology on strictly financial returns.

The HHC project was jointly managed by the management information systems (MIS) organization under Charlie Feld, vice president of MIS, and the field sales organization under Ron Rittenmeyer, vice president of sales operations and planning. Feld and Rittenmeyer described the importance of the MIS/business partnership to the project's success:

> We could not have implemented this project without joint leadership from the technology and business functions. The HHC was designed to change the sales process. As a result, sales leadership was essential. But the new technologies and massive redesign of our technology infrastructure also required strong technology leadership.

Both field and headquarters personnel accepted the HHC overwhelmingly. Most salespeople believed it made their jobs easier and more productive. Kevin Cotty, a route salesman who had been with Frito-Lay for four years, in late 1988 declared:

> I would never want to go back to the old way. The HHC is great. It has dramatically decreased accounting errors, which are charged directly to my take-home pay. Before the HHC, we used to check inventory every month, and it would take several weeks before accounting errors were cleared up. The few times I have a shortage now, I can quickly pinpoint the problem by checking inventory in the truck against book inventory, which we print off the HHC every week. Another great thing about not having to do the calculations manually is that I can use the time I save to talk to the person in charge of the store, which is a good way to generate additional volume.

"My biggest problem before the rollout," explained Don Kinney, a Frito-Lay route salesperson for 14 years, "was inventory shortages. Now the computer does all the calculations, so there are no margins for error. The HHC has also eliminated the need to write sales tickets and do calculations. On the sales end, it saves me about three hours a week. Instead of doing paperwork, which doesn't put any money in my pocket, I now spend those hours selling."

Armed with the information from the HHCs, the field salesforce set about to improve efficiency and effectiveness of sales operations. By late 1988, Frito-Lay was beginning to reap the benefits from its investment. Savings from better control of stales alone were more than $40 million per year. The number of distribution centers was cut by 10%. The number of salespeople was cut by 600, and, even with a leaner salesforce, revenues from domestic retail sales increased from $3 billion in 1986 to $4.2 billion in 1989. The company estimated that the system saved 30,000 to 50,000 hours of paperwork per year.

But Frito-Lay management also recognized that improved productivity was only one of the HHCs' potential benefits. The ability to use the information generated by the HHC to implement the micromarketing strategy was the initial driving force for the project, and those benefits had yet to be realized.

Building the Information Infrastructure

In the mid-1980s, Frito-Lay, like many companies, had learned the hard way that dramatically increasing the complexity of the business while simultaneously increasing the speed of decision making greatly increased the demand for information throughout the firm. Jordan and Feld recog-

nized that two types of information would be needed to support the micromarketing strategy (see Exhibit 3). First, improved information was needed to enable the company to streamline, integrate, and time-synchronize operating processes. A series of IT projects, collectively called the Pipeline Project, were initiated to support operating process redesign activities within and across functional units. Feld explained:

> After studying the current status of our operations, we found that different areas of our business operated at different speeds and varying levels of effectiveness. Because of the interdependence of these different components of the business, we could only be as effective and efficient as our weakest part. The information technology supporting our business operations showed the same varying levels of sophistication and effectiveness. Excellent, up-to-date systems mixed with old, outdated systems and manual processes. We wanted to redesign operations, and the information supporting them, to optimize across the whole business rather than to optimize each function.

The second major area needing to be addressed was the redesign of management processes—the structures, systems, and decisions that coordinated and controlled operations. Jordan noted:

> We needed to create management information systems that would enable us to integrate the strategic perspective of top management with the detailed knowledge of local market dynamics present in the field. This integrated view of the business would be provided to operating people and managers at all levels. I envisioned a more interactive management system in which corporate headquarters was much more closely connected to the field and decisions were made on a much more interactive and real-time basis.

By June 1989, the new operating and management information systems had been developed and 55 executive and functional

EXHIBIT 3   Frito-Lay's Business Cycle

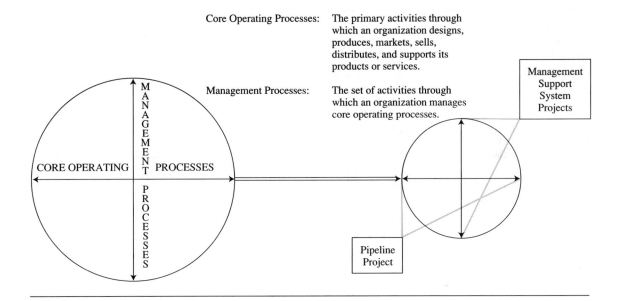

Streamlining the business cycle involves simultaneous redesign of
both organization and management processes

Core Operating Processes: The primary activities through which an organization designs, produces, markets, sells, distributes, and supports its products or services.

Management Processes: The set of activities through which an organization manages core operating processes.

manager workstations with about 350 information display panels had been rolled out to the senior management team.[4] In the late 1980s, Jordan commented on the use of information from the system:

> The last six months of 1989 were a time for senior managers at Frito-Lay to sharpen our understanding of what information we needed. Our focus was on learning how to use information to manage the business and create a shared understanding of the direction the company needed to take. The most helpful information for me during this time period was the internal information on regional and channel profitability and the external competitive information on market share and pricing. The internal information was thought provoking. I learned more about how our company works and understood better how our strategies and actions influenced our profitability. The external information served as an early warning signal of industry changes. As a senior management team, we believed we were better informed and able to manage and control the business in a much more timely and focused way. But the system's real benefit would not be realized until the information was also widely available to managers in the field to enable us to implement the micromarketing strategy.

By the end of 1989, senior managers at Frito-Lay were convinced that they had put in place the organization and information

---

[4]See *Frito-Lay, Inc.: A Strategic Transition, 1987–1989* (HBS No. 194-108) for further discussion of the information technology architecture development at Frito-Lay. In addition, a software demonstration of the Frito-Lay management support systems is available (see HBS No. 196-163).

infrastructures that would enable them to rethink the way they organized and managed the business. Targeted productivity and quality initiatives had returned the company to its former profitability level, but senior management believed that market share improvements would come only from implementation of a micromarketing approach to the business—a change in strategy that had been first identified over a decade before.

Redesigning the Organization

In January 1990, Jordan announced a major reorganization of North American operations into four regional headquarters offices known as area business teams (ABTs). Each of these teams was made up of six functional representatives—a director of marketing, vice president of zone sales, director of planning and control, vice president of manufacturing, vice president of logistics, and vice president of employee relations—who reported to an area general manager (AGM). The ABTs separated the North American market into four regions (West, South, Central, and North). The AGMs reported to Leo Kiely, senior vice president of field operations, who in turn reported to Robert Beeby, president of Frito-Lay, Inc. (see Exhibit 4).

Except in the West, where the Rocky Mountains made it more efficient to operate dedicated manufacturing facilities, Frito-Lay's existing plants served multiple ABTs. With the reorganization, all purchasing and manufacturing operations (including the factories in the West) continued to report centrally, with dotted line responsibility, to the AGM. The area VP of logistics and other functional managers reported to both their respective corporate functions and to the AGM. Ernest Harris, director of logistics for the Central area and a 20-year employee,

explained the reporting structure: "I still have a functional boss—and I also have an area team boss. Neither one is a dotted line. The good news is that both of these bosses are operating under the same profit objectives, so there have been few conflicts. It is interesting that before the reorganization my incentives were based on my ability to control functional expenses. I would have really fought many of the decisions that I now support because they would have influenced our bottom-line costs." In 1990, managers below the ABT level continued to be measured on performance against sales dollar volume and budgeted expense targets.

The first few months after the reorganization were spent attempting to put together new management systems to enable the ABTs to run their segments of the business. Though each AGM was given authority to define the management approach for his or her own area, Kiely had overall responsibility for helping the new ABTs develop the necessary management systems and for ensuring that the business remained profitable and in control during the transition. Prior to the announcement of the organization restructuring, Kiely had worked with Jordan and other members of the senior management team to develop a set of on-line information reports to help them manage the business. With the management changes in 1990, Kiely passed these reports on to the AGMs and authorized personal computer workstations for each member of the ABT. Kiely explained:

> I saw my major role as helping the new area business team managers learn to make decisions and take actions that were beneficial for the company. They needed to go beyond evaluating information based on their own personal goals to develop a business perspective that involved all parts of the business. Finally, they needed to use information to frame business decisions and not just observe information as

EXHIBIT 4   Frito-Lay Organization Structure (1989 & 1990)

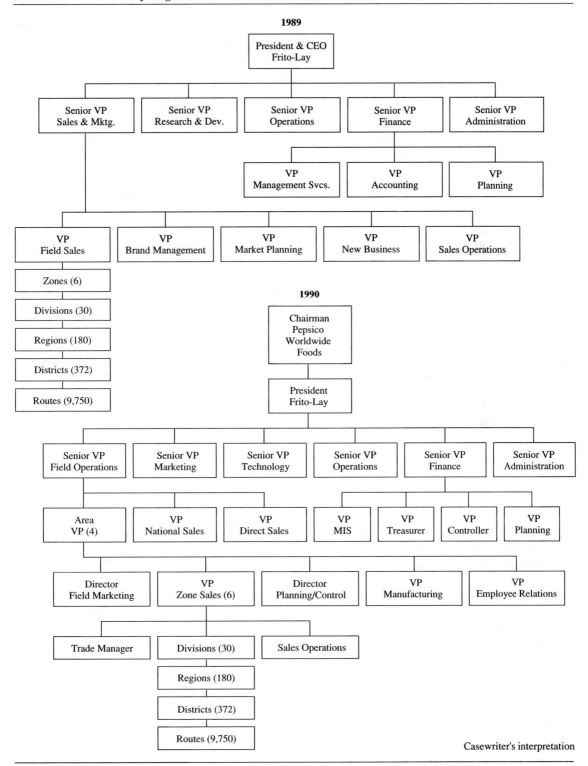

Casewriter's interpretation

an outcome. I call this "making the data actionable." When we first formed the teams, the new managers, who were used to just ensuring that we executed to plan, approached a problem by saying, "Boy, am I worried" and "So and so messed up and needs to fix it." I had to help them learn that you can't just be worried or blame someone else. You need to work together to solve the problem so that it goes away.

The second major initiative that Jordan and Kiely put in place to help senior management control the business and pass decision making down to the ABTs was a set of planning and control systems that would be timed to the business information cycle and would reflect the need for more rapid business decision making. Before 1990, Frito-Lay's annual planning cycle was tied to the creation of the Annual Operating Plan (AOP). Recognizing that the planning timeframe would need to be shortened to match the shorter decision-making cycles inherent in the micromarketing strategy, a trimester planning process was initiated (see Exhibit 5).

Because the ABTs were just learning to analyze and manage the business in an integrated way, using profitability rather than volume as the target, the 1990 plan continued to have a strong functional focus. By 1991, however, the ABTs were beginning to define targets that took into account the integrated cross-functional view of the business. George Legge, planning manager for the Central area, explained:

> One of the big improvements we accomplished in the 1991 plan was that, for the first time, with the help of a new system called CAPS, we linked our sales plan with our manufacturing plan. In the past, though those two targets would be close, manufacturing used different guidelines to come up with what they thought production would be, and there was no requirement that the target link to, or be the same as, the sales target. In the ABTs, however, we

found that the numbers needed to match. Before 1991, the manufacturing manager would report that production pounds were down at the same meeting that the sales manager would discuss the strength of sales. Even though these discrepancies didn't have a major impact on the day-to-day decisions on running the business, there was a huge disconnect that required endless discussions to understand whose numbers and analyses were correct.

The Period Review Process was developed to enable the ABTs to manage business operations to meet planning targets. When the ABTs were first formed, they adopted Frito-Lay's traditional management reporting process (see Exhibit 6). The year was broken down into 13 periods, each of which was four weeks long, and a formal business review was conducted by Leo Kiely and each of the AGMs at the end of each four-week period. In February 1990, the AGMs instituted weekly mini-reviews called the Breakfast Club (see Exhibit 7). Kiely explained:

> We have a very fast-moving business. But when we met only once a month, our thought cycle was once a month and our action cycle extended across several periods. By meeting weekly, we shortened both our thought cycle and our action cycle to be more in pace with the changes in the business. To make those weekly meetings effective, however, we needed weekly information.

By mid-1990, the new ABT managers were well aware of the challenges of managing a business rather than a function. Ernest Harris, logistics director for the Central area who had been with Frito-Lay for 20 years, explained:

> If you drew regionalization on a time continuum, we're at 2000 B.C.—we're growing and changing the organization but still struggling with our functional and business team roles. As managers we had always been very adept at functional management. I knew what

EXHIBIT 5   Frito-Lay's Traditional Planning Cycle

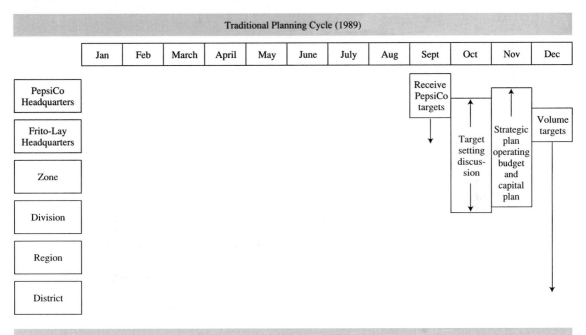

Traditional Planning Cycle (1989)

Trimester Planning (1990)

Step 1: Create the annual operating plan
in trimester 3

Step 2: Adjust plan in
trimesters 1 & 2

EXHIBIT 6 Frito-Lay's Traditional Performance Monitoring (Before 1990)

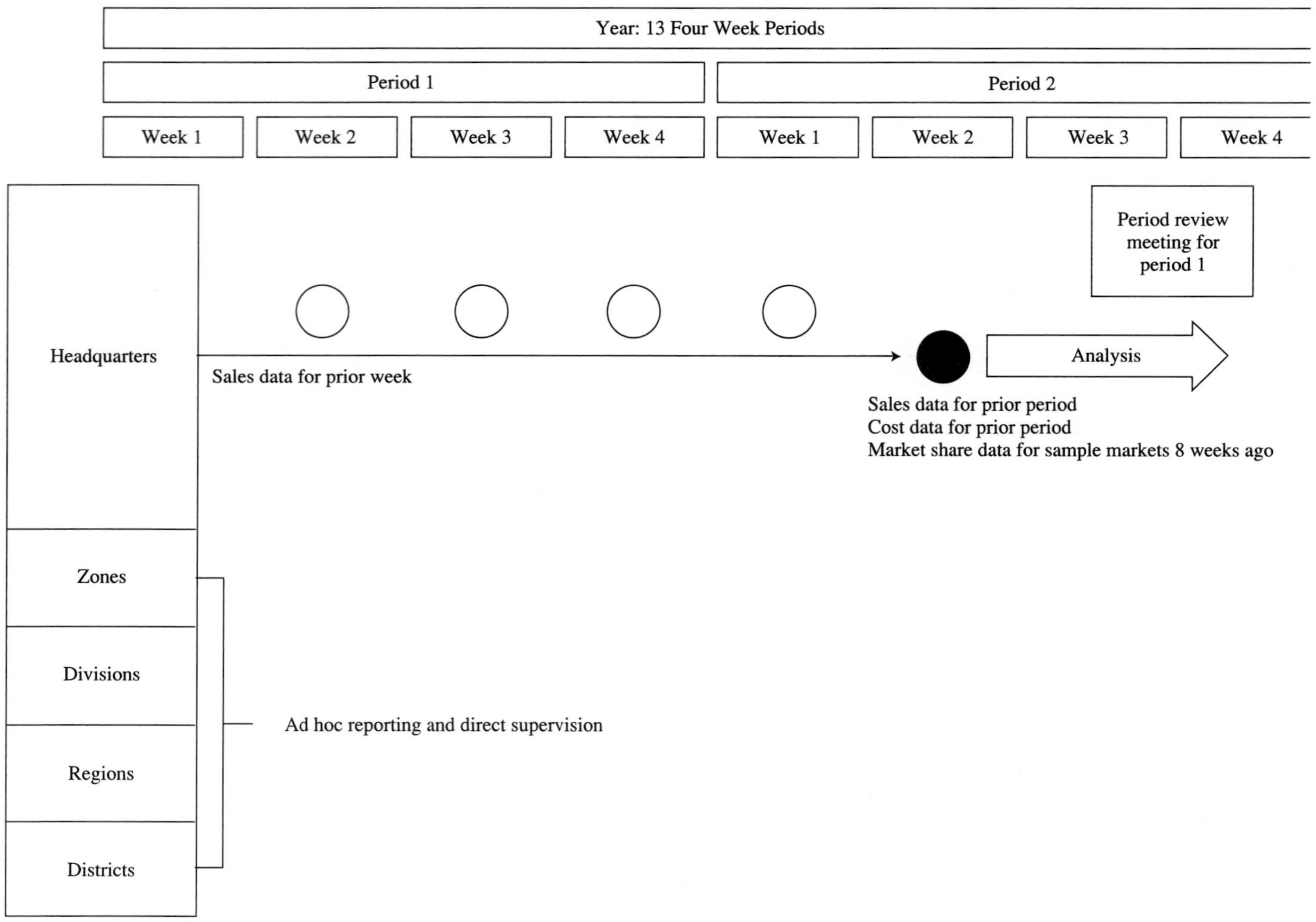

Year: 13 Four Week Periods

Period 1

Period 2

Week 1 | Week 2 | Week 3 | Week 4 | Week 1 | Week 2 | Week 3 | Week 4

Period review meeting for period 1

Analysis

Headquarters

Sales data for prior week

Sales data for prior period
Cost data for prior period
Market share data for sample markets 8 weeks ago

Zones

Divisions

Ad hoc reporting and direct supervision

Regions

Districts

Key: Shaded circles represent computer-generated reports
Nonshaded circles represent verbal telephone reports

EXHIBIT 7 The Period Review Process (1992)

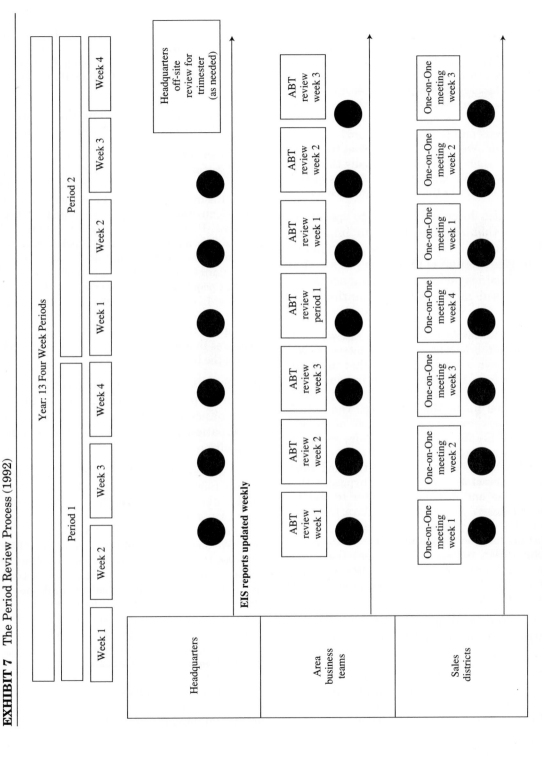

Key: Shaded circles represent computer-generated reports

information I needed to control logistics. I used to be able to tell you in detail what my cost structure looked like—if I tweaked here, what happened there, and so on. Where I struggle, and where I think all of my counterparts struggle, is on how to take functional data, decisions, and intuition and "transition" to a P&L approach. What we have learned over the past year is how to focus on the marketplace and on variable margin. We're learning to look at the business as a whole. My focus has totally changed; I am now beginning to think in terms of the marketplace rather than functional excellence.

Harris also described changes to operating processes that resulted from an improved understanding of the business, an understanding he attributed to working as a member of a business team and having access to more focused and timely information (see Exhibit 8):

We have dramatically changed the way we deliver our products over the past year. We used to have a single approach that involved shipping from the plants to a warehouse and then to a distribution center, where the product was picked up by the salesforce. The entire process took seven days or more out of the 35-day shelf life for our products. Now, we have two new approaches in addition to our traditional delivery process. The first, called Promotion Direct Delivery (PDD), bypasses the warehouse and distribution center to enable direct delivery, within one to two days, from the manufacturing plants to supermarkets to support products on promotion. The second, called Total Direct Delivery (TDD), uses the same direct delivery process to enable key accounts to receive the entire Frito-Lay product line within two days.

Andy Kerner, director of finance for the Central area, explained his impressions of the restructuring:

We are trying to better define what we do as a finance function. In early 1990, I began meeting with sales and marketing to figure out how to handle the overlap areas. There are some

people who like to work in distinct blocks—I do this and you do that—but that doesn't match our business. Between marketing, sales, and finance, there is a continuum—maybe 20% is proprietary functional work. Then there is this big gray area.

He went on to describe how the restructuring influenced his need for information:

There is so much information coming in that we are all getting swamped. I had to create a book, about one and a half inches thick, that contained the information I felt I needed to have on hand to answer questions and understand the business. It included not only the traditional finance information but also competitive, market, and sales information. I don't know where on my card it says that I am a marketing person, but people ask me marketing questions all the time. In our 1991 restructuring, we coined a new title—area performance manager—to encompass the broader scope of performance measures that we are now using to manage and control the business.

Bill Swanston, finance director for the South area, further described the evolution of the finance manager's role that resulted in the creation of the area performance manager position:

When we first had profit-and-loss data available in 1990, we felt like kids with a new toy. That lasted about one month—about the time it took us to realize we were using data dumps that gave us no analysis, explanation, or direction. We needed insights, not dumps. What good is a P&L statement when you can observe it as an outcome but not understand its causes? In finance, we found ourselves building a profit-reporting system that had virtually no analytical tools for supporting business decisions. Now, we're changing the role of finance from giving profit summaries to providing information on profit tradeoff decisions. For example, if you identify a profit growth problem that you think comes from a price/volume tradeoff, you have choices in merchandising, price, and promotions that can be used to

EXHIBIT 8 Frito-Lay's Product/Service Delivery Process (Before 1990)

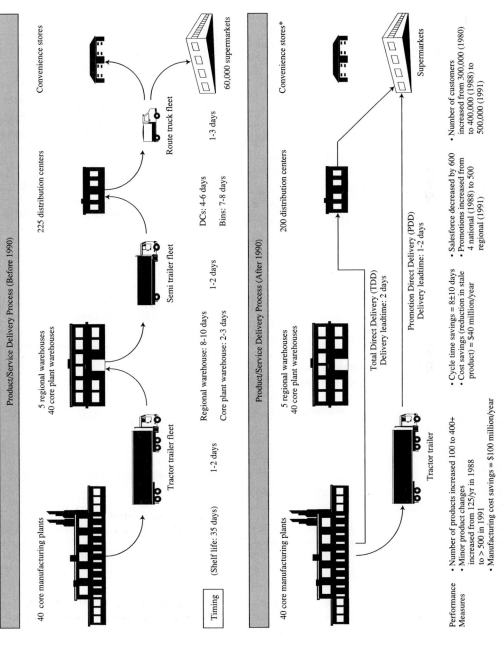

Product/Service Delivery Process (Before 1990)

40 core manufacturing plants

5 regional warehouses
40 core plant warehouses

225 distribution centers

Convenience stores

Tractor trailer fleet

Semi trailer fleet

Route truck fleet

60,000 supermarkets

Timing

1-2 days

(Shelf life: 35 days)

Regional warehouse: 8-10 days
Core plant warehouse: 2-3 days

1-2 days

DCs: 4-6 days
Bins: 7-8 days

1-3 days

Product/Service Delivery Process (After 1990)

40 core manufacturing plants

5 regional warehouses
40 core plant warehouses

200 distribution centers

Convenience stores*

Supermarkets

Tractor trailer

Total Direct Delivery (TDD)
Delivery leadtime: 2 days

Promotion Direct Delivery (PDD)
Delivery leadtime: 1-2 days

Performance Measures

• Number of products increased 100 to 400+
• Minor product changes increased from 125/yr in 1988 to > 500 in 1991
• Manufacturing cost savings = $100 million/year

• Cycle time savings = 8±10 days
• Cost savings (reduction in stale product) = $40 million/year

• Salesforce decreased by 600
• Promotions increased from 4 national (1988) to 500 regional (1991)

• Number of customers increased from 300,000 (1980) to 400,000 (1988) to 500,000 (1991)

* Total direct delivery and promotional direct delivery were only available for large accounts. Small accounts continued to be serviced in the traditional manner.

305

resolve it. The role of the finance manager evolved from just reporting outcomes to building a path from early warning symptoms to causes to responses. Feedback loops linking all of these pieces together are a critical component for creating an organization that learns and manages in real time.

Tuning the Information Infrastructure

Despite efforts to develop a flexible and comprehensive information infrastructure during the late 1980s, the new business teams found that gaining access to that information was a source of continual frustration. (See Exhibit 9 for a summary of changes to the scope of information available secondary to the implementation of the information infrastructure.) Rick Gunst, director of finance for the North area, summed up many of the ABT managers' feelings about the information systems available to them during 1990:

> One of our biggest assets was our information, and one of our biggest liabilities was our information. There was so much information it took weeks to analyze it. On-line information was available, which provided an easy way to look at information, but it gave us only a general view of the total business—not a detailed view of our local business. That was fine for corporate executives, but we also needed detail that was framed to address specific business decisions.

A market development manager clarified the problem further:

> As we worked together as a business team, we realized that we needed access to more information than the pre-formatted reporting systems provided. All the data that we needed were available, and, in fact, we had more data than we could possibly use, but trying to dig out the detail to answer a simple question was like looking for a museum in a foreign city. The museum may be only six blocks away, but the people you ask give you different directions and they all speak a different language.

Frito-Lay headquarters initially responded to ABT concerns about information access by instituting, in late 1990, a new position, the area information manager (AIM). These individuals, who had previously worked in the central MIS group, moved out to area offices to assist ABT managers and analysts with data-related concerns. They reported directly to the vice president of finance in the area and had dotted-line reporting responsibility to MIS. Jim Slatwa, the AIM for the North area, described his job:

> Analysts in this office were spending 80% of their time on data retrieval and 20% on data analysis. My job was to help them move toward 20% retrieval and 80% analysis. As a company, we did a good job of developing a huge corporate database. But to use it for answers to new questions, you needed to know specialized computer programming languages. Managers were beginning to understand how to use information to make business decisions. But we in MIS needed to understand how to help them get that information directly so that we were not in the middle.

The 1991 Restructuring

In addition to changing the information systems, Frito-Lay management also recognized that additional changes were required to the organization. On January 1, 1991, Roger Enrico, formerly with PepsiCola, was named CEO of Frito-Lay, Inc.[5] Immediately upon his arrival, Enrico hired a management consulting firm to study and make recommendations on the most appropriate structure for Frito-Lay. He appointed Charlie Feld, vice president of Frito-Lay's man-

---

[5]Michael Jordan, who had been CEO of Worldwide Foods since January 1987 and had supervised the 1990 Frito-Lay reorganization, was made CEO of PepsiCo International to define and execute the company's globalization strategy.

EXHIBIT 9 Changes in the Scope of Information

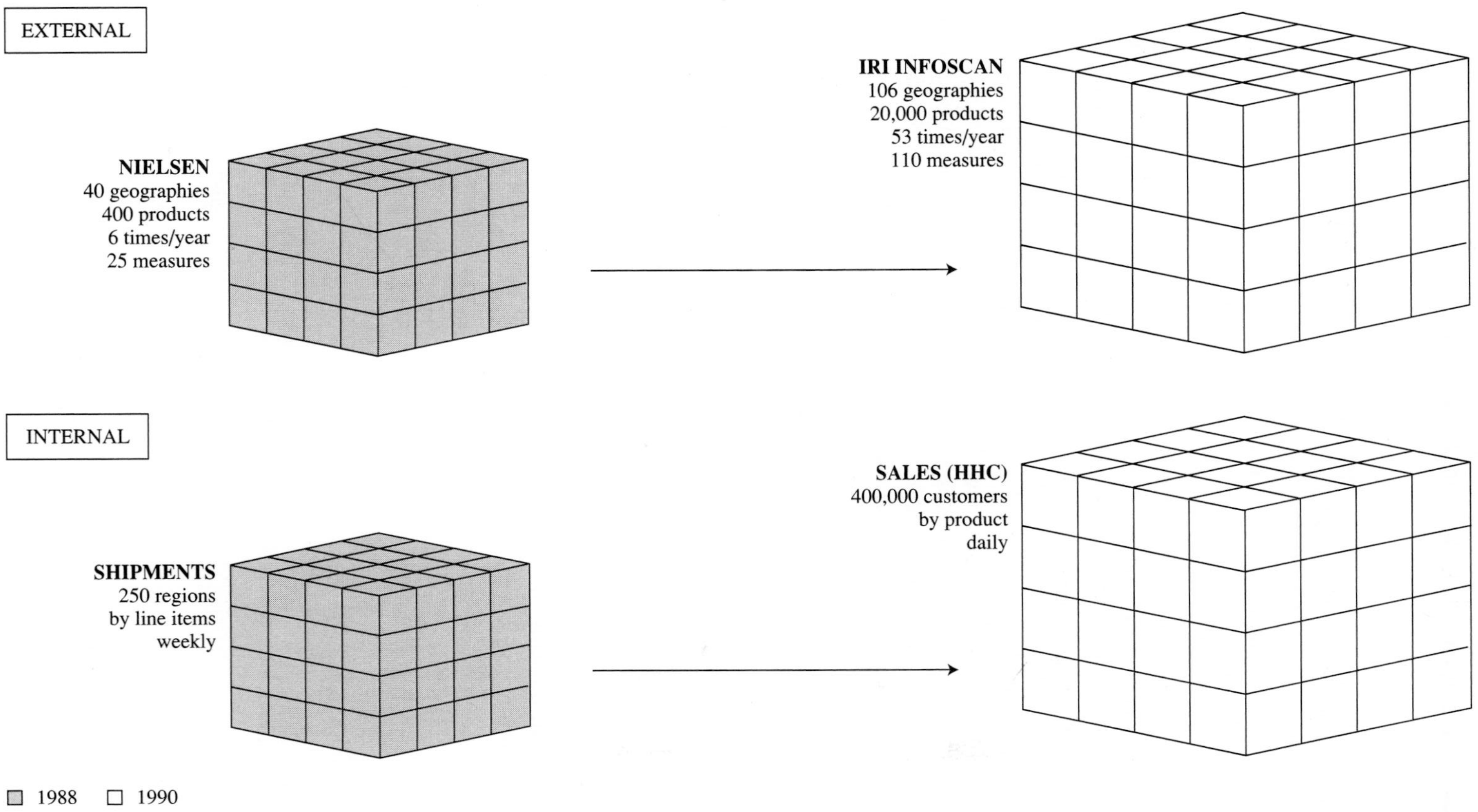

EXTERNAL

NIELSEN
40 geographies
400 products
6 times/year
25 measures

IRI INFOSCAN
106 geographies
20,000 products
53 times/year
110 measures

INTERNAL

SHIPMENTS
250 regions
by line items
weekly

SALES (HHC)
400,000 customers
by product
daily

■ 1988   □ 1990

agement information systems (MIS) organization, to head the organizational restructuring because of his broad knowledge of the organization, operations, and business dynamics. The results of the study, announced in September 1991, were implemented in a series of organizational changes that resulted in another companywide reorganization and the elimination of 1,800 positions (1,000 from corporate headquarters and 800 from the field). The AGM position was elevated to division president, and this new position reported directly to Enrico. To maintain consistency across PepsiCo, the four original area business teams were renamed divisions, and the regions were renamed zones. Twenty-two new area business teams, which corresponded to each of Frito-Lay's Market Areas (FLMAs), were created (see Exhibit 10). The 22 new area business teams reported to the four division presidents. They assumed general management responsibilities that previously had been the responsibility of the previous four business teams.

Where to Next?

As they contemplated the changes that the company had undergone, the division presidents recognized that the newly formed area business teams would need guidance and support as they assumed their new roles. "We wanted to help them learn from our mistakes," said one executive. Massive changes had taken place within the firm since the early 1980s but more would be needed to successfully implement the micro-marketing strategy. (See Exhibit 11 for a summary of organization changes between 1980 and 1992.) Competitors and large supermarket chains continued to exert pressure on the company to decrease prices while improving quality and service. (See Exhibit 12 for a summary of changes in profitability and market share.) "It's getting harder and harder to earn a dollar in the snack food industry," remarked a competitor at the annual Snack Food Association convention in 1991. "Today, the placid floors of your neighborhood supermarket have become a frenzied battleground of processor against processor . . . retailer against retailer . . . and processor against retailer fighting to steal dollars from the other's bottom line in what is essentially a no-growth industry."

EXHIBIT 10   Organization Structure (1992)

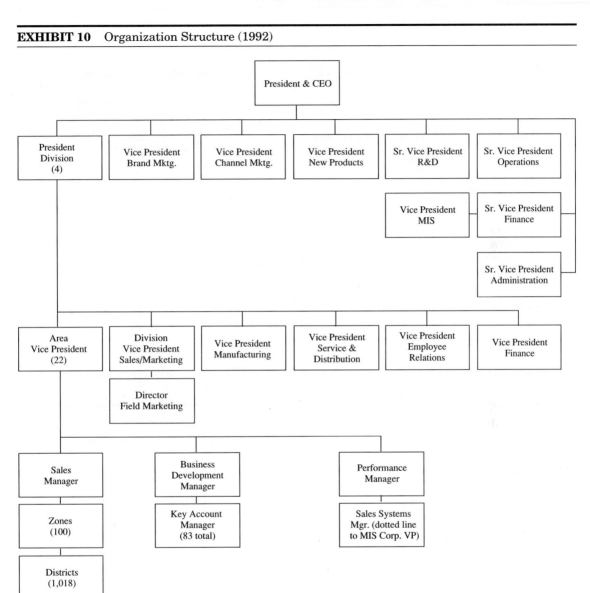

Casewriter's Interpretation

EXHIBIT 11   Summary of Organization Changes

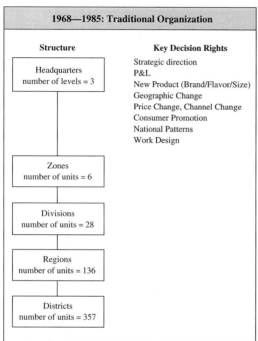

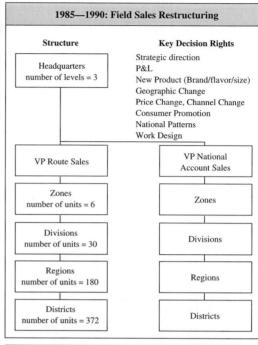

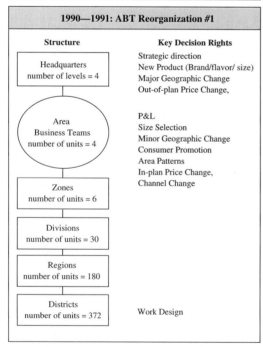

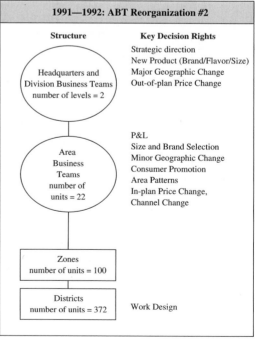

Note: Circles indicate team-based units; squares indicate hierarchical units.

EXHIBIT 12   Profitability and Market Share Changes over the 1980s and 1990s

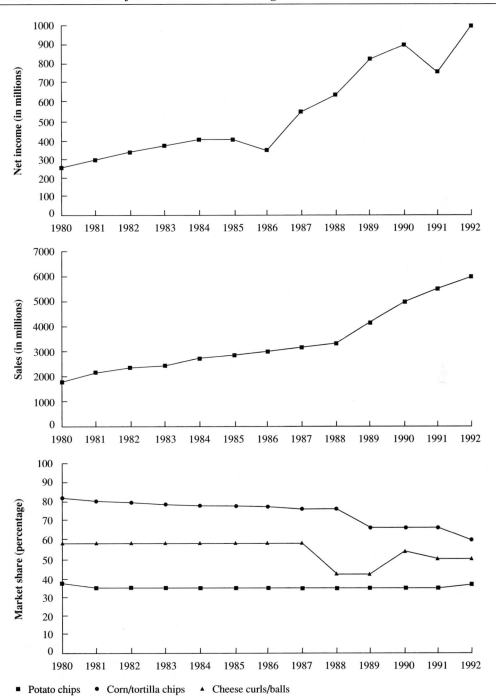

■ Potato chips   ● Corn/tortilla chips   ▲ Cheese curls/balls

Case 3–4

MICROAGE, INC.: ORCHESTRATING THE INFORMATION TECHNOLOGY VALUE CHAIN[1]

A virtual network of people, information and organizations, the MicroAge Information Technology Value Chain links together the products, resources and skills required to implement today's complex IT solutions.

In January 1998, MicroAge was a Fortune 300 full-line IT distributor, systems integrator and services provider for distributed computing solutions for corporations, government agencies and information technology (IT) resellers worldwide. From its headquarters in Tempe, Arizona, the MicroAge network of people, partnerships and information linked over 500 IT suppliers, who offer over 20,000 different products, to customers in 34 countries around the world (see Exhibits 1 and 2). MicroAge was one of only two IT companies founded in the 1970s that was still run by its founders; Microsoft was the other. In recognition of their entrepreneurial success, in 1995, Jeff McKeever (CEO and Chairman) and Alan Hald (President of MicroAge Enterprises) were named "Master Entrepreneurs of the Year" by *Inc.* magazine. Honors like this were not new. McKeever had been named one of the Top 25 Most Influential Executives in the Computer Industry by *Computer Reseller News* each year from 1985 through 1997, and in 1998, McKeever

was named "Best CEO" in the electronics industry by *Financial World* magazine.

MicroAge at a glance (1997)
www.microage.com

Founded:	1976
Traditional business focus:	IT distributor and master reseller
Revenues:	$4.4B
Operating income:	$70.7M
Employees:	2892

MicroAge's history and evolution paralleled the history and evolution of the IT industry. The company was founded in 1976 as the industry transitioned from the mainframe's centralized information management approach to the personal computer's decentralized approach. In the 1990s, MicroAge had embraced and championed the distributed, network computing model.

> We're on the brink of yet another flash point— a convergence of computer technology with telecommunications that will catapult us into an information-based society. The opportunities are so vast, they're difficult to quantify. We're truly entering a world with unlimited possibilities.
>
> Jeff McKeever, 1997

But as McKeever considered the future, he questioned whether the company was correctly positioned to exploit those opportunities. The past 5 years had been spent building the organizational capabilities that

---

This case was prepared by Professor Lynda M. Applegate and Research Associate Kirk A. Goldman.

[1]Copyright © 1998 by the President and Fellows of Harvard College.

Harvard Business School Case 398-068.

EXHIBIT 1   MicroAge Organization

Corporate Headquarters

Jeff McKeever Chairman and CEO, MicroAge, Inc.	Bob O'Malley President, MicroAge, Inc.	Alan Hald President, MicroAge Enterprise
Jim Daniel SVP and CFO MicroAge, Inc.		Jim Manton SVP, Operations, MicroAge, Inc.

Customer-Facing Business Units

Chris Koziol President, Distribution Group	John Lewis President, Integration Group

Capabilities-Based Business Units

John Andrews President, Logistics Group
Bob Mason CIO and President, Services Group
Katie Pushor President, EC Advantage

Biographies of management personnel are available in Appendix A at the end of the case.

senior management believed would be required to play a leadership role in the network computing era. By the beginning of 1998, however, senior management questioned whether further refinement of the business model would be needed. They were especially concerned by a recent market research study that confirmed what they already suspected; there was a great deal of confusion in the marketplace—and even within the organization—concerning Micro-

Age's hybrid business model. McKeever and O'Malley summarized the issues that the company faced in late 1997.

Over the past few years, people have been confused by and even skeptical of our decision to become both a full-line distributor and a value-added systems integrator and services company. Analysts have encouraged us to choose one or the other, and our stock has suffered, falling from $29 in September to $12½ in December 1997.

EXHIBIT 1 (continued)   MicroAge Organization

Business Unit	Description	Key Customers	Key Competitors	Strategic Initiatives 1997
Distribution group	Full line distributor of IT products	• Franchised and independent dealers and resellers • Value-added resellers • System integrators • Retail superstores, direct marketers • MicroAge resellers and branch offices	• Ingram Micro • Tech Data • Merisel • CHS	• Win share from weakened competitors • Target new markets and strengthen current markets through segmentation • Position company as full-line distributor (new technology products; new categories) • Strengthen relationships with suppliers, customers and partners through category management and ECadvantage
Integration group	Provide client-specific IT solutions and services including requirements definition, process reengineering, system design and development, operation and maintenance and asset management	• Fortune 2000 corporations • Global 50 • State and federal governments • Education institutions • Major systems integrators	• CompuCom • Vanstar • Inacom • GE ITS • Entex • EDS • IBM • Andersen Consulting	• Develop regional branch office structure • Develop global key account teams • Extend integration services capabilities (e.g., supply chain management, emerging technology solutions) • Develop consulting services
Logistics group	Provide services required to streamline and coordinate physical supply chain, including channel assembly, custom integration, warehousing and inventory management, physical distribution, and after-sales services (e.g., call center, help desk)	• Corporate outsourcers • Small businesses • MicroAge resellers and branch offices • Channel assembly partners	• FedEx Business Services • SCI • Dell • Gateway	• Expand channel assembly capabilities and vendor programs • Streamline, integrate and reduce the cost of supply chain activities for MicroAge and its business partners • Expand after-sales services offerings • Enable differentiation based on service quality

EXHIBIT 1 (continued)   MicroAge Organization

Business Unit	Description	Key Customers	Key Competitors	Strategic Initiatives 1997
ECadvantage	Internet-based electronic commerce platform providing electronic catalogs, system configuration, quote generation and ordering	• Corporate end users • Corporate purchasing • Value-added resellers • MicroAge resellers and branch offices	• Customer e-commerce activities • Partner e-commerce activities • Dell.com • Catalink	• Provide end-to-end secure, reliable, flexible e-commerce capabilities • Integrate web technology with legacy systems and databases • Penetrate user desktops quickly • Exploit the economic value of information and position as a market facilitator
Technology services	Comprehensive services to manage technology assets for electronic commerce and network computing, including operation, network management, asset replacement, disaster recovery and security	• Small to medium-size businesses • Value-added resellers • MicroAge resellers and branch offices	• Value-added resellers • System integrators	• Provide strategic direction and resources to newly-launched businesses • Expand internal organizational capabilities in technology asset management • Develop partnerships with network services providers

Despite the confusion, the company has been very successful over the past few years. In 1992, we had our first $1 billion year; in 1996, we had our first $1 billion quarter. We have grown our integration and services businesses from nothing in 1992 to over $2 billion in revenues in the past few years. Over the same period, we grew our distribution business from revenues of $1 billion to over $4 billion. In 1997, we set company records for revenue and net income. But as margins continue to erode on the distribution side of the business, we know we must concentrate our efforts on the higher margin integration and services businesses.

Today, our company is going through a period of intense strategic introspection. Should we continue to develop and refine our hybrid business model or should we rethink our decision to offer all of these services under our roof? If we decide to continue with the current model, how can we prevent brand confusion and the perceived conflict among the distribution and integration sides of the business? If we break up the company, can a stand-alone distribution or integration business survive against stronger, larger competitors such as GE Capital's Information Technology Services business on the integration side and Ingram Micro on the distribution side? No matter which model we choose, can we fulfill our vision of becoming an information intermediary, uniting all members of the IT channel? The answers to these questions will help us set

EXHIBIT 2 MicroAge Financial Information

Per Share Data ($)

(Year Ended Oct. 31)	1997	1996	1995	1994	1993	1992	1991	1990	1989	1988	1987
Tangible book value	13.39	11.56	10.96	11.11	13.48	6.32	4.87	4.27	3.66	3.37	3.00
Cash flow	.53	2.26	1.09	1.91	2.77	1.2	1.05	1.41	0.98	0.9	0.68
Earnings	1.40	0.89	0.02	1.22	1.15	0.59	0.5	0.97	0.64	0.62	0.47
Dividends*	N/A	N/A	N/A	N/A	N/A	N/A	N/A	N/A	N/A	N/A	N/A
Payout ratio*	N/A	N/A	N/A	N/A	N/A	N/A	N/A	N/A	N/A	N/A	N/A
Prices—High	29.25	25	15	32.5	26.63	10.5	10.13	12.38	7.13	6.13	7.63
Low	12.5	7.5	7.25	9.25	5.38	3.63	3.63	4.13	4.13	2.88	2.19
P/E ratio—High	24.3	28	NM	27	23	18	20	13	11	10	16
Low	10.9	8	NM	8	5	6	8	4	6	5	5

Income Statement Analysis (Million $)

	1997	1996	1995	1994	1993	1992	1991	1990	1989	1988	1987
Revenues	4,446	3,516	2,941	2,221	1,510	1,017	787	613	360	252	201
Operating income	70.7	56.8	41.1	41.8	25.1	13.4	10	4.7	6.2	6.5	4.8
Depreciation	N/A	20.3	15.4	9.3	6.4	4.8	3.5	2.9	2.2	1.8	1.4
Interest expense	N/A	1.3	3.4	1.3	0.7	1.6	1.6	0.3	1.4	1	0.8
Pretax income	43.3	23.1	1	27	17.5	7.8	5.8	11	7	5.9	4.8
Tax rate	42%	43%	78%	39%	40%	40%	44%	41%	40%	33%	42%
Net income	25.0	13.3	0.2	16.3	10.5	4.7	3.2	6.4	4.2	4	2.8

Balance Sheet and Other Financial Data (Million $)

	1997	1996	1995	1994	1993	1992	1991	1990	1989	1988	1987
Cash	24.0	20.5	13.7	11.1	20.2	23.2	14.7	2.5	3	2.6	3.1
Current assets	844	610	508	456	298	205	141	100	82	47	47
Total assets	974	690	573	510	323	227	162	113	92	54	54
Current liabilities	701	499	400	342	214	161	117	74	58	20	29
Long-term debt	35.2	3.9	4.1	2.1	1.2	9.3	11	9	6.4	10.1	5.3
Common equity	238	186	168	166	108	56.9	33.5	29.7	27	23.9	19.4
Total capital	N/A	190	173	168	109	66.2	44.5	38.5	33.4	34.1	24.7
Capital expenditures	N/A	24	22.9	17.6	7.9	4.9	8.4	4.9	1.6	2.2	1.2
Cash flow	N/A	33.6	15.7	25.6	16.9	9.5	6.8	9.4	6.3	5.8	4
Current Ratio	1.2	1.2	1.3	1.3	1.4	1.3	1.2	1.3	1.4	2.3	1.6
% LT debt of capital	12.8	2	2.4	1.2	1.1	14.1	24.7	22.9	19.2	29.7	21.4
% Net inc. of revenues	.6	0.4	NM	0.7	0.7	0.5	0.4	1.1	1.2	1.6	1.4
% Return on assets	2.9	2.1	0.1	3.7	3.3	2.1	2.4	6.4	5.7	7.2	2.7
% Return on equity	11.7	7.5	0.2	11.1	11.3	9.1	10.2	23.1	16.5	18	89.3

Note: Data as originally reported; before results of discontinued operations and/or special items.
N/A = not applicable, NM = not meaningful.
*MicroAge does not pay dividends to shareholders.

Source: Standard and Poors; Annual Reports.

EXHIBIT 3   Growth of Services Business in the Enterprise System Integration Segment

	Services Businesses as a % of Total Revenue*			Service Gross Profits as a % of Total Gross Profit Dollars		
	1995	*1996*	*1997*	*1995*	*1996*	*1997*
CompuCom	7%	9%	12%	18%	24%	33%
Entex	9%	10%	14%	16%	18%	30%
Inacom	4%	4%	6%	20%	19%	24%
MicroAge	NA	3%	4%	NA	18%	30%
Vanstar	11%	13%	15%	30%	33%	39%

Product Distribution vs. Service Margins

	Product Margins	*Service Margins*
CompuCom	9 to 10%	37%
Entex	9 to 10%	25%
Inacom	6 to 7%	30 to 40% (est.)
MicroAge	6 to 7%	30 to 40% (est.)
Vanstar	9 to 10%	37%

*Service activities include: system configuration (e.g., install memory, hard drives, accessories and software to customer specifications); design, build, install, and test business networks and systems (e.g., client-server systems, networked computing business solutions); asset tracking and management; lifecycle management and maintenance; help desk and call center support; and professional consulting (e.g., process reengineering).

Note: While each of these competitors also distributes product, only MicroAge and Inacom are positioning themselves as both a Full-Line Distributor and System Integrator.

Adapted From: Cal, Tom, "Computer Sales Channel Sector, 1998 Investment Perspective and Outlook," *SoundView Financial,* January 23, 1998.

priorities for how we invest our capital and will help us determine the kind of people we need to be successful.

> Jeff McKeever and
> Bob O'Malley,
> December 1997

See Exhibit 3 for a comparison of product and service margins for IT channel players.

Company and Industry Background

MicroAge—initially called the Phoenix Group, Inc.—was founded by Jeff McKeever and Alan Hald in August 1976. They bor-rowed $15,000 each and, in October 1976, opened a 1,000 square foot computer store, which they called "The Byte Shop." During their first year of operation McKeever and Hald sold $1.5 million worth of computer kits, priced at under $1,000 each, and opened three additional stores. Over the next three years they expanded the business, introducing mail-order catalogs in February 1977; forming MicroAge Wholesale in March 1977 (which assembled, then sold microcomputers to retailers); and, in July 1978, forming MicroAge International to distribute the computers they built in Tempe to the growing microcomputer reseller community in the U.S. and abroad. By 1979, revenues reached $30 million.

Anticipating the introduction of personal computers (PCs) for the business market, McKeever and Hald announced a national franchise program in December 1979 and set a goal to open 50 franchise stores per year during 1980 and 1981. Where The Byte Shop had been targeted at hobbyists, the new MicroAge Computer Stores were designed to meet the needs of small business owners and corporate accounts; business people came to the store to learn about computers and how to use them to make their businesses more successful. The stores also provided ongoing support and service. But a downturn in the economy made it difficult to meet their aggressive growth goals. By the end of 1980, only 8 new stores had been opened and the company posted a $1.3 million loss, its first ever. On December 29, 1981, the company filed for Chapter 11 bankruptcy. In 1982, an investor was found; the cofounders renegotiated their debt and emerged from bankruptcy ten months later. On January 11, 1983, they renamed the company MicroAge, Inc.—signifying a new beginning.

The business computer era was in full swing when McKeever and Hald began rebuilding the company. While continuing to concentrate on a full service approach, MicroAge now turned its attention to cultivating strong relationships with corporate desktop computer suppliers, which in the mid-1980s were dominated by IBM, Compaq, HP and Apple—the "Big Four." The strategy worked, and by 1985, MicroAge Computer Stores had evolved to a 149-store franchise chain with revenues of $142 million. On July 1, 1987, MicroAge went public on NASDAQ, raising $17 million. As fiscal 1987 came to a close, the company had 199 locations around the world and revenues over $200 million.

As they reinvented the company, McKeever and Hald also reinvented the industry, segmenting the channel. *Master Resellers,* such as MicroAge, became the sole distributors for brand name business computer systems; *Distributors,* having been excluded from selling brand name computers, offered a wide variety of peripheral products (e.g., printers, network equipment) and software. As low cost computer makers (for example, Dell and Gateway) entered the market in the late 1980s, *Retailers, Catalog,* and *Tele-sales* became important new channels for sales to consumers.

In the early 1990s, however, this neatly-segmented distribution model came under attack as PC clone and discount computer makers slashed prices and grabbed share. In an effort to stem the bleeding, Compaq shook the industry when, in 1992, they dramatically lowered their prices and abandoned their property design for commodity components and standard platforms. IBM and Apple followed shortly. By the end of 1993, the Big Four combined market share had decreased from over 80% (in the mid-1980s) to less than 20% and margins had eroded. By the mid-1990s "closed sourcing" of brand name computers (through dedicated Master Resellers, like MicroAge) had given way to "open sourcing."[2] As margins fell, Master Resellers expanded their product line and soon were selling a wide range of computer components, equipment, software, networks and peripherals. At the same time, they aggressively pursued opportunities to enter higher margin integration services businesses (e.g., system integration, call center, help desk, process reengineering consulting and outsourcing). By the late

---

[2]The decision by brand name business computer makers to enable full-line distributors, retail superstores and other channel players to sell their products was referred to as "open sourcing."

Two-Tiered IT Distribution Channel (1998)

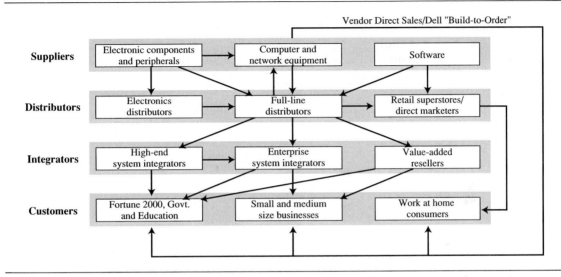

1990s, most channel players—MicroAge and Inacom were key exceptions—had focused on either becoming a Full-Line Distributor or a Corporate Systems Integrator. (See Appendix B for descriptions of key players and performance comparisons.)

Driven by Dell's success in penetrating the PC market—by 1997 it was the #2 computer maker in the US behind Compaq[3]—another major change in the way computers were built and distributed was also underway. Beginning in 1996, manufacturers such as IBM, HP, DEC, and Compaq had begun to shift from a "build-to-forecast" to a "build-to-order" model and started to collaborate with distributors in what is called "Channel

Assembly." In an August 25, 1997, report, Robinson-Humphrey stated: "The objective [of build-to-order and channel assembly] is to take over 10 points from the cost of a delivered PC." In addition to lowering the cost, the shift to build-to-order was also expected to result in further consolidation of the channel since only a handful of players had the required capabilities. "Only five or six reseller/integrators (Inacom, MicroAge, Vanstar, CompuCom and perhaps Entex and GE ITS) and two large distributors (Ingram Micro and Tech Data) have the systems and financial resources required to become high volume channel assemblers," the Robinson-Humphrey report continued. "Inacom and MicroAge are the clear leaders [in 1997]." (See Exhibit 4.)

After losing some large corporate customers to Dell in the mid-1990s, Compaq, HP and IBM began to win them back in 1997. For example, after losing the Delta Airlines contract to Dell in 1995, HP recaptured the business in 1997 when Delta designated HP

---

[3]By 1997, increasing consolidation within the enterprise computing segment of the market had resulted in the emergence of a new "Big Four"—Compaq, Dell, IBM and HP. These four boosted their combined market share from 27.1% in 1996 to 33.3% in 1997 (Francis, B., "Meeting Dell's Challenge," *InformationWeek*, December 15, 1997).

EXHIBIT 4   Comparison of IT Distribution Channel Models

Build-to-Forecast

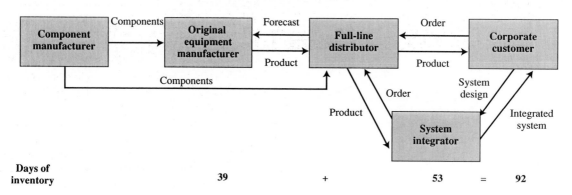

| Days of inventory | 39 | + | 53 | = | 92 |

Build-to-Order (Dell Direct)

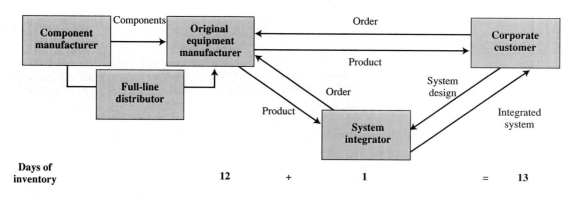

| Days of inventory | 12 | + | 1 | = | 13 |

Build-to-Order (Channel Assembly)

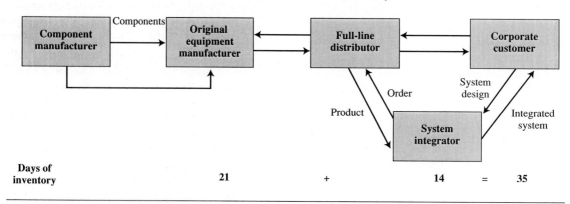

| Days of inventory | 21 | + | 14 | = | 35 |

Adapted from: "The Computer Sales Channel," Robinson-Humphrey, August 25, 1997.

EXHIBIT 4 (continued)   Comparison of IT Distribution Channel Models

Financial Performance: Dell vs. Compaq (1996)

Financial Performance Indicators	Dell	Compaq
Sales	$7.8B	$18.1B
Sales growth (93–97) CAGR	57%	36%
Market share	6.8%	13.1%
Gross margin	21.5%	23.1%
Profit margin	6.7%	7.18%
Inventory turns	30	12.1
Return on invested capital	85%	34.3%
Cash cycle (days)	−4	12.4
Inventory carrying costs (assumes 13% cost of capital)	$32.5M	$150M

Source: M. Mahoney and R. Sunder, "The Channel Strikes Back: How the Traditional PC Channel Is Fighting Back the Challenge from Dell," Final Paper for Coordinating and Managing Supply Chains, HBS, 1997.

Breakdown in the Delivered Cost of a PC

Time Frame	1991		Mid 1997	
Computer System	cost in $	% of delivery cost	cost in $	% of delivery cost
Microprocessor	$ 195	9%	$ 450	22%
Hard drive	$ 300	14%	$ 170	8%
Motherboard (excl. microprocessor)	$ 240	11%	$ 144	7%
Memory	$ 30	1%	$ 148	7%
Chassis, power, and packaging	$ 80	4%	$ 85	4%
CD-ROM	—	0%	$ 69	3%
Floppy drive, mouse, and keyboard	$ 75	3%	$ 35	2%
Controller/modem	$ 80	4%	$ 49	2%
Computer—Materials	$1,000	46%	$1,150	57%
Labor and assembly	$ 100	5%	$ 70	3%
Computer—Total	$1,100	50%	$1,220	60%
Monitor	$ 225	10%	$ 222	11%
System total	$1,325	60%	$1,442	71%
Manufacturer gross profit	$ 540	25%	$ 385	19%
Reseller gross profit	$ 330	15%	$ 203	10%
Delivered cost	$2,195	100%	$2,030	100%

1991 Computer System Configuration: CPU = 386DX, 1MB RAM, 60MB hard drive
1997 Computer System Configuration: CPU = 200MHZ, 32MB RAM, 2.6GB hard drive

Adapted from Robinson-Humphrey Company, Inc., The Computer Sales Channel, August 25, 1997, p. 14.

as its worldwide PC supplier. The cost efficiency, flexibility and speed provided by channel assembly were critical to winning the Delta contract. But even as traditional players gained ground in one area, Dell continued to push the industry forward in others. One particular area that had gained industry attention was Web sales. In December 1997, Dell did more than $6 million dollars per day of web sales, doubling its normal $3 million per day.[4] For large corporate customers such as Ford Motor Company and Boeing, Dell had a dedicated, secure Web site that enabled individual users within each company to configure and purchase workstations based on pre-approved, customized purchase orders and configurations. The ability to integrate and coordinate the enterprise computing supply chain through channel assembly and electronic commerce had become the new battleground in the late 1990s.

Shifting Strategy and Building Organizational Capabilities in the 1990's

As mentioned above, the shift from closed to open sourcing shook the foundations upon which the PC distribution channel was built. As margins dropped precipitously, MicroAge and other channel players responded. A summary of MicroAge strategic initiatives (1990–1997) is presented in the following sections of the case.

Becoming a Full-Line Distributor

Recognizing the threat to their current business, in 1992 McKeever and Hald created a new organizational unit that would target selling MicroAge's distribution services to the VAR community. Several years later

---

[4]B. Francis, "Meeting Dell's Challenge," *Information Week,* December 15, 1997.

new units were added to target sales to mail order, catalog, and retail accounts. These units were grouped together as the MicroAge Distribution Group.

During the 1990s, MicroAge also worked aggressively to expand its supplier base, By 1997, MicroAge provided over 20,000 products from over 500 suppliers, up from about 30 suppliers in 1990. In addition to expanding into networking, peripherals and software, MicroAge also expanded its product line to include powerful UNIX and NT servers, including those offered by IBM, Sun, Compaq and DEC.[5] In 1996, MicroAge announced expanded software licensing services; by 1997, MicroAge was authorized in all major software licensing programs, including Adobe, Borland, Corel, IBM, Lotus, Microsoft, Novell, and Symantec. Another major opportunity that MicroAge pursued was networking products. Sales in 1997 of these products were approximately $250 million, up from virtually zero in 1994.

During the first 8 months of 1997, MicroAge signed distribution agreements with more than 19 suppliers of emerging technologies, including Digital's AltaVista

---

[5]During the 1990s, the strict separation between desktop and data center computing began to erode. Initially, this erosion was due to the introduction of client-server computing; fueled by the popularity of the Internet, the growth of network computing spurred further development and use of the client-server model. In this model, "servers" stored and processed information and coordinated activities shared among many users, while "clients" stored and processed information and coordinated activities for an individual user. While servers could range in size from the largest mainframe to personal computers, most servers were high-end workstation machines. While servers could be any size, a key differentiator from a standard personal computer was the requirement that it support "multi-tasking"—the ability for the computer to process more than one task at a time. UNIX was an early multi-tasking operating system for desktop/workstation computers. In 1997, Microsoft's NT multi-tasking desktop computer operating system was rapidly gaining market share.

Internet Software lnc., CallWare Technologies, Inc., CoreData, Inc., Netscape Communications Corporation, PictureTel, Raptor Systems, Inc., Shiva Corporation, VST Technologies, Inc., and Vision Tek, Inc. In July 1997, MicroAge, Inc. announced an agreement with Lucent Technologies for national distribution of Lucent's most powerful communication system—Definity. "We're delighted to have MicroAge join the team distributing the entire Lucent Technologies product line," said Edison Peres, Vice President of Lucent Indirect Channel Management. "MicroAge has been a Lucent national distributor since 1987, providing resellers with communication solutions for small-to-medium sized businesses. By adding Definity systems to the mix, they offer resellers the ability to provide communication solutions that meet the needs of large companies as well."

In late 1996, MicroAge commissioned MSI, a market research firm, to conduct a market study of the VAR channel. As part of the study, MSI recommended that MicroAge segment the VAR channel into 9 market segments and develop a customized approach to working with each segment. (See Appendix C for findings from the MSI study and for customer evaluations of MicroAge products and services.)

Becoming a Systems Integrator

As they protected their distribution business, MicroAge senior management also expanded the company into higher margin activities. One key thrust was to develop closer links with large corporate customers. In late 1992, McKeever and Hald created the MicroAge Information Services (MIS) unit, appointing Chris Koziol as president. Through a series of acquisitions and strategic partnerships with independent resellers, MicroAge developed a network of company-owned and owner-managed branch offices

that provided enterprise computing business solutions to large corporations, government agencies and educational institutions worldwide. The MIS branch offices also became sub-contractors to large system integrators and outsourcers such as IBM, EDS, Andersen Consulting, and Computer Sciences Corporation. By 1997, MicroAge offered a full range of integration services (including business process reengineering system requirements definition, system development, project management and systems integration, asset management, disaster recovery, and maintenance) to large corporate customers such as Hewlett-Packard, Kodak, and Visa. In addition, MicroAge developed partnerships with value-added resellers (for example, Centric Resources, Inc.) that contracted with MicroAge to serve as MIS owner-managed branch offices.

In late 1996, MicroAge grouped all of their system integration activities under the Integration Group; John Lewis was appointed president, replacing Chris Koziol, who became president of the Distribution Group. In summer 1997, Lewis piloted a new organizational and operating model for the Integration Group based on a regional structure. Each region would provide support, services, and oversight for company-owned branches, owner-managed branch offices, and "agents" within a geographic region. McKeever believed that the agent model held particular appeal to MicroAge. "The insurance industry has used this model for many years. It provides tremendous flexibility for a company and enables efficient use of resources." Lewis elaborated, "We don't know exactly what services will be offered by regional offices or how many we will need today or in the future. We don't know how we will allocate accountability and authority between local branches, agents, regional offices and MicroAge corporate headquarters. We don't even know for sure whether this is the best model. We do know, however, that our customers—whether they are large corporations, public agencies, or the reseller community—are demanding that we provide more personalized, responsive, and consistent service."

In fall 1997, Lewis formalized the regional branch office structure and increased acquisitions to ensure that there were strong branch offices in each major market in the U.S. By early October 1997, MicroAge had 45 company-owned and 39 owner-managed branch offices providing integration services to corporate customers in the U.S. and alliance partners in 34 countries. (By comparison, at the end of August 1997, MicroAge had only 17 company-owned branch offices.)

Some independent VARs and owner-managed branch offices expressed concern over the company's aggressive acquisition stance. McKeever and Lewis attempted to assuage their fears. "We value our relationships with the VAR community and the owner-managed MIS branch offices, and will continue to strengthen our relationship with them," McKeever stated. "The current acquisitions," Lewis explained, "are necessary for us to maintain strong relationships with our suppliers. They are pushing us to have one company-owned branch office in each of our major markets to ensure account control." Still many of the VARs viewed MicroAge's acquisitions and resulting branch network as a competitive threat.

To satisfy the needs of global customers, who demanded that MicroAge provide consistent quality and services around the world, Lewis also created global account teams for the 50 largest global customers These teams would coordinate worldwide services for large global accounts and orchestrate support across the full spectrum of international alliance partners. In November 1997, MicroAge acquired InterPC, a Miami-based Latin America distributor. This acquisition gave MicroAgo Distribution a presence in North and South America.

Expanding into Value-Added Logistics Services

In an attempt to further solidify their position with corporate customers and to shift the focus of their business toward higher margin activities, MicroAge also spent the 1990s building their logistics services business. This transition took place in four major areas: (1) custom configuration and systems integration; (2) project management; (3) after sales services and support; and (4) channel assembly.

In 1991, MicroAge opened its first Quality Integration Center (QIC) in Tempe, Arizona. Corporate customers, dealers, and VARs could now order desktop computer equipment to meet individual requirements. Personnel in the QIC assembled the computers based on customer specifications, and integrated them with requested printers, modems, networks, software, and other equipment. They also loaded software, tested the equipment, and packaged it for delivery to the customer site, to a value-added reseller or to a MicroAge Integration Group branch office. If products were available in the warehouse, standard orders were configured and shipped within 48 hours from the time that the order was placed; orders could also be expedited to be configured within 8 hours, to arrive at the customer's door in 24 hours By 1997, the 135,000 square foot Tempe QIC built and shipped over 1,000 fully-configured systems per day. An additional center, in Cincinnati, Ohio, opened mid-year. Both centers, which operated at a 95%+ error free standard, had received ISO 9001 certification, the highest standard of quality.

Building on its QIC capabilities, in 1996 and 1997 MicroAge partnered with key suppliers to provide upstream value-added services through an innovative program called "channel assembly." The idea grew out of discussions between MicroAge President Bob O'Malley and John Andrews, Logistics Group President, and senior IBM management. During a series of meetings in late 1995 and early 1996, the two companies worked out a solution that would add value to both firms. Rather than buy pre-configured personal computer products and then take them apart and re-configure them for customers, MicroAge would take over final assembly of IBM desktop computer products in its QIC. By outsourcing computer assembly to MicroAge, IBM would reduce the cycle time for delivering its products to end customers, enable customization of IBM's products to meet customer specifications, and lower the cost for both IBM and MicroAge. A key factor in this lower cost was delayed procurement of Intel microprocessors. Since Intel was reducing prices aggressively, later procurement meant lower component cost. Over time, IBM hoped to be able to reduce its costs and cycle times to be competitive with Dell. By fall 1997, MicroAge and IBM had expanded their channel assembly relationship to include a wide variety of desktop and notebook computer products; MicroAge became the first channel player authorized to assemble IBM's servers. With its agreement with Fujitsu, Microsoft also became the first channel player authorized to assemble notebook computers.

By mid-1997, other suppliers—including Hewlett-Packard, Compaq, Panasonic, Digital, Acer, SUN, and Intel—had signed channel assembly agreements with MicroAge and agreements with a number of other suppliers were under negotiation. In announcing Digital's partnership with MicroAge in their "Seamless Supply Chain" (SSC) process (Digital's version of channel assembly), Bruce Claflin, vice president and general manager of Digital's Personal Computer Business Unit, remarked: "The SSC process greatly enhances the ease of doing business with Digital. Because Digital and MicroAge maintain a virtual supply pipeline, inventory investments and carrying costs are greatly reduced. [We] selected MicroAge as our first channel assembly partner for two reasons. MicroAge offers an industry-leading integration facility with proven ability to handle the volume of products and premium quality manufacturing Digital desired. Second, Digital and MicroAge have shared a long-term successful relationship through which the two companies have co-developed a number of innovative distribution and reseller programs."

During the mid-1990s, MicroAge introduced call-center and help desk services to provide 7 day per week, 24 hours per day customer service support, including technical trouble shooting, end user support, and tele-sales and marketing services (for example, direct mail follow-up, new product launches, market research, and special promotions). In 1997, profits from help desk and call center services accounted for 10% of the company's overall income.

Developing the Channel and Creating Demand

In addition to simply broadening the product line, in 1996 MicroAge began to actively pursue strategies designed to develop the channel and create additional demand. Central to this effort was a shift to category management—a business model that had been very successful in the supermarket industry. Category managers were considered general managers of a line of computer products that customers would use to create a business solution. They were responsible for understanding the product offerings of all suppliers in a category and for developing co-marketing programs to help the reseller community and MicroAge branch offices be as effective as possible in selling business solutions using those products. Jeff Hansen, Director of the Mobility Solutions Category, created educational materials describing how to create wireless e-mail solutions for mobile workers using Compaq's new wireless-enabled PC and Wireless Internet services from AT&T. In summer 1997, MicroAge announced the formation of two new Category Management groups: The Computer Telephony Integration Group would provide technical information, marketing support, and reseller certification for voice and data communications, mail, and video conferencing technologies; the MicroAge Internet Solutions Group provided similar services for Internet technologies.

Sample Performance Measures for
Category Managers

Revenue	Inventory on hand
Gross margin	Days on hand
Trade margin %	Fill rate
Rebates (gross)	$ > 60 days
Net profit contribution	% On hand > 60 days

"As we move upstream in the value chain, we've had to develop competencies in areas that we never considered before," said Hansen. "The shift to category management reflects our move away from the box picker mentality we had five years ago. Now we see ourselves as a sourcing company. We need to create strategic alliances with our suppliers and work with them to market solutions. It's easy to see how you add value on the Integration side of the business. But, how do you add value on the Distribution side? Category management is our strategy for

adding value both upstream (to our suppliers) and downstream (to the systems integrators), including the traditional VAR channel and MicroAge's Integration branch office network." (Appendix D provides sample materials developed by MicroAge category managers.)

Creating Electronic Commerce Capabilities and Exploiting the Economic Value of Information and Channel Relationships

A key strategic initiative between 1995 and 1997 was the development of the company's Internet-based electronic commerce capabilities. These initiatives extended efforts that had begun during the late 1980s. At that time, MicroAge had developed a PC-based system, called ZData, that allowed corporate customers, resellers, and MIS branches to access an on-line catalog of products available through MicroAge. Over the years the system was improved to enable on-line ordering, order status tracking, invoice history, and account status information. In 1995, MicroAge enhanced its marketing and customer support services by introducing its RealFax service through which customers could order thousands of documents on MicroAge products, services, and suppliers using their touch-tone phone. In late 1995, MicroAge launched POWERdisc, a CD-ROM version of the company's on-line product catalog that was updated on a monthly basis. In March 1996, under the leadership of O'Malley, MicroAge partnered with pcOrder.com to create ECadvantage—an Internet-based order fulfillment, quoting, and configuration tool that dramatically expanded power, reach, and ease of use of MicroAge's electronic commerce architecture (see Exhibit 5). ECadvantage was introduced in August 1996 and the product was shipped to corporate users, resellers, and MicroAge branch offices in late 1996. Within

EXHIBIT 5 ECadvantage Technical Architecture

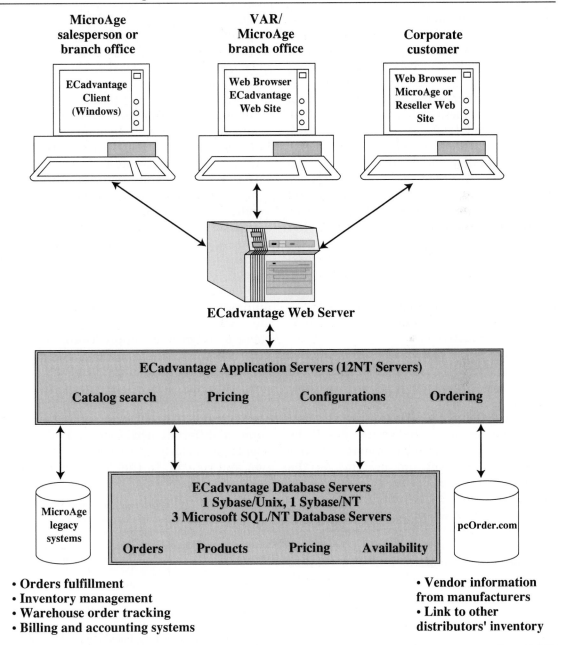

MicroAge
salesperson or
branch office

ECadvantage
Client
(Windows)

VAR/
MicroAge
branch office

Web Browser
ECadvantage
Web Site

Corporate
customer

Web Browser
MicroAge or
Reseller Web
Site

ECadvantage Web Server

ECadvantage Application Servers (12NT Servers)

Catalog search   Pricing   Configurations   Ordering

MicroAge
legacy
systems

ECadvantage Database Servers
1 Sybase/Unix, 1 Sybase/NT
3 Microsoft SQL/NT Database Servers

Orders   Products   Pricing   Availability

pcOrder.com

• Orders fulfillment
• Inventory management
• Warehouse order tracking
• Billing and accounting systems

• Vendor information
from manufacturers
• Link to other
distributors' inventory

Adapted from N. Engler, "A Wholesale Survivor." *Software,* August 1997.

the first 13 weeks, over 4,000 users had signed up for the service and over 300 online orders had been placed. By April 1997, over 8,000 users were registered. In December 1996, ECadvantage was set up as a separate division; Katie Pushor was named president of the new unit.

By December 1997, the number of ECadvantage users had increased to 28,000. The increased traffic strained MicroAge's network capacity and highlighted problems with reliability and performance on Internet-based ordering systems. Pushor also found that MicroAge's ability to expand its electronic commerce capabilities was limited by problems encountered as her group attempted to integrate ECadvantage with the company's order fulfillment warehousing, inventory tracking, and billing systems. Security issues also needed to be resolved before the company proceeded with more extensive Internet-based electronic commerce initiatives.

In fall 1997, Pushor and Bob Mason, MicroAge's newly-hired Chief Information Officer (CIO) and President of MicroAge Services, began to explore options for addressing the system integration and network management challenges posed by Internet-based electronic commerce. Pushor commented: "Getting our systems on the desktop of the resellers and corporate customers is critical. ECadvantage will enable us to reengineer the entire supply channel from the vendor to the end customers. It will strengthen our relationships with our customers, the vendors, and our reseller partners. Finally, it will provide us with information that will enhance our current business and serve as the foundation for new information-based products and services. We must penetrate quickly and then offer a steady stream of new products and services. We must resolve the systems integration and network problems immediately."

In early 1998, Mason and other senior managers in the company developed a Request for Information (RFI) to get quotes and feedback on a proposal to build the "most sophisticated, global network available today." Within weeks, the responses from some of the most sophisticated suppliers of networking equipment were being evaluated as the company worked to draft a Request for Proposal. In addition, Mason launched an initiative to unite the company's diverse electronic mail and internet initiatives into a single corporate-wide system. The company chose Microsoft as the vendor for development of a standardized suite of desktop, server, e-mail and commerce-related internet, intranet and extranet systems.[6] The company also signed agreements with Siebel Technologies to implement their state-of-the-art salesforce automation and customer support technologies and were in the final stages of an agreement with a supply chain management software vendor. "MicroAge's current information and communication technology platform is not flexible and robust enough to enable the company to execute its strategy," Mason said. "Today, stand-alone systems support different activities and it's up to people to perform the necessary coordination and control. In the future, we need to

---

[6]By late 1997, there was beginning agreement within the industry on terminology for internet-based systems. The *Internet* was the public internet network, accessible to all who had the required network connections and software. *Intranets* were systems that operated on a company's private, internal networks. These private networks used the internet standards of communication but they were specially protected so that they could only be accessed by company employees. *Extranets* were systems that operated on secure internet networks that could only be accessed by individuals who had been granted special permission bv the company. These secure networks were frequently used for business-to-business electronic commerce (for example, supply chain management).

have a robust and flexible information pipeline that enables us to integrate, streamline and time synchronize our operations. We also need robust, user-friendly information packaging and delivery tools to help individuals and teams get the information they need to make decisions and take action. We then need to extend these systems to link our suppliers and customers in a seamless information value chain." The ability to create this "seamless information value chain" required that the company develop a technology "architecture"[7] that would guide decisions concerning the development of MicroAge's information and communication infrastructure. (See Exhibit 6 for an overview of the company's proposed technology architecture scheduled to be in place by mid-1998.)

In addition to his role as MicroAge's CIO, Mason was also president of MicroAge Services. In this role, Mason was responsible for developing, launching and leading technology service companies that would provide small to medium-sized companies with the services and support required to design, operate and manage in a networked computing environment. Two such companies, launched by MicroAge Services in late

---

[7]Just as the blueprint of a building's architecture indicates not only the structure's design but how everything—from plumbing and heating systems to the flow of traffic within the building—fits and works together, the blueprint of a firm's IT architecture defines the technical computing, information management, and communications platform of the firm; the structures and controls that define how that platform can be used; and the categories of applications that can be created upon the platform. The IT architecture provides an overall picture of the range of technical options available to a firm, and, as such, it also implies the range of business options. Decisions made in building the technical IT architecture must be closely linked to decisions made in designing the IT organization that will manage the architecture, which, in turn, must be linked to the strategy and organization design of the firm itself.

1997 and early 1998, were NetGenuity and Technology Asset Management (TAM). The NetGenuity mission was to assist small to medium-sized firms with managing their IT assets by providing services such as IT architecture development, operations and network management, call center and help desk, technology update and replacement, network and data security services, and disaster recovery. TAM's mission was to provide a wide range of asset management and leasing services for large corporations. "MicroAge funds these new services companies and retains a share of the equity," Mason said. "I sit on the board of directors and provide ongoing oversight and guidance to the management team. These new businesses will partner with other MicroAge businesses to expand their capabilities (for example, call center services and logistics) and we will sell the technology services to our integration services branch offices. In fact, MicroAge's branch offices and owner-managed branches are among our best customers."

Revolution or Evolution?

Much has been written about how the Internet will cause disintermediation, bypassing the middle links of the supply chain as manufacturers gain direct access to customers. . . . No single industry is at as great a risk [for disintermediation] in the near term as the computer industry.

Gartner Group Report, June 9, 1997

In a recent report on supply chain management by the Gartner Group, MicroAge was profiled as a channel intermediary that had successfully positioned itself for survival—and success—as a market facilitator for the IT channel (see Exhibit 7). The report stated: "MicroAge's strategy maps directly

EXHIBIT 6   MicroAge Information Technology Architecture

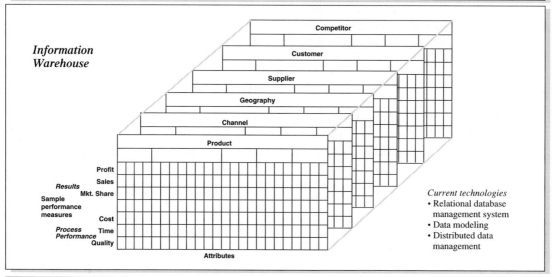

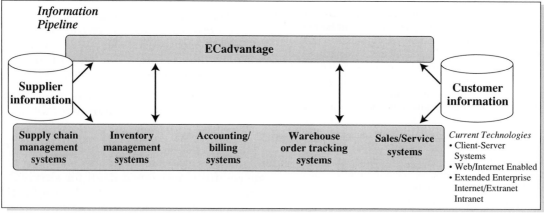

EXHIBIT 7   Gartner Principles for Wholesaler Survival and Assessment of MicroAge
Strategic Initiatives*

- *Enhance the Flow of Physical Goods:* MicroAge provides the services (for example, procurement, configuration, order fulfillment and tracking, delivery, installation, testing and maintenance) that are required to streamline the flow of physical goods through the IT supply channel. Working with suppliers and customers they have greatly increased the ability for customization and one-stop shopping, while decreasing cycle times from two months to two days and maintaining 95–99% accuracy.
- *Enhance the Flow of Information:* MicroAge was the first in the industry to provide non-proprietary, Internet-based configuration and electronic catalogs—not only for products in its warehouse, but also for products in competitor warehouses. The company is ahead of the pack in learning to use that information to add value.
- *Enhance the Rate of Consumption:* As they build the infrastructure to support both the physical flow of goods and the flow of information, MicroAge has begun to concentrate energy and resources on developing the organizational capabilities and infrastructure required to penetrate quickly. "In addition," the Gartner Group continued, "MicroAge has redefined the notion of the product it sells to customers."
- *Increase Item Value:* MicroAge has created additional value through the assembly and integration of multivendor products on a channel-wide basis, guaranteeing terms, price, and availability to customers.
- *Increase Process Management Value:* MicroAge has created additional value by re-engineering the procurement process for each customer, product, and channel, treating each as a unique client engagement with its own specific project management requirements. MicroAge has focused on the goals of reducing order cycle times and improving customer satisfaction.
- *Increase Services Value:* MicroAge has developed a portfolio of service offerings that it can uniquely configure for each product and customer relationship. Key areas of service include systems installation, training, help desk support, and client/server business recovery support. MicroAge also offers financing and leasing services to customers.
- *Increase Information Value:* MicroAge offers its customers a smorgasbord of information services that enable its customers to identify the "right" products for a given business requirement. Customers can use MicroAge's information services to identify available products, configure the required solutions, and manage the financial transactions between supplier and customers. MicroAge also offers an information service that provides technical product information to resellers, corporate customers, and MicroAge branch offices.

*Adapted from B. Enslaw, A. Mesher, and C. Smith, Gartner Group Strategic Analysis Report, June 9, 1997.

---

to Gartner's Model for Wholesaler Survival" in the age of the Internet. Despite the words of encouragement from Gartner, however, senior management at MicroAge knew that tough strategic decisions would need to be made before the company could capitalize on its early wins. Should the company continue on its current course or embark on yet another revolutionary change in its strategy and organization? No matter which approach was taken, senior management knew that the next year would be critical to the company's future.

Risk Assessment Scorecard

❏ Is the product in excess supply?	If so, it is already at or approaching commodity status and is ripe for dynamically priced open sourcing over the Internet.
❏ Does the product have low manufacturing content?	If so, it is easily imitated by competitors, including new entrants that use the Internet as a low-cost sales and marketing channel to achieve lower operating costs.
❏ Can the product be shipped by a small-package carrier?	If so, it can be globally sourced by buyers using Internet search agents and electronic marketplaces and can then be delivered overnight almost anywhere in the world.
❏ Is the product purchased on short-term contracts?	If so, the buyers are price sensitive and thus are likely to turn to the Internet for open sourcing.
❏ Is the product bought by customers with whom the enterprise has an informal business relationship?	If so, the buyers consider this to be a nonstrategic relationship and thus again are likely to turn to the Internet for open sourcing.
❏ Can the product be digitized?	If so, the actual physical role of distribution may be eliminated.
❏ Is the product consumed by computer-literate buyers?	If so, buyers will be apt to use the Internet for purchasing activities.
❏ Is the product assembled from commodity components using a non-asset-intensive conversion process?	If so, little money will be required to imitate.
❏ Is the product lifecycle short?	If so, local stocking will be avoided. If the product is also of high value, then inventory carrying costs will be significant, causing further avoidance of inventory build-up.
❏ Can the product be shipped by airplane?	If so, global sourcing will be feasible.
❏ Is the product of low value with no manufacturing content?	If so, the key role a distributor will play is to match buyers and sellers and/or guarantee delivery—services that can be provided through an electronic marketplace.

Strategic Planning Assumptions

Through 2002. The Internet will cause logistics activities to become key product differentiators.

By year-end 1998. Simply marketing items on the Internet will no longer be a competitive advantage for enterprises because virtually any organization will be able to post its products on electronic catalogs.

By mid-1999. 70% of enterprises that fail to incorporate logistics applications and content—such as inventory status and delivery dates—into their Internet management strategies will fail to gain a competitive advantage.

By 2002. 60% of wholesale distributors will earn a majority of their profits from post-sale service—for example, information services, delivery, installation, warranty, and training.

Adapted from B. Enslaw, A. Mesher, and C. Smith, Gartner Group Strategic Analysis Report, April 8, 1997.

Appendix A

KEY PERSONNEL BIOGRAPHIES

Jeff McKeever
Chairman and Chief Executive Officer

Jeffrey D. McKeever is chairman and chief executive officer of MicroAge, Inc., Tempe, Arizona. Prior to co-founding MicroAge in 1976, he was vice president at First Interstate Bank of Arizona, N.A., and served as a major in the United States Air Force.

McKeever was named Arizona Entrepreneur of the Year in 1984 by Arizona State University, Entrepreneurial Fellow at the University of Arizona in 1986, Distinguished Alumni by the National Junior Achievement in 1992, and, for the last 11 years, has been named one of the Top 25 Most Influential Executives in the computer industry by Computer Reseller News. In 1995 he was named Master Entrepreneur of the Year by *Inc.* magazine, recognizing a lifetime of entrepreneurial success. McKeever currently serves on the Board of Advisors of the Services Marketing Center at Arizona State University and he is a member of the Chief Executives Organization, Arizona Presidents Organization and Greater Phoenix Leadership. He received a bachelor's degree and master's in Business Administration from the University of Arizona.

Bob O'Malley
President, MicroAge, Inc.

Bob O'Malley is president of MicroAge, Inc. His direct responsibilities include overseeing two of MicroAge's four business groups, the MicroAge Logistics Group and the MicroAge Services Group. O'Malley joined the company in May 1995 as president of MicroAge Data Services, and was promoted to senior vice president Services in March 1996. He assumed his current position as MicroAge president in November 1996.

Prior to joining MicroAge, O'Malley spent 19 years with IBM, where he held positions in Large Systems Sales, Retail Industry Sales, Finance and IBM's PC business in the Americas and in Asia Pacific, Tokyo, Japan.

O'Malley has a bachelor's degree in Aeronautical Engineering from the University of Minnesota and an M.B.A. from Arizona State University. He also served as a T-38 instructor pilot in the USAF and completed service in 1973 as a Captain with 1,500 flying hours.

Alan Hald
President, MicroAge Enterprises

As co-founder of MicroAge, Inc., Alan Hald guided the growth of the company from a single location in 1976 to thousands of affiliated resellers worldwide. Between 1992 and 1996, he designed and ran MicroAge Infosystems. Currently, as president of MicroAge Enterprises, Inc., he is developing new IT businesses that have the potential to grow rapidly. He is chairman of the Board of Image Choice and MicroAge Federal subsidiaries.

Within the microcomputer industry, Hald is currently chairman of the Computer Technology Industry Association (CompTIA) and is shaping the Association's value chain focus. He also chairs CompTIA's Public Policy Committee and has been working on national legislative issues that impact the information industry. He also initiated the Association's electronic commerce initiatives.

Over the years Hald has received numerous computer industry awards, including Computer Reseller News' "Most Influential People in the Industry" and *Inc.* magazine's "Master Entrepreneur of the Year." In 1997 he received the Phoenix Community Forum's "Community Vision Weaver Award." His commitment to improving Arizona's climate for technologically innovative business was recently recognized by being named Arizona's "Entrepreneur of the Year" for supporting entrepreneurship. Hald is a graduate of Rensselaer Polytechnic University and has an MBA from Harvard University.

Jim Daniel
Senior VP and CFO

James R. Daniel is Senior Vice President and Chief Financial Officer of MicroAge, Inc. Daniel joined MicroAge in January of 1993. Prior to joining MicroAge, he served as Chief Financial Officer and Treasurer of Dell Computers, Inc. from 1991 to 1993. In this position he was responsible for treasury, tax, accounting, planning, investor relations, financial systems, internal audit, risk management, and facilities. From 1984 to 1991, Daniel served as Chief Financial Officer and Treasurer for SCI Systems, Inc. SCI is the world's largest electronic contract manufacturer. From 1981 to 1984, he served as Vice President, Treasurer and Controller of Lykes Bros. Steamship Company. He also served as Corporate Controller of Bio Rad Laboratories from 1979 to 1981, and as Director of Finance from 1974 to 1979 for the Hyland Therapeutics Division of Baxter International Inc.

Daniel is a Certified Public Accountant, with a B.S. in accounting from the University of Illinois, Champaign, Ill., and an M.B.A. from Loyola University, Chicago. He received the Loyola University Graduate School of Business Outstanding Alumnus award in 1995 and is a member of NASDAQ's Issues Affairs Committee.

Jim Manton
Senior VP, Operations

Jim Manton is Senior Vice President, Operations of MicroAge, Inc. The charter for Operations at MicroAge is to improve quality, lower costs, reduce cycle time and build strategic capabilities. Working with the senior management team, Manton's focus includes enterprisewide processes, structure and management systems.

Manton first worked for MicroAge from 1979 to 1989, becoming the Executive Vice President and COO in 1987. He left the company in 1989 to start his own businesses, which included a systems integration company as well as a cycle time reduction consultancy for high tech manufacturers. Returning in 1993, Manton led the development of the technical businesses at MicroAge, including configuration, support services, contract assembly and the emerging teleservices businesses. In 1996, Manton led a company-wide effort aimed at achieving operational excellence and overall process improvement. Prior to joining MicroAge, he held positions at Johnson & Johnson and White Motor Company. Manton earned his MBA from the University of Denver in 1973.

John Andrews
President, MicroAge Logistics Group

John H. Andrews is the President of MicroAge Logistics Group. MicroAge Logistics provides resellers, large organizations and technology suppliers world-class distribution and ISO 9001-certified integration services. The MicroAge Logistics Services Group includes MicroAge Quality Integration Centers and Channel Assembly services; MicroAge Service Solutions, which provides large volume inbound/outbound teleservices and call centers; Category Management, responsible for demand creation and the procurement and sourcing of products from over 500 technology suppliers; and Contract Logistics, which provides light assembly and other services to companies such as IBM, Compaq, Hewlett-Packard, Digital and Motorola.

Andrews has served as president of the MicroAge Logistics Services Group since July 1993. Prior to his current position, John served as Vice President and Chief Financial Officer from June 1990 to Jan. 1993, and Principal Accounting Officer and Corporate Controller from Dec. 1988 to June 1990. Prior to joining the Company in 1984, Andrews held various financial positions in the areas of Financial Accounting and Analysis with the Dial Corporation.

Andrews has a B.S. degree in Accounting from Arizona State University and is a certified public accountant.

Chris Koziol
President, MicroAge Distribution Group

Christopher J. Koziol serves as president of MicroAge Distribution Group and senior vice president of Sales at MicroAge, Inc.

Koziol joined MicroAge in 1985 and has served in several strategic sales and management positions. Prior to his current position, he served as president of MicroAge Infosystems Services (MIS). MIS provides systems integration services and distributed computing solutions to large organizations worldwide. Former positions include vice president of Sales for MicroAge Computer Centers, Inc. and director of Regional Support. As vice president of Sales, Koziol was instrumental in the development of the MIS organization.

A graduate of the University of Arizona and the Harvard Business School Program for Executive Development, Koziol also held sales and management positions with Pepsi-Cola Bottling Group and Western Office Systems, an agent for Exxon Office Systems and Wang Laboratories.

John Lewis
President, MicroAge Integration Group

John S. Lewis joined MicroAge's senior management team Jan. 1997 as president of the MicroAge Integration Group. In this position, John is responsible for global systems integration business, which includes MicroAge Infosystems Services and MicroAge Solutions. Prior to joining MicroAge, Lewis was chairman and CEO of First Interstate Bancorp Southwest until it merged with Wells Fargo on April 1, 1996.

Lewis has received recognition for numerous business achievements. In 1992, he was honored by the American Banker as one of "40 Top Bankers Under 40 Years of Age." He is a board member, and past president of the Arizona Bankers Association, and served as president of the Pacific Coast Banking School.

An active participant in the community, Lewis serves on the board of the Fiesta Bowl, and is a member of the Phoenix Leadership Council and chairman of the Phoenix Chamber of Commerce. He also is a member of the Dean's Council of 100 at Arizona State University's College of Business. Lewis has a bachelor's degree in business administration from the University of Nevada in Reno.

Bob Mason
President, MicroAge Technology Services Group and MicroAge, Inc. CIO

Robert W. Mason is president of the MicroAge Technology Services Group and chief information officer of MicroAge, Inc. The Technology Services Group is responsible for developing and growing the company's new IT services businesses, including network management, disaster recovery, security services and technology asset management. As chief information officer, Mason is responsible for directing client services, business systems development, and information technology functions for MicroAge headquarters and business units. Mason, who held Information Systems management positions at GE Lighting and Johnson & Johnson, most recently served as vice president and chief information officer at Anheuser-Busch Companies.

While CIO at GE Lighting in the 1980s, Mason led the implementation of an on-line order fulfillment service between GE and Wal-Mart that served as a prototype for the industry. Mason is an active member of several industry groups within the information systems field and holds an M.B.A. from Pace University in New York City.

Katie Pushor
President, ECadvantage, Inc.

Katie Pushor is president of ECadvantage, Inc., a wholly owned subsidiary of MicroAge, Inc. ECadvantage provides electronic commerce services and information to suppliers, distributors, integrators and corporate customers. Pushor joined MicroAge in 1989 and served as president of the Channel Services Division. In this capacity, she was responsible for managing the company's more than $300 million in inventory, the corporate and product marketing functions, and relationships with more than 120 manufacturers of hardware, software and related technologies.

Prior to joining MicroAge, Pushor worked at Coopers & Lybrand. During her 10-year tenure, she served on the audit staff and as director of Personnel, Finance and Administration. In 1990, Pushor was named one of the Top 25 Female Executives and Computer Reseller News recognized her as "One of 15 to Watch in 1991." In 1993, she was chosen as one of 100 women from the United States, Mexico and Canada to participate in the Leadership America program, and she was named to the National Board of Directors of the organization in 1995. In 1994 and 1995, she was named one of the Top One Hundred Arizona Women in Business by Today's Arizona Woman magazine. In 1996, Pushor accepted an appointment to the Finance Chair of the Arizona State Democratic Party.

Ms. Pushor is an honors graduate of the University of Colorado in Boulder, Colorado.

Appendix B

THE ENTERPRISE COMPUTING
DISTRIBUTION CHANNEL (1998)

**Electronic distributors sell
components to full-line distributors
and corporate system integrators**

Component
design and
manufacture › Electronic
distribution › Equipment
design and
assembly › Equipment
and component
distribution › Custom config.
and
business system
assembly › System design,
integration,
installation,
testing › Lifecycle
management
and support ›

**Component manufacturers sell
components to full-line distributors
and original equipment manufacturers**

MicroAge in 1990

| Master Reseller |

MicroAge in 1998

Full-line distributor

Channel assembly
and quality integration centers

Enterprise system
integration

Call center and
technology services

Category management

EC advantage

Key Players

Component Manufacturers (for example, Intel, Texas Instruments, Seagate, U.S. Robotics) design and manufacture electronic components and equipment, such as computer memory chips, processors, hard drives, and network cards.

Electronics Distributors (for example, Arrow) sell components Full-Line Distributors and Original Equipment Manufacturers.

Original Equipment Manufacturers (OEMs) design and assemble computer and network equipment. (Some OEMs, for example, IBM and HP, also manufactured some of their own electronic components.) By 1996, over 80% of the computers sold into the channel were broken down and reconfigured by Distributors, Value-Added Resellers (VARs) and System Integrators. In 1997, MicroAge pioneered a new concept called "Channel Assembly" in which OEMs sold a base system to channel players who then custom-configured and assembled a business system based on customer specifications.

Traditionally, *Master Resellers* (for example, MicroAge) sold brand name computers to a network of franchise dealers and small *Value-Added Resellers* (VARs), who then configured and installed personal computers and local area networks in small to medium-sized firms. Large corporations often bought their computers directly from the manufacturers. Until the early 1990s, *Full-Line Distributors,* having been excluded from selling brand name computers, sold primarily components (e.g., memory boards, drives, network cards) and peripherals (e.g., printers, network equipment, modems) to VARs and large corporate customers.

By the mid-1990s, closed sourcing of brand name computers had given way to open sourcing, and the distinction between Master Resellers and Full-Line Distributors began to blur. In addition, the rise of discount computer brands (for example, Dell, Gateway and Micron) had spurred the development of new distribution channels, including: Computer Retail Superstores, for example, CompUSA (1997 revenues = $4.6B) and Computer City (1997 revenues = $1.9B); and Direct Marketers, for example, Micro Warehouse (1997 revenues = $2.1B) and CDW (1997 revenues = $1.25B).

System Integrators buy computer equipment from distributors and work with corporate customers to develop, install, operate and maintain customized business systems. System Integrators are segmented by the size of their corporate customers and by the extent of system integration provided.

Value-Added Resellers (VARs) primarily service small to medium-sized companies and local business units of large companies.

Corporate System Integrators service large, global companies within two major market segments.

High-End Corporate System Integrators (e.g., EDS, Arthur Andersen, IBM Global Network Services) provide system integration and outsourcing services for a large firm's total information technology (IT) resources, including mainframe data centers and long distance network services.

Enterprise System Integrators (e.g., GE ITS, CompuCom, Entex and Vanstar) provide system integration and outsourcing services for desktop and local area network IT resources. By 1998, the lnternet had hastened the shift to a network computing environment in which a wide range of personal and portable computers connected to special purpose servers, at times including mainframe computers. As a result, High-End Corporate System Integrators often partnered with Enterprise System Integrators and/or Value-Added Resellers to provide total systems integration and outsourcing services to large corporate clients.

PERFORMANCE COMPARISON FOR IT CHANNEL PLAYERS (1997)

Hybrid Models (Full-Line Distributor and Enterprise Systems Integrator)

Selected Financial Measures	*MicroAge*	*Inacom*
Total revenues	$4.4B	$3.9B
Operating income	$70.7M	$78.9M
Net income	$25.0M	$29.5M
Gross margin ratio	.56%	.75%
Debt to equity	15.9%	43.5%
Return on assets	2.9%	3.3%
Return on equity	11.7%	11.7%
Current ratio	1.2	1.5
Asset turnover ratio	4.6	4.1
Earnings per share	$1.40	$2.48
1997 Stock prices H/L	29¼-12½	30⅜-20

Full-Line Distributor

Selected Financial Measures	*Ingram Micro*	*Tech Data*	*Merisel*
Total revenues	$16.6B	$7.1B	$4.0B
Operating income	$377.0M	$172.6M	N/A
Net income	$193.6M	$89.9M	−$15.8M
Gross margin ratio	1.2%	1.3%	−.4%
Debt to equity	108.2%	78.1%	1966.7%
Return on assets	4.7%	4.8%	−14.3%
Return on equity	20.4%	15.7%	−165.7%
Current ratio	1.6	1.4	1.4
Asset turnover ratio	3.4	3.3	5.5
Earnings per share	$1.43	$2.00	−$4.68
1997 Stock prices H/L	33 9/16-19⅜	50⅜-21⅝	5¼-1 1/16

Enterprise System Integrator (GE ITS is part of GE Capital, and Entex is a private company; separate data is not available)

Selected Financial Measures	*Vanstar*	*CompuCom*
Total revenues	$2.2B	$2.0B
Operating income	$68.3M	$67.0M
Net income	$30.0M	$35.2M
Gross margin ratio	1.4%	1.8%
Debt to equity	60.0%	51.4%
Return on assets	3.8%	6.1%
Return on equity	20.4%	19.5%
Current ratio	1.5	2.6
Asset turnover ratio	2.9	4.3
Earnings per share	$0.69	$0.75
1997 Stock prices H/L	24⅞-6¾	10⅞-5 3/16

Appendix C

SELECTED MARKET STUDIES

MSI Value-Added Reseller (VAR) Segmentation—1997 Selected Findings

- The U.S. VAR market reached approximately $33.5 billion in 1996.
- Specialists accounted for over half of all sales.
- Remaining sales were split almost evenly between networking resellers and generalists.
- The sample of 362 VARs (with revenues of <$20M) accounted for $1.34B in 1996 sales, or 4% of the overall market. VARs with $20 Million or less in annual revenue accounted for 78% of this study. (Note: 98% of all VARs have revenues of <$20M.)

VAR Market Sizing (U.S.)

	Fulfillment $8.5B	Integration $16.0B	Design $9.0B
Specialists $18.9B	Vertical resellers $4.2B	Vertical integrator $10.2B	Industry consultant $4.5B
Networking resellers $7.4B	Network resellers $1.4B	Network integrator $3.6B	Network consultant $2.4B
Generalists $7.2B	Box mover $2.9B	Business solution provider $2.2B	Technology consultant $2.1B

Specialization/Focus →

Value Add →

N=464

Source: Analysis of MSI 1995 VAR Study; 1/97 - 2/97 Reseller Interviews

COMPUTER RESELLER NEWS
PREFERRED DISTRIBUTOR
STUDY, 1997

Sourcing Trends: By Type of Distributor

Distribution	1996	1997
Full-line distributors	54%	45%
Master distributors*	22%	30%
Direct/manufacturers	14%	14%
Direct/mail order	5%	5%
Other resellers	5%	6%
Base:	3224	3198

Product Sourcing: By Product

	Computer Systems	Software	Mass Storage	Networking Products	Peripherals	Emerging Technologies
Full-line distributors	41%	43%	50%	41%	50%	44%
Master distributors	30%	28%	31%	37%	29%	27%
Manufacturer direct	19%	20%	8%	14%	10%	16%
Other reseller	5%	4%	7%	4%	6%	8%
Direct/mail order	5%	5%	4%	4%	5%	5%
Base	551	506	506	563	571	501

Evaluation Criteria: "Very Important"

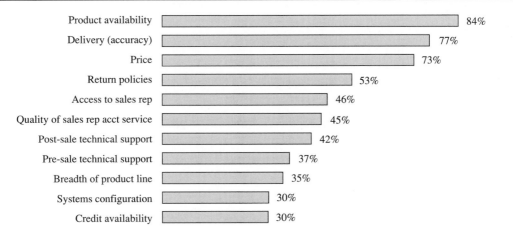

Product availability	84%
Delivery (accuracy)	77%
Price	73%
Return policies	53%
Access to sales rep	46%
Quality of sales rep acct service	45%
Post-sale technical support	42%
Pre-sale technical support	37%
Breadth of product line	35%
Systems configuration	30%
Credit availability	30%

Computer Reseller News separates the Distributor category into traditional Full-Line Distributors and Master Distributors. The latter are traditional Master Resellers who, in the advent of open sourcing, broadened their product line to include a more comprehensive range of items.

Summary of Preference Rankings

	Computer Systems	Software	Mass Storage	Networking Products	Peripherals	Emerging Technologies
Ingram Micro	1	1	1	1	1	1
Tech Data	2	2	2	2	2	2
Merisel	3	3	3	3	3	3
MicroAge	4	4	4	4	4	4
Gates/Arrow	6	5	5	5	5	6
Intelligent Electronics (IE)*	5	6	6	6	6	5

*Acquired by Ingram Micro

% of Resellers Rating Distributors "Excellent" on Key Criteria

	Ingram Micro	Tech Data	MicroAge	Merisel	Gates/Arrow	IE	Excellence Norm
Product availability	32%	26%	19%	20%	19%	14%	25%
Delivery (accuracy)	38%	37%	28%	25%	29%	19%	33%
Price	21%	19%	20%	15%	21%	29%	22%
Return policies	28%	26%	18%	18%	20%	13%	23%
Access to sales rep	27%	25%	20%	17%	20%	13%	25%
Quality of sales rep	25%	23%	20%	17%	23%	14%	23%
Post-sale tech support	16%	16%	12%	8%	10%	8%	14%
Pre-sale tech support	19%	18%	13%	10%	13%	7%	16%
Breadth of line	45%	32%	20%	27%	17%	20%	27%
Configuration/ integration	13%	12%	15%	8%	11%	10%	14%
Credit availability	27%	25%	23%	20%	27%	23%	24%

Source: *Computer Reseller News.*

1997 COMPUTERWORLD SURVEY OF PREFERRED SYSTEM INTEGRATORS

Overall Satisfaction   **Rating**

MicroAge, Inc.	1
Inacom Corp.	2
GE ITS*	3
US Connect, Inc.**	4
Entex Info. Services	5

Business Practice   **Rating**

MicroAge, Inc.	1
Inacom Corp.	2
US Connect, Inc.	3
GE ITS	4
Entex Info. Services	5

Project Management   **Rating**

MicroAge, Inc.	1
Inacom Corp.	2
GE ITS	3
US Connect, Inc.	4
Entex Info. Services	5

Technical Performance   **Rating**

MicroAge, Inc.	1
Inacom Corp.	2
US Connect, Inc.	3
GE ITS	4
Entex Info. Services	5

*Part of GE Capital.
**19 of 26 USConnect affiliates now owned by Ikon Technology Services.

Adapted from: *Computerworld,* July 28, 1997.

Appendix D

SAMPLE VENDOR
CO-MARKETING MATERIALS

Wireless E-Mail Solutions

Access your e-mail and company network while in the field with a Compaq® wireless-enabled notebook PC and Wireless IP service from AT&T Wireless Services.

Microsoft® Exchange® Users:
Add Remote Wireless Access To Your Server

Benefits
- Enhanced delivery of e-mail to personnel in the field
- Improved productivity of mobile personnel
- Better use of groupware resources like database and shared files
- Faster response to time-sensitive internal communications
- Leverage of current IS investments
- Easy application development
- Reduce administrative costs

If your business uses Microsoft Exchange, you already know how it empowers LAN users by giving them access to messaging, databases, and groupware applications on your corporate Intranet. Now access to those same applications can be made available to mobile workers on their Compaq laptop computers when they're out of the office—by using a CompaqSpeedPaq Cellular PC Card and Wireless IP (CDPD) from AT&T Wireless Services.

Mobile professionals can now take their offices with them when they go!
It's as easy to use as if they were physically connected to the LAN back in the office. Whether they're on the road, working at home, or meeting a client in a faraway city, they'll have seamless remote access to Microsoft Exchange functions wherever Wireless IP is available. Note: For coverage information visit our web site at www.att.com/wireless/data/ and select Coverage.

Contact Info

In the Original document, full Contact Information is provided for:

System Requirements

Integration services are available from MicroAge.

Recommended Software

- Microsoft Exchange Server on NT server
- Microsoft Outlook or Exchange Client on laptop PC
- Ericsson EVO Virtual Office Server software on NT server
- Ericsson EVO Virtual Office Client software on laptop PC
- TCP/IP enabled on both client and server
- Mircosoft dial-up networking capability enabled on your laptop PC

Recommended Hardware

- Compaq notebook PCs:
  Armada 7000 Family
  Armada 4100 Family
  Armada 1500 Family
- One Compaq SpeedPaq Cellular PC Card (single-card solution) per client or one Compaq SpeedPaq Cellular PC Card with SpeedPaq 336 Telephony Modem Kit (two-card solution)
- NT Server with a minimum of 32MB RAM to support Microsoft Exchange and Ericsson EVO (installations that support more than 100 users may require a dedicated server for EVO)

Network Connection

- Wireless IP service account with AT&T Wireless Service for each client
- Public gateway access to Internet or private network access to the AT&T Wireless Services network

This is a sample of the first and last pages of co-marketing materials available from the Mobility Solutions MicroAge Category Management team. The complete document is four pages.

Managing Information Assets

> *The process of managing technology in organizations is getting more complex as it becomes more important. . . . In the early years, the big job was to manage the technology—get it to work, keep it running, and thus reduce the cost of doing business. Later the main thrust was to manage the information resource of the organization, particularly to support management decision making by delivering information when and where it was needed. Today . . . the changes required to support the new [technologies] and organizational structures that are now emerging require a significant amount of well-coordinated business and IT executive leadership.*

> McNurlin and Sprague, 1998[1]

Once upon a time, not so very long ago, business computing was highly centralized and tightly controlled. Most business applications ran on central computer systems managed by management information systems professionals. Users had on their desks "dumb" terminals connected to computers in the machine room, located out of sight and out of mind. This centralized model of organizational computing offered a certain sense of order. Systems managers could readily control the environment from a single point in the system. End users performed their jobs without worrying about software updates, system backups, or network connectivity. Then personal computer (PC) and local area network (LAN) technologies entered the picture, and things changed. With high-performance computers on their desktops (or in their briefcases), managers now had direct access to the local data and the local computer processing power required to turn that data into useful

---

[1]B. C. McNurlin and R. H. Sprague, *Information Systems Management in Practice* (Englewood Cliffs, NJ: Prentice-Hall, 1998).

information. But these privileges did not come free. Now business users were forced to assume a more active role in operating the technology and implementing systems, and the ability to share information and to communicate with others got worse rather than better. Implementing networked computing environments that addressed these problems became a business imperative that by the late 1990s—enabled by the Internet and associated technologies—was becoming a reality. Effective deployment and management of new networked computing technologies requires another radical shift in approach—a transition as daunting for many firms as the transition in business strategy and organization.

Module 4 provides frameworks for organizing, managing, and leading the IT function and for implementing information systems. Recognizing that most firms have a "hodgepodge" of mainframe, independent PC, and new networked technologies in place, we discuss management issues from all three perspectives. Chapter 7, "Organizing and Leading the Information Technology Function," examines the issues that general managers face as they design the IT organization required for today's distributed, networked IT architectures. Chapter 8, "Managing IT Outsourcing," continues the discussion of IT organizational alternatives by examining the challenges and opportunities in outsourcing IT activities. Chapter 9, "IT Operations," and Chapter 10, "IT Management Processes," provide a detailed discussion of the activities performed by IT professionals as they deliver IT services. Chapter 11, "A Portfolio Approach to Information Technology Development," discusses the challenges of implementing complex information systems and of managing the risks inherent in these projects. The module ends with four cases—Xerox Outsourcing, General Dynamics and CSC Outsourcing, Singapore Unlimited, and the Denver International Airport Baggage-Handling System—that examine IT operating and management challenges and the role of general management, IT management, and business users in addressing them.

Chapter
7

Organizing and Leading the Information Technology Function

The preceding chapter noted that the management structures needed for guiding new technologies into the organization are quite different from those for older, established technologies. The corporation must encourage information technology (IT) staff and users to innovate with the newer technologies, while focusing on control and efficiency in the more mature technologies. In this chapter, we will discuss two rapidly changing aspects of IT management: the range of organizational alternatives that have emerged for effectively assigning responsibility for IT development and the coordination and location of IT policy formulation among users, IT, and general management.

ORGANIZING ISSUES IN IT DEVELOPMENT

Policies for guiding the deployment of IT development staff and activity in the future must deal with two sets of tensions. The first, as noted in the previous chapters, is the balance between innovation and control. The relative emphasis a firm should place on the aggressive innovation phase varies widely, depending on a broad assessment of the potential strategic impact of IT on the firm, general corporate willingness to take risk, and so on. If IT is perceived to be of great import in helping the firm reach its strategic objectives, significantly greater investment in innovation is called for than if IT is seen to be merely helpful. In 1998, the opportunities to many firms offered by the explosion of Enterprise and Intranet software has readjusted the balance toward more innovation.

The second set of tensions is between IT department dominance and user dominance in the retention of development skills and in the active selection of priorities. The user tends toward short-term need fulfillment (at the expense of long-term architectural IT structure and orderly development), while the IT department can become preoccupied with the mastery of technology and an orderly development plan at the risk of a slow response, or no response, to legitimate user needs. Balancing the roles of these two groups is a complex task that must be handled in the context of the corporate culture, IT's potential strategic role, and the urgency of short-term problem resolution.

Table 7–1 reveals some consequences of excessive domination by IT and by users, clearly indicating that very different application portfolios and

TABLE 7–1   Possible Implications of Excess IT and User Dominance

IT Dominance	*User Dominance*
Too much emphasis on database and system maintenance.	Too much emphasis on problem focus.
All new systems must fit data structure of existing system.	IT feels out of control.
All requests for service require system study with benefit identification.	Explosive growth in number of new systems and supporting staff.
Standardization dominates with few exceptions.	Multiple suppliers deliver services. Frequent change in supplier of specific service.
IT designs/constructs everything.	Lack of standardization and control over data and systems.
Benefits of user control over development discussed but never implemented.	Hard evidence of benefits nonexistent.
Study always shows construction costs less than outside purchase.	Soft evidence of benefits not organized.
Headcount of distributed minis and development staff growing surreptitiously.	Few measurements/objectives for new system.
IT specializing in technical frontiers, not user-oriented markets.	Technical advice of IT not sought; if received, considered irrelevant.
IT spending 80 percent on maintenance, 20 percent on development.	User buying design, construction, maintenance, and operations services from outside.
IT thinks it is in control of all.	User building networks to own unique needs, not to corporate need.
Users express unhappiness.	Some users are growing rapidly in experience and use, while others feel nothing is relevant because they do not understand.
Portfolio of development opportunities firmly under IT control.	No coordinated effort between users for technology transfer or learning from experience.
No strong user group exists.	Growth in duplication of technical staffs.
General management not involved but concerned.	Dramatically rising communications costs because of redundancy.
	Duplication of effort and input everywhere because different data, hardware, and communications will not allow seamless movement.

operating problems emerge in the two settings. Given the difficulty of antic-ipating the implications of introducing a new technology, this chapter will emphasize the need for experimentation, as illustrated by the following four cases.

Some Examples

Case 1: A Short-Term User-Need Situation, Strategically Important. A major textile company, over a four-year period, made a major investment in new systems to enable electronic commerce and fast-response ordering time inside its major divisions. By executing a few *very* large, centrally man-aged projects, the company's central IT unit implemented the projects by ensuring that appropriate companywide standards for software, communi-cations, and so on, were in place. The new applications were considered to be a success by all involved. However, in 1998, systems development activity was moved from the central IT unit to the divisions, involving some 80 peo-ple. This was done to align the development of new applications more quickly and effectively with the needs of senior divisional management. With the corporate-designed general management standards in place, the time was now appropriate to install this new structure to enable the divi-sions to innovate more rapidly around individual agendas. Early results suggest that this has been an extremely effective move and the central stan-dards have not been eroded at all (only the passage of time will show whether this latter posture can be maintained).

The number one priority in a large machine-tool manufacturer's engi-neering department was computer-aided design (CAD). Given its early suc-cess, the effort was significantly expanded; the digital information design output was modified to enable department personnel to control computer-driven machine tools directly. This work was deliberately kept independent of the bill of the materials/cost system, which was in a database format and maintained by the IT unit.

Short of staff to integrate the new system into the firm's Bill of Materials database structure, the user department decided to proceed—a decision that would result in major system integration problems in the future. The work was done over the objection of IT management, but the engineering depart-ment received full support from senior management because of the project's potential major and immediate impact on shortening the product develop-ment life cycle.

The engineers enthusiastically worked on the CAD project to make it work—the project slashed development time by half for new-product designs—while the IT unit remained decidedly lukewarm. Although IT data-base integration issues still exist, the firm is no worse off in that regard than it was before the CAD project.

Case 2: IT Control to Achieve Cost Reduction. A division of a large consumer products manufacturer substantially invested in desktop support with modest up-front cost-benefit justification. IT encouraged managers and administrative support personnel to "use" the systems, with only cursory direction and some introductory training on the desktop units made available. After four months, three product managers had developed support for sales-force activities. Two had developed a capability to use mainframe data spreadsheets, generating substantial savings; two others did little, but were encouraging their administrative support staff to try it out. The users were gaining confidence and pursuing new programs with enthusiasm.

Six months later, IT's challenge was to develop and evolve an efficient program with these seven "experienced" users; the IT manager estimated roughly two years would be needed to achieve this efficient integration. In retrospect, however, both he and divisional management felt that it would have been impossible to implement networked desktop support with a standard IT-dominated systems study and that the expense of the after-the-fact rationalization was an acceptable price for the benefits that accrued. The control over this first foray into desktop networks contrasted sharply with the strong central control IT was exerting over its mature data-processing technologies.

Case 3: Step-by-Step Innovation of a New Technology.   A large South African retail chain installed a system of point-of-sale terminals in all of their 50-plus stores. The retail division (with the support of the IT manager) had initially funded the installation to assist store managers in controlling inventory. The terminals were to be used exclusively within individual stores to accumulate daily sales totals of individual items and permit the stores to trigger reorders in case lots at given times. The planned inventory savings were quickly achieved.

At the initiative of corporate management, these IT systems then evolved into links to central headquarters. The links fed data from the stores to new corporate computer programs that measured product performance across the stores and provided the ability to manage warehouse stock levels chainwide much more efficiently. Because the communication protocols in the selected terminals were incompatible with those in the computer at headquarters, implementing this unplanned linkage was expensive.

Nonetheless, the possibilities and benefits of the resulting system would have been difficult to define in advance, since this eventual use was not considered important when the initial point-of-sale terminals were being installed. Further, in management's opinion, even if the organization had considered it, the ultimate costs of the resulting system would have been deemed prohibitive in relation to the benefits (in retrospect, incorrectly prohibitive). In an uncertain world, there are limitations to planning; in this case, the success of the first system laid the baseline for the next ones. The firm is now using the network to implement companywide a customer loyalty card to enable detailed understanding of who its key customers are and their individual buying habits to better target coupons and special discounting programs. Again, this was not anticipated at the beginning of the process.

Case 4: User Innovation as a Source of Productivity.   A large bank introduced an electronic mail system and a word processor system to facilitate preparation of loan paperwork. The two systems soon evolved to link the bank's loan officers (initially not planned to be clients of either system) to a series of analytical programs—an evolution that developed out of conversations between a loan officer and a consultant. Bundled with the word processor loan system was a powerful analytical tool that officers could use to analyze loan performance. Because of the bank's electronic mail system, loan officers (at headquarters and in branches) could easily access the analytical tool.

Three months later, the bank faced a series of internal tensions as the costs of both systems unexpectedly rose due to this added use. In addition, there were no formal means of reviewing "experiments" or evaluating unanticipated uses of the systems by participants not initially involved. Eventually, a senior-management review committee supported the new use of the two systems, and it was permitted to continue. Substantial enhancements were added to the word processing software to make it even more useful to the loan officers.

Implications

Typical of emerging new services supporting professionals and managers in doing work, the above examples powerfully convey our conviction that it is impossible to foresee in advance the full range of consequences of introducing IT systems. Excessive control and focus on quick results in the early stages can deflect important learning that can result in even more useful applications. In addition, because neither IT professionals nor users have outstanding records in anticipating how new technologies will affect organizations, a necessary general management role is to help facilitate this assimilation.

The material that follows is divided into three sections. The first discusses the pressures on users to gain control—not only over a system's development activities, but, when possible, over the resulting product so it can run on a networked basis from the department. The second section identifies the advantages of strong IT development coordination and the potential pitfalls of uncontrolled proliferation of user-developed systems. The third section identifies the core policies that must be implemented by IT management, user management, and general management, respectively, in order to ensure a good result. The general manager's role is particularly critical in creating an environment that facilitates technological change and organizational adaptation.

PRESSURES TOWARD USER DOMINANCE

A number of intense pressures encourage users to exercise stronger control over their systems development resources and acquisition of independent IT resources. These pressures can be clustered into five categories: pent-up user demand, the needs for staffing flexibility, competitive and service growth in the IT market, users' desire to control their destiny, and fit with the organization.

Pent-Up User Demand

The backlog of development work facing an IT systems development department is frequently very large in relation to its staff resources. The reasons for these staffing "crunches" are many. Existing systems, for example, require sustained maintenance to accommodate changing regulatory and other external business requirements. In addition, the number of automated systems continues to grow, the maintenance time for existing systems rises as ongoing customization increases system complexity and systems needs to be adapted to changes in the IT architecture (a current, widespread example is fixing Y2K problems), and installation of Enterprise software requires either additional development resources or the postponement of new work. This problem really emerged in the 1970s, when systems design philosophy shifted from one that incorporated data into programs to one that clearly separates data and their management from the processes that use the data. Enterprise software now formalizes this procedural change. Effecting these conversions has been very expensive in terms of staff resources and has starved some departments for resources.

Further, the most challenging, high-status, high-paying IT jobs in the industry tend to be with computer vendors and software houses, which puts great pressure on an organization's IT department, whose most talented staff are tempted to move to these jobs; indeed, it is often easier for IT systems development to secure budget allocations than to find the staff resources to use them. The delays caused by these factors have led to enormous user frustration and a strong desire to take matters into their own hands. It has also been a driver towards outsourcing.

Staff Flexibility and Growth

Because the central IT department appears to be unresponsive to users' demands, user-developed systems become attractive to users as a nonconfrontational way of getting work done. Deploying either their own staffs or those from outside software houses, users see that they are significantly speeding up the process of obtaining "needed" service.

Staff Professional Growth

An IT staff decentralized by both physical and organizational presence in the end-user department helps educate users to IT's legitimate potential; it also reduces communications problems between IT professionals and end users. Particularly important, it makes it easier to plan employee promotions that rotate IT staff to other (non-IT) jobs within the department, thus enhancing user-IT coordination. This also facilitates moving end users to IT positions.

Competitive and Service Growth in the IT Market

Thousands of stand-alone software packages are available for specific applications, ranging from simple accounts-payable systems to complete desktop support products. These systems appear to provide beguilingly easy solutions to short-term problems. Marketed by hardware and software vendors to end-user managers, the systems' functional features are emphasized, and any technical and software problems are soft-pedaled.

Frequently, the local solution also appears to be more cost-effective than work done or purchased by a central IT development group. Not only is there no cumbersome project proposal to be written and defended in front of IT technicians who have their own special agendas, but often a simple up-front price is quoted. Developed under user control, the project is perceived to be both simple and relatively free of red tape (by the time installation is completed, however, a very different perspective may have emerged as costs have run rampantly out of control).

User Control

The idea of regaining control over a part of their units' operations, particularly if IT is critical, is very important to users. In many cases, this reverses a trend that began 20 years ago in a very different technological environment. Control in this context has at least two dimensions.

Development.   Users can exercise direct control over systems development priorities. By using either their own staffs or self-selected software houses, which may offer highly specialized skills not present in the firm, users often hope to get a system with vastly improved support features functioning in less time than it would take to navigate the priority-setting process in the corporate IT department. A user systems staff is also seen as closer and more responsive to user needs because the local manager, rather than an outsider, sets priorities. Development mistakes made by a local group are more easily accepted than those made by a remote group, and they are rarely discussed; successes, by contrast, are often topics of conversation.

Maintenance.   Users gain control over systems maintenance priorities, since the work will be done either by themselves or by software houses that are dependent upon them for income. Users often overlook the importance of this point at the time of initial systems installation: their assumption is that maintenance will be no problem or that it can be performed by a clerk following a manual—a rare occurrence! Needs and desires relentlessly change, and they come to appreciate the need for major maintenance and desire to control it.

Fit with the Organization

As the company becomes more decentralized in structure and more geographically diverse, a distributed development function becomes a much better fit and avoids heavy internal marketing and coordination expenses. Among conglomerates, for example, only a few have tried to centralize development; most leave it with the original units. Heavily decentralized companies such as Pioneer Hi-Bred have closed down the central IT development unit and placed the IT developers in key divisions. Finally, should the corporation decide to divest a unit, the process will be easier to implement if its IT activities are not integrated with the rest of the company.

User Learning

Predicting the full ramifications of introducing a new technology is very difficult. On the one hand, enthusiastic user experimentation with work under their control can stimulate creativity and produce new approaches to troublesome problems. Systems developed by a central IT unit, on the other hand, must overcome greater user resistance in adoption. This IT challenge simply reflects research in the fields of organization development and control, which has identified organization learning as a principal benefit of organizing in multiple profit centers, rather than by function. As noted earlier, this is increasingly evident in office support and new professional support such as CAD.

Summary

In aggregate, these five pressures represent a powerful argument for a strong user role in systems development and suggest when that role might be the dominant one. The pressures driving users toward purchase, development, and/or use of local systems and software can be summarized as short-term user control. Stand-alone local Web-based development offers users more immediate solutions to the problems under their control and does so in a climate they perceive as enjoyable. While particular benefits associated with phase 1 and phase 2 learning can be achieved by using this approach, they may be gained with little regard for information hygiene and less regard for control, causing long-term problems, as discussed next.

PRESSURES TOWARD IT CONTROL

Countering the arguments of the previous section, pressures exist in many settings to consolidate a firm's IT development resource into a single unit or to at least keep it in two or more large clusters.

Staff Professionalism

As noted, a large central IT development staff enhances the organization's ability to recruit and retain (attract and keep challenged) specialized technical personnel. A central unit also provides useful support for a small division or unit that does not have its own IT staff and needs occasional access to IT skills.

Additionally, it is easier to modernize a centralized unit than one in which the development staff is scattered throughout the firm. For example, as the average age of many IT development staffs continues to rise, more employees are becoming comfortable and set in their ways (the graying of IT). The central unit is a useful fulcrum to insert a limited number of high-energy people to aid in recharging older staff and redirecting them to today's radically different technologies. The importance of this new talent is intensified by the fact that the existing staff's salary levels, individual interests, and perceived interpersonal relationships often make lateral movement out of the central IT system department undesirable. Many staff members either must be retrained or let go. The inability of some firms to manage this personal development is a key reason for the current popularity of outsourcing development to external vendors.

Developing and enforcing better standards of IT management practice is also easier in a large group. Documentation procedures, project management skills, and disciplined maintenance approaches are examples of critical infrastructure items in IT systems development departments. In 1988, a large chemicals organization faced with a deteriorating relationship between its central development department and key users was forced to distribute 80 percent of its development staff to four divisions, thereby changing both reporting responsibility and office location. Although the change has been generally successful in stimulating new ideas and better relationships with users (many development people better identified with users than with technical development issues), by 1993 the need for standards to control the costs of desktop proliferation became so intense that significantly tighter standards and management practices had to be instituted to bring order out of chaos. The basic decentralized structure, however, is still in place in mid-1998. Many organizations have experienced such periodic swings of the centralize/decentralize pendulum because the benefits of a change, over time, give way to new problems that require redirection.

Central staff expertise is particularly important for reviewing user-designed systems before they go live. Lacking practical systems design experience, the user often ignores normal data-control procedures, various corporate standards, and conventional costing practices.

For example, a large financial organization discovered that all the people involved in software design and purchase for three of the departmental systems used to process data on a daily basis had left the company. Further, no formal documentation or operating instructions had been prepared, and all source programs had been lost. What remained were disk files with object programs on them. The system ran, but why it ran no one knew; and even if the company's survival depended on it, changes would at best have been very difficult and time-consuming to execute. In 1998, with the Year 2000 (Y2K) problem ahead, this was a massive problem.

A recent study of a manufacturing firm showed that when their $16 million investment in networked personal computers was brought under central control and a corporate maintenance agreement was struck with a single provider, maintenance expenses dropped by 40 percent. Locally developed, rapidly evolving, and largely unmanaged, the distributed systems required more development money than the central development unit, which had extensive documentation and other controls. The situation was rectified before serious damage occurred.

Feasibility Concerns

A user-driven feasibility study may contain major technical mistakes that will result in the information system's being either inadequate to handle growing processing requirements or not easily maintainable. Because of inexperienced staff, the feasibility study may underestimate both the complexity of the software needed and the growth in the number of transactions to be handled by the system. (The risk increases if competent technical staff inputs to the feasibility study were limited and if the real business needs were not well understood.)

In addition, users often focus a feasibility study on a specific service without recognizing that successful first applications tend to generate unanticipated second applications, then third applications, and so forth. Each application appears to require only a modest incremental purchase price and, therefore, does not receive a comprehensive full-cost review. In consequence, fairly shortly, the hardware configuration or software approach selected cannot handle the necessary work. Unless the initial hardware selection and system design process has been carefully undertaken to allow for it, growth can lead to major business disruptions and very expensive software modifications.

User-driven feasibility studies are more susceptible to recommendations to acquire products from unstable vendors, who have some unusually attractive product features. However, significant numbers of software vendors continue to fail, and hardware manufacturers, such as Apple, are teetering on the edge. Accurate assessment of vendor stability is critical because many of these systems insinuate themselves into the heart of a department's operations. With software-intensive investments, failure of a special-features hardware vendor (on which the software depends) can mean both expensive disruption in the department's service and intensive, crisis-spending efforts to convert the software to another machine, unless an open systems approach has been established. In an open systems world, these vendor viability concerns are applicable to the packages and services provided by software suppliers. A single experience with a product from a failed software vendor can provide painful learning.

Particular care must be taken on local systems development projects, since uncoordinated user groups tend to buy or develop systems tailored to very specific situations, creating long-term maintenance problems. In many environments characterized by such local development, there is poor technology transfer between similar users and a consequent lack of corporate leverage, an issue of low importance to the local unit but a great concern from the corporate viewpoint.

A large forest products company, organized geographically, combined a system-minded regional manager with an aggressive growth-oriented IT manager who was responsible for all administrative support in the region. Within three years, the region's IT budget was double that of a comparable region; however, although their applications were extraordinarily effective, only one was exported to another region. Subsequent review indicated that nearly half of the systems developed were focused on problems of potentially general interest and could have been exported to other parts of the company.

Corporate Databases

A corporate database strategy involves both collecting a pointer file (or files) at a central location for reference by multiple users and developing client-server networks and procedures that allow users, regardless of physical location, to access these data files easily. A central development staff provides a focal point for both conceptualizing and developing the architecture of these systems to serve multiple users across the firm. The need for database sharing varies widely with the nature of the corporation's activities, of course. A conglomerate usually has much less need for data sharing across the firm than does a functionally organized, one-product company. However, electronic mail, videoconferencing, video streaming, and shared financial performance information have become legitimate needs in most organizations, and only a central department can cost-effectively develop and distribute such systems to users or coordinate a process whereby key parts of the system development efforts are outsourced to local development units in a way that ensures easy coordination between them.

Inevitably, when the issue of distributed development in several business units is raised, the first concern is that the company will lose the ability to manage and control its data flows. There is fear that data of significance to many people beyond those in the originating unit will be locked up in a nonstandardized format in inaccessible locations. While this is a valid concern in many settings, there are several mitigating factors.

Timing.   One mitigating factor is timing. In many cases, the argument raised against local data storage is the erosion of data as a corporate resource. Allegedly, in order to preserve flexibility for future database design, all files should be centralized. Often, however, such flexibility is not needed, as adaptive communication systems can provide control as well as access to distant users. In that context, a well-designed stand-alone system may be an equally good (if not better) starting point for these long-term systems as jumping directly from the present set of manual procedures. This possibility must be pragmatically assessed.

Abstraction of Data.   Another mitigating factor, often overlooked, is the ease of abstracting data from a locally managed system at planned frequent intervals and sending it directly to a central database. Often only a small portion of the information in a local file is relevant to or needed by other users. Indeed, often only a very small percentage is widely relevant to all users.

On the other hand, because locally designed data-handling systems can prove expensive to maintain and to link with each other, the firm must identify in operational terms the data requirements of the central files and provide guidelines for what can be stored locally and how accessible it should be to others. The problem is exemplified by the branch-office support systems that generate voluminous records in electronic format. Unless well designed, these files can be bulky, lock up key data from potential users, and pose potential security problems. For instance, a mail-order house discovered that each customer representative was using more than 200 disks per day and storing them in boxes by date of order receipt, making it impossible to collect aggregate customer information in a timely manner.

In certain sensitive situations, only by organizing electronic files centrally can appropriate security be ensured. Managing effective security—a topic of intense interest in a world of "hackers"—is usually easier when all files are in a single location rather than dispersed. However, some data are so sensitive that they are best kept off the network—the only way to ensure total security.

Fit with the Corporate Structure and Strategy

Centralized IT development's role is clearest in organizations character-ized by centrally managed planning and operational control. A large farm-equipment manufacturer with a tradition of central functional control from corporate headquarters successfully implemented a program wherein the corporate systems group developed all software for factories and distribution units worldwide. As the company grew in size, however, its structure became more decentralized; in turn, the cost of effective central systems develop-ment was escalating. The firm had to implement a marketing function to educate users on the virtues of central services and to decentralize some development functions. It is becoming increasingly common for centralized development groups to have an explicitly defined and staffed internal mar-keting activity to ensure appropriate coordination with the decentralized units.

Cost Analysis

Given its practical experience in other systems efforts, a centralized IT development group can usually produce realistic software development esti-mates (subject to the problems discussed in Chapter 10) that takes into account the company's overall interests. Software development estimates are problematic in user feasibility studies for two key reasons. Most new systems are more software-intensive than hardware-intensive; software costs are typically 75 to 85 percent of the total cost for a customized system. Few users have had experience in estimating software development costs, and an order-of-magnitude mistake in a feasibility study—particularly if it is an individually developed system and not a "turnkey" (i.e., general-purpose) package—is not unknown.

Users also lack understanding of the true operating costs of an existing ongoing service, particularly given complicated corporate IT charge-out sys-tems, many of which present calculations in terms of utilization of computer resource units that are completely unfathomable to the user; hence, each month or quarter, an unintelligible bill arrives, the amount of which is unpredictable. (In management control environments where the user is held closely responsible for variance from budget, this legitimately causes intense frustration.) For the user, a locally developed system, especially if it is for a networked, but locally managed, desktop device, is seen as producing both understandable and predictable costs. Further, since many corporate charge-out systems are designed on a full-cost basis, their charges to the end user seem high and thus offer great inducements to purchase locally.

Much of corporate IT is fixed cost in the short run, consequently appear-ing to the individual user, courtesy of the charge-out system, to be an oppor-tunity to reduce costs. However, in reality, individual user cost reductions may be a cost increase for the company—more hardware/software acquired locally and no possible savings at the corporate IT facility. Policies for ensuring that appropriate cost analyses for decentralized activities are prepared must be established.

Summary

The pressures toward centralized IT control can be summarized by the words *long-term information architecture building.* Inexorably, over the long run, most (but not all) stand-alone units will become part of a network and need to both receive and share data with other users and systems. In many respects, these pressures are not immediately evident when the system is installed but tend to grow more obvious with the passage of time. Policies for managing the trade-offs between the obvious short-term benefits and long-term risks are delicate to administer, but necessary.

COORDINATION AND LOCATION OF IT POLICY

The tension between IT and users can be effectively managed by establishing clear policies that specify the user domain, the IT domain, and senior management's role. Senior management must play a significant part in ensuring that these policies are developed and that they evolve appropriately over time. Both IT and users must understand the implications of their roles and possible conflicts.

IT Responsibilities

The following tasks constitute the central core of IT responsibilities— the minimum for managing the long-term information hygiene needs of an organization:

1. Develop and manage the evolution of a long-term architectural plan and ensure that new projects fit into its evolution as much as possible.
2. Establish procedures to ensure that, for potential IT projects of any size, internal development versus purchase is compared. If projects are implemented outside the firm or by the user, establish the appropriate professional standards for project control and documentation. These standards must be flexible since user-developed systems for desktop units pose demands quite different from systems to be run on large mainframe computers. Further, define a process for forcing adherence to the selected standards.
3. Maintain an inventory of installed or planned-to-be-installed information services.

4. Create and maintain a set of standards that establishes:
   a. Mandatory telecommunication standards.
   b. Standard languages for classes of acquired equipment.
   c. Documentation procedures for different types of systems.
   d. A corporate data dictionary with clear definitions of which elements must be included.
   e. Identification of file maintenance standards and procedures.
   f. Examination procedures for systems developed in local units to ensure that they do not conflict with corporate needs and that any necessary interfaces are constructed.
5. Identify and provide appropriate IT development staff career paths throughout the organization. These include lateral transfers within and between IT units, upward movement within IT, and appropriate outward movement from IT to other functional units. (Although this is more difficult in distributed units, it is still possible.)
6. Establish appropriate internal marketing efforts for IT support. These should exert catch-up pressure and coaching for units that are lagging and slow down units pushing too fast into leading-edge technologies they do not understand.
7. Prepare a detailed checklist of questions to be answered in any hardware/software acquisition to ensure that relevant technical and managerial issues are raised. These questions should ask:
   a. Does the proposed system meet corporate communication standards?
   b. For locally operated systems, has upward growth potential been addressed, and are adequate communication capabilities in place so that local files can be reached from other locations, if appropriate?
   c. Are languages being used appropriately and can they be maintained over the long term?
8. Identify and maintain relationships with preferred systems suppliers. Before entering a relationship with a vendor, the conditions for entertaining exceptions to established standards must be agreed on. For example, size, number of systems in place, and financial structure requirements should be clearly spelled out.
9. Establish education programs for potential users that communicate both the benefits and the pitfalls of a new technology and that define users' roles in ensuring its successful introduction in their departments.
10. Set up an ongoing review of systems for determining which ones have become obsolete and should be redesigned.

These issues apply with particular force to the design of systems that become embedded in the company's daily operations. Decision support systems do not pose quite the same problems, although the need to obtain data from the rest of the organization is rapidly putting them in the same situation.

These core responsibilities, of course, can be significantly expanded to impose much tighter and more formal controls if the situation warrants.

User Responsibilities

To assist in the orderly identification of opportunities and implementation of new IT services and to grow in an understanding of their use, cost, and impact on the organization, the following responsibilities should be fulfilled by the user of IT service:

1. Clearly understand the scope of all IT activities supporting the user. Increasingly, more experienced organizations have installed a user-understandable IT charge-out system to facilitate this.
2. To ensure satisfactory service, realistically appraise the amount of user personnel investment required for each new project, both to develop and to operate the system. These costs are often much higher than planned and are frequently ignored.
3. Ensure comprehensive user input for all IT projects that will support vital aspects of the unit's operations. This might include the nature of service, process of introduction, and level of user training for both staff and managers.
4. Realistically ensure that the IT-user interface is consistent with IT's strategic relevance to the business unit. If it is very important, the interface must be very close. If it is less important, more distance between the parties and more friction can be tolerated.
5. Periodically audit the adequacy of system reliability standards, performance of communications services, and adequacy of security procedures.
6. Participate in the development and maintenance of an IT plan that sets new technology priorities, schedules the transfer of IT among groups, and evaluates a portfolio of projects in light of the company strategy.

These represent the very minimum policies that the users should develop and manage. Depending on the firm's geography, corporate management style, stage of IT development, and mix of technology development phases, expanded levels of user involvement may be appropriate, including full-time assignment of their own staff. As these facets evolve, so will the appropriateness of certain policies.

General Management Support and Policy Overview

Distinct from the issues involved in the distribution of IT services is a cluster of broad policy and direction activities requiring senior management perspective. In the past, these activities were built into the structure of a central IT organization. Now, given the need to link IT to business, IT operations are frequently separated from IT planning. A chemical company, for example, reorganized in 1990 to establish a 500-person systems and operations department reporting directly to the head of administrative services, which works on corporate applications. (An additional 400 analysts and programmers are employed in the major divisional staffs.) This department does the company's implementation and operational IT work on a month-to-month, year-to-year basis. At the same time, a 25- to 30-person IT policy group reporting directly to the head of research works on overall IT policy and long-range IT strategy formulation for the firm. In a similar vein, a major conglomerate whose development staff and hardware are distributed to key users has a three- to four-person group at headquarters level. Firms that outsource most or all of their IT operations, development, and maintenance activities still need this policy group.

Key responsibilities of a corporate IT policy group should include:

1. Ensure that an appropriate balance exists between IT and user inputs across the different technologies and that one side is not dominating the other inappropriately. Initiate appropriate personnel and organizational transfers if the situation is out of balance. Establishing an executive steering committee, for example, is a common response to inadequate user input.

2. Ensure that a comprehensive corporate IT strategy is developed. A comprehensive overview of technology trends, current corporate use of IT, and linkage between IT initiatives and overall corporate goals is particularly important in organizations where resources are widely distributed. The resources to be devoted to this effort vary widely from organization to organization as IT's perceived contribution to corporate strategy, among other things, changes.

3. Manage the inventory of hardware and software resources, and assure that the corporate view extends to purchasing relationships and contracts. In most settings, the corporate group is the appropriate place to identify and manage standard policies for relationships with vendors.

4. Facilitate the creation and evolution of standards for development and operations activities, and ensure that the standards are applied appropriately. In this regard, the corporate policy group plays the combined role of consultant on the one hand and auditor (particularly if there is a weak or nonexistent IT auditing function) on the other. This role requires a technically competent and interpersonally sensitive staff.

5. Facilitate the transfer of technology from one unit to another. This occurs through recognizing the unit's common systems needs as well as stimulating joint projects. Actual transfer requires regular visits to the different operating units, organization of periodic corporate management information system (MIS) conferences, development of a corporate information systems newsletter, and other means.

6. Actively encourage technical experimentation. A limited program of research is a very appropriate part of the IT function; an important role of the corporate policy group is to ensure that research and scanning do not get swept away in the press of urgent operational issues. Further, the corporate policy group is in a position to encourage patterns of experimentation that smaller units might feel pose undue risk if they are the sole beneficiary.

7. Assume responsibility for developing an appropriate planning and control system to link IT firmly to the company's goals. Planning, system appraisal, charge-out, and project management processes should be monitored and (if necessary) encouraged to develop by the policy group. In this context, the group should work closely with the corporate steering committee.

As these responsibilities imply, the corporate IT policy group needs to be staffed with individuals who, in aggregate, have broad technical backgrounds and extensive practical IT administrative experience. Except in very limited numbers, it is not an appropriate department for entry-level staff members.

SUMMARY

This chapter has focused on the key issues surrounding the organization of IT development activities for the next decade. A significant revolution has occurred in what is regarded as good managerial practice in this field. Important contributors to this change have been the development of new hardware and software technologies and managerial experience with IT. These technologies not only permit quite different types of services to be delivered, but also offer the potential for quite different ways of delivering these services. Consequently, what constitutes best practice has changed considerably, and the evolution seems likely to continue; many IT organization structures that were effectively put together in the 1970s have been found inappropriate for the 1990s, and those that fit the early 1990s are inappropriate as we enter the world of the Intranet in the early 21st century.

Determining the appropriate pattern of distribution of IT resources within the organization is a complex and multifaceted subject. The general manager should develop a program that will encourage appropriate innovation on the one hand while maintaining overall control on the other. How these organization and planning issues are resolved is inextricably tied to non-IT-oriented aspects of the corporate environment. The leadership style of the person at the top of the organization and that person's view of the future provide one important thrust for redirection. A vision of tight central control presents a different context for these decisions than does a vision emphasizing the autonomy of operating units. Closely associated and linked to this is the corporate organizational structure and culture and the trends occurring within it. Also, the realities of geographical spread of the business units heavily affect IT organizational and planning possibilities; the corporate headquarters of a large domestic insurance company, for example, poses different constraints than do the multiple international plants and markets of an automobile manufacturer.

On a less global scale are the present realities of quality and location of existing IT resources (organizationally and physically), which provide the base from which change must be made. Equally important is how responsive and competent current users perceive these resources to be. The unit that is seen (no matter how unfairly or inaccurately) as unresponsive has different organizational challenges than the well-regarded unit. Similarly, the existing and the perceived-appropriate strategic roles of IT on the dimensions of the firm's applications portfolio and operations have important organizational implications. If the firm is in the "support" quadrant, for example, the IT policy unit must realistically be placed lower in the organization structure in order to deal with its perceived lack of burning relevance to corporate strategy.

In dealing with these forces, one is seeking an appropriate balance between innovation and control and between the inputs of the IT specialist and the user. Not only do appropriate answers to these questions vary among companies, but also different answers and structures are often appropriate for individual units within an organization. In short, there is a series of right questions to ask, and there is an identifiable but very complex series of forces that, appropriately analyzed, determine for each organizational unit the direction in which the correct answer lies—for now.

Managing IT Outsourcing[1]

Companies are increasingly outsourcing the management of information technology (IT) for reasons that include concern for cost and quality, lagging IT performance, supplier pressure, access to special technical and application skills, and other financial factors. The outsourcing solution is acceptable to large and small firms alike because strategic alliances are now more common and the IT environment is changing rapidly. This chapter identifies situations where outsourcing makes sense and the issues of how the resulting alliance should be structured and managed. In addition to clear successes, we have identified troublesome relationships and several that had to be terminated.

Long-term, sustained management of a strategic alliance is turning out to be the dominant challenge of effective IT outsourcing. From a relatively unusual entrepreneurial activity in the past, IT outsourcing has recently exploded across the global corporate landscape. Xerox, Delta Airlines, Commonwealth Bank (Australia), Dupont, and J.P. Morgan are the latest of these mega-alliances. Several years ago, Shell Oil outsourced its Brazilian IT activities. Like marriages, however, these arrangements are much easier to enter than to sustain or dissolve. The special economic technology issues surrounding outsourcing agreements necessarily make them more complex and fluid than an ordinary contract. Both parties must make special efforts for outsourcing to be successful.

Our purpose in this chapter is to provide a concrete framework to help senior managers think about IT outsourcing and focus on how to manage an alliance to ensure its success.

---

[1]This chapter is adapted from F. Warren McFarlan and Richard L. Nolan, "How to Manage an IT Outsourcing Alliance," *Sloan Management Review* 36, no. 2 (Winter 1995).

WHY OUTSOURCING ALLIANCES ARE SO DIFFICULT

Many outsourcing contracts are structured for very long periods in a world of fast-moving technical and business change. Eight to ten years is the normal length of a contract in an environment in which computer chip performance is shifting by 20 to 30 percent per year. (This standard contract length has emerged to deal with switching-cost issues and to make the economics work for the outsourcer.) Consequently, a deal that made sense at the beginning may make less economic sense three years later and require adjustments to function effectively.

Exacerbating the situation is the timing of benefits. The first-year benefits are clear to the customer, who often receives a one-time capital payment; the customer then feels relieved to shift problems and issues to another organization. Moreover, the tangible payments in the first year occur in an environment where the outputs most closely resemble those anticipated in the contract. In each subsequent year, however, the contract payment stream becomes less and less tied to the initial set of planned outputs (as the world changes) and, thus, more subject to negotiation and misunderstanding.

The situation from the outsourcer's perspective is just the reverse. The first year may require a heavy capital payment followed by the extraordinary costs for switching responsibility to them and executing the appropriate cost-reduction initiatives. All this is done in anticipation of a back-loaded profit flow. At precisely the time the outsourcer is finally moving into its earnings stream, the customer, perhaps feeling the need for new services, is chafing under monthly charges and anxious to move to new IT architectures. If the customer has not had experience in partnering activities before, the relationship can develop profound tensions.

A further complication is that only a few outsourcers have the critical mass and access to capital markets to undertake large contracts. Electronic Data Systems (EDS), Computer Sciences Corporation (CSC), IBM, and AT&T constitute the bulk of the current market. A much larger group of firms, such as Lockheed Martin, Perot Systems, and Cap Gemini, specializes in certain niches in the outsourcing market, fulfilling either special industry skills, small contracts, or specific subfunctions such as network operations. If an alliance is not working out, a company has limited options for resolving the situation, particularly because outsourcing is relatively easy but insourcing again is very difficult. The most common situation is typified by a major international packaging company, which was forced on short notice to transfer the relationship to another outsourcer when the original arrangement no longer fit the strategy of the outsourcer.

Finally, the evolution of technologies often changes the strategic relevance of IT service to a firm. From the customer's viewpoint, assigning a commodity service to an outsider is very attractive if the price is right. Delegating a firm's service differentiator is another matter. (This is increasingly being done and will be described later in this chapter.) The customer that made the original decision based on efficiency will judge it differently if using effectiveness criteria later.

OUTSOURCING IN RETROSPECT

Outsourcing IT has been popular for a long time—in the mid-1960s, for example, computer services bureaus ran a variety of programs, whose applications focused heavily on the financial and operations support areas (general ledger, payroll, inventory control, and so on). The programs were both customized and general-purpose, and the individual firm had to accommodate its operations to the standard options in the package. Customers of the service bureaus were mostly small and medium-sized firms, although some large firms used them for specialized needs or highly confidential items like executive payroll.

A good example of a provider in this industry then and now is ADP. ADP, which began as a small punch card payroll company in 1949, grew to a $4 billion organization by specializing in large-volume, standard transaction-type activities, such as payroll and handling proxy solicitations (almost 100 percent of the industry). Software contracting companies like Andersen Consulting in the private sector and CSC in the public sector developed large turnkey applications for organizations requiring either specialized staff or a large number of staff people, either of which the organization deemed inconvenient, imprudent, or impossible to retain. EDS, in the state and local government sector, provided full outsourcing for organizations whose cultures and salary scales made it impossible to attract people with the necessary skills in a competitive job market. These were the exceptions, however, to the general trend of developing IT in-house. Until 1990, the major drivers for outsourcing were primarily:

- Cost-effective access to specialized or occasionally needed computing power or systems development skills.
- Avoidance of building in-house IT skills and skill sets, primarily an issue for small and very low-technology organizations.
- Access to special functional capabilities. Outsourcing during this period was important but, in retrospect, largely peripheral to the main IT activities that took place in mid-sized and large organizations.

Kodak's decision in 1990 to outsource IT was the seminal event that really attracted public attention. Kodak's CIO at the time, who had been a general manager rather than a computer professional, took an aggressive position in outsourcing mainframes, telecommunications, and personal computers (PCs). Until then, outsourcing for medium-sized to large companies had been mostly a sideshow, and outsourcing was generally reserved for small and medium-sized companies with problematic, grossly mismanaged information services (IS) departments.

In the wake of Kodak's decision was a flurry of oversubscribed IS conferences on outsourcing, at which the Kodak CIO was often the featured speaker. The authors attended a number of these conferences and independently witnessed the hostility from many CIO participants (who perceived outsourcing as a terrifying threat to their status quo) toward the Kodak CIO as she explained her rationale. Even today, many of those very same CIOs quickly point out with some relief that only one (albeit the largest) of the three original Kodak outsourcing contracts was totally problem-free—although all three contracts are still in place and were reaffirmed in 1997. The Kodak experience can be deemed a real success.

OUTSOURCING IN THE 1990s

We have conducted more than eight years of case research on Kodak, General Dynamics, and over two dozen other outsourcing situations and have concluded that IT outsourcing is not a "flash in the pan" management fad. IT outsourcing is a harbinger of traditional IT department transformation and provides a glimpse at the emerging organizational structures of the information economy. Our research indicates that more than half of mid-sized to large firms have outsourced or are considering some type of outsourcing of their IT activities. And this phenomenon is not limited to the United States; for example, in 1997–1998, Novartis (Switzerland), ASDA (the United Kingdom), and the Australian government all outsourced substantial parts of their IT activities.

Two factors have affected the growth of IT outsourcing—the recognition of strategic alliances and the changes in the technological environment.

Acceptance of Strategic Alliances

The value of strategic alliances has been widely recognized, and their creation is motivated by interrelated forces. On one level, finding a strong partner to complement an area of weakness gives an organization an island of stability in a turbulent world. It is difficult to fight simultaneously on all fronts, and alliances allow a company to simplify its management agenda safely. Alternatively, alliances allow a firm to leverage a key part of the value chain by bringing in a strong partner that complements its skills. Such a partner may create an opportunity to innovate synergistically: the whole should become greater than the sum of the parts. Also, early, successful experiences with alliances increase a firm's confidence in undertaking new alliances in other parts of the value chain as a profitable way to do business. The early experience provides insight into how the likelihood of a successful alliance can be increased.

For an alliance to be successful and endure for the long term, both firms must believe that they are winners. Because of the synergistic potential of the relationships and the opportunity to specialize, both firms should legitimately feel that they are benefiting: this is not a zero-sum game. This usually means the economics of the arrangement must outlast the careers of the participants who put the deal together.

IT's Changing Environment

Today, firms are not focusing IT only on internal transaction processing systems; rather, in a networked fashion, they are integrating internal systems with those of their customers and suppliers so they can change their structure to more efficient forms for competing flexibly in the global marketplace. This integration places extraordinary pressures on firms trying to keep the old services running while developing the interconnections and services demanded by the new environment. Thus, outsourcing has become a viable alternative for these firms to get access to appropriate skills and to speed up the transition reliably and cost-effectively.

In fact, as shown in Table 8–1, the development of most of the code that companies now use is already outsourced. A distinct minority of the code in operating systems, e-mail systems, word processing packages, and spreadsheet software has actually been developed within the firm (with a much smaller percentage expected in the future). This trend, which occurred for obvious reasons of economies of scale and scarcity of competent staff, will only continue. Currently, Computer Associates, Lotus, IBM, Borland, and Microsoft are the de facto software providers to most companies. The internal IT organization is already a selector and integrator of code rather than a developer.

At the same time, many firms have a residue of 15- to 30-year-old systems primarily written in COBOL and PL/l, which are embedded with Year 2000 problems. Although this problem is particularly acute in the financial services industry and manufacturing, it is not confined to those areas. The cost-effective transformation of these systems to the client-server model (a key technology of the network era that separates the management of files and their integrity onto one machine, the server, from devices accessing these files, the clients) is an enormous challenge. On the one hand, firms are looking for low-cost maintenance of the old systems to ensure they operate reliably, while, on the other hand, gaining access to the new skills to permit their transformation to the new model. This shift is as significant today as the move from tabulating equipment 35 years ago in terms of providing new capabilities to the firm. A number of organizations see outsourcing as a way of bringing the appropriate specialized skills to this task (some by outsourcing the running/maintenance of the old code, while using internal staff to develop the new capabilities, while others are doing the opposite).

TABLE 8–1   IT Markets

Location	Physical Aspects	Information
Internal	*Automating:* Computerizing physical and clerical processes.	*Informating:* Leveraging knowledge workers with computers.
	• Dominant use of mainframe and minicomputers. • Operational level systems automated primarily with COBOL. • Process controls automated primarily with machine language. • Standard packages for payroll and general ledger. • Applications portfolio consists of millions of lines of code with 50% typically purchased from outside.	• User tasks leveraged through direct use of microcomputers enabled by graphical use interfaces (GUIs) and purchased software such as word processing, spreadsheet, graphics, and CAD/CAM. • Local area networks (LANs)—user-oriented software for e-mail, database sharing, file transfer, and groupware for work teams. • Microcomputer software consists of millions of lines of code—almost 100% purchased from other companies.
External	*Embedding:* Integrating computers into products and services.	*Networking:* "The Information Highway."
	• Specialized code embedded in products and services to enhance function. • Microcomputers in physical products such as automobiles and "smart cards" in services. • Thousands of lines of code developed by both specialized internal programmers and outside contract programmers.	• Wide-area networks (WANs) networking workers, suppliers, and customers. • Internet for commercial use. • Millions of lines of code, almost 100% purchased and maintained from outside software firms.

What Drives Outsourcing?

Although the mix of factors raising the possibility of outsourcing varies widely from one company to another, our research has revealed a series of themes that, in aggregate, explain most of the pressures to outsource.

General Managers' Concerns about Costs and Quality.   The same questions about IT costs and response times came up repeatedly when we talked to managers: Can we get our existing services for a reduced price at acceptable quality standards? Can we get new systems developed faster? We have uncovered the following ways an outsourcer can save money for a customer:

- Tighter overhead cost control of fringe benefits. On balance, the outsourcers run much leaner overhead structures than do many of their customers.
- More aggressive use of low-cost labor pools by creatively using geography. Frequently, the outsourcer moves data centers and portions of the development activity to low-cost areas (modern telecommunications makes this possible).
- Tough world-class standards applied to the company's existing staff, all of whom have to requalify for appointment at the time of outsourcing. Frequently, employees may have become lazy or are unskilled in leading-edge IT management practices.
- More effective bulk purchasing and leasing arrangements for all aspects of the hardware/software configuration through discounts and better use of capacity.
- Better management of excess hardware capacity. The outsourcer can sell or utilize underused hardware that would otherwise be idle by combining many firms' work in the same operations center. One small firm's on-line operations (a $27 million, 10-year contract) was transferred to a larger data center at no extra cost to the outsourcer. Capacity was simply better used.
- Better control over software licenses, both through negotiation and through realistic examination.
- More aggressive management of service and response time to meet, but not wildly exceed, corporate standards. Tighter control over inventories of paper and other supplies.
- Hustle. Outsourcers are professionals; this is their only business, and their success is measured by satisfied customers who recommend them to others, by bottom-line profitability, and by stock-market performance.
- The ability to run with a leaner management structure because of increased competence and critical mass volumes of work.
- The ability to access higher levels of IT staff skills, IT application skills (such as SAP, BAAN, and People Soft), or special customer industry skills.
- Creative and more realistic structuring of leases.

While the cumulative impact of these items can be significant, we issue a few cautionary notes. Until several knowledgeable bidders have closely analyzed an existing operation to propose an alliance, the true picture isn't revealed. An IT efficiency study funded by the IT department and performed by a consulting company hoping to get future business is simply self-serving and inadequate. Equally important is assessing whether the outsourcer can rapidly mobilize its staff for the quick-response development jobs when a customer needs to get products and services to market much faster.

Breakdown in IT Performance.   Failure to meet service standards can force general management to find other ways of achieving reliability. As we reflect on the past 30 years of computer growth in most companies, it is not atypical to find a company in which cumulative IT management neglect eventually culminated in an out-of-control situation the current IT department could not recover from. For example, Massachusetts Blue Cross and Blue Shield's decision to outsource to EDS was triggered by the failure of three major systems development projects (and losses in the tens of millions of dollars). It saw outsourcing as a way to fix a broken department. Similarly, a mid-sized bank's interest in outsourcing came after a one-day total collapse of its automated teller machine (ATM) network, caused by faulty internally designed software patches.

An additional driving factor is the need to rapidly retool a backward IT structure to maintain its competitiveness. In one firm, general managers thought the internal IT culture (correctly, in our judgment) was both frozen and backward; it needed to leap forward in performance. The general managers, who lacked both the time and the inclination to undertake the task personally, found outsourcing a good choice for making the transition from the Mainframe era to the Network era.

Intense Supplier Pressures.   Kodak's decision to outsource its data center and telecommunications to IBM, DEC, and Businessland was, as we noted, a flash point. Suddenly, all general managers saw outsourcing as a highly visible, if often misunderstood, alternative. At the same time, IBM and DEC were looking for new value-added services to reach their customer bases and compensate for declining hardware margins and sales. They moved aggressively into the field with expanded and highly energetic sales forces. EDS, the largest firm in the field, used its General Motors operations center to demonstrate its expertise. CSC, which was strong in the federal sector, built a bridge to the commercial sector with its General Dynamics contract. The visibility of these and other arrangements, combined with the suppliers' aggressive sales forces, enabled them to approach general managers with compelling reasons to outsource. Today, the industry is served by numerous large and small suppliers.

Simplified General Management Agenda.   A firm under intense cost or competitive pressures, which does not see IT as its core competence, may find outsourcing a way to delegate time-consuming, messy problems so it can focus scarce management time and energy on other differentiators. If managers perceive the outsourcer as competent and are able to transfer a noncore function to reliable hands, they will not hesitate to choose outsourcing. These IT activities must be done respectably, but long-term upside competitive differentiation does not come from the outsourcer executing them in an outstanding fashion.

Financial Factors.   Several financial issues can make outsourcing appealing. One is the opportunity to liquidate the firm's intangible IT asset, thus strengthening the balance sheet and avoiding a stream of sporadic capital investments in the future. An important part of many arrangements has been the significant up-front capital paid for both the real value of the hardware/software assets and the intangible value of the IT systems. General Dynamics, for example, received $200 million for its IT asset. Publicly held outsourcers with access to the capital markets have pushed this; partnerships like Andersen Consulting do not have such access (although their partnership with GE Capital has mitigated this). Up-front capital payments have been a less common aspect of recent deals.

Outsourcing can turn a largely fixed-cost business into one with variable costs; this is particularly important for firms whose activities vary widely in volume from one year to another or which face significant downsizing. The outsourcer can make the change much less painfully than the firm; it can broker the slack more effectively and potentially provide greater employment stability for the company's IT employees, who are there because of their ability to handle multiple operations. In fact, in several of the firms we studied, outsourcing was very positively received by the staffs. They saw themselves leaving a cost-constrained environment with limited potential for promotion and entering a growth company where IT (their core competence) was the firm's only business. In variable-cost arrangements, price deescalation clauses—rather than inflation protection clauses—should be negotiated in the sections of the contract that deal with IT hardware costs because of the dramatic downward changes in the technology costs. (In the current contracts, heavy reliance is being placed on industry benchmarking data to handle the evolving technology cost performance.)

Finally, a third-party relationship brings an entirely different set of dynamics to a firm's view of IT expenditures. It is now dealing with a hard-dollar expenditure that all users must take seriously (it is no longer soft-dollar allocation). There is a sense of discipline and tough-mindedness that an arm's-length, fully charged-out internal cost center has trouble achieving. Further, firms that do not see IT as a high-leverage function may perceive outside professionals as adding special value and, hence, as quite influential.

For a firm considering divestiture or outright sale of one or more of its divisions, outsourcing has special advantages. It liquidates and gets value for an asset unlikely to be recognized in the divestiture. It gives the acquirer fewer problems to deal with in assimilating the firm. And the outsourcing contract may provide the acquirer a very nice dowry, particularly if the firm is small in relation to the acquirer. The contract can be phased out neatly, and the IT transaction volume can be added to the firm's internal IT activities with little or no additional expense. This was the guiding rationale for outsourcing in several mid-sized banks we studied. It gave them access to reliable IT support while making their eventual sale (which they saw as inevitable) more attractive from the acquirers' viewpoint.

Corporate Culture.   A company's values can make it very hard for managers to take appropriate action, however. One firm we studied had several internal data centers, and there were obvious and compelling advantages to consolidating them. The internal IT department, however, simply lacked the clout to pull off the centralized strategy in what was a highly decentralized firm, built up over the years by acquisitions. The firm saw the decentralized culture as a major strength, not subject to reconsideration. Outsourcing, driven by very senior management, provided the fulcrum for overcoming this impasse, since it was not directly associated with any division or corporate staff. Similarly, an internal IT organization may fall behind the state of the art without being immediately attacked, while an outsourcer is forced to keep up with the latest technology to be successful.

Eliminating an Internal Irritant.   No matter how competent and adaptive existing IT management and staff are (and usually they are very good), there is usually tension between the end users of the resources and the IT staff. Often, this is exacerbated by the different language IT professionals use, lack of career paths for users and IT staff across the organization, perceived high IT costs, perceived unresponsiveness to urgent requests, and perceived technical obsolescence. In this context, the notion of a remote, efficient, experienced outsourcer is particularly compelling, even though the internal perceptions are not necessarily realistic.

Other Factors.   We found a variety of other drivers for outsourcing in specific situations. Some companies with a low-technology culture appeared to have trouble attracting and retaining high-technology IT staff. Outsourcing offered a way to gain these skills without getting involved in complex management issues.

A mid-sized high-tech firm needed to develop and run a series of critically important applications, for instance. Outsourcing gave it access to skills it could not attract to its organization. Managers felt that outsourcing had substantially reduced their corporate risk while providing needed access to specialized knowledge.

One large organization felt it was getting a level of commitment and energy difficult to gain from an in-house unit. For their rapidly growing outsourcer, good performance on the contract would provide a reference that was critical to achieving the kind of market growth it wanted.

Still another firm was frustrated by its inability to get its products to market faster. Its in-house resources, limited in size and training, were simply not moving quickly enough. Outsourcing gave it an adrenaline boost for building the IT infrastructure to achieve a two-thirds improvement in time to market.

WHEN TO OUTSOURCE IT

When do the benefits of outsourcing outweigh the risks? Our research suggests that there are five factors that tip the scale one way or the other. Each factor is fundamentally linked to the basic research models in the IT field.

Position on the Strategic Grid

Outsourcing operational activities is generically attractive, particularly as the budget grows and the contract becomes more important to the outsourcer. The more the firm is operationally dependent on IT, the more sense outsourcing makes. The bigger the firm's IT budget, however, the higher in the customer organization the decisions will be made, and thus the more careful the analysis must become. At the super-large scale, the burden falls on the outsourcer, which must show it can bring more intellectual firepower to the task.

When the application's development portfolio is filled with maintenance work or projects, which are valuable but not vitally important to the firm, transferring these tasks to a partner holds few strategic risks. However, as the new systems and processes increasingly come to deliver potentially significant differentiation and/or massive cost reduction, the outsourcing decision comes under greater scrutiny, particularly when the firm possesses a large, technically innovative, well-run IT organization. The potential loss of control and of flexibility and inherent delays in dealing with a project management structure that cuts across two organizations become much more binding and of greater concern. There are examples, like General Dynamics, where outsourcing was successful. The need for access to otherwise unavailable leading-edge technical applications skills has made outsourcing in these situations more interesting.

As shown in Figure 8–1, for companies in the support quadrant, the outsourcing presumption is yes, particularly for the large firms. For companies in the factory quadrant, the presumption is yes, unless they are huge and perceived as exceptionally well managed. For firms in the turnaround quadrant, the presumption is mixed; it may represent an unnecessary, unacceptable delegation of competitiveness, although conversely, it may be the only way to get these skills. For companies in the strategic quadrant, the presumption is also mixed; not facing a crisis of IT competence, some companies in the strategic quadrant have found it hard to justify outsourcing; others have found it indispensable in gaining access to otherwise unavailable skills. Also, having a subcritical mass in potentially core differentiating skills for the firm is an important driver that has moved companies to consider outsourcing.

For larger multidivisional firms, this analysis suggests that various divisions and clusters of application systems can legitimately be treated differently (e.g., strategic differentiated outsourcing). For example, an international oil company outsourced its operationally troublesome Brazilian subsidiary's IT activities while keeping the other country's IT activities in-house. Similarly, because of the dynamic nature of the grid, firms under profit pressures after a period of sustained strategic innovation (in either the turnaround or the strategic quadrant) are good candidates for outsourcing as a means to clean up their shop and procedures. This was true for one

---

FIGURE 8–1   Strategic Grid for Information Resource Management

---

High

Factory—uninterrupted service-oriented information resource management	*Strategic information resource management*
Outsourcing Presumption: Yes, unless company is huge and well managed.	*Outsourcing Presumption:* No.
Reasons to consider outsourcing: • Possibilities of economies of scale for small and mid-size firms. • Higher-quality service and backup. • Management focus facilitated. • Fiber-optic and extended channel technologies facilitate international IT solutions.	Reasons to consider outsourcing: • Rescue an out-of-control internal IT unit. • Tap source of cash. • Facilitate cost flexibility. • Facilitate management of divestiture.

Current Dependence on Information

Support-oriented information resource management.	*Turnaround information resource management.*
Outsourcing Presumption: Yes.	*Outsourcing Presumption:* No.
Reasons to consider outsourcing: • Access to higher IT professionalism. • Possibility of laying off is of low priority and problematic. • Access to current IT technologies • Risk of inappropriate IT architecture reduced.	Reasons to consider outsourcing: • Internal IT unit not capable in required technologies. • Internal IT unit not capable in required project management skills.

Low   ***Importance of Sustained, Innovative***   **High**
                                 Information Resource Development

---

large high-technology organization, which saved over $100 million by outsourcing.

Development Portfolio

The higher the percentage of the systems development portfolio in maintenance or high-structured projects, the more the portfolio is a candidate for outsourcing. (High-structured projects are those in which the end outputs are clearly defined, there is little opportunity to redefine them, and little or no organizational change is involved in implementing them.) Outsourcers with access to high-quality, cheap labor pools (in, for example, Russia, India, or Ireland) and good project management skills can consistently outperform, on both cost and quality, a local unit that is caught in a high-cost geographic area and lacks the contacts, skills, and confidence to manage extended relationships. The growth of global fiber-optic networks has made all conventional thinking on where work should be done obsolete. For example, Citibank does much of its processing work in South Dakota, and more than 150,000 programmers are working in India on software development for U.S. and European firms.

High-technology, highly structured work (e.g., building a vehicle tracking system) is also a strong candidate for outsourcing, because the customer needs staff people with specialized, leading-edge technical skills. These technical skills are widely available in countries such as Ireland, India, and the Philippines.

Conversely, large, low-structured projects pose very difficult coordination problems for outsourcing. (In low-structured projects the end outputs and processes are susceptible to significant evolution as the project unfolds.) Design is iterative, as users discover what they really want by trial and error. This work requires that the design team be physically much closer to consumers, thus eliminating significant additional savings. It can, of course, be outsourced, but that requires more coordination to be effective than the projects described above. One firm outsourced a large section of such work to a very standards-oriented outsourcer as a way of bringing discipline to an undisciplined organization.

Organizational Learning

The sophistication of a firm's organizational learning substantially facilitates its ability to effectively manage an outsourcing arrangement in the systems development area. A significant component of many firms' applications development portfolios comprises projects related to business process reengineering or organization transformation. Process reengineering seeks to install very different procedures for handling transactions and doing the firm's work. Organization transformation tries to redesign where decisions in the firm are made and what controls are used. The success of both types of projects depends on having internal staff people radically change the way they work and often involves significant downsizing as well. While much of this restructuring relies on new IT capabilities, at its heart, it is an exercise in applied human psychology, where 70 percent of the work falls disappointingly short of target in terms of impact on bottom-line profitability.

Responsibility for such development work (low structure by its very nature) is the hardest to outsource. A firm with substantial experience in restructuring will have less difficulty in defining the dividing line between the outsourcer and the company in terms of responsibility for success. Firms that have not yet worked on these projects will find that outsourcing significantly complicates an already difficult task. The more experience the firm has had in implementing these projects, the easier the outsourcing will be.

A Firm's Position in the Market

The farther a company is from the network era in its internal use of IT, the more useful outsourcing can be to close the gap. Firms still in the DP era and early micro era often do not have the IT leadership, staff skills, or architecture to quickly move ahead. The outsourcer, by contrast, cannot just keep its old systems running, but must drive forward with contemporary practice and technology. The advanced micro era firms are more likely to have internal staff skills and perspectives to leap to the next stage by themselves. The world of client-server architecture, the networked organization, and process redesign is so different from the large COBOL systems and stand-alone PCs of 1985 that it is often prohibitively challenging for a firm to easily bridge the 10-year gap by itself. For those in this situation, it is not worth dwelling on how the firm got where it is but, rather, how to extricate itself.

Current IT Organization

The more IT development and operations are already segregated, in the organization and in accounting, the easier it is to negotiate an enduring outsourcing contract. A stand-alone differentiated IT unit has already developed the integrating organizational and control mechanisms that are the foundation for an outsourcing contract. Separate functions and their ways of integrating with the rest of the organization already exist. Cost accounting processes have been hammered out. While both sets of protocols may require significant modification, a framework is in place to deal with them.

When there are no protocols, developing an enduring contract is much more complex because the firm must establish both the framework for resolving the issue and the specific technical approaches. This structure facilitated the General Dynamics implementation effort tremendously; the lack of this structure in another high-technology firm extended the resulting outsourcing process over a period of years, with a diminution of savings and a complex conversion.

STRUCTURING THE ALLIANCE

Establishing the parameters of the outsourcing arrangement at the beginning is crucial. The right structure is not a guarantee of success, but the wrong structure will make the governance process almost impossible. Several factors are vital to a successful alliance.

Contract Flexibility

From the customer's viewpoint, a 10-year contract simply cannot be written in an ironclad, inflexible way. The arrangements we have examined have altered over time—often radically. Evolving technology, changing business economic conditions, and emerging new competitive services make this inevitable. The necessary evolutionary features of the contract make the alliance's cognitive and strategic fit absolutely crucial. If there is mutual interest in the relationship and if there are shared approaches to problem solving, the alliance is more likely to be successful. If these do not exist, a troublesome relationship may emerge.

No matter how much detail and thought go into drafting the contract, the resulting clauses will provide imperfect protection if things go wrong. Indeed, the process of contract drafting (which often takes six to eight months) is likely to be more important than the contract. At this phase, one side gains insights into the other's values and the ability to redirect emphasis as the world changes. Kodak has repeatedly altered its outsourcing contracts as both business circumstances and technologies have changed. General Dynamics had eight contracts to provide for different divisions evolving in separate ways.

Standards and Control

One concern for customers is that they are handing control over an important part of the firm's operations to a third party—particularly if IT innovation is vital to the firm's success or if the firm is very dependent on IT for smooth daily operations. A company must carefully address such concerns in the outsourcing agreement.

Control, in some ways, is just a state of mind. Most organizations accustom themselves to loss of control in various settings, as long as the arrangement is working out well and the supplier is fully accountable. Moreover, vital parts of a firm's day-to-day operations have *always* been controlled by others. Electricity, telephone, and water are normally provided by third parties; and interruption in their support can severely cripple any organization in a very short time. Providing sustained internal backup is often impractical or impossible. For example, if a hotel's electricity or water fails for more than 24 hours, it will probably have to close until the situation is rectified. The managers at a major chemical company who were particularly concerned about loss of control were brought up short by one of us who asked to see its power-generating facilities and water wells (of course, they had neither).

Nevertheless, disruption of operations support has immediate and dramatic implications for many firms. It is also a short-term problem area where possibilities of adequate protection are capable of being structured once the need is clearly recognized. Conversely, putting innovation and responsibility for new services and products in the hands of a third party is correctly seen as a more risky, high-stakes game. As we discuss later, in outsourcing, these issues are much more capable of being resolved for the firms in the factory and support quadrants, where innovation is much less important, than for firms in the turnaround and strategic quadrants. A company must carefully develop detailed performance standards for systems response time, availability of service, responsiveness to systems requests, and so on. Only with these standards in place can the company discuss the quality of support and new trends.

Areas to Outsource

A company can outsource a wide selection of IT functions and activities. Data center operations, telecommunications, PC acquisition/maintenance, and systems development are all examples of pieces that can be outsourced individually. Continental Illinois outsourced everything, while Kodak kept systems development but outsourced, in separate contracts, data center operations, communication, and acquisition management of PCs. At its core, *outsourcing is more an approach than a technique.* As we noted earlier, significant portions of a firm's IT software development activities have been routinely outsourced for years. What is at stake here is a discontinuous major shift to move additional portions of a firm's IT activities outside the firm. Between the current situation and total outsourcing lie a variety of different scenarios. When assessing partial outsourcing, managers frequently ask the following questions:

- Can the proposed outsourced piece be separated easily from the rest of the firm, or will the complexities of disentanglement absorb most of the savings?
- Does the piece require particular specialized competencies that we either do not possess or lack the time and energy to build?
- How central are the proposed outsourced pieces to our firm? Are they either more or less significant to the firm's value chain than the other IT activities and, thus, deserve different treatment?

Total outsourcing is not necessary for attracting a supplier, but the portion to be outsourced must be sufficiently meaningful that the vendor will pay attention to it. Several organizations we studied had spun off bits and pieces of their activities to various organizations in a way that engendered enormous coordination costs among multiple organizations. These contracts were also very small in relation to the outsourcers' other work, and we had significant concerns about their long-term viability (in one case, the firm has already insourced again).

Cost Savings

Some CIOs believe that the firm's IT activities are so well managed or so unique that there is no way to achieve savings through outsourcing or for the vendor to profit. This may be true. But two caveats are important. First, only if several outsiders study outsourcing with senior management sponsorship is an honest, realistic viewpoint ensured. Having a study done objectively under the sponsorship of the local IT organization can be very difficult. The IT operation may see an outsourcing recommendation as so deeply disruptive that the study may be negatively biased from the start. Additionally, since consultants whom the IT organization retains are often dependent on it for future billing, either consciously or unconsciously, they may skew the results. One firm's internally initiated IT study, done by a consultant, purported to show that the firm was 40 percent more efficient than the average in its industry. Needless to say, IT's control of the evaluation process led to general management skepticism; the study was subsequently redone under different sponsorship, with very different results.

Disinterested professionals can make a real contribution in evaluating cost savings and negotiating a contract. A firm only outsources once, while the vendors do it continuously. It is consequently, without outside assistance, a very unbalanced negotiation between an amateur and a professional. The outsiders like TCI and TPI add real value. Doing a postaudit of the cost savings that were actually achieved is difficult. Because situations change rapidly and new priorities emerge, it is usually impossible to determine what the results would have been if the alternative had been selected. Thus, the IT organization may be tempted to anticipate internal efficiencies so that IT outsourcing does not appear to be viable.

Supplier Stability and Quality

How a supplier will perform over a decade is an unanswerable question, yet one of the most critical a customer must ask. In 10 years, technologies will change beyond recognition, and the supplier without a culture that encourages relentless modernization and staff retraining will rapidly become a liability as a strategic partner. The stability of the outsourcer's financial structure is also critical. Cash crunches and/or Subchapter 11, or worse, are genuine nightmares for customers. This issue is complicated by the reality that once a firm outsources, it is very hard to insource again, as the firm's technical and managerial competence may have evaporated. While it is difficult to move quickly from one outsourcer to another (usually the only practical alternative), if a firm considers the possibility in advance, the risks can be mitigated. Some of the best bids come from newcomers trying to crack the market.

Problems are intensified if the way a firm uses technology becomes incompatible with the outsourcer's skill base. For example, a firm in the factory quadrant that selects an operationally strong outsourcer may be in trouble if it suddenly moves toward the strategic quadrant and its partner lacks the necessary project management and innovation skills to operate there.

Finally, there is a potential, built-in conflict of interest between the firm and the outsourcer that must be carefully managed so that it does not become disabling. The outsourcer makes its money by lengthening leases, driving down operational costs, and charging premium prices for new value-added services. By contrast, the customer has no empathy for the joys of harvesting old technology benefits (one of the reasons it got out of the business in the first place) and also wants rapid access to cheap, high-quality project-development skills on demand. Managing this tension is complex, imperfect, and very delicate and must be covered in the contract. Both firms must make a profit. The more the customer moves to the strategic quadrant, however, the more challenging it is to design a good fit with an outsourcer.

Management Fit

Putting together a 10-year, flexible, evolving relationship requires more than just technical skill and making the numbers work. A shared approach to problem solving, similar values, and good personal chemistry among key staff people are critical determinants of long-term success. Various outsourcers have very different management cultures and styles. It is worth giving up something on the initial price to ensure that you find a partner with which you can work productively over the long term. The information gained in the tortuous six- to eight-month process of putting an alliance together is crucial for identifying the likelihood of a successful partnership. Of course, this chemistry is a necessary, but insufficient, condition for ultimate success. Realistically, it is corporate cultural fit that is most important, since, after several years, the key people in the initial relationship will have moved to other assignments, while the contract remains in place.

Conversion Problems

The period of time for an outsourcing study and conversion is one of great stress for a company's IT staff. Uncertainties about career trajectories and job security offer the possibility of things going awry. All the expertise a firm gains when acquiring another firm is vital during conversion. The sooner plans and processes for dealing with staff career issues, outplacement processes, and separation pay are dealt with, the more effective the results will be. Almost invariably, paralyzing fears of the unknown are worse than any reality.

MANAGING THE ALLIANCE

The ongoing management of an alliance is the single most important aspect of outsourcing's success. We have identified four critical areas that require close attention.

The CIO Function

The customer must retain a strong, active CIO function. The heart of the CIO's job is planning—ensuring IT resources are at the right level and appropriately distributed. This role has always been distinctly separate from the active line management of networks, data centers, and systems development, although it has not always been recognized as such. As noted, these line activities have been successfully outsourced in a variety of companies. In a fully outsourced firm, however, sustained internal CIO responsibility for certain critical areas must be maintained.

- *Partnership/contract management.* Outsourcing does not take place in a static environment. The nature of the technologies, external competitive situations, and so on, are all in a state of evolution. An informed CIO who actively plans and deals with the broad issues is critical to ensuring that this input is part of the alliance so it can continuously adapt to change. The evolving Kodak and J.P. Morgan contracts give ample evidence of this.
- *Architecture planning.* A CIO's staff must visualize and coordinate the long-term approach to interconnectivity. Networks, standard hardware/software conventions, and database accessibility all need customer planning. The firm can delegate execution of these areas—but not its viewpoint of what it needs to support the firm in the long term. A staff that is 5 percent of the size of the outsourced staff seems to be close to the norm, although there is a wide range of practice. In general, organizations err on the side of too much coordinating staff.
- *Emerging technologies.* A company must develop a clear grasp of emerging technologies and their potential applications. To understand new technology, managers must attend vendor briefings and peer group seminars and visit firms currently using the new technology. Assessing the hardware/software network alternatives and their capabilities requires knowing what is in the market and where it is going. This knowledge cannot be delegated to a third party or assessed by sitting in one's office.

    Similarly, identifying discontinuous applications and the opportunities and problems they pose is critical. At one large pharmaceutical organization, the CIO's staff was vindicated when it became clear that they had first spotted business process redesign as an emerging area, funded appropriate pilot projects (which were skillfully transferred to line management), and finally repositioned the firm's entire IT effort. (Users and an outside systems house executed the project, with the CIO playing the crucial initiator role.) Clearly, an outsourcer has an incentive to suggest new ideas that lead to additional work, but delegating responsibility for IT-enabled innovation in strategic and turnaround firms is risky because it is such an important part of the value chain.

• *Continuous learning.* A firm should create an internal IT learning environment to bring users up to speed so they are comfortable in a climate of continuous IT change. An aerospace firm felt this was so important that, when outsourcing, it kept this piece in-house.

Performance Measurements

Realistic measurement of success is generally very hard, so a company must make an effort to develop performance standards, measure results, and then interpret them continuously. Individual firms bring entirely different motivations and expectations to the table. In addition, many of the most important measures of success are intangible and play out over a long period of time. Hard, immediate cost savings, for example, may be measurable (at least in the short run), but simplification of the general management agenda is impossible to assess.

The most celebrated cases of outsourcing have evolved in interesting ways. Of Kodak's three selected vendors, while the major one remains intact, another has gone through several organizational transformations, triggered by financial distress. General Dynamics, in the first 18 months, spun off three of its divisions, along with their contracts. It is too early to determine the outcomes. EDS and General Motors (GM) took years to work out an acceptable agreement; ultimately, EDS was spun out as a separate company, and their share of GM's internal IT work has been shrinking.

A major power company postponed an outsourcing study for a year. Its general managers believed their internal IT staff and processes to be so bloated that, while outsourcing IT would clearly produce major savings, they would still be leaving money on the table. Consequently, in 1993, they reduced their IT staff from 450 to 250 and reduced the total IT expenditure level by 30 percent. With the "easy" things now done, they then entertained several outsourcing proposals to examine more closely what additional savings and changes in their method of operation would be appropriate. Similarly, Dupont did a major restructuring before outsourcing to get access to specialized technology, industry, and applications skills.

Mix and Coordination of Tasks

As we noted earlier, the larger the percentage of a firm's systems development portfolio devoted to maintaining legacy systems, the lower the risk of outsourcing the portfolio. The question becomes: Can we get these tasks done significantly faster and less expensively? The larger the percentage of large, low-structured projects in the systems development portfolio, the more difficult it becomes to execute a prudent outsourcing arrangement and the more intense the coordination work to be done. Large systems development projects using advanced technology play directly to the outsourcers' strengths. Conversely, issues relating to structure (and thus close, sustained give-and-take by users) require so much extra coordination that many outsourcing benefits tend to evaporate.

On the one hand, the costing systems, implicit in outsourcing contracts using hard dollars, force users to be more precise in their systems specifications early on (albeit a bit resentfully) and thus cut costs. On the other hand, evolving a sensible final design requires trial and error and discussion. Both the contract and the various geographic locations of the outsourcer's development staff can inhibit discussion and lead to additional costs if not carefully managed. Managing the dialogue across two organizations with very different financial structures and motivations is both challenging and, at the core, critical to the alliance's success. Concerns in this area led J.P. Morgan and Dupont not to outsource significant portions of their development activity. Other firms, such as British Aerospace, did, after careful analysis.

Customer-Outsourcer Interface

The importance of the sensitive interface between the company and the outsourcer cannot be overestimated. First, outsourcing can imply delegation of final responsibility to the outsourcer. The reality is that oversight simply is not delegatable, and, as we mentioned, a CIO and supporting staff need to manage the agreement and relationships. Additionally, the interfaces between customer and outsourcer are very complex and should occur at multiple levels. At the most senior levels, there must be links to deal with major issues of policy and relationship restructuring, while at lower levels, there must be mechanisms for identifying and handling more operational and tactical issues. For firms in the strategic quadrant, these policy discussions occur at the CEO level and occasionally involve the board of directors.

Both the customer and the outsourcer need regular, full-time relationship managers and coordinating groups lower in the organization to deal with narrow operational issues and potential difficulties. These integrators are crucial for managing different economic motivations and friction. The smaller the firm in relationship to the outsourcer's total business, the more important it is that these arrangements be specified in advance before they get lost in other priorities.

During the past ten years, an entirely different way of gaining IT support for outsourcing has emerged. While outsourcing is not for everyone, a number of very large and sophisticated organizations have successfully made the transition and the practice is rapidly growing. What determines success or failure is managing the relationship less as a contract and more as a strategic alliance.

IT Operations

A major investment banking firm operated all of its foreign exchange trading and other trading activities out of a large computing center containing $15 million worth of hardware, totally without backup. One Friday afternoon, the water main running vertically through the building burst on the floor directly above the computing center. In a half-hour, the computing-center floor was covered with three feet of water and all the equipment was destroyed. The company went into the weekend with many of its key trading positions uncovered—indeed, not even knowing what those positions were. Truly extraordinary efforts were made to replace all of the equipment in a 48-hour period in order to prevent massive balance-sheet erosion. Multiple sites, much tighter environmental measures, better controls, and new management were all parts of the solution.

As a result of a software glitch in May 1998, a major Boston bank's automated teller machine (ATM) network went down for several hours. The network was the key point of communication with the bank's customers, and a storm of customers' complaints and unfavorable newspaper publicity emerged.

The chief executive officer of an industrial products firm discovered that the delay in year-end financial closing was not due to reduced emphasis on close control of financial accounting, but to unexpected work and personnel difficulties in the information technology (IT) department. Increased use (and associated problems) of an on-line query system to provide salespeople and customers with detailed delivery and cost information had absorbed all available system support personnel. Consequently, no time was left for revising the accounting system for mandatory changes in tax laws before year-end closing.

The IT director of a large aerospace firm pondered whether to totally reorganize and consolidate 18 operations centers in order to save more than $50 million. Each center was configured to provide total support to a business unit; workloads were erratic, long response-time delays existed on some on-line systems, and the costs were high. In fact, the consolidated center produced annual savings in excess of $100 million.

Unusual problems? Hardly! Historically, the "glamorous" part of the IT function has been the technology-oriented new systems development activity. Systems maintenance and day-to-day operations and delivery of service have been distinctly secondary. Failures in the operations function, however, increasingly jeopardize entire organizations. In this chapter, the term *operations* is defined as the running of IT hardware, networks, data input devices, equipment scheduling, and workforces associated with these activities. The chapter also deals with the special challenges of security and privacy.

CHANGING OPERATIONS ENVIRONMENT

Both the management resources devoted to operations activities and the sophistication of management practices within the operations activity have often been inadequate for the growth and change companies have experienced in this area. Evolving technology is now triggering major changes in the way these activities are managed.

Move to On-Line Systems and Networks.   In the past decade, a significant increase in on-line technology applications and growing sophistication in operating systems have transformed a batch, job-shop environment with heavy human control into first a process-manufacturing shop and then a largely self-scheduled and -monitored 24-hour-a-day utility with networked servers and clients scattered across the firm, and with links to numerous customers and suppliers. This change in work flow has precipitated a total rethinking of what appropriate scheduling is and how adequate service levels are defined. These systems support thousands of internal devices and in many cases must provide "seamless" 7 by 24 service (7 days a week, 24 hours a day) links to customers and suppliers around the globe. Any problems in this area immediately reflect unfavorably on the firm as a whole.

Diversity of Performance Measures.   There is no such thing as an ideal standard IT operations management control system or an ideal measure of performance. How to balance the quality of service, the response time of on-line systems, the ability to handle unexpected jobs and costs easily, the installation of maintenance patches, and the ability to meet schedules on batch systems varies from one organization to another.

Efficiency-Effectiveness Balance.   Different IT operations environments must strike different balances between efficiency (low-cost production) and effectiveness in responding to unplanned, uneven flows of requests. IT operations cannot be all things simultaneously to all people, but must instead operate with the priorities of trade-offs established by corporate strategy. To implement these priorities, some large IT operations have reorganized into series of focused, single-service groups, each of which can be managed to serve quite different user service objectives.

Changes in Staffing Needs.   Many formerly valuable employees are unsuited for new tasks, and their relatively simple jobs have been "automated away." Complicating this dilemma is the fact that in many parts of the world, this function is unionized. In settings where operations centers are becoming "lights-out factories," however, the problem is relatively transitory.

Continued Change in Technology.   Evolving technology, while offering potential benefits of lower cost and new capabilities, poses significant problems of change as new equipment and new operating procedures are introduced. It is an unusual IT operations center that has the same hardware/software configuration from one month to the next.

These issues are similar to those involved in running a manufacturing facility characterized as utilizing highly volatile technology and specialized labor, serving dynamic markets, and operating within a changing industry structure. Consequently, much of the analysis in this chapter draws on work done in manufacturing management, particularly as it relates to efficiency-effectiveness trade-offs.

A Focused Service Organization Alternative—An Example

A key question stemming from the manufacturing analogy is how focused the department should be. Should it subdivide itself into sets of stand-alone services networked together as needed or be organized as a general-purpose IT service? The problem faced by the company mentioned at the outset of this chapter—of either closing its books late or providing continuous on-line service for queries from the sales force—stimulated a review of how responsive its operations were to the demands of new services. It was impossible, they realized, for that monolithic unit to respond adequately to such very different user needs.

To address the problem, the IT development and maintenance group was reorganized into four independent systems groups, each operating independently of the others and reporting to the IT manager. One group supported the on-line query systems, with its goals being to provide 10-second response, one-day change implementation, and hourly refreshment of all data. This query system was moved to a stand-alone server in the corporate data center to keep its volatility of demand from disturbing the rest of the company's operations.

The second group was devoted to the general ledger accounting system. Their goals were to keep the software up-to-date for month-end closing, to schedule work so as not to interfere with other systems, to ensure the quality and reliability of accounting data, and to close the books five days after the last working day of the month. This system ran on the data center's large mainframe computer.

The third group was responsible for all material-management systems. Their objectives were to ensure that all desired changes to the system were made and that all production control persons were well trained in use of the system in order to reduce rerun time dramatically.

The fourth group worked with the systems that supported new-product development. They were responsible for identifying system requirements of new products, maintaining the capacity simulator used in planning new-product development, establishing the data standards used to describe new products, and developing and performing analyses on new products as directed by the vice president of product development. Their systems also ran on the mainframe computer.

Each focused group included at least one user and two to three systems professionals, with the query group having its own server as well. All worked full time on their respective services, with the exception of the new-product group, which had spurts of work as new products hit the market and lulls after the market settled down. This structure has produced happier customers, significantly better perceptions of service, and increased employee morale.

Alternative Organizations

Historically, IT systems were developed to be run out of an integrated IT operations unit. As we have noted, some firms have reorganized IT development and operations in order to be more responsive to user needs. For example, many organizations have not only shifted application programmers to users, but have also allowed maintenance and operations to be decentralized around local systems. As IT's monopoly of system construction and make-or-buy decisions erodes and user control increases, IT operations become fragmented into a series of focused services (for example, using a standard word processing system for customer mailings). For some users and applications, this may be very effective. The services for other users, however, may be dependent upon an integrated set of data and a network, in which case severe coordination problems are created by a focused factory concept. The challenge is to identify where focus in operations (either within the central unit or distributed to the user) is appropriate and where it is not. Implementation of this is discussed in the section on production planning and control later in the chapter.

Intensifying this challenge is the fact that in all but the most decentralized corporations, central telecommunications networks have been developed for binding corporations' activities together. These include the capacity for electronic mail, document transfer, data file transfers, and so on. Including everything from local area networks to satellite links, many of the networks are both very large and highly sophisticated as they evolve links between fragmented services. For example, a large aerospace company initiated a total redesign of its network architecture after a confidential e-mail message from the president to the financial vice president wound up on the desk of a production planner in another country.

To build on the manufacturing strategy theme and develop an appropriate range of make-or-buy plans, the operations management discussion in this chapter is organized around these topics:

- Developing an operations strategy.
- Technology planning.
- Measuring and managing capacity.
- Managing the IT operations workforce.
- Production planning and control.
- Security.
- Privacy.

DEVELOPING AN OPERATIONS STRATEGY

The management team of an IT operations activity is trying to stay on top of a utility that is radically changing its production system, customer base, and role within the company. Twenty years ago, the manager and his staff could be described as monopolists running a job shop, where the key issues were scheduling (with substantial human inputs), ensuring that telecommunications were adequate, managing a large blue-collar staff, and planning capacity and staffing levels for future workloads with similar characteristics. Today, by comparison, they (1) operate an information utility that provides a 24-hour, seven-day-a-week service in support of thousands of terminals and personal computers (PCs)—perhaps located around the world—that must cope cost-effectively with uncertain short-term and long-term user demand; (2) manage a workforce far more highly skilled, more professional, and much smaller in numbers; and (3) evaluate external competing services that in many cases offer the potential to solve problems more economically and more comprehensively. Thus, while key issues for the IT operations manager continue to include staff, capacity, and telecommunications, they also entail appropriate assessment, assimilation, and integration of software and services emanating from outside the corporation in this new world of electronic commerce.

Senior management must assess the quality of IT operations and—depending on how critical it is to the overall strategic mission of the corporation—must be involved in determining its structure and the standards for its quality of service. The central question for both senior management and IT management is whether the current IT operations organization effectively supports the firm.

In this context, an operations strategy must address four key issues:

1. Ensure that an architecture has been conceived and is being implemented.

2. Ensure that new systems are developed in ways that appropriately address their long-term maintainability.
3. Ensure that internal/external sourcing decisions are carefully considered.
4. Determine the extent to which IT operations should be managed as a single entity or be broken into a series of perhaps more costly but more focused subunits that provide more customized user service than is possible with a single facility.

Effective IT operations hinge heavily on ensuring that the first step of the systems life cycle, the design phase, is well executed. The critical operations discussions for a system often occur early in the design phase. Both user and IT operational personnel should be intimately involved in the early design of significant processing systems. Strong IT operational input ensures that operational feasibility issues are given high priority from the beginning. It is easy for a development group to overlook such issues as appropriate restart points in case of hardware failures, adequate documentation and support for operational personnel when a program abnormally ends, and so on. They further need to ensure that inappropriate shortcuts are not taken during development and that the details of the conversion from the old system to the new system have been conceived appropriately. These issues are particularly complex if an external package is sourced.

TECHNOLOGY PLANNING

Technology planning for operations is a process whereby potential obsolescence and opportunities are continually reviewed. The scope and effort of this review should be determined by the nature of the business and the state of IT: for a bank it should be across many technologies and be very extensive; a mail-order business may concentrate on office support technology (although the Web now offers a whole new set of channels); a wholesale distributor may primarily focus on computing and telecommunications technologies. To be effective, the review must involve high-caliber, imaginative staff. It should regard today's IT possibilities in the context of the potential available two or three years in the future. This potential must be based on technological forecasting.

If a company is trying to distinguish itself from the competition through its application of information technologies, the resources dedicated to technological planning should be quite extensive. If a firm is trying to just stay even with competitors and sees its IT activity primarily as "support," simple comparison with the operations of competitors or leaders in particular fields may be sufficient. Some firms periodically solicit bids from different vendors to help ensure that their IT department is fully up-to-date or do benchmarking studies. For example, a large insurance company whose IT department is dominated by the technology of one vendor has annually asked a competitor of the vendor to bid an alternative system, even though they have not perceived a need for change. As a result of these bids, however, they recently switched to another vendor's PCs, and on another occasion they installed a large machine purchased from a different vendor. These moves have kept the annual bidding process honest. (Obviously if no moves are made, eventually the process becomes corrupt as nonserious bids are received.)

The objective of the review is to determine—relative to available and announced systems—how cost-effective and adequate for growth the existing installed technologies are. The review should generate an updated priority list of technologies to be considered as replacements. Such lead time is critical; technology replacements or additions planned two years in advance cause a small fraction of the disruption that those planned only six months in advance do. (Realistically, of course, breakthrough announcements limit the precision of advance planning.) In order to better define the architecture of the future information service, the planning activity should include field trips to vendors, education sessions, and pilot studies as vehicles for obtaining an understanding of emerging technologies.

A useful approach to a technology review is categorizing the applications portfolio of operations systems by length of time since development or last total rewrite of each system. Discovering that a significant percentage of IT systems were designed a decade or more ago often indicates that a major redesign and rewrite will offer great opportunities for reduced maintenance and improved operational efficiency.[1] When a large international bank recently performed such a review, it discovered that 60 percent of its central processing unit (CPU) utilization and 50 percent of its systems effort were devoted to maintaining and running transaction processing systems constricted in the second era (see Figure 9–1).

If a new technology involves hardware replacement, or the new systems use existing hardware more effectively, implementation may be transparent to the user. Other replacement technology, however, affects users consciously by providing different or improved service—as do report writers for databases or new PCs. These technologies basically support users rather than change their operations style. Still other replacement technologies affect user habits so dramatically that user leadership must drive the implementation effort if it is to succeed. Each implementation situation requires careful planning to ensure that service is not interrupted and that the affected individuals understand how to operate with the new service. Figure 9–1 summarizes the tensions and forces that must be managed in IT innovation.

Good technology planning includes an ongoing appraisal of user readiness, an inventory of how existing technology is used, an awareness of where technology is going, and a program of appropriate pilot technology projects. A large consumer products company, for example, has an IT unit

---

[1]Martin Buss, "Penny-Wise Approach to Data-Processing," *Harvard Business Review,* July–August 1981.

FIGURE 9–1   Forces to Be Managed in IT Innovation

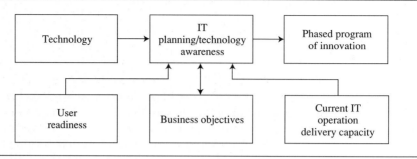

Source: Martin Buss, "Penny-Wise Approach to Data Processing," *Harvard Business Review,* July–August 1981.

with a very strong emerging-technology group; for each division and function, it maintains an updated log of services in use and an assessment of current problems. They are currently introducing a Windows '95–based program of office support that includes a large portfolio of applications in a pilot division. Scheduled over 24 months, the detailed program for this division includes benchmarks and reviews for evaluating benefits, operating problems, and progress. Such pilot testing stimulates broader organizational awareness of the opportunities and operational issues associated with new technology and permits better planning for full-scale implementation in the other divisions.

As the above example suggests, a new, explicitly separate organization unit to address innovation-phase technology exploitation and management appears to be a promising approach. Called the "emerging-technology (ET) group," it often resides initially in the IT organization on a level equal with applications development and operations departments. A historical analysis of 12 firms found that the key difference between leading and lagging financial institutions, airlines, and manufacturers was the early formation of an ET group. In some large, strategic IT organizations, the ET unit has been placed outside the IT department to avoid its being swamped by the IT control philosophy.

Three issues must be dealt with by general management in structuring the ET group: organization, management control, and leadership (see Table 9–1). The following paragraphs address these three issues in relation to the innovation and control phases. Because the innovation phase is more troublesome for most organizations, it is discussed in more detail.

Innovation Phase

The ET group might explore such current technologies as interorganizational video-streaming modeling software. The atmosphere within the ET

TABLE 9–1   Characteristics of Effective Management of Emerging-Technology (ET) Groups by Phase

Management Issue	Characteristic	
	Innovation-Phase Effectiveness	*Control-Phase Efficiency*
Organization	Organic (ET)	Mechanistic (traditional IT)
Management control	Loose, informal	Tight
Leadership	Participating	Directive (telling, delegating)

group is experimental; the organizational structures and management controls are loose and informal. Cost accounting and reporting are flexible (though accuracy is essential), and little or no requirement exists for pro forma project cost-benefit analysis. The leadership style resembles what Hersey and others[2] refer to as participating; that is, the distinctions between leaders and subordinates are somewhat clouded, and the lines of communication are shortened. The level of attention to relationships is high compared to that of task orientation. This informality is key to innovation and organizational learning.

A study of the tobacco industry[3] referred to such informality as organizational slack and stated that "the creation or utilization of slack normally requires the temporary relaxation of performance standards." In the effective companies, standards of efficiency were greatly reduced during the early testing phases of a new IT innovation. Organizations strategically dependent on IT should view innovation-phase activities as an integral part of their ongoing response to pressures to adapt to changing environments, and should fund them appropriately.

In addition, ET contributes to the broad-based learning of a company by being responsible for "interorganizational technology transfer." This refers to designing and managing the phase 2 introduction and diffusion of the targeted technology throughout the firm. ET must first facilitate the development of user-oriented, creative pilot applications of the new technology; it then participates in discussions about how the new applications can best be developed and implemented, the education and training needs of users and IT professionals for using the new technology, and the changes in strategy or structure that may result from implementing the new technology and associated applications.

After the ET group develops the ability to support the new technology, general management then decides whether to provide additional resources

---

[2]P. Hersey and K. H. Blanchard, *Management of Organizational Behavior,* 3rd ed. (Englewood Cliffs, NJ: Prentice-Hall, 1977).

[3]R. Miles, *Coffin Nails and Corporate Strategies* (Englewood Cliffs, NJ: Prentice-Hall, 1982).

to continue the diffusion of the technology (phase 2). With requisite support of senior management, the ET group begins to teach others throughout the organization how to utilize it and encourages experimentation. A chief concern of the ET manager at this point becomes how to market it effectively. (In some organizations, the job of selling the new technology is easy because the organizational culture encourages innovation and experimentation.) In the words of March and Simon, innovation in such companies is "institutionalized."[4]

Again, the cultural differences between laboratory and operations are important. Part of the task of successfully selling this technology to other parts of the organization is finding a way to translate the unique language associated with the technology into a language compatible with the larger organizational culture. A study of the electronic industry suggested that these cultural differences exist more in the minds of the organizational participants than in any objective reality. The artifacts identified in the study resulted from the natural tendency of people "when faced with problems in human organizations of an intractable nature, to find relief in attributing the difficulties to the wrong-headedness, stupidity, or delinquency of the other with whom they had to deal."[5]

The issue is not, however, whether the cultural differences exist only in people's minds but, rather, given that they do exist somewhere, what can be done about them. The study identified two useful solutions employed by the sample companies. One was assigning members of the design department to supervise production activity and production personnel to supervise the design activity. For IT, this means assigning responsibility for user implementation work to ET staff, as well as putting the user in charge of ET group projects. To be effective, this solution must be implemented with consideration for the wide gaps in technical expertise between subordinates and their managers. (That is, subordinates usually know more about the technology or business process than the manager does.) However, this has proven to be a viable approach when the key individuals are chosen carefully.

A second solution was effective in other settings: creating special intermediaries to serve as liaison between the design department and production shops. IT steering committees and user department analysts are examples of these intermediaries that have worked effectively in the IT environment. This strategy unfortunately tends to increase bureaucracy, but for many organizations, it has proven to be a very effective way of improving communication.

ET managers must analyze existing or potential resistance to the changes the new technology elicits. Resistance to change often stems from the reluctance of organization members to disturb delicately balanced power and status structures. ET managers need to adopt a "selling" leadership style

---

[4]J. March and H. Simon, *Organizations* (NY: John Wiley & Sons, 1958).
[5]T. Burns and G. Stalker, *Management Innovation* (London: Tavistock Publishing, 1979).

characterized by high task orientation and high levels of interpersonal interaction. Major organizational change threatens long-established power positions and opens up opportunities for new ones to develop. The new technology advocate who is insensitive to the political ramifications of the new system will face unpleasant, unanticipated consequences.

Once the range of potential uses has been ascertained and appropriate users are acquainted with the new technology, management must decide whether to put the technology permanently into place. At this juncture, the assimilation project moves from the innovative phases to the control phases.

Control Phase

The focus of the control phase is to develop and install controls for the new technology. Whereas the main concern during the innovation phase was effectiveness of the technology, control-phase management is concerned with efficiency. In installing the necessary controls, management's task is to define the goals and criteria for technology utilization. The most effective leadership style here is one of "informing," with lower interpersonal involvement relative to task orientation. During this phase, the organizational users (non-IT staff) are better able to judge the appropriateness and feasibility of the new technology to their tasks than they were during the innovation phase. The traditional IT organization and associated administrative systems are generally appropriate for this task.

For technologies in the later part of the control phase, IT managers typically exhibit a "delegating" leadership style. Interpersonal involvement and task orientation are low. With operation procedures now well understood and awareness high, effective managers let subordinates "run the show."

MEASURING AND MANAGING CAPACITY

The less one knows about computer hardware/software/networking technology, the more certain one tends to be in matters of capacity. In reality, the various hardware/software/network elements tend to interact in such a complex way that diagnosing bottlenecks and planning long-term capacity require a high degree of skill. To understand capacity and its key changeability, we must consider these factors:

1. Capacity comes in much smaller, less-expensive increments than it did a decade ago. In many organizations, this has created an "asymmetric reward structure" for capacity excesses versus shortages; that is, a shortage of capacity in critical operating periods is very expensive, while the cost of extra capacity is very low. For these organizations, a decision to carry excess capacity is sound.

2. A capacity "crunch" develops with devastating suddenness. During one six-month period, for example, a mid-sized sign manufacturer operated with few difficulties with a 77 percent load on the CPU during peak demand. Senior management refused to listen to IT management's warning that they were on the edge of a crisis and would not permit the ordering of additional equipment. During the next six months, the introduction of two new minor systems and the acquisition of a major contract brought the CPU load during the first shift to 85 percent. This created a dramatic erosion in on-line systems response time and a steady stream of missed schedules on the batch systems. Working through weekends and holidays failed to alleviate the situation. To the untutored eye, the transition from a satisfactory to a thoroughly unsatisfactory situation occurs suddenly and dramatically.

3. There has been an explosion of diagnostic tools, such as software monitors and simulation packages, that assist in identifying systems' capacity problems. These tools are analytical devices and thus are no better than the ability of the analyst using them and the quality of the forecasts of future demands to be placed on the systems. In firms where operations play a vital role, these tools and their contributions have led to significant growth in both the number and quality of technical analysts in the IT operations group.

4. A dramatic increase has occurred in the number of suppliers of computer peripherals, as well as an explosion of open systems architectures. This has sharply reduced the number of firms that are totally committed to a single vendor's equipment. Additional features, coupled with attractive prices of specialist manufacturers, have pushed many firms in the direction of IT vendor proliferation. Combined with the integration of telecommunications and office support, this phenomenon makes the task of capacity planning more complex and increases the need to referee vendor disputes when the firm's network fails.

5. Complex trade-offs must be made between innovation and conservatism. Companies in which IT offers significant (in terms of overall company profitability) cost reductions or the possibility of significant strategic offensive or defensive competitive advantage should push innovation much harder than other firms. Similarly, firms very dependent on smooth minute-to-minute operation of existing systems must be more careful about introducing new technology into their networks than other firms. Unanticipated interaction with existing systems could jeopardize reliable operation of key parts of the organization. (That was at the root of the bank network collapse noted at the beginning of the chapter. Inadequately tested software to provide new ATM features interacted in an unexpected way with the rest of the network's software.)

6. The cost and disruption caused by change may outweigh the specific advantages associated with a particular technology. Therefore, skipping a generation of change is desirable in some circumstances, although this must be examined carefully from two perspectives:

a. The system design practices of the 1960s and early 1970s were quite different from those of today. Some firms, eager to postpone investment, have stayed too long with the older systems and have exposed themselves to great operational risk when they have tried to implement massive change in impossibly short periods of time. In many cases, the results have been disastrous. (These time pressures were triggered either by external vendor decommitment of key components of an operating hardware/software configuration or by an urgent need to modify software drastically to meet new competitive needs.) Software, like a building, depreciates. Because industry accounting practices, except for those of software companies, do not recognize this, it is very easy for general managers to overlook the problems of this aging asset. Fundamentally, too many operating managers mistakenly think of IT development as an annual operating expense as opposed to a capital investment or asset maintenance activity.

b. Certain changes in the hardware/software configuration are critical if the firm is to be competitive; other changes cannot legitimately be considered essential. Investments in this latter category clearly can be postponed.

7. As investments in the products of small software and hardware vendors increase, the issues of vendor viability and product maintainability become important. The mortality rate among these small suppliers has been high since the early 1970s. When evaluating hardware vendors, the questions to consider are: If they go under, is there an acceptable, easily convertible alternative? Is it easy to keep existing systems going in both the short term and the long term? and What are the likely costs of these alternatives? In evaluating software vendors, the question is: Does the contract provide for access to source programs and documentation if the vendor goes out of business? An additional area of complexity is the vendor's posture toward program maintenance. This includes error correction and systems enhancements. How will these changes be charged? As noted earlier, experienced IT operations thinking is critical in these negotiations. When either the user or the systems and programming department purchased software without understanding the long-term operating implications, all too often the results have been very unhappy.

8. Finally, a hidden set of capacity decisions focuses on appropriate infrastructure backup—such as power, height above the flood plain, and adequate building strength for the weight of the equipment. The importance of the reliability of these items is often underassessed. For example, the temperature in a large metropolitan data center rose from 78 degrees to 90 degrees in a two-hour period, shutting down the entire operation. A frantic investigation finally found that, three floors down, a plumber had mistakenly cut off a valve essential to the cooling system room. In another setting, a once in a century flood imperiled a data center built underground to be protected from tornadoes. No one thought about floods in building the center.

All the above points clearly show that capacity planning is a very complex subject requiring as much administrative thinking as technical thinking. Few organizations in the 1990s are building a new "factory"; rather, they are implementing a continuous program of renovation and modernization of their operations. This is a formidable and, unfortunately, often seriously underestimated task.

MANAGING THE IT OPERATIONS WORKFORCE

Personnel issues in the operations function have changed significantly in the past few years. Most dramatic has been the major reduction, and in *most* cases elimination, of the data input and preparation departments. The introduction of on-line data entry has not only changed the type of tasks to be done (keypunching, key verification, job-logging procedures, etc.), but has permitted much of this work to be transferred to the department that originates the transaction. Indeed, the work is often transferred to the *person* who initiates the transaction or it is a by-product of another activity (such as cash register sales of bar-coded items). This trend is desirable because it locates control firmly with the person most directly involved and reduces costs. The large centralized data-entry departments have faded into history.

At the same time, jobs in the computer operations section are being altered significantly. For example,

1. Database-handling jobs are steadily being automated. The mounting of tapes and disks has been automated, and many firms have successfully automated the entire tape library function.
2. The formerly manual functions of expediting and scheduling have been built into the computer's basic operating system, eliminating a class of jobs.
3. Consolidation of data centers allows significant staff reductions as well as reductions in software site rentals. In one company, a recent consolidation of 10 large data centers reduced the staff from 720 to 380.
4. Establishing work-performance standards in this environment has become less feasible and less useful. As the data input function disappears and the machine schedules itself rather than being paced by the operator's performance, the time-and-motion performance standards of the 1960s and 1970s are now largely irrelevant. Inevitably, evaluating the performance of the remaining highly technical individuals has become more subjective. These people are either trouble-shooting problems or executing complex operating systems and facilities changes.

As these factors imply, the composition of the operations workforce has changed dramatically. The formerly large, blue-collar component has been virtually eliminated, while the technical and professional components have been increased significantly. In an environment of continuous technological change, the skills of these staff members must continually be upgraded if they are to remain relevant.

Career Paths.   In this environment, career-path planning is a particular challenge. At present, three major avenues are available for professionals. Those with technical aptitude tend to move to positions in either technical support or systems development. A common exit point for console operators is as maintenance programmers. As a result of operations experience, they have developed a keen sensitivity to the need for thorough testing of systems changes. The second avenue is a position as a manager in operations, particularly in large organizations where management positions ranging from shift supervisors to operations managers are filled mostly through internal promotions. (The number of these jobs, however, is steadily decreasing.) Finally, in banks and insurance companies, in particular, there have been a number of promotions out of IT operations into other user positions in the firm. In the manufacturing sector, this avenue of opportunity has been rare. Any of these promotion paths, if given the proper attention, can make the operations environment an attractive, dynamic place to work.

Unionization.   Although the trade union movement has been relatively inactive in the U.S. IT environment, it has been quite active in Europe and portions of western Canada. Organizing this department gives the union great leverage in many settings, because a strike by a small number of individuals can virtually paralyze an organization. For example, strikes by small numbers of computer operations staff in the United Kingdom's Inland Revenue Service have caused enormous disruptions in its day-to-day operations in the past. Changes in the skill mix that favor highly professional and technical staff suggest that this concern will be less important in the future.

In thinking about the potential impact of unionization, these points are important:

1. The number of blue-collar jobs susceptible to unionization has dropped dramatically. In the technology of the past generation, IT shops were more vulnerable to being organized than in the current or future generation.
2. The creation of multiple data centers in diverse locations tends to reduce a firm's vulnerability to a strike in one location. The networks of the future will reduce the risk even further. This has been a factor, although generally not the dominant one, in some moves toward distributed processing.
3. The inflexibilities that accompany unionization can pose enormous problems in this type of organization, given the frequency and unpredictability of operating problems and the need for high-technology skills. Further, the dynamics of technical change continuously transform IT operating functions and jobs. If the technology were ever to stabilize, the inflexibilities presented by organized labor would be of less concern.

Selection Factors for Operations Manager and Staff

Selecting the appropriate IT operations manager and key staff is crucial. Several factors generate the need for particular skills in different environments.

Scope of Activities. As scope widens from on-line satellite to knowledge-based systems, the IT operations' activity demands greater diversity of staff, and the complexity of management increases dramatically. Significantly more sophisticated managerial skills are required.

Criticality of IT Operations Unit.   Firms that are heavily dependent on IT operations (factory and strategic) are forced to devote higher-caliber professional staff resources to this area. Uneven quality of support is very expensive for such companies.

Technical Sophistication of the Shop.   A shop heavily devoted to batch-type operations (there are still some around) with a relatively predictable workload and a nondynamic hardware/software configuration requires less investment in leading-edge management than does a shop with a rapidly changing workload in a volatile technical environment. The latter type of shop requires staff members who can effectively lead such efforts as upgrading operating systems.

These factors suggest the impossibility of describing a general-purpose IT operations manager. Not only do different environments require different skills, but over time the requirements within an individual unit shift. The overall trend of the last decade is toward demand for an even higher quality of manager even as the number of staff members has been reduced. The tape handler or console operator of the early 1970s has often proven inadequate for the job.

Human Issues in Managing the Workforce

A series of long-term human issues must be dealt with in managing the workforce effectively.

1. The problem of staff availability and quality is a long-term challenge for IT operations. In an environment demanding small numbers of highly skilled workers, intensified efforts are needed to attract quality individuals to the IT operations group. Career paths and salary levels require continuous reappraisal. In factory and strategic companies, IT operations must not be treated as less important and prestigious than the development group.
2. IT operations must develop appropriate links to both the users and the development group. The linkage to development is needed for ensuring that standards are in place so that both new systems and enhancements

to existing ones are operable (without the development staff being present or on call every time the system is run) and that no unintended interactions with other programs and data files occur. Establishing a formal IT operations quality-assurance function is a common way to deal with this. No system is allowed to run on the network until it has been certified by the IT operations unit as meeting the company's standards. The user linkage is critical for ensuring that when an operating problem occurs, the user knows who in the IT operations unit can solve it—and for avoiding endless rounds of finger-pointing.

3. A long-term IT operations staff development plan that includes specific attention to training should be generated.
4. Issues concerning the quality of work life must be addressed continuously. These include such items as flexible time, three- or four-day workweeks, shift rotation, and so on. (These are still issues for the large shops.)

No single ideal policy or procedure can address these issues. Rather, a continuous reassessment must occur to ensure that the best of current practice is being examined and that the unit does not inadvertently become frozen in obsolete work practices.

PRODUCTION PLANNING AND CONTROL

Setting Goals

Operations production planning is complicated by the multitude of goals an IT operations function may have. Among the most common goals are these:

- To ensure a high-quality, zero-defect operation. All transactions will be handled correctly, no reports will be lost or missent, and so forth.
- To meet all long-term job schedules (or to meet them within some standard).
- To be able to handle unanticipated, unscheduled jobs, processing them within x minutes or hours of receipt provided they do not consume more than 1 percent of the CPU resource.
- To provide an average response time on terminals for key applications during the first shift of x seconds. No more than 1 percent of transactions will require more than y seconds.
- To limit day-to-day operating costs to specified given levels. Capital expenditure for IT equipment will not exceed the budgeted levels.

Establishing Priorities

By and large, IT operations goals are mutually conflicting: all of them cannot be optimized simultaneously. Where IT operations support is critical to achieving corporate missions (factory and strategic), establishing priorities requires senior management guidance. In environments where it is less critical, these goals can be prioritized at a lower level. Failure to set priorities in a manner that makes for widespread concurrence and understanding of the trade-offs to be made has been a primary cause of the poor regard in which some operations units have been held. When their goals were not prioritized, their task has been impossible.

A firm's priorities give insight into how it should address two other items: organization of the capacity and ensuring consistent operating policies.

Organization of Capacity.   Whether to have a single, integrated computer configuration or a series of modular units, either within a single data center or in multiple data centers, is an important strategic decision—assuming the nature of the workload allows a choice. Setting up modular units ("plants within a plant") allows specialized delivery of service for different applications and users. These multiple factories also allow for simpler operating systems and enable quite different types of performance measures and management styles to be implemented for each. This focused factory concept has been too often overlooked in IT operations.

Consistent Operating Policies.   Uncoordinated management specialists, each trying to optimize his or her own function, may create a thoroughly inconsistent and ineffective environment. For example, in a large insurance company, the following policies were simultaneously operational:

- An operator wage and incentive system based on meeting all long-term schedules and minimizing job setup time.
- A production control system that gave priority to quick-turnaround, small-batch jobs that had certain technical characteristics.
- A quality-control system that focused on zero defects, ensuring that no reruns would have to take place.
- A management control system that rewarded both low operating budgets and low variances from the operating budgets. Among other things, this control incentive had pushed the company toward a very constrained facilities layout as a means of minimizing costs.

While each policy might make sense individually, collectively they were totally inconsistent and created tension and friction within the IT operations group. Not surprisingly, the key users' perceptions of service varied widely.

Strategic Impact of IT Operations

The management focus brought to IT operations depends on the IT function's role in the firm. IT operations in the "support" and "turnaround" categories can appropriately be oriented toward cost efficiency. Deadlines, while important to meet, are not absolutely critical to these organizations' success. Quality control, while important on the error dimension, can be dealt with in a more relaxed way. It is appropriate to take more risks on the capacity dimension for both job-shop and process-type IT operations in order to reduce the firm's financial investment. Less formal, less expensive back-up arrangements are also appropriate. Finally, corners can safely be cut in user-complaint response mechanisms.

The factory type of operation poses very different challenges, because IT is integrally woven into the ongoing fabric of the company's operations. Zero-defect accuracy, fast response time, and prompt schedule meeting are absolutely critical. Capacity to meet various contingencies is also critical, because severe competitive damage may occur otherwise. Consequently, the issue of capacity needs to be managed more carefully, and more reserve capacity for contingencies usually needs to be acquired. New operating systems and hardware enhancements must be very carefully evaluated and managed to avoid the danger and financial damage of downtime. More investments in help desk and fast-cycle repair arrangements need to be made. These factors cause a company to make any necessary cost-reduction decisions more carefully than in organizations less dependent on IT service.

The strategic operation faces all the issues of the factory operation, plus several others. Capacity planning is more complicated because it involves major new services, not simply extrapolating figures for old services with new volume forecasts. A stronger liaison must be maintained with users in order to deal with the potential service disruptions associated with adding new technology and new families of applications. These factors suggest the need for more slack in both capacity and budget to protect vital corporate interests.

Implementing Production Control and Measurement

The issues raised in the previous section show why only an evolutionary, adaptive control and reporting structure will work. The indexes, standards, and controls that fit one organization at a particular time will not meet their own or other organizations' needs over an extended period of time as both the technology and the organization evolve more toward on-line systems.

Within the appropriate goals for the operations department, there is a critical need to establish both performance indexes and performance standards. This allows actual data to be compared against standards. Performance indexes should include items in the following areas:

- Cost performance, both aggregate performance and the performance for different IT services.
- Staff turnover rates.
- Average and worst 5 percent response times for different services.

- Quality of service indicators, such as amount of system downtime, by service.
- Number of user complaints, by service.
- Number of misrouted reports and incorrect outputs.
- Usage of services—such as word processing, electronic mail, and computer utilization—and peak hours.
- Surveys of user satisfaction with service.

While the data generated may be quite voluminous, the data (including trends) should be summarizable in a one- to two-page report each week or month. Such quantitative data provide a framework for making qualitative assessments of performance against the standards that reflect the department's goals.

SECURITY

One of the emotional topics related to IT operations is how much security is necessary for protecting the site and how much actually exists. This complex subject is discussed briefly here in order to call attention to its nature and importance. Exhaustively covered in other sources, the breadth of the issue is defined by the following points:

1. Perfect security is unattainable at any price. The key need is to determine the point of diminishing returns for an organization's particular mission and geography. Different units in the organization and different systems may have distinctly different security requirements.
2. Smaller organizations for which the IT activity is critical have found it desirable to go to something like the SUNGUARD solution, in which a consortium of firms funded the construction and equipping of an empty data center. If a member firm incurs a major disaster, this site is available for use. Backing up networks, today's major challenge, has made it much more complex to shift to these arrangements.
3. Large organizations for which IT activity is fundamental to their functioning and existence appropriately will think about this differently. Such firms will be strongly motivated to establish multiple remote centers (to avoid the investment bank's experience described at the beginning of the chapter). Duplicate data files, extra telecommunications expense, and duplicate staff and office space all make this an expensive (although necessary) security measure. These firms have concluded that if they do not back themselves up, no one else will. The architecture of these networks is extraordinarily complex to design in an efficient, yet responsive, fashion.
4. For organizations in which the IT operation is less critical, appropriate steps may include arranging backup with another organization, which is very hard in a networked world. Another alternative is to prepare a

warehouse site with appropriate wiring, telephone lines, air conditioning, and so on. (In a real emergency, locating and installing the computer is the easiest thing to do. Locating and installing all the other items consumes much more time.) Backing up the network is much more complex than just data centers. The insurance company in the example at the beginning of the chapter now has two entirely separate networks with two carriers and carefully allocates work between them in order to reduce their operational vulnerability. Reuters News Service has processing nodes around the world with multiple paths out of each node. If one path fails, the network is not imperiled; if a node fails, the network degrades but does not fail in all respects.

5. Within a single site, a number of steps can be taken to improve security. Listed here are some of the most common, each of which has a different cost associated with it.

   a. Limiting physical access to the computer room. Methods from simple buzzers to isolated "diving chamber" entrances can be used.

   b. Complex, encrypted access codes that serve to deny file and system entry to unauthorized personnel through the network. External hackers have successfully penetrated a large number of organizations that have not paid attention to this item.

   c. Surrounding the data center with chain-link fences, automatic alarms, and dogs. Monitoring access to inner areas by guards using remote TV cameras.

   d. Ensuring an uninterrupted power supply, including banks of batteries and stand-alone generators.

   e. Storing a significant number of files off-site and updating them with a high level of frequency.

   f. Using a Halon inert gas system to protect the installation in case of fire.

   g. Systematically rotating people through jobs, enforcement of mandatory vacations (with no entry to building allowed during vacation time), and physical separation of IT development and operations staff.

   h. Rigorous procedures for both certifying new programs and change in the existing programs.

This is merely an illustrative list and in no sense is intended to be comprehensive. Sadly, it is extremely difficult to fully secure files in a world of PCs, viruses, and floppy disks that go home at night.

PRIVACY

An explosive issue that cuts across the IT applications world of the 1990s is IT's increasing intrusiveness into privacy. (The 1998 controversy surrounding American Express's decision to sell a portion of its database on customer purchasing habits to a focused marketing mail-order house shows the emotions and sensitivities surrounding this type of activity.) This issue transcends all aspects of the field of IT and is included in this chapter only as a matter of organizational convenience. Consider the following examples.

A consumer foods company uses information from redeemed coupons and rebate forms to create a database for targeted marketing. It is assailed in a national consumer-advocacy publication with the headline "Smile—You're on Corporate Camera!"

An entrepreneur realizes that he can easily tie together several credit bureau databases and some other sources of information (such as motor vehicle records) about individuals. When he begins to market this service to small businesses for credit checking and preemployment screening, the state assembly passes a bill that would significantly regulate his activities.

Many credit bureaus offer services in which mailing lists are "prescreened" according to a customer's stated criteria. In addition, some credit bureaus transfer selected information from their credit files to marketing databases, from which mailing lists are sold for targeted marketing. These policies became major topics of discussion in a House of Representatives subcommittee hearing, where there were many calls for additional federal legislation.

These examples demonstrate an increasing challenge to managers in the late 1990s. Societal concerns about information privacy—the belief that limits are needed on access to information about individuals—are increasing, and these concerns could erupt in the next decade with considerable force. Unless proactive steps are taken, firms will find themselves grappling with these anxieties in two forms: public-opinion backlash against various computerized processes and a tightened legal environment with additional governmental control.

The Roots of the Privacy Issue

Two forces are behind this focus on privacy in the 1990s: the new technology capabilities that allow these new applications and the vacuum surrounding the distinction between "right and wrong."

Technological Capabilities.   Much more information is in computer-processable form today. Information that was previously stored in hand-written or typed paper files is now digitally encoded and electronically accessible from thousands of miles away.

Owing to less-expensive storage devices, faster processors, and the development of relational database techniques and structured query languages, it has become both more feasible and vastly more economical to both store and cross-classify information. Likewise, passing and correlating information between organizations is now relatively inexpensive and easy to accomplish. As networks become commonplace, new strategic applications pool data from different sources.

In addition to the potential intrusiveness of this pooling is the almost unsolvable issue of correcting errors in information. In many cases, it is virtually impossible to stop the trickle of errors as data pass from firm to firm.

Not only have both the speed/cost of computing and network availability undergone phenomenal improvements in the last decade, but the trend is accelerating; thus, in the future, it will be even easier and more economical to search for information and store it. As personal computers and local area networks proliferate across organizations in the hands of nonsystems personnel, people will propagate uncontrolled databases (on personal hard disks and file servers), and the number of people accessing networks will increase.

Add to this the growing use of artificial intelligence. As more decision rules are automated in expert systems, perceptions of these problems may be amplified as mistakes are inexorably carried to their logical conclusion in a documented form.

Taken together, these technological trends could easily and inexpensively lead to applications that would create unacceptable intrusions into people's privacy.

Ethical Concerns.   The technological forces operate in a large vacuum regarding right and wrong. Situations have been created for which the rules of behavior that worked well in earlier decades do not offer meaningful guidance. We are confronting a new set of policy decisions. While it is true that individuals and organizations may be inappropriately harmed by certain applications and activities, the degree of the impact is uneven. Some practices can be deeply damaging to people, while many others lie in the category of "merely inconvenient." Some inconvenient results of increased information gathering—such as mailbox clutter—are accepted by many as the "cost of progress," but society will eventually draw a line to protect against other applications that are recognized as more damaging.

For example, tenant-screening services, which allow landlords to exchange information about problems with former tenants, can lead to the unjust refusal of an individual's rental application if incorrect information is in the database or if mistaken identification occurs.[6] More often than not, however, such services protect landlords from losses incurred in renting to tenants who have already proven to be bad risks, and they thereby facilitate lower rents. Will society demand that such screening services be restrained?

---

[6]Some of the examples used here are adapted from *The Privacy Journal,* an independent monthly newsletter based in Washington, DC.

The Implications

Questions for Organizations.   Firms must anticipate potential privacy problems as they make decisions and take action to avoid negative public opinion and extreme legislative responses to inflammatory charges. Good planning may help your firm avoid the cost of adapting to new rules. Some critical questions regarding privacy issues are discussed here.

Storage of Information.   *Is there any information in the organization's files that should not be there? If it were brought to light that such information was being collected and stored, would there be a public backlash?* For example, several insurance firms have recently struggled with this issue as it applies to AIDS test results and where and how this information should be disseminated. Some advocates became outraged when they learned that individuals' files contained notations about positive test results. Lawsuits and numerous pieces of legislation (mostly at a state level) followed quickly.

Use of Information.   *Is information being used for the purposes individuals believed it was being collected to serve?* Many individuals who provide information for what they believe is one purpose become angry when they learn it has been used for another. For example, a credit card issuer came under legal scrutiny when it installed a computer system that could evaluate cardholders' purchasing histories for the purpose of enclosing targeted advertising material with their monthly statements (a mild reaction in relation to the earlier example of American Express). In another example, a car dealership installed an interactive computer system that asked potential customers to answer questions about their personalities and attitudes. The computer printed a "recommended car profile" for each customer. It also printed—with a different printer, in a back room—suggested sales strategy for the salesperson, based on the customer's answers. Had the potential customers known about this back-room printer, they might never have entered the dealer's showroom.

Sharing of Information.   *Are pieces of information about individuals being shared electronically with other organizations? If so, would individuals approve of this sharing if they knew about it?* Certainly, extraordinary opportunities for gaining strategic advantage have come through such sharing activities (micromarketing strategies). However, some people object when a company with which they do business sells their names and addresses, purchasing histories, and other demographic details to other companies. If the shared information is highly sensitive—if, for example, it concerns individuals' medical or financial histories—the reaction to having it shared—sold even—is dramatically exacerbated. On the other hand, some people would be happier if their "mailbox clutter" contained a much higher percentage of relevant items.

Human Judgment.   *Are decisions that require human judgment being made within appropriate processes?* Individuals legitimately become upset and request governmental protection when decisions that they feel require human judgment are being made without it. For example, an insurance company's decisions on whether to accept or reject new applicants—made within prescribed formulas and without direct human involvement—caused considerable difficulties when it was blindly applied in extraordinary situations that had not been contemplated when the rules were formulated.

Combining Information. *Are pieces of personal information from different sources combined into larger files?* The concerns of individuals and lawmakers are heightened when disparate pieces of information—even if innocuous in themselves—are pulled together. The possibility of creating a single profile of an individual's life is, to many, a threatening prospect. The entrepreneur who tied together several databases in order to provide "one-stop shopping" for several types of information through one vehicle faced this perception.

Error Detection and Correction. *Are appropriate procedures in place for preventing and correcting errors?* At issue here are both deliberate and inadvertent errors. Deliberate errors, which include unauthorized intrusions into databases, are often subject to audit controls. Inadvertent errors, on the other hand, are much more subtle and stubborn. They include misclassifications, data-entry errors, and the sorts of errors that arise when information is not updated as circumstances in people's lives change. It is impossible to achieve 100 percent error-free operation, but observers may reasonably ask whether the trade-offs a company makes for assuring accuracy are reasonable. If your organization were examined by lawmakers or consumer advocates, would you appear to be making the "correct" trade-offs?

An example from the public sector comes from the National Crime Information Center, a nationwide computer system linked to many state criminal-justice information systems. Outstanding warrants, parole violations, and other criminal data are often entered into local systems and are later "uploaded" to the national system. Law-enforcement agencies can then query the system to learn if individuals are wanted in other areas. Unfortunately, for a long time, problems with inaccurate data and mistaken identities were not uncommon, leading to improper arrests and incarcerations, and a number of lawsuits.

Other Issues. An audit of the questions we have enumerated often reveals several items for action in the organization. Additional issues to be considered by firms include the following:

Long Term versus Short Term. Line management should carefully think through each new use of information before they embrace it. In some cases, a "quick hit" for short-term profitability can yield disastrous results later. For example, an insurance company sold a list of its policyholders to a direct-marketing firm, earning a healthy fee. However, many policyholders determined that the company had done this—because of unique spellings of their names and other peculiarities—and were unhappy about it. The company received an avalanche of mail complaining about this use of their names and addresses, as well as a nontrivial number of policy cancellations, which brought the CEO to vow "never again." The short-term gain was not worth the long-term fallout.

Education.   Problems can be avoided through appropriate education initiatives. An organization's clients (customers or other individuals about whom information is stored) should be informed regarding the corporation's use of information about them when it strays from the narrow purpose for which it was collected. Clients should be told (1) what type of information about them is permanently stored in the corporation's files, (2) what is done with the information they provide, and (3) whether additional information from external sources is added to their files. This education process can take place in several forums, including inserts with monthly statements, special letters, and press releases. Corporations in particularly sensitive industries might provide toll-free telephone lines for clients' questions about information use.

Organizational Mechanism.   Through an initial audit and on a continuing basis, the internal and external uses and distribution of data should be given close scrutiny—especially if the firm is in an industry where such data sharing is likely to occur, such as consumer marketing or financial services. In very sensitive situations, a standing Data Distribution Committee can provide a forum for evaluating these issues. Such a committee should have high visibility and comprise senior executives. It could also be augmented by outside advisers (such as corporate directors) to ensure that objective viewpoints are provided and that problems are approached with sufficient breadth.

As laws and public opinion change in the next decade, it will be necessary to check current and planned applications against evolving policies and attitudes. Data files should be organized in ways that facilitate such ad hoc evaluations. For example, one might be called upon to list all data elements that are exchanged between internal organizational entities and with external entities. Could your organization construct this list in a quick and credible way?

Conclusions.   Our discussion of these issues indicates the complexity of the privacy concerns growing up around IT use. Chief information officers and other members of senior management should brace themselves for intense scrutiny of their activities by both legislators and privacy advocates. No doubt, there will be more focus on commercial IT activities than on governmental ones in the coming years. The tension between the effective functioning of commerce and individuals' rights to privacy will certainly become more pronounced. It is far better for the business community to be taking a voluntary, proactive stance now than to have to adopt a reactive posture later.

SUMMARY

IT operations management is a complex, evolutionary field. This is partly due to a changing technology that continually makes obsolete existing IT service delivery processes and controls, partly due to the continuing questions related to in-house operation versus outsourcing of the service, and partly due to the changing profile of the IT workforce. Major insights for dealing with these issues come from applying the understandings gained in managing technological change and manufacturing to this very special type of high-technology endeavor. Most large firms now know how to schedule and control multiprocessing batch computer systems working on numerical data from decentralized input stations. Building upon this base to include word processing, electronic mail, computer-aided design (CAD), image processing, links to outside customers and suppliers, and a host of more decentralized IT activities is an extraordinarily challenging task. Underlying this, the most critical need for operations success is for recruiting, training, and retaining knowledgeable people to operate, maintain, and develop IT services. Finally, of course, there are the issues of privacy, what forms of data files should be kept, what forms of cross-correlation are acceptable, and who should have access to them.

Chapter

10

IT Management Processes

The management processes linking information technology (IT) activities to the rest of the firm's activities are extraordinarily important. IT planning systems ensure that IT activities are congruent with other organizational activities; management control systems highlight potential operating problems; and project management systems ensure that disciplines likely to optimize the success of individual pieces of work are in place. This chapter emphasizes the first two processes—the IT management control and planning systems.

MANAGEMENT CONTROL

The IT management control system, which integrates IT activities into the rest of the firm's operations, ensures that IT is being managed in a cost-efficient, reliable fashion, on a year-to-year basis. The planning process, conversely, takes a multiyear view in ensuring technologies and systems are developed and assimilated to match the company's evolving needs and strategies. Finally, the project management system *guides* the life cycle of individual projects (many of which last more than a year).

The management control system builds on the output of the planning process to develop a portfolio of projects, hardware/software enhancements and additions, facilities plans, and staffing levels for the year. It then monitors their progress, raising red flags for action when necessary. The broad objectives of an effective IT management control system are to:

1. Facilitate appropriate communication between the user and the provider of IT services and provide motivational incentives for them to work together on a day-to-day, month-to-month basis. The management control system must encourage users and IT to act in the best interests of

the organization as a whole—to motivate users to use IT resources appropriately and help them balance investments in this area against those in other areas.

2. Encourage effective utilization of the IT department's resources and educate users in the potential of existing and evolving technologies. In so doing, the management control system must guide the transfer of technology consistent with strategic needs.

3. Provide the means for efficiently managing IT resources and provide necessary information for investment decisions. This requires developing the standards for measuring performance and the methods for evaluating performance against the standards to ensure productivity; it should also help to facilitate "make" or "buy" decisions and make sure that existing services are delivered in a reliable, timely, error-free fashion.

In the 1960s and 1970s, IT management control systems tended to be very cost performance focused, for example, relying heavily upon ROI (return-on-investment) evaluations of capital investments. Where the technology was installed on a cost-displacement justification basis, these systems proved workable; however, where the technology was used for competitive reasons, where it was revenue generating, or where the technology was pervasively influencing industry structure or operations (such as in retailing and airlines), cost analysis and displacement alone did not provide appropriate measurements of performance. Thus, developing additional management control techniques has been necessary.

Several years ago, for example, a large metropolitan bank instituted an expensive, complex charge-out system for improving user awareness of costs. Poorly thought out in broad context, the system generated a surge in demand for "cheap" minicomputers of multiple types and little or no investment in integrating network services; it triggered an overall decline in quality of central IT support in comparison with leading-edge banks and ultimately created market image and sales difficulties for the bank as a whole. It also led to soaring support/maintenance costs. The system ultimately had to be completely restructured to provide seamless, reliable, low-cost service.

Four special inputs now appear to be critical to an IT management control system structure for an organization:

1. The IT control system must be adapted to very different software and operations technology in the late 1990s than that existing in the 1970s. An important part of this adaptation is becoming sensitive to the mix of phases of information technologies in the company. The more mature technologies may be managed and controlled in a tighter, more efficient way than those in early phases, which need protective treatment similar to that of a research development activity.

2. Specific corporate environmental factors determine what is workable in an appropriate IT management control system. They include users' IT

sophistication, geographic dispersion of the organization, stability of the management team, the firm's overall size and structure, nature of the relationship between line and staff departments, and so on.

3. The design of the organization's overall management control system and the philosophy underlying it influence what is appropriate for the IT control systems.

4. The IT control system is affected by the perceived strategic significance of IT, in both the thrust of its applications portfolio and the ever more-important dependence on existing automated systems in many settings.

IT EVOLUTION AND MANAGEMENT CONTROL

Software Issues

Software support expenditures are divided between small project routine maintenance and the very large bulletproof transition of existing software systems to new architecture.

A second software issue concerns outside sourcing. As the percentage of development money devoted to outside software acquisition grows, management control systems designed for an environment where all sourcing was internal are often inappropriate for environments dominated by external software sourcing alternatives.

Operations Issues

For IT operations, management control is complex because measuring and allocating costs in a way which encourages desired behavior is difficult. In the short term, overall operations costs are relatively fixed, yet the mix of applications running on a day-to-day basis is volatile. This means that the same job can cost radically different amounts, depending on when it is run. The operations cost control problem is further complicated by the cost behavior of IT over time. Today, a replacement computer generally has 4 to 10 times the capacity and costs less than its predecessor. This has created an interesting control issue: Should the cost per unit of IT processing be lower in the early years (to reflect the lower load factor) so that it can be held flat over the life of the unit while permitting full (but not excessive) recovery of costs? Conversely, as utilization grows over the years, should the user's cost per unit of IT processing decline?

Selecting a particular method of cost allocation varies with the firm's experience with technology. In many organizations, the current control system gives broad management of desktop support to the user and complete management of networks to the IT department. As we have noted, however, desktops and telecommunications are so interrelated that such a separation is becoming ever more highly suspect and expensive.

Growth in User Influence.   A major stimulant to growth in IT usage has been the emergence of users who are familiar with problem solving using IT—although today's users are vastly different from those of even four years ago. After 20 years, it is clear that effective user applications generate ideas for additional applications. This is desirable and healthy, provided a control system exists to encourage appropriate appraisal of the new use's potential costs and benefits (broadly defined) to the organization. The absence of such controls can result in explosive growth (often unprofitable and poorly managed), requiring inefficient cost structures—or, alternatively, in little growth, with frustrated users obtaining necessary services surreptitiously (and also more expensively). Both situations erode confidence in the IT delivery process and its management control system. Also, for many of the new generation of user demands, articulating benefits is more difficult than determining costs. In repeated situations, the control system has given the hard cost of an applications implementation undue weight against the soft, but often very strategic, management benefits.

The control of information services thus presents a paradox: while the area is technologically complex, its effective, efficient use depends on human factors. This seemingly poses very familiar management control challenges; however, since both technology and user sophistication are continually changing, the types of applications are also changing. Many individuals are sufficiently set in their ways and find change difficult to implement, and thus resist it. As a by-product, these users' perceptions of the change agent (IT staff) are often unnecessarily poor.

External and Internal Factors.   Forces of change also exist in external items such as patterns of external computation and in numerous internal strategic items. Internal changes include the addition of new customers and products, new office locations, and modifications in the organization. A well-designed management control system recognizes these changes and handles them appropriately.

Geographic and Organizational Structure.   Other important control aspects relate to the organization's geographic dispersion and size. As the number of business sites grows and staff levels increase, substantial changes may be needed in organizational structure, corporate management control, and IT management control. Informal personnel supervision and control appropriate for a more limited setting can fall apart in a larger, more dispersed setting. Similarly, the nature of relationships between line and staff departments within the company influences expectations about the evolving IT-user relationship and thus the appropriate IT management control.

An important aspect of the IT management control architecture is the firm's organizational structure. Over time, it becomes increasingly difficult to manage with good results an IT organization whose control architecture is sharply different from that of the rest of the firm. A firm with a strong functional organization that maintains the central service function as an unallocated cost center may find it appropriate to keep IT as an unallocated cost center. Conversely, a firm that is heavily decentralized into profit or investment centers or that traditionally charges out for corporate services is propelled down the path of charging for corporate IT activities—and may go as far as setting it up as a profit or investment center.

Corporate Control Process

In concept, then, the IT management control system should be similar to that of the corporation. Ideally, as mentioned later in the chapter, there is a multiyear plan linked to the overall business strategy, which, in turn, is linked to a budget process that allows the responsible managers to negotiate their operating budgets. As such, IT budgeting should be compatible with the overall business budgeting. If business planning primarily consists of an annual budget with periodic follow-up of performance during the year, however, a very difficult environment exists for IT management control. Implementing many sizable IT changes can easily take two or more years—including as much as a year to formulate, select, and refine the appropriate design approach. Thus, an IT organization often must maintain at least a three-year view of its activities to ensure that resources are available to meet these demands. In many cases, this extends the IT planning horizon beyond the organization's planning horizon.

To be useful, IT project plans must systematically and precisely identify alternative steps for providing necessary service. For example, to upgrade reservation service in a large hotel chain, the IT department, in concert with key hotel managers, had to project the type of service the hotels would need four years hence in order to select the proper desktop computers and provide an orderly transition to the new system over a 30-month period. A major bottleneck in this massive, one-time, 1,000–desktop computer installation was a corporate planning and control approach that extended only one year into the future.

This combination of short corporate time horizons, long IT time horizons, and rapid technical innovation can generate intense corporate management control conflicts. These conflicts, which can only be resolved by repeated judgments over time, raise two major clusters of managerial issues.

1. How congruent/similar should the IT management control architecture and process be with that of other parts of the organization? Where differences exist, how can the dissonance best be managed? Should it be allowed to exist in the long term?
2. How can the tension between sound control and timely innovation best be balanced?

Control typically depends on measuring costs against budgets—actual achievements versus predictions—and returns against investments. Innovation calls for risk taking, gaining trial experience with emerging technologies; it relies on faith and, at times, moving forward despite unclear objectives. A portfolio excessively balanced in either direction poses grave risks. (As will be discussed in Chapter 11, different companies balance their IT portfolios quite differently.)

Strategic Impact of IT on the Corporation

An important consideration in determining how closely the IT control system should match the business's planning/control process is the strategic importance of IT systems developments for the next three years. If these developments are very strategic, then close linkage between corporate control and IT control is important, and any differences between the two will cause great difficulty. Additionally, IT investment decisions and key product development innovations must be subject to periodic top-management review.

The control system for these strategic environments must encourage value-based innovations, even if there is substantial implementation risk. Often, the key challenge is to encourage the generation, evaluation, and management of suggestions for new services from multiple unplanned sources while maintaining adequate control. Several now-defunct brokerage houses and soon-to-be-merged banks were unable to do this.

If IT is not strategic to the business but is more a "factory" or "support" effort, congruency of links to the rest of the business planning and control activities is not as critical. IT can more appropriately develop an independent control process to deal with its need to manage changing user demand and the evolving technology. A factory environment, for example, must emphasize efficiency controls, while a "turnaround" should focus on effective utilization of new technology.

A useful way of looking at management control was developed by Ken Merchant,[1] who suggested that controls can be grouped into three categories: results controls, personnel controls, and action controls.

- *Results* controls focus on the measurement of concrete results; they include such measurements as a percentage of variance from the budget, number of items procured/hour versus the budget, amount of downtime, and the like.
- *Personnel* controls focus on hiring practices, types of training and testing in place, personnel evaluation procedures, and so on.
- *Action* controls involve the establishment and monitoring of certain protocols and procedures; examples include segregation of duties, establish-

---

[1]Kenneth A. Merchant, *Control in Business Organizations* (Marshfield, MA: Pitman Publishing, 1986).

ment of certain task sequences, control of access to certain areas, creation of firewalls, and so on.

All of these are important in the IT context. Because of the special managerial problems historically associated with results control issues, the rest of this chapter pays particular attention to them.

Looking Ahead: Other Aspects of Control

To achieve desired results, the specific approach to IT management control is tailored to an organization, based on one or more of the dimensions discussed. Further, as circumstances change, it will evolve over time. The remainder of the chapter describes additional key factors that influence selection of control architecture (financial), control process (financial and nonfinancial), and the audit function. Briefly introduced below, each aspect of control is discussed in depth later in the chapter.

Control Architecture.   *Should the IT function be set up as an unallocated cost center, an allocated cost center, or a profit center?* Each alternative generates quite different behavior and motivation, and each decision is a fundamental one; once made, it is not lightly changed. Finally, what nonfinancial measurements should be designed to facilitate effective use of IT?

Control Process, Financial and Nonfinancial.   *What form of action plan is most appropriate?* Typically, this is represented by the annual budget and drives both operations and project development. What forms of periodic reporting instruments and exception (against budget targets) reporting tools are appropriate during the year? These forms change much more frequently than architectural forms.

Audit Function.   Issues here include ensuring that an IT audit function exists, that it is focused on the right problems, and that it is staffed appropriately.

RESULTS CONTROL ARCHITECTURE

Unallocated Cost Center

Establishing the IT activity as an unallocated cost center is a widely used approach offering many advantages. When IT is essentially free to users, user requests are stimulated and user experimentation is encouraged. This climate is particularly good for technologies in phase 1 or 2 of their assimilation into the firm, or where there is extreme urgency to generate/execute strategic applications. The lack of red tape makes it easier for the IT department to sell its services, and all the controversy and acrimony over the IT charge-out process is avoided, since no charge-out system exists. Further, expenditures for developing and operating IT accounting procedures are very low.

In aggregate, these factors make this a good alternative for situations in which the IT budget is small. Innovation and change are facilitated in settings where financial resource allocation is not a high-tension activity. A large bank, operating as an unallocated cost center, for example, introduced electronic mail, spreadsheets, and word processing over a two-year period. The most senior levels had resolved that this infrastructure was critical and strategic to long-term operational viability and competitiveness; the lack of an end-user charge-out system was seen as an important facilitator to its introduction.

On the other hand, treating IT as an unallocated cost center can pose significant problems. With no financial pressure, the user can quickly perceive IT as a free resource, and everyone wants a piece of the action. This perception can rapidly generate a series of irresponsible user requests for service and features that may be difficult to turn down. Further, where staff or financial resources are short, the absence of a charge-out framework may excessively politicize IT resource-allocation decisions.

The unallocated cost center also insulates the IT department from competitive pressures and external measures of performance, permitting operational inefficiencies to develop or to be hidden. Further, this approach fits the management control structure of some firms poorly (e.g., firms with a strong tradition of charging out corporate staff services to users). Finally, by blurring important revenue/cost trade-offs, an unallocated cost center poses particular problems for organizations where IT charges are perceived to be both large and strategic. In combination, these pressures explain why many firms that start with an unallocated cost center approach evolve another approach, at least for their more mature technologies and users.

One approach widely followed is to keep IT as an unallocated cost center but to inform users through memos what their development and operations charges would be if a charge-out system were in place. Without raising the frictions (described next) associated with charge-out procedures, this shows users that they are not using a free resource of the corporation and gives them an idea of the magnitude of their charges. The approach is often adopted as a transitional measure when a firm is moving IT from an unallocated cost center to some other organizational form. Unfortunately, however, a memo about a charge does not have the same bite as the actual assignment of the charge.

Allocated Cost Center and Charge-Out

From a corporate perspective, establishing the IT activity as an allocated cost center has the immediate virtue of helping to stimulate honesty in user requests. This approach fits rather well the later phases of technology assimilation, where the technology's usefulness has been widely communicated within the firm. While it may open up heated debate about costs, it avoids controversy about whether an internal IT activity should be perceived as a profit-making entity. An allocated approach particularly fits environments that have a strong tradition of corporate service charges. (It should be noted that outsourcing forces these changes to be identified and codified.)

Allocation Problems.   The allocated cost center introduces a series of complexities and frictions, however, since such a system necessarily has arbitrary elements in it. The following paragraphs suggest some practical problems that come from allocating IT department costs to users (whether in a cost center or via some other approach).

The first problem is that the IT charges will be compared to IT charges prepared both by other companies in the same industry and by outside service organizations, raising the possibility of misleading and invidious conclusions. The words *misleading* and *invidious* are related, because the prices prepared by other organizations often have one or more of the following characteristics:

1. The service being priced out is being treated as a by-product rather than as a joint costing problem, and thus the numbers may be very misleading.
2. IT is being treated under a management control system different from that of the company making the evaluation (that is, a profit center in one organization and a cost center in the other); thus, the cost comparison is highly misleading because the charges have been developed under very different bases. Communication costs, for example, are treated very differently across organizations, with many firms literally not knowing what their full communications budget is.
3. An independent IT services firm or an in-house operation selling services to outside customers may deliberately produce an artificially low price as a way of buying short-term market share; thus, their prices may be perceived as fair market when in fact they are nothing of the sort over the long term.

Since the prices produced by other companies are not the result of an efficient market, comparing them to in-house prices may easily produce misleading data for management decisions.

Another issue of concern is innovation. Unless carefully managed, the charge-out system tends to discourage phase 1 and phase 2 research projects or truly strategic applications, whose benefits are real but hard to quantify. These activities must be segregated and managed differently from projects utilizing the more mature technologies. In our view, nothing necessarily useful is accomplished by charging 100 percent of all IT costs to the users. Segregating as much as 15 to 25 percent as a separately managed, emerging-technology function and including it in corporate overhead (after careful analysis) can be a sound strategy. Similarly, strategic investments being segregated and accounted for centrally may also make sense.

On a more technical note, in the majority of companies charging out IT costs today, two major concepts underlie the charge-out process:

1. The charge-out system for IT operations costs uses a very complex formula (based on use of computer technology by an application) that spreads the costs in a supposedly equitable fashion among the ultimate users. Featuring terms such as *EXCP,* the concept is that users should bear computer costs in relation to their pro-rated use of the underlying resource.
2. The charge-out system ensures that all costs of the activity are passed to consumers of the service. Not infrequently, this involves users' reimbursing all IT operations costs the firm incurs each month and certainly by year-end.

Rigorous application of these concepts has led to a number of unsatisfactory consequences from the user's perspective. Most important, in many cases the charges are absolutely unintelligible and unpredictable to the end user, as they are clothed in technical jargon and highly affected by whether it has been a heavy or light IT-activity month. There is no way for the user to predict or control the charges short of disengaging from the IT activity entirely. This was one reason for the explosion of stand-alone minis and desktops in the early and mid-1980s.

Not infrequently, the charges are highly unstable. The same application processing the same amount of data run at the same time of the week will cost very different amounts from week to week depending on what else happens to be running on the network during the week. In addition, if all unallocated costs are charged out to the users at the end of the year, they are often hit with an entirely unwelcome and unanticipated surprise, which generates considerable hostility.

The charges tend to be artificially high in relation to incremental costs. As mentioned earlier, this can cause considerable IT-user friction and encourage the user to examine alternatives that may optimize short-term cost behavior at the expense of the long-term strategic interests of the firm.

In addition, in both operations and development, this approach makes no attempt to hold IT uniquely responsible for variances in IT efficiency. Rather, all efficiency variances are directly assigned to the ultimate users, which creates additional friction and allegations of IT irresponsibility and mismanagement. Finally, administration of a charge-out system of this type frequently turns out to be very expensive.

These factors in combination have generated a number of charge-out systems that do not satisfactorily meet the needs of many organizations. We believe this is a direct result of the technical and accounting foundations of the system. For most situations, technology and accounting are the wrong disciplines to bring to the problem. The task can be better approached as a problem in applied social psychology: What type of behaviors do you want to trigger in the IT organization and the users? What incentives can be provided to help assure that as they aim for their individual goals, they are moving in a more or less congruent fashion with the overall goals of the corporation?

The design of such a system is a very complex task, requiring trade-offs along many dimensions. As the corporation's needs change, the structures of the charge-out system will also have to change. Critical questions to ask include:

1. Should the system be designed to encourage use of IT services (or components thereof), or should it set high barriers for potential investments?
2. Should the system encourage IT to focus on efficiency or on effectiveness? The answer to this question may well evolve over time.
3. Should the system favor the use of internal IT resources or outside resources?
4. What steps must be taken to ensure that the system is congruent with the organization's general control architecture, or if it is not, to ensure that the deviation is acceptable inside the firm?

Desirable Characteristics.   While the answers to these questions will dictate different solutions in different settings, some generalizations fit most settings and represent the next step in the evolution of a charge-out system. First, for an IT charge-out system to be effective, users must understand it—that is, the system needs to be simple. Again and again, evidence suggests that a charge-out system that grossly distorts the underlying electronics but that users can understand is vastly preferable to a technically accurate system that no one can comprehend. Put another way, user understanding that encourages even partial motivation and goal congruence is better than no motivation or goal congruence. In this context, systems that are based on an agreed-upon standard cost per unit of output are better than those that allocate all costs to whoever happened to use the system that particular week. Even better (and a clear trend today) is designing these standards, not in IT resource units, but in transactions that users understand (for example, so much per paycheck, so much per order line, so much per Web page), where the prices of these transactions are established at the beginning of the budget year.

A second desirable characteristic of an IT operations charge-out system is that it should be perceived as fair and reasonable on all sides. In an absolute technical sense, it does not have to *be* fair; it is enough that all involved believe that it is fair and reasonable. In this vein, the IT operations charge-out system should produce replicable results; processing a certain level of transactions at 10 AM every Tuesday should cost the same amount week after week. If it does not, skepticism sets in and undermines the system's credibility.

A third desirable characteristic of an IT operations charge-out system is that it should distinguish IT efficiency issues from user utilization of the system. IT operations should be held responsible for its inefficiencies. Charging month-end or year-end cost-efficiency variances to the user usually accomplishes no useful purpose—it only raises the emotional temperature. After appropriate analysis of the causes for the variances, they normally should be charged directly to corporate overhead.

IT Maintenance and Development Charges.   The issues involved in charging for IT maintenance and systems development are fundamentally different from those of IT operations and must be dealt with separately. In advance of development and maintenance expenditures of any size, a professional contract should be prepared between IT and the users (as though it were a relationship with an outside or systems integration company). Elements of a good contract include:

1. A provision indicating that estimates of job costs are to be prepared by IT and that IT is to be held responsible for all costs in excess of those amounts.
2. Procedures for reestimating and, if necessary, canceling the job if job scope changes.
3. A provision that if a job is bid on a time-and-materials basis (very frequent in the systems integration industry), a clear understanding must be reached with the user, in advance, about what significant changes in scope would make the contract be reviewed.

For many systems (e.g., database systems), the most challenging, and sometimes impossible, task is to identify the definable user (or group thereof) with which to write the contract. Moreover, if the contract is written with one group of users but others subsequently join, are the new users charged at incremental cost, full cost, or full cost plus (because they have undertaken none of the development risks and are buying into a sure thing)? Neither easy nor general-purpose solutions to these issues are possible.

Example.   One company approached these issues in an effective way, in our judgment. It provided computer services to 14 user groups, many of which had very similar needs, spreading operations expenses as follows:

1. Every time a piece of data was inputted or extracted on a computer screen, a standard charge was levied on the user, irrespective of the type of processing system involved. This charge was understandable to the user.
2. Since all costs from the modems out (terminal, line) could be directly associated with a user in a completely understandable fashion, these charges were passed directly to the end user.
3. All report and other paper costs were charged to the user on a standard cost-per-ton basis, irrespective of the complexity of the system that generated them.

4. All over- or under-recovered variances were analyzed for indications of IT efficiency and then closed directly to a corporate overhead account, bypassing the users.

With respect to maintenance and development cost, the following procedures were used:

1. Items budgeted for less than 40 hours were charged directly to the users at a standard rate per hour.
2. Projects budgeted to take more than 40 hours were estimated by the IT organization. If the estimate was acceptable to the user, work would be done. Any variances in relation to the estimate were debited or credited to the IT organization, with the user being billed only the estimated amount.
3. A job-reestimating process handled potential changes in job specification, with the users having the option of accepting the new costs, using the old specifications, or jettisoning the job.
4. The IT organization budgeted research and development projects separately. IT was accountable to corporate for the costs of these jobs, and the users were not charged for them.

Over a several-year period, these procedures were remarkably successful in defusing tensions in user-IT relationships, enabling the groups to work together more easily.

Profit Center

A third frequently discussed and used method of management control is to establish the IT department as a profit center. Advocates of this approach note that it puts the inside service on the same footing as an outside one and brings marketplace pressures to bear; it also hastens the emergence of the IT marketing function, which, if well managed, will improve relationships with users; thus, the IT function is encouraged to hold costs down through efficiency and to market itself more aggressively inside the company. Further, IT management tends to deal promptly with excess IT capacity and is willing to run more risks on the user service side. (Interestingly, this is the de facto structure for the outsourcing vendor in an outsourcing relationship.)

Excess capacity also encourages the IT department to sell services to outside firms—often a mixed blessing. When priced as incremental sales (rather than on a full-cost basis), these services are unprofitable; in addition, many IT departments—excited by the volatile "hard" outside dollars as opposed to the captive "soft" inside ones—begin to give preferential treatment to outside customers, with a resulting erosion of service to inside users.

Establishing IT as a profit center may generate other problems. First, significant concern is often raised within the organization about the appropriateness of an inside "service department" establishing itself as a profit center, particularly when it does not sell any products outside the company. "Profits should come from outside sales, not service department practices" is the dominant complaint. The problem is exacerbated when, because of geography, shared data files, and privacy and security reasons, users do not have the legitimate alternative of going outside (unless the entire IT department is outsourced). Therefore, users perceive the argument that the profit center is subject to normal market forces as spurious. (Although in a world of outsourcing alternatives, this argument has more validity.)

At least in the short run, setting up the IT activity as a profit center can lead to higher user costs, because a profit figure is added to user costs. Not only can this create user hostility, but also in many settings it prevents the user from having legitimate full-cost data from the corporation for external pricing decisions.

Overall, the above issues must be addressed before an organization adopts a profit center approach. A deceptively intriguing idea on the surface, it has many pitfalls (although, as will be seen later, the practice of outsourcing IT is growing rapidly).

Summary.   Although many potential IT results control architectures are possible, none represents a perfect general-purpose solution. The challenge is to pick the one that best fits the company's general management control culture, current user-IT relationships, and current state of IT sophistication. The typical firm has approached these issues in an evolutionary fashion, rather than having selected the right one the first time.

Financial Reporting Process

Budget Objectives.   A key foundation of the IT results control process is the budgeting system. Put together under a very complex set of trade-offs and interlocked with the corporate budgeting process, its first objective is to provide a mechanism for appropriately allocating financial resources. While the planning effort sets the broad framework for the IT activity, the budgeting process ensures fine-tuning in relation to staffing, hardware, and resource levels. A second objective of budgeting is to trigger a dialogue that ensures that organizational consensus is reached on the specific goals and possible short-term achievements of the IT activity; this dialogue is particularly important in organizations without a well-formed planning process. Finally, the budget establishes a framework around which an early warning system for negative deviations can be erected. In the absence of a budget, it is difficult to spot deviations in a deteriorating cost situation in time to take appropriate corrective action.

Budget Process.   The budget system must involve senior management, IT management, and user groups. Its primary outputs include establishing the planned service levels and costs of central operations, the amount of internal development and maintenance support to be implemented, and the amount and form of external services to be acquired. The planned central IT department service levels and their associated costs must flow from review of existing services and the approved application development portfolio as well as user desire for new services. In addition, these planned service levels must take into account long-term systems maintenance needs. The budget must also ensure that there are appropriate controls on purchased IT services for the firm as a whole (software and hardware, such as desktop devices). The practices that organizations have assembled to understand the totality of their IT expenditures are very uneven. A dialogue between users and the IT department regarding anticipated needs and usage for the budget year helps clarify the IT department's goals and constraints and iteratively leads to generating a better IT plan and clarifying users' plans.

Example.   A leading chemical company asks users and the IT department each to develop two budgets, one for the same amount of dollars and headcount as the preceding year and one for 10 percent more dollars and 2 percent more headcount. In recent years, the IT department's proposals have involved an expansion of networks and desktop devices. To help ensure a dialogue, the main descriptions of key items are stated in user terms—such as the number of personnel records and types of pension planning support—with all the jargon relating to IT technical support issues being confined to appendixes. Both groups are asked to rank services of critical importance as well as to identify those that are of lower priority or that are likely to be superseded. A senior management group then spends a day reviewing a joint presentation that examines the budget in terms of probable levels of expenditure and develops a tentative ranking of the priority items. This meeting allows senior management to provide overall direction to the final budget negotiations between the two groups. The IT manager then consolidates priorities established in these discussions for final approval. This modified, zero-based budgeting approach is judged to have provided good results in this setting.

Budget Targets.   The IT budget should establish benchmark dates for project progress, clarify the type and timing of technical changeovers, and identify needed levels and mixes of personnel as well as set spending levels. A further mission is to identify important milestones and completion dates and tie them to the budget. This helps to ensure that periodic review will allow for early detection of variances from the plan. Budgeting key staff headcount and levels is a particularly important management decision. A major cause of project overruns and delays is lack of talent available to support multiple projects in a timely manner. Shortage of personnel must be dealt with realistically in fitting projects together—and should be done periodically through the year as well.

An important benefit of involving users and suppliers in the budget process is education. The IT department can understand each user department's particular needs for IT support and assess them relative to other departments' needs. At the same time, users become aware of what is possible with available technology and can better define their potential needs. In one financial institution, the budget process is heavily used as a stimulus for innovation. During budget preparation, both users and IT staff take many trips to other installations and receive information from their hardware/software suppliers to generate thinking on potential new banking services. This activity has significantly improved the relationship between the two groups over the past several years.

Periodic Reporting.   Effective monitoring of the department's financial performance requires a variety of tools, most of which are common to other settings. These normally include monthly reports highlighting actual performance versus the plan and exception reports as needed; design and operation of these systems are rather routine. Obvious issues to consider include: (1) Are budget targets readjusted during the year through a forecasting mechanism? (2) If so, is the key performance target actual versus budget or actual versus forecast? (3) Are budgets modified for seasonal factors, or are they prepared on a basis of one-twelfth of the annual expense each month?

The IT financial reporting task is a bit different because an IT organization requires a matrix cost reporting system as it grows in size. One side of the matrix represents the IT department structure and tracks costs and variances by IT organizational unit. The other side of the matrix tracks costs and variances by programs or projects.

Whether budget numbers and actual results should be reported in nominal dollars or in inflation-adjusted dollars is an issue of major importance for corporate management control systems today, particularly for multinational firms. It is, however, beyond the scope of this book.

Nonfinancial Reporting Process

At least in an operational sense, the nonfinancial controls are more important than the financial ones in assuring management that the IT function's day-to-day and month-to-month activities remain on target. One critical item here is regularly surveying (every six months) users' attitudes toward the IT support they are receiving. Such surveys identify problems and provide a benchmark against which progress can be measured over time. Their distribution to the users for completion also clearly communicates that IT is concerned about user perception of service. Problems surfacing in surveys need to be acted on promptly if the instrument is to be an effective control.

Another category of controls relates to staff. Reports monitoring personnel turnover trends can provide critical early insight into the problems of this notoriously unstable group. These data allow timely action on such items as sensitivity of leadership, adequacy of salary levels, and workplace climate. In the same vein, formal training plans and periodic measurement of progress are important management tools for ensuring a professionally relevant group and maintaining morale.

Reports and other procedures generating absolute measures of operational service levels are very important in IT operations. These include data on such items as trends in network uptime, ability to meet schedules on batch jobs, average transaction response time by type of system, number of missends and other operational errors, and a customer complaint log. To be effective, these systems must be maintained and adhered to; when quality-control errors are allowed to creep in, performance appears better than it actually is.

In relation to systems development, reports on development projects in terms of elapsed time and work-months expended (vis-à-vis budget) provide a crucial early warning system for assessing overall performance. The type of data needed and available varies widely by company. The company's maturity in dealing with IT, the relative strategic role of IT development and operations, and the corporation's general approach to managerial control also influence both the form these issues take and the detail with which they are approached.

IT AUDIT FUNCTION

Located as a part of the office of the general auditor, the IT auditor function provides a vital check and balance on IT activity. Given "worms," interorganizational systems, and electronic fraud, it is hard to overstate the importance of this function, which forms the front line of defense in an increasingly complex networked world. There are three basic elements of the audit function mission. The first is ensuring that appropriate standards for IT development and operations have been developed and installed consistent with the control architecture. With changes in both technology and the organization's familiarity with it, developing these standards is not a one-time job but requires continuous effort.

The second element is ensuring that operating units adhere to these standards in order to help reduce operations errors and omissions and increase user confidence and satisfaction. This activity includes both regular progress reviews and surprise audits. Such audits should reduce fraud and loss; they also serve as a prod toward improving operating efficiency.

The third element is active involvement in the systems design and maintenance functions to ensure that systems can be easily audited and that maintenance changes do not create problems. Such involvement clearly compromises the supposedly independent mission of the auditor but is a necessary accommodation to the real world. It helps ensure the smooth running of the final system.

Successful execution of the above mission elements helps to reduce the amount of outside assistance needed by the firm; yet these seemingly straightforward tasks are very difficult to implement in the real world—for the following reasons.

1. Maintaining necessary auditing staff skills is difficult. Operating at the intersection of two disciplines (IT and auditing), good practice demands thorough mastery of both. Unfortunately, because IT auditing is frequently a "dead end" career path, staff members who are retained may be sufficiently deficient in both disciplines to be ineligible as practitioners in either. Higher salaries and visibly attractive career paths are essential preconditions to reversing this situation.
2. The "art" of IT auditing continually lags behind the challenges posed by new technologies. Understanding methodologies for controlling batch systems for computers, for instance, is not very relevant for a world currently dominated by complex operating systems, networks, and on-line technologies. Managing catch-up for such lags poses a significant IT auditing challenge for the future.
3. Management support for IT auditing has been uneven. Partly owing to the lack of formally defined requirements from an outside authority, support for a strong IT auditing function tends to be very episodic, with periods of strong interest following conspicuous internal or external failure. This interest, however, tends to erode rapidly once the calamity has been corrected.

Overall, the role of the IT auditing function is poorly defined in most organizations at this time. Typically part of the internal auditing organization, and often not reporting to senior management, this function, in fact, deserves serious consideration at that management level.

Summary   Although many IT management control issues resemble general management control concerns, there are several different aspects to them. The first arises from the rapid changes in the underlying technology and the long time span required for users to adapt to new technologies.

Phase 1 and phase 2 technologies require a commitment to R&D and user learning that directly conflicts with the charge-out techniques appropriate for phase 3 and phase 4 technologies. It is very easy for an organization to become too uniform in its control system, standardizing in order to use systems "efficiently" and stamping out innovation as a by-product. In most organizations today, different divisions (at varying stages of learning and using varying mixes of technologies) necessitate quite different control approaches. Further, as organizational learning occurs, other control approaches become appropriate; thus, quite apart from any breakthroughs in the general area of IT control methods, their practice in an organization undergoes continual evolution.

As IT becomes more firmly established in an operation, the penalties for uneven performance of technology may impose very severe consequences for the organization as a whole: action controls become vital. As a company, department, or system evolves from "turnaround" to "factory" to "support," very different control philosophies become appropriate.

Adding these issues to those concerning the changing corporate environment and evolving corporate control processes (in a world shifting from "make" to "buy" in software), the full complexity of the IT management control problem is apparent. Different organizations must adopt quite different control approaches, which then must evolve over time to deal with a changing corporate environment, changing strategic role of IT, and changing technologies.

PLANNING—A CONTINGENT FOCUS

Organizations launch IT planning efforts with great hope and often witness positive early results. Subsequently, however, many of these efforts run into difficulty. This section explores key managerial issues surrounding IT planning and provides guidelines to help assure success.

As IT applications have grown in size and complexity over the past two decades, developing a strategy for assimilating these resources into firms' operations has grown steadily more important. A primary vehicle for strategy development is a sensitive architecture planning process, which, to be effective, must deal simultaneously with the realities of the firm's organizational culture, corporate planning culture, and various technologies, and the importance of IT activities to the corporate goals.

Many studies have shown a positive correlation between user perception that IT activities are effective and a focused, articulated, appropriate planning process.[2] Since good standards do not exist for measuring the overall effectiveness of the IT activity, however, the evidence linking its effectiveness with planning processes is necessarily diffuse and fragmentary.

The material in this section is organized around four topics:

1. External and internal pressures generating the need for an articulated IT planning process.
2. Pressures limiting the value derived from IT planning.
3. The relationship between IT planning and corporate strategy formulation.
4. Corporate factors influencing the effectiveness of IT planning—tailoring the IT planning process to a specific firm.

---

[2]Philip Pyburn, "Information Systems Planning—A Contingency Perspective," DBA thesis, Harvard Business School, 1981.

PRESSURES TOWARD IT PLANNING

External (Corporate) Pressures

Although a variety of external pressures define the need for IT planning, the most important ones are discussed here.

Rapid Changes in Technology.   Hardware and software continue to evolve rapidly, providing substantially different and potentially profitable IT applications from year to year. This requires continual interaction between IT staff and management groups in order to identify the technology changes significant to the company and develop appropriate plans and pilot projects. IT staff must make potential users, such as office managers and analytical staffs, aware of the implications (including the possible problems) of these new technologies so they can identify those potential new applications in their areas of responsibility that IT staff might not recognize.

As technology changes, planning grows increasingly important in order to avoid the problems of incompatible systems and inaccessible data files. The networked organization is becoming reality, and developing network linkages frequently requires implementation schedules of up to four years.

For example, an insurance company instituted a two- to three-year program for placing a portable personal computer (PC) containing expert financial counseling software into the hands of each of its 5,000 agents. A detailed plan was absolutely critical to maintaining senior management's confidence in the integrity of the program and the sales force's effectiveness and good morale during the implementation.

Personnel Scarcity.   The scarcity of trained, perceptive analysts and programmers, coupled with their long training cycles, continues to restrain IT development and to demand that planning priorities be established. As discussed, these appear to be long-term difficulties rather than cyclical problems and are forcing larger amounts of software and electronic support to be sourced from outside and necessitating tough internal resource allocation decisions.

Scarcity of Other Corporate Resources.   Limited availability of financial and managerial resources is another planning pressure. IT is only one of many strategic investment opportunities for a company, and the potential financial return of investment in it must be weighed against alternatives. Most U.S. companies' financial accounting practice, which charges IT expenditure against the current year's earnings, even though much of it is actually a capital expenditure, intensifies this problem. Reviewing the effectiveness and the efficiency of these expenditures is of great importance, as resource availability is a crucial limiting factor for new projects—particularly in companies under profit or cost pressures.

Trend to Database Design and Integrated Systems. An increasing and significant proportion of the applications portfolio involves the design of relational data architecture for supporting sophisticated applications that link different parts of the firm as well as its customers and suppliers. A long-term view of the evolution of applications is critical to appropriately selecting database contents, the methods for interrelating them, and the protocols for updating them.

Validation of Corporate Plan. In many organizations, new marketing programs, new-product design, and introduction and implementation of organizational strategies depend on the development of IT systems. Indeed, the new technologies may drive fundamental changes in the company's strategy if it is to survive. For example, the large bookstore, Barnes & Noble, had to pioneer a Web-based distribution system to counter the attack from Amazon.com, the Internet bookseller (whose sales in 1998 were approaching $500 million). Similarly, IBM is being forced to deal with the fact that Dell Computer will sell $1 billion of PCs across the Internet in 1998. Understanding these points of dependency is also vital. If IT limitations or opportunities render corporate strategy infeasible, corporate management must hear that message loud and clear; the problem must be faced and resolved while alternatives are still available.

In organizations where IT products and processes are integral to elements of the corporate strategy (or even shape the strategy), this linkage is very important. A large paper company, for example, was forced to abandon its planned new billing discount promotions—a key part of its marketing strategy—because its IT function was unable to translate the very complex ideas into the existing computer programs with the present level of staff skills. Advance coordination between IT and marketing management would have identified the problem much earlier and permitted satisfactory solutions to be identified.

Internal (IT Process) Pressures

At various points in the evolution of an IT, the balance between these pressures shifts and planning serves substantially different purposes. Reflecting upon the advent and growth of business data processing, databases, distributed systems, fiber optics, image processing, and other new technologies (as noted in earlier chapters) one can identify four distinct phases of technology assimilation, each imposing different pressures.

Phase 1: Technology Identification and Investment. In the initial phase of a new technology, the basic planning focus is on both technology identification and the need for new human resource skills. Problems include identifying appropriate technologies for study, preparing the site, developing staff skills, identifying potential product champions, and managing initial pilot applications.

Phase 2: Technological Learning and Adaptation. The basic thrust of planning in this second phase is making potential users aware of the new technology and communicating how it can be useful to them. Sequencing projects and ensuring good coordination between team members are also important as the company continues to master the technology's nuances. The effectiveness of this phase's planning can be measured by a series of user-supported pilot projects.

As a secondary output, the planning process in this phase identifies the number of staff and the skills to be acquired.

Since technology will continue to evolve for the foreseeable future, there will normally be a phase 2 flavor to some part of a company's IT development portfolio. Our observations of successful planning in this phase suggest clearly that:

1. A new technology is best introduced by starting with a pilot test to generate both IT staff and user learning, rather than by spending years on advance introspection and design without any practical hands-on experience.
2. Attracting the interest of potential users on their terms and stimulating their understanding about what the technology can do for them are critical to success, and success here leads to later requests for service; pilot users become important allies.
3. Planning during this phase (and phase 1 as well) involves a program of planned technological innovations, encouraging users to build upon their past experience and organizational receptivity to change. There is a desirable "softness" in the tangible and intangible benefits specified for these projects.

Phase 3: Rationalization/Management Control. Effective planning for technologies in this phase has a strong efficiency focus; the emphasis shifts to getting the results of the successful pilot projects implemented cost-efficiently. Whereas planning for technological learning and adaptation (phase 2) has a long-range (though not terribly accurate) perspective, planning for phase 3 technologies has a short-term, one- to two-year efficiency focus. Activities include identifying and completing applications, upgrading staff to acceptable knowledge levels with the new technology, reorganizing to develop and implement further projects using the technology, and efficiently utilizing the technology. For technologies themselves, the objective in this phase is to set appropriate limits on the types of applications that make sense and to ensure that they are implemented cost-efficiently. In terms of

Robert Anthony's framework,[3] effective planning for phase 3 technologies has a much stronger management and operational control flavor and a weaker strategic planning thrust.

Phase 4: Maturity/Widespread Technology Transfer. The final phase is one of managed evolution, whereby the technology is transferred to a wider spectrum of applications. With organizational learning essentially complete and a technology base with appropriate controls in place, it is time to look seriously into the future and to plot longer-term trends in exploitation of the technology. If one is not careful, however, such planning—based on the business and technology as they are now understood—can be too rigid. Unexpected quirks in the business and evolution of technology alike may invalidate what has been done during phase 4 planning as the technology is superseded by a still better one.

Given the current dynamic state of IT, technologies in all four planning phases are normally present simultaneously in a typical firm—suggesting that uniformity and consistency in IT planning protocols throughout the firm are inappropriate. Instead, the organization is dealing with a portfolio of technologies, each of which poses a different planning challenge.

For example, one manufacturing company studied was in phase 4 in terms of its ability to conceptualize and deal with enhancements to its on-line MRP-II production scheduling system (soon to be phased out). At the same time, it was in phase 3 in terms of driving its new CAD system across the entire engineering and product development functions. Finally, it was just launching an SAP Enterprise software evaluation to replace most existing code; it was clearly in phase 1 in respect to this technology. The firm's plans for the MRP-II system were detailed and crisp, whereas the SAP project was essentially ill informed, and no coherent view existed as to where it was going.

In summary, "planned clutter" (as opposed to consistency) is desirable in a firm's approach to IT planning. Similarly, the approach to IT planning for different organizational units within a company should vary, since each unit often has quite different familiarity with specific technologies.

LIMITATIONS ON IT PLANNING RESULTS

As new products appear, as the competitive environment shifts, as laws and corporate strategies change, and as mergers and spin-offs take place, the priorities a company assigns to its various applications evolve. Some previous low-priority or unconceived applications may become critically

---

[3]Robert Anthony, *Planning Control Systems: A Framework for Analysis* (Boston: Division of Research, Harvard University Graduate School of Business Administration, 1965).

important, while others once seen as vital will diminish in significance. This volatility places a real premium on building a flexible management framework that permits orderly and consistent change to meet evolving business requirements.

In a similar vein, every IT planning process must make some very specific assumptions about the nature and role of technological evolution. If this evolution occurs at a different rate from the one forecast, then major segments of the plan may have to be reworked, both in scope and in thrust. For example, the recent explosion of Extranet, a potential new way of communicating with and providing service to customers, has caused many firms to rethink their priorities.

Planning as a Resource Drain

Every person and every dollar assigned to IT planning represent resources diverted from such activities as new systems development; the extent to which human and financial resources should be devoted to planning is always in question. Just as the style of planning changes over time as parts of the organization pass through different phases with different technologies, so should the commitment of resources to planning also change. This phenomenon too suggests that the instability in an IT planning process relates positively to its role of stimulating a creative view of the future. If not carefully managed, IT planning can become a mind-numbing, non-creative process of routinely changing the numbers, as opposed to a sensitive focus on the company's real opportunities and problems.

Fit to Corporate Culture

An important aspect of IT planning is implementation within the realities of the corporate culture. For example, in organizations with a very formal corporate planning process actively supported by senior management, the internal user-management climate typically supports formal approaches to IT planning. Other organizations, however, have quite different cultures and approaches to corporate planning. These factors significantly alter both the form and the degree of commitment that can be expected from users of an IT planning process, as is discussed later in the chapter.

Strategic Impact of IT Activities

As we have noted, IT activities are of strategic importance in some organizations, while playing a cost-effective, useful, but distinctly supportive role in others. The latter organizations should not expect senior managers to devote the same amount of thinking to IT items as in organizations of the former type. Moreover, the IT function that hitherto held little strategic importance may, because of its new-technology-enabled applications portfolio, suddenly assume great significance in the future. Thus, IT planning may become very important to the firm at some time, and in the process it must face and surmount the challenge of breaking the habits and molds of the past.

In an environment of management turmoil, high turnover, and reassessment, one is unlikely to find the intensity and commitment to IT planning possible in a stable environment, where people are emotionally attached to the organization. Although such negative factors limit the benefits of planning and make the process more complex, they do not eliminate the need for it. Rather, they increase the multidimensional complexity of the planning task and diminish reasonable expectations of the output's quality.

For other organizations, the opposite is true. While IT now plays an important operational role, future applications may not offer great payoffs or significance. If this occurs, a less intensive focus on IT strategic planning will be in order, and different people will be involved than when it was more significant.

Mismatches: Using the Strategic Grid

Selecting the appropriate planning approach is further complicated when a mismatch exists between where an organization is on the grid (see Figure 10–1) and where senior management believes it should be. In such a case, more planning is needed for energizing the firm to make appropriate adjustments, as is illustrated in Figure 10–1. A large international financial institution's senior management was very comfortable with the company's IT performance, although the issue infrequently appeared on their agenda. The IT management team, however, was deeply concerned that their senior IT managers lacked a thorough understanding of how IT was changing the firm's business, what its products would be four to five years hence, and the types of new organization structures and controls required. IT management knew that senior IT managers needed this input if the emerging IT architecture was going to be able to support the firm's goals.

The institution had a very sophisticated but closely held corporate planning activity. In a world of major shifts in what financial institutions can and should do, top management was greatly concerned about the confidentiality of planning information, and only a handful of individuals (four or five) knew the full scope of it. Since neither the IT manager nor his boss was among this handful, IT was substantially in the dark about the organization's direction and could only crudely assess it by trying to guess why some projects were funded and others were not.

FIGURE 10–1 Information Technology Strategic Grid

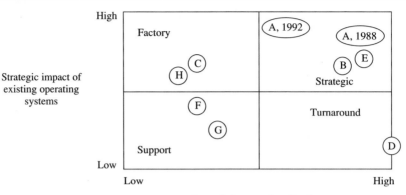

Key:
A. Major bank 1988–1992
B. Major insurance company
C. Medium-size grocery chain
D. $100 million distributor
E. Major airline
F. Major chemical company
G. Major process industry manufacturers
H. Insurance broker

The company's full-time IT planning manager had three assistants and reported to the IT manager. For the past two years, IT planners had worked closely with middle management users and information technologists to develop strategies and applications portfolios that both sides perceived as relevant to their needs. Because there was little formal or informal linkage between the IT planning activity and the corporate planning department (which had repeatedly communicated, "Don't call us, we'll call you"), the IT staff had two overriding concerns:

1. The plans and strategies developed for IT may be technically sound and meet the needs of user management as they understand them today, but they may be unproductive or indeed counterproductive if they do not support the corporate thrust.
2. Corporate plans are developed "at the top" by a few executives completely isolated from IT and its issues. This could unwittingly place onerous or unworkable support requests on IT in the future.

At this stage, senior management perceived IT as a factory, believed it was being staffed and managed appropriately, and had no concerns about the IT planning process. IT saw itself as strategic but could not sell the concept to anyone.

This frustration was resolved when an outside review of the institution's overall strategy (initiated by the chairman) noted in its conclusions that IT, a strategic force in similar firms, was not being so treated in this firm and was moving in an unproductive direction. Given the outside reviewer's credibility, senior management readily acknowledged that they had misunderstood the role of IT and that IT should indeed be treated as strategic. Unfortunately, they perceived IT management as inadequate for this newly defined (i.e., newly recognized) challenge, and many senior IT staff did not survive the transition.

On the surface, based on the written plan, IT planning had looked good; in fact, however, it had failed to come to grips with the realities of the corporate environment. Consequently, an organization for which IT activities were of significant strategic importance had been left in a state of potential unpreparedness and risk. When IT activities were belatedly recognized as critical, the result was fatal for the IT planners—they were held accountable for this state of affairs.

The extent to which IT is strategic for the company as a whole and for individual business units and functions must be assessed. IT's impact typically varies widely by unit and function, and thus the IT planning process must be adapted to deal with these differences. Those units where IT is of high impact require much more intense IT planning than those units for which it is of low impact, of course. This makes the planning more complex, but it also makes it more useful.

Table 10–1 suggests that a firm's position on the strategic grid not only influences its IT planning needs, but has numerous other implications, including the role of the executive steering committee, the placement of IT in the organization, the appropriate IT management control system, and so on. Further, since organizational units may be in different quadrants of the grid, the planning, organization, and control approaches suitable for one unit may be inappropriate for another. Finally, an IT planning approach that is suitable at one time may be totally wrong if the firm's position on the grid changes.

Corporate Environmental Factors That Influence Planning

Research has identified four corporate environmental factors influencing how IT planning must be structured to improve its likelihood of success.[4]

Perceived Importance and Status of the CIO.   The CIO's status must align with the role that IT plays, or should play, in the overall operation and strategy-formulating process of the company. If IT has strategic or turn-around importance, a low-status IT manager (low status in reporting level

---

[4]Pyburn, "Information Systems Planning," op. cit.

TABLE 10–1   Managerial Strategies for "Support" and "Strategic" Companies

Factor	"Support" Company	"Strategic" Company
Steering committee	Middle-level management membership. Existence of committee is less critical.	Active senior management involvement. Committee is key.
Planning	Less urgent. Mistakes in resource allocation not fatal	Critical. Must link to corporate strategy. Careful attention to resource allocation is vital.
Project portfolio risk profile	Avoid high-risk projects because of constrained benefits. A poor place for corporate strategic gambles	Some high-risk, high-potential-benefit projects are appropriate if possibility exists to gain strategic advantage.
IT capacity management	Can be managed in a looser way. Operational headaches are less severe.	Critical to manage. Must leave slack.
IT management reporting level	Can be low.	Should be very high.
Technical innovation	A conservative posture one to two years behind the state of the art is appropriate.	Critical to stay current and fund R&D. Competitor can gain advantage.
User involvement and control over system	Lower priority. Less heated debate	Very high priority. Often emotional.
Charge-out system	Managed cost center is viable Charge-out is less critical and less emotional.	Critical that it be sensitively designed.
Expense control	System modernization and development expenses are postponable in times of crisis.	Effectiveness is key. Must keep applications up to date; save money other places.
Uneven performance of IT management	Time is available to resolve problems	Serious and immediately actionable.

and/or compensation) will have difficulty getting the necessary information from general management in the planning process. If the corporate communication culture (style) at the top is informal, this low status can be fatal, as the CIO will be outside the key communication loop. If the corporate culture is more formal, development and management of appropriate committees and other formal processes can significantly alleviate this potential problem.

In a company where IT is and should be serving a support function, lower status may be appropriate for the CIO, and less effort is needed to align IT and corporate strategy. A lower level of investment (in dollars and type of staff) in IT planning is also appropriate for such situations. These factors are apparent in the comments of a director of strategic planning for a large process-manufacturing company: "We relate to IT by giving them insight on the corporate goals and the elements and forms of a good planning system. Because of their role in the company, we do not solicit feedback from them as to 'the art of the possible.' The nature of their operation is such that they can provide no useful input to decisions of corporate strategy."

Physical Proximity of the Systems Group and the General Management Team.   In an organization where many important decisions are made informally in ad hoc sessions and where IT has strategic or turn-around importance, key IT management staff should be physically close to the senior line manager; literally, their offices should be nearby. Regardless of the CIO's status, being an active member of the team in this type of organization is difficult when one is geographically distant from the other members of the team (unless the entire team is scattered). According to a manager in one such company, "The people who are around when a problem surfaces are the ones who solve it. We don't wait to round up the missing bodies." When the prevailing management culture is more formal, physical proximity is less important. In these situations, formal written communications and scheduled formal meetings largely replace the informal give-and-take.

In informal organizations in which IT is strategic or turnaround, it is critical that the CIO, and preferably a small staff, be at corporate headquarters, even if their systems development groups must be located many miles away. For support and factory organizations with informal cultures, location at corporate headquarters is much less critical.

Corporate Culture and Management Style.   In an organization where the management culture is low key and informal and the relationship between the CIO and senior management is informal and personal, formal IT planning procedures do not appear to be critical to effective planning. The relationship is typically fostered by geographic proximity and the CIO's status. As an organization becomes more formal, however, disciplined IT planning becomes more significant, even in a systems environment that is not highly strategic.

Organizational Size and Complexity.   As organizations increase in size and complexity and as IT applications grow larger and more complex, formal planning processes help ensure the kind of broad-based dialogue essential to creating an integrated vision of IT. This point relates to the previous comments concerning management culture and style, for greater size and complexity typically necessitate more formal practices. If the business unit size is small and relatively simple, formal planning approaches are less critical, irrespective of other factors. Similarly, for a smaller business unit where the systems environment is primarily "support," IT planning can safely be more informal. However, as the portfolio of work increases in size and integration across user areas, planning must be more disciplined and formal.

In aggregate, these corporate environmental items explain why recommendations on how to do IT planning "in general" almost always are too inflexible for a specific firm. Even within a firm, these issues often force considerable diversity of practice among organization units. The following illustrates how these issues have shaped the planning process in a billion-dollar manufacturing organization.

An Example.   This company has a medium-sized corporate IT facility and stand-alone IT facilities of some significant size in its six U.S. divisions. The divisional IT facilities report "straight-line" to their respective divisions and "dotted-line" to the corporate IT function. The corporate IT group is part of a cluster of corporate staff activities, and considerable power has traditionally been located at the corporate level.

The corporate planning activity reports to the vice president of corporate IT, who has enjoyed a long personal and professional relationship with both the chairman of the board and the CEO. IT responsibility was initially given to this vice president because operational and developmental problems had reached crisis proportions. Under normal circumstances, IT had a "support" role, but these difficulties had pushed the firm into the turnaround category.

While the company's management culture is informal, the closeness of relationships between division general managers and their IT managers varies widely. The size of the divisions' application portfolios in relation to their overall size also varies considerably, with IT activities playing a more significant role in some divisions than in others.

IT planning at the divisional level begins when the corporate IT group gives a division some rather loose guidelines concerning technological direction; it culminates in a division IT plan. The planning processes and dialogues vary widely from division to division in terms of line manager involvement. In some divisions, the line managers are intimately involved in the process of developing the plan, and the division general manager invests considerable time in final review and modification. Elsewhere the relationship is less close: IT plans are developed almost entirely by the IT organization, and general management review is very limited. These differences seem to reflect IT's respective contributions to individual divisions' strategic functioning.

Critical to the IT planning process is an annual three-day meeting of the vice president of corporate IT and his key staff, in which the divisional IT managers present their plans. The vice president plays a major role in these sessions, critiquing and suggesting modifications to the plans to ensure their fit with corporate objectives. His thorough understanding of the corporation's plans, the thinking of the divisional general managers, and the thinking of the chairman and president enable him immediately to spot shortfalls in IT plans, especially in those of divisions with weak IT–line management relationships.

As a result, emerging IT plans fit the organization's real business needs, and the IT activity is well regarded. A set of planning processes that might lead to disaster in other settings has worked well here, given the vice president's special qualities and the style of communication between him and general management that is appropriate to this firm's culture.

SUMMARY

Research evidence continues to show a correlation between effective IT planning and user perception of effective IT activity. Effective execution of IT planning, however, has been found to be far more subtle and complex than envisioned by earlier authors. In addition to generating new ideas, a major role of the IT planning process is to stimulate discussion and exchange of insights between the specialists and the users. Effectively managed, this is an important element in averting potential conflicts in the firm.

In this context we conclude that:

1. Organizations in which IT activity is integral to corporate strategy implementation have a special need to build intense, two-way communication links between IT and the corporate strategy formulation process. Complex to implement, this requires dialogue and resolution along many dimensions. Key aspects of the dialogue are:
    a. Testing elements of corporate strategy to ensure they are possible within the existing IT resource constraints and capabilities. Sometimes the resources needed are obtainable; in other settings, they are unavailable and painful readjustments must be made. Conversely, formulators of corporate strategy must understand the potentials of new technologies because they may suggest new ways of competing (even radically different ways).
    b. Transfer of planning and strategy-formulation skills to the IT function.
    c. Ensuring long-term availability of appropriate IT resources. In "support" and "factory" settings such linkage is less critical. Over time, the nature of this linkage may change as the firm's strategic IT mission evolves.
2. As an organization grows in size, systems complexity, and formality, IT planning must be directly assigned to someone in order to retain focus and avoid having significant pieces "drop between the cracks." The job is

subtle, not simple. The planner must possess a strong set of enabling and communication skills to relate to all individuals and units affected by this technology and cope with their differing familiarity with it. Ensuring the involvement of IT staff and users for both inputs and conclusions is key. The great danger is that planners will define the task with more of a "doing" orientation than an "enabling" one and inappropriately interpose their own priorities and understandings. To overcome this problem, many organizations define this job as a transitional one rather than a career one.

3. "Planned clutter" in the planning approach is appropriate, because the company's applications portfolio should contain technologies in different phases with different strategic payouts to different units of the firm at different times. While planning all technologies for all business units at the same level of detail and schedule may appear superficially attractive and orderly, in reality this would be inappropriate.

4. IT planning must be tailored to the realities of the organization's environment. The CIO's importance and status, the physical placement of senior IT staff in relation to general management, the corporate culture and management style, and organization size and complexity all influence how IT planning should be carried out.

5. The planning process must incorporate and integrate a broad range of technologies—internal and external electronic communications, data processing, database management software, personal computers, and so forth.

Chapter

11

A Portfolio Approach to Information Technology Development

In 1998, a major medical devices company abandons the conversion of its distribution system to a new software package and takes a major writedown. The existing systems were not Year 2000 compliant, and the risk that the new package would not be completed in time was too great for the firm to go forward with the project. A massive redirection of the project occurs to ensure that the existing systems will be Year 2000 compliant, with significant postponement of new functionality.

A major manufacturing company is suddenly told by its outsourcer that in 12 months, the outsourcer will no longer support its service. The firm has 12 months to launch a project with a new vendor and ensure that the existing systems will be Year 2000 compliant.

A significant manufacturing company consolidates over 50 plant, customer contacts, and order entry activities into a national telecommunications center. Only after the center is built and plant conversions are well under way does the company realize that the average operator has to wait 25 seconds after data is inputted to confirm an order. Management's judgment is that anything over a 2-second response time will make the system inoperative.

Two major insurance companies attempt to install the same software package to solve the same problem with their field sales forces. In one company, all the money expended turned out to be totally wasted, and $600 million was written off with no benefit. The other company, using a different installation process, uses the new technology to generate a 46 percent increase in sales from one year to the next.

Horror stories from the stage 1 and stage 2 days of the late 1960s and early 1970s? Hardly! All but one of these examples come from the late 1990s.

Although it is disturbing to admit, the day of the big disaster on a major information technology (IT) project has not passed—and given business's nearly 40 years of IT experience, the question becomes, Why? An analysis of these cases (all of them domestic companies, although we could have selected equally dramatic tales from overseas) and firsthand acquaintance with a number of IT projects in the past 10 years suggest three serious deficiencies that involve both general management and IT management: (1) failure to assess the implementation risk of a project at the time it is funded; (2) failure to consider the aggregate implementation risk of the portfolio of projects; (3) failure to recognize that different projects require different managerial approaches.

These aspects of the IT project management and development process are so important that we address them in this separate chapter. Chapter 7 discussed the influences of corporate culture and the technology's perceived strategic relevance on the balance of control between IT and the user over the various stages of the project management life cycle. Since many projects have multiyear life cycles, these project management issues must be dealt with separately from those of the management control system with its calendar-year focus.

PROJECT RISK

Elements of Project Implementation Risk

In discussing risk, we assume that the IT manager has brought appropriate methods and approaches to bear on the project—mismanagement is obviously another element of risk. Implementation risk, by definition here, is what remains after the application of proper tools. Also, we are not implying that risk itself is bad. Rather, higher-risk projects must have potential for greater benefits to offset the risk.

The typical project feasibility study exhaustively covers such topics as financial benefits, qualitative benefits, implementation costs, target milestone and completion dates, and necessary staffing levels. Developers of these estimates provide voluminous supporting documentation, conveyed in clear-cut terms. Only rarely, however, do they deal frankly with the risks of slippage in time, cost overrun, technical shortfall, or outright failure: more usually, they deny the existence of such possibilities by ignoring them. They assume the appropriate human skills, controls, and other critical factors are in place to ensure success.

Consequences of Risk.   Risk, we suggest, implies exposure to such consequences as:

1. Failure to obtain all, or any, of the anticipated benefits because of implementation difficulties.

2. Much higher-than-expected implementation costs.
3. Much longer-than-expected implementation time.
4. Resulting systems whose technical performance is significantly below estimate.
5. System incompatibility with selected hardware and software.

In the real world, of course, these risks are closely related, not independent of each other.

Project Dimensions Influencing Inherent Risk.   Three important project dimensions (among others) influence *inherent* implementation risk:

Project Size.   The larger the project in monetary terms, staffing levels, elapsed time, and number of departments affected, the greater the risk. Multimillion-dollar projects obviously carry more risk than $50,000 efforts and tend to affect the company more if the risk is realized. Project size relative to the normal size of an IT development group's projects is also important: a $1 million project in a department whose average undertaking costs $2 to $3 million usually has lower implicit risk than a $250,000 project in a department whose projects have never cost more than $50,000.

Experience with the Technology.   Because unexpected technical problems are more likely, project risk increases as the project team's and organization's familiarity with the hardware, operating systems, database handler, and project application language decreases. Phase 1 and phase 2 technology projects are intrinsically more risky for a company than phase 3 and phase 4 technology efforts. A project posing a slight risk for a leading-edge, large-systems development group may be highly risky for a smaller, less technically advanced group. (The latter could reduce its risk by purchasing outside skills for an undertaking involving technology in general commercial use. This rapidly growing market for outside skills is served by the major systems integrators such as Arthur Andersen, Computer Science Corporation, Electronic Data Services, and IBM, as well as a host of smaller competitors.)

Project Structure.   In some projects, from the moment of their conceptualization, the nature of the task completely defines the outputs; these are fixed, not subject to change during the project's lifetime. Not only is the task fixed, but it does not involve the same degree of organization change as do those whose outputs, being subject to user-manager's judgment and learning, are more vulnerable to modification.

An insurance company's automating the preparation of its agents' rate book for use on a laptop exemplifies a highly structured project. At the project's beginning, planners reached agreement on the product lines to be included, the layout of each page screen, the process of generating each number, and the type of client illustration that would be possible. Throughout the life of the project, there was no need to alter these decisions.

Consequently, the team organized to reach a stable, fixed output rather than to cope with a potentially mobile target. The key risk, effectively managed, was training the agents to operate in these new ways.

Project Categories and Degree of Risk

Figure 11–1, which combines in a matrix the various dimensions influencing risk, identifies eight distinct project categories with varying degrees of implementation risk. (Figure 11–2 gives examples of projects that fit this categorization.) Even at this grossly intuitive level, such a classification is useful to separate projects for different types of management review. Innumerable IT organizations have used the matrix successfully for understanding relative implementation risk and for communicating that risk to users and senior executives. The matrix helps to address the legitimate concern that all people viewing a project will have the same understanding of its risks.

Assessing Risk of Individual Projects

Figure 11–3 displays excerpts from a questionnaire a company developed for assessing project implementation risk: a list of 42 questions the project man-

---

FIGURE 11–1   Effect of Degree of Structure, Company-Relative Technology, and Project Size on Project Implementation Risk

		Low Structure	High Structure
Low Technology	Large Project	Low risk (very susceptible to mismanagement)	Low risk
	Small Project	Very low risk (very susceptible to mismanagement)	Very low risk
High Technology	Large Project	Very high risk	Medium risk
	Small Project	High risk	Medium-low risk

FIGURE 11–2   Comparison of Project Implementation Risk by Degree of Structured and Company-Relative Technology—Examples

	Low Structure	High Structure
Low Technology	Spreadsheet support for budgeting	Manufacturing inventory control
High Technology	On-line graphic support for advertising copy	Expert system bond trading

ager[1] answers about a project prior to senior management's approval and then several times during implementation. The company drew up the questions after analyzing its experience with successful and unsuccessful projects. Although no analytic framework underlies the questions and they may not be appropriate for all companies, they provide a good starting point—and a number of other companies have used them in developing their own instruments for measuring implementation risk.

These questions not only highlight the sources of implementation risk but also suggest alternative routes to conceiving the project and managing it to reduce risk. If the initial aggregate risk score seems high, analysis of the answers may suggest ways of lessening the risk through reduced project scope, more routine technology, breaking the project into multiple phases, and so on. Thus, managers should not consider risk as a static descriptor; rather, its presence should encourage better approaches to project management. Questions 5 and 6 in the "Structured Risk Assessment" section are particularly good examples of questions that could trigger changes.

The higher the assessment score, the greater the need for very senior approval. Only the executive committee in this company approves very risky projects. Such an approach ensures that top managers are aware of significant hazards and are making appropriate trade-offs between risk and strategic benefits. Managers should ask themselves:

1. Are the benefits great enough to offset the risks?
2. Can the affected parts of the organization survive if the project fails?
3. Have the planners considered appropriate alternatives?

---

[1]Actually, both the project leader and the key user answer these questions, and then they reconcile differences in their answers; of course, the questionnaire data are no better than the quality of thinking that goes into the answers.

FIGURE 11–3 Project Implementation Risk Assessment Questionnaire (sample from a total of 42 questions)

Size Risk Assessment

Risk Factor			Weight
1. Total development work-hours for system[a]			5
100 to 3,000	Low	1	
3,000 to 15,000	Medium	2	
15,000 to 30,000	Medium	3	
More than 30,000	High	4	
2. Estimated project implementation time			4
12 months or less	Low	1	
13 months to 24 months	Medium	2	
More than 24 months	High	3	
3. Number of departments (other than IT) involved with system			4
One	Low	1	
Two	Medium	2	
Three or more	High	3	

Structure Risk Assessment

Risk Factor			Weight
1. If replacement system is proposed, what percentage of existing functions are replaced on a one-to-one basis?			5
0% to 25%	High	3	
25% to 50%	Medium	2	
50% to 100%	Low	1	
2. What is the severity of user-department procedural changes caused by the proposed system?			5
Low		1	
Medium		2	
High		3	
3. What is the degree of needed user-organization structural change to meet requirements of the new system?			5
None		0	
Minimal	Low	1	
Somewhat	Medium	2	
Major	High	3	
4. What is the general attitude of the user?			5
Poor; against IT solution	High	3	
Fair; sometimes reluctant	Medium	2	
Good; understands value of IT solution		0	
5. How committed is upper-level user management to the system?			5
Somewhat reluctant, or unknown	High	3	
Adequate	Medium	2	
Extremely enthusiastic	Low	1	
6. Has a joint IT-user team been established?			5
No	High	3	
Part-time user representative appointed	Low	1	
Full-time user representative appointed		0	

FIGURE 11–3 *(continued)*   Project Implementation Risk Assessment Questionnaire (sample from a total of 42 questions)

Technology Risk Assessment

Risk Factor			Weight
1. Which of the hardware is new to the company?[b]			5
None		0	
CPU	High	3	
Peripheral and/or additional storage	High	3	
Terminals	High	3	
Mini or macro	High	3	
2. Is the system software (nonoperating system) new to IT project team?[a]			5
No		0	
Programming language	High	3	
Database	High	3	
Data communications	High	3	
Other (please specify)	High	3	
3. How knowledgeable is user in area of IT?			5
First exposure	High	3	
Previous exposure but limited knowledge	Medium	2	
High degree of capability	Low	1	
4. How knowledgeable is user representative in proposed application area?			5
Limited	High	3	
Understands concept but has no experience	Medium	2	
Has been involved in prior implementation efforts	Low	1	
5. How knowledgeable is IT team in proposed application area?			5
Limited	High	3	
Understands concept but has no experience	Medium	2	
Has been involved in prior implementation efforts	Low	1	

[a]Time to develop includes system design, programming, testing, and installation.
[b]This question is scored by multiplying the sum of the numbers attached to the positive responses by the weight.

Note: Since the questions vary in importance, the company assigned weights to them subjectively. The numerical answer to the questions is multiplied by the question weight to calculate the question's contribution to the project's risk. The numbers are then added to produce a risk score for the project. Projects with risk scores within 10 points of each other are indistinguishable in their relative risk, but those separated by 100 points or more are very different in their implementation risk to even the casual observer.

Source: This questionnaire is adapted from the "Dallas Tire" case, No. 180-006 (Boston: Harvard Business School Case Services, 1980).

Periodically, the questionnaire is used again to reveal any major changes as the project unfolds. If assessments are positive, the risk continually declines during implementation as the number and size of remaining tasks dwindle and familiarity with the technology increases.

When senior managers believe a project has low implementation risk, yet IT managers know it has high implementation risk, "horror stories" sometimes result. IT managers may not admit their assessment because they fear that senior executives will not tolerate such uncertainty in information systems projects and will cancel a project of potential benefit to the organization even after risk is taken into account. The questionnaire data, however, encourage a common understanding among senior management, IT, and user managers about a project's relative implementation risk.

PORTFOLIO RISK

In addition to determining relative risk for single projects, a company should develop a profile of aggregate implementation risk for its portfolio of systems and programming projects. Although a universally appropriate implementation risk profile for all firms does not exist, different types of companies and strategies offer different appropriate risk profiles.

For example, in an industry where IT is strategic (such as retailing and catalogs), managers should be concerned if no high-risk projects are in evidence. Such a cautious stance may open a product or service gap for competition to step into. On the other hand, a portfolio loaded with high risk projects suggests that the company may be vulnerable to operational disruptions if projects are not completed as planned. In "support" companies, heavy investment in high-risk projects may not be appropriate; they should not be taking strategic gambles in the IT arena. Yet even these companies should have some technologically challenging ventures to ensure familiarity with leading-edge technology and maintain staff morale and interest.

These examples suggest that the aggregate implementation risk profiles of the portfolios of any two companies could legitimately differ. Table 11–1 lists the issues that influence a company toward or away from high-risk

TABLE 11–1   Factors That Influence Implementation Risk Profile of Project Portfolio

	Portfolio Risk Focus	
Factor	*Low*	*High*
Stability of IT development group.	High	Low
Perceived quality of IT development group by insiders.	High	Low
IT critical to delivery of current corporate services.	No	Yes
IT important decision support aid.	No	Yes
Experienced IT systems development group.	Yes	No
Major IT fiascoes in last two years.	No	Yes
New IT management team.	No	Yes
IT perceived critical to delivery of future corporate services.	No	Yes
IT perceived critical to future decision support aids.	No	Yes
Company perceived as backward in use of IT.	No	Yes

efforts. (The risk profile should include projects executed by outside systems integrators as well as those of the internal systems development group.) As the table shows, IT's aggregate impact on corporate strategy is an important determinant of the appropriate amount of implementation risk to undertake.

Summary

It is both possible and useful to assess a project's implementation risk at the feasibility study stage. Discussing implementation risk is important to those working on the project and to the user departments as a whole. Not only can this systematic analysis reduce the number of failures, its power as a communication link helps IT managers and senior executives reach agreement on the risks to be taken in relation to corporate goals.

PROJECT MANAGEMENT: A CONTINGENCY APPROACH

Much of the literature and conventional wisdom suggest that there is a single right approach to project management. A similar bias holds that managers should apply a cluster of tools, project management methods, and organizational linkages uniformly to all such ventures.

While there may indeed be a set of general-purpose tools (and we describe some later), the contribution each device makes to project planning and control varies widely according to the project's characteristics. Further, the means of involving the user—through steering committees, representation on the team, or as leader—should also vary by project type; in short, there is no universally correct way to run all projects.

Management Tools

The general methods (tools) for managing projects are of four principal types:

- *External integration* tools include organizational and other communication devices that link the project team's work to users at both the managerial and the lower levels.
- *Internal integration* devices, which include various personnel controls, ensure that the team operates as an integrated unit.
- *Formal planning* tools help structure the sequence of tasks in advance and estimate the time, money, and technical resources the team will need for executing them.
- *Formal results-control* mechanisms help managers evaluate progress and spot potential discrepancies so that corrective action can be taken.

Results controls have been particularly effective in the following settings:[2]

1. Clear knowledge of the desired results exists.
2. The desired result can be controlled (at least to some extent by the individuals whose actions are being influenced).
3. The controllable result areas can be measured effectively.

Highly structured projects involving a low degree of technology satisfy these conditions very well; formal results-control mechanisms are very effective in these settings. For low-structured projects involving a high degree of technology, none of the above conditions applies; consequently, results control can make only a limited contribution. In those settings, major contributions are derived from internal integration devices (personnel controls).

Table 11–2 gives examples of commonly used types of integration and control tools. The following paragraphs suggest how the degree of structure and the company-relative technology influence the selection of tools.

Influences on Tool Selection

High-Structure–Low-Technology Projects.   Highly structured projects that present familiar technical problems are not only lower-risk endeavors but also are the easiest to manage (see Figure 11–1). Year 2000 compliance work fits clearly into this category. These projects are the least common as well. High structure implies that the nature of the task clearly defines its outputs and that the possibility of users changing their minds about the desired outputs is essentially nonexistent. Project leaders, therefore, do not have to create extensive administrative processes to get a diverse group of users to agree to a design structure and then stick to their decision. Such external integration devices as assigning IT systems analysts to user departments, heavy representation of users on the design team, and formal user approval of design specifications are cumbersome and unnecessary for this type of project. Other integrating devices, however, such as training users to operate the system, remain important.

Since the system's concept and design are stable in this environment, and since the technology involved is familiar to the company, the project can proceed with a high percentage of people having only average technical backgrounds and experience. The project leader does not need extraordinary IT skills. This type of project readily provides opportunities to the department's junior managers, who can gain experience applicable to more ambitious tasks in the future.

---

[2]Kenneth A. Merchant, *Control in Business Organizations* (Marshfield, MA: Pitman Publishing, 1985).

TABLE 11–2 Tools of Project Management

Integration Tools, External	*Integration Tools, Internal*
Selection of user as project manager.	Selection of experienced IT professional to lead team.
Creation of user steering committee.	
Frequent in-depth meetings of user steering committee.	Frequent team meetings.
	Regular preparation and distribution of minutes within team on key design evolution decisions.
User-managed change control process.	
Frequent and detailed distribution of project team minutes to key users.	Regular technical status reviews.
	Managed low turnover of team members.
Selection of users as team members.	Selection of high percentage of team members with significant previous work relationships.
Formal user specification approval process.	
Progress reports prepared for corporate steering committee.	Participation of team members in goal setting and deadline establishment.
User responsibility for education and installation of system.	Outside technical assistance.
User management decision on key action dates.	

Formal Planning Tools	*Formal Control Tools*
PERT, "critical path," etc.; networking.	Periodic formal status reports versus plan.
Milestone phases selection.	Change control disciplines.
Systems specification standards.	Regular milestone presentation meetings.
Feasibility study specifications.	Deviations from plan.
Project approval processes.	
Project postaudit procedures.	

With their focus on defining tasks and budgeting resources against them, project life-cycle planning concepts—such as PERT (Program Evaluation and Review Technique) and "critical path"—force the team to develop a thorough and detailed plan (exposing areas of "soft" thinking in the process). Such projects are likely to meet the resulting milestone dates and adhere to the target budget. Moreover, the usual results-control techniques for measuring progress against dates and budgets provide very reliable data for spotting discrepancies and building a desirable tension within the design team to work harder to avoid slippage.

An example of this type of highly structured project is the insurance agents' rate-book project mentioned earlier. A portfolio in which 90 percent of the projects are of this type should produce little unplanned excitement for senior and user managers. It also requires a much more limited set of skills for the IT organization than would be needed for portfolios with a different mixture of project types.

High-Structure–High-Technology Projects. Vastly more complex than high-structure–low-technology projects, high-structure–high-technology projects involve significant modifications of practices outlined in project management handbooks. A good example is converting one computer manufacturer's systems to another's, with all the code being rewritten with no enhancements. Another example is converting a set of mainframe procedures into a client-server architecture with the main objective being performing the same functions more quickly and cheaply.

The normal mechanisms for liaison with users are not crucial here; the outputs are so well defined by the nature of the undertaking that both the development of specifications with user inputs and the need to deal with systems changes that users request are unimportant aspects. However, a liaison with users is nevertheless important in two respects: (1) to ensure coordination on any changes in input/output or any other manual procedure changes necessary for project success and (2) to deal with any systems restructuring that must follow from unexpected shortcomings in the project's technology.

In this kind of project, it is common to discover during implementation that the selected technology is inadequate for the task, which forces a long postponement while either new technology is chosen or vital features of the system are modified to make the task fit the available technology. This was true of the firm at the beginning of the chapter which consolidated the calls from over 50 plants into a national call center. Similarly, an industrial products company had to convert some computerized order-entry procedures back to a manual basis so the rest of an integrated materials management system could be shifted to already purchased hardware.

In cases in which system performance is much poorer than expected, user involvement is important both to prevent demoralization and to help implement either an alternative approach (less ambitious in selection of technology) or to attain a mutual agreement to end the project.

The skills leading to success in this type of project, however, are identical to those that effectively administer projects involving any technical complexity. The leader needs a strong background in high-technology projects (preferably, but not necessarily, in an IT environment) plus administrative experience. The leader must also "connect" to technicians. By talking individually and collectively with the project team members at various times, the ideal manager will anticipate difficulties before the technicians understand they have a problem. In dealing with larger projects in this category, the effective manager must establish and maintain teamwork through meetings, develop a record of all key design decisions, and facilitate subproject conferences as needed.

Project life-cycle planning methods identify tasks and suitable completion dates. Their predictive value is much less in high-structure–high-technology projects than in high-structure–low-technology projects. The team will not understand key elements of the technology in advance; thus, seemingly minor bugs will have a curious way of becoming major financial drains of consequence.

Roughly once an hour, an on-line banking system in one company, for example, generated "garbage" (Os and Xs) across all computer screens. Although simply hitting a release key erased this "ghost," four months and more than $200,000 were dedicated to actually eliminating it. That involved uncovering a complex interaction of hardware features, operating system functions, and application traffic patterns; indeed, the vendor ultimately had to redesign several chips. Formal results-control mechanisms have limits in monitoring the progress of such projects, and personnel controls become more important.

In summary, technical leadership and internal integration are the keys in this type of project, and external integration plays a distinctly secondary role. Formal planning and control tools give projections that intrinsically may contain major inaccuracies, and the great danger is that neither IT managers nor high-level executives will recognize this. They may believe they have precise planning and close control, when in fact they have neither.

Low-Structure–Low-Technology Projects.   When low-structure–low-technology projects are intelligently managed, they present low risk. Again and again, however, such projects fail because of inadequate direction. (In this respect they differ from the high-structure–low-technology project, where more ordinary managerial skills could ensure success.) The key to operating this kind of project lies in effective efforts to involve the users.

Developing substantial user support for only one of the thousands of design options and keeping the users committed to that design are critical. Essential aspects of this process include:

1. A user as either project leader or the number two person on the team.
2. A user steering committee to evaluate the evolving design periodically.
3. Breaking the project into a sequence of very small, discrete subprojects.
4. Formal user review and approval on all key project specifications.
5. Distributing minutes of all key design meetings to users.
6. Adhering, when possible, to all key subproject time schedules. Low managerial and staff turnover in the user areas is vital in this respect, since a consensus on approach with a user manager's predecessor is of dubious value.

The importance of user leadership increases once the design is finalized. At that stage, users almost inevitably will state some version of "I have been thinking . . . " Unless the alternatives they suggest imply critical strategic significance (a judgment best made by a responsible, user-oriented project manager), the requests must be postponed for consideration in some formal change process. Unless this control is rigorous (a problem intensified by the near impossibility of distinguishing between the economies of a proposed alternative and those implicit in the original design), users will make change after change, with the project evolving rapidly to a state of permanent deferral, its completion forever six months in the future.

If the project has been well integrated with users, the formal planning tools will be very helpful in structuring tasks and in removing remaining uncertainties. Target completion dates will be quite firm as long as the system's target remains fixed. Similarly, the formal results-control devices afford clear insight into progress to date, flagging both advances and slippages (as long as the systems target remains fixed). Personnel controls also are vital here. If integration with user departments is weak, for example, excessive reliance on results controls will produce an entirely unwarranted feeling of confidence in the project team. By definition, however, the problems of technology management are usually less difficult in this type of project than in the high-technology ventures, and a staff with a normal mixture of technical backgrounds should be adequate.

In almost every respect, in fact, effective management of a low-structure–low-technology type of project differs from that of the previous two. The key to success is close, aggressive management of external integration, supplemented by formal planning and control tools. Leadership must flow from the user rather than from the technical side.

Low-Structure–High-Technology Projects.   Because these projects' outputs are not clear at the start and they also carry high technical complexity, their leaders require technical experience along with the ability to communicate with users. The same intensive effort toward external integration needed for low-structure–low-technology projects is necessary here. Total user commitment to a particular set of design specifications is critical; and again, they must agree to one out of the many thousands of options.

Unfortunately, however, an option desirable from the user's perspective may turn out to be not feasible in the selected hardware/software system. In the past several years, such situations have occurred, particularly with network designs, and they commonly lead either to significant restructuring of the project or to its elimination. This makes it critical that users be well represented at both the policy and the operations levels.

At the same time, technical considerations make strong technical leadership and internal project integration vital. This kind of effort requires the most experienced project leaders, and they need wholehearted support from the users. Before undertaking such a project, managers must intensely explore the possibility of dividing it into a series of much smaller subprojects and/or employing less innovative technology.

While formal planning and results-control tools can be useful here, at the early stages they contribute little either to reducing overall uncertainty or to highlighting overall problems. In addition, while planning tools do allow the manager to structure the sequence of tasks, unfortunately, in this type of project, new tasks crop up with monotonous regularity, and those that appear simple and small can suddenly become complex and protracted. Further, unsuspected interdependencies between tasks often become apparent. Time, cost, and resulting technical performance are almost impossible

TABLE 11–3   Relative Contribution of Tools to Ensuring Project Success by Project Type

		Contribution			
Project Type	*Project Description*	*External Integration*	*Internal Integration*	*Formal Planning*	*Formal Results Control*
I	High structure–low technology, large	Low	Medium	High	High
II	High structure–low technology, small	Low	Low	Medium	High
III	High structure–high technology, large	Low	High	Medium	Medium
IV	High structure–high technology, small	Low	High	Low	Low
V	Low structure–low technology, large	High	Medium	High	High
VI	Low structure–low technology, small	High	Low	Medium	High
VII	Low structure–high technology, large	High	High	Low+	Low+
VIII	Low structure–high technology, small	High	High	Low	Low

to predict simultaneously. In NASA's Apollo moon project, for example, technical performance achievement was key, and cost and time were secondary, which in the private sector is usually unacceptable.

Relative Contribution of Management Tools

Table 11–3 shows the relative contribution each of the four groups of project management tools makes to maximizing potential project success. It reveals that quite different management styles and approaches are needed for managing the different types of projects effectively. Although the framework could be made more complex by including more dimensions, it would only confirm this primary conclusion.

SUMMARY

The usual corporate handbook on project management, with its single-minded prescriptive approach, fails to deal with the realities of the tasks facing today's managers, particularly those dealing with information technology. The right approach for managing a project flows from the specific characteristics of the project.

Additionally, the need to deal with the corporate culture within which both IT and the project team operate further complicates the project management problem. Formal project planning and results-control tools are much more likely to produce successful results in highly formal environments than in ones where the prevailing culture is more personal and informal. Similarly, the selection and effective use of integrating mechanisms is very much a function of the corporate culture. (Too many former IT managers have made the fatal assumption that they were in an ideal position to reform corporate culture!)

The past decade has brought new challenges to IT project management and new insights into the management process. Our conclusion is threefold:

1. Firms will continue to experience major disappointments as they push into new application areas and technologies. Today, however, the dimensions of implementation risk can be identified in advance, and this information can be included in the decision process. Inevitably, if a firm only implements high-risk projects, it will sometimes fail.
2. A firm's IT development projects in aggregate represent a portfolio. Just as financial fund managers calculate and manage the risks within their portfolios, general management must make critical strategic decisions on the aggregate implementation risk profile of the IT portfolio.
3. Project management in the IT field is complex and multidimensional; to succeed, different types of projects require different clusters of management tools.

Case 4–1

XEROX: OUTSOURCING GLOBAL INFORMATION TECHNOLOGY RESOURCES[1]

In June 1994, Jagdish Dalal, head of Xerox's global outsourcing team, finalized a 10-year, $3.2 billion contract with Electronic Data Systems (EDS). Reflecting on the hard work this effort involved, Dalal was pleased with what his team had accomplished and confident that the agreement they had crafted would allow Xerox to quickly create the information infrastructure needed to support its new business processes. The new outsourcing model Xerox was pioneering would automatically adjust to environmental changes while keeping EDS's and Xerox's incentives aligned.

The deal was noteworthy both for its facts and figures and for the way it was to be managed. This was reputed to be the largest computer outsourcing deal in history, and the first to be implemented on a global scale. Few vendors could support such a contract. The size and complexity drove the management philosophy; the contract would not be used as an instrument to define organizational boundaries and limitations. As noted by Dalal:

The term *outsourcing* is inappropriate. This is really more of an integration of two separate

This case was prepared by research associate Kevin Davis under the supervision of Professor Lynda M. Applegate.

[1]Copyright © 1995 by the President and Fellows of Harvard College.

Harvard Business School case 195-158.

businesses. We wanted to take the best parts of each culture and put them together. The same goes for structure, strategy, and people. We will realize substantial economic value if we can achieve commitment to a high degree of integration. It is the spirit of the agreement that creates this commitment; there are no "mechanisms" that can be put into place as a substitute for the spirit.

Finally, for some observers, Xerox's outsourcing had an additional message. Xerox possessed substantial technological prowess within the digital and computer arenas. Xerox PARC[2] had, among other things, invented the first graphics-oriented monitor, the first "mouse" input device, the Ethernet protocol, the first laser printer, and the applications "windowing" concept. Hence, Xerox's outsourcing seemed to signal that even at companies where digital technologies were important core competencies, the IT function could be outsourced.

Company Background

Xerox, a global enterprise addressing the worldwide document processing market, developed, manufactured, marketed, serviced, and financed a complete range of products and services designed to make offices around the world more productive. It marketed copiers, duplicators, digital production publishers, electronic printers, facsimile products, scanners, workstations, networks, computer software and supplies in more than 130 countries using a direct sales force and a network of dealers, agents, and distributors.

Company History

After spending more than a decade perfecting the xerographic (copying/duplicating) process, Xerox introduced its model 914 copier in 1959; sales went from $32 million

in 1959 to $1.1 billion in 1968; employment surged from 900 in 1959 to 24,000 in 1966. By 1970, Xerox held a 95 percent share of the plain-paper copier market. Gross margins for many products in 1970 ranged from 70 to 80 percent. (See Exhibit 1 for selected Xerox financial information.) At the same time, Xerox's phenomenal growth and profitability attracted federal lawsuits. In 1975, Xerox reached a settlement with the Federal Trade Commission: Xerox was forced to forfeit patent protection and had to license its competitors.[3]

From 1976 to 1982, Xerox's share of U.S. copier installations dropped from an estimated 80 percent to 13 percent, due to competition provided by such Japanese companies as Canon, Minolta, Ricoh, and Sharp. Licensing also dramatically increased new product introductions: between 1971 and 1978, 77 different plain-paper copiers were introduced in the United States; between 1978 and 1980, another 70 arrived (see Exhibit 2).

After struggling to develop a strategy to address its newly competitive environment, in 1980 Xerox began to aggressively pursue benchmarking and employee involvement.[4]

---

[2]Palo Alto Research Center.

[3]Xerox executives recount how the proliferation of lawsuits began to have a chilling effect on company strategy. For example, Xerox became less aggressive in its pricing policies; lawyers began to accompany managers when they met with other companies in order to ensure that there was no hint of illegal collaboration; managers were coached on what they could say—words such as "annihilate" were outlawed. In addition, costs in terms of legal fees and executive time (the CEO, for example, lost an estimated thirty or forty days a year) were substantial. See Gary Jacobsen and John Hilkirk, *Xerox: American Samurai* (New York: Macmillan, 1986), especially pp. 69–75 and 196–200.

[4]"The company issues a little red booklet on benchmarking to employees. You see it in offices everywhere. It explains how each department and employee can determine what to benchmark, how to benchmark, and how to use that information to improve Xerox." Jacobsen and Hilkirk (1986, p. 233).

EXHIBIT 1 Xerox Financial Highlights

	1993	1992	1991	1990	1989	1988	1987	1986
				Operations				
Operating revenues (sales, service)	$13,384	$13,460	$12,734	$12,542	$11,602	$11,029	$10,320	$9,355
Cost of sales, service, and rentals	$7,230	$7,126	$6,661	$6,656	$6,237	$5,778	$5,382	$4,814
SGA	$4,585	$4,779	$4,497	$4,286	$3,929	$3,847		
Research and development expenses	$883	$922	$890	$848	$809	$794	$722	$650
Income from document processing	*($193)	$562	****$436	$599	$488	##$148	$353	$316
Income from insurance operations	$4	**($779)	$2	$11	$154	$181	$188	#$129
Income from continuing operation	*($189)	**($217)	$438	$610	$642	$329	$541	$445
Net Income	*($126)	***($1,020)	****$454	##$243	$704	##$388	$578	$465
				Financial Position				
Total document processing assets	$18,158	$17,140	$15,178	$14,421	$13,488	$12,415		
Total insurance assets	$15,418	$15,479	$15,552	$14,579	$14,864	$13,036		
Long-term debt	$7,386	$8,105	$7,825	$8,726	$9,247	$6,675		
Shareholder equity	$3,972	$3,875	$5,140	$5,051	$5,035	$5,371	$5,105	$4,687
				Per Share				
Net income per common share###	($2.46)	($3.32)	$3.91	$5.51	$6.56	$3.50	$5.35	$4.52
Dividends per common share	$3.00	$3.00	$3.00	$3.00	$3.00	$3.00	$3.00	$3.00
Document processing employees at year end	97,000	99,300	100,900	99,000	99,000	100,000	99,032	100,367

* Includes the following special pretax charges: Severance pay and other employee separation benefits ($843 million); lease cancellation and site consolidation ($258 million); write-down of various assets ($94 million); litigation settlements ($278 million).

** Includes insurance operations restructuring charge ($778 million after tax).

**** Includes the following special after tax charges: Insurance operations restructuring ($778 million); adoption of FASB SFAS 106, related to employee benefits ($606 million); adoption of FASB SFAS 109, relating to income taxes ($158 million).

***** Includes a $101 million after-tax charge for the costs of a work-force reduction.

Includes a before-tax charge of $375 million as a provision for real estate losses. In 1990 the company discontinued its real estate operation and related real estate financing operations.

Includes several special pretax charges: Write-off of excess electronic typewriter manufacturing capacity ($140 million); overhead and employment reductions ($100 million); revaluation of assets ($35 million).

Before results of discontinued operations of $0.62 per share in 1993, −3.84 in 1990, −0.67 in 1986, +0.98 in 1985, and special items of −7.97 in 1992 and +0.43 in 1986.

Source: Xerox Annual Reports and Standard and Poor's Reports.

EXHIBIT 2   Pace of Xerox Product Introductions

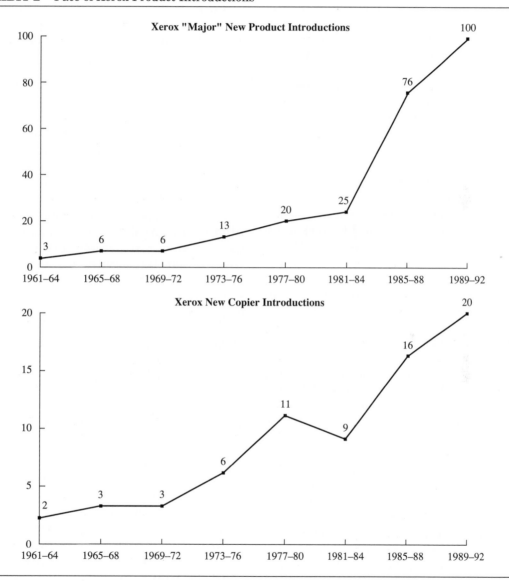

Source: Xerox 1993 Factbook.

In addition, under the leadership of CEO David T. Kearns, Xerox embraced quality as its basis for competition, instituting a program called Leadership Through Quality. These three directions—participation, benchmarking, and quality management—worked in unison. "Benchmarking," Kearns noted, "spread like wildfire through the company. We were fast closing in on our goal of having every department in the company measuring its performance against similar operations at other companies."[5] "We had begun to build long-term relationships with our best vendors," he explained. "We began to treat our vendors as part of an extended family and to train them in the principles of Leadership Through Quality."[6] Xerox's efforts to improve quality earned the company several prestigious awards: In 1989, it earned the national Malcolm Baldrige Quality Award; shortly afterward, Xerox Canada won the Canadian National Quality Award; and, in 1992, Xerox became the first winner of the European Quality Award.

The emphasis on participation, benchmarking, and quality seemed to work in the marketplace as well; between 1984 and 1993, Xerox's market share in low-end copiers rose from 8 percent to 18 percent, while for mid- and high-end copiers its share rose from 26 percent to 35 percent.[7]

Corporate Restructuring

Despite improvements in market share, overall corporate performance declined in the early 1990s. In 1992 Xerox's CEO, Paul Allaire, announced a major reorganization: Xerox would create nine divisions along market segment lines and three customer operations along geographic lines[8] (see Exhibit 3). The nine market segment divisions were created to move decision making closer to the customer. According to the 1992 Annual Report, "Each Xerox division [has] 'end-to-end' responsibility for a set of products and services, a set of primary market segments, an identifiable set of competitors and an income statement and balance

sheet."[9] Allaire, determined to do more than just change the formal structure, explained, "Many times people will change just the structure and reporting relationships. But if you want to change a company, you'd better change more than that. There's the formal structure and then there's the way the company really works. You have to change the way it really works."[10]

Reorganizing the corporation along customer lines meant redefining both operational and management processes. The company also focused on its core competencies, as underlined by its moves to sell its financial businesses. In January 1993, Allaire announced, "We've decided to disengage from our remaining Insurance and Other Financial Services businesses. . . . With the decision to exit from financial services, we can now focus clearly and unencumbered on our Document Processing business."[11] Finally, Xerox announced in 1993 that it would be reducing the size of its document processing workforce by 10,000, approximately 10 percent, over the next two to three years.

Information Management (IM) at Xerox

Xerox established corporate information management (CIM) in the early 1970s[12] to be responsible for managing data centers and networks; in 1987, however, these were moved to a separate division called the general services division (see Exhibit 4). Patricia Barron, appointed director of CIM in June 1987, explained CIM's new mission: [We were] to develop the information technology strategy for

---

[5]See David T. Kearns and David A. Nadler, *Prophets in the Dark* (New York: HarperCollins, 1992), p. 238.

[6]Ibid., p. 256.

[7]Subrata Chakravarty, "Back in Focus," *Forbes,* June 6, 1994.

[8]Ibid. (also see Xerox 1992 Annual Report, p. 4.)

[9]Xerox 1992 Annual Report, p. 9.

[10]Chakravarty, "Back in Focus," p. 76.

[11]Xerox 1992 Annual Report, p. 6.

[12]See Harvard Business School Case, *Xerox Corporation: Leadership of the Information Technology Function (A),* No. 188-133.

EXHIBIT 3   Global Process and Information Management Structure

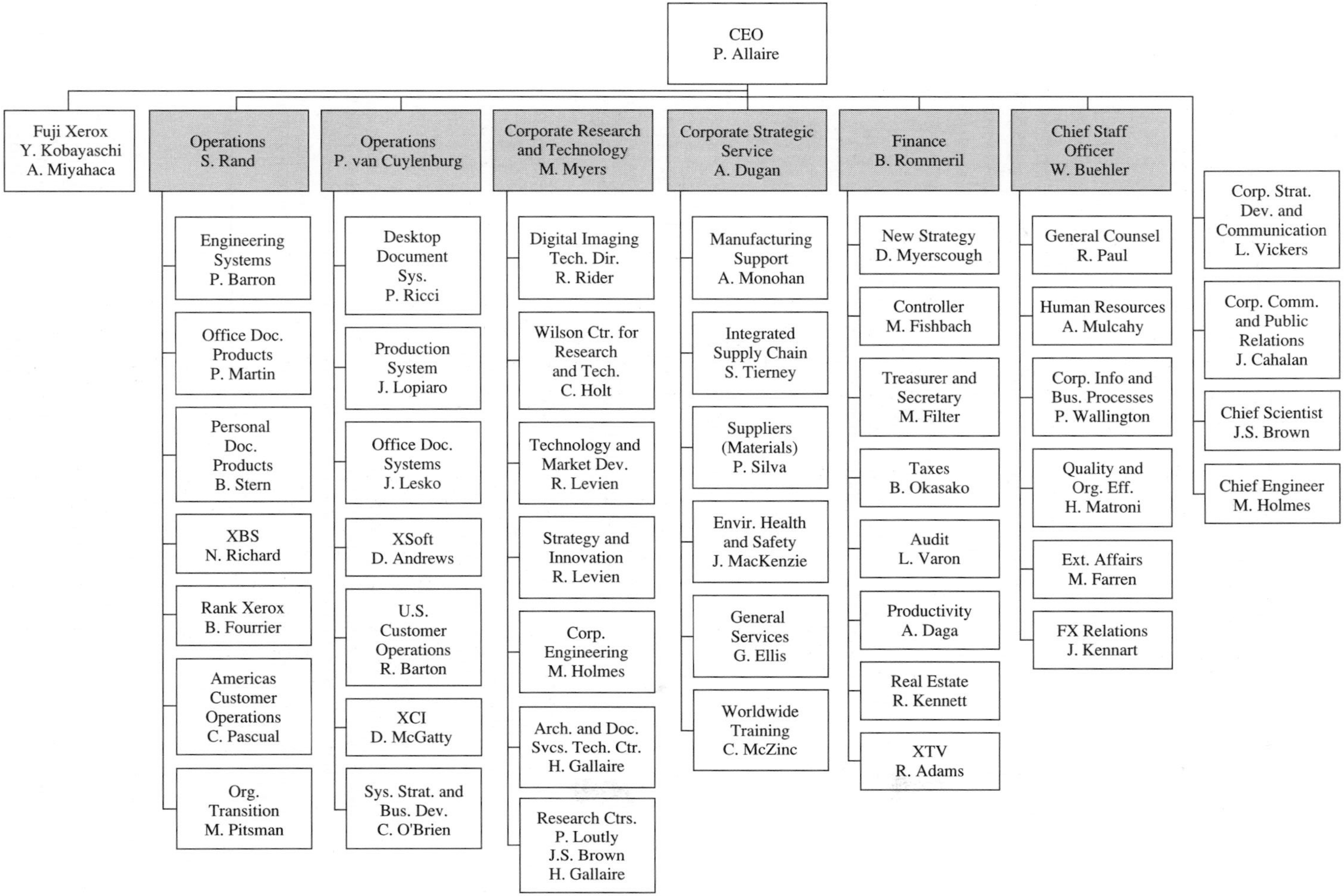

CEO
P. Allaire

Fuji Xerox
Y. Kobayaschi
A. Miyahaca

Operations
S. Rand
- Engineering Systems — P. Barron
- Office Doc. Products — P. Martin
- Personal Doc. Products — B. Stern
- XBS — N. Richard
- Rank Xerox — B. Fourrier
- Americas Customer Operations — C. Pascual
- Org. Transition — M. Pitsman

Operations
P. van Cuylenburg
- Desktop Document Sys. — P. Ricci
- Production System — J. Lopiaro
- Office Doc. Systems — J. Lesko
- XSoft — D. Andrews
- U.S. Customer Operations — R. Barton
- XCI — D. McGatty
- Sys. Strat. and Bus. Dev. — C. O'Brien

Corporate Research and Technology
M. Myers
- Digital Imaging Tech. Dir. — R. Rider
- Wilson Ctr. for Research and Tech. — C. Holt
- Technology and Market Dev. — R. Levien
- Strategy and Innovation — R. Levien
- Corp. Engineering — M. Holmes
- Arch. and Doc. Svcs. Tech. Ctr. — H. Gallaire
- Research Ctrs. — P. Loutly, J.S. Brown, H. Gallaire

Corporate Strategic Service
A. Dugan
- Manufacturing Support — A. Monohan
- Integrated Supply Chain — S. Tierney
- Suppliers (Materials) — P. Silva
- Envir. Health and Safety — J. MacKenzie
- General Services — G. Ellis
- Worldwide Training — C. McZinc

Finance
B. Rommeril
- New Strategy — D. Myerscough
- Controller — M. Fishbach
- Treasurer and Secretary — M. Filter
- Taxes — B. Okasako
- Audit — L. Varon
- Productivity — A. Daga
- Real Estate — R. Kennett
- XTV — R. Adams

Chief Staff Officer
W. Buehler
- General Counsel — R. Paul
- Human Resources — A. Mulcahy
- Corp. Info and Bus. Processes — P. Wallington
- Quality and Org. Eff. — H. Matroni
- Ext. Affairs — M. Farren
- FX Relations — J. Kennart

- Corp. Strat. Dev. and Communication — L. Vickers
- Corp. Comm. and Public Relations — J. Cahalan
- Chief Scientist — J.S. Brown
- Chief Engineer — M. Holmes

Note: This chart is illustrative only and does not show all organizations or reporting relationships.

471

EXHIBIT 4   Xerox Corporation: IT Management Organization, 1988

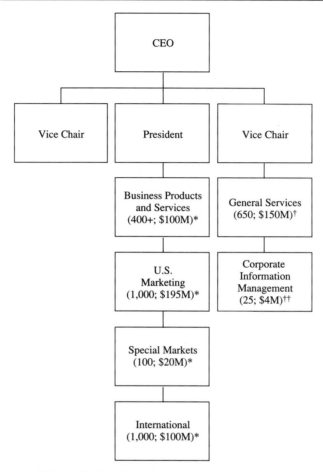

* Information Management (IM) was highly decentralized with autonomous information management organizations located within each division. The numbers in parentheses represent IM headcount and budget.

** The General Systems Division included the data center and telecommunications services units.

*** The Corporate Information Management unit provided information management leadership for Xerox Corporation. In addition, a small system development group was responsible for corporate application development and corporate data management.

Xerox and ensure that it was implemented in all the business units." Added Bill Glavin, vice chairman in the late 1980s, "We expected CIM to provide the overall information technology leadership to the company."

Yet as Barron worked to provide this leadership, she found she would not be able to fulfill this mission without substantial organizational changes. "While senior management expected CIM to ensure that the $500 million information technology budget was well spent, the business unit managers regarded attempts to audit expenditures as unnecessary," Barron observed. In order to assess IM at Xerox, in 1988 she brought in an IT strategy consulting firm—and it found numerous areas of concern. In particular, the diffusion of authority in IT decision making had created many IT problems at Xerox. The consultants elaborated:

> There was no overall coordination or management of the hundreds of millions of dollars spent each year and no corporatewide management of IM investment priorities. The CIM organization at Xerox was not positioned, chartered, or staffed to perform many of the CIO functions. Overall, CIM was a peripheral player in the IT management picture because they were not chartered to direct or manage infrastructure nor resourced to furnish leadership.
>
> The IT function at Xerox possessed a narrowly focused IM talent pool, reported to senior managers who viewed IT infrastructure investment as an expense to be avoided, required redundant and overlapping efforts to find or reconcile the most basic information, and lacked effective staff development mechanisms.

It was clear that the 1989 Xerox IM infrastructure could not support the company's strategic direction in the 1990s.

Centralizing Xerox IM

In 1993, in order to align IM with the direction the company was taking, Patricia Wallington,[13] head of corporate information management, asked for and received direct authority over IM worldwide. (See Exhibit 5 for the new IM organization implemented by Wallington.) For several years IM managers had been addressing the problems Barron and the consultants had identified, but change had been slow. Thus, as the IM workforce tried to support the new Xerox divisional structure, it became obvious that the

existing information systems infrastructure was inadequate. IM was simply unable to provide the data needed to support Xerox's new divisions.

After investigating the extent of the problems facing IM, Wallington presented her findings at the Xerox Presidents Council meeting in April 1993. Xerox had spent $670 million on IM during 1992, a figure that was forecast to grow to $1 billion by the end of the decade, she noted. IM personnel were well aware that the division presidents did not feel they were getting an adequate payback from what amounted to 3.7 percent of total Xerox revenues. Suzanne Higgins, head of IM management processes, commented on Wallington's presentation: "She actually pulled together all this information; it was a real eye-opener. At that point the Presidents Council said we needed to get control of these dollars. There was a sense from the division presidents that they were not getting what they needed for the dollars being spent."

The IM 2000 Project

To address IM problems, CIM started the "IM 2000" reengineering project in mid-1993. An initial IM 2000 design team was formed to identify IM problem areas and recommend strategies to address them. Projects supporting these strategies would be implemented by transitional teams, which would ultimately move IM to a new information systems infrastructure.

Salient IM problems. Xerox possessed an aging applications portfolio built on proprietary technologies created to support the previous, functionally structured organization.[14] IM appeared to be "trapped in a spending spiral on outdated legacy

---

[13]Wallington was appointed head of CIM in 1992; Barron, the previous head, was promoted to president of the newly created office document products division as part of the 1992 reorganization.

[14]*IM 2000,* Issue 2 (a Xerox internal publication), December 1993, p. 13.

EXHIBIT 5   Xerox Information Management Organization, December 1993

```
          P.M. Wallington*
          Vice President and        Executive
          Chief Information         Assistant
              Officer


   Business Process          Global Integrated
     Management              Business Solutions


     Technology
      Services                 IM Controller


         IM                         IM
   Quality Strategies         Human Resource
                                Operations


    Information
    Management              Global Data
     Strategy               Management
```

* Corporate Officer:
Note: This chart shows reporting relationships only and is in no
     way intended to reflect relative importance.

---

systems."[15] The corporate change to a divisional structure had exposed the inflexibility of existing information systems. Janice Malaszenko, head of the CIM strategy function, explained:

The company had reorganized the previous year to a divisional, product line focus, versus what primarily had been a regional or geographic focus. Where our systems essentially fell apart was in not being able to supply information about how a particular division's products were doing globally. We were jury-rigging a lot of systems and a lot of data to try to

respond to this new divisional structure. The division presidents were not getting the information they needed to run their businesses. We needed better access to information and flexible solutions that would be relevant even if the number of divisions changed.

Dalal noted that, in part, Xerox's "legacy"[16] systems prevented IM from addressing division needs. "I spent 110 percent of my time on

---

[15]Ibid., p. 5.

[16]"Legacy" refers to transaction processing systems designed to perform a specific function, which, over time, may not accurately reflect business information needs. In addition, as hardware and software improvements occur in the information systems marketplace, older IS solutions may be more costly to operate and maintain.

legacy systems; there was not enough time to implement new ideas," he commented. "You had to maintain the old systems. It took a lot of resources and a lot of time. It was like an additional weight on your shoulders and prevented you from moving quickly forward," he continued.

There were financial challenges as well. "We were a support function in a company operating in a very competitive industry, and we had a hard time competing for the investments we needed in tools and training," noted Dick Bailey, a member of the core outsourcing team.

Finally, Xerox's culture, with its emphasis on autonomy, had allowed significant duplication of effort in IM across functional areas. "We had no consolidated list of applications—what their technology was, what development methods were used, or what business process they supported," one manager observed.

Design Team Strategies. After studying IM's problems, the IM 2000 design team recommended specific strategies whereby IM could quickly develop the IT infrastructure and capabilities required to provide Xerox's business divisions with the information they needed. (See Exhibit 6 for a graphical depiction of these strategies, representing the Xerox IM 2000 vision.) The four strategies follow:

1. *Reduce/Redirect.* IM would seek to reduce overall costs by reigning in the expense of legacy systems. A part of any savings would be retained by IM to fund new applications and infrastructure able to support new Xerox business processes.
2. *Infrastructure Management.* IM would move to an industry-standard infrastructure that would be managed centrally in order to increase interoperability and sharing of solutions and information worldwide. A major objective of the infrastructure strategy was to move to a client/server environment.

3. *Leverage Worldwide IM Resources.* IM was to create a library of shareable core modules, centrally developed or purchased, which could be used locally to create solutions. Central monitoring of solutions would limit redundancy.
4. *Business Process Driven Solutions.* The current portfolio of applications (legacy systems) was to be retired or replaced with solutions supporting new Xerox business processes.

The Information Systems Outsourcing Decision

Xerox's earlier drive for quality had created a change in the corporate culture by promoting a sense of partnership with suppliers. Hence, given the company's experience with outsourcing and creating alliances, the Presidents Council instructed top IM staff to contemplate outsourcing as a way to change IM radically. Malaszenko recalled:

> The presidents, very specifically in their request to us, documented that we should be considering radical and significant moves, including outsourcing. They [the division presidents] might be outsourcing pieces of their product; they might be outsourcing distribution; they might be outsourcing some of their sales through channels. The term *outsourcing* was not foreign. Why not consider using the same concept and how it might apply in an IM world?

At first, many IM managers felt that outsourcing was unnecessary; they could accomplish the needed changes internally. The IM design team quickly realized, however, that many internal obstacles would not be easily overcome.

First, any attempt to solve IM problems internally would also have to contend with the relationships between IM and its customers, the business divisions—which apparently did not fully appreciate the problems IM faced. Top IM managers found that, after

EXHIBIT 6   The Xerox IM 2000 Vision

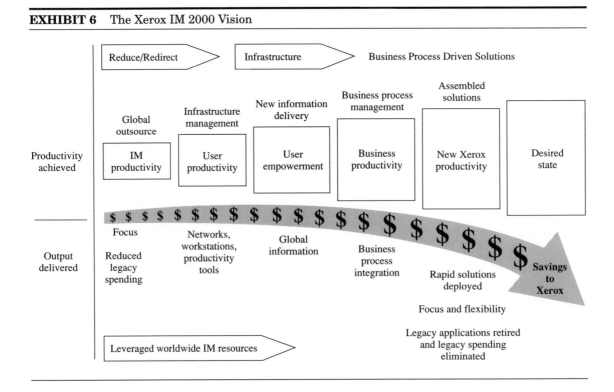

addressing business requests for current systems, they had little time or money to address future infrastructure and process redesign issues. And as long as IM was internal, they knew they would always be asked to satisfy more demands than they could support. There was a feeling that an outside change agent might introduce some welcome discipline into the process. Bailey explained:

> By doing business with an external vendor in a business-like fashion, with real money changing hands, we hoped to get some sharper decision making as to how much money was spent and on what. We hoped to reduce the tendency of a captive in-house organization to queue up an enormous backlog of things for it to do. This made it very difficult to determine an appropriate spending level.

Other managers agreed. For example, one manager noted, "When you began to spend the money outside, you were much more con-

scious of how much money you were spending; you questioned all of those quick [information systems applications] changes."

Funding constraints added to the impossibility of an internal solution. The implementation costs for the IM 2000 strategies were expected to be substantial. "The costs internally were prohibitive, with $55 million just for hardware, much more when applications development and training and reskilling were included," Dalal explained. Bailey pointed out that such an expense was unlikely to be funded internally: "We had enormous pressures on profit margins and we couldn't expect our top executives to divert this level of investment into what they probably considered to be an expense center."

Nevertheless, IM executives felt that given enough time they *could* successfully transform their information systems internally; unfortunately, IM required immediate improvement. Xerox businesses were facing an increasingly competitive environment and were being forced to adapt quickly (as evidenced by the increase in product introductions in Exhibit 2). To provide the information the business divisions needed, IM managers knew they had to rebuild the IM infrastructure rapidly while radically changing the processes IM personnel used. Top IM managers began to realize they would not be able to change quickly enough without outside help. Many managers admitted that modest change efforts in the past hadn't been particularly successful, as Audrey Pantas, the CIO's executive assistant during the outsourcing effort, explained:

> It wasn't as if we hadn't tried to implement change internally; we had tried—with varying degrees of success. Unfortunately, the business required us to change more rapidly. The real key to outsourcing was that Xerox would be able to move towards the future quickly. We were focused on building the new solutions; EDS was focused on supporting the legacy systems and the desktop infrastructure. Without the change in focus, it would have taken us years to implement the required changes. The business could not wait; speed was critical.

It was the need for rapid movement toward the IM 2000 vision that ultimately convinced Xerox IM managers to outsource.

A global outsourcing team was created to formally examine the benefits and feasibility of outsourcing. If outsourcing was found to be feasible, the team was to find a partner and create a contract. Dalal, Xerox's lead outsourcing manager, enlisted Dick Bailey, an IM manager from the U.S. customer operations division, and Charles Gilliam, senior corporate counsel, to assist him in the recruitment of an outsourcing team. These three served as the "core" Xerox outsourcing team. Over time, the number of people working on the outsourcing effort grew to 50. The group was managed informally, without a definitive organizational structure. As the

need for expertise arose, team members approached new people who could provide it. Areas of expertise included: Tax, Treasury, Human Resources, Finance, Audit, and Security. Most team members worked on outsourcing in addition to their normal duties.

Outsourcing Benefits

Based on first-level feasibility studies, completed in November 1993, the team, having identified numerous potential benefits, decided to pursue an outsourcing arrangement.

Financial benefits from outsourcing included rapid funding of new systems development and economies of scale and scope. According to Dalal, "As part of the transaction, IT assets were sold. This gave Xerox an opportunity to renew their asset base and accelerate growth towards the new infrastructure." Xerox's internal experience with consolidation convinced the outsourcing team that even greater economies could be achieved by an external vendor. A Xerox manager observed, "Xerox has consolidated some internal data centers in the last few years. Through these consolidations we experienced cost reductions in hardware/software licensing, facilities, and support headcount. An outside vendor will be able to attain further economies by continuing this consolidation effort."

The team also expected to capitalize on an outside vendor's extensive IT problem-solving knowledge. Malaszenko, for example, stated that she "wanted to be able to draw on the vendor's expertise to say, 'how are you approaching it with some of your other customers?'" The vendor's additional expertise derived, in part, from investment in IT. As Dave Skotnicki, who worked with potential bidders to define Xerox's information management needs, noted, "An outside vendor had the ability to get more of the technology that came out. They could spend money on investments which we couldn't afford internally. That opened up a lot more avenues to future technologies."

IM managers also believed that an outside vendor would manage the IT function more efficiently. Another Xerox manager pointed out that a vendor's "main competency was managing computer systems. Through their skills, leverage, and economies of scale, they could provide a level of efficiency that we could not achieve at Xerox." Bailey agreed: "This was their core competence. And a combination of that and their focus allowed them to harness all that energy and be more effective. The top outside vendors had standardized approaches. In this company, every pocket of systems expertise had a tendency to do it their own way and march to a different drummer."

Perhaps most important, outsourcing allowed internal IM managers to focus on the development of a new IT infrastructure. Underlying the outsourcing effort, according to Bailey, was a fundamental strategy: "to offload legacy applications and operations so we could focus on developing new strategic applications to support the global business processes which were being reengineered." Skotnicki agreed: "The idea was to outsource all of our existing legacy applications. We were going to screw down spending on legacy, enabling Xerox to focus on new development."

Bailey summarized the benefits of outsourcing this way:

> Many people thought the only reason you would outsource was because your company was in trouble and you needed immediate cash or your information management organization was considered a hopeless failure. Our reasons for looking at outsourcing were quite different: One, we wanted to control and drive down spending on our "legacy" IM environment to provide investment funds for new strategic systems and infrastructure; two, we wanted to improve both the quality and cost of our IM services; and, three, we wanted to focus the company's resources on

our primary mission as "The Document Company." We believed outsourcing would help us address all three objectives.

The Outsourcing Process

Choosing a Partner

The outsourcing team began by inviting numerous companies to bid. (See Exhibits 7, 8, and 9 for diagrams of the selection and project processes.) One manager who worked on the outsourcing recounted how they decided whom to invite: "We opened it up to some of the companies we've done business with or do business with, as well as major customers that we've had that might have some options for pursuing this, and left it open to them to refuse."

The size and complexity of the deal, however, forced most potential bidders to walk away: only two vendors and one vendor team formally responded. "They weeded themselves out," recalled Bailey. Added Skotnicki, "You're not just looking at running a data center or supporting business applications, you're also including network and infrastructure solutions on a worldwide scale."

The team then created a list of criteria (see Exhibit 10) providing a general sense of how potential vendors would be judged. [Such] scoring allowed us to eliminate one [vendor]," noted Dalal. Next, following intense negotiations with the remaining two vendors, Xerox chose EDS, based on several factors. "First," Dalal explained, "global presence was extremely important and EDS was believed to have a superior global presence." Xerox was also quite interested in ensuring a good transition for outsourced employees. Dalal described EDS as, "more willing to tailor their human resource program for our folks." Finally, EDS entered a very competitive bid, and Dalal was confident EDS could make money on that bid: "Our intention was not to have EDS lose money. The best partner is a viable, strong

EXHIBIT 7   Outsourcing Vendor Selection Process

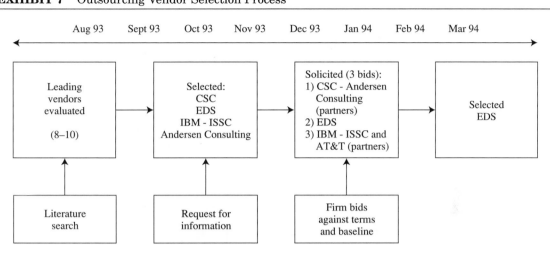

partner," he explained. He also felt that it was irrelevant to ask whether EDS would be losing money during the first year or two. "You really couldn't make money in one year, whether it was early or late. You really had to look at the whole deal."

Interestingly, the outsourcing team felt that another vendor actually offered the best "cultural match." IM managers considered the advantages of a vendor with a different background, however; they felt "out-of-box" thinking was needed—and that would be facilitated by partnering with a firm with a different culture.

The Contract
In June 1994, Xerox signed a $3.2 billion, 10-year deal with EDS. (Exhibit 11 shows contract highlights; Exhibit 12 provides a generic outsourcing contract checklist.) EDS was responsible for running mainframes, maintaining legacy systems, and handling worldwide voice and data communications in 19 countries. (See Exhibit 13 for a summary of the deal's scope.) Approximately 1,900 Xerox IM personnel, and about $170

million in assets, were transferred to EDS. Xerox retained control of strategic and architectural information management functions and new applications development; 700 IM workers were retained to work on these functions. According to Wallington, the mission for those staying on at Xerox was clear: "We want to focus our internal staff on moving us to the environment that will support us tomorrow."[17]

EDS's share of the Xerox IM budget was forecast to be 70 percent in the first year of the contract and shrink to 30–35 percent by the final year. According to Dalal, by the end of the 10-year contract, "We will have rebuilt all of our applications systems, and our legacy that we are outsourcing to EDS will no longer exist." However, even without legacy retirements, the IT expense was expected to decline. According to lawyer John Halvey, an outsourcing expert from Milbank Tweed who worked on the Xerox contract:

---

[17]*Computerworld* 20 (June 1994), p. 12.

EXHIBIT 8   Outsourcing Process

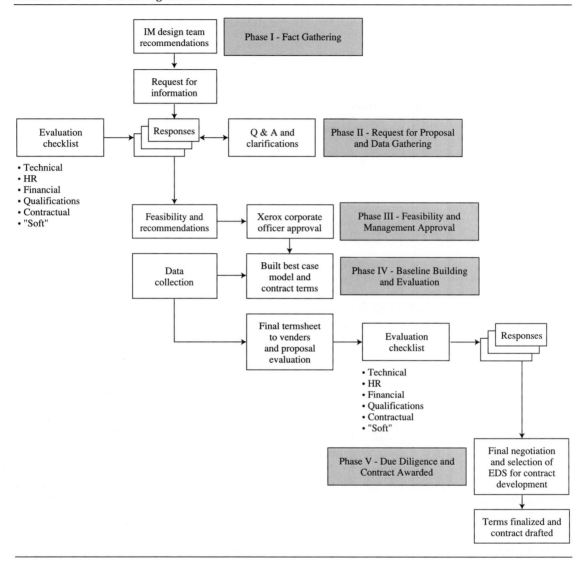

Source: Adapted from Xerox presentation by J. Dalal.

There were several reasons why IM executives at an outsourcing company expected their I/T processing volume and expenses to decline. First, they believed that, over time, the vendor would increase overall I/T efficiency. Second, personnel and hardware expenses were expected to decrease for any given level of I/T capacity as new technologies became available. Third, many companies were downsizing and expected their I/T usage curve to fall as they began to concentrate on core competencies, and stopped trying to do everything else.

EXHIBIT 9   Benchmarking Completed during Phase I of the Outsourcing Process

Extensive Benchmarking was conducted resulting in information on:

- Outsourcing strategies
- Outsourcing processes
  - •• Contracting
  - •• Transitioning
  - •• Ongoing management of the relationship
- Vendor references
- Human resource impact

Companies used in the Benchmarking process included:

Salomon Brothers	Equifax	AT&T
KF (Sweden)	First Boston Corporation	Kodak
General Dynamics	McDonnell Douglas	Sun
British Home Stores	KugelFischer (Germany)	Europcar
General Motors	British Aerospace	

Source: Xerox presentation by J. Dalal.

Though confident that they had created a robust agreement, IM managers knew they had to keep the transition from the legacy environment to a new information infrastructure on track. Confirming the importance of a timely transition, Dalal remarked, "The goal was, after 10 years, to replace the legacy systems with new business solutions. We ran a risk of increasing costs if we did not achieve our systems retirement plan."

The "Spirit" of the Contract

As they hammered out an agreement, Xerox's core outsourcing team (Dalal, Bailey, and Gilliam) met frequently with EDS's core team (see Exhibit 14). According to Dalal, it quickly became evident that the outsourcing relationship required something more than negotiations with a traditional IT supplier. Reed agreed: "This is not a client/vendor relationship; this is not a supplier relationship; this is not a win/lose situation; this is a strategic relationship." But both sides realized that integration

could only be achieved if they developed a high degree of cooperation.

The first obstacle to be overcome was what Dalal termed "fear of publication." In order to achieve the level of honesty required to attempt an integration, participants had to be assured that what was said in the core meetings would not be shared beyond the members of the core team. Only after creating an environment of trust could the six (who came to view themselves as a single team) work to understand each corporation's objectives. Dalal described how an open environment and sharing of objectives were accomplished:

Each side made two lists. First we wrote down our company's objectives; then we wrote down what we thought were the other company's objectives. All of the objectives were then put on flip charts. This procedure allowed us to quickly identify disconnects. In order to ensure complete honesty, we went a step further and the two of us who led the team put up our personal objectives as well; right down to what

EXHIBIT 10   Xerox Vendor Selection Criteria

Vendor Qualifications

- Global presence
- Capability to manage "globally"
- Experienced in large-scale outsourcing
- "Core" strengths in various frameworks*
- Desire to "create a different outsourcing environment" (for Xerox)
- Management processes and strength

Human Resources

- Treatment of Xerox employees
- Human resource values

Technical Solutions

- Overall productivity commitment: % and credibility
- Support for existing Xerox diverse environments
- Capability to help "migrate"

Financial

- Translation of productivity savings to Xerox
- Flexibility in meeting Xerox financial requirements (globally)
- Experience in "engineering" financial environment (worldwide)

"Soft" Criteria

- "Congruence" with positive Xerox cultural traits
- Provide benchmark for desired Xerox cultural traits

*"Frameworks" included data center, telecommunications, infrastructure support, and applications.

Source: Xerox presentation by J. Dalal.

EXHIBIT 11   The Xerox-EDS Contract

Contract Highlights

"Evergreen" contract terms: a new concept.
The objective was to create a contract that would automatically adjust to current global needs. Mechanisms used to achieve this evergreen concept included:

- Schedules and exhibits
- Terms that have "built in" renewal processes (e.g., pricing)
- Terms and performance separated for management purposes (e.g., Service Responsibility Manual, Operations Manual)
- Global terms for the life of the contract separated from transition terms to facilitate on-time transition activities.

Other contract terms, some of which are unique, included:

- Global contractual terms
- Human resource terms
- Pricing mechanism: benchmarking and indices
- Service level management: "Service Level Variance" Concept (Adaptation of Xerox Quality processes/tools)
- Ongoing relationship terms built on "partnership" rather than establishing a "supplier/buyer" model
- Future business relationship terms

Source: Xerox presentation by J. Dalal.

would get us promoted and fired. That session got us extremely close to one another. After the discussion we threw the charts away, but as the negotiations progressed, these objectives were always in the back of our minds.

Once the team reached an understanding of the "spirit" of the relationship, the rest of the negotiations proceeded smoothly. To ensure that the spirit persisted, they worked hard to capture a sense of it within the final contract. Dalal explained how the contract was used to capture the spirit and maintain a focus on IM 2000 objectives:

Article one of the contract covers the spirit of the agreement. It stresses the vision of IM 2000 and what makes us successful. The objective was not to outsource but to accomplish IM

2000. Outsourcing is simply the first in an integrated set of strategies. It provides the savings that help to deliver the rest of the strategies. If EDS doesn't help us by delivering on the agreement, we cannot achieve the IM 2000 vision.

Yet the very length and complexity of the contract made transmitting the "spirit" of the deal difficult. Global issues alone demanded more than 50 pages of contractual language. According to Dalal, the team responded to this problem by "creating a summary of the contract that was circulated among senior Xerox management to ensure that everyone understood the spirit of the relationship." Dalal also held one-day sessions with IM managers to ensure "that they understood not only the contract but also the spirit of the agreement."

The team attempted to use the contract as a repository of corporate memory, instead of as an instrument to define organizational boundaries and limitations. Hence, long-time employees would be able to use the contract to refresh their memories as to the nature and spirit of the agreement; new employees could use the contract to learn about the EDS/Xerox relationship. The team expected the spirit to evolve over time in response to changing environmental realities. They agreed to change the contract as needed to ensure that it mirrored any changes in the spirit.

Two sets of contractual issues presented a significant challenge in maintaining the relationship: divorce issues and pricing issues. The pricing issue was solved by an intricate mechanism. Dalal recalled:

> Xerox built on its quality and benchmarking heritage and devised a unique methodology. The contract required annual price benchmarking. Therefore, the contract guaranteed both to Xerox and EDS that current prices would always be at benchmark levels worldwide. Our price benchmarking would be based on forty-odd price elements rather than aggregate

prices. We had found an appropriate benchmark or index for each of these price elements. The contract ensured that we wouldn't have to worry about I/T price swings that occurred during the duration of the contract. The contract would not have to be reopened to adjust pricing; the contract renewed itself.

Divorce concerns were addressed by including clauses in the contract that would adequately protect each party if a split became necessary. "The contract had certain checkpoints and conditions along the way that provided the capability for moving out," Malaszenko explained. Nevertheless, Xerox IM managers realized that once the two companies became integrated, divorce would be difficult. For example, Malaszenko noted, "Restaffing would be complex, as transitioned employees might not be available or interested in returning to work in their previous capacity."

The actual negotiation of the divorce clause was apparently not very difficult, due to the team's insistence on understanding each other's objectives up front, as Dalal stated:

> The termination portion of the agreement was where the objectives helped most. We tried to ensure that corporate and personal objectives would live through any termination of the relationship. The termination negotiation did not take long; I think we did it in a couple of hours one morning.

Dalal underlined the importance of not dwelling on divorce issues: "You cannot drive your commitment based on disintegration." Other IM managers expressed similar views. For example, one manager commented, "If we didn't have a real strong feel that it was going to work, we wouldn't have gone into it at all." And Bailey commented, "I believed it was very important to approach both the contract and the relationship with a win-win attitude because it was important that the relationship was a healthy one."

EXHIBIT 12   Checklist of Clauses for an Outsourcing Agreement (Listing below does not imply that Xerox-EDS agreement includes these clauses.)

Note: This material represents a checklist of items to be included in a typical outsourcing agreement. It is not necessarily complete, and all such contracts should be tailored to the specific objectives of the customer and the vendor. The list is deliberately in random sequence in order to avoid any imputation of importance to any particular clause.

1. Description of base services.
   - Data processing
   - Data communication
   - Voice communication
   - Application development and maintenance
2. Miscellaneous services to be provided.
   - Mail
   - Messenger
   - Consulting
   - Training
   - Reports
3. Service levels.
4. Initial term of agreement.
5. Renewal term of agreement.
6. Fees and charges.
7. Payment schedule.
8. Adjustments to charges based on volume.
9. Price protection.
   - Percentage cap on increases
   - CPI/GNP inflator
   - Most Favored Nation
10. Verification of costs.
11. Annual adjustments to charges.
12. Expenses.
   - Cap on expenses
   - Documentation of expenses
   - Customer policy in respect of expenses
13. Miscellaneous expenses—paper, supplies, messenger, duplication, binding, etc.
14. Third-party contracts.
   - Required consents
   - Transfer fee
15. Third-party software contracts
   - Required consents
   - Transfer fees
16. Third-party equipment leases.
   - Required consents
   - Transfer fees
17. Change procedures—programming and processing.
18. Data center.
19. File ownership.
20. Data ownership.
21. Media ownership.
22. Security procedures at data center.
23. Auditor access at data center.
24. Access at data center.
25. Hiring of employees.
26. Transfer of personnel.
27. Arbitration.
28. Insurance.
29. Back-up system availability.
30. Back-up files and programs.
31. Disaster recovery procedures.
32. Liquidated damages for failure to achieve service levels.
33. Confidentiality.
34. *Force majeure.*
35. Default and termination.
36. Termination for convenience.
37. Termination upon sale of business.
38. Post-termination assistance.
39. Continuity during dispute.
   - Pay fees into escrow account
40. Correction of errors.
41. Assignment.
42. Relationship.
43. Staff to be assigned.
44. Staff caliber.
45. Project manager.
46. Right to change staff.
47. No solicitation.
48. Indemnification.
   - By customer
   - By vendor
49. Survival.
50. Limitation of liability.
51. Severability.
52. Notices.
53. Amendments.

EXHIBIT 12 *(concluded)*　　Checklist of Clauses for an Outsourcing Agreement (Listing below does not imply that Xerox-EDS agreement includes these clauses.)

---

53. Amendments.
54. Headings not controlling.
55. Entire agreement.
56. Governing law.
57. Breach not waiver.
58. Publicity.
59. Management committee.
60. Taxes.
61. Representations and warranties.
    - No infringement

- Meet service levels
- Qualified personnel
62. Disclaimer
63. Performance review.
64. Counterparts.
65. Exhibits.
    - RFP, proposal, description of services, service levels, payment schedule, third-party contracts, customer software, employee list.

Source: John K. Halvey, Milbank, Tweed, Hadley and McCloy.

By focusing on the spirit of the relationship, and solving pricing and divorce issues early, the team had created an agreement that would allow them to integrate the two companies. Early indications of this success were noted by Dalal, who observed, "Today, in any meeting, you cannot tell who is from Xerox and who is from EDS. And it doesn't matter who leads the meeting because the objective is a common objective." Reed, too, addressed the success of integration: "Our check on what we do is always measured by 'is this providing value to Xerox?' We will not take additional revenue opportunities that don't provide value for Xerox."

Global Complexities

The global nature of the contract added greatly to its complexity. The team had to ensure that overseas Xerox units would be satisfied with the outsourcing deal. As noted by Halvey, global outsourcing deals were extremely complex:

There are additional concerns in any global deal. First, different countries have different human resource laws; these laws affect a wide variety of employee issues. For example, virtually all of these contracts contained some kind

of a COLA[18] provision. But if you were a vendor doing work in Brazil, where inflation could be 100 percent in a day, a typical COLA clause might have been unworkable. Second, the effect of a "force majeure"[19] event is a significant issue in all outsourcing contracts. While this is a problem at the domestic level as well, on a global basis firms faced a much greater degree of risk, particularly in terms of political instability and labor disputes. Third, asset transfer laws are different in each country. These differences can make it difficult to transfer hard assets like real estate. And, in many nations, the transfer of intellectual property, such as software, could create unexpected legal liabilities. Finally, dealing with the local telephone companies could be a challenge. . . . The list just goes on and on. The bottom line is, if you are going to do a global deal with someone, you have to trust them. I tell my clients that I can get them a state of the art termination clause, but if they have to use it, they are in a lot of trouble. In these kinds of deals legal victories are Pyrrhic.

---

[18]Cost of living adjustment.
[19]Force majeure events, resulting from certain contingencies, may excuse the vendor from contract performance. Examples of possible force majeure events include: delays caused by the other party, acts of God, war, labor disputes, and third-party nonperformance.

EXHIBIT 13   Scope of the Xerox/EDS
Outsourcing Deal

Data Center Operations

Operations and management of data centers
- Monroe County, NY (serving the United States, Canada, and Mexico)
- London, England
- Brazil
- Various "decentralized"

All print operations—centralized and decentralized—EDS in turn outsourced print operations to Xerox Business Systems on a subcontract

Network Operations

Operations and management of:
- Worldwide voice
- Worldwide data/video—WAN and LAN

Legacy Applications Maintenance and Enhancements

Production support of applications worldwide
Limited enhancements of applications worldwide

Infrastructure Support

Support of Information Management activities for the above platforms: includes worldwide desktop devices and Local Area Networks (6085s, Personal Computers)
- Help desk
- Software and hardware support (move, add, change)

Source: Xerox presentation by J. Dalal.

To ensure that global issues were adequately addressed, Graham Rudge, director of global process and information management and CIO of Rank Xerox, the company's European subsidiary, was added to the outsourcing team. In the end, Xerox was able to create a single global contract that could be implemented locally in each of the 130 countries in which the company operated. For example, in order to contend with currency fluctuations, Xerox created a "price book"

EXHIBIT 14   The Core Xerox and EDS
Outsourcing Teams

The Core Xerox Outsourcing Team

Jagdish Dalal	Lead Outsourcing Manager, Xerox
Richard Bailey	Formerly an IM manager in Xerox's U.S. Customer Operations Division
Charles Gilliam	Corporate Counsel

The Core EDS Outsourcing Team

Mike Reed	Lead Outsourcing Manager, EDS
Will Clark	Proposal Manager
John Funk	Corporate Lawyer

---

system that dynamically adjusted IM prices to ensure that Xerox groups in other countries were better off after implementation of the outsourcing agreement. For most services, prices for each country were in local currencies, not dollars, and were benchmarked against the local economy. IM managers felt that if they allowed groups in other countries to become dissatisfied with outsourcing efforts, significant problems could result. As Bailey noted:

> Theoretically, we could have told them that this was how it was going to be. But if we screwed it up and it messed up their business results, they'd be impossible to control. It was in our own self-interest to make sure they were involved and taken care of properly.

Implementing the Outsourcing Agreement

In mid-1994, the integration of EDS and Xerox was proceeding smoothly, largely because of the sense of partnership. Reed commented on the process:

> In a typical outsourcing deal the announcement is made one day, and the people are told,

"Tomorrow you all work at EDS." That is the wrong way to outsource. It can take you a year to try to get everyone back up to speed because you just destroyed their trust. What we did at Xerox was identify the leadership that would be transitioning to EDS, and then empowered them to participate in the transitioning and integration of their employees. This made the transition date, when the people and assets from Xerox officially moved to EDS, unimportant because everything had already begun to move forward.

Within Xerox the outsourcing effort was to be implemented as part of the overall IM 2000 reengineering effort. For example, a portion of the money saved via outsourcing was to be used to move the company away from legacy systems. Suzanne Higgins, leader of the IM 2000 project's management processes team, explained, "This [fund] was for new projects; new things, nothing that would be enhancing the legacy systems would be funded out of these dollars." The 700 IM professionals who remained at Xerox would focus their efforts on the four recommended IM 2000 strategies (identified earlier) as they moved forward.

EDS had created a separate global strategic business unit dedicated solely to Xerox. Reed was trying to structure this unit in a non-hierarchical way. He knew that he needed to create an environment that fostered cooperation because, "when you have a globally diverse group, you have no alternative; you must cooperate, or you can't operate."

According to Dalal, it was important to differentiate among three outsourcing terms: "Transition is the event of officially moving IM over to EDS; migration refers to the activities and process that lead to a successful transition; integration is the process of bringing the two companies together over time" (see Exhibit 15). Dalal and Reed knew that long-term success depended on the degree of integration achieved by the two organizations. According to Dalal:

> For the integration to be successful five dimensions had to be addressed: culture, strategy, structure, people, and process. We created a set of EDS/Xerox teams to focus on each of these dimensions from a quality perspective. For example, we have a team that identified current and future processes; their challenge is to work on the transition from one to the other. To capture the relationship's potential economic value we must emphasize integration. My organizing model for systems integration uses "degree of integration" on one axis and "opportunity for integration" on the other. Our agreement with EDS contains a lot of opportunity for integration; therefore, we will realize substantial economic value if we can achieve commitment to a high degree of integration. It is the spirit of the agreement that creates this commitment; there are no "mechanisms" that can be put into place as a substitute for the spirit. For example, after we were done with the pricing mechanisms, we discovered that there was a whole class of users that we had not priced correctly. We sat down with EDS and constructed a whole new set of prices and published them. The word *outsource* does not really describe this relationship. Mike Reed and I believe that what we have done is hand a Xerox function over to EDS, which they now manage for us. And Xerox doesn't really have an outsourcing management organization; EDS was enfranchised by our commitment to integration.

Issues To Be Clarified
While the outsourcing process had been a valuable learning experience (see Exhibit 16 for a "lessons learned" list), the integration process was only beginning in late 1994. The partners were working on many important issues, including:

1. *Structure.* Both sides were still working on their organizational structures. (See Exhibit 17 for the initial Xerox

EXHIBIT 15   Xerox*EDS Integration

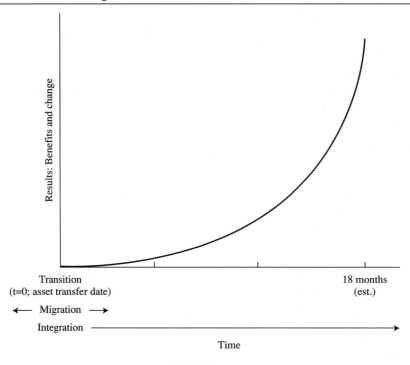

Definition:

Transition: Specific point in time at which accountability and ownership are transferred to EDS

Migration: Actions that support changes in strategy, structure, people, process, and culture designed to create the new X*EDS organization

Integration: Gradual alignment of strategy, structure, people, process, and culture

Source: Xerox presentation by J. Dalal.

post-outsourcing IM structure.) In response to this need for initial governance mechanisms, Xerox IM had set up what it called "framework teams." "There's a framework team around applications, there's a framework team around telecommunications, there's a framework team around infrastructure. They are jointly being run," explained a manager. But the details of how the IM 2000 transition teams and framework teams were

to interact with EDS still had to be worked out. As Dalal noted, "We're working on details that relate to the fine line of how some groups relate." The goal, according to Bailey, was to create "an integrated organization which would continue to serve Xerox, but under EDS management."

2. *IM operating processes.* Xerox and EDS were working together to define IM processes. Higgins explained, "We're

---

EXHIBIT 16   Lessons Learned

General Lessons

- The quality process works for outsourcing
- Good understanding of objectives and "what you want" is essential for good results
- A multidisciplinary team is a necessity
- A full-time project manager (with IM and business backgrounds) is a key success factor
- Activities and efforts take longer than expected
- A good contract requires a tremendous amount of data
- Collection and identification of pre-outsourcing cost data is critical
- Employee communication is a key success factor
- The vendor management process must be subject to strict discipline

Global Lessons

- Global integration of IM is necessary for a global contract
- Acceptance of a global IM strategy is a necessity for common contract development
- Global consistency of IM measurement is a necessity
- Economic differences prevent a global pricing methodology without significant effort on part of both the companies
- Vendors/Consultants are not yet experienced in managing a global outsourcing contract
- Local legal requirements (for Human Resources and billing) require thorough research and understanding before a global outsourcing contact is developed

Critical Success Factors

- Existence of a multiyear, total IM strategy
- Corporate commitment to the IM strategy
- Corporate commitment to outsourcing, where the process defines the results
- Quality culture and "Team Xerox" attitude
- Not being bound by "this is how it is done"

Source: Xerox presentation by J. Dalal.

---

taking the best practices from both. [If] EDS has a process that they've already got defined and working, we'll examine it."

3. *Management processes.* While the contract specified, in part, the measures to be used to judge EDS's effectiveness, the actual management processes to be used required finalization. In addition, incentive systems for the relationship still needed to be worked out.

4. *Human resource management.* The roles of IM workers would be further clarified as management and business processes were selected. For example, to what extent would IM managers need to become negotiators and coaches in addition to their duties as technologists or administrators?

Since these areas were interdependent, it was believed that the relationship would take many months to reach a stable form.

EXHIBIT 17   Global Process and Information Management Structure as of January 1995

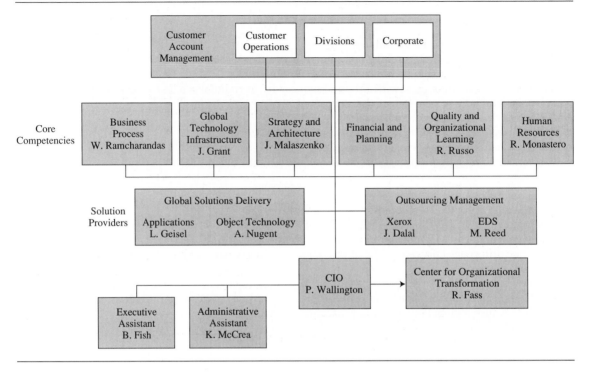

Case 4–2

GENERAL DYNAMICS AND COMPUTER SCIENCES CORPORATION: OUTSOURCING THE IS FUNCTION (A+B, ABRIDGED)[1]

It was June 1991, just over a year since Computer Sciences Corporation (CSC) and

This case was prepared by Research Associate Katherine N. Seger under the supervision of Professor F. Warren McFarlan.

[1]Copyright © 1993 by the President and Fellows of Harvard College.

Harvard Business school case 193-178.

General Dynamics had first come into contact at a conference on information systems outsourcing. Now, the two companies were attempting to negotiate what could be the largest information systems outsourcing deal in history, dwarfing the 1989 Kodak outsourcing mega-contract both in size and complexity.

In the proposed arrangement, General Dynamics would sell its information systems organization, the Data Systems Division (DSD), to Computer Sciences Corporation; in addition, the staff of DSD would be transferred to CSC to continue to operate the data center assets. CSC would then use this capacity to provide information services to General Dynamics as well as other clients.

It was an excellent opportunity for General Dynamics to continue to get superior information services at even lower cost while monetizing fixed assets and providing more flexibility for the future. In addition, General Dynamics considered the arrangement to be a valuable career opportunity for the employees of the Data Systems Division to enter a growth business in information services by joining CSC. The deal provided a brilliant opportunity for CSC to significantly enter the commercial information systems outsourcing market and achieve its corporate goal of gaining more commercial clients.

Ace Hall, corporate vice president, information systems and administrative services, and Larry Feuerstein, vice president planning and quality assurance, were the managers of the General Dynamics Data Systems Division who had been involved in developing the deal with Van Honeycutt, president of CSC's Industry Services Group. Over 15 long months, these executives and their staffs had worked together to develop a plan that could benefit both companies.

Now, they were entering more serious negotiations, and they focused on defining a plan for outsourcing the Data Systems Division which could be presented at the next General Dynamics Board of Directors meeting.

General Dynamics Company Background

General Dynamics, headquartered in St. Louis, Missouri, was the second-largest defense conglomerate in America. It provided tactical military aircraft, submarines, missile and electronics systems, armored vehicles, and space launch vehicles to the U.S. government. Its high-tech weapons systems included the Trident submarine, the M-1 tank, the F-16 fighter plane, and the Tomahawk cruise missile. In addition, General Dynamics owned and operated several smaller commercial subsidiaries. In the years of Cold War defense buildup, General Dynamics enjoyed a thriving defense market and sales grew to an all-time high of $10.2 billion in 1990.

In 1991, General Dynamics was composed of seven aerospace and defense divisions (Exhibit 1). Its four core defense groups were Space Launch Systems, Missiles and Electronics, Military Aircraft, and Marine and Land Systems. In addition, the company had two non-defense operations—the Resources group and Cessna Aircraft. Finally, General Dynamics defined its own information systems organization as a separate division—the Data Systems Division.

- The Space Systems Division designed, manufactured, and supported space launch vehicles that carried defense and communications satellites into orbit around the earth.
- The Missiles and Electronics Group was mainly composed of two separate businesses. The Missile Systems business designed and manufactured air defense products such as the Tomahawk cruise missile, the Advanced Cruise Missile, the Sparrow, the Stinger, and the Phalanx gun system. The Electronics business produced avionics test equipment and provided information systems for the U.S. Air Force and radio systems for the Army. In addition, it designed and manufactured digital imagery and signal processing equipment for intelligence information gathering.

EXHIBIT 1 General Dynamics Divisions, 1991

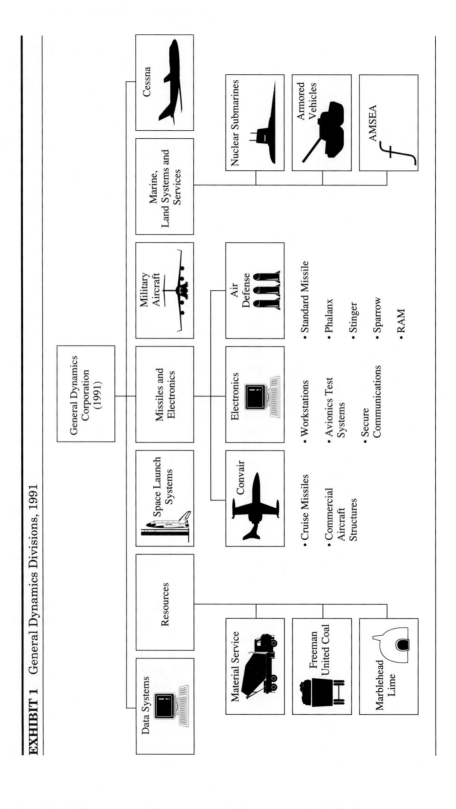

- The Military Aircraft Group designed and manufactured tactical aircraft. Its strongest product was the F-16 fighter, which served as the backbone of America's tactical aircraft fleet and was sold to other nations around the globe. In addition, the division had an equal share with Lockheed and Boeing in the design of the F-22 fighter, the next generation of tactical aircraft.
- The Marine and Land Systems Group was composed of two businesses. The Electric Boat Division was the nation's leading designer and builder of nuclear submarines. In 1991, the U.S. Navy awarded Electric Boat the contract to build SSN22, the second ship in the *Seawolf* class. The Land Systems Division designed and built land defense systems such as M1Al Abrams main battle tank
- The Resources Group was composed of three commercial operations. The Material Service Corporation produced aggregates, ready-mix concrete and concrete pipe. Marblehead Lime produced lime for use in the steel industry and building materials. Freeman United Coal was a coal mining operation.
- Cessna Aircraft was a subsidiary that designed and manufactured small private business jets.
- The Data Systems Division (DSD) supported the company's corporate information systems and provided information services to all of General Dynamics's aerospace and defense divisions. (See below for more detail on DSD.)

The Board of Directors of General Dynamics totaled 16 members, comprising seven General Dynamics insiders and nine outsiders. The chairman and chief executive officer of the company was William A. Anders, who had joined General Dynamics in 1990 as vice chairman and then became chairman in January of 1991. Prior to joining GD, Anders had been an astronaut on the Apollo 8 mission around the moon, the executive secretary of the National Aeronautics and Space Council, chairman of the Nuclear Regulatory Commission, ambassador to Norway, and an executive at two large industrial manufacturing companies.

The fall of the Berlin Wall in 1989 marked the beginning of the end of the Cold War. In 1991, communism collapsed in the Soviet Union; by 1992, the Soviet Union had crumbled into a federation of independent states. With the end of the Cold War, a growing federal deficit, and a troubled domestic economy, the United States government began to reduce procurement spending on military power from a high of $96.8 billion in fiscal 1985 to $54.4 billion in fiscal 1993,[2] causing the market for defense products and weapons to shrink dramatically. (See Exhibit 2 for a 100-year history of defense spending.)

This reduction in the defense market led to extreme overcapacity among suppliers and financial troubles for companies throughout the defense industry. In 1990, General Dynamics posted a loss from continuing operations of $674 million. (See Exhibit 3 for financial summaries.) There seemed to be two major strategies for surviving this sharp decline in the defense market: (1) diversify capacity into commercial markets, or (2) downsize to a level that could be supported by a smaller defense market.

1991 GD Corporate Strategy

In 1991, Anders's top priorities for General Dynamics were to increase shareholder value and build financial strength and

---

[2]Eric J. Savitz, "Hold the Taps for Defense Stocks," *Barron's* 72 (August 3, 1992).

EXHIBIT 2   100 Years of U.S. Defense Spending*

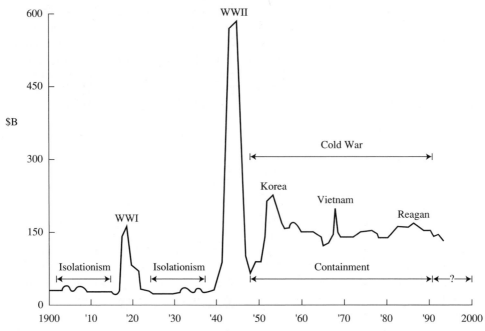

*In 1982 dollars.

flexibility for the uncertain future. In this year's annual report, Anders wrote,

> Studies by outside consultants and by us clearly show that diversification by defense companies into commercial enterprises histori- cally has had unacceptably high failure rates. . . . We believe that the process of widespread conversion of defense resources to commercial use at General Dynamics, while an alluring concept, is generally not practical. Instead, we are sticking to what we know best, and are therefore focusing more sharply on our core defense competencies.

This policy was part of Anders's philoso- phy of defense industry rationalization which he had refined during his first year as General Dynamics's CEO. Anders believed that defense companies could survive the changing marketplace only if the industry sufficiently downsized to meet the reduced

demand. Overcapacity must be shed (not merely diversified) and the industry must consolidate so that individual companies could obtain a "critical mass" of the market in order to maintain profitability.

In his 1991 letter to shareholders, Anders outlined three criteria for maintaining the strength of General Dynamics' individual businesses. For a business to remain viable, it must be within GD's core defense compe- tency, it must be no. 1 or no. 2 in its field, and it must have a "critical mass" to ensure effi- ciency, economies of scale, and financial strength given the future business volumes available.[3] For businesses that did not fit these criteria, Anders's policy was "Buy, Sell, or Merge." In addition, Anders launched an aggressive campaign to increase General

---

[3]From *GD 1991 Annual Report.*

EXHIBIT 3   General Dynamics Financial Highlights

General Dynamics Financial Highlights
(dollars in millions, except per share and sales per employee amounts)

	1991	1990	1989
Summary of Operations			
Net sales[a]	$ 8,751	$ 9,457	$ 9,442
Operating costs and expenses	8,359	10,374	8,934
Interest, net	−34	−62	−73
Provision (credit) for income taxes	−43	−366	134
Earnings (loss) from continuing operation	374	−674	269
Net earnings (loss) per share			
Continuing operations[a]	8.93	−16.17	6.44
Discontinued operations	3.13	2.31	0.57
Capital expenditures[a]	82	306	411
Research and development[a]			
Company sponsored	162	353	438
Customer sponsored[b]	601	510	506
Total	$ 763	$ 863	$ 944
At Year End			
Total backlog[a]	$ 25,597	$ 22,151	$ 27,688
Shareholders' equity	1,980	1,510	2,126
Total assets	6,207	5,830	6,049
Number of employees	80,600	98,100	102,200
Sales per employee[a]	116,200	101,700	96,400
Other Information			
Purchases of property, plant, equipment	82	306	411
Depreciation, depletion, and amortization	303	370	352
Salaries and wages	$ 3,204	$ 3,433	$ 3,311

[a]Data exclude Cessna Aircraft Company.
[b]Data exclude A-12 R&D expenditures.

Dynamics' shareholder value. He instituted an executive compensation plan with heavy rewards for increased stock prices, and he sought out opportunities to monetize assets and generate more cash

Larry Feuerstein commented on the power of Anders's corporate strategy within General Dynamics:

Anders was *really* pushing his strategy out to all the executives and managers in the company. This was *the* business strategy of General

Dynamics, and it was reinforced daily for every employee Anders ever came in contact with. This was his singular focus.

It was with this corporate strategy in place that Larry Feuerstein and Ace Hall of GD's Data Systems Division began to look at outsourcing as a possible option for the future of the company's IS organization. As Feuerstein noted,

General Dynamics is in the defense business, and data processing, admittedly, is not one of

EXHIBIT 3 (continued)   General Dynamics Consolidated Balance Sheet

General Dynamics Consolidated Balance Sheet (dollars in millions)

	31-Dec	
	1991	*1990*
ASSETS		
Current Assets:		
Cash and equivalents	$ 513	$ 109
Marketable securities	307	—
	$ 820	$ 109
Accounts receivable	444	353
Contracts in process	2,606	2,843
Other current assets	449	288
Total current assets	$4,319	$3,593
Noncurrent Assets:		
Leases receivable—finance operations	$ 266	$ 287
Property, plant and equipment, net	1,029	1,411
Other assets	593	539
Total noncurrent assets	$1,888	$2,237
	$6,207	$5,830
LIABILITIES AND SHAREHOLDERS' EQUITY		
Current Liabilities:		
Current portion of long-term debt	$ 455	$ 1
Short-term debt-finance operations	61	65
Accounts payable and other current liabilities	2,593	2,279
Deferred income taxes	—	326
Total current liabilities	$3,109	$2,671
Noncurrent Liabilities:		
Long-term debt	$ 168	$ 619
Long-term debt-finance operations	197	264
Other liabilities	753	766
Total noncurrent liabilities	$1,118	$1,649
Shareholders' Equity:		
Common stock	$ 55	$ 55
Capital surplus	25	25
Retained earnings	2,651	2,195
Treasury stock	−751	−765
Total shareholders' equity	$1,980	$1,510
	$6,207	$5,830

our core businesses. This is a great example of MIS really getting in line with corporate strategy. You read a lot about this, but rarely find such crisp examples of it really happening.

IT at General Dynamics: The Data Systems Division

Information technology was critically important to the operations of General Dynamics. Larry Feuerstein described computer technology as "the lifeblood" of GD's product units. Sophisticated computer systems were used in the operating units for product engineering, simulation, and manufacturing. Many of GD's products (such as "smart" cruise missiles) also had microcomputers installed directly within them. These proprietary embedded systems offered strategic advantage for GD's product lines. In addition, large computer systems were used to manage the company's business data in areas such as accounting, payroll, and inventory management. Information technology supported all aspects of General Dynamics operations; the quality and reliability of these information systems were crucial to the success of the company.

Prior to 1972, the information systems capabilities of General Dynamics were widely dispersed in the various business units of the company. In 1972, a study by Arthur Andersen recommended the consolidation of these facilities into regional centers to achieve more efficient and effective use of these resources. By 1976 this consolidation was complete, and the resulting organization—Data Systems Services—comprised three regional centers in San Diego, California; Fort Worth, Texas; and Norwich, Connecticut. At this time the organization had 1,488 employees and was operated solely as a cost center. (See Exhibit 4 for DSD growth history.)

Larry Feuerstein joined the Data Systems Services management staff in 1976 at the Norwich center as it was being formed. Feuerstein recalls his experience at this time of organizational change as being excellent preparation for his role in the CSC outsourcing decision and implementation: "There was major turmoil. I saw the pain of changing relationships, fundamental restructuring, and consolidation. It was an important experience which I've drawn on throughout this CSC deal."

In 1981, the Data Systems Services organization was elevated to the status of an operating business unit, and its name was changed to Data Systems Division (DSD). The charter for the DSD stated:

> The Data Systems Division provides corporatewide guidance for, direction to, and management of the company's information resources and the information services required by the company's business units.

The DSD Management Vision stated:

> Working together as part of the General Dynamics Team, our people are recognized leaders in providing high-quality, cost-effective, information solutions to make our Company's processes and products the best in the world, improve competitiveness, and enhance shareholder value.

The Data Systems Division had two main areas of responsibility: (1) the companywide direction of information resource strategies, policies, procedures, and standards; and (2) the provision of a full range of information services to General Dynamics operating units, including computer systems development, data processing for business systems, computer-aided design and manufacturing systems (CAD/CAM), engineering systems, and development of software that is embedded and delivered in General Dynamics products.[4]

---

[4]From GD company records.

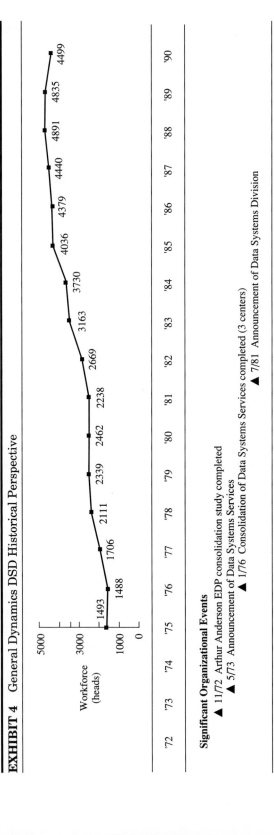

EXHIBIT 4 General Dynamics DSD Historical Perspective

Significant Organizational Events

▲ 11/72 Arthur Anderson EDP consolidation study completed

▲ 5/73 Announcement of Data Systems Services

▲ 1/76 Consolidation of Data Systems Services completed (3 centers)

▲ 7/81 Announcement of Data Systems Division

Source: General Dynamics Company Records.

498

The Data Systems Division facilities were located in the 3 large regional centers and 28 smaller service sites around the country. Hardware included 13 IBM mainframes, 3 Amdahl mainframes, a Univac mainframe, 2 Cyber scientific mainframes, a Cray scientific supercomputer, and 440 minicomputers. In addition 3,700 engineering workstations and over 15,000 desktop microcomputers were scattered throughout the company's divisions. DSD operated three interconnected network layers—wide area, campus area, and work group. Capabilities included CAD/CAM, manufacturing, business applications, logistics, systems integration, electronic data interchange (EDI), distributed processing, and training total processing capacity for DSD was more than 1,000 MIPS (millions of instructions per second). The write-off lifetime for these fixed assets was a five-year accelerated depreciation for computer equipment and a five-year linear depreciation for software. In 1991, the DSD assets (including real estate, equipment, computer hardware, and licensed software) had a net book value of $140 million.

The Data Systems Division was staffed by highly skilled professional computer technicians and programmers. Their educations and careers were in information systems, and their salaries and benefits were competitive with IS professionals in other companies and industries. The majority of the DSD staff was located at the three regional centers or satellite service centers, with only a few (2 to 50) information systems people at each of GD's product division sites. These people served primarily as liaisons to the DSD service providers in the regional centers. When Ace Hall came in from General Dynamics' Corporate Planning Department to become general manager of the division in 1984, DSD had grown to 3,730 employees. In 1989, DSD reached its peak of 4,835 employees. By 1991, the staff had been reduced to 3,400.[5] The DSD staff had been downsized in response to the shrinking defense market, mainly through attrition, reduced recruitment and hiring, and the elimination of selected positions. According to Larry Feuerstein, "We saw the market conditions and we knew we were going to have to cut costs. We tried to manage downsizing in an orderly way, to avoid having to reduce the head count abruptly."

Each of the three regional data centers (West, Central and East) served mainly the operating units in its region, giving each its own unique "clientele." A sophisticated charge-back billing system enabled the DSD to operate as a self-liquidating cost center. (See Exhibit 5 for DSD cost flow chart.) Larry Feuerstein commented on the meticulous accounting of costs in DSD's billing system:

> DSD was a cost center operation for General Dynamics, but it was organized and managed like an independent business. We knew where to charge every cost we incurred. Most "garden variety" in-house IS departments are not organized like this. They have all kinds of costs commingled and buried in the "overhead" category.

DSD identified four main categories of costs within its structure—Professional Services, Computer Utility, Dedicated Resources, and Overhead Costs:

Professional Services included human services such as systems development, programming, consulting, and CAD/CAM.

Computer Utility was data processing on shared mainframe systems. These two categories were "rated"—GD divisions were charged at a given rate per unit of work for the amount of these resources consumed.

---

[5]Of this number, approximately 800 individuals were assigned specifically to the development and installation of technology directly embedded in GD's products.

EXHIBIT 5   General Dynamics DSD Sample Flow Chart (1987)

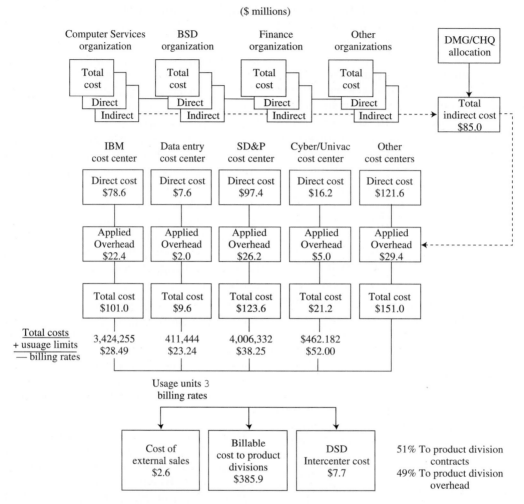

Notes:

Direct Costs are services directly consumed by GD business units.

Indirect Costs are DSD overhead costs.

The organizations across the top of the chart are departments of DSD which incur costs.

- The **Computer Services Organization** manages the computer utility.
- The **Business Systems Division (BSD) Organization** manages Professional Services.
- The **Finance Organization** managed DSD finances, and was considered an overhead department; it thus had "direct costs" of zero.

The middle portion of the chart shows various cost categories for billing purposes.

- The **IBM Cost Center** contains Computer Utility Costs for GD business systems.
- The **Data Entry Cost Center** contains non-professional data entry services. These costs are rated by man-hour, in the same way as Professional Services.
- The **SD&P (Systems Development and Programming) Cost Center** contains Professional Services costs.
- The **Cyber/Univac Cost Center** contains Computer Utility costs for GD scientific and engineering systems.

EXHIBIT 5 *(concluded)*   General Dynamics DSD Sample Flow Chart (1987)

The bottom of the chart shows the different consumers who are billed for DSD services.
- The majority of DSD services are used by **GD Product Divisions.** Of these billed costs, 51% were charged directly to government contracts; the remaining 49% were considered product division overhead. This 51% figure was very favorable by industry standards.
- DSD provided limited services to outside clients as **External Sales,** but these sales were negligible.
- **DSD Intercenter Costs** accounted for work done by one DSD data center for another DSD data center. It was an accounting elimination tool to eliminate double charges.

Source: General Dynamics company records.

The rates[6] in these categories were determined by dividing the total cost to DSD in each category by the total units used in each. (The units used to define Professional Services rates were work-hours; the units used to define Computer Utility were volume units of processing resources.) The rate was then charged to each division for the particular amount of each cost category it consumed. These rates were reviewed monthly and adjusted at least quarterly by data center finance managers. Throughout the year, the divisions were charged at these *estimated provisional rates.* At the end of each year, the *actual rate* was calculated, and the divisions were charged or credited accordingly. According to Feuerstein, "The job of a good financial manager is to make sure the estimated rates are as close to the actual rate as possible. The division managers (our 'clients') want the adjustment at the end of the year to be small—and they want it to be a credit, not a charge. Generally, our financial managers were good at their estimate adjustments."

Dedicated Resources included dedicated, division-unique (not shared) computer

equipment and resources. These costs were "non-shared"; each business unit was charged directly at DSD cost incurred for these specific devices.

Finally, DSD *Overhead Costs* were fully allocated to the divisions as a percentage of total direct costs in each cost category. DSD divided its total overhead costs by the total of their direct service costs to get the overhead percentage. All of DSD's overhead was then applied at this percentage to the other cost categories and included in the determination of rates charged to the divisions. In the non-rated category, overhead was applied as a percentage of the division's non-rated costs.

Describing the charge-out structure of DSD, Feuerstein commented on the success and importance of this complex system:

> This was a system that was well understood and accepted by the product division managers. They were used to it, they were generally comfortable with it, and it was predictable. In addition, the government accepted it. The Defense Contract Audit Agency looks over these charges with a fine-toothed comb, and they were comfortable with the existing structure.

DSD's total billable costs in 1991 were $375 million. Projected costs for 1992 were $370 million.[7] The breakdown of these 1992

---

[6]Within the Computer Utility cost category, DSD identified eight different rates for resources such as disk usage, tape drive usage, and processor usage. In the Professional Services category, however, DSD identified only one rate per hour of professional time without differentiating the skill level or specific task of the professional.

[7]These DSD cost figures did not include the 800 programmers located in GD product divisions who developed product-embedded software. These software engineers were considered product division overhead.

costs by category (including overhead, which was projected to be 18% of direct costs) was as follows:

Professional Services ("rated"): systems development, CAD/CAM, consulting	$ 80 million
Computer Utility/Processing Services ("rated"): mainframe resources, tapes, disks	$ 82 million
Dedicated Resources ("non-rated"): dedicated division-unique resources and equipment	$208 million
TOTAL COST to GD	$370 million

General Dynamics Data Systems Division was widely considered to be a highly successful operation. For example, in 1989 and 1990, *Computerworld Premier 100* rated DSD number one in the aerospace industry based on its "clearly stated IS management vision, strong commitment to IS quality, strong user role in defining applications, and advanced factory-automation applications."[8] In spite of its outstanding service, however, DSD suffered, along with the rest of General Dynamics, from the sharp decline in the defense market. The reductions in the DSP head count and billings reflected this downturn in the industry.

With the new realities of the shrinking defense market, Hall began in 1990 to evaluate the future viability of the Data Systems Division. To address this issue, GD brought in a major general management consulting firm to do a strategic assessment of General Dynamics' information systems organizational structure.

Prior to the inception of this study, Ace Hall had sent Bob DeLargy, DSD vice president of finance, and Ken Wang, DSD direc-

tor of systems integration, to a March 1990 conference on information systems outsourcing, which was emerging as an important trend in the information services field. Since the landmark 1989 Kodak outsourcing arrangement in which Kodak outsourced a large part of its business systems to three vendors, outsourcing had gained much attention and recognition as an important alternative solution for managing information services in the competitive economy of the 1990s. As more and more companies struggled to downsize and focus on their core businesses, outsourcing offered them a way to meet their information services needs without having to own and operate an information services business. Outsourcing was seen as an opportunity for companies to transform fixed overhead into variable costs, and free themselves from capital expenditures on information systems in an environment of rapidly changing technology. Companies found that they could receive better services at a lower cost while freeing up precious financial resources by outsourcing their IS needs to information systems experts At the outsourcing conference, Dekargy and Wang heard a presentation by a corporate senior vice president of Computer Sciences Corporation who introduced CSC's outsourcing framework.

CSC Company Background

Computer Sciences Corporation, headquartered in El Segundo, California, was a leader in the information technology systems and services industry, with clients in both the federal and private sectors. The company described its business as follows:

> Computer Sciences Corporation (CSC) solves client problems in information systems technology. Its broad-based services range from management consulting in the strategic use of information and information technology to

---

[8]Mitch Betts, *Computerworld Premier 100,* October 8, 1990.

the development and operation of complete information systems. A leader in software development and systems integration, CSC designs, integrates, installs, and operates computer-based systems and communications systems. It also provides multidisciplinary engineering support to high-technology operations and specialized proprietary services to various markets. The company manufactures no equipment.[9]

In 1991, CSC had over 23,000 employees and was composed of four major business groups: the Systems Group, the Industry Services Group, the Consulting Group and CSC Europe.

The Systems Group was CSC's largest operating entity and major technological resource. It provided software, systems development, and systems operations primarily to the U.S. government. This federal client base consisted of hundreds of contracts with a wide range of the government's administrative, scientific, and military agencies, including NASA, the EPA, the National Weather Service, the Postal Service, the Air Force, the Navy, and the Army. The Systems Group had extensive experience specifically in the development of software for aerospace and defense systems, satellite communications, intelligence, logistics, and related high-technology fields. In 1990, the Systems Group's federal contracts accounted for 66 percent of CSC's total revenue. CSC was known as the premier contractor of information systems services to the U.S. government. With the Systems Group as its largest unit, the company had developed much of its expertise on large-scale government systems.

CSC's commercial customers were served primarily by its Industry Services Group and its Consulting Group. The Industry Services Group handled information ser-

vices, including facilities management and systems operations, for health care, insurance, and financial-services customers. The Consulting Group (comprising subsidiaries such as CSC Index and CSC Partners) worked with businesses to develop strategic plans for information technology and to design and implement integrated computer and communications systems that would fully support the customer's management objectives. (See Exhibit 6 for CSC organization chart.)

CSC was a successful and strong company. In 1991, the company set records in revenue and earnings from operations. Worldwide commercial revenue increased 32 percent from $508 million to $668 million, and federal revenues increased 8 percent from $993 million to $1.07 billion, resulting in a total revenue of $1.74 billion in 1991, up 16 percent from the previous year's $1.5 billion. (See Exhibit 7 for financial summaries.) CSC also had an excellent record of capturing new business opportunities. Over the period 1985–1990, the company won 54 percent of new federal contracts it bid on.

CSC's success was due to three decades of experience in software development and information systems management, combined with comprehensive knowledge of the information and application requirements of various industries and highly specialized government activities. The company had a deep and rich base of knowledge to bring to bear on information problems in both the public and private sectors. In addition, CSC differentiated itself in the information services market by its strong focus on quality and client satisfaction. According to William Hoover, chairman, president, and CEO,

Performance management and client satisfaction are the dominant factors that have differentiated CSC in the industry. We have a high reputation for quality performance and

---

[9]From CSC Annual Report, 1990.

EXHIBIT 6   CSC Organization Chart

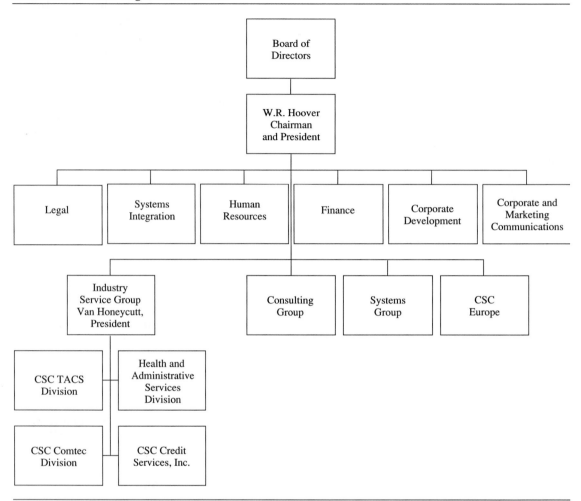

delivering the systems that our clients ask us to build.[10]

In 1991, Computer Sciences Corporation was governed by an eight-person Board of Directors, comprising three CSC insiders (President William Hoover, the chief financial officer, and the president of the Systems Group) and five members from other organizations.

CSC Corporate Strategy

1991 marked the end of a five-year period in which CSC's main goals had been to improve its financial strength and increase its presence in the commercial information services market.[11] Over the period, the company had succeeded in steadily increasing its revenue every year by an average of 15 to 16 percent.

---

[10]From an interview with William Hoover in *CEO Interviews,* May 1, 1989.

[11]Cowan and Company, *Perspectives,* August 1989, p. 2.

EXHIBIT 7   Computer Sciences Corporation—Consolidated Balance Sheet (in thousands except shares)

	March 29, 1991
ASSETS	
Current assets:	
Cash and cash equivalents (note 1)	$ 73,304
Short-term investments, at cost	63,674
Receivables	443,447
Prepaid expenses and other current assets	37,403
Total current assets	$ 617,828
Investments and other assets:	
Excess of cost of businesses acquired over related net assets	$ 174,689
Purchased credit information files	34,664
Purchased software	9,918
Other assets	35,235
Total investments and other assets	$ 254,506
Property and equipment—at cost:	
Land, buildings and leasehold improvements	$ 92,520
Computers and related equipment	104,297
Furniture and other equipment	54,709
	$ 251,526
Less accumulated depreciation and amortization	117,039
Net property and equipment	$ 134,487
	$1,006,821
LIABILITIES AND STOCKHOLDERS' EQUITY	
Current liabilities:	
Notes payable to banks	$ 28,864
Current maturities of long-term debt	3,828
Accounts payable	53,785
Accrued payroll and related costs	98,536
Other accrued expenses	56,611
Federal, state, and foreign income taxes	113,339
Total current liabilities	$ 354,963
Long-term debt, net of current maturities	$ 108,867
Other long-term liabilities	$ 16,765
Total stockholders' equity	$ 526,226
	$1,006,821

EXHIBIT 7 (continued)   Computer Sciences Corporation—Consolidated Statement of Earnings
(in thousands except per-share amounts)

	Fiscal Year Ended		
	March 29, 1991	*March 30, 1990*	*March 31, 1989*
Revenues	$1,737,791	$1,500,443	$1,304,414
Expenses			
Costs of services	$1,436,052	$1,230,930	$1,067,189
Operating overhead	131,512	118,594	98,885
Depreciation and amortization	40,203	34,014	31,090
	$1,607,767	$1,383,538	$1,197,164
Operating income	130,024	116,905	107,250
Corporate general and administrative expenses	23,376	20,945	19,416
Other expense (income)—net	4,106	(7,240)	3,370
	$ 27,482	$ 13,705	$ 22,786
Income before taxes	102,542	103,200	84,464
Taxes on income	37,551	37,668	31,982
Net earnings	$ 64,991	$ 65,532	$ 52,482
Earnings per common share	$ 4.02	$ 4.07	$ 3.28

The company had also made significant progress in increasing its commercial business. In 1989, U.S. commercial revenue accounted for 19 percent of CSC's total revenue; in 1990, U.S. commercial revenue rose to 21 percent; and in 1991, it was at 24 percent of the company's total revenue. (See Exhibit 8 on revenue distribution by markets.) As William Hoover predicted in 1989,

> We're going to see a shift in our customer mix from the federal sector to the non-federal sector. We have a strong emphasis right now in taking our technology base and our project management base that we developed in the federal sector in communications/computer systems integration and applying that to the emerging needs of commercial organizations in the United States and Europe—the Fortune 500 and large corporations that have broad, diversified information systems requirements.[12]

---

[12]From an interview with William Hoover in *CEO Interviews,* May 1, 1989.

While the company's revenue distribution in commercial markets was growing, CSC still was not considered a dominant leader in commercial information services in 1991. As Van Honeycutt described it, "Whenever anyone listed the top providers of information services to commercial industry, CSC seldom made the elite list." One reason for CSC's slowness in entering this market, according to Honeycutt, was actually a positive—its long history and reputation as the premier provider of information services to the U.S. government. According to its 1991 annual report, the company's goal in the commercial sector was to be one of the industry's top three professional services firms.

The General Dynamics deal was a brilliant opportunity for CSC because it would allow the company to achieve this goal. A contract of that size would immediately place CSC among the top four providers of information services to commercial industry. In addition, company officials believed that

EXHIBIT 8   Computer Sciences Corporation—Revenue Distribution by Market

Fiscal Year	*1991*	*1990*	*1989*
Defense Department	32%	35%	39%
NASA	14	16	17
Civil agencies	16	15	17
Total federal government	62%	66%	73%
Commercial	24	21	19
State and local governments	2	3	3
International	12	10	5
Total for continuing operations	100%	100%	100%

Revenues by Group

In millions	*Federal Government*	*Commercial*	*State and Local Governments*	*International*	*Total*
Fiscal 1991					
Systems Group	$1,029.9	$ 12.2	$ 0.6	$ 3.3	$1,046.0
Consulting Group	9.8	151.4	8.7	201.0	370.9
Industry Services Group	30.3	259.4	31.2		320.9
Total	$1,070.0	$423.0	$40.5	$204.3	$1,737.8
Fiscal 1990					
Systems Group	$ 952.5	$ 12.5	$ 0.7	$ 0.5	$ 966.2
Consulting Group	9.9	108.6	10.7	146.8	276.0
Industry Services Group	30.4	196.7	31.1		258.2
Total	$ 992.8	$317.8	$42.5	$147.3	$1,500.4
Fiscal 1989					
Systems Group	$ 863.9	$ 9.6	$ 3.9	$ 3.7	$ 881.1
Consulting Group	2.4	80.9	1.8	58.7	143.8
Industry Services Group	29.9	144.1	31.3		205.3
Continuing Operations	$ 896.2	$234.6	$37.0	$ 62.4	$1,230.2
Operations Sold	25.2	32.9	0.1	16.0	74.2
Total	$ 921.4	$267.5	$37.1	$ 78.4	$1,304.4

the new assets acquired from GD would enable CSC to attract other new commercial customers.[13]

---

[13]Pauline Yoshihashi, "Computer Sciences Signs Pact to Provide Technical Services to General Dynamics," *Wall Street Journal,* September 24, 1991, p. A9:1.

History of Outsourcing Business at CSC

In the late 1980s, at the same time CSC was trying to grow its presence in commercial markets, information systems outsourcing was beginning to emerge as an important business trend. The landmark 1989 Kodak outsourcing arrangement in which Kodak outsourced a large part of its business systems to three vendors was, according to Honeycutt, the "big bang, the point from which outsourcing really took off." As outsourcing began to emerge in the information services industry, CSC had to decide how to address this new trend. It was definitely a business that the company wanted to be in, for it offered an excellent opportunity to serve commercial clients. But how to enter this new market?

In 1990, CSC decided to develop its outsourcing business in the part of the company which provided information services to commercial clients—the Industry Services Group. The Industry Services Group had a staff of approximately 3,500 professional information systems technicians and programmers operating in 5 data centers across the country. Their skills in data center management closely matched the skills needed to succeed in the outsourcing business. While CSC's Consulting Group had more commercial contacts, their skills were in strategic planning and development of information systems, not in the actual operation of those systems. It was the Industry Services Group that provided extensive, ongoing information processing services to commercial clients in such areas as insurance, financial services, and health care.

The two commercial groups in CSC, for example, worked with Bay State Health Care, the fastest-growing HMO in Massachusetts, to build an open systems architecture that would allow better customer service, faster communications, streamlined paperwork, and lower operating costs by mixing a wide range of technologies. They also enabled a leading Midwest lending firm to revamp its mainframe-driven, centralized system to create a decentralized, distributed system that put more computing power in the hands of users. A major West Coast insurance company drew on the Industry Services Group's systems and software expertise to speed the handling of claims for more than 250,000 members who submit an average of 100,000 claims per month. Hewlett-Packard turned to CSC to develop a logistics system to improve the efficiency of its repair parts operation. The system improved the availability of parts by streamlining the ordering and delivery process and improved methods of tracking inventory.

Van Honeycutt, president of the Industry Services Group, began by putting together a special marketing team to call on CSC Partners and Index customers. He recalled:

> We had several false starts, and no takers. There was a container company, for example, who decided to outsource their IS needs, but they ended up going to IBM because they were concerned about our government background. We stirred up a lot of dust, but no contracts.

Eventually CSC had the opportunity to buy a small IS outsourcing company in North Carolina called CompuSource, which served commercial clients. According to Honeycutt, "We bought it and added it to the Industry Services Group. This gave us some additional credibility in the commercial outsourcing market."

Honeycutt also worked with his marketing team to develop an outsourcing framework that would appeal to Fortune 500 companies. "We pretended we were a Fortune 500 company in trouble or looking to improve information systems effectiveness. What would we want to hear? What are our critical needs?" Out of this thinking, Honeycutt and his marketing team developed a framework for CSC's outsourcing service. They recognized that there were many vendors in the market who provided "outsourcing" with different definitions of the word. Most information services providers were "functional outsourcers" or "partial outsourcers"; they took on only one system or one portion of a company's overall information technology needs. Honeycutt decided to distinguish CSC in the market as the "total outsourcer." In an outsourcing agreement CSC would provide total information services to its clients by becoming a company's "information services partner." As Honeycutt explained,

> Outsourcing with CSC would be a transaction not at the functional level, but at the CEO and boardroom level. We become an integral partner of the company's senior management as we take over all responsibility for the company's information services needs. We become their IT resource.

After developing this marketing framework, Honeycutt worked to increase CSC's visibility in the outsourcing arena. CSC representatives gave speeches, participated in panels, and attended conferences to try to sell their outsourcing framework to the commercial market.

General Dynamics' Bob DeLargy, DSD vice president of finance, and Ken Wang, DSD director of systems integration, attended one such conference in March of 1990 where they heard one of Honeycutt's colleagues present CSC's outsourcing framework. This presentation was so compelling that DeLargy and Wang invited CSC to address the next DSD strategic planning meeting later that month to present their outsourcing framework as another potential option for the future of DSD.

The Outsourcing Decision

General Dynamics' interaction with CSC officially began when CSC was invited to present its "total outsourcing" framework to DSD management at its strategic planning session in March 1990. After this meeting, DSD management was impressed with CSC

and agreed that outsourcing as a possible solution for General Dynamics' information services needs warranted further study.

1990

Over the next several months, several key managers from CSC and DSD continued a dialogue on the subject of outsourcing, and eventually, the idea evolved into a proposed joint venture project between CSC and General Dynamics. In August of 1990, Van Honeycutt formally presented the joint venture concept to Ace Hall. He proposed a shared-equity business venture of which CSC would have the majority interest; the new business would provide information services to General Dynamics and other clients. Through the end of 1990, Hall, Feuerstein, and other DSD managers remained interested in the CSC proposal and arranged several meetings with Honeycutt and other CSC managers to refine the details of the concept.

January 1991

In January of 1991, William A. Anders became General Dynamics' new CEO after having spent a year as vice chairman. His top priorities as CEO were to increase shareholder value and build financial strength and flexibility to ensure the survival of General Dynamics in the shrinking defense market. To drive his corporate strategy, Anders brought in Harvey Kapnick as GD vice chairman. In addition, Anders formed a Corporate Executive Council of GD's top executives and division heads for the purpose of instilling his strategy throughout the company. For the Council's first meeting, in March of 1991, Anders assigned "homework" for each member—he asked them to bring to the meeting innovative ideas for implementing his corporate strategies and managing GD in the shrinking defense market of the future.

March 1991

At this council meeting, Ace Hall presented the idea of a joint venture with CSC to provide information services to GD and other clients. Anders and the Executive Council were interested in the proposal, and Jim Mellor, GD president and chief operating officer, asked Hall to present the CSC option at an upcoming meeting in May, at which the consulting firm was scheduled to present their findings and recommendations for GD's future information services structure.

May 1991

In what Larry Feuerstein described as "an *intense* six-hour session," Jim Mellor and other GD corporate managers heard first from the consulting firm. The consultants recommended maintaining the information systems facilities within General Dynamics, but eliminating the centralized Data Systems Division and returning the IS capabilities to the individual business groups. This plan was estimated to result in a cumulative savings of $243 million over a four-year period. Feuerstein noted, however, that he was skeptical of their numbers and wary of their plan:

> I thought their numbers were probably overstated, and their implementation plan made me nervous. They wanted us to go back to the IS structure we had in 1973, before we consolidated into a centralized data systems organization. But that kind of a structure wouldn't work for us today. Our IT capabilities had become so specialized that I doubted the operating units had enough expertise to manage them well. In addition, by being centralized, we had achieved economies of scale that would be lost if DSD was broken up and parceled out to the other divisions. Finally, it would not have been good for our people. Frankly, IS professionals are seen as "second-class citizens" by the product engineers in the operating units. Spread out across these units, they would lose the professional community and career development

opportunities that DSD was able to offer. We would end up losing our best people to other companies that could offer them a better career path.

With the consulting team still at the conference table, Feuerstein then presented the CSC idea, which he called "Another Potential Option for Information Systems Structural Change." He explained the history of the joint venture proposal and gave background on CSC, highlighting its strong financial position and extensive experience in government information systems. He identified the benefits for GD as cost reductions for information services, a large cash infusion (since CSC would purchase GD's IS facilities for the new business), and the opportunity to participate in the growth market of commercial outsourcing. The risks, however, were the loss of GD's full control over its IS resources, the potential failure of the new business, and the uncertain growth of the commercial outsourcing market. Feuerstein's main goal in this meeting was to learn whether or not there was enough interest on the part of corporate headquarters to explore this option further.

At the end of the meeting, and much to the surprise of the consultants, Mellor was very enthusiastic about the CSC option. As Feuerstein later noted, "It was critical that Mellor was positive. We would never have done this deal without operating management's buy-in." Mellor suggested that Hall and Feuerstein present the plan to Harvey Kapnick, GD vice chairman, whom Anders had brought in to drive his corporate restructuring strategy. As Feuerstein explained,

> Kapnick was Anders's shareholder-value-enhancement and divestiture guy. It was an incredible bit of fate, too, because Kapnick had been a top executive of another computer services firm, and so he understood the intricacies

of MIS and was immediately drawn to this plan. This was an important subtle nuance in this whole process.

Kapnick was interested in the concept and agreed to meet with top CSC people to discuss the proposed business venture. On May 22, Ace Hall, Larry Feuerstein, and Harvey Kapnick met for dinner at the St. Louis Club with Van Honeycutt, CSC CEO William Hoover, and a CSC corporate senior vice president. As Honeycutt described it,

This was Harvey Kapnick's "get-to-know-you meeting." The first thing Kapnick wanted to know was whether we had the kind of money for a deal like this. He really wanted the cash. Next, he wanted to know who from CSC would be in charge. Again, he was testing our level of commitment to this deal. It was critical that we had Hoover there; we were pitching the whole company, and his presence gave us credibility. After that, things settled down and went very smoothly. There seemed to be a good personality fit around the table. Kapnick and one of our guys had a mutual past experience before coming to GD, so they shared an immediate connection. At the end of the evening, Kapnick said that he would work with us, provided we get Jim Mellor [GD's president and chief operating officer] on board.

It was critical that Jim Mellor and his operations managers be behind this deal because IS runs throughout all of GD's business divisions. They were the DSD customers, and they would become CSC customers if this plan went through. They had to be convinced that we could do the job for them.

As Feuerstein described it,

It was a very positive meeting. Harvey [Kapnick] and Bill [Hoover] hit it off very well. And since Kapnick and a member of the CSC team had some mutual experience, there was instant common ground. They traded names and stories for a long time, helping to set a positive tone. The group was congenial; there was an immediate "fit." This was a critical "chemistry test." Had that meeting not gone so well,

the whole idea might well have gone straight to the filing cabinet. After dinner, Harvey said to Ace and me, "These are good guys; I could work with them." And that was our go-ahead.

June 1991

Throughout early June, various teams of GD and CSC people traded visits to one another's facilities. Feuerstein noted that:

CSC has an extremely good ability to muster a companywide team of great, intelligent, experienced people. The right individuals were there within 48 hours. They really know how to respond to a deal and pull it off.

Feuerstein invited a CSC review team to "come out and kick the tires" at DSD's regional data centers. According to Feuerstein, they were impressed with the IS facilities and personnel. Jim Mellor and several GD senior operations managers visited CSC offices and facilities to assess CSC operational capabilities. According to Honeycutt,

We had to convince General Dynamics not only that we had the technical capability to handle their needs, but also that we had the right industry experience to be a good fit with their business. It's ironic that our extensive government and defense experience—which had previously been our obstacle to gaining commercial outsourcing clients—was now our selling point to GD. It was exactly what they were looking for. We spoke their language.

According to Feuerstein,

The GD operations guys came away satisfied that CSC had the capability to serve their information needs. They saw that CSC had not only the technological capability, but also the "product fit" because of their extensive experience with government clients and weapons systems. CSC grew up in the same defense business as we did. They know the regulations and the critical success factors. We would have had to teach other vendors the rules of the defense environment before they could do the work.

With their knowledge of the defense and high-tech industries, CSC was able to speak our language. This was another critical litmus test. Because IS runs throughout all of GD's operating units, we had to get the business units' buy-in. Mellor liked what he saw in the CSC facilities, and the operations managers were confident too. So he gave Kapnick the thumbs-up.

Later that month, Hall, Feuerstein, Kapnick, and GD's chief financial officer met with Honeycutt and Hoover to discuss terms for the proposed business venture. The main concern at this meeting was how to value the sale of GD's IS business. Honeycutt recalled this meeting:

We did extremely good due diligence on this deal. We had some appraisals done of GD's technical assets, facilities, equipment, and real estate, and we knew this hard investment to be carried at some $140 million. We offered about $100 million for the division, and we proposed a 10-year contract with an annual charge for IS services that offered a slight savings over DSD's current charges. Kapnick told us in no uncertain terms, however, that our figure was totally unacceptable. He told us to get back to him when we could "clean up our numbers."

According to Feuerstein,

This was the point where the deal began to crash and burn. The problem is that there is no precedent for valuation of this kind. There is no "used-car blue book" to understand how to value these assets. The net book value for the assets was $140 million; but because of the award-winning service DSD maintained, we also expected some premium above book value. Harvey Kapnick had worked in information services before, so he was very familiar with computer systems and facilities. He looked at the data we had and estimated the value of our business at perhaps $200 million. We went in to the meeting with CSC hoping to get near this amount. They offered us a 10 year contract with

an annual charge for IS services that offered a slight savings over DSD's current charges. But the purchase price of $100 million they offered us for the business was not acceptable.

Both sides left the meeting with this issue unresolved and the future of the joint venture uncertain.

Over the next month, Harvey Kapnick continued to think about the plan and finally decided that a joint-venture business was not the best solution at all—a 100 percent sale and pure outsourcing agreement would be better for both parties. In an outsourcing partnership, CSC could purchase outright all of GD's IS facilities and business (except product-embedded technology development)[14] and then provide information services to them. This solution fit beautifully with Anders's corporate strategy—General Dynamics would get a large cash infusion from this sale, could divest a non-core business division (DSD), and would not have to worry about the future risks of being involved in a new non-core high-technology business. Other GD top executives agreed with Kapnick that the better plan was an outsourcing agreement, and not a joint business venture.

According to Honeycutt,

This looked great from our perspective: 100% ownership of an outsourcing business was much better for us than a joint venture with GD. We were trying to build a reputation as a commercial outsourcer. In retrospect, the last thing we needed was a joint venture with a government defense contractor. Acquiring GD's IS capacity would put us on the elite list of commercial outsourcers, and it could give us

---

[14]GD's product-embedded hardware and software technology was never up for sale in this negotiation. This proprietary technology was crucial for GD's innovative product strategies. As such, this technology fell under the auspices of GD "product development," rather than "information services."

facilities that we could use to serve other commercial clients.

This change of mind-set sparked renewed interest in the negotiation, but the purchase price was still an unresolved issue. In order for this deal to go through, a purchase price for the business would have to be agreed upon, and then Hall, Feuerstein, and Honeycutt would have to work with CSC to put together a plan for outsourcing the Data Systems Division which could then be presented to the GD Board of Directors at their next meeting in August—less than two months away. If the Board approved the outsourcing concept, the two companies would then work to create a detailed contractual agreement.

At this point, Hall and Feuerstein had several critical issues on their minds: Clearly, the cash infusion generated by the sale of the DSD would be very valuable to GD, but how much was "enough"? How much cash did they have to get for the sale of the DSD business to make the transaction worthwhile? In addition, the flexibility and savings afforded by outsourcing was a great advantage, but were the advantages of outsourcing worth the risks? How much cost savings should they demand? Or would it be enough for GD to pay CSC an amount equal to their own DSD charges for the benefit of cash and flexibility? How could GD maintain enough control over its information systems? How "operationally transparent" could this transfer be? How could they minimize the trauma to the organization and the people? How would employees be treated by this deal? Could they take their pensions, vacations, and fringe benefits with them as they transferred from GD to CSC? What would happen to the CSC contract in the future if GD decided, according to Anders's corporate policy, to divest any of its business units?

At the same time, Honeycutt had several critical issues on his mind: It was clear that GD wanted a significant cash infusion, but how much should CSC, a publicly held company, prudently pay for this business? This was a brilliant opportunity for CSC to leverage its strength in government information systems to enter the commercial market. The publicity from the deal would boost CSC's visibility in the commercial outsourcing market substantially. But how much was this opportunity really worth?

Equally important was the question of how much slack was in the Data Systems Division to be squeezed out while maintaining GD performance requirements. Could CSC make a healthy profit managing the organization?

An additional imponderable was how much excess capacity was in the DSD facilities for CSC to use serving other clients. Honeycutt expected that CSC could respond to General Dynamics requirements and still have resources available to attract and serve new commercial clients.

With General Dynamics' corporate strategy of "Buy, Sell, or Merge," Honeycutt was concerned with the future viability of an outsourcing contract if GD chose to divest any business units. How could a contract be structured to protect CSC if GD divested one of its business units in the future?

Finally, Honeycutt thought about the transfer of employees from GD to CSC. The expectation was that the professional IS staff would be happy to make the move to CSC because CSC could offer a better career path for IS professionals in a growth computer business than GD could offer in a declining defense market. These individuals had similar backgrounds and professional skills as CSC's own employees, and Honeycutt thought that in the future, they would even be able to move out into CSC's other units.

Case 4–3

SINGAPORE UNLIMITED: BUILDING THE NATIONAL INFORMATION INFRASTRUCTURE[1]

By adopting the Singapore Unlimited philosophy [the country] empowered itself to see beyond its physical limitations and to view the world as the playing field. . . . Singapore will become an Intelligent Island, a global center of excellence for science and technology, a high-value location for production and a critical strategic node in global networks of commerce, communications and information.

Singapore Unlimited, published by Singapore's Economic Development Board[2]

After leading Singapore's transformation from a "jungle island" into one of the world's most prosperous economies, Lee Kuan Yew stepped down as prime minister in 1990, clearing the way for a new generation. Observers wondered how Singapore could keep up its record economic performance, marked by annual growth rates of nearly 10% for the past 30 years.[3]

Twenty-six years after the country declared its independence, the fiber-optic cables are laid, the skyscrapers are built, the computers are buzzing. But the days of hyperactive growth are over. . . . The question now is whether the new generation can come up with a second act.[4]

The government of Singapore, now headed by Prime Minister Goh Chok Tong, was quick to respond to this challenge. Its December 1991 *Strategic Economic Plan: Towards a Developed Nation* summarized Singapore's goal for the Next Lap—to become a "first league developed country" in terms of economic dynamism, quality of life, national identity and global reach. This would require Singapore to sustain growth rates close to 7% in Gross Domestic Product (GDP) despite a domestic market of 2.8 million, a lack of natural resources, and persistent shortages of labor. The report warned that "the economic strategies for Singapore needed to evolve from the past single dimensional type to the multi-dimensional type in order to remain viable in an increasingly complex environment."[5]

The Strategic Economic Plan was presented by the Economic Planning Committee (see Exhibit 1), comprising key individuals in private, public and academic sectors organized in eight committees. Their work was supplemented by 100 roundtable discussions and 13 industry workshops (see Exhibit 2).[6] The Strategic Economic Plan provided an overview of the economic landscape over the next 20 to 30 years; it defined eight strategic thrusts and 19 programs through which they could be implemented (see Exhibit 3). One of the strategic thrusts was to further increase the role of information technology in Singapore's development.

In April 1992, Singapore's National Computer Board and the IT2000 Committee (see Exhibit 4) published the *IT2000 Report: A Vision of an Intelligent Island*. The vision called for the creation of a National Information Infrastructure (NII), which would be leveraged to enable Singapore to compete at home and abroad. The report explained what the National Information Infrastructure meant to Singapore both at home and in the international arena. The NII would make Singapore a more efficient switching center for goods, services, capital, information and people. The goal of the IT2000 initiative was simple yet powerful: to sustain substantial increases in productivity with limited physical and human resources. In a document entitled *Singapore: The Next Lap,* Goh reminded his fellow citizens:

> We must keep trying to stay ahead in the race of nations . . . never forget the basics . . . stay united, work hard, save, look after each other, be quick to seize opportunities and be vigilant.[7]

---

[6]The 13 industry "clusters" were Commodity Trading, Shipping, Precision Engineering, Electronics, Information Technology, Petroleum and Petrochemical, Construction, Heavy Engineering, Finance, Insurance, General Supporting Industries, Tourism, and International Hub.

[7]*Singapore: The Next Lap,* Government of Singapore, 1991, p. 15.

What Is a National Information Infrastructure?

Singapore's development had been marked by successful major infrastructural developments. Initially, the NII was compared to Singapore's road network or public utilities infrastructure. The *IT2000 Report* explained: "Just as transportation and land-use planning had been the *de facto* social planning movement of the 1960s and 1970s, information infrastructure planning is likely to become the social planning of the early 21st century. We need the equivalent of the land-use master plan . . . for information infrastructure planning."

However, there were major differences between planning for and building a road and planning for and building the NII. First, the technology underlying the design, implementation, and maintenance of a road or water network, for example, did not change at the break-neck speed of IT in the 1990s. Second, NII experimentation and prototyping would have to occur at home. There was no blueprint and no "best practice" for what Singapore had set out to do. Third, the NII would serve as a general platform for information sharing and communication. It would make possible the provision of new forms of information, educational, entertainment and transactional services. Furthermore, the development of Singapore's urban infrastructure was chiefly under the jurisdiction of the Urban Redevelopment Authority. Similarly, the Port Authority of Singapore managed the country's port installations. In contrast, the NII required a multi-agency effort.

The NII was defined around three core components—conduit, content and compute—each of which was under the purview of several government agencies and involved many players in the private and public sectors. *Conduit* referred to the physical "pipelines" (e.g., voice and data lines,

EXHIBIT 1   Members of the Economic Planning Committee, 1991

Main Committee	*Resource Persons*
Chairman: Mah Bow Tan Minister for Communications	Associate Professor Lin Chin Department of Business Policy, NUS
Government Members Dr. Andrew Chew Head Civil Service, PSD (for Phase 2)	Dr. Tan Kong Yam Vice Dean, Faculty of Business Administration, National University of Singapore

Lam Chuan Leong
Permanent Secretary, Ministry of Trade and
   Industry
	Dr. Linda Low
	Senior Lecturer, Economics and Statistics
	   Department, National University of Singapore

Philip Yeo Chairman, Economic Development Board	Dr. Toh Mun Heng Senior Lecturer, Economics and Statistics Department, National University of Singapore
Yeo Seng Teck Chief Executive Officer, Trade and Development Board	Wong Seng Hon Board Secretary, National Computer Board (up to July 1990)
Tan Chin Nam Chairman, National Computer Board	COL (Res) Lai Seck Khui Deputy Secretary, Ministry of Trade and Industry
COL (Res) Quek Poh Huat Chairman, Singapore Institute of Standards and Industrial Research	Liew Heng San Director, Ministry of Trade and Industry
Professor Cham Tao Soon President, Nanyang Technological University	Peter Connell Vice President, Arthur D. Little
Koh Beng Seng Deputy Managing Director, MAS	*Secretariat* Daniel Selvaretnam Ministry of Trade and Industry/Economic Development Board
Private Sector Members Robert Chua Executive Chairman, ACE Daikin	LTC (Res) Francis Yuen Singapore Institute of Standards and Industrial Research (for Phase I)
Leong Chee Whye President and Chief Executive Officer, UIC	Balagopal Nair Trade Development Board (up to September 1990)
Lim Ho Kee Executive Vice President, Union Bank of Switzerland	Sonny Tan Economic Development Board
Rafiq Jumabhoy Managing Director, Scotts Holdings	Judy Tan Economic Development Board (for Phase 2)
Cheng Hong Kok President and Chief Executive Officer, SPC	Yong Yaw Nam Economic Development Board (for Phase 2)

EXHIBIT 2   Sample Sectoral Analyses for the Strategic Economic Plan, 1991: IT Industry Cluster

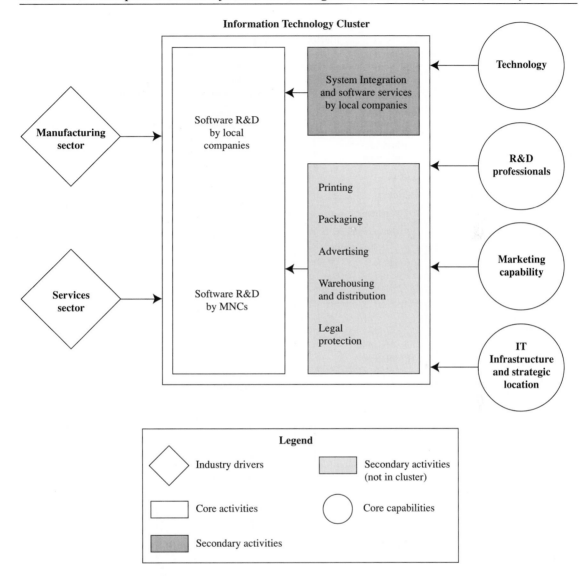

Cluster Analysis Summary

1. Cluster: Information Technology
2. Lead agency: National Computer Board

Other agencies with major involvement:
   • Economic Development Board
   • Trade Development Board

3. Vision statement:
   • To support Singapore as an effective exploiter of information technology.

   • To be a competitive exporter of software products and services focusing on strategic sectors and capitalizing on niche technologies.

4. Desired upgrading of cluster to achieve Strategic Economic Plan objectives:
   • Develop competence in core application technologies.

(continued)

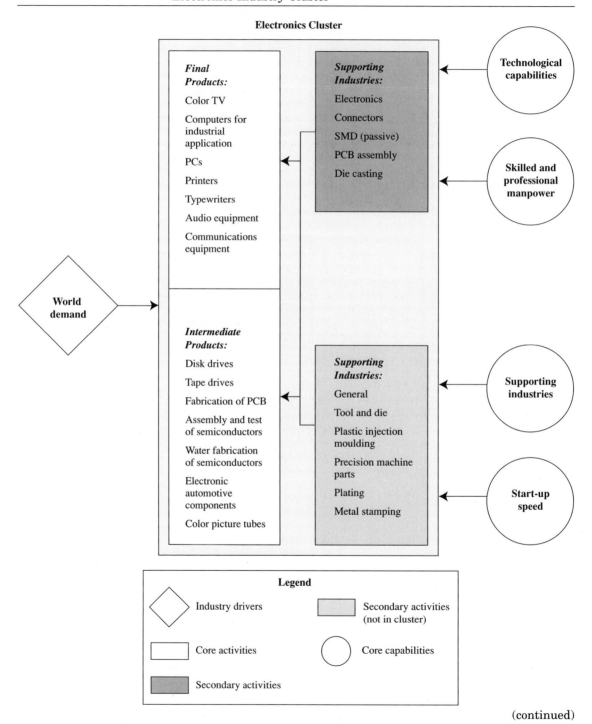

Electronics Cluster

Final Products:
- Color TV
- Computers for industrial application
- PCs
- Printers
- Typewriters
- Audio equipment
- Communications equipment

Supporting Industries:
- Electronics
- Connectors
- SMD (passive)
- PCB assembly
- Die casting

Technological capabilities

Skilled and professional manpower

World demand

Intermediate Products:
- Disk drives
- Tape drives
- Fabrication of PCB
- Assembly and test of semiconductors
- Water fabrication of semiconductors
- Electronic automotive components
- Color picture tubes

Supporting Industries:
- General
- Tool and die
- Plastic injection moulding
- Precision machine parts
- Plating
- Metal stamping

Supporting industries

Start-up speed

Legend

- Industry drivers
- Core activities
- Secondary activities
- Secondary activities (not in cluster)
- Core capabilities

(continued)

518

EXHIBIT 2 (concluded)   Sample Sectoral Analyses for the Strategic Economic Plan, 1991:
Electronics Industry Cluster

Cluster Analysis Summary

1. Cluster: Electronics

2. Lead agency: Economic Development Board

Other agencies with major involvement:
   - National Science and Technology Board
   - Singapore Institute of Standards and Industrial Research

3. Vision statement:
   - To excel in selected specialized technologies.
   - To establish Singapore as a premier manufacturing center of high value-added electronic products/components as well as an R&D and product management center for the Asia Pacific region.
   - Higher value-added and higher quality products with a high level of precision engineering and knowledge content.

4. Desired upgrading of cluster to achieve SEP objectives
   - Higher value-added activities such as R&D and product management.
   - More automated with higher software/intelligence content.
   - Improved resource efficiency in the utilization of water.

---

broadcast and cellular transmission) that carried information flows, or *"content"* (e.g., payment instructions, multimedia courseware, entertainment programs, government database records, stock price information). *Compute* referred to the processing of content (e.g., user authentication, billing, processing of permit documents) (see Exhibit 5). The NII's strategic framework required the orchestration of telecommunications networks, common network services, technical standards, national IT applications projects and an appropriate policy and legal framework (see Exhibit 6).

A press release accompanying the IT2000 report described "A Day in the Life of the Intelligent Island" through the fictional Tay family. The Tays' world was enabled by voice-controlled, wide-screen, high-definition TV that served as picture phone, interactive tutor, and electronic place of business. The Tays used "smart-cards" instead of money for identification and medical records.

Portable cellular data screens helped them avoid traffic jams and recommended the best itineraries. Furthermore, the NCB and several government agencies as well as private companies and IT vendors co-sponsored a "Singapore 2000" exhibit. The exhibit, which also addressed national development issues, attracted 350,000 visitors and sought to provide a collective visualization of what NII and Singapore could be like in the year 2000.

By the mid 1990s, Singapore was poised to become the world's first fully networked society—one in which all homes, schools, businesses, and government agencies would be interconnected in an electronic grid. A member of one of the original sectoral committees that had contributed to the *IT2000 Report* commented:

A lot of work went into IT2000. Tons and tons of work. I think what it represents today is the vision. It puts very vague ideas into a common language which people must eventually know and use. And it represents a piece of work that

EXHIBIT 3 The Strategic Economic Plan: Implementation Plan

Strategy	Lead Agency	Programs	Key Success Factors
Enhancing human resources	Economic Development Board	1. International Manpower Program	• Attractiveness of Singapore's intellectual environment for overseas Asian talent. • Availability of suitable job opportunities.
Promoting national teamwork	Ministry of Trade and Industry	2. Establishment of an Economic Panel	• The Economic Panel must be accepted within the government as having a valid role in discussing issues involving ministries other than the Ministry of Trade and Industry, and that it does so in an objective and neutral manner. • The Economic Panel must also be accepted by labor movement and business groups as a forum where their views are taken seriously and where government is prepared to consider meaningful responses to the issues raised.
Becoming internationally oriented	Economic Development Board	3. Preparing Singaporeans for international assignments	• Any overseas posting will cause some inconvenience and Singaporeans who are very comfortable in their present positions may not be willing to go overseas unless the incentives are substantial. • The willingness to adapt to a foreign cultural environment is important if Singaporeans are to be effective in their overseas assignments.
Becoming internationally oriented	Economic Development Board	4. Promoting the Growth Triangle and business alliances in the region	• The ability of Singapore management to cope with handling new start-ups, particularly in environments with different social and business cultures.
Becoming internationally oriented	Economic Development Board	5. Developing information infrastructure	• Effective promotion of business-related activities.

EXHIBIT 3 (*continued*) The Strategic Economic Plan: Implementation Plan

Strategy	Lead Agency	Programs	Key Success Factors
Creating a conducive climate for innovation	National Productivity Board	6. Reviewing government rules that hinder innovation	• The ability of government bureaucracy to be flexible and yet not lose its focus or efficiency.
Developing manufacturing and service clusters	Lead agencies for respective clusters	7. Implementation of cluster-based development plans	• Acceptability of the plans to the private sector and their level of commitment to it. This can be enhanced by close consultation with the private sector in the development of these plans.
Developing manufacturing and service clusters	Lead agencies for respective clusters	8. Cluster workshops	• Willingness of both government and business to discuss detailed plans openly.
Developing manufacturing and service clusters	Ministry of Labor	9. Improving the bond between employers and employees	• Ability to provide an attractive incentive to the employees.
Developing manufacturing and service clusters	Ministry of Trade and Industry	10. Improving the overall balance between supply and demand of labor	• Technical ability to produce usable forecasts. • Flexibility of incentives or other fiscal measures to be used in this particular way.
Developing manufacturing and service clusters	Economic Development Board with administrative support from the National Productivity Board	11. Multi-agency task force on economic redeployment	• Management ability and educational and skill levels of the workforce limit the extent to which potential upgrading and redeployment can be successfully implemented. • Willingness of companies in an industry to work together. • Companies may not have the motivation to change existing practices in the absence of serious business challenges.
Maintaining international competitiveness	Ministry of Industry and Trade	12. Establishment of a Competitiveness Monitoring Group	• No significant problems envisioned.

Source: Strategic Economic Plan.

521

EXHIBIT 4   Members of the IT2000 Committee, 1992

Chairman:

Tan Chin Nam
Chairman
National Computer Board

Members:

Arthur Berg Partner Ooi Clinic	Lim Swee Say General Manager National Computer Board
Bernard Tan Dean of Science Faculty National University of Singapore	Liu Thai Ker Chief Executive Urban Redevelopment Authority
Daniel Selvaretnam Director (Planning) Economic Development Board	Noel Hon Chairman Singapore Federation of the Computer Industry
Goh Kim Leong Permanent Secretary Ministry of Information and the Arts	Patrick Daniel Managing Editor The Straits Times
Hang Chang Chieh Deputy Chairman National Science and Technology Board	Patrick Yeoh Chairman Association of Banks in Singapore
Juzar Motiwalla Director Institute of Systems Science	Pek Hock Thiam Executive Director Singapore Tourist Promotion Board
Ko Kheng Hwa Deputy General Manager National Computer Board	Robert Chua President Singapore Manufacturers' Association
Lee Chee Yeng Director (Operations) Port of Singapore Authority	Steven Goh Chairman Singapore Retail Merchants Association
Lee Tsao Yuan Deputy Director The Institute of Policy Studies	Sung Sio Ma Executive Vice President Singapore Telecom
Lim Hock San Director-General Civil Aviation Authority of Singapore	

Secretariat:

Foong Tze Foon Director (Planning) National Computer Board	Wong Seng Hom Division Director (Special Duties) National Computer Board
Michael Yap Program Manager National Computer Board	

EXHIBIT 5   Components of the National Information Infrastructure (NII)

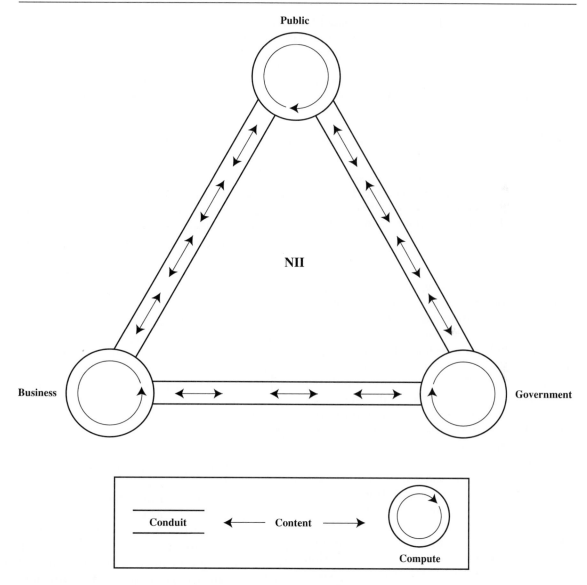

The **Telecommunication Networks** consisted of both cable and wireless networks, partly under the purview of Singapore Telecom and partly under the Singapore Broadcasting Corporation. The **National IT Application Projects** consisted of applications that could be implemented using telecommunications networks of the early 1990s and those that would require the higher bandwidth and wireless features of future networks.

Common Network Services were value-added services implemented mainly through software. They imposed the standards necessary to enable users to exchange information and perform

(continued)

EXHIBIT 5 (continued)   Components of the National Information Infrastructure (NII)

---

transactions in a secured, reliable, and compatible environment. These included user authentication, user and service directories, network security, and central billing.

Technical Standards, based mostly on international standards, were applied to the telecommunication networks, the common network services, and the national IT application projects. They ensured seamless and harmonious interaction across the infrastructure.

The **Policy and Legal Framework** would help address non-technological issues such as data protection and intellectual property rights (see Exhibit 6).

Source: *IT Report,* published by the National Computer Board, April 1992.

---

people can point back to and say, well, we all participated in creating this, now let's build one more small block of the vision. When will it happen? A lot more work remains to be done.

Singapore in 1995

Singapore—an island republic off the tip of the Malay peninsula of , across the Singapore Strait from Indonesia (see Exhibit 7)— had been at the crossroads of trade routes for nearly 200 years. It has a Chinese majority in a Malay and Muslim world, and is one of the world's most densely populated countries with 2.94 million inhabitants in 622 square kilometers, an area roughly the size of the city of Chicago. Annual population growth, including immigration, approached 2%; 23% of the population was under the age of 15, and half was under the age of 25. The entire population lived in urban areas, and 85% of the jungle that originally covered the island had been cleared. The capital city occupied land reclaimed from the sea. Only 1% of the population worked in agriculture, 61% in industry/commerce, and 38% in services; 17% of Singapore's workers belonged to a union.[8]

From 1990 to 1994, real GDP growth averaged 8.4%, inflation 3.1%, and the country boasted a strong current account balance of $2.82 billion. Income per capita exceeded $21,000 in 1994, which was second only to Japan in the region and one of the highest in the world, giving Singapore the status of a newly industrialized economy (NIE). GDP growth in 1993–1994 was led by 28% growth in the electronics manufacturing sector. Financial services grew by 14%, manufacturing by nearly 13% and construction by 12%. An 8% real GDP growth rate and 2.7% inflation rate were expected for 1995. Until the year 2000, real GDP growth was expected to average 6.8% and inflation 2.9%.[9] Singapore's success and vulnerability came from its strategic position as trade site guarding the Pacific entrance of the straits of Malacca.

Prime Minister Goh, benefiting from his party's strong political control and the country's excellent economic performance, stood a good chance of winning the next election, which he could call any time before August 1996. Although the president was the head of state, the prime minister exercised executive authority and headed the government with his cabinet. He reported to a unicameral parliament. This compact, single-tiered government system maximized efficiency and expediency (see Exhibit 8). Singapore's civil service was known for its commitment to economic development, efficiency, and a

---

[8]*Singapore—Geographic Report,* Political Risk Services, IBC USA, January 1, 1995.

[9]Ibid.

EXHIBIT 6   Overall Organizational Framework for National Information Infrastructure (NII)

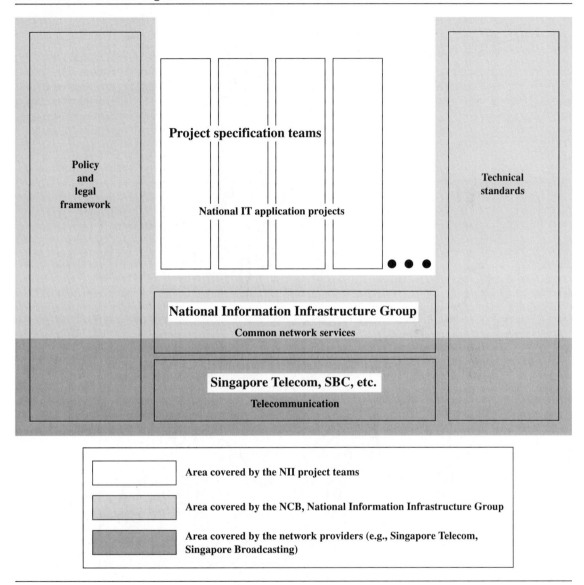

Source: *A Vision of an Intelligent Island: IT2000 Report,* Singapore: National Computer Board, April 1992.

strict code of ethics. Civil servants were highly trained. The civil service targeted the top 3% of college graduates for intensive recruitment. Government employees received bonuses based on the performance of the domestic economy. A 7% growth rate could result in a bonus equivalent to as much as three months' salary. Public-sector salaries were expected to increase 7% to 8% in 1995.[10]

———
[10]Ibid.

EXHIBIT 7   Map of Singapore and Surrounding Region

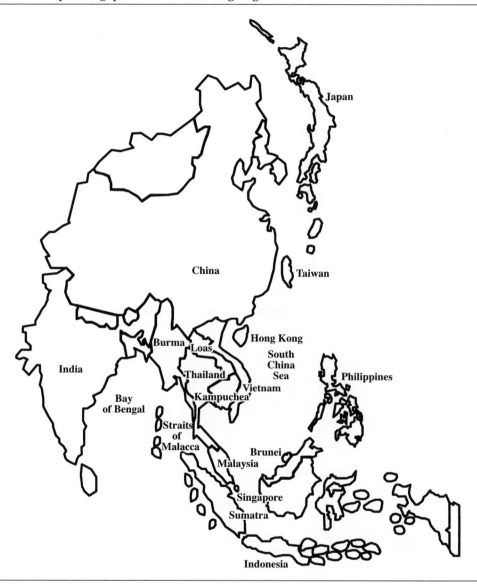

Before stepping down as prime minister in 1990, Lee Kuan Yew had been reelected eight times and had exercised a degree of control rarely seen in successful economies. He was widely credited for the "Singapore Miracle." The Cambridge-educated lawyer and brilliant strategist had been the central figure in Singapore's history since its independence in 1965 from the Federation of Malaysia. At the time, a Western magazine had predicted that "with the links to the natural riches of Malaysia severed, Singapore

---

EXHIBIT 8　　Fact Sheet: Republic of Singapore

Constitution	August 9, 1965
Head of State	President Ong Teng Cheong (1993)
Head of Government	Prime Minister Goh Chok Tong (1990)

Cabinet Officials

Senior Minister	Lee Kuan Yew
Deputy Prime Ministers	Lee Hsien Loong
	Tony Tan
Communications	Mah Bow Tan
Community Development	Abdullah Tarmugi
Defense	Tony Tan
Labor	Lee Boon Yang
Education	Lee Yock Suan
Finance	Richard Hu Tsu Tau
Health and Information	George Yeo
Home Affairs	Wong Kan Seng
Law	Shunmugan Jayakumar
National Development	Lim Hng Kiang
Trade and Industry	Yeo Cheow Tong
Environment	Teo Chee Hean

Legislature: Unicameral, 81-member Parliament. The president is elected in a presidential election for a six-year term. The president formally appoints the prime minister and the cabinet. Parliamentary elections are to be held at least once every five years.

Distribution of seats in 1995: People's Action Party (PAP), 77 seats; Singapore Democratic Party (SDP), 3 seats; Workers' Party, 1 seat.

Currency exchange system: managed float; exchange rate in July 1995, US$1 = 1.4 Singapore dollars.

Principal exports: Machinery and equipment, petroleum products, rubber, manufactured goods, processed foods, coconut oil, palm oil, tin, and copra; mainly to the United States, Japan, Vietnam, Malaysia, Thailand, Hong Kong, Australia, and Germany.

Principal imports: Machinery and equipment, mineral fuels, chemicals, manufactured goods, and food; mainly from Japan, the United States, Malaysia, the European Community, and Saudi Arabia.

Source: Data, which were mainly drawn from Political Risk Services, IBC USA, January 1, 1995, were updated to reflect status as of August 1, 1995.

---

was doomed to live on the wits of its people."[11] Singapore combined four ethnic groups, religions and official languages.[12]

While the multicultural makeup of the country had once led to racial conflicts, the government had been remarkably successful in

---

[11]John Andrews, "Lee's Legacy: A Survey of Singapore," *The Economist,* November 22, 1981, p. 4.

[12]Ethnic groups in 1994: Chinese (77%), Malay (15%), Indian (6%), other (2%). Main religions in 1994: Buddhist (29%), Christian (19%), Muslim (16%), Taoist (13%). Languages: Malay, Chinese, Tamil, and English

were all official languages. Malay was the national language, while English was the language of administration and instruction and was widely used in science, technology, commerce and tourism. In the past decade, the study of Mandarin had been encouraged in the expectation of growing trade with China.

promoting unity. To build social cohesion, Lee had emphasized common Confucian values which included discipline, hard work, and a strong sense of duty to the state and the family. Most Singaporeans identified themselves as Singaporeans first, and as Chinese, Malay or Indian second.

To admirers, Lee embodied all that was good about Asia. Singapore's rapid economic progress was accompanied by litter-free streets, a low crime rate, a high literacy rate, and a high level of public amenities and services. Critics, however, pointed out that the price for Singapore's success had been strict laws and government control. Under Lee, radio and television facilities were operated by the government, satellite dishes were prohibited (except for commercial purposes), and newspapers were privately owned but had to be licensed.

Reduced to its essentials, Singapore's strategy had been straightforward: leveraging its single natural advantage of strategic location by establishing world class transportation and materials handling facilities; providing ancillary financial and other services by establishing a sophisticated communication and information technology infrastructure; continuously upgrading the skills of its work force; and monitoring and absorbing relevant global technological improvements.[13] In particular, the government's centralized approach to economic and infrastructural development had focused on the creation of a business infrastructure that would attract multinational corporation (MNC) dollars. This was the base from which the country planned to launch the Next Lap.

The Foundations

Infrastructure: 1. An underlying base or supporting structure. 2. The basic facilities, equipment, services and installation needed for the growth and functioning of a group, country, or organization. 3. A governmental or administrative apparatus.[14]

Singapore's highly modern airport was consistently ranked as the best in the world by business travelers and had the highest number of airlinks in the Asia Pacific. Over 55 international airlines provided 2000 weekly flights to more than 110 cities in 53 countries. Two more international terminals and a third international runway were in planning. Singapore operated one of the world's busiest ports, served by 800 shipping lines to more than 750 ports around the world. Almost every international logistics company was represented, including Federal Express, UPS, TNT Express Worldwide, AIE, Burlington, and DHL. The government had committed $1.1 billion to upgrade and expand two existing container terminals as well as add a third one offshore. These developments in physical infrastructure would be complemented by the installation of state-of-the-art telecommunications and a new nationwide electronic data interchange (EDI) designed to turn Singapore into an "Intelligent Logistics Hub."

The island was linked to Thailand and Malaysia by road. The extensive road system was well maintained, and the urban population was served by one of the world's most modern and user-friendly subway systems; most city dwellers lived within one kilometer of a station. As in all Singaporean infrastructure projects, Singapore's downtown, four-regional centers, sub-regional centers, town centers and neighborhood centers were defined to be modular, scaleable, and extremely flexible. By 1990, nearly 90% of Singaporeans lived in high rises, and most of them owned their flats. Liu Thai Ker, Singapore's former chief urban planner,

---

[13]Rajendra Sisodia, "Singapore Invests in the Nation-Corporation," *Harvard Business Review,* May–June 1992, p. 4.

[14]*The American Heritage Dictionary of the English Language,* 1976 ed.

explained that through a combination of foresight, pragmatism and patience, "Singapore has tasted the sweet fruits of investing in infrastructure and should continue to do so":

> When it comes to providing infrastructure, it should best be done in a logical sequence, according to a comprehensive plan. With infrastructure provided, the pace of development can proceed rapidly with a minimum waste of time. When it comes to creating the urban environment, we strive to create variety within this small island. Variety, however, must be based on some kind of order. Variety without order may lead to chaos. The story of urban development in Singapore is one where, having learned the principles from the West, we have had to develop our own guidelines and models. In doing so, we have had to stand up to many years of criticism by many people. It takes clear vision, experience, conviction, and courage for us to solve our problems in the best way we know.

Funding for infrastructure projects had come mostly through government channels, and once a decision had been made to proceed with a particular project, funds were provided until completion. The government relied mostly on internal sources of capital and regularly accumulated a budget surplus. Singapore benefited from one of the world's highest savings rates, thanks in part to a system of mandatory contribution to a Central Provident Fund. From a negative savings rate in 1960, Singapore's domestic savings grew to 18% of GDP in 1970, 38% in 1980 and 47% in 1991. Contribution rates, equally split between employees and employers, rose from 16% in 1970 and peaked at 50% in 1980. After providing up-front capital investments for infrastructure projects, the government set up agencies and so-called statutory boards to operate them and recover operating costs. Statutory boards were created by enabling legislation which usually tied them to a Ministry but

were not government departments.[15] As not-for-profit corporations whose directorship consisted of a mix of leaders from government, the private sector, and labor organizations, they generally operated without government subsidies and could retain surplus earnings to expand their programs. In fact, most boards were expected to make money, and the government used a "tax" to retrieve excess funds from boards that operated with a substantial surplus. In 1994, Teo Chee Hean, the chairman of the National IT Committee and a Senior Minister of State, described Singapore's infrastructural planning and investment process:

> When we opened the first container berth [at the Port] in 1971/1972, containerization was not yet a major aspect of trade. Now we are one of the world's largest container ports. [In 1993, we started planning] a new container terminal that can handle three to four times the capacity we can handle today. This will provide us with the capacity we expect to handle for the next 30 to 40 years. . . . Similarly we decided to move the airport to Changi in the mid-1970s because Changi provided the space for future growth. We are now planning for our third and fourth terminals even though the second airline terminal was opened recently and is adequate for our needs in the next few years. We have consistently allocated 60% of the government's budget to development expenditure—mainly infrastructure investments for the future.

Commitment to infrastructural development did not mean that budgetary approval was simple. Productivity gains had to be demonstrated, often in terms of labor savings or more recently in terms of

---

[15]Statutory boards were responsible for vital utilities (e.g., Telecommunication Authority of Singapore), major installations (e.g., Civil Aviation Authority of Singapore and the Port Authority of Singapore), major construction enterprises (e.g., the Urban Redevelopment Authority), and analytical functions (e.g., the Economic Development Board charged with attracting foreign investment to Singapore).

improvement in quality of life. Singapore used its industrial development formula—provide the infrastructure, some subsidies, and let market forces take over—to manage large projects such as the Esplanade, a massive performing arts center to be opened in the year 2000. The project would be partly financed through the sale of adjacent land for commercial purposes, commercial sponsorship, and an endowment fund.

Wong Hung Khim, deputy chairman, Singapore Telecom, explained how national goals also guided the development of the world's best telecommunications infrastructure:[16]

> First we look at the broad objective [and see] how investments will help us achieve our work, corporate objectives, and national goal—to be the communication hub for the region. For example, we will see how strategically the submarine cable or satellite will help us meet this objective. Then we evaluate earning potential and technical viability. Once these are ascertained, it becomes a project and we go through the financial evaluation.

Under the guidance of the Telecommunications Authority of Singapore, Singapore Telecom exercised its exclusive license to provide national and international phone services until 2007 and cellular phone and paging services until 1997. The Telecommunications Authority of Singapore regulated the quality and price of Singapore Telecom's telecommunications services. Singapore Telecom retained the surplus generated on its operations. This arrangement was considered to be one of the most favorable schemes enjoyed by any telecommunications company worldwide. Singapore Telecom officials pointed out that Singapore Telecom had been consistently profitable

while offering low-cost, high-quality service, as well as investing in innovations.

Singapore Telecom's prices on regulated services tended to be below average rates for similar services provided by other regional and global communications centers and NIEs. In 1993, Singapore Telecom's international direct dial rates were among the lowest in the world, comparable to Hong Kong's and about 30% lower than Japan's. By 1994, Singapore had three telephone exchanges, six satellite antennae and nine submarine cables supporting its international services. The phone network was fully digitized. Fiber to the curb was available to certain commercial buildings and a fiber-to-the-home project was well under way. Singapore Telecom had developed a national intelligent network capable of supporting advanced value-added services. Singapore Telecom also provided leased circuit service with high availability to MNCs who needed to transport large information volumes. Singapore Telecom managed, monitored and serviced its associated equipment through a scheme known as Facility Management Service, which released MNCs from having to own and maintain their facilities. Furthermore, it was involved in 25 telecom projects in 13 countries. Singapore Telecom had invested over $1 billion in capital expenditure since 1989 and planned to spend another $2.3 billion by the close of the century (see Exhibit 9).

In October 1993, Singapore Telecom was listed on the Singapore Stock Exchange.[17] Few changes were made to Singapore Telecom's organization because it had already been reorganized to operate more

---

[16]According to the *1991 World Competitiveness Report.*

[17]In the early 1990s, the scope of government involvement—mostly in transportation, communications, oil refining, and housing—was being reduced, with the government selling minority shares in state firms, such as Singapore Telecom.

EXHIBIT 9   Milestones in the Development of Singapore's Telecommunication Infrastructure

---

1966   First submarine cable was laid.

1970   First satellite earth station was installed.

1970s Telephone installation program reduced waiting time for telephone service from over six months to less than three. In 1994, there was no waiting time.

1977   "Live" traffic was carried through optical fibers.

1982   Global satellite communications services (INMARSAT) was launched.

1983   Automatic paging and cellular mobile phone services were introduced.

1984   The "push button for all" program was completed, making telebanking possible, for example.

1987   Optical fiber digital local access network for high-speed leased circuits became available.

1988   Cellular mobile phones could be used in the subway.

1989   Caller Identity was introduced in paging services.

1990   Teleview, the nationwide interactive photo-videotext system, was launched.

1991   Skyphone, a worldwide aeronautical satellite voice communication service, became available on Singapore Airlines.

1991   A public videophone booth enabled users to send and receive full-motion and full-color video of themselves to 10 cities in Japan.

1991   Fiber-to-the-curb for telephone and data services became available.

1991   Optical fiber submarine cable system was introduced.

1992   CT/2 Service became available. The system bridged current cellular technology and personal communications networks (PCNs), which would tie phone numbers to individuals rather than locations.

1992   Customer Services and Information System was commissioned to provide fully integrated, on-line customer service facilities.

1993   All overhead cables were buried.

1994   Analog switching equipment was replaced by digital switching equipment.

Source: Singapore Telecom documents and a variety of published sources.

---

like a private company than a government organization. Citizens received credit toward the purchase of newly issued shares. Wong explained that "the main objective [of the privatization] was to make sure that people have a stake in the country."

Open for Business

Singapore's transportation, communication and financial infrastructure ranked with the best in the world.[18] Investing in a world class infrastructure, high quality civil service, and an educated work force enabled

---

[18]Singapore had a well-developed financial infrastructure. It was home to more than 290 financial institutions, including 132 banks (13 local banks and more than 119 foreign banks), 75 merchant banks, 27 finance companies and 10 international money brokers. It had the world's fourth-largest foreign exchange trading center, after London, New York and Tokyo.

Singapore to consistently attract and manage MNC investment dollars, technologies, and skills. Foreign direct investment, mostly in electronics, totaled $2.6 billion in the first half of 1994, well on the way to exceeding the 1993 record of $3.9 billion.

Starting in the mid-1960s, the Economic Development Board (EDB), charged with promoting foreign investment, convinced companies such as HP to relocate assembly and commercial operations to the island, taking advantage of its strategic location and low labor rates. Over the years, improvements in business infrastructure compensated for rising wages, and Singapore authorities sought to shift the investment from manufacturing to a "total business emphasis." Generous incentives packages were offered to MNCs for different types of activities. These incentives evolved over the years in accordance with the national economic strategy. For example, the mid-1980s "Operational Headquarters Incentive Scheme" led to the "Regional Headquarters Incentive Scheme." In February 1994, the EDB introduced a "Business Headquarters Program" that would provide tax and investment incentives to companies that locate in Singapore and provide business, technical, and professional services to firms outside the country.

Though MNC investment remained a *Leitmotif* of Singapore's development, the nature of MNC presence, role, and clout evolved constantly. In the early 1990s, over 3,000 MNCs had operations in Singapore. A U.S. Department of Commerce study estimated that American companies achieved a rate of return of 31% in Singapore, compared with an Asian average of 23% and a world average foreign direct investment ROI of 14%.[19] In the first quarter of 1994 alone,

investments in manufacturing by U.S. companies topped $460 million out of total commitments of $600 million. According to the EDB, these investments would yield a gross-value-added per worker of almost $190,000, or four times the current average for the manufacturing sector. Attracting MNCs in the IT sector played a fundamental role in the country's IT strategy. In 1992, MNCs manufactured most of the country's disk drives, printers, and other peripherals. Most MNCs used local subcontractors. Computers and peripherals, in turn, accounted for more than a third of Singapore's total electronics exports, and close to a fourth of its GDP.[20]

The shortage of labor was the main constraint on business; unemployment fell to an all-time low in 1990 and, after increasing in 1993, declined again to just 1.5% in 1994. This led the government to ease restrictions on foreign workers in the manufacturing sector. Higher wage rates than those prevailing in neighboring countries also constrained business. This problem was eased temporarily by the slowdown in economic growth in 1992, when real wage growth fell to 5.2% from 8.9% in 1990. However, the strong economic expansion of 1993 and 1994 once again pushed up wages in a tight labor market (see Exhibit 10).

"Information Arbitrage" and Global Connections

By the late 1980s, strengthening currencies and rising labor costs had begun to slow the growth of Asia's NIEs—Hong Kong, Singapore, South Korea and Taiwan. By 1989, their growth rate was surpassed by the growth rate in the region's four largest economies—Indonesia, Malaysia, the Philippines, and Thailand, known as the

---

[19]Quoted by Prime Minister Goh Chok Tong in his keynote address to the Singapore Forum held in London, April 19, 1994.

[20]"Is Singapore Becoming an Intelligent Island?" *East Asian Executive Reports* 15, no. 5, May 15, 1993, p. 8.

EXHIBIT 10 Comparative Regional Performance Indicators, 1991

	East Asia				Southeast Asia		
	Hong Kong	Japan	South Korea	Taiwan	Indonesia	Malaysia	Singapore
Production							
Per capita GNP (US$)	13,430	26,930	6,330	8,788	610	2,520	14,210
Total GNP 1990–1991 (US$M)	77,894	3,336,627	274,089	179,763	110,593	45,864	39,788
Total GDP (US$M)	67,555	3,362,282	282,970	175,396	116,476	46,980	39,984
Agriculture (% GDP)	0.0	3.0	8.0	3.7	19.0	NA	0.0
Industry (%)	25.0	42.0	45.0	42.5	41.0	NA	38.0
of which: manufacturing (% GDP)	17.0	25.0	28.0	34.4	21.0	NA	29.0
Services and other (% GDP)	75.0	56.0	47.0	53.8	39.0	NA	62.0
Average Annual Growth 1980–1991							
GDP (%)	6.9	4.2	9.6	7.6	5.6	5.7	6.6
Agriculture (%)	NA	1.2	2.1	4.7	3.1	3.7	−6.6
Industry (%)	NA	4.9	12.1	11.7	5.9	7.7	5.8
of which: manufacturing (%)	NA	5.6	12.4	11.8	12.3	9.6	7.0
Services, and other (%)	NA	3.7	9.3	13.7	6.8	4.7	7.3
Structure of Demand							
Government consumption (% GDP)	8.0	9.0	11.0	17.9	9.0	14.0	11.0
Private consumption (% GDP)	60.0	57.0	53.0	54.3	55.0	56.0	43.0
Gross domestic investment (% GDP)	29.0	32.0	39.0	22.8	35.0	36.0	37.0
Gross domestic savings (% GDP)	32.0	34.0	36.0	27.3	36.0	30.0	47.0
Exports (% GDP)	141.0	10.0	29.0	43.4	27.0	81.0	185.0
Money and Prices							
Money supply (% GDP)	NA	183.1	52.3	NA	40.5	NA	126.0
Average growth 1980–1991 (%)	NA	8.9	21.3	20.8	26.2	12.6	13.5
Average inflation 1980–1991 (%)	7.5	1.5	5.7	4.5	8.5	1.7	1.9
Nominal deposit rate (%)	NA	3.3	10.0	6.8	23.3	7.2	4.6
Nominal interest rate (%)	NA	7.5	10.0	8.6	20.6	8.1	7.6

(continued)

EXHIBIT 10 (continued) Comparative Regional Performance Indicators, 1991

	East Asia				Southeast Asia		
	Hong Kong	Japan	South Korea	Taiwan	Indonesia	Malaysia	Singapore
Public Finance							
Surplus/deficit (% GDP)	NA	-1.6	-1.7	2.7	0.4	-2.3	11.2
Government expenditures (% GDP)	NA	15.8	17.3	18.0	20.7	30.6	22.1
Defense (% expenditures)	NA	NA	22.2	26.8	8.2	NA	24.0
Education (% expenditures)	NA	NA	15.8	20.7	9.1	NA	19.9
Health (% expenditures)	NA	NA	2.0	3.6	2.4	NA	4.6
Housing and welfare (% expenditures)	NA	NA	11.3	7.3	1.8	NA	8.2
Economic services (% expenditures)	NA	NA	19.2	22.7	27.1	NA	16.8
Other (% expenditures)	NA	NA	29.5	0.9	51.5	NA	26.5
Government revenues (% GDP)	NA	14.5	17.4	20.7	21.1	28.1	27.7
Income and capital gains (% revenues)	NA	69.2	31.3	NA	61.8	33.1	25.6
Social security tax (% revenues)	NA	0.0	5.0	NA	0.0	0.0	0.0
Sales or VAT tax (% revenues)	NA	16.9	33.3	NA	23.7	20.9	16.0
Tariffs (% revenues)	NA	1.3	9.2	NA	6.4	18.0	2.0
Other taxes (% revenues)	NA	7.4	10.9	NA	2.7	2.4	13.8
Nontax revenues (% revenues)	NA	5.2	10.4	NA	5.4	25.6	42.6

EXHIBIT 10 (concluded)   Comparative Regional Performance Indicators, 1991

	East Asia				Southeast Asia		
	Hong Kong	Japan	South Korea	Taiwan	Indonesia	Malaysia	Singapore
Foreign Trade							
Total exports (US$M)	29,738	314,395	71,672	76,178	28,997	34,300	58,871
Average growth 1980–1991 (% total)	4.4	3.9	12.2	14.3	4.5	10.9	8.9
Fuels, minerals, metals (% total)	2.0	1.0	3.0	1.9	43.0	17.0	18.0
Other primary (% total)	3.0	1.0	4.0	0.3	16.0	22.0	8.0
Machinery and transportation equipment (% total)	24.0	66.0	38.0	11.5	2.0	38.0	48.0
Textiles and clothing (% total)	40.0	2.0	21.0	20.4	14.0	6.0	5.0
Other manufacturers (% total)	72.0	31.0	55.0	65.9	39.0	23.0	26.0
Total imports (US$M)	100,255	234,103	8,251	62,855	25,869	35,183	65,982
Average growth 1980–1991 (% total)	11.3	5.6	11.1	14.5	2.6	7.2	7.2
Food (% total)	6.0	15.0	6.0	3.5	5.0	6.0	6.0
Fuels (% total)	2.0	23.0	16.0	5.1	9.0	4.0	14.0
Population							
Total population (M)	5.8	123.9	43.4	20.6	181.3	18.2	2.8
Estimated 2000 (M)	6	127	47	22	206	22	3
Health							
Years life expectancy	78	79	70	74	60	71	74
Persons per physician 1990	NA	610	1,370	870	7,030	2,700	820
Infant mortality rate (per 1000)	7	5	16	5	74	15	6
Education							
Primary students 1990 (% age group)	106.0	101.0	108.0	98.7	117.0	93.0	110.0
Secondary students 1990 (% age group)	NA	96.0	87.0	86.2	45.0	56.0	69.0
Tertiary students 1990 (% age group)	NA	31.0	39.0	21.0	NA	7.0	8.0
Social							
PPP[a] adjusted GDP per capita (US=100)	83.7	87.6	37.6	NA	12.3	33.4	71.2

[a] Purchasing power parity.
Note: All data for 1991 unless otherwise noted

Sources: Far Eastern Economic Review's Asia 1994 Yearbook.

ASEAN Four.[21] Average monthly manufacturing wage rate in the four Asian NIEs was estimated at $695 in 1989, or four and a half times that of the ASEAN Four. The latter were expected to grow by 5% to 7% until the turn of the century, mostly through infusion of foreign investment.[22] Malaysia planned to be a developed nation by 2020. As the Singapore economy matured and development accelerated in the Asia-Pacific region, Singapore's leaders realized that they could use their infrastructure development and foreign investment management skills to participate in and benefit from the region's growth. In a 1991 advertisement in the international business press, Singapore presented itself as "Business Architect with Global Connections." Goh explained this approach during a worldwide tour in 1994:

> We have always played the role of a "business architect"—helping companies, Singaporean and foreign alike, plan their business strategies and configure their activities for maximum return. We carry out a form of "global knowledge arbitrage." First, in information— Singapore's familiarity with East and West means we will be able to fill informational gaps and create the business opportunities which can arise if these gaps are filled. . . . This is where Singapore's industrial parks in China, India and elsewhere will prove useful. They provide conducive business environments that international investors are familiar with. At the same time, they satisfy the host country's needs, aspirations, and concerns. Second, different countries have advantages which are suited for different activities. Companies may find that there is not one location which fits all their needs. This is where knowledge arbitration of location comes in.[23]

The establishment of a "growth triangle" comprising Singapore, the Malaysian state of Johore, and Indonesia's Riau Islands, announced in the mid-1980s, was an example of "location arbitrage." Singapore would provide the management expertise, technology, telecommunications, and transportation infrastructure while Malaysia and Indonesia offered land and low-cost labor. Malaysia and Indonesia would retain sovereignty, but Singapore had substantial freedom to administer the development. Furthermore, a Singapore consortium had taken a 40% stake in a joint venture to build a $180 million information technology park in a province of India. IBM and AT&T were reportedly interested in the project. Singapore was also helping Chinese authorities develop an industrial township in Suzhou, near Shanghai. It would eventually be home to 600,000 people and create 360,000 jobs. Singapore would build the infrastructure for the 70-square-kilometer township, occasionally referred to as "Singapore II," help establish businesses there, and train Chinese administrators—under a so-called "software transfer program." Singapore planned to invest $1.6 million a year in public money over the next three to five years for the software transfer program and bring a consortium of 19 companies, most with links to the government, to invest another $200 million in the venture in exchange for a 65% stake. In fact, Singapore authorities planned to invest up to 30% of its reserves, close to $15 billion, in regional projects.

---

[21]ASEAN: Association of the Southeast Asian Nations, which grouped Brunei, Indonesia, Malaysia, the Philippines, Singapore, and Thailand, a total of 350 million people. Vietnam was expected to join in July 1995. ASEAN had a potential market of 480 million when all 10 Southeast Asian countries—including Cambodia, Laos, Myanmar, and Vietnam—joined the group.

[22]Friedrich Wu, "The ASEAN Economies in the 1990s and Singapore's National Role," *California Management Review,* Fall 1991, pp. 103–114.

[23]Prime Minister Goh Chok Tong, keynote address to the Singapore Forum held in London, April 19, 1994.

NII Prototyping

What is the Singapore NII effort? The NII is in its early evolution, with little agreement on what it is and much less how it should be built. Possibly, the only agreement is that it should, in a vendor neutral manner, bring about electronic services to the masses.[24]

Michael Yap, assistant director, NII Group, NCB, September 1994

In 1994, in collaboration with several IT vendors and research facilities, the NCB proposed a Proof of Concept prototype of the NII. NII was defined as a "common electronic platform for efficient delivery of information and services." It would initially use current telecommunications infrastructure, but maximum flexibility was to be built into the system to migrate to future technologies. It would provide a basic set of NII core services such as a distributed computing environment, directory services, groupware, multimedia e-mail, and development toolkits. The services that could be run on the NII would be "multimedia in nature, providing customers with an utmost total sensory experience." Because the "NII [could] only be as good as the services it offered," NCB was developing trigger applications in education, library, government, and leisure, among others (see Exhibit 11A). The NII would tap into the existing systems in Singapore's civil service. The NCB continued to work with key users within the civil service to design, build, and operate many government computer systems. Many government systems, from information and licensing, that were already linked with the business sector would become accessible to the public at home. For instance, in 1993, NCB launched 11 new government services on Teleview.[25] (See Exhibit 11B for a description of Teleview.)

Meanwhile, Singapore's tertiary institutions were experimenting with small-scale versions of the "Intelligent Island" concept. For example, Ngee Ann Polytechnic commissioned a campus-wide fiber-optic network in the fall of 1993. The S$9 million project, called NPNet, linked 15,000 students and 1,500 staff in 31 buildings, 21 lecture halls and an auditorium. It was Singapore's first polytechnic to implement a campus-wide fiber-optic network using the sophisticated FDDI network protocol.[26] Concurrently, the Singapore Polytechnic was developing a 20,000-user, S$17 million Intelligent Computing Environment. The 20-month project was scheduled for completion in mid-1995, at which point the integrated, campus-wide network system and networking services would form the foundation of Campus 2000, the borderless and nearly paperless campus of the future.

In 1994, NCB Chief Executive Ko Kheng Hwa summed up the process to date on the three core components of the NII—conduit, content, and compute:

Attention in the early 1980s was focused on basic computerization, the first "c." The 1986 plan added another "c," communications. . . . IT2000 is about making multimedia contents available and accessible. . . . We are looking at technologies that have not been tried before. Many standards are not even defined. We need all kinds of skills and expertise. We need to coordinate and collaborate on both national and international scales.

---

[24]Michael Yap, "Singapore NII: Beyond the Information Highway," *Information Technology, Journal of the Singapore Computer Society,* September 1994, p. 12.

[25]Through these applications, the public could bid on-line for their Certificate of Entitlement to buy a motor vehicle, file income tax returns, tender for government projects, and book Arts Festival tickets.

[26]The Fiber Distributed Data Interface (FDDI) network protocol enabled improved network communication efficiency for distributed and multi-media information.

EXHIBIT 11A   Selected NII Projects

Four of NCB's projects that would form some of the core services of the NII were already well-advanced in late 1994: the Construction and Real Estate Network (CORENET), the Education Information Infrastructure (EDUNET), the Library of the Future Project, and the CashCard.

CORENET   This integrated network would link together public-private organizations in the construction and real estate sector to facilitate, among other things, the exchange and processing of required documentation for regulatory approval and the automation of the construction procurement process. The system would also offer a suite of information services from property prices to land development information. A business process reengineering was carried out for the development approval process. CORENET was expected to reduce the costs of doing business through shortened approval cycles and enhance Singapore's ability to attract foreign investments due to faster turnaround time for factory construction authorizations. Stringent checks throughout the approval process would enhance building safety. The CORENET Steering Committee, led by the Chairman of the Construction Industry Development Board and the director-general of the Public Works Department, brought together members of the industry.

EDUNET   Its objective was to make it possible to access student data which was deemed vital for education planning. It was based on the creation of an integrated student Data Bank which would hold a student's profile and track his or her progress through school. It managed education data centrally and linked existing information systems such as the Joint Polytechnic Admissions System, Teacher Admissions System and Tuition Grant Scheme. In collaboration with the Education Ministry, the NCB had developed the Student's and Teacher's Workbench that provided access to local and international resources and learning materials in multimedia format. Students and teachers could access the "borderless classroom" at school, at the library, or at home. The system was expected to enrich learning, enhance teaching and teaching effectiveness as well as instill IT fluency at an early age. Workbench was a joint project of the Education Ministry and NCB. A pilot project would run in six schools from July 1994 to December 1996. R&D funding for the pilot project was provided by the NSTB while the Education Ministry funded the infrastructure costs at the pilot schools.

In June 1994, the Internet was introduced to the Ministry of Education's headquarters and junior colleges. According to the NCB's annual report, connecting schools to international resources would enable students and teachers, for example, to "look at pictures from museums, browse through the United Nations' press releases or read scientific journals from all over the world [as well as] share ideas or work on joint projects with their overseas counterparts."[a] When dial-in services became available, some schools also gained access to the Internet. There were plans to introduce the Internet to all secondary schools through local area networks over the next few years. On July 1, 1994, the Internet was opened to the public.

Library 2000   This project highlighted the central role that libraries would play in creating and supporting the knowledge acquisition and dissemination process that was imperative to Singapore's ambition to be a "learning nation." To demonstrate what a highly sophisticated education and information center could look like, the NCB set up a prototype library of the future at the Tampines Regional Library (TRL). The TRL's advanced high-speed network infrastructure supported multimedia programs, cable television, international databases, and access to the library from home. TRL would also pilot a range of new services such as self-service loan terminals, home delivery of books, computerized audio visual systems, an IT gallery to show the latest IT products and services, library club, multimedia kiosks on government services, and other community based activities and programs. The first SingaTouch public information kiosks were also introduced at National Public

---

[a]*The NCB Yearbook 1993/1994*, p. 15.

EXHIBIT 11A (continued)   Selected NII Projects

Library branches. A new statutory board would be set up to expand the pilot project at the country level.

CashCard   A common stored-value card had been recommended by the financial services sector during the IT2000 project. The NCB had been working with various public and private organizations to develop a vision of the common card infrastructure and card management system using smart card technology. In 1995, citizens were awaiting the nationwide launch of the common stored-value CashCard, which would work like an "electronic purse." It would be used to make daily transactions such as buying fast food, making phone calls, buying tickets to a movie and paying entrance fees at the local swimming pool. The CashCard system was announced by the Network for Electronic Transfers (S) Pte Ltd (NETS) and would complement the existing NETS system. A pilot project was launched in late 1994 in the central financial district with participating movie theaters, sports complexes, fast food outlets, polytechnics and libraries. In July 1994, the National University of Singapore launched the Campus Card, based on the CashCard infrastructure.

Source: *NCB Yearbook 1993/1994.*

EXHIBIT 11B   Singapore Teleview Service

In the mid-1980s, when TradeNet was being discussed, Singapore Telecom announced plans to invest $40 million in R&D to develop a national Teleview system which would provide applications like home shopping, travel services, and access to databases. According to Singapore Telecom documents, Teleview's "primary objective was to provide a quantum leap in national productivity and to improve the quality of life for the average Singaporean." By 1992, Singapore Telecom offered the only photo/video/audio/text system available at the time and the only interactive system that came close to realizing the multimedia promise. Text data was transmitted via phone lines. By using broadcast technology for the transmission of high resolution photographs, Teleview optimized on both time and transmission quality. In late 1993, Teleview had 15,000 users and more than 120,000 pages, when a 131% surge in the use of its stock market and investor services forced Singapore Telecom to open a waiting list. Singapore Telecom later expanded the network.

At the end of March 1995, Singapore Telecom reported 32,000 Teleview business and home subscribers. Numerous databases gave subscribers a variety of information services and resources online. Citizens used Teleview to pay bills, check stock prices, exchange mail, compute income taxes and pick stocks. They could get medical advice, submit passport applications, make airline and hotel reservations, download recipes, and shop. Subscribers had to agree not to use the service to send "any message which [was] offensive on moral, religious, communal, or political grounds."

By early 1995, progress had been made on several elements of the NII. The key players, who had already massively invested in Singapore's information infrastructure, defined their place in the NII to ensure a return on their investment. The implementation of the NII required the participation of, and had an impact on, many government departments and statutory boards. Several issues of institutional coordination had to be resolved. All agreed that a highly coordinated and consensual approach was imperative to derive synergies and avoid duplications (see Exhibit 12).

A crucial element of the NII, Singapore's telecommunication networks, which consisted of both cable and wireless networks, was partly under the purview of Singapore Telecom and partly under the Singapore Broadcasting Authority.[27] Singapore Telecom's control of the telecommunications network and the Singapore Broadcasting Authority's control of the country's broadcasting and cable television networks were being challenged by the technological convergence of telecommunications and broadcasting. A taskforce had been formed to analyze the situation and clarify issues regarding control, access, and pricing, as well as organizational leadership over, and investment in, future developments. At the time of the case, Singapore Telecom and Singapore Cablevision were sharing the development and management of the backbone fiber-optic networks, with Singapore Cablevision wiring homes to provide cable TV services.

The evolution of existing and future common network services also involved several players. Singapore Network Services[28] had developed a sophisticated network infrastructure and had provided high customer service while purposely keeping prices low. Chan was confident that Singapore Network Services could continue to develop and manage commercial IT networks. Like Singapore Network Services, recently privatized

Singapore Telecom had broad national and international ambitions to become a "full service provider" in a range of technologies. Singapore Telecom was interested in increasing its 15% stake in Singapore Network Services.

In the area of national IT applications, Singapore Telecom had massively invested in developing Teleview Projects. Singapore Network Services had also launched its own version of a public network, Comet. Furthermore, during the preparation of the IT2000 report, sectoral groups had identified over 60 IT applications for 11 strategic sectors. Finally, the National IT Committee and the NCB had established committees to examine non-technological issues ranging from intellectual property rights to censorship and to recommend an appropriate *policy and legal framework* (see Exhibit 13). The NCB was also involved in setting and monitoring Technical and Data standards as they evolved. The National IT standards Committee had already proposed standards for barcoding, EDI and Smart Card technologies.

In the spring of 1995, the initial excitement over IT2000 had given way to specific project developments that deliver NII applications and services—student and teacher's workbench in school, common library network for science and technology, electronic medical record systems, construction systems, cashcard, etc. Although progress had been made on several fronts, NCB estimated a 15-year time frame for implementation. At least that much time was necessary just to upgrade the country's phone lines to accommodate broad-band telecommunications. Speed was becoming an issue for two reasons. First, Singapore was not alone in the IT race; Taiwan and Hong Kong, for example, were working on their own version of IT2000. Second, expectations for the NII had been raised and more services were awaited.

---

[27]Singapore Broadcasting was privatized in 1994. The regulatory functions were taken over by the Singapore Broadcasting Authority, a new statutory board. Four private companies were formed to take over the delivery of existing TV and radio services. They are part of a new holding company, Singapore International Media Pte. Ltd.

[28]Singapore Network Services was incorporated in March 1988 to initiate and manage the creation of value-added network services for trade and commerce arising out of the government sponsored TradeNet project.

EXHIBIT 12 Key NII-Related Institutions, 1994

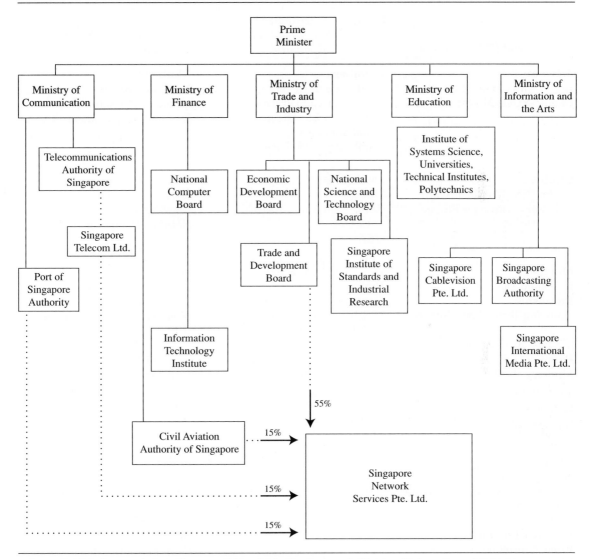

Source: Published sources include *Singapore 1994,* published by Singapore's Ministry of Information and the Arts.

Building the NII also posed coordination problems with agencies that were not directly involved in IT activities. Singapore's former chief urban planner lamented the fact that NII proponents were unable to provide usable information on items that influence urban infrastructure, ranging from telecommuting to the cost of accommodating sprawling telecommunication infrastructure within and outside of dwellings.

Most observers agreed that the physical and even institutional aspects of realizing

EXHIBIT 13   Members of the National Information Technology Committee

National IT Committees	Information Technology Institute (ITI) International Advisory Committee	ITI/ISS* Common Management Board
Advisor BG (NS) Lee Hsien Loong Deputy Prime Minister	**Members** Mr. Laszlo A. Belady Chairman and Director Mitsubishi Electric Research Laboratories Cambridge, MA, USA	**Chairman** Mr. Lim Swee Say Managing Director Economic Development Board
Chairman RAdm (NS) Teo Chee Hean Minister of State for Finance and Defense	Dr. John Seely Brown Director Xerox Palo Alto Research Center USA	**Deputy Chairman** Mr. Ko Kheng Hwa Chief Executive National Computer Board
Members Dr. Cham Tao Soon President Nanyang Technology University Mr. Goh Kim Leong Permanent Secretary Ministry of Information and the Arts Chairman Singapore Broadcasting Authority Mr. Moses Lee Deputy Chairman Singapore International Media Pte. Ltd. Professor Lim Pin Vice-Chancellor National University of Singapore Mr. Tan Chin Nam Chairman National Computer Board	Dr. Clarence A. Ellis Professor Department of Computer Science, University of Colorado (Boulder) USA Professor Herbert Weber Director Fraunhofer Institute for Software and Systems Technology Germany	**Members** Mr. Pearleen Chan Managing Director Singapore Network Services Pte. Ltd. Dr. Christopher Chia Director Information Technology Institute Mrs. Chin Tahn Joo Senior Director Industry and Technology Division National Computer Board Professor Chong Chi Tat Head Dept. of Information Systems and Computer Science National University of Singapore Professor Goh Thong Ngee Dean of Engineering Faculty of Engineering National University of Singapore

---

EXHIBIT 13 (continued)   Members of the National Information Technology Committee

National IT Committees	Information Technology Institute (ITI) International Advisory Committee	ITI/ISS* Common Management Board
Mr. Ngiam Tong Dow Permanent Secretary (Budget and Review Divisions) Ministry of Finance		Mr. Noel Hon Managing Director NEC Singapore Pte. Ltd.
Mr. Koh Boon Hwee Chairman Singapore Telecom		Mr. Takuyo Kogure Director of AV/Info Research Centre Asia Matsushita Electric (S) Pte. Ltd.
Mr. Tjong Yik Min Permanent Secretary Ministry of Communications		

*In Exhibit 12, the Information Technology Institute (ITI) reports to the NCB while the Institute of System Sciences (ISS) reports to the Ministry of Education.

Source: *IT2000 Report.*

---

the NII would be easier to manage than its social, political, and economic ramifications. Singapore was clearly at a crossroads. The direct capital cost of TradeNet's development (i.e., the contract cost to IBM and other contractors) exceeded $10 million. This did not include the investments made by the various ministries and statutory boards in conceiving the project, developing the requirements and specifications, managing the contracting process, and establishing Singapore Network Services.

The IT2000 committees had identified 11 strategic sectors and proposed over 60 strategic IT applications. Though commercial exploitation of technology was a key thrust, priority would be given to projects with the highest impact on achieving the Next Lap and the potential to benefit a large cross-section of the population, such as those in education, healthcare and transportation. A balance also had to be sought between projects that exploited available IT and telecommunication infrastructure with projects that involved advanced technology and high-speed networks. Funding approval for IT2000 projects would be made on a case-by-case basis with detailed justifications from project specification and feasibility studies. The government planned to fund only those projects that were not commercially viable but strategic and highly beneficial to the country. Projects with commercial potential would be open to foreign and domestic private sector participation.

Finally, without broad participation, the return on Singapore's information and physical infrastructure would not be realized. Indeed, the vision of the "Intelligent Island" depended on the far-reaching use of IT by Singaporeans to improve their businesses, make their work easier, and enhance their personal and professional lives. Building the NII would test Singapore's legendary ability to learn, "create its future," and select only "the best elements" of the West.

NCB and its 1,500 employees felt prepared to carry out their mission to "drive Singapore into the information age" (see Exhibit 14). NCB's Michael Yap felt that Singapore had "a real opportunity to lead the world in the conceptualization and implementation [of an NII]."[29] Its chairman, Tan Chin Nam, explained how past experience and investments would help NCB and Singapore transform the "Intelligent Island" dream to reality:

> In 1981, the original computerization effort, which led to the establishment of the NCB, called for the development of core competence in computer software technology. In 1986, the National IT Plan set out to integrate this budding software competence with communication technology to create world class IT applications. In 1991, the IT Masterplan [integrated] the computing and communications technologies . . . to generate a vision of Singapore as an Intelligent Island with advanced information infrastructure. Every stage of masterplanning was a major organizational learning experience for the NCB. . . . We welcome the "learning, relearning, and unlearning challenge" posed by the emerging knowledge economy.[30]

Singapore's prime minister was equally confident:

> The [IT2000] plan reaffirmed the strategic role IT will play in the Next Lap of Singapore's development, and showed that because the country dared to dream it will become a reality. . . . It is our lot in life that we continue running in the fast lane to keep up with changes in the new world economy.[31]

---

[29]Michael Yap, "Singapore NII: Beyond the Information Highway," *Information Technology, Journal of the Singapore Computer Society,* September 1994, p. 7.

[30]The Chairman's Statement, *NCB Yearbook: Dedicated to Making a Difference,* 1992–1993.
[31]Goh Chok Tong quoted in the *Strait Time,* September 27, 1991.

EXHIBIT 14 National Computer Board Organization Chart

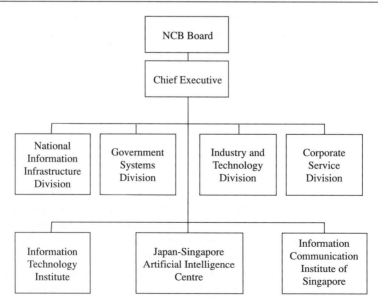

In addressing a forum of European business leaders in London in April 1994, Prime Minister Goh articulated the role that Singapore desires to have in the expected Asian economic expansion:

> Investing in the region, or "Going Regional" as we call it, is part of our long-term strategy to climb up the economic ladder. Regionalization means that we will be able to participate in the growth of the region to interlock the regional economies with our domestic economy. We thus expand our economic space, and through this expansion strengthen our domestic economy, especially the manufacturing sector. Building an external economy is a national imperative.

In May 1995, the Organization for Economic Cooperation and Development announced that Singapore would be upgraded to "developed nation" status in January 1996. At that time, Singapore would lose the special tariff preferences and eligibility for soft loans for development that came with "developing nation" status. Some observers wondered whether a tiny island distant from most of the industrialized world could make the transition from manufacturing to marketing and high technology—from catching up to keeping up to leading.

EXHIBIT 14 (continued)   National Computer Board Income Statement, 1991–1994 (in thousands of Singapore $)

	For Fiscal Year Ended March 31,			
	1991	*1992*	*1993*	*1994*
Operating income	3,653	4,500	13,443	61,264
Operating expenditures	32,284	27,901	45,346	102,142
Deficit/surplus before grants	(28,631)	(23,401)	(31,903)	(40,878)
Grants				
Operating grants				
Government	17,268	24,390	10,228	19,721
statutory boards	5,095	5,932	16,045	16,046
Deferred capital grants amortized				
(government and statutory boards)	5,434	5,263	6,183	6,996
	27,706	35,616	32,567	42,763
Deficit/surplus after grants	(836)	2,213	665	1,885
Deficit/surplus after taxation	(836)	2,213	665	1,885
and before ITI retention surplus	(36)	(51)	(56)	—
Net deficit/surplus for year	(871)	2,162	609	1,885
Accumulated surplus as of April 1	2,338	1,467	3,629	4,238
Accumulated surplus as of March 31	1,467	3,629	4,238	6,123

Note: Totals may not add up exactly due to rounding.

Source: National Computer Board Annual Reports.

Case 4–4

BAE AUTOMATED SYSTEMS (A): DENVER INTERNATIONAL AIRPORT BAGGAGE-HANDLING SYSTEM[1]

No airport anywhere in the world is as technologically advanced as the Denver International Airport.[2]

It's dramatic. If your bag [got] on the track, your bag [was] in pieces.[3]

In November 1989 ground was broken to build the Denver International Airport (DIA). Located 25 miles from downtown Denver, Colorado, it was the first major airport to be built in the United States since the opening of the Dallas–Fort Worth Airport in 1974. In 1992, two years into construction, the project's top managers recommended inclusion of an airport-wide integrated baggage-handling system that could dramatically improve the efficiency of luggage delivery. Originally contracted by United Airlines to cover its operations, the system was to be expanded to serve the entire airport. It was expected that the inte-

grated system would improve ground time efficiency, reduce close-out time for hub operations, and decrease time-consuming manual baggage sorting and handling. There were, however, a number of risks inherent in the endeavor: the scale of the large project size; the enormous complexity of the expanded system; the newness of the technology; the large number of resident entities to be served by the same system; the high degree of technical and project definition uncertainty; and the short time span for completion. Due to its significant experience implementing baggage-handling technology on a smaller scale, BAE Automated Systems Inc., an engineering consulting and manufacturing company based in Carrollton, Texas, was awarded the contract.

Construction problems kept the new airport from opening on the originally scheduled opening date in October 1993. Subsequently, problems with the implementation of the baggage system forced delays in the opening of the airport another three times in seven months. In May 1994, under growing pressure from shareholders, the business community, Denver residents, Federal Aviation Administration (FAA) com-

Assistant Professor Ramiro Montealegre and research associate H. James Nelson of the University of Colorado at Boulder, research associate Carin Isabel Knoop, and Professor Lynda M. Applegate prepared this case.

[2]Fred Isaac, Federal Aviation Administration regional administrator, quoted in "Denver Still Working Out Kinks as Its First Birthday Arrives," *USA Today,* February 28, 1996, p. 4b.

[3]Fred Renville, United Airlines employee, quoted in ibid.

missioners, and the tenant airlines and concessionaires, Denver mayor Wellington Webb announced that he was hiring the German firm Logplan to help assess the state of the automated baggage system. In July, Logplan issued an 11-page report to the City of Denver that characterized BAE's system as "highly advanced" and "theoretically" capable of living up to its promised "capacities, services and performances," but acknowledged mechanical and electrical problems that "make it most improbable to achieve a stable and reliable operation." Logplan suggested that it would take approximately five months to get the complete BAE system working reliably. It also suggested that a backup system of tugs, carts, and conveyor belts could be constructed in less than five months.

In August 1994, Mayor Webb approved the construction of a backup baggage system. At the same time, he notified BAE of a $12,000-a-day penalty for not finishing the baggage system by DIA's original October 29, 1993, completion date. Webb also demanded that BAE pay for the $50 million conventional tug-and-cart baggage system. Gene Di Fonso, President of BAE, knew that his company could demonstrate that flaws in the overall design of the airport and an unsystematic approach to project changes had affected implementation of the integrated baggage system. He wondered whether he should just cancel the contract and cut his losses, or attempt to negotiate with the city for the support required to finish the system as specified, despite the severe deterioration in communication and rising hostility. Could the problems with the automated system be overcome with the dedication of additional resources? Given that the system represented a significant departure from conventional technology, would reducing its size and complexity facilitate resolution of the problems that plagued it? And, if the city

could be persuaded to accept a simplified system, would the tenant airlines, particularly those with hubbing operations that had been promised more advanced functionality and better performance, be likely to sue?

Building the Most Efficient Airport in the World

Until about 1970, Denver's Stapleton Airport had managed to accommodate an ever-growing number of airplanes and passengers. Its operational capacity was severely limited by runway layout; Stapleton had two parallel north-south runways and two additional parallel east-west runways that accommodated only commuter air carriers.

Denver's economy grew and expanded greatly in the early 1980s, consequent to booms in the oil, real estate, and tourism industries. An aging and saturated Stapleton Airport was increasingly seen as a liability that limited the attractiveness of the region to the many businesses that were flocking to it. Delays had become chronic. Neither the north-south nor east-west parallel runways had sufficient lateral separation to accommodate simultaneous parallel arrival streams during poor weather conditions when instrument flight rules were in effect. This lack of runway separation and the layout of Stapleton's taxiways tended to cause delays during high-traffic periods, even when weather conditions were good.

Denver's geographic location and the growing size of its population and commerce made it an attractive location for airline hubbing operations. At one point, Stapleton had housed four airline hubs, more than any other airport in the United States. In poor weather and during periods of high-traffic volume, however, its limitations disrupted connection schedules that were important to maintaining these operations. A local storm could easily congest air traffic across the entire United States.[4]

The City and County of Denver had determined in the mid-1970s that Stapleton International Airport was in need of expansion or replacement. In July 1979, a study to assess the airport's needs was commissioned by the City of Denver to the Denver Regional Council of Governments. Upon completion of the study in 1983, a report was issued saying that, due to its size and geographic location, and strong commitments by United and Continental Airlines, Denver would remain a significant hub for at least one major U.S. carrier. The study recommended expansion of Stapleton's capacity.

Political Situation[5]

The City of Denver's 1983 mayoral race precipitated initiatives to improve the airfield infrastructure. Three candidates were vying for mayor: Monte Pascoe, Dale Tooley, and Frederico Peña. Pascoe, a prominent Denver attorney and former State Democratic Party co-chair, seized upon the airport issue, forcing other candidates to adopt stronger positions on airport expansion than they might have otherwise.[6] Peña and Tooley, however, drew the highest numbers of votes in the general election, and were forced into a runoff. At the persistent urging of the Colorado Forum (a collection of 50 of the state's top business executives), Peña and Tooley signed a joint statement committing

themselves to airport expansion. Peña won the runoff. Committed by a public promise that could have been enforced, if necessary, by the most highly motivated members of the region's business leadership, Peña immediately restated his intent to expand Stapleton.

The City of Denver and neighboring Adams County began to develop plans for long-term airport development in 1984. In 1985, a new site northeast of Denver was chosen. Consummation of the airport siting issue, however, was left to Adams County voters, who had to vote to permit the City of Denver to annex property therein. The city hired a consulting firm to help organize its resources and its efforts to work through the legal process. The data that was gathered through the master planning and environmental assessment later proved useful for public education.

An "Annexation Agreement" between Adams County and the City of Denver was reached on April 21, 1988. Adams County voters approved a plan to let Denver annex 43.3 square miles for the construction of an airport. In a special election on May 16, 1989, voters of Denver endorsed a "New Airport" by a margin of 62.7% to 37.3%. According to Edmond, "Those two referendums passed largely on the merits of the economic benefits: jobs and sales tax revenues."

Economic Considerations

A number of trends and events in the mid-1986s alarmed bank economists and others of the region's business leaders in the mid-1980s. The collapse of oil shale ventures between 1982 and 1986 saw mining employment fall from 42,000 to 26,000 jobs, while service support jobs fell from 25,300 jobs to 13,700.[7] Construction jobs fell from 50,700

---

[4]According to James Barnes [1993], "By 1994, Stapleton was one of the top five most constrained airports in the United States. There were over 50,000 hours of delay in 1988, and by 1997 the FAA had projected that Stapleton would experience over 100,000 hours of delay per year."

[5]Extracted from S.T. Moore, "Between Growth Machine and Garbage Can: Determining Whether to Expand the Denver Airport, 1982–1988," Annual Meeting of the Southern Political Science Association, Atlanta, Georgia, November 4, 1994.

[6]Ibid.

---

[7]*Colorado Business Outlook Forum,* University of Colorado School of Business, 1990.

to 36,600 jobs, and the value of private construction plummeted from $24 billion to $9.5 billion.[8]

A lackluster economy led many government officials in counties and municipalities as well as in Denver to embark upon an unprecedented policy of massive public construction to save the region from what was regarded in 1987 as an economic free-fall. A $180 million-plus municipal bond was issued for public improvements, including a new downtown library, neighborhood and major roadway improvements, and a host of overdue infrastructure investments. During the same period, the Peña administration moved decisively to confront an increasingly aggressive Chamber of Commerce leadership that was promoting airport relocation.

The determination of the "pro-New-Airport" clan was growing. The project was being marketed as a technologically advanced, state-of-the-art structure to draw businesses, import federal capital, and fund the creation of new jobs with bonded debts to overcome the short-term decline in the economy. The airport was to become a grandiose project to revive the Colorado economy and a master showcase for the Public Works Department. "The entire business community," recalled a member of the Mayor's administrative team:

> Chamber of Commerce, members of the city council, the mayor, and state legislators, participated in informational discussions with other cities that had recently built airports. [This enabled] everybody to understand the magnitude of the project. So we studied the other two airports that had been built in the United States in the last 50 years and said, "Tell us everything that you went through and all the places you think there will be problems." We were not going into it blindly.

---

[8]*Small Area Employment Estimates: Construction Review,* U.S. Department of Commerce, 1990.

Forecasts of aviation activity at Stapleton by the Airport Consultant team, the FAA, and others, however, did not anticipate events such as a new phase of post-deregulation consolidation, the acquisition in 1986 of Frontier Airlines by Texas Air (the owner of Continental), significant increases in air fares for flights in and out of Stapleton, and the bankruptcy of Continental. Consequently, the level of aviation activity in Denver was overestimated. Instead of rising, Stapleton's share of total U.S. domestic passenger enplanements fell 4% per year from 1986 through 1989.[9]

The Master Plan

The City of Denver's approach to preparing a master plan for the airport was typical. "One hires the best consultants on airfield layout, noise impacts, terminal layout, on-site roadways, off-site roadways, cost estimating, financial analysis, and forecasting," observed DIA administrator Gail Edmond. "They brainstorm and generate as many alternate layouts as possible." Alternatives were discussed and eliminated at periodic joint working sessions, and a technical subcommittee was organized to gather input from the eventual airport users, airlines, pilots, and the FAA. "Everybody knows how to begin an airport master plan," Edmond added.

Following a bid, the consulting contract was awarded to the joint venture of Greiner, Inc., and Morrison-Knudsen Engineers for their combined expertise in the fields of transportation and construction. The

---

[9]Furthermore, when selling the project to voters, planners at one point forecast up to 36 weekly flights to Europe by 1993. The number recorded in 1993, however, was four. The number of passengers departing from Denver was to rise from 16 million in 1985 to some 26 million by 1995. The 1994 figure, however, was about the same as the number of passengers in 1985, or half of Stapleton's capacity.

consulting team, working under the direction of the DIA Director of Aviation, focused first on four elements: site selection; the master plan; the environmental assessment and developing support by educating the public on economic benefit. The final master plan presented to the city by the team in the fall of 1987 called for the construction of the world's most efficient airport. It was to be created from the ground up with no predetermined limitations.

The plan was to allow the airport to grow and expand without compromising efficiency. Twice the size of Manhattan at 53 square miles, the nation's largest airport was to be designed for steady traffic flow in all weather conditions. It was to comprise a terminal with east and west buildings joined by an atrium structure, three concourses, an automated underground people-mover, and five parallel 12,000-foot-long runways on which as many as 1,750 planes could take off and land daily. Its flow-through traffic patterns would allow planes to land, taxi to concourse gates, and take off again all in one direction. The ultimate buildout, projected for the year 2020, was to include up to 12 full service runways, more than 200 gates, and a capacity of 110 million passengers annually. Estimated cost (excluding land acquisition and pre-1990 planning costs) was $2 billion. By the end of 1991, the estimated cost had increased to $2.66 billion. Plans called for the project's completion by the fall of 1993.

In September 1989, Federal officials signed a $60 million grant agreement for the new airport, which was to be financed in multiple ways—by issuing revenue bonds and securing federal grants—supplemented by a sizable investment by the city [County of Denver 1991]. Estimated federal grants for the new airport originally totaled $501 million. Portions of these were forthcoming from the FAA, for federal fiscal year 1996 in

the amount of $90 million and for federal fiscal year 1991 in the amount of $25 million. The remainder of the $501 million letter of intent was to be received on an annual basis through fiscal year 1997. The revenue bonds assumed the "Date of Beneficial Occupancy" (DBO) to be January 1, 1994, with bond repayments to begin on that date. At that time, the city determined that DIA would meet the DBO no later than October 31, 1993. A member of the Mayor's administrative team described the approach:

> What we did was plan the DBO date and then we planned an extra six months just in case there was a lag in the opening, which, in essence, allowed us to create stability in the market. The other thing we did was that we conservatively financed and filled every reserve account to the maximum. So we borrowed as much money as we could at the lower interest rate and were able to average the debt cost down, not up, as we thought it would be.

A Build-Design Project

By the time construction began at DIA in November 1989, a transfer of authority was taking place in the City of Denver. Wellington Webb was elected the new mayor. According to one of his assistants, the Peña administration had announced that the airport would be operational in October 1993. "This was a build-design project, which means that we were building the airport [while] we were designing it," he explained. "Because of the delays early on in the project, we had to accelerate construction immediately. There was a lot of pressure and too many players. This was an airport built by committee. We had regular meetings to straighten things out but it didn't always work."

Although the Webb administration inherited the airport project without a commitment on the part of the major carriers, the support and input of concerned airlines were absolutely key, not only financially but also in terms of input on overall airport layout, scope, and capacity, and supporting systems such as fueling and baggage handling. Denver launched the DIA program without specific commitments from either of Stapleton airport's two major tenant airlines, United and Continental, which together accounted for more than 70% of existing passenger traffic. Continental committed to the new airport in February 1990, United in December 1991. Fundamental changes were made to the airport layout plan and facilities (some already under construction) to accommodate the operational needs of these carriers.

The Webb administration followed the predecessor administration's emphasis on assuring that the project's greatest beneficiaries would be local businesses. The desire was to involve as many individual firms as practicable and to use Denver-area talent. It was reasoned that local talent was easily accessible to the program management team (PMT), knew Denver building codes and practices, and had available the necessary professional labor pool to accomplish the design in accordance with the demanding schedule. In addition, existing law stated that 30% minority-owned firms and 6% women-owned firms had to participate in a public works program. The result was a contracting philosophy that maximized opportunities for regional businesses and the local workforce to compete for the work. At least five of 60 contracts awarded for the design of DIA went to Denver-area firms. These 60 design contracts generated 110 construction contracts. Eighty-eight professional service contracts also had to be coordinated. Many local firms had to be hired, and the program was chopped up into many small projects. Involvement totaled 200 to 300 firms and reached 400 during the construction phase. Five different firms

designed the runways, four the terminal. The city's emphasis on encouraging everyone to compete and yet be part of the project increased the potential for interface and coordination problems.

Denver's flat economy led the administration to keep construction money within the city. Although this benefited the city, it introduced an additional burden on administration. As many as 40–50 concurrent contracts involved many interrelated milestones and contiguous or overlapping operational areas. The estimated daily on-site workforce population exceeded 2,500 workers for a 15- to 18-month period beginning in mid-1991 and peaked at between 9,000 and 10,000 in mid-1992. Adding to the human resource coordination problems was a forecasted 4,000 deliveries daily. Construction volume for six months in mid-1992 exceeded $100 million per month.

The prolonged period of assessment and negotiation prior to final approval of the project, and the financial plan selected (which required that bond repayments begin on January 1, 1994), pressured the PMT to push the project ahead at all cost. Because the project had to assume the characteristics of a "fast-track" project early in the construction startup, the compressed design period precipitated a more dynamic construction effort than might be anticipated for a "competitively bid, fixed price" program. Reliance on a design/build method for the project was, according to one DIA official, "unusual because projects this complex normally happen during separate stages. For example, you need to finish up the site selection before you begin the master planning."

Moreover, communication channels between the city, project management team, and consultants were neither well defined nor controlled. "If a contractor fell behind," a resident engineer who reported to one of the area managers said, the resident engineer would alert the contractor and document this. The resident engineer would document what would have to be done and what additional resources were necessary to get back on schedule and finish the contract on time. As a public agency it was enormous, the amount of documentation that we did. I don't know how many trees we cut down just for this project. The resident engineer had about five to eight 12-drawer filing cabinets of documentation, and this was nothing compared to what the area manager had. It was just incredible. There were at least four to six copies of everything.

The scheduling manager described the evolution of the tracking system that was used:

One of the biggest problems we had was keeping track of all the changes. So we developed a database system that was installed at each one of the resident engineer's trailers, and each contract administrator was then charged with keeping that system up to date and feeding us disks, which we would then merge together periodically to produce an integrated report. But every party had developed their own tracking system before the start of the project. That worked well for each group, but there was no way to take each one of these divergent systems and combine it into one, comprehensive report. So when we introduced the change tracking system everybody said, "fine, that's wonderful, and I'll update it when I get to it and when I get time." It took three years to implement the tracking system.

Project Management

In a fast-moving, ever-changing environment such as the development of a new airport, the management structure must be able to rapidly produce engineering alternatives and the supporting cost and schedule data.[10] But because DIA was financed by many sources and was a public works program, project administrators had to balance administrative, political, and social imperatives.[11]

The City of Denver staff and consultant team shared leadership of the project and coordinated the initial facets of DIA design. "The initial thought," reflected one staff member, "was that the city staff would do their thing and the consulting staff do theirs, and later we would coordinate. It became evident within a very short time that we were doing duplicate duties, which was inefficient. Finally the city decided to coordinate resources."

The city selected a team of city employees and consultants and drafted a work scope document that clearly separated the city's from the consultants' responsibilities. The elements the city did not delegate to consultants included ultimate policy and facility decisions, approval of payments, negotiation and execution of contracts, facilitation of FAA approvals, affirmative action, settlement of contractor claims and disputes, selection of consultants, and utility agreements. The city delegated some elements, such as value engineering, construction market analysis, claim management, on-site staff and organization, and state-of-the-art project control (computerized management of budget and schedule). Exhibit 1 depicts the DIA management structure.

The program management team became the organization dedicated to overseeing planning and development for the new airport. Headed by the associate director of aviation, the team was partially staffed by city career service employees. To add experience and capability, the city augmented the PMT

---

[10]The DIA project used the so-called "fast-tracking" method, which made it possible to compress some activities along the critical path and manage the construction project as a series of overlapping tasks.

[11]These included considerations such as affirmative action, local participation, neighborhood concerns, civic pride, input from the disabled community, art, secondary employment benefits of contract packaging, concern for the environment, and political interest.

EXHIBIT 1 Organization Chart

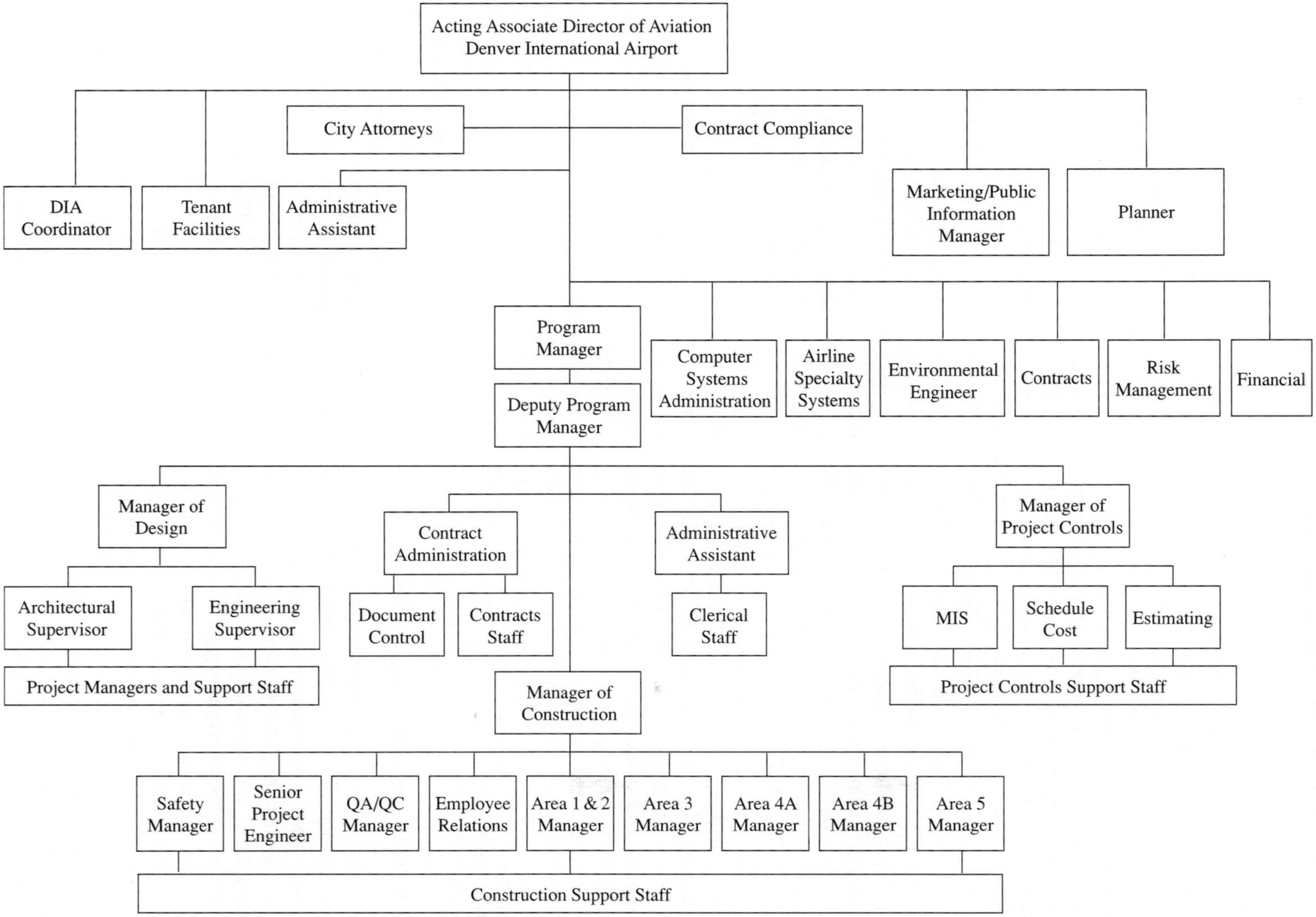

Source: City and County of Denver, Colorado, Airport System Review Bonds, Series 1991D, October 1991.

with personnel from the joint venture of Greiner Engineering and Morrison-Knudsen Engineers, the consulting team. Observed one program management team member, "This working partnership of the City of Denver and consulting joint venture team developed into a fully integrated single organization, capitalizing on the best to be offered by all participants, and optimizing the use of personnel resources."

DIA's operational project structure comprised five different areas subdivided into smaller units. The working areas were: site development (earthmoving, grading, and drainage); roadways and on-grade parking (service roads, on-airport roads, and off-airport roads connecting to highways); airfield paving; building design (people-mover/baggage-handler, tunnel, concourses, passenger bridge, terminal, and parking); and utility/special systems and other facilities (electrical transmission, oil, and gas line removal and relocation). An area manager controlled construction within each area. Area managers were responsible for the administration of all assigned contracts and, in coordination with other area managers, for management of the portion of the overall site in which their work took place.

United Airlines' Baggage System

From the public's perspective, the "friendliness" of any airport is measured by time. No matter how architecturally stimulating a new airport structure, the perception of business or leisure travelers is often registered in terms of efficiency in checking luggage at the departure area or waiting to claim a bag in the arrival area. The larger the airport, the more critical the efficient handling of baggage. Remote concourses connected by underground tunnels present special problems for airport planners and operators because of the great distances passengers and baggage must travel. The purpose of an airport being to move passengers as efficiently as possible, moving bags as quickly is part and parcel of that responsibility. Rapid transport of frequent flyers accomplishes very little if bags are left behind.

DIA's Concourse A, which was to house Continental Airlines, was situated some 400 meters, and United Airlines' Concourse B nearly 1,000 meters, north of the main terminal. Concourse C, home to other carriers, including American, Delta, Northwest, America West, and TWA, sat parallel to the other two concourses more than 1,600 meters north of the main terminal. The initial project design did not incorporate an airport-wide baggage system; the airport expected the individual airlines to build their own systems as in most other American airports.[12] United Airlines, which in June 1991 signed on to use DIA as its second-largest hub airport proceeded to do just that.

Needing an automated baggage-handling system if it was to turn aircraft around in less than 30 minutes, United, in December 1991, commissioned BAE Automatic Systems, Inc., a world leader in the design and implementation of material-handling systems, to develop an automated baggage-handling system for its B Concourse at DIA. The contract, which included engineering and early parts procurement only, was valued at $20 million; and the task was estimated to be completed in two and one-half years. "We began working at DIA under a contract directly with United Airlines," recalled Di Fonso. "Obviously, United Airlines has experience with airports. They concluded that the schedule had gotten totally out of control from the standpoint of baggage, and they

---

[12]G. Rifkin, "What Really Happened at Denver's Airport," *Forbes*, SAP Supplement, August 29, 1994.

acted to serve their own needs, basically to protect themselves. We contracted with United and were already designing their portion of the system before the city went out for competitive bidding."

BAE was founded as a division of Docutel Corporation in 1968. Docutel, which had developed the Telecar (a track-mounted automated baggage system), constructed an automated baggage system for United Airlines at San Francisco airport in 1978. When Docutel ran into financial difficulties during this installation, United asked Boeing, a major supplier of its aircraft, to take over the company. Boeing agreed, and the new company, a wholly owned subsidiary dubbed Boeing Airport Equipment, completed the San Francisco installation. In 1982, Boeing sold the company to its senior management, which renamed it BAE Automated Systems. In August 1985, BAE became an operating unit of Clarkson Industries, a wholly owned subsidiary of London-based BTR plc. BTR plc (formerly British Tire and Rubber), was a $10 billion conglomerate with global interests in building, paper and printing products, and agricultural and aircraft equipment.

In 1994, BAE's 365 employees worked on projects across the United States and in Europe and Australia. In-house engineering, manufacturing, and field support capabilities enabled BAE to develop, design, manufacture, install, and support every project it undertook from start to finish. BAE also provided consulting, engineering, and management services for airport projects and a variety of material-handling applications.

With sales of $100 million in 1994, up from approximately $40 million in 1991, BAE accounted for 90% of U.S. baggage-sorting equipment sales. Between 1972 and 1994, the company had successfully designed, manufactured, and installed nearly 70 automated baggage-handling

systems (worth almost $500 million) at major airports in the United States, in New York, Dallas–Fort Worth, Chicago, San Francisco, Atlanta, Miami, Newark, and Pittsburgh. It had also installed systems in Vancouver and London and was selected, in 1992, as a consultant to the $550 million main terminal for the New Seoul Metropolitan Airport in South Korea.

BAE was a very self-contained, integrated company structured along two business lines: manufacturing and engineering. Its approximately 200,000 square foot manufacturing facility was capable of producing nearly all of the components required by BAE systems save motors, gearboxes, and bearings. The engineering department was structured according to major projects. Each project was assigned a project manager who reported directly to the company president.

Implementing an Integrated Baggage-Handling System

BAE had already commenced work on United's baggage system when the PMT recognized the potential benefits of an airport-wide integrated baggage system. Moreover, as one DIA senior manager explained, "Airlines other than United simply were not coming forward with plans to develop their own baggage systems." Airport planners and consultants began to draw up specifications, and the city sent out a request for bids. Of 16 companies contacted, both in the United States and abroad, only three responded. A consulting firm recommended against the submitted designs on the grounds that the configurations would not meet the airport's needs.

BAE was among the companies that had decided not to bid for the job. BAE had installed the Telecar system at a number of other airports, and the basic technologies of the Telecar, laser barcode readers, and conveyor belt systems were not new. What was new was the size and complexity of the system. "A grand airport like DIA needs a complex baggage system," explained Di Fonso:

> Therefore, the type of technology to be used for such a system is the kind of decision that must be made very early in a project. If there is a surprise like no bidders, there is still time to react. At DIA, this never happened. Working with United Airlines, we had concluded that destination-coded vehicles moving at high speed was the technology needed. But quite honestly, although we had that technology developed, its implementation in a complex project like this would have required significantly greater time than the city had left available.

A United project manager concurred: "BAE told them from the beginning that they were going to need at least one more year to get the system up and running, but no one wanted to hear that." The City of Denver was getting the same story from the technical advisers to the Franz Josef Strauss Airport in Munich. The Munich Airport had an automated baggage system but one far less complex than DIA's. Nevertheless, Munich's technical advisors had spent two years testing the system, and the system had been running 24 hours a day for six months before the airport opened.

Formulating Intentions

As BAE was already working on United's automated baggage-handling system and enjoyed a world-wide reputation as a superior baggage system builder, Denver approached the company. BAE was asked to study how the United concept could be expanded into an integrated airport system that could serve the other carriers in the various concourses. BAE presented the City of Denver with a proposal to develop the "most complex automated baggage system ever built," according to Di Fonso. It was to be effective in delivering bags to and from passengers, and efficient in terms of operating reliability, maintainability, and future flexibility. The system was to be capable of directing bags (including suitcases of all sizes, skis, and golf clubs) from the main terminal through a tunnel into a remote concourse and directly to a gate. Such efficient delivery would save precious ground time, reduce close-out time for hub operations, and cut time-consuming manual baggage sorting and handling.

Although an automated system was more expensive initially than simple tugs and baggage carts, it was expected that it would reduce the manpower which was required to distribute bags to the correct locations. Bags unloaded from an aircraft arriving at a particular concourse would barely be touched by human hands. Moved through the airport at speeds up to 20 mph, they would be waiting when passengers arrived at the terminal. To prove the capability of its mechanical aspects, and demonstrate the proposed system to the airlines and politicians, BAE built a prototype automated baggage-handling system in a 50,000 square foot warehouse near its manufacturing plant in Carrollton, Texas. The prototype system convinced Chief Airport Engineer Walter Slinger that the automated system would work. "[The City of Denver] approached us based on one core concept," recalled Di Fonso. "They wanted to have a fully integrated, airport-wide baggage system. The city had two major concerns. First, they had no acceptable proposal. Second, United was probably going to go ahead and build what it needed and the rest of the airport would have been equipped with something else." Di Fonso continued:

> When we arrived on the scene, we were faced with fully defined project specs, which obviously in the long run proved to be a major planning error. The city had fallen into a trap, which historically architects and engineers

tend to fall into as they severely underplay the importance and significance of some of the requirements of a baggage system, that is, arranging things for the space into which it must fit, accommodating the weight it may impose on the building structure, the power it requires to run, and the ventilation and air conditioning that may be necessary to dissipate the heat it generates.

In April 1992, BAE was awarded the $175.6 million contract to build the entire airport system. According to Di Fonso, company executives and city officials hammered out a deal in three intense working sessions. "We placed a number of conditions on accepting the job," he observed:

> The design was not to be changed beyond a given date, and there would be a number of freeze dates for mechanical design, software design, permanent power requirements and the like. The contract made it obvious that both signatory parties were very concerned about the ability to complete. The provisions dealt mostly with all-around access, timely completion of certain areas, provision of permanent power, provision of computer rooms. All these elements were delineated as milestones.

Denver officials accepted these requirements and, in addition, committed to unrestricted access for BAE equipment. Because of the tight deadlines, BAE would have priority in any area where it needed to install the system. Di Fonso elaborated:

> When we entered into the contract, Continental Airlines was still under bankruptcy law protection. The city was very concerned that they would be unable to pay for their concourse. They only contracted for about 40% of the equipment that is now in Concourse A, which was the concourse that Continental had leased. Beyond that, Concourse C had no signatory airlines as leaseholders at the time. The city, therefore, wanted the simplest, most elementary baggage system possible for Concourse C. The outputs and inputs were very, very crude, intentionally crude to keep the

costs down because the city had no assurance of revenue stream at that point in time. The city did not get the airlines together or ask them what they wanted or needed to operate. The approach was more along the lines of "we will build the apartment building, and then you come in and rent a set of rooms."

Project Organization and Management

No major organizational changes to accommodate the new baggage system were deemed necessary, although some managerial adjustments were made on the DIA project. Design of the United baggage system was frozen on May 15, 1992, when the PMT assumed managerial responsibility for the integrated baggage system. The direct relationship with BAE was delegated to Working Area 4, which also had responsibility for building design efforts such as the peoplemover, airside concourse building, passenger bridge main landside building complex and parking garage, and various other smaller structures. The area manager, although he had no experience in airport construction, baggage system technologies, or the introduction of new technologies, possessed vast experience in construction project control management.

BAE had to change its working structure to conform to DIA's project management structure. Di Fonso explained:

> There was a senior manager for each of the concourses and a manager for the main terminal. The bag system, however, traversed all of them. If I had to argue a case for right of way I would have to go to all the managers because I was traversing all four empires. In addition, because changes were happening fast at each of these sites, there was no time to have an information system to see what is Concourse A deciding and what is Concourse B deciding. We had to be personally involved to understand what was going on. There was no one to tie it all together and overlap all these effects because the basic organization was to manage it as discrete areas. It was pandemonium. We

would keep saying that over and over again. Who is in charge?

For the first two years of the project, Di Fonso was the project manager. The project was divided into three general areas of expertise: mechanical engineering, industrial control, and software design. Mechanical engineering was responsible for all mechanical components and their installation, industrial control for industrial control design, logic controller programming, motor control panels, and software design for writing real-time process control software to manage the system.

At the time the contract with BAE was signed, construction had already begun on the terminal and concourses. Substantial changes had to be made to the overall design of the terminal, and some construction already completed had to be taken out and reinstalled to accommodate the expanded system. Installation of the expanded system was initially estimated to require more than $100 million in construction work. Walls had to be removed and a new floor installed in the terminal building to support the new system. Moreover, major changes in project governance were taking place during the baggage system negotiations. In May 1992, shortly after the baggage system negotiations commenced, the head of the DIA project resigned.

The death in October 1992 of Chief Airport Engineer Slinger, who had been a strong proponent of the baggage system and closely involved in negotiations with BAE, also exerted a significant impact on the project. His cooperation had been essential because of the amount of heavy machinery and track that had to be moved and installed and the amount of construction work required to accommodate the system. His replacement, Gail Edmond, was selected because she had worked closely with him and knew all the

players. Her managerial style, however, was quite different from Slinger's. A Public Works manager recalled his first reaction to the change: "[The airport] is not going to be open on time." A United Airlines project manager summarized Edmond's challenge thus:

> Slinger was a real problem solver. He was controversial because of his attitude, but he was never afraid to address problems. He had a lot of autonomy and could get things done. Gail was in a completely different position. Basically, she had a good understanding of how the project was organized and who the key players were, but didn't know much about the actual construction. Also, the city council didn't give her anywhere near the autonomy and the authority that Slinger had, and she had to get approval from the council on just about all decisions. They really tied her hands, and everyone knew it.

Di Fonso echoed the project manager's assessment:

> Walter [Slinger] understood that one of the things we had to have was unrestricted access. I think he clearly understood the problem the city was facing, and he understood the short timeframe under which we were operating. He was the one that accepted all of the contractual conditions, all the milestones of the original contract. He really had no opportunity to influence the outcome of this project, however; because he died within months after the contract was signed. I think Gail did an excellent job [but] she was overwhelmed.[13] She just had too much. The layers below focused inward, worrying about their own little corners of the world.

"Not only did we not get the unrestricted access that was agreed upon," Di Fonso emphasized, "we didn't even have reason-

---

[13]In addition to her role as Chief Airport Engineer, Edmond kept her previous responsibilities as Chief of Construction and Acting Director of Aviation.

able access." Ten days after Slinger's death, a BAE millwright found a truck from Hensel Phelps, the contractor building Concourse C, blocking her work site. She asked someone to move the truck or leave the keys so it could be moved. According to a BAE superintendent, "she was told that 'this is not a BAE job and we can park anywhere we please: is that clear?'" Elsewhere, BAE electricians had to leave work areas where concrete grinders were creating clouds of dust. Fumes from chemical sealants forced other BAE workers to flee. Di Fonso pleaded with the city for help. "We ask that the city take prompt action to assure BAE the ability to continue its work in an uninterrupted manner," he wrote. "Without the city's help, the delays to BAE's work will quickly become unrecoverable."[14]

To further complicate matters, the airlines began requesting changes to the system's design even though the mechanical and software designs were supposed to be frozen. "Six months prior to opening the airport," Di Fonso recalled, "we were still moving equipment around, changing controls, changing software design."

In August 1992, for example, United altered plans for a transfer system for bags changing planes, requesting that BAE eliminate an entire loop of track from Concourse B. Rather than two complete loops of track, United would have only one. This change saved approximately $20 million, but required a system redesign. Additional ski-claim devices and odd-size baggage elevators added in four of the six sections of the terminal added $1.61 million to the cost of the system. One month later, Continental requested that automated baggage-sorting systems be added to its west basement at an additional cost of $4.67 million. The ski

---

[14]*Rocky Mountain News,* January 29, 1995.

claim area length was first changed from 94 feet to 127 feet, then in January 1993, shortened to 112 feet. The first change added $295,800, the second subtracted $125,000, from the cost. The same month, maintenance tracks were added to permit the Telecars to be serviced without having to lift them off the main tracks at an additional cost of $912,000. One year later, United requested alterations to its odd-size baggage inputs—cost of the change: $432,000.

Another problem was the city's inability to supply "clean" electricity to the baggage system. The motors and circuitry used in the system were extremely sensitive to power surges and fluctuations. When electrical feedback tripped circuit breakers on hundreds of motors, an engineer was called in to design filters to correct the problem. Although ordered at that time, the filters still had not arrived several months later. A city worker had canceled a contract without realizing that the filters were part of it. The filters finally arrived in March 1994.

A third, albeit disputed, complication related to Denver's requirement, and city law, that a certain percentage of jobs be contracted to minority-owned companies. The City of Denver had denied BAE's original contract because it did not comply with hiring requirements, whereupon BAE engaged some outside contractors in lieu of BAE employees. Di Fonso estimated that this increased costs by approximately $6 million, a claim rejected by the Mayor's Office of Contract Compliance. Then, in September 1993, BAE's contract negotiations with the City of Denver over maintenance of the system resulted in a two-day strike of 300 millwrights that was joined by some 200 electricians. BAE negotiated with Denver for maintenance workers to earn $12 per hour on certain jobs that the union contended should be worth $20 per hour. As a result, BAE lost the maintenance contract.

Project Relations

Much of the effort for implementing the baggage system was directed within one of the four working areas. "The relationship with the management team was very poor," recalled Di Fonso:

> The management team had no prior baggage-handling competence or experience. This was treated as a major public works project. The management team treated the baggage system as similar to pouring concrete or putting in air-conditioning ducts. When we would make our complaints about delays and access and so forth, other contractors would argue their position. The standard answer was, "Go work it out among yourselves." . . . With contractors basically on their own, this led almost to anarchy. Everyone was doing his or her own thing.

Another perspective was offered by a project manager from Stone & Webster, a consultant to the PMT, reflecting on the work done by BAE: "This contractor simply did not respond to the obvious incredible workload they were faced with. Their inexperienced project management vastly underestimated their task. Their work ethic was deplorable."[15] PMT management insisted that access and mechanical issues weren't the problem. "They were running cars in Concourse B all summer [1993]," Edmund observed. "The problem was that the programming was not done and BAE had full control of the programming."[16]

Lawsuits and a Backup Baggage System

In February 1993, Mayor Webb delayed the scheduled October 1993 airport opening to December 19, 1993. Later, this December date was changed to March 9, 1994. "Everybody got into the panic mode of trying

---

[15]*Forbes,* ASAP Supplement, August 29, 1994.
[16]Ibid.

to get to this magical date that nobody was ready for," a senior vice-president for BAE recalled. In September 1993, the opening was again postponed—this time until May 15, 1994. In late April 1994, the City of Denver invited reporters to observe the first test of the baggage system, without notifying BAE. Seven thousand bags were to be moved to Continental's Concourse A and United's Concourse B. So many problems were discovered that testing had to be halted. Reporters saw piles of disgorged clothes and other personal items lying beneath the Telecar's tracks.

Most of the problems were related to errors in the system's computer software, but mechanical problems also played a part. The software that controlled the delivery of empty cars to the terminal building, for example, often sent the cars back to the waiting pool. Another problem was "jam logic" software, which was designed to shut down a section of track behind a jammed car, but instead shut down an entire loop of track. Optical sensors designed to detect and monitor cars were dirty, causing the system to believe that a section of track was empty when, in fact, it had held a stopped car. Collisions between cars dumped baggage on tracks and on the floor; jammed cars jumped the track and bent the rails; faulty switches caused the Telecars to dump luggage onto the tracks or against the walls of the tunnels.

After the test, Mayor Webb delayed the airport's opening yet again, this time indefinitely. "Clearly, the automated baggage system now underway at DIA is not yet at a level that meets the requirements of the city, the airlines, or the traveling public," the mayor stated. The city set the costs of the delay at $330,000 per month. Recognizing that his reputation was staked on his ability to have a baggage system performing to a point at which the new airport could be opened, Mayor Webb engaged, in May 1994, the German firm Logplan to assess the state of the automated baggage system. In July, Logplan isolated a loop of track that contained every feature of the automated baggage system and intended to run it for an extended period to test the reliability of the Telecars. Jams on the conveyor belts and collisions between cars caused the test to be halted. The system did not run long enough to determine if there was a basic design flaw or to analyze where the problems were. Logplan recommended construction of a backup baggage system, and suggested using Rapistan Demag, a firm it had worked with in the past. Construction of a backup system was announced in August 1994. The system itself cost $10.5 million, but electrical upgrades and major building modifications raised the projected cost to $50 million.

In the meantime, the City of Denver, as well as many major airlines, hired legal firms to assist with negotiations and future litigation. "We will have enough legal action for the rest of this century," a city administrator mused. The City of Denver had to communicate with such parties as the United States federal grand jury, Securities Exchange Commission, and the General Accounting Office. The federal grand jury was conducting a general investigation concerning DIA. The SEC was investigating the sale of $3.2 billion in bonds to finance DIA's construction, and GAO the use of Congressional funds.

Di Fonso, reviewing Mayor Webb's letter and requests that BAE pay a $12,000-a-day penalty for missing DIA's original October 29, 1993, completion date, as well as assuming the costs of building the $50 million conventional tug-and-cart baggage system, summed up the situation thus: "We have gotten to the point with the city that literally we are not talking to each other. Consultants recommended a backup baggage system, and the minute that the decision was made, the city had to defend it. We are left out in limbo."

Special Topics

In turbulent times, an enterprise has to be managed both to withstand sudden blows and to avail itself of sudden unexpected opportunities. This means that in turbulent times the fundamentals have to be managed, and managed well.[1]

Companies exerted significant effort during the 1980s and 1990s reorganizing to meet the challenges highlighted by the cases in this book. But as the millennium draws to a close, many are being forced to face the reality that the 21st century will demand even more radical change. Thomas Kuhn's[2] analysis of scientific revolutions suggests that crisis is a necessary precondition to the emergence of new theory. But when presented with crisis, most people do not immediately reject existing models. Instead, they attempt to relate new evidence to their existing theories. They attempt incremental adjustments that, over time, begin to blur the boundaries between old and new. Practitioners are often the first to lose sight of the details of the old models as the familiar rules for solving problems are called into question. At some point, total reconstruction from new fundamental principles is required. This appears to be the point at which many of the companies described in the book find themselves. A crisis, largely driven by a fundamental mismatch between environmental demands and organizational capabilities, has called into question many of the fundamental assumptions of traditional industry, organizational, and IT models.

Module 5 addresses two topics—global issues and the IT business—that synthesize the models and frameworks discussed throughout the book. Four integrative cases—Colliers, www.springs.com, Providian Trust, and Southwire—are included in this final module. These cases, when analyzed with the cases in other modules of the book, help advance our understanding of the industry, organization, and IT infrastructure required to successfully manage in the information age.

---

[1]P. Drucker, *Managing in Turbulent Times* (New York: Harper & Row, 1980)

[2]T. Kuhn, *The Structure of Scientific Revolution* (Chicago: University of Chicago Press, 1970).

Chapter

12

Global Issues

In a major chemical company, the executive vice president of administrative services received a proposal to shut down their European data center and, using channel extender technology, to run the entire network of 1,000 European terminals out of the U.S. center. According to the proposal, this would save $3 million a year in operating costs plus provide better backup and faster response time to the *European* operations. Several other organizations had recently made a similar move, he was told. After the proposal was executed, all savings and service improvement goals were achieved.

A large pharmaceutical company was reviewing its software development experiences in India. Five projects had been developed there in the previous year. Three had been outstanding successes, with the software being delivered for roughly 50 percent of its cost domestically; the other two were conspicuous disasters, with all the invested money wasted. Apparently, specification changes and the distance of the India development group were the major causes of these disasters. The IT manager was uncertain how to proceed, given this information.

Asea Brown Boveri (ABB) developed, in the early 1990s, a worldwide personal computer-based network that allowed it to close all books around the world in 10 working days and have all financial and operating data available both to corporate and country management. In a major article, ABB's chairman noted that his firm was a massive, information-intensive organization that could not operate without such support.

These stories illustrate two major shifts in the 1990s: (1) the management of a transnational organization has been dramatically impacted by new technologies, allowing new controls and the placement of work in very different locations; (2) the development of IT support for organizations has likewise changed dramatically.

In the past, investigating transnational information technology (IT) issues has been neglected; it seemed too specialized and technical to the scholars of international business, and, for their part, scholars of IT management have been highly national (i.e., United States) in their orientation. However, significant new work is being done in the field, exemplified by Peter Hagstrom's *The 'Wired' MNC*[1] and the four-year-old *Journal of Global Information Management: Information Technology Impact on Transnational Firms.*

Not only is transnational IT management evolving dramatically, but its issues will become even more significant in the coming years. Managing the forces (described as six trends in Chapter 2) driving transition in IT is complicated in the international arena by the wide diversity in cost, quality, and maturity of national IT infrastructures (e.g., those of Germany versus those of Hungary), local manufacturing and distribution technologies, and the scope and sophistication of IT applications. Building on the concepts of strategic relevance, culture, contingent planning, and managing diffusion of technology, this chapter focuses on aspects of transnational business influenced by IT and the new ways of delivering IT service internationally.

IT coordination issues for international operations are vastly more complex than purely domestic ones because they involve all the issues of domestic operations plus many additional difficulties. During the coming decade, IT will continue to be challenged by the opening of Eastern Europe and Asia to private enterprise, the need to share technologies within a firm for common problems around the world, and the continued evolution of transnational firms in both products and structure. The cross-border flows of research, goods, and materials are accelerating, requiring new and complex information infrastructures.

Financial and human resources for global operations require extremely coordinated management. Many firms have growing pools of staff needing extensive global coordination and development, including the underlying electronic support. Finally, technology skills, expertise, and intelligence all require much tighter coordination in the multinational realm. IT is central to accomplishing this.

Additional complexity comes from wide differences in cultures, labor and technology costs, products, and the need for and viability of IT support in different areas of the world. India, for example, with its cheap labor and good telecommunications gateways, is a highly cost-effective location to do certain kinds of software development. Its marginal in-country telecommunications, however, realistically pose fundamentally different integration issues for in-country operations than those faced by firms in Singapore, with its high-cost labor, high-quality telecommunications, and small geography.

---

[1]Peter Hagstrom, *The 'Wired' MNC: The Role of Information Systems for Structural Change in Complex Organizations,* Stockholm School of Economics, Institute for International Business, Stockholm, Sweden, 1991.

Likewise, technology advances have significantly affected firms' overall organization structures, permitting tasks to be moved cost-effectively around the globe while maintaining tighter control and facilitating new ways of defining and doing work.

The first section of this chapter reviews IT's impact on the operations of transnational firms. The second section examines national characteristics determining what type of IT support is both possible and appropriate for a firm's operations within a country. Environmental issues that influence how a firm can develop IT support in another country are explained in the third section, while company-specific issues helping corporations develop and coordinate IT activity internationally are discussed in the fourth section. The final part reviews some IT policies firms have adopted and discusses their appropriateness in particular settings.

INFORMATION TECHNOLOGY IMPACT ON TRANSNATIONAL FIRMS

The new technologies of the past decade have affected the ways in which and places where firms do work in many ways, and their impact will be even greater in the coming decade as the technologies evolve and firms gain experience in implementing the changes enabled by them. Organization structures, control procedures, and tasks are being altered, albeit with great effort and expense.

Geographic Transfer of Work

The new technologies have facilitated the physical movement of work from areas with high-cost labor pools to areas where labor pools are both high quality and low cost. A domestic U.S. example is Citibank's moving its credit card operation from high-cost New York City to Sioux Falls, South Dakota. (Citibank achieved enormous savings.) In the same vein, American Airlines has moved a significant amount of its data entry work out of Dallas, where the company is headquartered. Documents are now keyed in Barbados, and the resulting outputs are transmitted electronically back to Dallas. Opportunities to source engineering and design activities internationally have also emerged. Several years ago a U.S. insurance company developed a significant systems development and programming unit in Ireland. This allowed the company to access the much less-expensive, high-quality Irish labor pool, effecting important savings. An added bonus was the firm's ability to use the third shift of domestic computer operations for debugging because of the five-hour time difference between Ireland and the United States. Similarly, a number of software organizations with more than 150,000 employees have developed in India; these organizations compete aggressively for Western European and American systems development activities, particularly for highly structured tasks and ones with medium to high technology. In a world where the economy is increasingly service oriented and where telecommunications costs continue to drop, such trends will accelerate.

Global Networking and Expertise Sharing

Firms like IBM and Price Waterhouse have developed very sophisticated international electronic mail, groupware, and conferencing technology and procedures. Tens of thousands of professional support staff around the world now have direct electronic access to each other. Global sources of knowledge can be quickly tapped, the barriers of time zones swept away, and the overall response time to problems sharply altered. (Today, marketing representatives routinely assemble documentation from around the world and can prepare a large, multimillion-dollar project proposal in 24 hours.) As overseas markets, manufacturing facilities, and research facilities proliferate, these coordinating mechanisms become vitally important in a world where competition is time-based. Inexpensive, broadband, fiber-based global communication provides important opportunities for sharing and managing designs, manufacturing schedules, and text. Identifying expertise and then sharing it globally are allowing some transnational firms to differentiate themselves in the late 1990s. The new capabilities and costs made possible by optical fiber are only accelerating this trend. This is particularly easy for companies, such as VeriFone, which have grown up in the information age and thus have not had to go through wrenching cultural transformation.

Global Service Levels

The standards constituting world-class service are sharply increasing. Several years ago, for example, a major U.S. trucking company could tell you where each of its trucks was and what was on it (e.g., a truck had just left the Kansas City depot carrying a certain load and should arrive in San Francisco in 36 hours). The truck's location at a precise moment was unknown, however, and there was no way to direct the driver to cities in between for emergency pickups. (None of its competitors could perform any better.) Today, on top of each of the company's trucks is a small satellite dish containing a computer. The firm now knows exactly where each truck is (within a city) and at any time can send instructions to drivers to alter their routes as customer needs emerge and change. Today's upmarket American cars are tracked by satellite, and if, for example, an air bag pops open, emergency road service from the nearest service facility is immediately dispatched.

In the overseas transportation business, global information links have allowed U.S. carriers such as American President Lines to survive in a world dominated by low-cost competitors. Since the 1970s, this firm has used IT to provide a highly customized and differentiated electronic-based service for its customers around the world. It has thereby neutralized its competitors' significant labor cost advantage by providing a highly valuable customer service, which includes up-to-the-minute cargo locations, reliable delivery promises, and flexibility in handling emergencies. Such advantages, of course, do not endure forever, and the pressure to maintain this edge through innovation is constant. The U.S. Postal Service is identifying service bottlenecks by mailing letters which contain small emitting chips and then tracking their progress.

Time-Based Competition

The required response time in the global community is dramatically shrinking. Automobile manufacturers and large construction firms, for example, have been able to shave months—even years—off the design cycle as local computer-aided design (CAD) equipment is linked internationally to CAD equipment owned by them, their suppliers, and their customers. In financial services, the question repeatedly arises, "Is two-second response time enough, or are we at a significant disadvantage?" A speaker at a telecommunication conference noted that within a week after the opening of the new London stock exchange, which allows automatic electronic tracking, firms using satellites had shifted to optical fiber because the 50-*millisecond* delay put them at a distinct competitive disadvantage.

In between these extremes, of course, are situations where taking weeks off order entry, order confirmation, and manufacturing cycles is the issue. A British chemical company's $30 million investment in manufacturing and IT transformed what had been a 10-week order entry and manufacturing cycle to one or two days. Needless to say, this changed the rules of industry competition and put unbearable pressure on some competitors. In the words of one of our colleagues, "Competing on the basis of time is done not just by speeding up the mess, but by enabling the construction of very different infrastructures that challenge every aspect of the firm's procedures." Global time-based competition will be a major item for world business in the next decade. ("The sun never sets on the British Empire" has new meaning for today's global firms, which are able to operate continuously around the globe.)

Cost Reduction

Much tighter information links between overseas operations, customers, and suppliers allow a firm to eliminate significant slack from its manufacturing systems, resulting in significant reductions in buffer inventories and staffing levels and a general acceleration in asset utilization. At the extreme, these links enable the creation of "hollow" global corporations such as

Benetton, which owns virtually nothing but a sophisticated global information system that connects the activities of its franchises with its suppliers.
VeriFone, the credit card transaction authorization company, is another
example of a firm which easily coordinates 30 global manufacturing and
sales operations.

In sum, IT has enabled the transformation of the very structures of
transnational organizations, the type of work they do, and where they do the
work; it has also meant massive disruptions in existing patterns of work.
More important, the new technologies assure that this impact will continue
to evolve. The dark side of this trend, of course, is a huge increase in operational dependence on networks, central processors, and so on. In consequence, firms have had to build high levels of redundancy into their
networks, creating alternative paths for information flow to back up their
computing centers and so on. Reuters, as we have seen, provides more than
a dozen electronic information paths from any one part of the world to
another. For many organizations, these issues are so fundamental and of
such potential strategic impact that the IT activity is positioned near the top
of the firm and is intimately involved in all strategic planning activities to
ensure it can fully support the firm's plans.

COUNTRY DIVERSITY

A number of factors inherent in a culture, government, and economy determine which IT applications are feasible within the country, how they should
be implemented, and how (if at all) they should be directed by a corporate IT
function located in another country. The most important factors are discussed here.

Sociopolitical

A country's industrial maturity and form of government are particularly
important factors when considering the use of IT. Developing countries with
high birth rates and low labor cost structures have views and opportunities
far different from those of mature industrialized nations with their shrinking labor populations, financial resources, and well-established bureaucra-
cies that provide the necessary stability for developing communication
systems. In some countries, investments in technical infrastructure are
made at the expense of such other national priorities as food and medical
care. This was a driving force for Malaysia, for example, to privatize their
telecommunications so they could gain access to the capital markets to continue their rapid growth. In countries like Hungary, investments in land
lines are so inadequate (and such significant amounts of time will be needed
to rectify this) that cellular networks have taken over the dominant role.

Language

A common spoken language facilitates technical communication and the sharing of relevant documentation. When that is lacking, the potential for errors, mishaps, or worse is greatly increased. Frequently, senior managers of international subsidiaries are fluent in the language of the parent company, but lower-level managers and staff technicians are not. Asea Brown Boveri, the large Swiss-Swedish pharmaceutical/chemical company, for example, has made a major effort to establish English as the companywide language, but, realistically, full fluency lies only at the senior management and staff levels. Internet homepages have to display product information and other data in multiple languages.

Local Constraints

A multitude of local cultural traditions can inhibit the development of coordinated global systems and orderly technology transfer between countries. Differing union agreements, holidays, tax regulations, and customs procedures all force major modifications of software for applications like accounting and personnel. Further, differences in holidays, working hours, and so on, complicate coordination of reporting and data gathering.

Also important are issues relating to geography and demographics. For example, a large music company centralized its order-entry and warehouse management functions for France in Paris, because doing so fit the structure of that country's distribution system. In Germany, however, the company had to establish multiple factories and distribution points and a quite different order-entry system for serving the German market, because that structure reflects the realities of German geography and prevailing distribution patterns. Unfortunately, this meant that the software and procedures used in the French subsidiary were inappropriate for German operations.

Economics

Serving the interests of different national cultures in a transnational IT organization often means building country-specific solutions. A mature industrial economy, for instance, normally has an available pool of well-trained, procedurally oriented individuals who are well paid relative to world standards. Further, the economic incentive to replace clerical people with IT systems is complemented by a limited availability of well-trained clerical staff. In countries with low wage rates, however, perhaps dependent on one or two main raw material exports for currency, both human talent and some of the economic incentive toward IT are lacking. (In the microchip world, however, this has changed quickly.) Logistics management improvements (better asset utilization, etc.) are global phenomena. Within these countries, organizations need to develop reliable sources of information and more conducive environments for IT use.

Currency Issues

Currency restrictions and exchange-rate volatility also complicate the operation of international information service activities. A sharp change in exchange rates may make the supposedly cost-effective location for providing service to neighboring countries suddenly cost-ineffective. The late 1998 collapse of the East Asian currencies suddenly invigorated the prospects of Singapore-based systems integrators.

Autonomy

The drive for autonomy and feelings of nationalism also represent important issues. The normal drive for autonomy in units within a country is intensified by differences in language and culture as one deals with international subsidiaries. In general, more integration effort is needed to coordinate foreign subsidiaries than domestic ones. Coordination difficulties increase with the subsidiary's distance from corporate headquarters as its relative economic importance to the corporation decreases and if different spoken languages are the norm.

National Infrastructure

The cost and availability of utilities (particularly telecommunications utilities), reliable electric power, and a transportation system can place important constraints on feasible alternatives. On the other hand, their absence may provide an opportunity to experiment with certain emerging technologies. For example, to overcome one country's unpredictable transportation and communication systems, a South American distributor developed a private microwave tower network to link the records of a remote satellite depot with the central warehouses. Direct ground links to satellites and cells can bypass the need for expensive ground line installation. This set of issues has been diminishing in importance over the past decade.

Summary

These factors in aggregate make coordinating international IT activities more complicated than domestic IT activities; indeed, the complications are so deep-rooted as to provide enduring challenges. Consequently, most multinationals have had to develop special staff and organizational approaches for these issues. Over the past decade, as global information velocity has been enabled by new technologies, in general, much stronger information sharing and global coordination have emerged.

NATIONAL IT ENVIRONMENT ISSUES

In addition to the many differences among countries, some specific IT issues make coordinating and transferring IT from one country to another particularly challenging. These are due in part to the long lead times necessary for building effective systems and in part to the changing nature of the technology. The most important of these issues are discussed in this section.

Availability of IT Professional Staff

Inadequate availability of systems and programming resources, a worldwide problem, is more severe in some settings than others. Further, as soon as people in some less developed English-speaking countries develop these skills, they become targets for recruiters from more industrialized countries where salaries are higher—a particular problem in the Philippines and India, for example.

If local IT staff is supplemented by people from corporate headquarters, the results are often not totally satisfactory. The expatriates can provide an initial outburst of productivity and an effective transfer of new technology and skills. This may result in local staff resentment. It can also lead to broken career paths for the expatriates, who find they have become both technically and managerially obsolete when they return to corporate headquarters. Management of IT expatriates' reentry to their home offices has generally been quite inadequate.

This personnel shortage has led to the growth of India-based software companies such as Tata and HCL (Hindustani Computers Limited), which take advantage of India's high skill levels and very low wage rates to bid effectively on overseas programming jobs. Obviously, geographic distances limit the types of work these companies can bid on. Highly structured applications are much easier to develop remotely than those with less structure, which require much closer interaction between end user and developer during the systems development phase.[2]

Central Telecommunications

The price, quality, and availability of telecommunications support vary widely from one country to another. On all three dimensions, the United

---

[2]See "The Indian Software Industry," Harvard Business School case 9-398-164, for further background material.

States sets the standard. In many European countries, the tariffs on these services are an order of magnitude higher than those in the United States (although with recent deregulation, this is changing rapidly). Also, lead times to get extra land lines, terminals, and so forth, can stretch to years instead of weeks in many countries—if they are available at any price (thus, the move to cellular and satellite links). Conversely, the service may be outstanding to international gateways and terrible inside the country. Finally, communication quality, availability, and cost differ widely among countries. As a consequence of varying line capacity, costs, and uptime performance, profitable home-country on-line applications can become cost-ineffective, inadequate, or unreliable in other countries. The new bandwidth needs, plus major first-world investments in this area, suggest this gap will continue to be an enduring challenge.

National IT Strategy

In some countries, development of a local computer manufacturing and software industry is a key national priority. This has been true of France, Germany, Singapore, and the United Kingdom in the past and more recently for India and the Philippines. In these situations, subsidiaries of foreign companies can view buying the products of the local manufacturer both as evidence of good citizenship and as an opportunity to build credit for later dealings with the government. This motivation creates a legitimate need for local deviation from corporate hardware/software standards. In the global economy of the late 1990s, this is not as dominant a factor as it was in the past.

General Level of IT Sophistication

The speed and ease with which companies can implement or develop an IT activity are linked to the general level of IT activity in the country. A firm located in a country with a substantial base of installed state-of-the-art electronic-based information systems and well-trained, mobile labor can develop its IT capabilities more rapidly and effectively than if these conditions did not exist. Countries with limited installed electronic-based information systems require substantially more expatriate labor to implement IT work, as well as great effort and time to educate users in the idiosyncrasies of IT and how best to interface with it. Careful investigation of the staff mobility factor is particularly important, because bonding arrangements and cultural norms may place considerable rigidity on what appears to be a potentially satisfactory labor supply. In all but the least developed of countries, however, the past decade has seen a surge of IT skills and expertise.

Size of Local Market

The size of the local market influences the number of vendors who compete for service in it. Thus, in small markets, a company's preferred international supplier for particular hardware and for software may not have a presence, thereby complicating service. Global desktop standards around Microsoft have softened some of these issues. Further, the quality of service support varies widely from one setting to another; vendors who provide good support in one country may give inadequate support in another. Also important is the availability and quality of local software and consulting companies (or subsidiaries of large international ones). A thriving, competent local IT industry can offset other differences in local support and staff availability.

Data Export Control

Since the mid-1980s, significant publicity has been given to the issue of how much information about people and finances may be transmitted electronically across national boundaries. It has been driven both by concerns about individual privacy and the often weak security and low-quality controls over these data.

A relatively benign point of discussion in the 1980s, it is rearing its head much more vigorously in the late 1990s. The use of personal data generates a wide range of sensitivities in different societies. In general, it is of most concern in Western Europe today, particularly in the Scandinavian countries, and is of less concern in the United States, although this is changing. Existing legislation and practice vary widely among countries, as do criteria for evaluating and resolving these issues. The business community should not misread current apparent lack of interest in these issues; they are deep and emotional, and the spotlight will eventually make this a burning topic. What is seen in one environment as a sharp consumer micromarketing implementation may be seen as deeply intrusive and immoral in another. Increasingly, the word *Orwellian* has become a label for some new IT applications that use personal data.

Technological Awareness

Awareness of contemporary technology spreads very rapidly around the globe because IT magazines, journals, and consultants are distributed internationally. This awareness poses problems for effective applications development in less IT-sophisticated countries because it leads subsidiaries to promote technologies that they neither understand, need, nor are capable of managing. Conversely, late starters with a high degree of IT awareness have advantages because they can pioneer distinctly different and faster paths for exploiting IT in the subsidiaries than are used in home offices.

Summary

For a transnational firm, the factors described above severely constrain the way in which policies and controls can be implemented in its international activities, particularly in less developed countries. Rigid policy cannot be dictated effectively from corporate headquarters, which often are located a vast distance from the subsidiary's operating management. Because there are many legitimate reasons for diversity, local know-how must be brought to decisions.

CORPORATE FACTORS AFFECTING IT REQUIREMENTS

Within the context of the different national cultures and the current state of the IT profession in different countries, numerous factors inside a company influence how fast IT can be transferred internationally and how centralized its control of international IT activity should be. As we have stressed, more control must be delegated in an international environment than in a domestic one. Important opportunities exist for technology transfer; however, service and cost issues can arise if these opportunities are not managed. The more important company-specific factors are discussed here.

Nature of the Firm's Business

Some firms' businesses demand that key data files be managed centrally so that they are accessible, immediately or on a short delayed-access basis, to all units around the world. Airline reservation files for international air carriers require such access. A United Airlines agent in Boston confirming a flight segment from Tokyo to Hong Kong needs up-to-the-minute access to the flight's loading to make a valid commitment, while other agents around the globe need to know that a seat is no longer available for sale. Failure to have this information poses risks of significant loss of market share, as customers perceive the firm to be both unreliable and uncompetitive.

American President Lines, an international shipping company, maintains a file, updated every 24 hours, comprising the location of each of its containers, its status, and its availability for future commitment by regional officers in 20 countries. Without this information, the firm would most likely make unfulfillable commitments, which would present an unreliable image to present and potential customers. In another example, the standards of international banking have evolved to where the leaders provide customers with an instantaneous worldwide picture of clearances, and so on, thus opening the door for more sophisticated cash management—for which the banks charge significant fees. Those firms not providing such services find themselves increasingly at a competitive disadvantage.

Other firms require integration and on-line updating of only some of their files. A European electronics firm attempts to provide its European managers with up-to-date, on-line access to various key operational files on such items as production schedules, order status, and so forth. This is done for its network of 20-plus factories in order to manage an integrated logistics system. International client-server architecture is up and running. No such integration, however, is attempted for key marketing or accounting data, which essentially are processed on a batch basis and organized by country. While developing such integration is technically possible, at present the firm sees no operational or marketing advantage in doing so.

Still other firms require essentially no integration of data, and each country can be managed on a stand-alone basis. A U.S. conglomerate, for example, manages each division this way. Eight of its divisions have operations in the United Kingdom, and by corporate policy they have no formal interaction with each other in IT or any other operational matters. (A single tax specialist who files a joint tax return for them is the sole linking specialist.) The company's staff generally perceives this to be an appropriate way to operate, with nothing of significance being lost. Such examples suggest the impossibility of generalizing about how transnational IT activities should be organized.

Strategic Impact of IT

If IT activity is strategic to the company, tighter corporate overview is needed to ensure that new technology (with its accompanying new ways of operating) is rapidly and efficiently introduced to outlying areas. One of the United States' largest international banks, for example, has a staff of more than 100 at corporate headquarters to develop software for their international branches and to coordinate its orderly dissemination to them. The bank feels the successful use of IT is too critical to the firm's ultimate success to be managed without technical coordination and senior management perspective. At the other extreme is a reasonably large manufacturer of chemicals that sees IT as playing an important but clearly a supportive role. At least twice a year, the head of the European IT unit and the head of corporate IT exchange visits and share perceptions. The consensus is that there is not enough potential payoff to warrant further coordination (other than for their broadband networks, which support design sharing, e-mail, and Lotus Notes).

Corporate Organization

As its international activity grows, a firm adopts different structures, each requiring quite different levels of international IT support and coordination.

The earliest phase of an export division generally requires only limited numbers of overseas staff, who need little if any local IT processing and support. As the activity grows in size, it tends to be reorganized as an international division with a larger number of marketing, accounting, and manufacturing staff people located abroad. At this stage, an increasing need for local IT support may arise. A full-blown level of international activity may involve regional headquarters (in Europe, the Far East, and Latin America, for example) to coordinate the activities of the diverse countries.

Coordinating such a structure is very complex. Not only are there vertical relationships between corporate IT and the national IT activities, but cross-border marketing and manufacturing integration requirements create the need for relationships between individual countries' IT units. Appropriate forms of this coordination, of course, vary widely. A multibillion-dollar pharmaceutical firm was discovered to have very close links between corporate IT and its major national IT units (defined by the firm as those with budgets in excess of $5 million). None of the IT unit managers, however, knew the names of their contemporaries or had visited any of the other units. Since little cross-border product flow existed and none was planned for the near future, this did not appear to present a significant problem.

At the most complex level are firms organized in a matrix fashion—with corporate IT activity, divisional IT activities (which may or may not be located at corporate headquarters), and national IT activities. Here, balancing relationships is a major challenge. Divisions having substantial vertical supplier relationships with each other and substantial integration of activities across national borders possess even more complicated relationships. In such cases, the policies that work for the international divisions are too simplistic.

Company Technical and Control Characteristics

Level of Functional Control.   An important factor in effective IT control structures is the corporation's general level of functional control. Companies with a strong tradition of central control find it both appropriate and relatively easy to implement line IT control worldwide. A major manufacturer of farm equipment, for example, has for years implemented very strong management and operational control over its worldwide manufacturing and marketing functions. Consequently, it found considerable acceptance of similar controls for the IT organization. Most of the software that runs the overseas plants has been developed and is maintained by the corporate IT headquarters group.

At the other extreme is a 30-division, multibillion-dollar conglomerate with a 100-person corporate staff involved mostly in financial and legal work associated with acquisitions and divestitures. This company has totally decentralized operating decisions to the divisions, and the number of corporate staff is deliberately controlled as a means of preventing "meddling." At present, a two-person corporate IT "group" works on only very broad policy and consulting issues. Effective execution of even this limited role is very challenging.

Technology Base.   A company's technology base is another important factor. High-technology companies with traditions of spearheading technical change from a central research and engineering laboratory and disseminating it around the world have successfully used a similar approach with IT. Their transnational managers are used to corporately initiated technical change. Firms without this experience have had more difficulty assimilating information technology in general, as well as more problems in transplanting IT developed in one location to other settings.

Corporate Size.   Finally, corporate size is also relevant. Smaller organizations, because of the limited and specialized nature of their application, find transferring IT packages and expertise to be particularly complex. As the scope of the operation increases, however, it becomes easier to discover common applications and facilitate transfer of technology—perhaps because the stakes are higher.

Other Considerations

Other factors also influence IT coordination policies. Is there substantial rotation of staff between international locations? If so, is it desirable to have common reporting systems and operating procedures in place in each subsidiary to ease the assimilation of the transfers? Do the firm's operating and financial requirements essentially demand up-to-the-week reporting of overseas financial results? If not, consolidating smaller overseas operations on a one-month, delayed-time basis is attractive.

TRANSNATIONAL IT POLICY ISSUES

As the preceding sections explain, great diversity exists in the policies for coordinating and managing international IT activities. This section identifies the most common types of policies and relationships and briefly addresses key issues associated with the selection and implementation of each. The scope of these policies and the amount of effort needed to implement them are influenced by the degree of needed central control, corporate culture and policies, strategic importance of information technologies, and other factors.

Guidance on Architecture

The most important central IT role is to facilitate the development and implementation of a view on appropriate telecommunications architecture, operating systems, and database standards. The firm must pragmatically move to ensure that these standards are installed in all of its operations. There are no substitutes in this task for pragmatism and the ability to listen. Ideas that make perfect sense in Detroit may need selective fine-tuning in Thailand—if indeed they are viable there at all.

The opportunity to transmit data electronically between countries for file updating and processing purposes has created the need for a corporate international data dictionary. Too often, this need is not addressed, leading to clumsy systems designs and incorrect outputs. Where data should be stored, the form in which they should be stored, and how they should be updated are all considerations requiring a centrally managed policy—operating, of course, within the framework of what is legally permissible.

Similarly, central guidance and coordination in the acquisition of communication technology are important. At present, communication flexibility and cost not only vary widely from country to country, but they are shifting rapidly.

Effectively anticipating these cost and flexibility changes requires a corporate view and broad design of telecommunications needs for meeting the demands of growth and changing business needs over the coming decade. The service levels and the technologies to be utilized must be specified. Such a plan requires capable technical inputs and careful management review. An important by-product of the plan is guidance for corporate negotiation and lobbying efforts on relevant items of national legislation and policies regarding the form, availability, and cost of telecommunication.

Central Hardware/Software Concurrence or Approval

The objectives of a central policy for acquiring hardware and software are to ensure that cost-effective global networking is acquired, that obvious mistakes in vendor viability are avoided, and that purchasing decisions achieve economies of scale. Other benefits include the bargaining leverage a company gains by being perceived as an important customer, the reduction of potential interface problems between national systems, and the enhancement of applications software transferability between countries. Practical factors demanding sensitive interpretation and execution of central policy include:

- Corporate headquarters' awareness of the vendor's support and servicing problems in the local country.
- The local subsidiary's desire to exercise its autonomy and control its operations in a timely way. The Korean subsidiary of a large bank, for example, wanted to buy a $25,000 word processing system. Its request for approval took six months to pass through three locations and involved one senior vice president and two executive vice presidents. Whatever

benefits standardization might have achieved for the bank in this situation seemed to be more than offset by the cost and time of the approval process.

- The need to maintain good relationships with local governments. This may involve patronizing local vendors, agreeing not to eliminate certain types of staff, and using the government-controlled IT network.
- The level and skill of corporate headquarters people who set the technical and managerial policies. A technically weak corporate staff dealing with large, well-managed foreign subsidiaries must operate quite differently from a technically gifted central staff working with small, unsophisticated subsidiaries.

Central Approval of Software Standards and Feasibility Studies

Central control of software standards can ensure that software is written or sourced in a maintainable, secure way so that the company's long-term operational position is not jeopardized. Control of feasibility studies can ensure that potential applications are evaluated in a consistent and professional fashion. Practical problems with this policy of central approval revolve around both the level of effort required and the potential erosion of corporate culture.

Implementing such standards can be expensive and time-consuming in relation to the potential benefits. The art is to be flexible with small investments and to review more closely the investments that involve real operational exposure. Unfortunately, this approach requires more sensitivity than many staffs possess.

Further, a decentralized company's prevailing management control system and the location of other operating decisions may directly conflict with central control. The significance of this conflict depends on the size and strategic importance of the investment. Relatively small distinctly "support" investments in decentralized organizations should clearly be resolved in the local country. Large strategic investments, however, should be subject to central review in these organizations, even if time delays and cost overruns result.

Central Software Development

In the name of efficiency, reduced costs, and standard operating procedures worldwide, some firms have attempted to develop software centrally, or at a designated subsidiary, for installation in subsidiaries in other countries. The success of this approach has been mixed. Most companies that have succeeded have well-established patterns of technology transfer, strong functional control over their subsidiaries, substantial numbers of expatriates working in the overseas subsidiaries, and some homogeneity in their manufacturing, accounting, and distribution practices. Success has also resulted when the IT unit responsible for the package's development and installation has carried out very intensive marketing and liaison activities.

When these preconditions have not been present, however, installation has often been troubled. The reasons most commonly cited by IT managers for the failure include:

- The developers of the system did not understand local needs well enough. Major functions were left out, and the package required extensive and expensive enhancements.
- The package was adequate, but the efforts needed to train people to input data and handle outputs properly were significantly underestimated (or mishandled). This was complicated by extensive language difficulties and insensitivity to existing local procedures.
- The system evolution and maintenance involved a dependence on central staff that was not sustainable in the long run. Flexibility and timeliness of response were problems.
- Costs were significantly underestimated. The overrun on the basic package was bad enough, but the fat was really in the fire when the installation costs were added.

Such statements seem to reflect the importance of organizational and cultural factors. In reality, an outside software house, with its marketing orientation and its existence beyond the corporate family, often does a better job of selling standard software than does an in-house IT unit in a decentralized transnational environment. Finally, in many settings, the sheer desire on both sides for success is the best guarantee of success.

IT Communications

Although they are expensive, investments in improving communications between the various national IT units often pay big dividends. Several devices have proven useful.

1. *Regular interunit meetings*—An annual or biannual conference of the IT directors and the key staff of the major international subsidiaries. For organizations in the "turnaround" or "strategic" categories, these meetings should occur at least as frequently as do meetings of international controllers. Small subsidiaries (IT budgets under $1 million) probably do not generate enough profitable opportunities to warrant inclusion in this conference or to have a separate one.

   The conference agenda should combine planned formal activities (e.g., technical briefings, application briefings, and company directives) with substantial blocks of unplanned time. The informal exchange of ideas, initiation of joint projects, and sharing of mutual problems are among the most important activities of a successful conference.

2. *Corporate-subsidiary exchange visits*—Regular visits of corporate IT personnel to the national organizations, as well as of national IT personnel to corporate IT headquarters. These visits should occur at planned intervals, rather than only when an operational crisis or technical problem arises. Less contact is needed with the smaller units than with the larger ones.

3. *Newsletters*—A monthly or bimonthly newsletter to communicate staffing shifts, new technical insights, major project completions, experience with software packages and vendors, and so forth.

4. *Education*—Organizing joint education programs where possible. This may involve the creation and/or acquisition of audiovisual materials to be distributed around the world. A large oil company recently supplemented written communications about a radically different IT organization structure with a special film, complete with sound track in five languages.

One of the largest British chemical components has literally a one-person corporate IT "department," who continuously travels the world, helping to facilitate education and training sessions and identifying appropriate topics and sources of expertise for IT staff in far-flung places. The individual is a member of the firm's most senior general management and clearly adds substantial value. General management and middle management staff awareness programs remain a central challenge for this leader.

Developing stronger psychological links between the national IT units is fundamental. These links can be as important as the formal ties between the national IT units and the parent company's IT unit.

Facilitating the development of centers of systems expertise in many parts of the world is another important need. A single-system unit in the parent company's home country is not necessarily the best way to operate. Many jobs can usefully be split over three or four development centers. One of the large entertainment companies recently assigned large portions of its financial systems, marketing systems, and production systems to its British, German, and French development units, respectively. While each unit was enthusiastic about leading their part of the effort, they also knew that if they did not cooperate, they in turn would not receive the cooperation necessary to assure the success of their unit's output. This approach tapped new sources of expertise and was successful because of the shared interdependencies of leadership and innovation.

Staff Rotation

Rotating staff between national IT units and corporate IT is an important way of encouraging communication; at the same time, the practice can generate problems. Both advantages and disadvantages are addressed below.

Advantages

- Better corporate IT awareness of the problems and issues in the overseas IT units. As a corollary, the local IT units have a much better perspective on the goals and thinking at corporate headquarters because one of their members has spent a tour of duty there.
- More flexibility in managing career paths and matching positions with individual development needs. Particularly to someone working in a crowded corporate IT department, an overseas assignment could seem very attractive.
- Efficient dispersion of technical know-how throughout the organization.

Disadvantages

- People can jeopardize their career paths by moving from corporate headquarters to less IT-developed parts of the world. The individuals bring leading-edge expertise to the overseas installation and have a major positive impact for several years. When they return to corporate headquarters they may find themselves completely out of touch with the contemporary technologies being used. Also, some of these people have been dropped out of the normal progression stream through oversight.
- Assigning people overseas not only involves expensive moving allowances and cost-of-living differentials, but it also raises a myriad of potential personal problems. These problems, normally of a family nature, make the success of an international transfer more speculative than a domestic one.
- Transfers from corporate to smaller overseas locations may cause substantial resentment and feelings of nationalism in the overseas location: "Why aren't our people good enough?" Such problems can be tempered with appropriate language skills and efforts on the part of the transferred executives, corporate control over the number of transfers, local promotions, and clearly visible opportunities for local staff to be transferred to corporate.

Appropriately managed with reasonable limits, the advantages far outweigh the disadvantages.

Consulting Services

Major benefits can come from a central IT group's providing foreign subsidiaries with consulting services on both technical and managerial matters. In many cases, corporate headquarters is not only located in a technically sophisticated country, but its IT activities are bigger in scope than those of individual foreign installations. Among other things, this means that:

1. Corporate IT is more aware of leading-edge hardware/software technology and has had firsthand experience with its potential strengths and weaknesses.
2. Corporate IT is more likely to have experience with large project-management systems and other management methods.

In both cases, the communication must be done with sensitivity in order to move the company forward at an appropriate pace. All too often, the corporate group pushes too fast in a culturally insensitive fashion, creating substantial problems. Movement through the phases of technology assimilation can be speeded up and smoothed, but no phase should be skipped.

As an organization becomes more IT intensive, effective IT auditing becomes increasingly important for shielding the organization from excessive and unnecessary risks. IT auditing is a rapidly evolving profession that faces a serious staff shortage. The shortage is more severe outside the United States and Europe. Thus, the corporate audit group of a transnational frequently must take responsibility for conducting international IT audits and for helping to develop national IT audit staffs and capabilities.

Central IT Processing Support

The extent to which IT should be pushed toward a central hub or a linked international network depends on the firm's industry and the dimensions along which it chooses to compete. At one extreme is the airline industry, where being unable, on a global basis, to confirm seats represents a significant competitive disadvantage. Originally, international airlines were driven to centralize as an offensive weapon; now it is a defensive one. At the other extreme is a company with a network of operations for converting paper (a commodity). Transportation costs severely limit how far away from a plant orders can profitably be shipped. Thus, the company handles order entry and factory management on a strictly national basis, with a modest interchange of data between countries. Even here, however, substantial economies have come from international standardization of packages and corporate purchasing agreements.

Technology Appraisal Program—An Example

An international appraisal can provide perspective, allowing greater coordination of overseas IT efforts. A U.S.-based transnational company with a long history of European operations discovered that its operations in the Far East and South America were posing increasingly complicated information problems. General management initiated a three-year program for bringing the overseas operation under control. The first step was to appraise the condition of each national IT unit and its potential business, which was conducted by a three-person IT team with multilingual abilities. It was followed by a formulation of policies and appropriate action programs at the annual meeting of company executives.

Originally planned as a one-time assessment of only 11 national IT units, the effort was considered so successful that it was reorganized as an established audit function. The team learned to appraise locally available technology and to guide local management in judging its potential. This required at least one week and often two weeks in the field, typically in two trips. The first visit appraised existing services and raised general concerns that local management could effectively pursue. The second visit assessed problems of:

1. Government restrictions.
2. Quality and quantity of available human skills.
3. Present and planned communications services.

Alternatives to the present means of service were examined further, and economic analyses of at least three standard alternatives were prepared. The three standard alternatives were:

1. Expansion of the present system.
2. Transfer of all or portions of IT work to a neighboring country.
3. Transfer of all or portions of IT work to regional headquarters.

Local managers' enthusiasm for this review was not universal, and, in several countries, long delays occurred between the first and second visits. However, in 7 of the original 11 units, the appraisals succeeded in generating appropriate change by bringing better understanding of the potential impact of uncertainties—such as changing import duties, planned market introduction of new technologies by U.S. suppliers, and a new satellite communications alternative. This organized appraisal significantly increased senior management's awareness and comfort concerning IT. The activity became an ongoing effort for the company, and several persons were added to the appraisal team.

SUMMARY

Coordinating international IT is extraordinarily complex. Corporate IT management may have maximum responsibility for, but only limited authority over, distant staff and technologies. Leadership demands persuasion and cajoling, plus being well informed on new technologies, the corporate culture, and the wide diversity of cultures existing in the world. The job requires very high visibility and an appropriate reporting structure inside the firm. The latter is particularly important, given the need to lead through *relationships.*

If IT is globally strategic, the IT leadership must be represented at the very top of the firm, where acquisition, divestiture, and other components of corporate strategy are developed. The IT department's effectiveness crucially depends on its being heard in this forum. However, the interpretation of the function varies widely by industry, global reach, and size of firm. For example, the international airline business requires a large central hub to manage a global database. The IT leadership role in this industry consequently has a very strong global line management component. The earlier described chemical company's operations, on the other hand, are contained within individual, autonomous national units; hence, an entirely different structure of central IT is appropriate for that company, and IT corporate leadership involves more limited line responsibility but high-placed coordination.

International IT development must be managed actively to avert major long-term difficulties within and between national IT activities. Doing so is complicated because the assimilation of IT in countries is often more heavily influenced by local conditions such as infrastructure and service availability. Overcoming obstacles presented by the local conditions demands much more than simply keeping abreast of technology: a long view is required to succeed.

Chapter

13

The IT Business

The previous chapters in this book have presented frameworks for viewing the information technology (IT) activity and the functions of IT management; taken together, they specify how to conduct an IT management audit. This final chapter highlights the impact of the book's six major themes:

1. The strategic importance of IT evolves over time and is different for individual organizations.
2. Computing, telecommunication, and desktop technologies have merged into a single whole.
3. Organizational learning is important to technology assimilation.
4. Make-or-buy decisions are shifting toward much greater reliance on external sources of software, administrative, and computing support.
5. The systems life-cycle concept continues to be valid, although the timing and process of executing the pieces have changed dramatically.
6. The pressures of the three constituencies—IT management, user management, and general management—must be continuously balanced.

"THE IT BUSINESS" ANALOGY

We have chosen to view an organization's IT activity as a stand-alone "business within a business" and, in particular, have chosen to apply the concepts of marketing-mix analysis. This permits us to synthesize the concepts of organization, planning, control, and strategy formulation for IT. Using this analogy, we will speak of the business's strategy formulation as its marketing mix, its steering committee as the board of directors, and its IT director as the chief executive officer. These items are particularly relevant to the sensitive and critical interface between the IT business and its host, or parent, organization—the firm.[1] We will not explain the details of operating strategy, since the general aspects of IT operations management were covered earlier; nor do we discuss here the issues of internal accounting and control within the IT organization, as they do not impact directly on the interface between the two businesses. For similar reasons, we discuss only those IT organizational issues dealing with external relations of the IT business.

IT is a high-technology, fast-changing industry. A particular "IT business" in this industry may grow rapidly, remain more or less steady, or decline. Its territory encompasses the development, maintenance, and operation of all information technologies supporting a firm, regardless of where they are located and to whom they report.

The scope of IT technologies to be coordinated has expanded tremendously as computers, telecommunications, external databases, and desktop devices have merged, and its product offerings are exploding into such new consumer areas as electronic mail, groupware, editing, and computer-aided design/computer-aided manufacturing. The complexity of implementing projects, the magnitude of work to be done, and the scarcity of human resources have forced the IT business to change from a business that primarily produced things to one that identifies and distributes things; a significant percentage of its work now involves coordinating the acquisition of outside services for its customers to use. This shift has forced major changes in its approach to planning and controls in order to deal effectively with these new products and new sources of supply.

Implicit in this view of the IT business is that, at least at a policy level, the overwhelming majority of firms require an integrated perspective and approach to IT. The IT activities include not just the corporate IT center and its client-server networks, but also desktop devices, distributed systems development activities, outside software company contracts, computer service bureaus, and so on. Many users of IT services—its customers—possess options to buy services from providers other than the central IT organization—the business within the business.

We believe this analogy is useful for applying management principles and theories to the IT business in a way that generates important insights. Similarly, we believe that the analogy we draw between general management and a board of directors is useful in conceptualizing a realistic role for an executive steering committee.

Like all analogies, this one can be pushed too far and some caution is in order. For example, the financing of the IT business is not analogous to the corporate capital markets, since its capital support comes directly from the firm (with no debt analogy), and its revenues—exclusively, in many cases— also come directly from the firm. In many respects, the customer bases of the

---

[1]Throughout this chapter, the term *firm* refers to the parent holding company of the IT business.

IT business and the firm are dependent on common files, and so on, so that customers cannot be treated as entirely independent. Similarly, the IT business is free from many of the legal and governmental constraints on the firm. Other legal and governmental constraints—such as the Equal Employment Opportunity Commission (EEOC), for instance—are placed on it in the context of the firm's total corporate posture, and there is little possibility or need for the IT business to strike an independent posture.

The rest of this chapter is devoted to three topics related to managing the IT business:

- The IT marketing mix.
- The role of the IT board of directors.
- The role of the IT chief executive officer.

THE IT MARKETING MIX

The Products

The IT product line is continuously evolving. Table 13–1 summarizes the key aspects of change. Some of the dynamism of the product line is due to

TABLE 13–1   Changes in IT Product Line

	Focus	
Factor	*The Past*	*The Future*
Product obsolescence.	Developing new products.	Heavy maintenance of old products to meet new challenges of obsolescence.
Source.	Most products manufactured inside.	Significant percent sourced outside.
Dominant economic constraint.	Capital intensive (hardware; economy of scale).	Personnel intensive (economy of skill).
Product mix.	Many large, few medium, many small products.	Some large, many medium, thousands of small products.
Products/benefits.	Good return on investment.	Many projects have intangible benefits.
New-product technologies.	New technologies	New technologies and grouping of old ones.
Services.	Structured, such as automated accounting and inventory control.	Unstructured, such as executive decision support and query systems.

the enormous proliferation of opportunities afforded by the economics of new technology. Other dynamic elements include changing customer needs as a result of ordinary shifts in business and new insights (phase 2 learning) into how technology can be applied to specific operations.

In terms of development time and complexity to operate, IT products range in size from very small to enormous. A large product's development period can be so lengthy that it may not even meet the current customers' needs when it is completed. (Four years—for truly megaprojects—is not uncommon.) The introduction of some products can be delayed with only limited damage to the host firm; however, if delays of any magnitude occur in the development of other products, the damage to consumers (users) may be severe. In terms of day-to-day operations, the importance of tight cost control, good response time, quality control, and so on, varies widely from one firm to another, as well as within different parts of the firm.

Product Obsolescence.   Product obsolescence is a major headache in the IT business. Products rapidly become clumsy in the changing technology environment, and introducing the necessary enhancements—styling changes—to keep them relevant can be very expensive. Eventually, major factory retooling is necessary. Emerging consumer needs (which can only be satisfied by new technologies) and the need to install those new manufacturing technologies combine to put sustained pressure on the IT business.

Sources, Marketplace Climate.   The method of delivering IT products is shifting as the IT customer makes many more of the sourcing decisions. An increasing percentage of IT development expenditures is going to software houses, systems integrators, and database vendors, while more of the production expenditures is related to client-server as opposed to mainframe systems. Formerly, IT was primarily a developer and manufacturer of products; now it is becoming a significant distributor of products manufactured by others, including being a complete distributor in outsourcing situations (e.g., at Xerox and British Aerospace). The distributor role involves identifying and evaluating products and professionally evaluating those that customers identify, with a view to ensuring that the costs and services of the firm as a whole are fully competitive.

IT products run the gamut from those where customers clearly and correctly understand the need in advance (such as point-of-sale terminals) to those for which there is no perceived need (although ultimately great need may exist) and, consequently, considerable, extended sales efforts must precede a sale. Products range from those that are absolutely essential and critical to the customer (inventory control systems, for instance) to those that are desirable but whose purchase can essentially be postponed (e.g., standard industry databases for spreadsheet files). Obviously, products at the two extremes require quite different sales approaches.

Sourcing decisions are complicated by differences in the maturity of IT suppliers. A relatively stable competitive pattern exists among suppliers of large mainframe computers, for instance, but the Internet software and middleware software markets are far more turbulent; in fact, it is not clear which companies will survive and what form their products will take five years from now. Although a competitive pattern is emerging, the Justice Department lawsuit against Microsoft, cellular innovations, and new Internet software firms—among other factors—will confound the nature of competition for the foreseeable future.

In the past, monopoly control over product delivery gave IT businesses considerable discretion in timing their new-product introductions. The changed climate of competition and nature of products among IT suppliers imply that the IT business has lost control over the marketing of new products in many organizations.

Profits/Benefits.   IT products range from those whose benefits can be crisply summarized in a return-on-investment (ROI) framework for the customer to those whose benefits are more qualitative and intangible and, thus, extremely hard to justify analytically. Again, products at the ends of the spectrum require different marketing approaches. Some products are absolutely structured (e.g., certain types of accounting data), while others are tailored to individual tastes and preferences. Further, in many instances, purchasers may not easily comprehend a product's complexity and the inherent factors influencing its quality. Finally, some products require tailoring during installation and thus need specific field support and distribution staffs whose costs are not easily estimated in advance.

Implications for Marketing.   The above description of evolving IT product characteristics highlights the complexity of the IT marketing task. Other businesses attempt to streamline the product line in order to facilitate economy and efficiency in manufacturing and distribution; many IT businesses' inability to do this has contributed to turbulence in their management. Too often, they are trying to deliver too many products from their traditional monopoly-supplier position with weak promotion, surly sales, and a fixation on manufacturing—as opposed to focusing on service and distribution. What works for one set of products may not work for another. Recognizing the need for and implementing a differentiated marketing approach is very difficult, particularly for a medium-sized IT business.

The IT Consumer

Description of the Consumer.   The IT consumer's needs and sophistication are changing, as Table 13–2 summarizes. After 20 years of working with mature technologies, older consumers have become sensitive to the problems of working within constraints; at the same time, many of them are quite unaware of the newer technologies and the enormous personal and organization behavioral modifications they must make in order to use them

TABLE 13–2   Changes in IT Consumer Profile

Factor	Consumers	
	Older	*Younger*
Experience with traditional technologies.	Experienced.	Inexperienced.
Attitude toward newer technologies.	Leery.	Enthusiastic and unsophisticated (but they do not recognize their lack of sophistication).
Visibility.	Identifiable as consumers.	Often unidentifiable as consumers; numerous at all levels in organizations.
Attitude toward IT unit.	Willing to accept IT staff as experts.	Many are hostile because they want to develop their own solutions.
Self-confidence.	Low confidence in their own abilities (often cautious because of cost).	High confidence in their ability and judgement (often unwarranted).
Turnover rate.	High.	High.

properly. These older consumers often bring their old purchasing habits to the new environment without understanding that it is new. Younger consumers, on the other hand, have close familiarity with Graphical User Interfaces (GUI), personal computing, and surfing the Internet and tend to be intolerant when they are unable to get immediate access to whatever they need. They also, however, tend to be naive about the problems of designing and maintaining IT systems that must run on a regular basis. In general, both classes of consumers have major educational needs if they are to become responsible consumers.

The new user-friendly technologies have made the problem more complicated because many consumers see the opportunity to set up their own businesses, withdrawing from reliance on the IT business. Propelling them in this direction are their own entrepreneurs or purchasing agents (i.e., decentralized systems analysts), who are long on optimism and short on practical, firsthand expertise and realistic risk assessment. This go-it-alone, no-standards approach has turned out to be very expensive in many situations.

In such an environment, the IT marketing force particularly needs to target potential new consumers and reach them before they make independent sourcing decisions. New application clusters and groups of consumers keep surfacing. This ever-changing composition of consumer groups sustains the need for a field sales force. An effective job of educating people does no good if they subsequently move on to other assignments and are replaced by people unaware of current technologies and the sequence of decisions that led to the present status of the organization.

Firsthand personal computing experience and a barrage of advertising have substantially raised consumers' expectations and their general level of self-confidence in making IT decisions. Unfortunately, this confidence is often misplaced; there seems to be a lack of appreciation for subtle but important nuances and for the IT control practices necessary to ensure a significant probability of success in a new system. This also increases the need for sustained direct sales and follow-up.

In today's environment, the number of service alternatives for customers, some of which appear to have very low prices, has exploded. It is confusing to consumers when products essentially similar to those available in-house appear to be available at much lower prices out-of-house (by conveniently forgetting the long-term costs of maintenance and interchangeability). Great consumer sophistication is needed to identify a *real* IT bargain.

Implications for Marketing. The above factors have substantially complicated the IT marketing effort. An unstable group of consumers with diversified, rapidly changing needs (often linked among customers in ways they don't understand) requires a very high level of direct-selling effort. Intensifying the need to spend promotion money on these customers is the low regard for the IT business's management in many settings. Consumers who are hostile about the perceived quality of IT support welcome solutions that will carry them as far away as possible from reliance on the IT business management. Trained to respond correctly to many of yesterday's technologies, these managers are inappropriately trained for today's technologies. Underinvestment in the marketing necessary for dealing with these realities has been a major cause of dissatisfaction among users.

Costs

Cost Factors. From a marketing viewpoint, significant changes are occurring in the costs of producing and delivering systems, as summarized in Table 13–3. On the one hand, the cost of many IT hardware elements has decreased dramatically and is likely to continue to drop significantly. On the other hand, reducing the cost of software development is likely to progress slowly for some time (although object-oriented technology and Enterprise software are changing this very rapidly). Moreover, the ability to accurately estimate the development, production, and maintenance costs for large, high-technology, low-structure systems continues to be disappointing.

The steady increase in the cost of maintaining installed software (either self-developed or purchased) is a critical component of cost explosion. These expenses are usually not factored in carefully at the time of purchase, and

---

TABLE 13–3   Changes in Consumer Costs

Cost Factor	Changes in Consumer Costs	
	The Past	*The Future*
Hardware.	Very expensive.	Very expensive.
Economies of scale.	Major in large systems; user stand-alones not feasible in most cases.	Limited in large systems; user stand-alones very attractive.
Software systems development.	Expensive.	Less expensive in some cases.
Software acquisitions.	Limited cost-effective outside opportunities.	Attractive cost-effective opportunities.
Development and production.	Hard to estimate.	Hard to estimate.
Maintenance.	Underestimated.	Soaring.

---

they tend to grow as the business grows and changes over the years. In the short term, these costs can be deferred with apparently little damage. In the long term, however, neglecting them can cause a virtual collapse of the product. Similarly, a purchased or rented package generates a never-ending stream of upgrades to be handled, which can generate considerable costs and time delays.

The proliferation of systems integrators and software packages and their overall cost reductions have accelerated the movement of the IT business into the distributor role. It is now cost-effective to purchase specialized databases and software useful to many users that would be utterly uneconomical if developed and maintained by single users for their own purposes. Not all efforts in developing shared software have been successful, however. For example, a consortium of 25 regional banks funded a joint $13 million software development project (in areas such as demand deposit accounting and savings accounts). The consortium's inability to manage the project doomed it to failure. Additionally, the failure rate of fledgling software package companies is quite high. Another change is the growing number of users who have their own computer capacity. At many business schools, for instance, 100 percent of the students and nearly all of the faculty own personal computers. The schools may or may not own this equipment, but facilitate its acquisition by the students and faculty and identify the standards it must conform to if it is to be attached to a school's networks and provide optimal value to the students.

As will be discussed in the section on pricing, identifying potential or actual total costs for a particular product or service is difficult—in part because data clusters or software modules often support multiple products and consumers. This raises the issue of whether costs should be treated as joint costs or by-product costs. Another complicating factor is the extent to which previously spent R&D costs (to get to today's skill levels) should be treated as part of a product's cost.

While cost management and control are a critical component of the IT business strategy, how they are executed varies significantly among IT settings. High-growth, product-competitive environments place more emphasis on new services and products with less emphasis on IT efficiency and cost control than do environments where the firm's products are more stable and competition is cost-based; in these settings, IT efficiency and cost control can be paramount.

Implications for Marketing.   In summary, the changing cost structure of IT products has forced the IT business to reconsider its sourcing decisions and has pushed it to assume a much stronger distribution role as opposed to simply a manufacturing one. The relative emphasis an IT business places on cost control, product-line growth, quality, and service depends on its business strategy; thus, wide variances exist.

Channels of Distribution

As described in earlier chapters, the number of channels of distribution (to users) and their relative importance have been shifting rapidly. Table 13–4 shows some of the important changes in this domain. Historically, the major channel for both manufacturing and delivering the IT product has been the IT business itself; in most firms it has had a complete monopoly. Changing cost factors and shifts in user preferences have placed great pressure on this channel, causing deep concern inside the IT business as it has adapted to the new challenges of a competitive market—which it cannot totally serve in a cost-effective fashion from its manufacturing facility. Adapting to a new mission, the IT business is now not the sole channel for service and manufacturing but, rather, one of many sources of manufacturing. It has assumed the major new role of identifying products in other channels and assessing their cost, quality, and so on, bringing them to their customers' attention. Adapting to this new role has made many IT businesses very uncomfortable psychologically as they have struggled with such incorrect notions as loss of power.

Risks in Using New Channels.   Successful, rapid adaptation by the IT business is critical to the health of its present and future consumers. The new channels, while offering very attractive products and cost structures, introduce sizable risks in many cases. The most important of these risks include:

1. Misassessment of the real development and operations costs of the products in the channel. Important short-term and more important long-term

TABLE 13–4   Changes in the IT Channels of Distribution

Distribution Factor	*The Past*	*The Future*
Development by central IT.	Heavy.	Shift to packaged software and service providers.
Direct purchase of hardware/software by user.	Limited.	Major.
Service source for individual user.	Limited to service from large, shared system.	Can obtain powerful independent system.
Service bureaus.	Sell time.	Sell products and time bundled together.
Use of external databases via time-sharing.	Limited.	Major.
Number of software and processing services.	A few; crude.	Many.
Software development by users.	Limited.	Major (facilitated by packages and user-friendly languages).
Reliance on external contract analysts/programmers.	Very significant.	More significant; full outsourcing is a real alternative.

cost factors may be completely overlooked. The first work on the annual cost of supporting a networked personal computer (PC) came as a shock to many IT customers, who had underestimated it by an order of magnitude.

2. Consumer vulnerability to abuse of data by failure to control access, install documentation procedures, and implement data updating and management disciplines.

3. Financial vulnerability of the supplier. If the possibility of failure exists, the consumer's fundamental interests need to be protected through identifying an appropriate exit path from the supplier's services.

4. Obsolescence of products. If the supplier is not likely to keep the products modernized (at some suitable cost) for the consumer over the years, alternatives (if modern products are important) should be available. (Obviously, a financial-transaction processing system may be more vulnerable to obsolescence than a decision support model.)

The IT business must employ considerable marketing efforts and adjust its internal perspectives if its consumers are to feel they can rely on the staff to evaluate alternative channels objectively—instead of pushing their own manufacturing facility at every opportunity. Failure to think through and execute these issues will ultimately cripple the IT business's effectiveness in servicing its customers' needs. The results will be fragmentation of data needed by many consumers, redundant development efforts, and an increase in poorly conceived and managed local factories.

Competition

The IT marketing-mix analogy is weakest in describing administrative practice and problems in the area of competition. The IT business faces two principal competitive obstacles:

1. Potential consumers independently seeking solutions without engaging the IT business in either its manufacturing or its distribution capacity.
2. Potential consumers failing to recognize they have problems or opportunities that IT can address.

In the first case, competition normally arises because of the IT business's poor performance. An inability to formulate and implement sensible, useful guidelines to assist consumers in their purchase decisions represents IT's failure to adapt its product line to meet the needs of the changing times. For the broad purposes of the firm, it may be useful to run this aspect of the IT business as a loss leader. Loss of manufacturing business to other channels in a planned or managed way should not be seen as a competitive loss to the IT business, but simply as a restructuring of its product line to meet changing consumer needs.

With regard to the second case, competition—really the cost of delayed market opportunity—arises as a result of ineffective management of price, product, or distribution policies; the result is consumers, in an imperfect market, allocating funds to projects that may have less payoff than IT products. The IT business has a monopoly responsibility: sometimes it produces a product; other times it stimulates consumer awareness of appropriate external sources of supply. The notion of aggressive external competition hurting the IT business through pricing, product innovation, and creative distribution is not appropriate.

Promotion

The rapid changes in IT and consumer turnover make promotion one of the most important elements of the marketing fix to manage: unlike the previously discussed elements, promotion is largely within the control of IT management. Phase 2 learning by consumers is at the core of a successful IT business; thus, even as today's consumers take delivery of mature technologies, tomorrow's consumers must be cultivated by exposing them to tomorrow's products. Price discounts (introductory offers), branch offices (decentralized analysts), and a central IT sales force are key to making this happen.

A multinational electronics company, for example, has a 400-person central IT manufacturing facility near its corporate headquarters. Included in this staff are five international marketing representatives who constantly promote new IT products and services. They prepare promotional material, organize educational seminars, and frequently visit overseas units to build and maintain close professional relationships with IT consumers. These relationships permit them to effectively disseminate services and to acquire insight into the performance of the existing products and the need for new ones. This level of effort is regarded as absolutely essential to the IT business.

In large part, the need to adapt is due to the recent shift in the industry. From the industry's beginning to the late 1970s, large information systems suppliers sold primarily to IT managers. Most vendors that initially had a strong industrial marketing approach have now added a retail marketing one. Desktop hardware and software suppliers have not only opened retail stores, but they also now sell directly to end users. This has forced the IT business to promote the validity of its guidelines within the firm to protect its firm's users from disasters.

A number of IT businesses have organized both their development and their production control activities around market structure, as opposed to manufacturing technology. In other words, rather than having a traditional development group, a programming group, and a maintenance group, they assign development staffs to specific clusters of customers. This structure promotes close, long-term relationships and better understanding and action on operation problems as they arise.

IT newsletters containing announcements of new services and products—that is, advertising and promotional material—should be sent to key present and potential business consumers regularly. Similarly, the IT business can conduct consumer educational seminars or classes and publicize appropriate external educational programs to assist the marketing effort. Complemented by appropriate sales calls, this can accelerate phase 2 learning.

The ideal mix of these promotional tools varies widely by organizational setting. Just as industrial and consumer companies have very different promotion programs, so also should different IT businesses. The strategic relevance of products to consumers, customer sophistication level, and geographic location are some factors that affect appropriate promotion.

Price

The setting of IT prices—an emotional and rapidly changing process—is a very important element in establishing a businesslike, professional relationship between the IT business and its customers. Aggressive, marketing-oriented pricing policies legitimize the concept of the stand-alone IT business. Issues that influence pricing are discussed here.

Inefficient Market.   Establishing rational, competitive criteria is complicated by several factors:

1. Product quality is largely hidden and is very elusive to all but the most sophisticated and meticulous customer. Prices that on the surface appear widely disparate may actually be quite comparable if analyzed carefully.

2. Hardware/software vendors differ in their goals, product mixes, and stability. A small vendor trying to buy into a market may offer a very attractive price to defuse questions about its financial viability or to gain what it considers a strategic customer relationship.
3. Vendors may price a service as a by-product of some other necessary business—resulting in a more attractive price than that of a pricing system that attempts to charge each user a proportionate share of the full cost of the manufacturing operation. This practice explains the bargains available when organizations try to dispose of excess capacity in return for some "financial contribution." Long-term stability should be a concern to the customer. (What if my output became the main product and the other consumer's output the by-product?)
4. Excess-capacity considerations may allow attractive short-term marginal prices (a variant is a bargain entry-level price). Once captured, however, the customer is subjected to significantly higher prices. This pricing practice is particularly prevalent for large, internally developed telecommunications systems.

Introductory Offers.   To stimulate phase 2 learning and long-term demand, deep discounts on early business are often appropriate. This can generate access to long-term profits at quite different price or cost structures as volumes build.

Monopoly Issues.   Senior management review and regulation of pricing decisions are sometimes needed, given the IT business's de facto monopoly. Highly confidential data and databases needed by multiple users in geographically remote locations exemplify IT products that normally cannot be supplied by providers other than the firm's IT business. The prices of these services should be appropriately regulated to prevent abuses.

"Unbundling."   The pricing strategy should incorporate two practices that are not widely used. The first is "unbundling" development, maintenance, operations, and special turnaround requirements into separate packages, each with its own price. Establishing these prices "at arm's length" in advance is critical to maintaining a professional relationship with the customers. The IT business must negotiate the prices with as much care as outside software companies exercise in their negotiations with these customers. This negotiation can be useful in educating users on the true costs of service.

Making prices understandable to the customers is the second desirable practice, which is accomplished by stating prices in *customer* units such as price per number of report pages, per number of customer records, per invoice, and so on, rather than as utilization of such IT resource units as central processing unit (CPU) cycles and millions of instructions per second (MIPS). The added risk (if any) of shocking a potential customer with the facts of economic life tends to be more than offset by much better communication between the IT business and the customer.

Profit.   A final pricing issue, which also strains the independent-business analogy, is how much emphasis should be placed on showing a profit. In the short term (in some cases, even for the long term), should an IT business make a profit or even break even in some settings? IT businesses in firms where consumers require significant education and where much phase 1 and 2 experimentation occurs may appropriately run at a deficit for a long time. This issue must be resolved before the pricing policy is established.

Establishing an IT pricing policy is one of the most complex pricing decisions made in industry. An appropriate resolution, critical to a healthy relationship with the IT consumer, weaves a course between monopolistic and genuine competitive issues, deals with imperfect markets, and resolves ambiguities concerning the role of profits.

THE ROLE OF THE BOARD OF DIRECTORS

The appropriate relationship of the firm's general management to the IT business, a topic first raised in Chapter 1, can be usefully compared to the role of a board of directors in any business. (Many firms give this de facto recognition by creating an executive steering committee.) Viewed this way, the key tasks of general management can be summarized as follows:

1. Appoint and continually assess the performance of the IT chief executive officer (normally a function of the nominating committee).
2. Assure that appropriate standards are in place and are being adhered to. This includes receiving and reviewing detailed reports on the subject from the IT auditor and a more cursory review by the firm's external auditors (normally a function of the audit committee).
3. Ensure that the board is constructed to provide overall guidance to the IT business from its various constituencies. Unlike the board of a publicly held firm, the IT board does not need a representation of lawyers, bankers, investment bankers, and so forth. However, it does need senior user managers who can and are willing to provide user perspective. (As the strategic importance of the IT business to the firm decreases, the level of these managers should also decrease.) At the same time, people from research and development (R&D) and technology planning and production (people who have IT development and operations backgrounds) need to be present to ensure that suggestions are feasible.
4. Provide broad guidance for the strategic direction of the IT business, ensuring that comprehensive planning processes within the IT business are present and that the outputs of the planning processes fit the firm's strategic direction. In practice, the board will carry out this surveillance through a combination of:

    a. IT management presentations on market development, product planning, and financial plans.

b. Review of summary documentation of overall direction.

c. Formal and informal briefings by selected board members on how the IT business is supporting the firm's business needs.

d. Request for and receipt of internal and external reviews of these issues as appropriate.

The above description of the board's role addresses the realities of the members' backgrounds and available time for this kind of work. Focusing on operational or technical detail is unlikely to be suitable or effective. In many settings, periodic (every one to two years) education sessions for the board members have been useful for making them more comfortable in their responsibilities and for bringing them up-to-date on trends within the particular IT business and the IT industry in general.

THE ROLE OF THE IT CHIEF EXECUTIVE OFFICER

Historically a high-turnover job, the IT chief executive position is difficult and demanding, requiring a steadily shifting mix of skills over time. It is critical that the IT CEO:

1. Maintain board relationships personally. This includes keeping the board appropriately informed about major policy issues and problems and being fully responsive to their needs and concerns. A strong link between the board and the customers, not present in many other settings, is critical.

2. Ensure that the strategy-formulation process evolves adequately and that appropriately detailed action programs are developed. As in any high-technology business, high-quality technical review of potential new technologies and new channels of distribution is absolutely essential. Its interpretation is crucial and may well lead to major changes in organization, product mix, and marketing strategy. Without aggressive CEO leadership, the forces of cultural inertia may cause the IT business to delay far too long, with the parent firm's general management eventually taking corrective initiatives as a result.

3. Pay close attention to salary, personnel practices, and employee quality-of-life issues. In many firms, the IT workforce is far more mobile and difficult to replace than many of the firm's other employees.

4. Give high priority to manufacturing security, which is more important in an IT business than in many other businesses. A single disgruntled employee can do a vast amount of damage that may go undetected for a long time. Similarly, an external hacker can reach across the switched network and damage the firm's files.

5. Assure an appropriate management balance between the marketing, manufacturing, and control parts of the IT business. Of the three, marketing—in its broadest sense—is the one most often neglected. CEOs who have begun their careers in manufacturing and dealt with operating

difficulties tend to be most sensitive to manufacturing issues. However, since their manufacturing experience was gained at a particular time with a particular mix of technology assimilation problems and a particular set of control responses, even their perspectives in these areas may not be very appropriate for today's manufacturing challenges.

6. Develop an IT esprit de corps. A key factor of success in the IT business is the belief in IT's value to the firm. Senior IT managers must develop team spirit and lead their organizations into new ventures with enthusiasm. At the same time, they must earn the confidence of the board by exhibiting good judgment—not only taking risks, but also making wise decisions on how to limit the market and when to forgo a useful technology. They must balance keeping abreast by accurately reading the market's receptiveness.

SUMMARY

This chapter has discussed several important complicating aspects of the IT business. Complex and shifting products, changing customers, new channels of distribution, and evolving cost structures have forced and will continue to force a major reanalysis and redirection of IT's product offerings and marketing efforts. The changed marketing environment has forced significant changes in IT manufacturing, organization, control systems, and, most fundamentally, in its perception of its strategic mission.

Ted Levitt's classic article, "Marketing Myopia,"[2] best captures this idea. Levitt noted that the great growth industry of the 19th century—the railroads—languished because the owners and managers saw themselves in the railroad business, rather than the *transportation* business. Similarly, IT is not in the electronic-based computer, telecommunications, and desktop support business. Rather, it is in *the business of bringing a sustained relevant stream of innovation in information technology to companies' operations* and, in many cases, *products.* Far too many people in the IT business myopically believe they are running a computer center! Failure to perceive and act on their broader role can lead to a collapse of their operations, loss of jobs, and great disservice to the customer base.

When IT is defined in this way, the dynamic, successful marketing mix for the 1990s suddenly snaps into focus. To rely on an existing product structure and attempt to devise more efficient ways to deliver the old technology within old organizational structures or even new technologies within the old organizational structure will certainly lead to dissolution of the IT business. The IT organization has been an agent of change for its customers for 30 years. The change agent itself also must change if it is to remain relevant.

---

[2]Theodore Levitt, "Marketing Myopia," *Harvard Business Review,* September–October 1975.

Case 5–1

COLLIERS INTERNATIONAL PROPERTY CONSULTANTS, INC.: MANAGING A VIRTUAL ORGANIZATION[1]

The single biggest thing we have to deal with today is our organization,[2] we need to create the right organization to drive a global company. The crux of the matter is the following: how do we streamline the organization and maintain our network philosophically? A key challenge for us will be to manage the tremendous variety of cultures—social, business, organizational—that we have. We have to ensure that this diversity continues to be the source of our strength and dynamism.[3]

John R. McLernon[3]

In 1995, Colliers International Property Consultants, Inc., a commercial real estate corporation with 184 offices and approximately 4,400 professionals in 34 countries, provided a wide range of real estate services.[4] Colliers members managed close to 300 million square feet around the world, reported 1994 total worldwide revenues of $485 million (a 50% increase over 1993), and completed transactions valued at $16.8 bil-

lion.[5] Nearly 55% of its revenues were generated in North America, 26% in Europe and 18% in Asia-Pacific. Colliers had expanded from 97 offices in 12 countries in 1990 to almost twice as many offices in approximately three times as many countries in 1995. Individual member firm revenues ranged from $500,000 to $80 million. While some firms were over 150 years old, others had not yet celebrated their first anniversary.

At the same time that Colliers was expanding, clients' expectations of real estate service providers was changing. Colliers International Chairman John McLernon and a significant number of Colliers leaders believed that the real estate landscape was evolving from one in which clients needed services for single transactions in local markets to one in which clients demanded advisory services on a broader scale, and often

---

Research associate Carin Isabel Knoop prepared this case under the supervision of Professor Lynda M. Applegate.

[1]Copyright © 1996 by the President and Fellows of Harvard College.

Harvard Business School case 396-080.

[2]According to *Webster's Dictionary,* "an organization is a number of persons or groups having specific responsibilities and united for a particular purpose."

[3]John R. McLernon, International Chairman, interviewed by casewriters in May 1995.

[4]1993 revenue breakdown by specialization: office sales and leasing (approximately 21% of worldwide revenues), industrial sales and leasing (19%), property management (16%), investment sales (8%), appraisal and consulting (13%), retail sales and leasing (6%), land sales (5%), development (4%), as well as other services (8%).

[5]Colliers International will be referred to as "Colliers." Member firms will be referred to as "members" or by their names.

across national borders. Clients wanted not only a proposal for a new location, but also advice on relocation. At the May 1995 International Meeting, McLernon argued that a litmus test of Colliers' ability to compete would be the number of national or international contracts—which he referred to as "value-added business"—Colliers firms could win by year-end.

McLernon sought to transform Colliers from a global federation of real estate services providers to a leading global provider of professional real estate services with worldwide revenues of $850 million in the year 2000. But the International Meeting yielded more questions than answers as Colliers leaders tried to decide what steps were required to achieve their vision. What form and structure would Colliers need to have in the 21st century? Which new competencies were required? How could leaders of a worldwide loosely knit federation make sure that the headquarters organization and individual firms possessed the necessary commitment, skills, structures, and systems? How could they improve Colliers' ability to support investments in training and technology to respond to the growing competition from within and beyond the real estate field? What were the main trade-offs they had to manage? What role did and could technology play in binding together Colliers' diverse firms? Finally, what was necessary to preserve the entrepreneurial and cooperative spirit credited for Colliers' success while deriving financial and knowledge economies of scale from an ever-expanding global organization?

Building Colliers

In the early 1970s, Robert McCuaig, a Sydney-based British chartered surveyor, and his colleague David Collier merged their real estate firm with a firm in Melbourne and one in Adelaide. 'We dropped the names

of our own firms and kept Colliers," explained McCuaig. "It was high in the alphabet, easy to spell and pronounce." In 1974, three firms in three cities used the Colliers name. McCuaig recalled the next step:

> When clients told us that Colliers was good locally but did not have any international contacts, we set about building this organization on a worldwide basis. First, we believed that it was the only way that we could maximize our potential. None of us wanted to be just local estate agents. Second, we had an insatiable desire to be the best. Third, we loved to travel! We approached our task with missionary zeal. But instead of spending 225 years establishing ourselves, as Jones Lang Wootton, one of our competitors, had done, we took the Price Waterhouse model and formed a worldwide federation. We identified prominent real estate business leaders and then we met them.

One of these leaders was Canadian real estate businessman John McLernon, whose firm in 1984 became Colliers Macaulay Nicolls.[6] McLernon recalled, "At that point Colliers was like a club because most of its leaders were real estate professionals and none had any training in running a company. In 1985, we decided that if we wanted to expand, we had to provide funding.[7] This marked a watershed in our thinking about building an organization."

After a false start, the American Realty Services Group, a national association cre-

---

[6]Colliers Macaulay Nicolls' strategy was to buy at least 50% of a prospective Colliers firm. Firms acquired by Colliers Macaulay Nicolls Canadian firms adopted the Colliers colors and the name Colliers Macaulay Nicolls. In 1994, Colliers Macaulay Nicolls acquired majority ownership of a Colliers firm in Portland, Oregon, in Seattle, Washington, and in San Francisco, California.

[7]Until the mid-1980s, new members paid a joining fee that was split among existing firms. The joining fee was then converted to annual dues, and starting in 1990 members paid both a joining fee and annual dues.

ated in Boston in 1979 by 14 real estate industry leaders and headed by Boston-based Stewart Forbes in the role of chairman, became the U.S. Colliers member in February 1985. Subsequently, Forbes became president of Colliers Worldwide and his office became Colliers headquarters. Parts of the Hong Kong and Singapore real estate operations of Jardine Matheson Ltd. teamed up with Colliers in the late 1980s. In 1991, the Australia and New Zealand offices of Colliers merged with Jardine Pacific to form Colliers Jardine.[8] Then came Western Europe and another false start before London-based Erdman and Lewis and Paris-based Auguste Thouard decided to join in 1995. As shown in Exhibit 1, by 1994, Colliers had members all over the world.

The Rules of the Game

The procedure for becoming a member firm was simple. Cross-ownership of shares with existing Colliers firms was neither obligatory nor expected. Colliers looked for firms that sought to grow and specialize and saw joining Colliers as a way to reach these goals. After approval by the existing membership, a firm could become a Colliers shareholder. New firms signed a Stockholders Agreement and purchased stock in a Delaware Corporation called Colliers International Property Consultants, Inc., that was set up primarily to own and protect the "Colliers" name, logo and performance standards. Members agreed to annual dues ranging from $10,000 to $60,000 depending on market size and potential.[9] In addition, Colliers North American firms paid a fee of 5% to headquarters on commissions for transactions generated through Colliers.[10]

Although Colliers issued fee-splitting guidelines, firms negotiated compensation for referrals on a case-by-case basis and percentages ranged from 10% to 50% depending on the type of deal and firms involved (see Exhibit 2). Members were expected to refer their clients to Colliers' affiliates, but had the option not to do so as long as they informed the Boston office and any concerned firms. Revenues from fees, dues, and referrals supported headquarters activities—communication, coordination, and the organization of conferences, as well as other operating expenses such as legal and advisory services. Exhibit 3 contains selected financial statements.

After paying the joining fee, a new member in the United States was required to put its Colliers affiliation on its letterhead within one year, as well as use the Colliers logo and colors in compliance with the "Visual Identity Guidelines."[11] One staff member within each member firm had to be appointed "Colliers manager" to act as a point of contact with members and headquarters. The firm was expected to participate in Colliers meetings and adhere to the performance standards set forth in the Guidelines for Colliers Standards and Recertification. When a firm decided to leave Colliers, it surrendered use of the name. Although firms joined for different reasons and at different stages in their development, they all had an interest in sharing information, market knowledge, and access to clients and business opportunities. Colliers firms pointed out that they shared a "depth

---

[8]Colliers Jardine was owned 50% by Jardine and 50% by Colliers employees.

[9]A new fee structure was under discussion at the time of the case.

---

[10]The fee was paid by the Stockholder which benefited from the referral. In 1994, the volume of referral business was $6 million, compared to $2.5 million in 1988.

[11]When American Realty Services Group joined Colliers in 1985, Colliers members were allowed to keep their firm names. The requirement that all firms adopt the Colliers name was approved in the early 1990s.

EXHIBIT 1   Offices of Colliers Members Worldwide, 1994

THE AMERICAS

Argentina
- Buenos Aires

Brazil
- São Paulo

Canada
- Calgary
- Edmonton
- Montreal
- Ottawa
- Toronto
- Vancouver
- Victoria
- Winnipeg

Chile
- Santiago

Mexico
- Mexico City

United States
- Allentown
- Akron
- Atlanta
- Baltimore
- Boston
- Charleston
- Chicago
- Cincinnati
- Cleveland
- Columbus
- Dallas
- Dayton
- Denver
- Detroit
- Ft. Lauderdale
- Grand Rapids
- Greenwich
- Hartford

- Houston
- Indianapolis
- Kansas City
- Los Angeles
- Louisville
- Memphis
- Miami
- Milwaukee
- Minneapolis
- New Jersey
- New York
- Norfolk
- Oakland
- Philadelphia
- Phoenix
- Portland
- Raleigh
- Richmond
- St. Louis
- Sacramento
- San Diego
- San Francisco
- San Jose
- Savannah
- Seattle
- Washington, D.C.

Venezuela
- Caracas

EUROPE

Austria
- Vienna

Belgium
- Brussels

Czech Republic
- Prague

England
- Birmingham

- Leeds
- London

France
- Paris

Germany
- Frankfurt
- Hamburg

Greece
- Athens

Hungary
- Budapest

Italy
- Milan
- Rome

Netherlands
- Amsterdam

Northern Ireland
- Belfast

Poland
- Warsaw

Portugal
- Lisbon

Russia
- Moscow

Scotland
- Edinburgh
- Glasgow

Spain
- Barcelona
- Madrid

Turkey
- Istanbul

AUSTRALASIA

Australia
- Adelaide

- Brisbane
- Canberra
- Darwin
- Hobart
- Melbourne
- Perth
- Sydney

New Zealand
- Auckland
- Christchurch
- Wellington

ASIA

China
- Beijing
- Shanghai

Hong Kong

India
- Bangalore
- Bombay
- New Delhi

Indonesia
- Jakarta

Japan
- Tokyo

Malaysia
- Kuala Lumpur

Philippines
- Manila

Singapore

Taiwan
- Taipei

Thailand
- Bangkok

Vietnam
- Ho Chi Minh City

---

of knowledge of their market, long experience in the real estate business, strong ethics, and a sense of fairness."

McLernon explained that Colliers was a collection of firms "with very different people in very different companies" and Colliers meant different things to different member firms (see Exhibits 4 and 5). Because most members provided a wide range of real estate services with different strong points, professionals within most firms differed in terms of experience, profile, and remuneration. On the advisory side, for example, professionals were usually on retainer, and sometimes worked with success fees, contingency fees, or a retainer offset against a success fee. Brokers were usually paid on straight commission.[12] Furthermore, brokers tended to work alone and in the United States completed close to 10 transactions per year. In contrast, advisory services often required

---

[12]Most Colliers firms followed an independent contractor system, in which salespeople received a commission of approximately 50% of the revenue generated from a transaction.

EXHIBIT 2   Sample of Fee-Splitting Guidelines

These guidelines shall apply to all intercompany referrals in North America. The following are to be considered Colliers transactions, which shall require compensation to be paid to Colliers from the participating firms:

A. Colliers, USA shall receive 5% fee on all brokerage deals between Colliers firms where the gross commission received by Colliers firms are $2,000 or more. Transactions where the gross commissions to Colliers firms are less than $2,000 shall be reported for informational purposes only.

   Colliers, USA shall receive 5% of the total commissions due to Colliers firms, net of non-Colliers co-broke commissions. Such commissions shall be payable when and as received by sending or receiving Colliers firms, or both, as the case may be. The firm receiving the Colliers commission shall be responsible for paying the Colliers, USA portion from the total fee. If the receiving and sending firms are paid separately, each shall pay to Colliers, USA 5% of their individual commission amount.

Example:

   In the event of a co-broke deal where the Colliers firm is paid directly by the co-broker or client, the appropriate distribution would be as follows:

Total Commission	**$100,000**
Less: co-broke fee of 50%	(50,000)
Subtotal (Colliers Transaction)	**50,000**
Paid to Colliers sending firm (10%)	5,000
Paid to Colliers receiving firm (90%)	45,000
Payable to Colliers, USA from Colliers sending firm	250
Payable to Colliers, USA from Colliers receiving firm	2,250
Total payable to Colliers, USA	2,500
Total payable to sending firm	4,750
Total payable to receiving firm	42,750
	$ 50,000

B. Where a member firm significantly uses the personnel of other Colliers firms in soliciting business, negotiating a deal, or marketing a property, Colliers shall receive a 5% fee from any resulting commissions, as provided in the previous paragraph. The firms shall agree among themselves on the appropriate division of resulting fees.

C. Where a referral results in management, appraisal, or consulting business, Colliers shall receive a fee of 2.5% of the generated fees paid quarterly, provided no such fee shall be paid unless fees generated to member firms exceed $5,000 per year or unless the assignment requires competitive bidding, or in which case the Colliers fee shall be waived.

EXHIBIT 3 Colliers International Statement of Income, Year Ended December 31, 1994

	Amount	Percent
Income:		
Referrals	$ 303,348	17.20%
Dues	944,517	53.57
Services	105,463	5.98
Interest, miscellaneous	30,420	1.73
Conferences	228,059	12.93
International contribution	85,000	4.82
Special assessment	50,250	2.85
Consulting	12,329	0.70
Reimbursables	3,821	0.22
Total income	$1,763,207	100.00%
Cost of sales:		
Promotional products	41,891	2.38
Presentation products	23,297	1.32
Brochure	27,424	1.56
International communications	32,359	1.84
General promotion	88,734	5.03
Miscellaneous promotion	12,734	0.72
National account program	25,267	1.46
Total cost of sales	$ 251,706	14.31%
Gross Profit	$1,511,501	85.69%
Operating expenses:		
Organizational development	$ 203,339	11.53%
Direct sales	3,226	0.18
Marketing	110,876	6.29
Information management	113,107	6.41
Research	44,331	2.51
Legal	41,912	2.43
Office overhead	526,230	29.86
Travel and entertainment	75,452	4.28
International contribution	71,595	4.08
Colliers group health	34,637	1.96
Conferences	242,725	13.77
Consultants	1,537	0.09
Depreciation	28,266	1.60
Bad debts	22,088	1.25
Total operating expenses	$1,519,321	86.24%
Loss before taxes	(9,381)	0.53
Taxes		
State corporate tax	459	(0.03)
	(9,840)	(0.56)%
Retained deficit, beginning balance	(141,715)	
Retained deficit, ending balance	$(151,555)	

teamwork, client management, and longer sales cycles. History and regional idiosyncrasies further accentuated diversity. "In most cases U.S. firms are established family businesses and do not want to change," McCuaig explained. "I respect that. But we could not operate that way in Asia-Pacific because we need a much greater commitment to the organization because we are doing so much business with a few clients that need service in multiple locations all at once."

Within Colliers Jardine, revenues were almost equally split between the advisory and transaction areas, while for some U.S. firms, 90% of revenues came from brokerage activities. While Colliers Jardine held 100% of the Hong Kong office, 70% of its Singapore office, and 50% of its Tokyo and Taiwan offices, most U.S. firms were owned by individual members who met twice a year—once at an Owners' Meeting and once at the Sales Conference. For Colliers Jardine, client loyalty was key to profitability; repeat business represented just 20% of each U.S. firm's activity in 1994. Colliers Jardine enforced the "2 + 2 rule," which amounted to asking every client two additional questions: "what else can we do for you today?" and "where else in the world can we help you?" A U.S. director described how diversity influenced inter-firm collaboration:

The way our business works in the United States is quite different from the way it works

---

EXHIBIT 4   What Is Colliers?

"A comprehensive consultancy real estate company that provides all the various services related to real estate. Marketing, advisory, research, representation, valuation."

"A federation of similar quality of real estate service providers. It is not a franchise."

"Number 1."

"It is a network."

"A real estate corporation. A virtual corporation."

"An arrangement among real estate service providers."

"We view Colliers as a platform for people and firms to exploit their services for their own good and the good of the organization."

"It is a stock federation."

"Colliers is a federation that enjoys global marketing from a centralized source."

"Colliers is a collection of entrepreneurs in various subgroups. They come together at different levels with a common goal—do deals, do business. There are local, national, regional, global levels of contact."

"Colliers is, by and large, determined by what is needed by the client."

"Colliers is a network—I know we are not supposed to use the word network. . . . I'd say we are a worldwide network of commercial real estate firms. They are not owned by a particular firm."

"A combination of competition and cooperation. So Colliers allows you to be your own personal best, develop and work on your particular individual skill. Colliers lets you be an individual athlete but your talents need to be coordinated as a team."

Source: Casewriter interviews of Colliers members.

abroad. U.S. brokers often need to provide some form of market information before dealing with a client, for example, market rates in the central business district of a particular capital. The Colliers member in that country may

EXHIBIT 5   North American Colliers' Shareholders Ranked by Revenues and Number of Professionals, 1994

1994 Revenue	1994 Professionals
$81,540,000	766
76,581,495	450
60,000,000	500
42,000,000	495
21,000,000	42
17,091,500	125
11,200,000	35
11,000,000	56
10,800,000	32
10,200,000	40
10,013,000	51
9,200,000	56
8,722,000	20
8,550,000	22
7,900,000	40
7,830,000	34
6,831,000	20
5,598,254	29
5,008,000	17
4,881,226	27
4,712,010	20
4,660,366	33
4,600,000	40
4,458,770	25
4,380,000	32
4,200,000	24
4,050,000	26
3,724,058	28
3,000,000	8
2,850,000	9
2,600,000	11
2,550,000	11
2,200,000	18
1,908,000	10
1,622,081	15

be reluctant to respond immediately to such requests. They need to trust the person asking for the information.

Another source of tension could be the perception that one Colliers firm was poaching in another's territory. In 1995, for example, a U.S. member was doing transactions in South Korea, Colliers Jardine's backyard. Also, fee-sharing negotiations could be intense and difficult. One manager believed that over the past five years clients had been "forcing us to put the fee issues aside and put service first. Clients will again drive the changes to the year 2000. They will force us to grow trust internally." Colliers firms pointed out that they had several things in common, including "depth of knowledge of their market, long experience in the real estate business, strong ethics, and a sense of fairness."

Structure and Systems

Colliers was organized along regional lines and governed by an international chairman, a president and a board, the International Governing Committee. McLernon, chairman of the board since 1987, ensured that the entire organization worked towards the same goals. One young broker spoke for many Colliers members when he described McLernon as "the glue that holds it all together. He has the vision. He has no problems taking someone else's idea, buying into it, refining it and then disseminating it. He is a great communicator." McLernon presided over the International Governing Committee.

As the overall governing entity, the International Governing Committee set strategy, monitored standards and performance of member firms and reinforced agreed codes of practice and conduct. In 1994, Colliers created a regional structure—Asia-Pacific, the Americas, and Europe—under three boards responsible for formulating strategy, monitoring member conduct, and reviewing new firms. (See Exhibit 6 for data per region.) The boards reported to the International Governing Committee, and each region had two representatives on the board (see Exhibit 7). Regionalization was seen as a way to put members in close contact, allow them to share information on related markets, provide central marketing contacts, and build commonality. Wally Pinkard (Principal, Colliers Pinkard, Baltimore and former U.S. chairman and International Governing Committee member), added:

EXHIBIT 6   Regional Data

Region	1994 Fee Base	1994 Number of Offices	1994 Number of Personnel	2000 Estimated Fee Base ($ millions)
Europe (approx. 17 countries)	$130 million	51	1,300	$200
Asia-Pacific (approx. 13 countries)	$ 70 million	38	1,100	150
The Americas (approx. 33 members)	$250 million	95	2,000	500

Source: Colliers document.

EXHIBIT 7   Colliers Organizational Structure

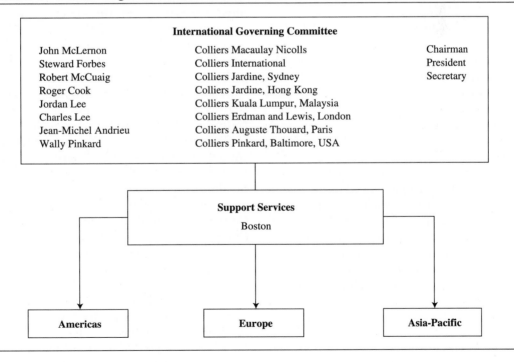

The rationale behind regionalization was to economize on management time and talent. We decided to have driver firms in each region. It is also easier to manage conflict in three spots instead of in a central one. Another reason we wanted a regional organization is that while many multinationals have one central real estate decision point, they also have one person in charge for Europe, one for Latin America, etc. So being regional for us made sense.

Colliers firms in Canada, the United States, and Central and South America reorganized into the Americas region. The existence of prior structures as well as the diversity of the 33 member firms involved posed a significant challenge to implementing a regional organization. Pinkard explained that the U.S. region had created an executive committee that met on a bimonthly basis in 1994. But in July 1995, the U.S. Regional Committee had yet to meet but had decided to meet on an as-needed basis. Members McLernon, Houston, and Pinkard spoke regularly on the phone. The Colliers offices in Canada reported to Colliers Macaulay Nicolls, headed by McLernon. Canada and the U.S. together oversaw the rest of the Americas. Colliers Macaulay Nicolls also owned 50% of the Colliers firm in Mexico. At the time of the case, Forbes had been screening firms in the region and working on creating a Colliers Latin America.

Implementing regional structures was easier for the European and Asia-Pacific regions, where there were mostly larger firms. The European Regional Committee met for the first time in September 1994, decided to meet on a quarterly basis, voted on centralizing some pan-European marketing, financial/budgeting, and business development functions, and defined its regional strategy. The United Kingdom and France, as major firms, accepted the joint role of "drivers" of the European region and as such would seek to develop cross-border business.

It was decided that London would provide a scaled-down version of the Boston operation (i.e., information, communications, research focused on the European region). The costs of this operation would be shared by the European members. The London office also provided a Secretariat, directed by Wilf Dawkins, who was also charged with developing business within the region, and hosted Colliers Manager Craige Coren, who worked out of the London office to develop business across the Atlantic. Representatives of member firms in Europe would meet two to three times a year.

Dawkins attributed Europe's rapid response to regionalization to the lack of pre-existing structure. "With the growth of international business, we realized that we needed to have very efficient structures as soon as possible," he explained. "It was an underlying principle that if we were to join Colliers, that we, as main European firms, would retain control of our operations and have a major say in the strategic development and operations of the region. We felt that it was important for each region to determine its own strategy and for the global strategy to reflect this."

In contrast to Europe, where no organization existed, regionalization in Asia essentially confirmed the approach taken by Colliers Jardine. Chief Executive Cook continued to report to his Board and shareholders, and Colliers Jardine's corporate headquarters in Hong Kong continued its oversight and support functions. In 1994, Colliers Jardine focused on expansion, with the opening of several new offices in mainland China and the finalization of joint ventures in India and Vietnam.

"The Boston Office" and the President

The Boston office was the headquarters of the U.S. region as well as the central office for Colliers worldwide. As part of their annual dues, members received the Annual Sales

Directory, Annual Report, newsletters, flyers, two International Office Market Surveys, International Office Leasing Guidelines, and a Global Market Overview (see Exhibit 8). Boston also provided a variety of informational services and searches from client and proprietary databases. These were billed at cost when specifically requested by a member of a Colliers firm. Use of e-mail and database queries were billed on an as-used

---

EXHIBIT 8　Services of Colliers International Headquarters

Organizational Development and Promotion Program
Coordinator and Manager Support
Legal, Administrative, and Finance Planning and Policy

Marketing and Communications

- **PRODUCE**
  For External Distribution
  Newsletters
  Sales Flyers
  Case Histories—Success Stories
  Annual Report
  Presentation Materials

  For Internal Distribution:
  Sales Directory
  Sales Associate Guide

- **PROMOTE TO**
  National Association Meetings
  New Owners
  • North America
  • Europe
  • Pacific Rim
  Owners
  Sales Associations
  Prospects
  Clients
  Trade and Business Press

Information Management

- **DOCUMENT**
  Firm Capabilities
  Individual Skills
  Corporate Relationships
  Transaction Experience
  Referrals

- **MAINTAIN**
  Database
  Prospect Information
    Value Line
    Dun & Bradstreet Reports
    Dow Jones News Retrieval

- **TRAIN/SUPPORT**
  Telecommunications Operators

- **ORGANIZE**
  Owners' Meetings
  Annual Sales Conference
  Meetings:
    Annual Owners
    Colliers Managers
    Regional Sales
    Specialists (Peer Groups)

Research and Program Development

- **PRODUCE**
  International Office Market
    Report (Semi-Annual)
  North American Office Market
    Report (Quarterly)
  North American Industrial Market
    Report (Quarterly)

- **MAINTAIN**
  Resource Library
  Market Information

- **SCREEN AND CATALOG**
  System/Software
  Presentations
  Publications
    Trade
    Economic
    Business

basis. Other custom promotional, technical, and research tasks were quoted on an hourly- or fixed-fee basis. International activities took about one-third of the Boston office's time.

Colliers president, Forbes, compared his role to that of a chief operating officer—to "facilitate and increase the productivity and market share of participating firms by developing the goals, strategy, and consensus necessary for implementation as well as documenting and making accessible the collective resources of the organization." Boston's role was to convince, not sell. Forbes saw an "ability to listen, objectively establish facts, and develop commitment to shared goals" as necessary prerequisites for this job.

To improve information flows between members and with Boston, Forbes strongly encouraged that Colliers managers be non-owners "so that Colliers does not become tenth [on the list of priorities]." Ideally, the managers should function as "spokespeople to the sales associates or to the clients" and provide input from the field to headquarters. McLernon believed that headquarters needed to be more involved in the global community. For Forbes, headquarters performance could be assessed by looking at cross-firm referrals and firm revenues as well as the level of complaints from owners.

Intra- and Inter-Regional Links

In 1994, peer groups formed in all three regions. In the United States, for example, the property managers group was formed in mid-1994 out of an eight-firm effort to respond to a request for proposals. It had already met twice and planned to meet again in June 1995. In contrast, an investment sales group was dormant for eight months and was regenerated by Forbes through a memo with an agenda for discussion on "how we are going to market ourselves." Forbes believed that successful groups had to remain small, around a dozen professionals of the same caliber. While most peer groups in the United States met informally, the sharing of best practices was more formal on the other side of the Pacific. In 1994, Colliers Jardine senior professionals tasked with codifying and spreading best practices in areas such as valuation, property management, etc., began to meet at regional conferences. Within the European region, several working groups developed cross-border opportunities in valuation, retail, investment, business space, and hotels.

Furthermore, according to Pinkard, Colliers leaders had been "developing relationships among the strongest firms, first through stronger business relationships, such as referrals, and then through cross-ownership and equity participation." To build such bridges, Colliers Jardine kept a manager director in the United Kingdom. He and his team of five shared offices with Colliers Erdman Lewis. In 1994, Colliers Jardine nominated Kevin Manning as its managing director in the United States. Manning had previously been with the Colliers member in San Jose, California. "One of my jobs," he explained, "is to make sure that the system works globally, especially in the Asian arena. I am the conscience, the ombudsman for that process. Recently, we noticed that some United States clients want to see United States interlocutors when they go abroad. In other cases clients want to see locals. So we have to change the look and feel of our site in different countries."

While Manning helped promote and coordinate Asia-Pacific services to U.S.-based corporations, Coren worked on developing business across the Atlantic. At the International Governing Committee Meeting, an ERC member suggested that "without Craige [Coren] nothing would get done between the United Kingdom and the United States." Pinkard pointed out, however, that "in the United States, few people know that Kevin [Manning] exists."

Responding to the shift away from individual transactions and towards advisory services, account management, and process-oriented activities, individuals from 15 different Colliers firms in the United States formed the Colliers Corporate Services Group. Set up in 1994, the Group described itself as a reliable and accountable long term partner that could provide multidimensional services on a multinational basis. Most members of the Colliers Corporate Services Group were seasoned professionals who were put on salary for a minimum of three years by their respective "hosting firms," an unusual procedure in the United States, where most Colliers professionals were on commission. Hosting firms in turn hoped to have access to large corporate business and expand their client base.

The Colliers Corporate Service Group's steering committee was composed of six members of different U.S. Colliers firms. The group reported to Forbes and was supported by headquarters resources in exchange for its promise to "expand the market potential for all Colliers firms." Forbes underlined that the Colliers Corporate Services Group "should be seen by member firms as an additional resource, as a SWAT team they could call in for specific assignments, but that they would not take over a relationship and take it away from the originator. That is the difficult balance we are trying to strike." The Colliers Corporate Service Group had ambitious goals for year-end 1995: perform services for 30 to 40 clients, generate $1 million in fees, and grow to 20 professionals.

To provide seamless service, Colliers Corporate Services Group members would coordinate client services wherever and whenever they were required and provide a single Colliers point of contact and unique account management system to provide maximum accountability. Ultimately, Colliers Corporate Services Group members and their clients would be electronically linked through a proprietary software system enabling minute to minute reporting and real time client access to assignment status report. Colliers' technological capability was a central part of the Colliers Corporate Services Group's sales pitch. The Colliers Corporate Services Group selected Lotus Notes at its communication platform, and the group started using it in October 1994.

Interestingly, Colliers Corporate Services Group was not the first group of its type within Colliers in the United States. In fact, in 1990, Ian Stuart, a British chartered surveyor, started a Colliers Advisory Group at Damner Pike in San Francisco. Its members—who did not work on commission—"provided strategic real estate planning and implementation at a local, national, and international levels" to Bay area clients, such as Oracle Corp. Stuart recalled the internal and external challenges of building his group:

> At first we had a tough time convincing clients that they needed us. Then we had to get used to presenting ourselves differently. We found that it was difficult to establish a centralized contact both within Colliers and with the client. Finally, we faced the challenge of convincing others [within Colliers] that we could help grow their business; [we ran into] the what-can-you-do-for-me mentality that used to be typical in the real estate world.

Colliers was not a pioneer in formalizing corporate account management: one of its major U.S. competitors, the New America Network, established a Corporate Services Group in 1987.[13] Although Manning

---

[13]New America Network Aims to Meet the Needs of Corporate America," *National Real Estate Investor* 33, no. 4 (April 1991), p. 99.

believed that sophisticated U.S. corporations favored this type of advisory service over the speculative, intermediary brokerage process, he described the Colliers Corporate Service Group as "an unproven bet." Pinkard felt that "new challenges, such as the continuing investment in heretofore unprofitable corporate services work, threaten to strain our management capabilities." Forbes was nevertheless "convinced that the right combination of structure, management, technology, capital and leadership [could] put Colliers at the top of the industry."

Responding to Changes in the Real Estate Industry

In the late 1980s, corporations that owned real estate became more concerned about maximizing the value of their property and minimizing operational expenses. Also, occupancy rents became a major expense for corporate tenants. For many companies, real estate remained the second largest line item after payroll and related benefits. Real estate started to receive top management attention. By the 1990s, real estate portfolios were being examined from a global perspective as firms relocated and rationalized operations around the world. According to the managing director of CB Commercial's international department, "meeting multinationals' growing real estate space requirements and investment appetite will determine which firms lead the real estate business in the next century."[14]

Once "local," clients were starting to require national and global services. In 1994, Colliers registered a 30% increase in multi-city assignments over 1993. At the same time, winning international business was becoming a way to obtain local business. A Colliers member recounted:

> You finally get to see the general manager of a large U.S. firm's subsidiary in Brazil, say, and they tell you that they like you and Colliers but that you have to go to headquarters in New York because that is where real estate decisions are now being made. You've wasted time and money. So we have to ask ourselves: how do we find out about how decisions are made at potential "local" clients, and how do we make sure that we are the ones selected as the real estate partner by New York?

Although Colliers' competitors varied in type, and from region to region, Colliers' members agreed that in all their markets competition had increased "exponentially." The number of competitors offering corporate real estate services ranged from relatively small, boutique-type firms in individual markets to large U.S. and international real estate service organizations. Main competitors were other large international real estate companies. Colliers also competed against specialized service providers such as developers. Since the late 1970s, less obvious threats had emerged in the guise of professional services firms (i.e., accountants, lawyers, and merchant bankers). Competitors differentiated themselves by size and geographic coverage, international expertise, financial expertise, facility and portfolio management capabilities, advisory services, and strategic planning, systems, and technology.

The need to gain the necessary "critical mass" both in terms of expertise and geographic coverage led to the creation of major global real estate partnerships. In October 1994, ONCOR International, one of the oldest U.S. brokerage firms, and Hillier Parker International, together with leading European firms including France's Bourdais S.A., announced a partnership to create the world's largest full-service commercial real

---

[14]*National Real Estate Investor* 37, no. 1 (January 1995), p. 6.

estate organization, with 6,000 real estate professionals in 29 countries in every continent. "Our philosophy is to think and act in terms of global real estate strategy, implemented locally by leading real estate firms in every marketplace," declared Hillier Parker's chairman.[15]

In January 1995, the United States' two largest real estate service providers both announced they were forming separate worldwide alliances. The first, Cushman & Wakefield Worldwide, combined 39 Cushman & Wakefield offices with 34 Healey & Baker offices in Europe, along with one of Canada's leading real estate services firms, a multiservice real estate firm based in São Paulo, Brazil, and the Marlin Land Corp. that would provide real estate services throughout Asia from its Hong Kong base. Within a couple of days, Los Angeles-based CB Commercial Real Estate Group announced that it was forming a Latin American alliance, after setting up partnerships in Europe, the Middle East, Asia and Australia. By early 1995, the firm had forged 23 alliances, including South America, with over 160 offices worldwide.

At the International Meeting, McLernon commented that growing competition at the global level meant that Colliers could no longer rely on the lead it once had in terms of combining "geographic coverage with local knowledge" to win large contracts and bid for value-added business. Competing for and delivering on such contracts required a "new way of running and doing business at Colliers." Headquarters reported that negative feedback from external customers tended to center around the issue of accountability, the inability to document a capability, the failure to obtain information, and the existence of different standards and systems in each

market, leading clients to conclude that Colliers was not a "seamless organization."

The Best of All Worlds?

The move towards regionalization 1994 and the flurry of initiatives at the International Meeting brought to the surface the multiplicity of views within Colliers about ownership structure, the meaning of membership, the optimal profile of the real estate professional, as well as the need to expand or slow down geographic coverage. Members speculated on the impact on the organization and individual firms of the decision to provide global real estate services in contrast with providing real estate services in every part of the globe. Some argued that Colliers was trying to change too fast; others felt that "Colliers could not change fast enough."

Organizational Issues

Colliers ownership structure was seen as both an asset and a liability by potential and existing members. Some members commented that lack of common equity ownership was occasionally used by the competition as a point against Colliers. Their argument was that firms with fully owned subsidiaries were better able to guarantee quality, enforce standard, and provide seamless service. David Houston, President, David Houston Co., New Jersey and chairman of the U.S. region of Colliers, explained that it was important to tailor the sales pitch to the region, point of contact, and type of company; for example, larger, integrated firms often required more clarification and details on Colliers structure. He elaborated:

> What is important in marketing Colliers is that you give people a structure that they understand, that is close to what they can relate to. Because of business and culture differences, it is nearly impossible to explain the organization in the same way to everyone around the world.

[15]"History Made with the New International Alliance," *Real Estate Weekly* 41, no. 12 (October 26, 1994), p. 13.

When we market Colliers in the United States, we do not use the term "network" because I do not think that it is a concept that many of our corporate clients understand. Instead, we refer to Colliers as a cooperative corporation with decentralized profit centers. That is terminology they can understand. We have a president, a board of directors. But instead of headquarters owning all the offices, the offices own the headquarters.

For McCuaig, the ideal structure had to be "fairly decentralized, but totally accountable. There is inevitably a bit of bureaucracy. Also, the bigger the organization, the more expensive it becomes to run because you have to build bigger systems." Although McCuaig agreed that Colliers' tendency to be more entrepreneurial and less bureaucratic was a competitive advantage, he did not see consolidation as a threat to the existing culture. For McCuaig, further consolidation meant "greater quality control and better internal relationships:"

> If you are asking someone in another company to do something, no matter how much you may love them and they love you, they may not do it. It's human nature. I just think you get more reliable service when you are with one company. In that case, you do not have to ask someone to do something, you can expect them to do it. [Yet] each office remains a profit center so the referral business remains the same. It makes it easier to refer because the systems are consistent.

Colliers' co-founder was convinced that "modern day management structures could achieve anything, provided the right people were running the show." Through "high quality, simple systems" Colliers could preserve the benefits of small entrepreneurial firms with the economies of scale of a large organization. "If you had the right culture of service, in which the client comes first, second, third and fourth, then everything would fall into place." But Jordan Lee, whose firm

in Malaysia had joined Colliers in 1984, suggested that "good or bad [service was often] a matter of opinion" and that there was "no yardstick to measure good service. I have to believe that my colleagues have provided what *they believe* is the best possible service."

Forbes believed that Colliers Jardine, Colliers Macaulay Nicolls, and Colliers Europe were all pulling together, but the United States did not see the advantage of doing so. Pinkard felt that in the United States efforts to unite the independent firms were perceived as a threat to the sovereignty of individual member firms. Pinkard also worried that disparate levels of service capability would worsen as stronger firms were pushed to higher levels of performance by increasingly sophisticated clients. Cook responded that smaller firms had no choice but to raise their standards. To him, "improving standards across the board [was] the only issue [because] our weakest link was the one most visible to clients." For this reason, Colliers Jardine had decided in 1994 to obtain the ISO9001 accreditation for services, which required adhering to certain internal and external audit requirements. In the process, Colliers Jardine was surveying staff and customers to identify quality gaps. By having common standards and systems, Colliers Jardine could expand and bring new firms up to speed rapidly. Nevertheless, although within Colliers Jardine the reporting structures were identical, the accounting, the remuneration system, and quality standards were not all the same. Moreover, it was essential, according to a Colliers Jardine executive, to ensure that no firm's self-interest, however large and significant, predominate. Finally, regional autonomy had to be preserved.

While most members seemed to approve of the regional structure, they wondered about overlaps in authority. "The European

Regional Committee's decisions are final," a Committee member ventured, "though perhaps they could be reconsidered. The International Governing Committee's decisions are final, although if a majority of members are opposed to a decision, it will not be implemented. It has not happened yet." Pinkard was not surprised by the confusion:

> Control of Colliers has been somewhat haphazard, particularly at the international level, because of the role of the Boston office. We need to refine that role or find a substitute approach—perhaps a stronger chairman's office with some international funding. This organization needs more management and structure. More importantly, it needs to follow up on goals and objectives.

Managing Member Expectations

Members had widely different views of what the Boston office's role and services should be. While some members were very demanding, others never called. Most believed that the central office should provide public awareness of the organization and a forum for exchange of ideas and other services, for example, training and information systems. According to McCuaig, member firms wanted "information on basic standards, a library of best practice, and, most importantly, information on who had done what to whom, when, where, why, and for how much." Other members saw marketing and promotion initiatives as a way to reimburse their dues. Forbes pointed out that in the past Boston had relied on local firms to be the primary interface with the market. Members had complained about the quality of some services—information that was dated, inapplicable, incomplete or not in the expected format and level of detail (e.g., a list of transactions instead of a comprehensive presentation). Some members also felt that headquarters did not have enough field

and real estate related experience. They also resented having to pay for customized services and being unable to get immediate service or to use e-mail. Finally, members often blamed headquarters more than themselves when they had "missed something."

Those who used and promoted the name and colors of Colliers argued that Boston should at a minimum guarantee strict worldwide enforcement of the visual identity guidelines. While a director in Malaysia expected Boston to provide expertise upon request, she did not want Boston to "police" individual firms. In contrast, a Colliers Jardine executive in Singapore argued that Boston had to ensure that if he referred a client to another Colliers office, "the client would come back happy, [and that everything would occur] without too much red tape, discussion, and negotiation." Also, he believed Boston should take the lead in setting software and hardware standards for Colliers to make it possible to "carry a diskette to any member firm around the world and be able to use it." Furthermore, while Dawkins felt that "it would be wrong for Boston to propose a new member in Europe," others approved of Boston's initiatives in other parts of the world.

In response, Colliers had worked on organization-wide technology solutions. In late 1994, Colliers recommended that member firms adopt Lotus cc: Mail and Notes as the organization-wide communication platform. This would change the way Colliers professionals exchanged information internally as well as with clients. "The older folks still believe that cold calling is the way to do it," one U.S. principal explained. "The new school will e-mail the client, who will already have replied by the time the other guy makes it past the reception desk. Some new school brokers may also have other types of experiences and bring these to the real estate business."

Furthermore, Colliers began a training program, leveraging training programs and staff at Colliers Macaulay Nicolls' in-house training group. Participants at the March 1995 North American Owners Meeting attended a workshop on "Business Planning" that covered operational as well as strategic issues. Delivered locally or regionally by headquarters staff, the two-day session on "How to use Colliers" targeted approximately 25 new recruits or professionals needing updating. "How to build Multi-City Assignments," to be held four times a year by a training company, targeted professionals with five to seven years of experience. In 1996, "How to build Relationships" would cater to individuals with consultative activities.[16]

Colliers was also considering the development of a common worldwide training for young recruits—common practice in most international accounting, consulting, and banking firms. Some Colliers real estate competitors held rookie training camps, which provided mostly networking opportunities. A Colliers member discussed some of the problems of common worldwide training:

> In audit, for example, you can go through a common training, but [within Colliers] people have different skills, cultures and backgrounds, and provide different real estate services. While we cover a broad span, some U.S. firms do mostly brokerage, emphasizing valuation. The atmosphere is very different from offices where brokers learn to "sell, sell, sell." These differences make it hard to do a common training and sometimes to communicate.

To Forbes, the challenge was not so much diversity as commitment:

---

[16]Delivery of training and support tools were to be funded by local firms and individuals. Based on groups of 20 to 25 professionals, total cost for the 2½ day training sessions, complete with research materials, sales tools, manuals and tapes, came close to $1,300 per person.

> It was tough to convince people that it was in their interest to attend Colliers training, especially when their domestic market was booming. People agreed that training was good but it could be put off if things were going well. I do not know how much training we will be able to motivate. But we are committed to training and see it as a critical element to achieve the effectiveness we need.

More fundamentally, Pike added, it was a matter of responding to member needs. "While [Colliers] began as a group of people who met largely on a social basis, the younger generation wants new tools and databases and are interested in the educational aspect of the conferences instead of the social ones," he explained. The need to invest in training and technology in turn explained his "bias for a more centralized organization. The investments are so large that we have to make sure that we derive economies of scale from them." Doing so also required standards, and, Pike believed, "the implementation of standards [required] a stronger executive body. We can all talk about standards, but someone needs to enforce them. By standards, I mean nearly everything. Accounting, reporting, statistics, stationery, logo, etc. One thing is inevitable—the centralization of ownership. The larger firms will have to be the driving forces."

Leveraging Product and Service Range

Although most Colliers members believed that broad, multi-location, long-term contracts could be very profitable, they expected the costs of selling and servicing such relationships to rise as clients and competitors became more and more sophisticated. In June 1994, Sprint International, through its real estate department, retained Colliers to provide comprehensive property services in Europe and Asia. An account manager was responsible for the entirety of the transaction, ensuring that the Colliers' representatives were performing. During 1994 and early 1995, Colliers had been negotiating similar regional agreements with companies such as Ford, General Motors, and Hughes Electronics. An internal memo regarding Sprint pointed out some of the risks and opportunities that long-term, open-ended, outsourcing-type client relationships entailed:

> It is hard to estimate the amount of work we will receive from Sprint over the next year. The real estate department reacts to various departments in Sprint, and in some cases Colliers may be asked to provide cost analysis for a project that never happens, or, on the other hand, Colliers could be requested to make an evaluation of the whole property portfolio of a company with which Sprint is considering a merger. Not only does Sprint need Colliers to negotiate on its behalf in foreign markets, but it also needs us to outline various characteristics of the local market, to enable [the relationship manager at Sprint] to explain to the legal department why his or her department is committed to various issues.

The level of information sharing and the scope of activities required by such contracts contrasted with the "broker's natural instinct to guard knowledge and data jealously," Dawkins underlined from experience. "To convince a broker with significant local remuneration to participate in and contribute to international assignments is challenging. Meetings are the best ways to build trust and confidence in each other's abilities. Ultimately, the [membership] agreement says that we have to cooperate."

McLernon responded:

> When people tell me that big national contracts may not be good business, I tell them that every business is good business. Or we have to make it good business. When a new product area is significant, we have a management challenge to come up with a system. It won't be easy. We will have to decide who will make the selling presentation. To whom? On what bases? When? Who will quote our price? Who will decide how commissions are shared? How do we split the cost if we lose? What do we do once we win? Who does what where? These are the real questions. But what matters most is to win.

Several Colliers leaders felt that value-added business meant higher selling expenses, greater specialization, and investment in systems, for example, for project management and financial analysis. Consequently, some felt that Colliers should be run more like a business than an association of top professionals. The 1995 Business Plan for the U.S. region explained that dues would have to be raised to cover a 28% increase in the operating expenses at Colliers headquarters, mostly because of increasing demand for services such as training, IT support, and marketing.

As Colliers expanded its product portfolio and hosted a growing number of specialized business units, some wondered whether Colliers could be all things to all people while at the same time striving to provide seamless service or come across as one organization to the increasing number of clients that came in contact with several Colliers members. Pike wondered:

> Indeed, there is a broker Colliers, an institutional Colliers, a small town Colliers. In some respect it can be dangerous because you set up competition that can be unhealthy. Also, you cannot allow some people to think that they have higher skills than others. And, we must avoid free riders benefiting from the Colliers network. We must continue to invest in the Colliers brand without diluting it.

At this juncture, McCuaig and Cook felt that it was crucial to enforce the common name and logo policy. According to Cook, the U.S. region was still debating name, color, logo, and recruiting issues while "Canada and Colliers Jardine have resolved these issues and now, as united entities, have pursued new ones." The U.S. 1995 Business Plan reminded U.S. owners that Colliers

USA would have spent nearly $112,000 in 1994 and 1995 to promote the Colliers name while close to 50% of the firms either did not use or promote the Colliers name and were thus in technical violation of the Visual Identity Guidelines. The noncomplying U.S. firms were given until June 1996 to comply. Some found it irresponsible to risk losing some valuable members over the name issue.

Decisions

Forbes was fond of saying that Colliers did not dictate to members how to run their business. Nevertheless, at the May 1995 International Meeting, McLernon gave Colliers one year to develop worldwide public relations initiatives at the inter-office, inter-region, and worldwide levels. Also, each region would identify 20 prospects for international contracts and five presentations would be made. "This," he told the delegates, "is not a topic of debate but a matter of commitment." A task force would propose an approach for selling and managing such contracts to the International Governing Committee by September 1995. Finally, McLernon told delegates that each member firm was to schedule Lotus Notes training sessions for its IT department and one salesperson as soon as possible. He told the delegates, "We have to move to electronic communication. Those who do not get on Notes, for example, won't get the next International Directory. It is no longer a matter of choice, it is a matter of must." Many agreed that this was a new approach for Colliers. McLernon explained:

> To drive Colliers into the 21st century, we have to agree on what we are prepared to do to ensure a commitment in capital and a common plan. The big question is whether or not we are compatible enough to actually affect those changes if we undertake them?

When the meeting was over, an attendee mused, "We have never been short of good ideas. The problem is in the implementation."

Case 5–2

WWW.SPRINGS.COM[1]

Business Week's June 1997 "Rising Star" profile of Springs Industries' President and Chief Operating Officer, Crandall Bowles, reported that she was poised to become one of the top two or three women executives in the country.[2] In November 1997 the company announced Bowles' appointment to the position of Chief Executive Officer as of January 1998. A priority on her agenda as CEO was to hone in on the company's information systems (IS) strategy and determine both the breadth of expenditures and the pace of innovation necessary for the coming years.

Professor F. Warren McFarlan and research associate Melissa Dailey prepared this case.

[1]Copyright © 1997 by the President and Fellows of Harvard College.

Harvard Business School case 398-091.

[2]*Business Week*, June 23, 1997, p. 132.

Springs Industries Inc.—a $2.2 billion textile company headquartered in Fort Mill, South Carolina, 20 miles south of Charlotte, North Carolina—produces home furnishings under such well-known brand names as Wamsutta and Springmaid and major licenses such as Disney, Liz At Home, and Bill Blass. Springs' home furnishings segment, which accounted for 82 percent of the company's 1996 revenue, is a leading U.S. producer of bedding products and also produces a broad selection of bath products (including towels, rugs, and shower curtains), baby products, and window hardware and coverings. The balance of the company's revenue was generated by the specialty fabrics segment, which produced fabrics for the apparel industry, home sewing outlets, and industrial users (see Exhibits 1 and 2).

A book documenting the first hundred years of the company's history pictured company founder Samuel White, Bowles' great-great-grandfather, in his Confederate uniform standing in front of the monument to the Confederate Soldiers of Fort Mill District. Determined to help re-build the economy of the South in the aftermath of the Civil War, White raised capital from local farmers, built cotton mills, and, in 1887, founded Fort Mill Manufacturing Company, later Springs Industries.

Family members are Springs Industries' largest shareholders. A graduate of Wellesley College and Columbia University's MBA program, Crandall Bowles worked for Morgan Stanley & Co. and spent 14 years managing the family's nontextile operations through a privately held investment company before joining Springs in 1992. After demonstrating her management abilities in corporate planning, textile manufacturing, and bath products, she stepped into the role of President and COO in January 1997, and information technology became one of her major areas of responsibility.

Chairman Walter Y. Elisha, who would retire in December 1997, had piloted Springs through a period of leveraged buyouts and bankruptcies in the home furnishings industry that had left it with fewer but larger companies better able to meet the mounting demands of powerful retailers and price sensitive consumers. Springs' balance sheet was the industry's least-leveraged—long-term debt was just 22.5 percent of shareholder equity. Since 1992, however, Springs' sales had risen just 13.6 percent to $2.2 billion in 1996 and operating earnings, at $113 million, were the same as they were in 1992. By contrast, competitor WestPoint Stevens' operating earnings were $196 million on sales of just $1.7 billion.[3]

In the home furnishings industry, profits are tied to fast and flexible product development, short production cycles, and the ability to replenish stock quickly. Springs' capital expenditures had approached $1 billion over the past ten years as it moved to develop these capabilities. Planned capital spending for 1997 was $100 million, up from $75 million in 1996, much of it targeted at new technology to help the company produce higher quality products at the lowest possible cost. The complexity of making these changes was enormous as Springs had 54 plants and warehouses predominantly located in the southeast. These plants included Grace finishing plant, the largest finishing plant in the country, located 30 miles from corporate headquarters, four additional finishing plants, several fabrication operations, and a number of fabrics manufacturing plants.

Springs' customers, mega-retailers such as Wal-Mart, Kmart, and Target, expected suppliers to keep inventories precisely tuned to consumers' purchasing trends.

---

[3]Ibid., p. 134.

EXHIBIT 1 Springs Industries' Annual Balance Sheet ($ millions)

	Dec. 1996	Dec. 1995	Dec. 1994	Dec. 1993	Dec. 1992
Assets					
Cash and equivalents	30.719	2.606	0.769	2.79	4.033
Net receivables	350.83	351.669	312.739	315.834	298.807
Inventories	370.896	384.73	264.161	267.842	263.041
Prepaid expenses	0	0	0	0	0
Other current assets	37.177	30.3	39.335	40.073	37.122
Total current assets	789.622	769.305	617.004	626.539	603.003
Gross plant, property and equipment	1,320.40	1,380.66	1,253.06	1,195.84	1,168.43
Accumulated depreciation	785.836	766.7	697.81	645.938	609.123
Net plant, property and equipment	534.564	613.959	555.25	549.905	559.305
Other investments	0	0	0	0	0
Intangibles	2.011	2.363	1.699	0	
Other assets	71.759	141.917	115.09	115.687	87.995
Total Assets	1,397.96	1,527.54	1,289.04	1,292.13	1,250.30
Liabilities					
Long-term debt due in one year	6.921	13.078	21.318	20.511	20.943
Notes payable	0	21.9	11.1	61.42	46.014
Accounts payable	103.841	103.737	83.232	73.64	79.164
Taxes payable	0	0	0	0	0
Accrued expenses	141.727	124.275	128.306	117.439	128.693
Other current liabilities	0	0	0	0	0
Total current liabilities	252.489	262.99	243.956	273.01	274.814
Long-term debt	177.64	326.949	265.384	293.028	273.551
Deferred taxes	5.495	26.608	30.731	27.914	34.264
Investment tax credit	0	0	0	0	0
Minority interest	0	0	0	0	0
Other liabilities	181.553	176.475	164.881	154.986	79.616
Equity					
Preferred stock—redeemable	0	0	0	0	0
Preferred stock—nonredeemable	0	0	0	0	0
Total preferred stock	0	0	0	0	0
Common stock	5.064	5.062	4.429	4.428	4.427
Capital surplus	110.352	109.84	11.413	11.144	10.887
Retained earnings	667.741	622.069	570.851	530.406	575.698
Less: Treasury stock	2.378	2.449	2.602	2.785	2.954
Common equity	780.779	734.522	584.091	543.193	588.058
Total Equity	780.779	734.521	584.091	543.192	588.058
Total Liabilities and Equity	1,397.96	1,527.54	1,289.04	1,292.13	1,250.30
Common Shares Outstanding	20.148	20.137	17.595	17.582	17.571

Source: Standard & Poor's, Compustat.

Exhibit 2 Springs Industries' Annual Income Statement ($ millions, except per share)

	Dec. 1996	Dec. 1995	Dec. 1994	Dec. 1993	Dec. 1992
Sales	2,243.33	2,233.05	2,068.91	2,022.82	1,975.69
Cost of goods sold	1,749.45	1,743.94	1,552.79	1,541.34	1,507.61
Gross profit	493.878	489.111	516.122	481.48	468.079
Selling, general, and administrative expense	299.326	270.989	300.58	281.539	277.174
Operating income before depreciation	194.552	218.122	215.542	199.941	190.905
Depreciation, depletion, and amortization	80.8	84.6	79.7	78.086	77.744
Operating profit	113.752	133.522	135.842	121.855	113.161
Interest expense	22.064	32.035	29.253	30.256	31.418
Nonoperating income/expense	−3.343	−3.754	0.123	−7.786	−1.748
Special items	16.174	13.2	0	0	0
Pretax income	104.519	110.933	106.712	83.813	79.995
Total income taxes	16.086	39.307	44.485	36.557	35.465
Minority interest	0	0	0	0	0
Income before extraordinary items and discontinued operations	88.433	71.626	62.227	47.256	44.53
Preferred dividends	0	0	0	0	0
Available for common	88.433	71.626	62.227	47.256	44.53
Savings due to common stock equivalents	0	0	0	0	0
Adjusted available for common	88.433	71.626	62.227	47.256	44.53
Extraordinary items	−3.552	0	0	−72.543	0
Discontinued operations	0	0	0	0	0
Adjusted net income	84.881	71.626	62.227	−25.287	44.53
Earnings per share (primary)— excluding extra items and discounts	4.32	3.71	3.5	2.65	2.5
Earnings per share (primary)— including extra items and discounts	4.15	3.71	3.5	−1.42	2.5
Earnings per share (fully diluted)— excluding extra items and discounts	4.32	3.71	3.5	2.65	2.5
Earnings per share (fully diluted)— including extra items and discounts	4.15	3.71	3.5	−1.42	2.5
EPS from operations	3.15	3.27	3.5	2.65	2.5
Dividends per share	1.32	1.26	1.2	1.2	1.2

Source: Standard & Poor's, Compustat

Many suppliers were developing sophisticated information technology (IT) systems for analyzing mega-retailers' point of sale (POS) data. To increase profitability, Springs had to quicken the pace of its application of new technology and sources of information to marketing, customer service, and inventory management. Elisha and Bowles were navigating the 110-year-old company through massive change as it entered a business environment where electronic commerce and marketing were key sources of competitive differentiation.

Confronting the Competition

Since the early 1980s, Springs had been shifting away from commodity textiles for apparel, which foreign competitors could produce more cheaply, to home furnishings sold directly to retailers as finished products. This enabled them to capitalize on the trend in home fashions toward highly designed, coordinating products for the bedroom and bathroom. The sale of its Clark-Schwebel fiberglass subsidiary in 1996 illustrated the company's determination to become a focused supplier of products used in and around the home. The nearly $200 million proceeds of the sale allowed Springs to reduce its long-term debt and provided funds for its aggressive capital programs as well as acquisitions that fit into its long-term marketing strategy.

At the same time, to improve its position with consumers and retailers and increase market share, Springs acquired companies that would enable it to introduce new complementary products. For example, in 1995 Springs acquired a towel manufacturer and a shower curtain manufacturer to expand its existing bath products. Bowles led the integration of towelmaker Dundee Mills and Dawson Home Fashions, a maker of shower curtains, into the existing Bath Fashions Division. During the same year, Springs also acquired Nanik Window Coverings, a maker of wood blinds and interior shutters. These acquisitions posed not only an ongoing challenge of integrating new businesses into Springs' operations, but also a daunting IT challenge. The company's bold directive to "Present One Face to the Customer" presented many management complexities as the company worked to consolidate the back-office, administrative, and marketing efforts of its acquisitions.

In addition to broadening its product lines by expanding its manufacturing capacity, Springs sought to improve the speed and efficiency of its existing manufacturing systems by upgrading its technology—installing new weaving machines, faster fabrication equipment and new information technology systems to enable more flexible and cost effective use of existing capacities. The company consolidated several manufacturing facilities and moved the production to modernized plants capable of producing greater quantities of fabric with lower overhead.

While Springs was making headway in its efforts to overhaul its manufacturing and systems infrastructure, rival WestPoint Stevens was already reaping the benefits of a five-year strategy of reducing costs while investing heavily in marketing and technology. Although WestPoint Stevens had incurred huge debts fending off hostile takeover attempts, new management decided in 1992 to reinvest $100 million a year into the business. By 1997 the company had a track record of five consecutive years of strong earnings growth (see Exhibits 3 and 4). The industry trade magazine *Textile World* awarded its coveted annual Model Mill award to WestPoint Stevens in 1997, a title Springs had held in 1975 and 1987. "The massive spending program allows the company to rapidly expand capacity," reported *Textile World*. The magazine predicted that WestPoint Stevens would expand

EXHIBIT 3   Financial Comparison of Springs Industries with Key Competitors

	1992	*1993*	*1994*	*1995*	*1996*
Operating income					
Springs Industries	190.9	199.9	215.5	218.1	194.5
Pillowtex	20.6	27.9	24.6	48.5	50.9
Fieldcrest Cannon	118.1	97.61	100.4	52.1	67.2
WestPoint Stevens	235.8	246.0	257.4	263.6	272.6
Net income					
Springs Industries	44.5	−25.3	62.2	71.6	84.9
Pillowtex	10.9	12.8	7.79	11.5	14.1
Fieldcrest Cannon	15.3	−42.9	30.7	−15.7	1.6
WestPoint Stevens	397.4	−402.3	−203.4	−129.9	57.7
Sales					
Springs Industries	1,975.7	2,022.8	2,068.9	2,233.1	2,243.3
Pillowtex	273.5	292.2	351.9	474.9	490.7
Fieldcrest Cannon	1,217.3	1,000.1	1,063.7	1,095.2	1,092.5
WestPoint Stevens	1,496.1	1,501.0	1,596.8	1,649.9	1,723.8
Return on sales					
Springs Industries	2.3	2.3	3.0	3.2	3.9
Pillowtex	3.1	4.4	2.2	2.4	3.0
Fieldcrest Cannon	1.7	1.5	2.5	−1.8	−0.3
WestPoint Stevens	−53.6	−21.4	−12.7	−7.9	3.3
Return on assets					
Springs Industries	3.6	3.6	4.8	4.7	6.3
Pillowtex	6.4	7.1	2.4	3.5	3.9
Fieldcrest Cannon	2.4	1.9	3.4	−2.5	−0.4
WestPoint Stevens	−40.5	−21.3	−16.1	−11.4	4.9
Return on equity					
Springs Industries	7.6	8.7	10.7	9.8	11.3
Pillowtex	118.8	18.4	10.1	13.3	14.7
Fieldcrest Cannon	7.2	7.5	11.4	−9.4	−1.6
WestPoint Stevens	−345.7	NA	NA	NA	−12.8
Price/earnings					
Springs Industries	14.5	14.2	10.6	11.2	9.9
Pillowtex	NA	15.5	13.4	10.8	12.9
Fieldcrest Cannon	13.1	19.9	8.4	−7.2	−41.8
WestPoint Stevens	NA	−1.9	−2.4	− 5.5	16.5
Earnings per share					
Springs Industries	2.5	2.7	3.5	3.7	4.3
Pillowtex	1.3	1.3	0.7	1.8	1.4
Fieldcrest Cannon	1.8	1.2	3.2	−2.3	−0.4
WestPoint Stevens	−27.6	−10.0	−6.2	−4.0	1.8
Book value per share					
Springs Industries	33.5	30.8	33.2	36.5	38.6
Pillowtex	1.1	6.5	7.2	8.3	9.4
Fieldcrest Cannon	23.8	22.5	26.4	24.5	23.6
WestPoint Stevens	8.1	−4.2	−10.2	−15.8	−14.6

Source: Standard & Poor's, Compustat.

bath capacity by 12 percent in 1997 and bedding by 15 percent by mid-1998.[4]

In September 1997, Pillowtex, a $490 million manufacturer of pillows and blankets, announced its acquisition of Fieldcrest Cannon, a leading U.S. producer of towels and bedding products. The transaction, valued at over $700 million, created a third big player in the home furnishings industry. The acquisition made Pillowtex the nation's third largest home furnishings maker; its combined annual 1996 sales exceeded $1.5 billion, which compared with Springs' $2.2 billion and WestPoint Stevens' $1.7 billion. The Pillowtex–Fieldcrest Cannon combination, with its portfolio of many of the industry's best recognized brands, constituted a formidable competitor for Springs. Springs' attempted hostile takeover of Fieldcrest Cannon in 1993 had been rebuffed. Like Springs, Pillowtex could now offer a broad array of products and cross-merchandise its bed and bath product offerings. Observed the *Charlotte Observer,* "Pillowtex would have a broader mix of basics—from pillows and mattress pads to sheets and towels— than the other two. Analysts say Pillowtex also has great depth within its lines. A strong product lineup is critical because retailers increasingly want to buy from fewer suppliers."[5]

---

[4]"Catering to Consumers' Dreams—WestPoint Stevens," *Textile World,* June, 1997, p. 41

[5]"WestPoint and Springs May Be Forced to Grow," *The Charlotte Observer,* September 13, 1997.

EXHIBIT 4   Textile Home Furnishings Industry Monthly Stock Price— January 1995–September 1997

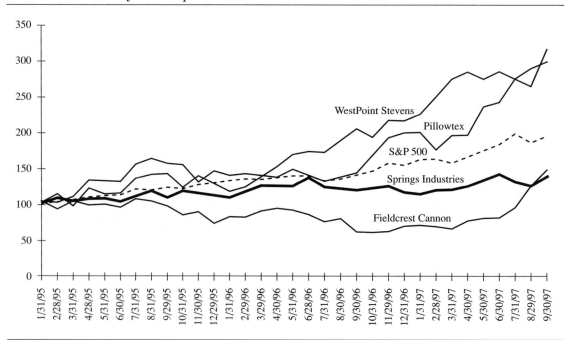

Source: Datastream International.

The Rise of the Mega-Retailer

We're no longer identifying ourselves as a textile company. We're identifying ourselves as a consumer products company. To be successful and viable we need to be consumer focused and consumer driven. In dealing with Wal-Mart and Kmart, we are no longer competing for shelf space with other textile manufacturers. We are competing against an apparel manufacturer or an appliance dealer, even with a Rubbermaid or Coca-Cola.

Robin Torkildsen,
IS Director of Sales
and Marketing

EXHIBIT 5

*Top Ten Home Textile Retailers
(based on 1996 sales)*

JC Penney
Wal-Mart
Kmart
Target
Sears
Bed, Bath, Beyond
Linens 'n Things
Mervyn's
Spiegel
TJ Maxx/Marshalls

Note: Eight of these firms were among Springs' top ten customers.

Mega-retailing pioneers Wal-Mart, Kmart and Target had significantly increased their market share of home textile products in the 1990s (see Exhibit 5). A litany of traditional department stores had merged or closed over the years as superstores attracted new "precision shoppers," mostly working mothers looking for competitive prices and a broad array of merchandise in one location according to Standard & Poor's retail industry report.[6]

In 1997 Wal-Mart was the world's largest retailer with almost 3,000 Wal-Mart Supercenters, Wal-Mart discount stores, and Sam's Club warehouse stores worldwide and plans to open additional stores in China and Central and South America. When it went public in 1970, Wal-Mart had only 18 stores and sales of $44 million. Management subsequently invested in two strategic technology initiatives to increase efficiency: an automated distribution system that cut shipping costs and time and a computerized inventory system that increased the speed of check-out and re-ordering. In 1980, one decade after its IPO, Wal-Mart had 286 stores and sales of $1.2 billion.[7]

Sophisticated computerized inventory management systems were becoming the retailing standard in the late 1990s, with many retailers collecting point of sale (POS) data, including dollar amounts of purchases, categories of merchandise, color, vendor, and SKU number. By forming alliances with vendors, retailers could get the fastest-selling inventory onto the shelves and achieve higher sales. In an ideal partnership, suppliers would have access to the retailer's POS data in order to be able to identify sales trends early and resupply fast-selling items. Wal-Mart's Retail Link technology afforded 3,200 vendors access to its POS data for purposes of replenishing inventory at some 2,000 stores. For example, workwear clothing inventory at each store was customized by the vendor according to demographics, regional tastes, and weather patterns. As a result of this practice, Wal-Mart recorded in

---

[6]"Retailing: General Industry Survey," Standard & Poor's, July 24, 1997, p. 12.

[7]*Hoover's Handbook of American Business 1997,* pp. 1416, 1417.

May 1996 a 25 percent reduction in SKUs and a 15 percent increase in sales.[8]

With retailers passing much of the responsibility for inventory data analysis and management to suppliers, vendor managed inventory (VMI) was increasingly becoming the standard; vendors that offered inventory management services improved their chances of winning the best supplier contracts. Springs, with a majority of its 1996 sales derived from its top ten customers, had to move from a supplier's response system to pro-active data analysis and efficient supply chain manufacturing and distribution. An active participant in Wal-Mart's Retail Link program, Springs was negotiating similar VMI programs with other customers.

Competitor WestPoint Stevens, which had launched a vendor managed inventory program in 1995, was gaining a reputation for its ability to replenish stock based on current sales results and adjust production schedules to retail sales projections. The company's management claimed not only to collect information on every sale from every cash register of its major customers, but also to have the customer service and technological power to analyze inventory data and respond appropriately. Remarked WestPoint Stevens president and COO Thomas Ward in *Textile World*'s profile of his company: "We know what's selling on a daily basis at the point of sale. That's extremely important." Moreover, the implementation of a company Web site (http://www.westpointstevens.com) served notice that management might plan to provide direct to consumer sales via the Internet.

Springs was coming to grips with the fact that electronic commerce would be a key source of competitive differentiation in the near future. "The ability to receive, transmit, and translate a geometrically increasing amount of data into useful information will be critical to a company's survival," stated a Springs' planning document entitled, *Vision 2002: A View of the Future and Implications to Springs*. The Internet Web site (http://www.springs.com) the company had established to communicate its public image to prospective employees and external markets was one step in a shift towards electronic enablement. Wal-Mart, Kmart, and other major national chains that had launched Web sites incorporating features such as search engines, electronic order forms, and savings coupons appeared to be preparing for an anticipated surge in on-line shopping.

Towards a Network Architecture

> *Modular, dynamic, user-oriented computing platforms have been found to best support and enable new ways for organizing and managing work. The ability to align the various components of information technology architecture with more streamlined and modular approaches for conducting business operations is the main business driver for network computing.*
>
> —*Paradigm Shift: The New Promise of Information Technology*[9]

EVP and President of Diversified Home Products Group Stephen Kelbley (then CFO) hired Vice President of Information Systems Jim Wood in 1992 to implement information technology projects that would improve manufacturing flexibility and efficiency and reduce cycle time (see organizational chart in Exhibit 6). Springs had long been an

---

[8]"Retailing: General Industry Survey," Standard & Poor's, July 24, 1997, p. 17.

[9]Don Tapscott and Art Caston, *Paradigm Shift: The New Promise of Information Technology* (New York: McGraw-Hill, 1993), p. 127.

EXHIBIT 6 Organizational Chart

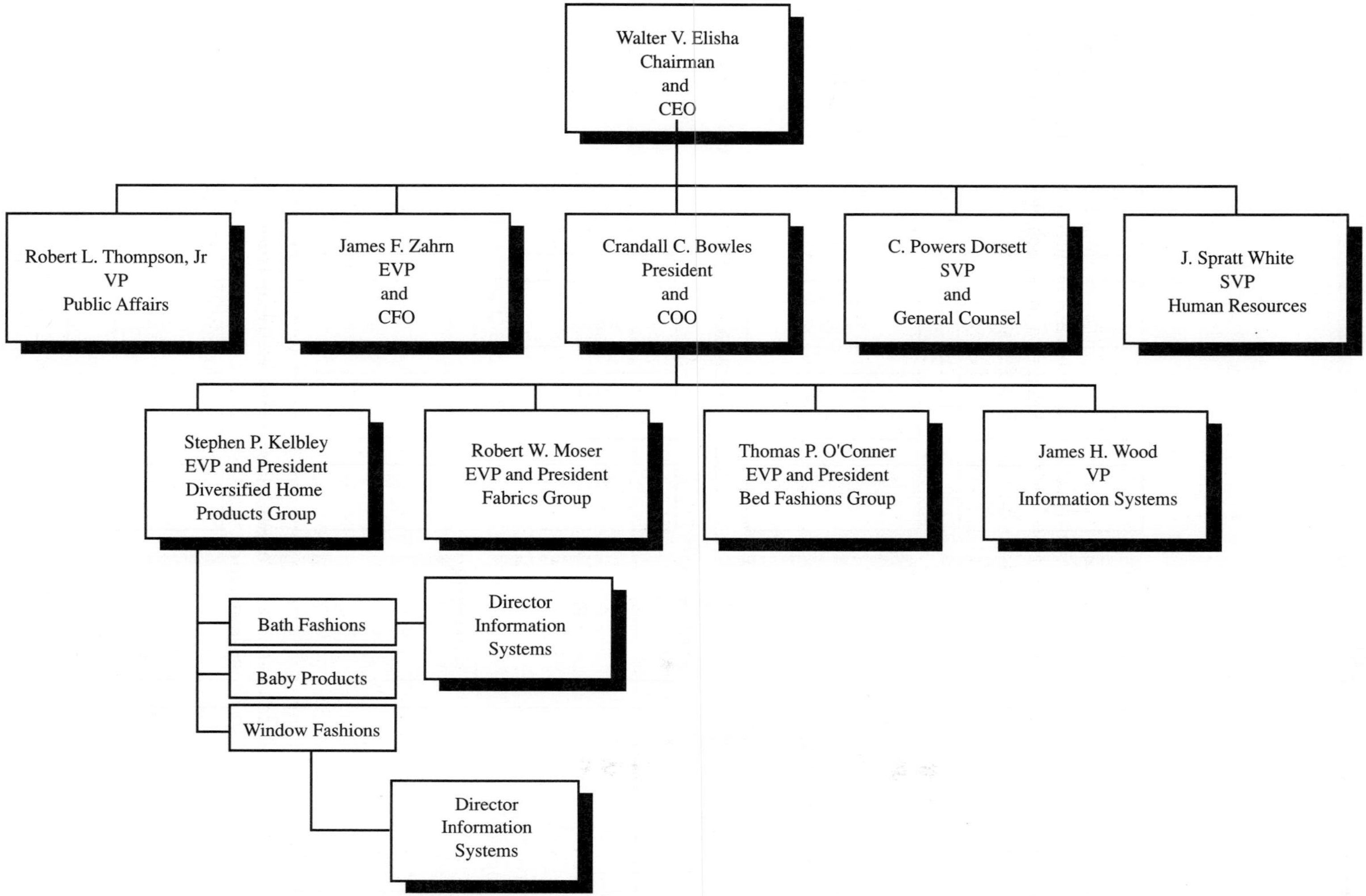

Walter V. Elisha
Chairman
and
CEO

Robert L. Thompson, Jr
VP
Public Affairs

James F. Zahm
EVP
and
CFO

Crandall C. Bowles
President
and
COO

C. Powers Dorsett
SVP
and
General Counsel

J. Spratt White
SVP
Human Resources

Stephen P. Kelbley
EVP and President
Diversified Home
Products Group

Robert W. Moser
EVP and President
Fabrics Group

Thomas P. O'Conner
EVP and President
Bed Fashions Group

James H. Wood
VP
Information Systems

Bath Fashions

Baby Products

Window Fashions

Director
Information
Systems

Director
Information
Systems

(continued)

EXHIBIT 6 (continued)   Organizational Chart—Information Systems

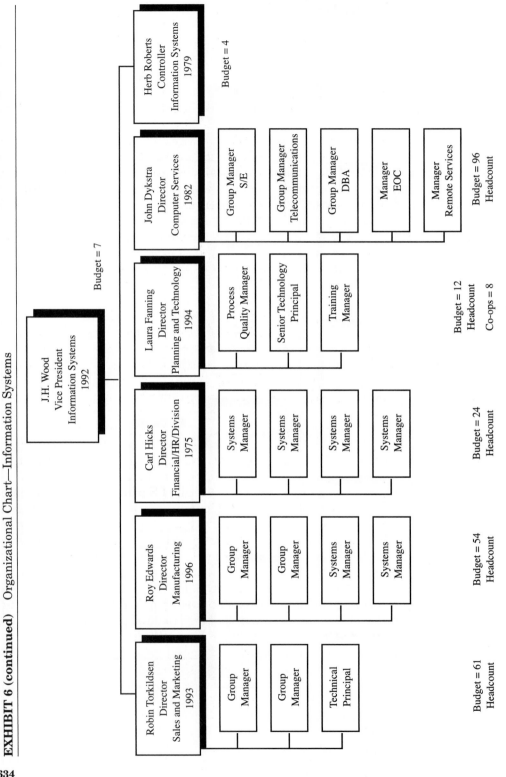

J.H. Wood
Vice President
Information Systems
1992

Budget = 7

Herb Roberts
Controller
Information Systems
1979

Budget = 4

John Dykstra
Director
Computer Services
1982

Group Manager
S/E

Group Manager
Telecommunications

Group Manager
DBA

Manager
EOC

Manager
Remote Services

Budget = 96
Headcount

Laura Fanning
Director
Planning and Technology
1994

Process
Quality Manager

Senior Technology
Principal

Training
Manager

Budget = 12
Headcount
Co-ops = 8

Carl Hicks
Director
Financial/HR/Division
1975

Systems
Manager

Systems
Manager

Systems
Manager

Systems
Manager

Budget = 24
Headcount

Roy Edwards
Director
Manufacturing
1996

Group
Manager

Group
Manager

Systems
Manager

Systems
Manager

Budget = 54
Headcount

Robin Torkildsen
Director
Sales and Marketing
1993

Group
Manager

Group
Manager

Technical
Principal

Budget = 61
Headcount

Employment start dates appear beneath management names.

Source: Springs company document, September 16, 1997.

intensive user of IT and had been the first manufacturing company to install an IBM 650 in 1956. Wood was asked to develop a long-range information systems strategic plan, and cautioned that the company could accommodate evolutionary, but not revolutionary, change. An external report written before Wood's arrival had noted that Springs did not have a clear IT vision and was lacking IT leadership, project management methodology, and skilled technicians. "The organization had not evolved over time," explained Wood. "Throughout the 1960s and 1970s no formal development methodology had been implemented. The programmers were writing programs in the afternoon and dropping them into production the same night without adequate testing or quality review."

In 1992, much of Springs computing power was centralized in one data center filled with massive mainframes. A limited number of Springs employees could connect to the data center via "dumb terminals" to access information, a process complicated by the fact that the mainframe controlled the interaction and provided data in a character-based format. As users' needs expanded, Springs' programmers created and installed on the mainframe hosts monolithic software applications, resulting in a computing environment that was inflexible, unstable, and difficult to manage. "We were fighting to stay alive," recalled Wood. "We couldn't run the computer center. We had to literally de-install and re-install everything we had." Wood worked with Director of Computer Services John Dykstra to re-skill the technicians, re-wire several buildings and factories, and standardize on IBM's enterprise servers and mid-range platforms, utilizing DB-2 as their relational database and CASE tools from Sterling Software. Through an intense quality effort, nightly ABENDS (abnormal endings of a program) were

reduced from hundreds to a consistent record of between 0 and 1. In 1997, Compass, an external benchmarking firm, rated Springs' data center the "best of the best" in relation to other businesses of the same size.

Whereas Springs' mainframe systems had once functioned as the company's computerized brain, advanced microprocessor technology would enable the distribution of computer intelligence to employees' desktops. Springs' migration from mainframe host computing to a more complex enterprise server and mid-range server structure supporting multiple clients began with Jim Wood's arrival in 1992 and was still in progress in 1997 (see Exhibits 7 and 8). With continued expansion of its business operations and increased complexity of its administrative tasks, Springs computer processing power—measured in millions of instructions per second (MIPS)—jumped from 85 in 1992 to 956 in 1997. As the mid-range environment expanded, manufacturing applications were moved to the mid-range servers and the enterprise servers supported high volume transactions such as order fulfillment.

By 1995, all of Springs' facilities were tied into a wide area network (WAN) and 60 local area networks (LANs), enabling workgroups to share computer services such as laser printers, file servers, and e-mail. "As a consequence of lingering technology," explained Dykstra, reflecting on the 500 Springs associates still using aging "286" terminals that had not been updated since desktop computers were first introduced in 1983, "we have software issues, networking issues, and ultimately, network stability issues. Some units are operating very old versions of gateway software to connect to the data center. If they're left on all the time, they continue to spawn new threads on our gateways to the point where the line can crash and

EXHIBIT 7 Springs Industries, Inc., Information Technology Architecture

Description	1992	1995	1997
IT architecture	Host based systems with many terminals and limited PC emulation. Host systems typically used nonrelational databases. Single mainframe system.	Host based systems using relational databases, use of midrange platforms which are extensively integrated. Client/server based systems and extensive use of PCs for multi-system access. Multiple mainframe images in parallel.	Host and midrange based systems integrated using real-time message queuing between platforms. Most platform access via networked PC. Multiple mainframe images in parallel.
Wide area network (WAN)	No WAN. Multiple low speed, redundant links to manufacturing and administrative facilities.	All facilities served by a routed WAN. Mix of line speeds from 56kb to T1. Redundant links not needed for network diversity are eliminated.	Frame relay, dedicated circuits, private fiber, and SONET ring with ATM in production to support host access, midrange access, Internet, Intranet, and mail. Real-time network management platform and reporting capabilities.
Local area networks (LANs)	12	60	75
Desktop computers	1,000	2,500	3,600
Desktop applications	Word processing, spreadsheets, database, and terminal emulation.	E-mail, word processing, spreadsheets, presentation graphics, database, terminal emulation, query.	Extensive e-mail, word processing, spreadsheets, presentation graphics, database, terminal emulation, query, groupware, Internet browser.
Mainframe MIPS[a]	42	235	381
Midrange MIPS	43	160	575

[a]Millions of instructions per second.

EXHIBIT 8 Springs Industries, Inc., Technical Architecture, 1992

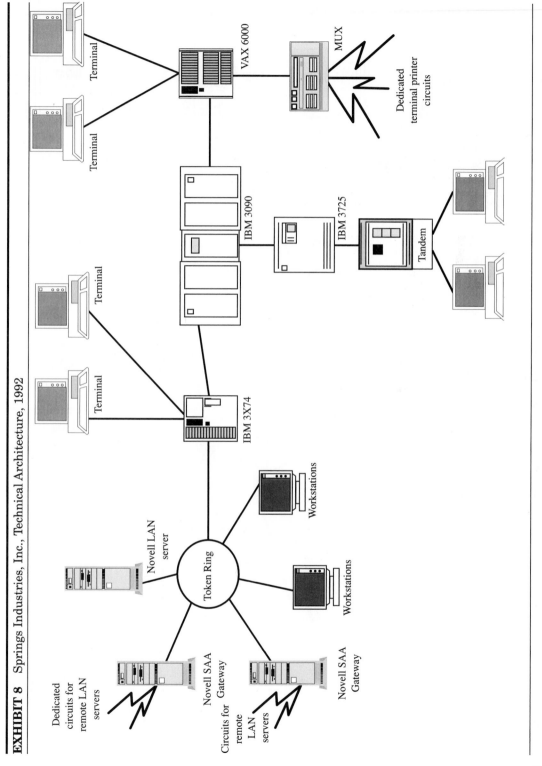

EXHIBIT 8 (continued) Springs Industries, Inc., Technical Architecture, 1992

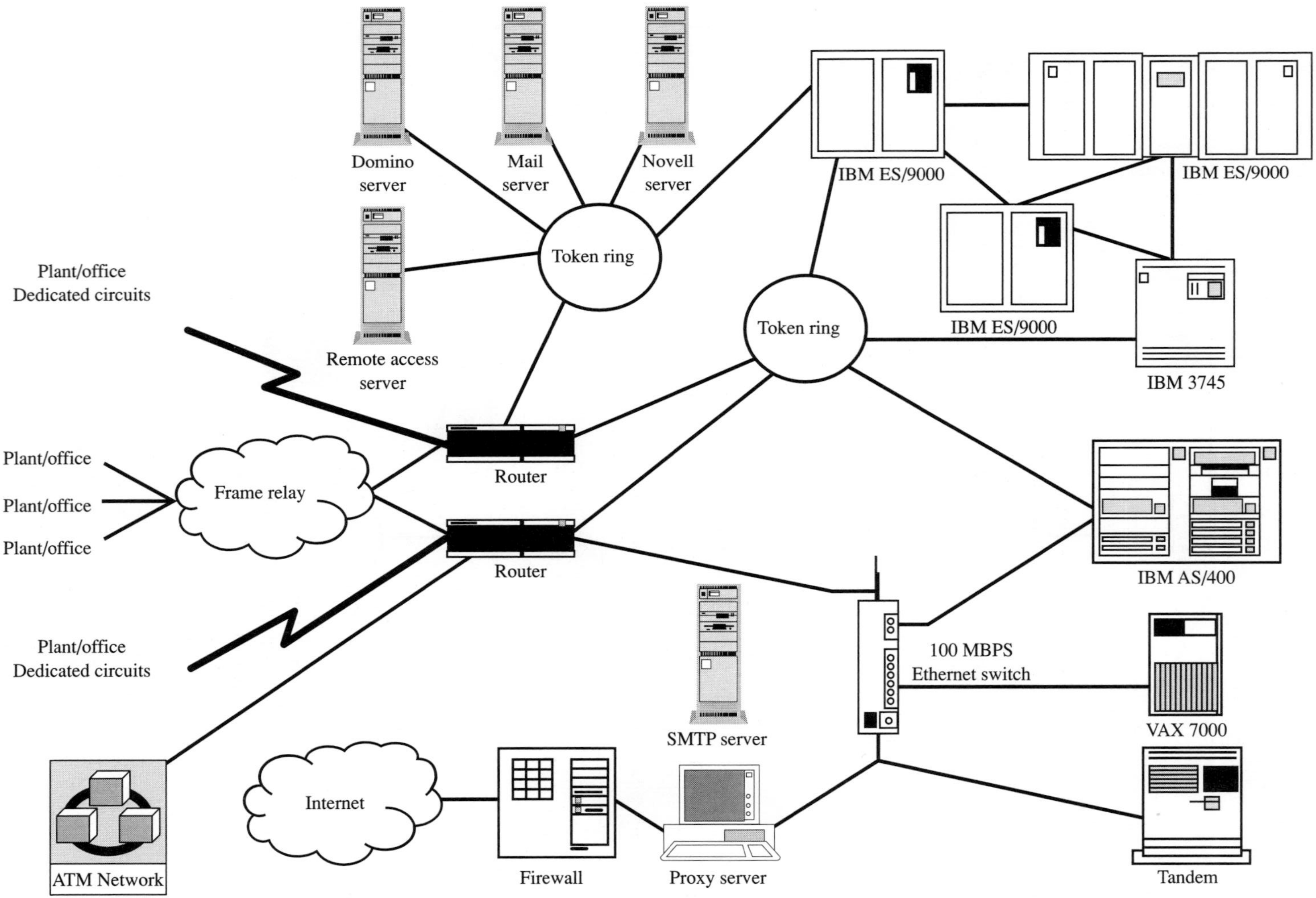

IBM ES/9000

IBM 3745

IBM ES/9000

IBM ES/9000

IBM AS/400

VAX 7000

Tandem

100 MBPS
Ethernet switch

Token ring

Token ring

Novell
server

Mail
server

Domino
server

Remote access
server

Router

Router

SMTP server

Proxy server

Firewall

Internet

Frame relay

ATM Network

Plant/office
Dedicated circuits

Plant/office

Plant/office

Plant/office

Plant/office
Dedicated circuits

leave a segment of our user base without service." Moreover, the multitude of software configurations frustrated Springs technicians, who had to support more than 40 different desktop configurations.

A Desktop Operating Committee—which drew representatives from legal, financial, human resources, sales and marketing, customer service, distribution, manufacturing operations, and all of the product divisions—recommended after considerable debate that the company standardize on Windows 95 and, because it already had a significant investment in Lotus applications, on Lotus Smart Suite '97 rather than Microsoft Office '97. Organizational change, business strategy, and cost of conversion were also key considerations in the recommendation by the committee. Following a planned desktop pilot program that had involved the installation of 200 PCs, Springs was preparing for a company-wide roll-out through 1998. Approval of the nearly eight digit price tag, which included hardware and software installation and training, was still pending. Wood anticipated approval. "If people in the company are using different software packages or different versions of software," he observed, "they can't share documents and collaborate. This frustration ultimately impacts productivity, cycle time and customer service—so desktop standardization should be a pretty easy sell."

Wood envisioned for Springs a united, networked enterprise that would enable organizational units to work together and with business partners. Networked computing would require the further adoption of enterprise-wide application and architecture standards. Wood's priority was to bring all of Springs' divisions into a corporate suite of applications within the enterprise server architecture, from which a Web-enabled architecture would emerge.

Creating a Corporate Suite of Tools

Implementation beats strategy nine times out of ten. If you cannot implement, strategy means nothing.

Jim Wood,
Vice President of Information Systems

Springs' first IT strategic plan adopted an enterprise-wide perspective and was treated as "a living document" that was to be reviewed and updated frequently. Because IT initiatives would have a direct impact on all divisions of the company, Wood developed a project management model that involved partnerships between users and technicians. All projects were to be approved not only by him, but also by the heads of the divisions that would adopt the new systems. In fact, the head of the division or organizational unit that would adopt the new IT system was responsible for presenting and selling proposed IT projects to the corporate management committee and, for projects budgeted at over $5 million, the Board. "IT was becoming a change agent," recalled Wood. "The largest problem we had was 'evolution versus revolution.' We could bring about changes faster than the human organization could adjust to them." An essential part of the challenge, change management, involved a phased approach to project implementation and the involvement of users from inception to completion.

"After we developed a long-range IS plan, the next step was to develop the ability to implement the plan," said Wood. "We had to establish a new IS management team, upgrade skills, and bring in new people." With a skilled IS team in place, Wood was able to lead the development of several major IS projects that were larger and more fundamental than any project attempted previously; some required over $10 million in expenditures and would be designed and implemented over two to four year periods (see Exhibits 9 and 10). Wood also began an intense effort to develop and to utilize project management standards (see Exhibit 11).

The implementation of a fundamental Materials Resources Planning (MRP) system called PACER was already well underway when Wood arrived. He analyzed it at great length and saw major design and project management flaws in the effort. "The design called for the MRP system to be run on-line, instantaneously, at any moment. Technically, that's impossible. They were doing the design and the programming simultaneously: the programmers sat in one room, the designers sat in the other room; both were to complete their project at a point in time. The people running the project were from manufacturing and had not been given the tools and training to do large-scale development," explained Wood. Because major investments had already been made in PACER, Wood's team continued the system roll-out into all of Springs' fabrication plants and eventually realized the system's benefits. By providing material and capacity visibility, the system improved manufacturing's planning and scheduling capabilities. Wood decided to "encapsulate" PACER and planned to upgrade the system with more advanced software over a two-year period.

The first phase of Springs' order management system (OMS) came on-line in 1995, marking the beginning of a new era of strategic alliances with retailers. OMS encompassed 16 separate applications ranging from order receipt, to pricing, to customer data base, to product shipment. The order management system—which was the largest single IT project ever accomplished in the history of the company, involving 120 associates directly during the peak design period—had over 10 million lines of code at the time of the first installation and, due to proper testing and quality control, ran error-free for six months before the first software bug was discovered and corrected. OMS expanded Springs' ability to efficiently process an order from receipt through shipping and invoicing, provide the information necessary to respond to customer order status inquiries, acknowledge orders, determine the available inventory and necessary production time, and commit to prompt delivery dates. The task of integrating OMS across Springs' divisions was complicated by the necessity of simultaneously replacing multiple systems that had been used by acquired companies.

"Five years ago all of our data was internally focused, as opposed to customer focused," said Torkildsen. "Now we are partnering with the retailers; we need to work with the same data and the same measurements because, ultimately, we serve the same consumers." For the first time in the company's history, Springs' technology supported the internal buyer/purchasing function of the retailer. With OMS to service customers and the manufacturing division's PACER directly interfaced, Springs was able to electronically tie order fulfillment directly with factory planning and scheduling. When initial roll-out of Kmart's Martha Stewart line of home furnishings took place, Dykstra and Torkildsen were able to use OMS and parallel processing capability to complete the order in record time and in Wood's words, "enable a highly successful Martha Stewart roll-out."

The speed of the delivery of information from Springs' enterprise servers had improved by 1995, with the development of relational databases such as the Information Engine. Former databases had stored information in long lists or hierarchies, while "relational" databases organized data into tables with corresponding rows and columns, so that it took less time for the

EXHIBIT 9 Information Systems Strategic Plans, Past and Future

I/S Strategic Plan—1993–1997

	1993	1994	1995	1996	1997
★ **Phase I: Assesment and Vision**	██████████				
➤Assess environment					
➤Assess immediate business needs					
➤Structure IS to support clients					
➤Develop infrastructure standard					
★ **Phase II: Execution**			████████		
➤Implement systems					
➤Implement infrastructure					
➤Develop future marketing outcomes					
★ **Phase III: Receive Investment's Benefits**					
➤Improve operational efficiency					
➤Enhance revenue generation					
➤Improve linkages to customers					

I/S Strategic Plan—1997–2002

➤**Implement, Enhance and Maintain Standard Applications**

—Financial/human resource   —Planning and scheduling

—Purchasing   —Cost management

—Order management   —Warehouse and distribution

➤**Differentiate Company in Marketplace**

—Electronic commerce   —Integrated marketing

—Product management   —Brand development

—Decision support   —New markets

—Demand planning   —New channels

➤**Prepare for Next Century**

—Year 2000 compliance   —Re-skill associates

—Upgrade infrastructure   —Implement new applications

—New acquistitions   —International

Source: Springs company documents, September 16, 1997

EXHIBIT 10 Information Systems Development Strategy, Past and Future

Enterprise Development Strategy 1993–1997

Standard Application	Division A	Division B	Division C	Division D	Division E
Human resources/payroll	✔	✔●	✔●	✔	✔
Financials	✔	○	✔	●	✔
OMS	✔	●	○	●	○
Electronic commerce	✔	●	○	●	○
POS	✔	●	○	●	○
Inventory replenish	●	●	○	●	○
Planning and scheduling	✔○	○	●	●	○
Warehouse management	●	○	○	●	○
Purchasing	○	○	○	●	○

Enterprise Development Strategy 1997 to 2002 (as of 2002 with 1997 information)

Standard Application	Division A	Division B	Division C	Division D	Division E
Human resources/payroll	✔	✔	✔	✔	✔
Financials	✔	✔	✔	✔	✔
OMS	✔	✔	✔	●	✔
Electronic commerce	✔	✔	✔	✔	✔
POS	✔	✔	✔	✔	✔
Inventory replenish	✔	✔	✔	✔	✔
Demand planning	○	○	○	○	○
Planning and scheduling	✔●	✔	✔	●	✔
Warehouse management	✔	✔	✔	●	✔
Purchasing	✔	✔	✔	●	✔

Key:

✔ Implemented

● Decision made without standard

● Decision made with standard

○ Decision to be made

Source: Springs company documents, September 16, 1997.

computer to find requested records. Springs' Information Engine, a data warehouse, provided consolidated sales and inventory data to support management decisions. Programmers were also making use of the intelligence of the PC to provide easy-to-use graphical user interfaces to company data. Though enterprise servers were still in control of processing the information for applications such as OMS and the Information

---

EXHIBIT 11   Project Management Checklist

1. Require a feasibility study to be conducted prior to a project starting to establish scope, resource requirements, a timeline, and a business case. Do not allow a project to start until this has been accomplished, reviewed, and approved.
2. Present a project for Capital Appropriations Committee approval with the entire scope of effort and resources estimated but request funding for the project in phases. Calculate the return using the total resource estimate and total benefits and not individual phases. Give value to soft items such as better information and meeting customer requests. Understand that increasing the revenue stream has a much greater impact on the business than reducing a cost line.
3. Organize a project to provide a series of measurable deliverables over the entire life of the effort. These deliverables should be measured about every 6–12 months.
4. Require detailed work plans for a project and measure the hours expended and earned during the life of the project as well as estimated hours for completion.
5. Provide extensive training for the entire project team (IS and business users) with special emphasis on project management and team coordination and work style.
6. Organize a project team with both information systems and business users assigned full-time for the life of the project and place them in the same physical location. Treat assignments to a project as a reward and a perk for a business user.
7. Each large-scale project must have a business champion and an information systems project manager assigned full-time as leaders. The business champion must have the authority to speak for the business and the ability to access top executives to obtain a decision when required.
8. Establish a formal change management program for the project and properly fund and support the effort within the business area receiving the new system. The impact new applications have on the daily activities of associates is large and this must be managed and activities re-engineered as appropriate if associates are to gain the benefits of the investment.
9. Conduct outside third party quality reviews on a regular basis with written reports going directly to executive management and the executive sponsor. Use the reports to improve the project and not to punish the associates who report the difficulties.
10. Understand benefits happen over time after implementation, not installation, and business users are accountable for delivery of benefits. Benefits occur when business users change and use the new tools and processes provided.
11. Maintain control of project efforts by company associates and hold them accountable for delivered results. Do not turn over the accountability for deliverables to a consulting firm.
12. Maintain scope control of project and do not allow change except with executive committee approval and a revised estimate of resource requirements and a new timeline.
13. Be willing to cancel a project when benchmarking, pilots, and prototyping (etc.) show major difficulties that probably cannot be overcome.
14. Establish programs that provide recognition to the team for their efforts and reward individuals. Provide continual positive feedback to the team.

Engine, the complexities of the system were hidden from the end user.

IT Director for Financial and Human Resources Carl Hicks led the implementation of a real-time on-line human resources system to replace three outdated and isolated databases. Its purpose was to make accurate, consolidated human resources information accessible from all Springs locations and divisions. Hicks also led the implementation of a consistent technical infrastructure across financial systems, resulting in improved efficiency in payroll and other administrative functions, error-free month-end closings, compilation of the year-end statements and better customer support. In the first wave of the system implementation, the IS team installed the payroll software for 16,000 associates with no disruption to business.

Just as Springs' new IS team was proving its project management skills, one major project, a product planning and scheduling system for the finishing plants, proved to be a difficult and costly implementation. IT Director of Manufacturing Roy Edwards led technology, manufacturing, and planning associates in a team effort to stabilize the system, and the company received the planned benefits, albeit on a delayed basis.

Due to persistent demand for IT professionals in the marketplace, Wood's main concern in 1992 continued to be his main concern in 1997: how to recruit and retain the human resources capability to implement the evolving strategic plan. There was an average 19–25 percent turnover rate in IS organizations, compared with Springs' 16 percent turnover rate in 1996, according to Springs' research. "The market is crazy," Wood emphasized. He estimated the average cost of turnover per person to be $100,000, not including productivity loss.

An attitude survey commissioned by Wood and conducted by Human Resources Manager Carl Vincent in 1997 found that for 25 percent of IT staff polled, the greatest dissatisfaction was lack of adequate training. "Associates must be trained effectively and quickly in new and innovative ways," Vincent reported. "Part-time work, telecommuting, and flex-time need to be investigated as work alternatives. Associates must be given multiple avenues to enhance and develop careers." Due to a focus on critical strategic initiatives, the average number of training days for IT associates had declined from 11 in 1995 to seven in 1996.

Financing the IT Future

Do you need a calculator to count the number of different information technology systems supporting your core business functions? Do you shudder at the cost of supporting and interfacing this tangled patchwork of legacy systems? Are you feeling pressured to replace your systems with a more modern platform? For many sewn products companies faced with the reality of an aging, inflexible and costly IT platform, major change is becoming a critical business imperative. . . . For some, the cost of remediation of a Year 2000 problem weighed against its benefit to the business is the driver. For others the driver is simply trying to get the IT systems simplified and unscrambled across the enterprise so that they can cost effectively respond to the requirements of doing business in the '90s and beyond.

Bobbin magazine[10]

"One would think that the sophisticated, consumer-driven apparel industry would be planning some really nifty strategic IT stuff," surmised the trade magazine *Bobbin* upon completing a survey of IT expendi-

---

[10]Paul Schottmiller, "So, Your IT System is Outdated?" *Bobbin,* July 1997, p. 22.

tures. "Guess again." The trade magazine reported that apparel companies—which generally led the way for trends in home furnishings—were still trying to get IT systems simplified and unscrambled across the enterprise. Apparel companies with sales of more than $100 million spent an average of 1.56 percent of sales on IT in 1996, according to the *Bobbin* survey.[11]

Springs' IT expenditures, in the vicinity of one and a half percent of 1996 sales, were consistent with other manufacturing companies. The fact that investments had increased every year since 1992 was an indication that Springs' management believed information technology had the potential to revitalize operations throughout the enterprise (see Exhibit 12).

The approach to spending was cautious, however. Wood and project leaders had to win financial approval for proposed projects from the Capital Appropriations Committee, which included Bowles and other senior executives. "If we get projects back that have not been approved, it's because the plans do not include the information that committee members want to see," emphasized Financial Controller Herb Roberts. "We have to determine how we're going to save money or make money if we do the project. We have to have a complete estimate of costs. There's a lot of justification work in our projects." One of Roberts' major responsibilities was to help IT directors benchmark their project financial goals on a regular basis. "They all want to go a hundred miles an hour," he explained.

One IT investment that could not be avoided was preparation for the numerical transition to the year 2000. Work had begun on this problem at Springs as early as 1993.

___

[11]Mike Barnes, "The Cost of Systems: What We're Spending," *Bobbin,* July 1997, p. 26.

All applications had to be updated to indicate a day, month, and year so that when the millennium arrived, systems would not automatically assume the year to be 1900. "A lot of computer systems calculate, process, or sort based on dates," explained IS Director of Planning and Technology Laura Fanning, who was coordinating the effort to update Springs' systems. "Discrepancies could impact business significantly. The problem is bigger than Springs," she added. "Even if we fix all of our data problems, if we have a customer or a supplier who has not, they could send us misinformation and corrupt our systems."

As of October 1997, 30 consultants were helping Springs prepare for the transition to a new millennium. That number was expected to peak at 55 in 1998. An end user study that involved site visits to every facility and an inventory of every piece of equipment indicated that 87 percent of Springs' equipment could be left untouched. If a date routine was in the process-logic controller but Springs was not using that function, it was not considered a problem. Technicians were in the process of figuring out mitigation strategies for the 13 percent of equipment that was not Year 2000 compliant by consulting with vendors, devising internal solutions, or putting new equipment purchases into the 1998 capital budget. The planned enterprise-wide upgrade of desktop computers to the Windows 95 operating system would help to ensure Year 2000 compliance at the user level. Fanning was also designing a training and remediation strategy that would make employees responsible for their own business data at the desktop, assisted by IS as needed.

One difficulty for Bowles in assessing IT spending was that the Year 2000 issue and routine infrastructure expenditures would not have a return. "Are we spending too much?" Bowles wondered:

EXHIBIT 12 Springs Industries, Inc., Information Systems Operating Expenses[a]

Description	Budget 1998	Budget 1997	ACT/EST 1997	Actual 1996	Actual 1995	1994	1993	1992	1991	1990
Total compensation	210.7	139.5	164.4	133.1	130.2	113.3	105	91.6	88.67	100
Hardware and property	283.5	247.7	252.5	242.7	218.2	184.3	125.9	102.6	105.4	100
Telecommunications	88	64.2	75.2	75.7	82.4	107.3	102.3	90.6	89.3	100
All other	383.6	234.4	259	247.5	149.2	188.5	59	52.5	81.9	100
Total	238.3	177.1	196.1	171.9	162.2	141.7	116.8	99.7	98.6	100
% for prior year actual	21.5%	3.0%	14.1%	4.9%	14.5%	21.3%	17.1%	1.1%	-1.4%	-4.7%
Capital approvals[b]	226.9	83.7	87.4	87.4	177.5	122.9	100	—	—	—

[a]1990 = 100.
[b]1993 = 100.

Are we spending too little? I don't know. We try to benchmark but that's hard to do because it's difficult to get a handle on what our own IT expenditures are, much less anybody else's. There's a level of discomfort, but it's basically from lack of familiarity with the types of investments, the technologies, and the rapid changes. We try to quantify the returns from incremental sales or cost savings, but it's very hard to do for some of these projects which basically improve productivity. I think the returns are longer term than we would like to think. We can get the information out there, but getting people to fully utilize new systems and run their businesses differently is a larger challenge.

Conclusion

With major applications implemented across the enterprise, Springs was now in a position to begin implementing electronic enablement technologies. Beyond the marketing and sales implications of the Internet, the Intranet and Extranet were perceived to have long-term implications for Springs. The Intranet would be key to improving productivity and service by facilitating the sharing, instantaneously across the internal parts of the company, of standards and procedures and significant amounts of data. The Extranet would enable selected customers and suppliers to access

Springs' database and perform value-added hookups to relevant data. "Our customers want to move beyond standard, typical EDI (electronic data interchange)," explained Torkildsen. "Extranets will provide visibility into our systems. Customers are going to ask for it, and we need to be in a proactive mode as opposed to a responding mode." Springs perceived skyrocketing demand for EDI to be an indication of a larger trend towards newer forms of electronic commerce (see Exhibit 13). In 1997, Springs' managers began to acknowledge that Internet technologies would also become a critical element in manufacturing and distribution activities.

In only five years Springs' Information Systems Department had become a key enabler of business strategy. In Wood's words: "We are the hammer that is driving the change to a certain extent." As Springs moved into the information age, Bowles knew that the standard approach to IT project development would no longer work. Simply achieving buy-in from users and involving them in systems development would not suffice. With the reality of electronic commerce fast approaching, Bowles realized that she and professionals across the enterprise would have to start thinking strategically about information technology

EXHIBIT 13   Business Changes—Springs' Growth in Electronic Commerce

Electronic Commerce	*1988*	*1993*	*1996*	*1997E*	*1998F[a]*
Document	3	13	23	31	33
Trading partnerships	26	266	369	460	550
Partner documents	30	425	875	1,100	1,550
Document volume (millions)	.06	5.6	9.8	19.2	28.8
COLT—Order Fulfillment Life Cycle					
Time (days) (bedding)	35	21	10	5	

[a]Includes projections for incorporation of Baby, Bath and Custom Designs.

Source: CSC Data Center, September 16, 1997.

on a daily basis. One of Bowles' first decisions as COO was to establish and chair a new corporate IS committee: each month she and the group presidents, the CFO and Wood, met to review strategy and performance. In 1998 they would address the following questions:

1. Has Springs focused its IT efforts appropriately between 1992–1997?

2. As Crandall Bowles becomes CEO, how should she direct Springs' IT strategy in terms of:

   - Types of applications
   - Expenditure levels
   - Sourcing decisions
   - Other

Case 5–3

PROVIDIAN TRUST: TRADITION AND TECHNOLOGY (A)[1]

A New CEO

Within two weeks of accepting the position of CEO of Providian Trust Company, Stephen Walsh, a lawyer by training, faced an unusual corporate conflict and he would have to play the role of judge. There was an extraordinary difference of opinion between Providian Trust's internal auditor, Peter Storey, and the leaders of a major information technology (IT) project in the trust division. "Peter's extremely vocal point ran to the issue of documentation, that it was incomplete and should be brought up to speed," explained Walsh. The conflict reached a climax during an Audit Committee meeting on May 13, 1995, when members of the committee, who were all on the Providian Trust Board of Directors,

Research associate Melissa Dailey prepared this case under the supervision of Professor F. Warren McFarlan.

[1]Copyright © 1997 by the President and Fellows of Harvard College.

Harvard Business School case 398-008.

expressed to Walsh that they had lost confidence in the internal auditor and recommended that the external auditor, Steinman & Smith, do an analysis of the project documentation prior to implementation.

The purpose of the project was to convert the trust division's outdated information system into a more efficient system using Access Plus, new trust and custody management software made by Select One. The project had been initiated in 1993 under a former CEO who had been dismissed by the board, and had continued under an interim CEO. By the time Walsh arrived on the scene, over two-thirds of the $18 million budget had been invested in the implementation of the IT project and Providian Trust had built up expectations among clients that the new system would dramatically improve service. Though the company had experienced transitions in leadership at the CEO level, the Access Plus project had stable leadership under the direction of senior vice president of Trust, Investment and Treasury Michael LeBlanc. It was LeBlanc who had argued before the board in April, 1994 that the information technology project was critical to the business future of the trust division, winning its unanimous approval to move forward with the plan. Storey, who had criticized the project from day one, was regarded by some Providian Trust executives as having a tendency to "cry wolf." Walsh, working on a five year strategic plan for Providian Trust, emphasized that he did not have time to become intertwined in a political knot:

> I'm the new CEO. I have no credibility yet with this board other than my C.V. It's the Audit Committee that's expressing reservations about this project. So, in addition to satisfying myself about whether or not this is a go, who better than the external auditors to satisfy the Audit Committee in terms of the appropriateness of continuing the project? My solution was to have Steinman & Smith send in one of their people, and I asked that person to join the Implementation Committee, to be involved in the project and tell me what the story was here.

Transforming Tradition

> *The trust profession is an old and noble one. Its origins go back centuries and are based upon some of the highest values known— trust, integrity, and honesty. It was built upon a foundation of taking care of the grantor's needs and providing the services that he or she wanted. To put it in modern day language, it was about customer service, customer service that meant doing the*

right thing, at the right time, in the right way for the customer.

Trust & Estates[2]

Providian Trust, headquartered in New York, delivered financial and fiduciary services through a network of 216 branches. The company's lending products—including residential and commercial mortgages and consumer and corporate loans—were the principal source of its revenue (see Exhibit 1). Intense competitive pressures and client demands were driving the need for improvements in the quality of trust services. In 1994 Providian Trust managed $49.4 billion in trust assets with a staff of 840 full-time employees (FTE). Sixty percent of the company's fee income and nine percent of gross earnings were generated by its fiduciary business that year. All three areas of the trust division—Pension and Institutional Trust Services (PITS), Personal Trust Services, and Trust Operations—reported to LeBlanc (see Exhibit 2).

The Pension and Institutional Trust Services business had $42.7 billion in assets in 1994. "We were the tenth largest provider, and we were losing money. We had outdated reporting systems as far as our clients were concerned," explained LeBlanc. The institutional custody business was becoming

---

[2]Sam F. Lewis, Jr. "Trust Professionals Must Keep Their Eyes 'On the Target'" *Trust & Estates*, April 1997, p. 20.

Trust Divisions' Assets Managed and FTE in 1994

	Total	Pension and Institutional Trust (PITS)	Personal Trust	Trust Operations
Assets managed	$49.4B	$42.7B	$6.7B	
No. full-time employees (FTE)	840	300	240	300

EXHIBIT 1 Four Year Financial Review

	1995	1994	1993	1992
Year-End Position (in thousands)				
Assets				
Cash and short-term investments	$ 2,141,428	$ 2,262,157	$ 2,123,444	$ 806,510
Securities	762,637	881,843	805,798	911,778
Mortgages	12,982,370	12,563,718	12,766,391	13,546,999
Other loans	3,016,258	3,090,782	3,064,751	3,200,840
Other assets	287,178	266,977	229,742	213,727
Total	$19,189,871	$19,065,478	$18,990,126	$18,679,854
Liabilities				
Demand deposits	$ 4,339,858	$ 3,742,219	$ 4,248,367	$ 4,558,691
Term deposits and other borrowings	13,447,114	13,950,570	13,532,132	14,184,486
Other liabilities	180,940	215,544	98,454	52,292
	17,967,911	17,908,333	17,878,954	18,795,469
Capital Funds				
Subordinated notes	225,947	225,947	225,947	225,947
Shareholders' equity	951,013	931,198	885,226	858,439
	1,176,960	1,157,144	1,111,172	1,084,386
Total	$19,144,871	$18,105,478	$19,879,855	$43,525,811
Assets under administration	$50,036,288	$50,279,732	$45,629,868	$43,461,011
Results for the Year (in thousands)				
Investment income	$ 1,545,920	$ 1,482,524	$ 1,522,976	$ 1,897,861
Interest expense	1,144,602	1,076,926	1,258,602	1,521,344
Net investment income	401,318	405,599	384,374	376,517
Provision for loan losses	77,174	42,881	95,848	115,500
Net investment income after provision for loan losses	324,144	362,718	288,527	261,017
Fees and other income	148,241	156,296	145,187	123,668
Total income	472,385	519,230	433,714	884,685

(continued)

EXHIBIT 1 (continued) Four Year Financial Review

	1995	1994	1993	1992
Expenses				
Salaries and benefits	196,013	192,833	172,699	173,130
Premises	67,757	58,022	56,174	53,549
Other operating expenses	162,469	165,119	123,155	112,636
Total operating expenses	426,239	415,974	352,028	339,314
Income before income taxes	46,146	103,256	81,685	45,371
Income tax provision	7,210	33,976	24,569	– 1,774
Net income	$ 38,936	$ 69,281	$ 57,116	$ 47,144
Financial Statistics				
Return on average shareholders' equity	0.04%	0.08%	0.07%	0.06%
Net investment margin	2.26	2.27	2.12	2.06
Net investment spread	2.00	2.02	1.89	1.80
Productivity ratio	77.56	74.00	66.48	67.83
Other Statistics				
Common shares outstanding (in thousands)	43,803.60	42,786.00	42,087.60	41,715.60
Number of branches	216	229	228	232
Number of full-time equivalent employees	4,496.40	4,936.80	4,740.00	4,950.00
Statistics per Common Share				
Net income	$ 1.08	$ 1.97	$ 1.63	$ 1.37
Dividends	1.06	1.06	1.06	1.06
Shareholders' equity	26.05	26.11	25.24	24.70

Source: Providian Trust Annual Report.

651

EXHIBIT 2 Providian Trust Management Committee, July 1994

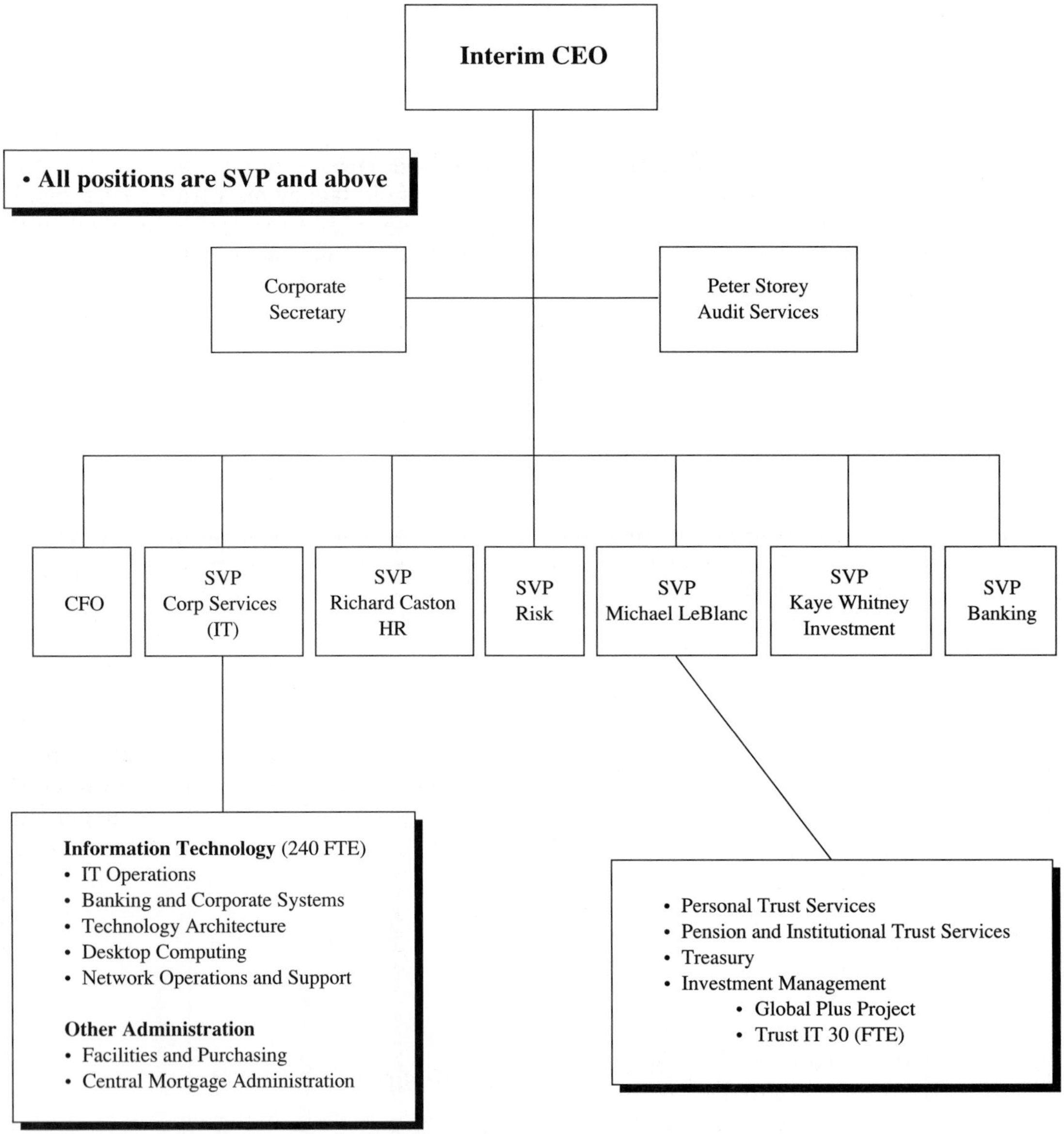

extremely technology-intensive, with some of the larger players outsourcing their entire backroom function in order to make large operations more effective.

Personal Trust Services managed $6.7 billion in assets for 10,000 clients and was only marginally profitable, observed LeBlanc: "It wasn't the stuff that 15 percent return on equity (ROE) was made of." Personal Trust Services included the administration of estates, trusts and agencies, will and estate planning, self-directed registered savings plans, and dealer trustee services. Investment management services were provided through Kaye Whitney Investment Management Limited, the company's investment counsel and portfolio manager.

Management regarded the trust division as the most isolated and change-resistant area of the company. The majority of trust officers had 20–30 years of experience with Providian Trust and had always managed their clients' affairs on a personal level, calling them regularly and generating and correcting financial statements with the help of administrative support staff. Trust officers often compensated for late or inaccurate statements by discounting or waiving fees, costing the company an estimated $2–5 million per year, according to LeBlanc.

> Every statement that was prepared for our 10,000 Personal Trust clients had to be reviewed by a trust officer, corrected by the trust officer, and then mailed out to the client. They had total control over what went out. The clients were relatively happy, although there were some grumblings about having to wait two or three months for a statement. Our research on competitors showed that we were hopelessly behind in terms of number crunching.

The trust officers working in PITS and Personal Trust were considered "front office" people because they were client driven and managed clients' accounts. The 250 personnel in the Trust Operations Department, or the "back office," were responsible for handling, settlement, and record-keeping for securities. "The administrative functions were being done both by the front and back offices," explained LeBlanc. "We had an environment where everybody could point a finger at everybody else if something went

wrong. The trust officers blamed the operations people, and the operations people blamed the trust officers. It had been running this way forever."

LeBlanc believed that intense client demand, especially on the part of Pension and Institutional Trust clients, dictated that Providian Trust quickly upgrade the trust division's old legacy mainframe systems. He also believed that the lack of control in the trust division had persisted for too long and that it was time for the company to remove control of clients' accounts from the trust officers' hands. An improved computerized trust system would enable management to centralize and control the numbers, thereby forcing the discipline that had been lacking in the division for decades. In the proposed new environment, the operations people, who were generally experienced with computers, would assume the trust officers' administrative duties, including the generation of client statements. Not only would trust officers lose control of their clients' financial information in the new environment, they would also have to learn how to use the new software system in order to access the computerized data. Few of the trust officers had ever touched a personal computer (PC). "Your average trust officer was covered in 17th century cobwebs," said one executive. "They're completely averse to technology, uncooperative, and they leave at five to five."

The Business Impact Report

> *I'm sort of a bull-headed person, and the only way I could see this not getting lost in a quagmire of internal politics and bickering was to run and run and run it as hard as I possibly could.*
>
> Michael LeBlanc, Senior Vice President of Trust, Investment and Treasury

In April 1994, LeBlanc argued before the Providian Trust board that the capabilities of trust and custody management software provided the technological precondition for the redesign of business processes. He estimated that the installation of hardware and software, the conversion of all trust financial data, and the transformation of the operating environment could be achieved by December 1995 through a phased implementation process. Total project costs were estimated at $18 million. Once fully implemented, annual savings of approximately $9.2 million were expected to result from reengineering the business processes and capitalizing on the new system's functionality, while reducing FTE from 840 to 660 (see Exhibit 3). The board unanimously approved the implementation of the new operating environment for trust defined in the Business Impact Report.

A year-long review of 12 software vendors had resulted in the recommendation that Select One's Access Plus asset management system be acquired. Customizing a proven, off-the-shelf system was viewed by LeBlanc as the quickest way to get the most advanced technology for the bank's trust operations. Ten financial institutions, including one competitor, were using the Access Plus software at the time.

LeBlanc chaired the project Steering Committee, which originally included vice presidents from Corporate Services, Finance, Trust Operations, and Audit Services. Internal auditor Peter Storey said that he repeated "like a broken record" at both Steering Committee and Audit Committee meetings that the proper management controls were not in place to ensure the project's success. The fact that the senior vice president of Corporate Services, who headed up Providian Trust's force of 240 IT personnel, was not asked to help lead the Access Plus project had served to intensify tension on the Steering Committee. (The company had two IT departments: a group of 240 IT personnel who supported retail banking and an additional 30 IT personnel in the Operations Department.) Being riddled with political tension, the Steering Committee had little effect on the Access Plus rollout.

With the Steering Committee disintegrating, it fell to the Implementation Committee, which was also chaired by LeBlanc, to provide a guiding and protective hand for almost all of the project team's activities. The Implementation Committee included vice presidents from each of the departments upon which the Access Plus system implementation was expected to have an impact (see Exhibit 4).

LeBlanc decided that forceful and decisive management was required to make changes in a change-resistant environment. Certain that the historically antagonistic front and back office divisions would not cooperate in the reengineering of business processes, he selected the back office to drive the project. LeBlanc designated Todd Benari, the vice president of Trust Operations, to lead the Access Plus implementation. The project managers and project management team reported directly to Benari. The team included 15 representatives, ten from Trust Operations, two from Personal Trust Services, and one each from: Pension and Institutional Trust Services, Kaye Whitney Investment Management, and Audit Services. The Business Impact Report emphasized that collectively the core project team had over 70 years of trust experience. "I wanted people in this group who had been in the trenches, in the lines dealing with clients, and who could look at the project from a relationship manager's perspective," explained LeBlanc. He guaranteed that team members' positions would be made available to them again at the end of the project and that they would lose no seniority.

EXHIBIT 3   Investment Summary for Proposed Trust Operating Environment

Hardware

Central system server, including system software	$ 2,034
Communications network and local servers	530
Workstations—personal computers, related software, and printers	3,100
Total hardware	5,664
Anticipated recoveries from sale of existing equipment	− 180
Net hardware	**$ 5,484**

Application software and implementation

Access Plus application software	$5,292
Information management application software	684
Select One implementation charges, including expenses	2,377
Business impact review	563
Customization	1,739
Total application software and implementation	**$10,655**
Providian Trust effort	**$ 1,800**
Training of staff	**$600**
Net investment	**$18,539**

Annual returns

Cost deductions

Data center operations	$ 455
Application software maintenance	2,068
Paper reduction	108
Staff savings	7,200
Total cost reductions	**$ 9,831**

Revenue increases

New business	$1,200
Avoidance of loss business	600
Total revenue increases	**$ 1,800**
Total annual returns	**$11,630**

Annual operating costs

Hardware maintenance	92
Select One remote computing option fees	584
Disaster recovery	168
Select One application software maintenance	1,049
Select One dedicated application support	534
Total annual operating costs	**$ 2,427**
Net annual returns	**$ 9,201**

Source: Business Impact Report, Providian Trust. Amounts are reported in thousands.

EXHIBIT 4   Committee Structure

Audit Committee

Executive and Risk Management Committee

Steering Committee

Chair: Michael LeBlanc

Senior Vice President, Corporate Services
Senior Vice President, Chief Auditor
Senior Vice President, Chief Financial Officer
Vice President, Trust Operations

Implementation Committee

Chair: Michael LeBlanc

V.P./S.V.P. Personal Trust	(3)
V.P. Pension and Institutional Trust Services	(2)
V.P. Trust Operations	(1)
V.P. Kaye Whitney Investments	(1)

Project Team

Chair: Todd Benari

Representatives:

Trust Operations	(10)
Personal Trust Services	(2)
Pension and Institutional Trust Services	(1)
Kaye Whitney Investment Management Investments	(1)
Internal Audit Service	(1)

Although LeBlanc was known for his keen knowledge of the trust market, he had no project management experience and would depend to a large extent on Benari's team to orchestrate the reengineering effort. The Operation Department's 30 IT professionals would assist in the complete overhaul of the trust division's technology environment, including the installation of desktop computers in the head and branch offices and new servers to support the intense networking activity planned for the proposed new trust operating environment. Previously, Operations had never attempted an information technology initiative that exceeded a half million dollar budget.

Reengineering a New Operating Environment

I reviewed your update on the trust project. The major issue will be the culture shift inherent in moving to a dramatically different way of managing the business. While extensive training will help, it is my experience that organizational cultures function from very deep-seated norms, values, and attitudes, which are not easily changed despite reengineering efforts. Good luck!

Richard Caston
Senior Vice President of Human Resources

in a memo to Todd Benari copied to Michael LeBlanc, February 17,1995

The Business Impact Report stated that "business processes would be revised based on effectively using technology as an enabling mechanism." The project team sought input from 30 key employees in order to match 17 business processes with Access Plus software functions. The team's proposed business model for the trust division included detailed diagrams of how the software would streamline information flow for each of the 17 processes (see Exhibit 5). The expectation was that cycle time for information processing would be reduced, resulting in faster and improved service for the customer.

Administration would be consolidated and centralized in the proposed operating environment. All existing trust information would be converted to the Access Plus system, and the Operations group would become the primary caretakers of the data, taking over sole responsibility for trust account administration. As the paper was removed from their desks and filing cabinets, the trust officers' traditional role would be transformed—they would become "client relationship managers," providing a full range of fiduciary services and retail banking products to their existing and future client base. LeBlanc explained that while Trust Operations would become centralized, the client relationship managers, sales teams, and portfolio managers would be decentralized to enable them to proactively sell to their clients.

We knew that there was no point buying a new trust system or improving the technology unless we concurrently also completely rebuilt the culture and provided the training incentives to customer relationship people to completely revisit how they approach their clients. They needed to be trained in relationship management skills and become more focused on the bottom line, cross-selling products to clients, a whole range of skills upgrading to become more sales and service oriented rather than simply bureaucrats responding to client phone calls.

Concerns Communicated

In early 1995, as the project implementation picked up speed, Personal Trust managers started raising concerns. According to Personal Trust vice president David Brown, the project team had decided that it would "drive the project through" with very little

EXHIBIT 5   Design of the New Trust Operating Environment, Based on 17 Access Plus Software Functions

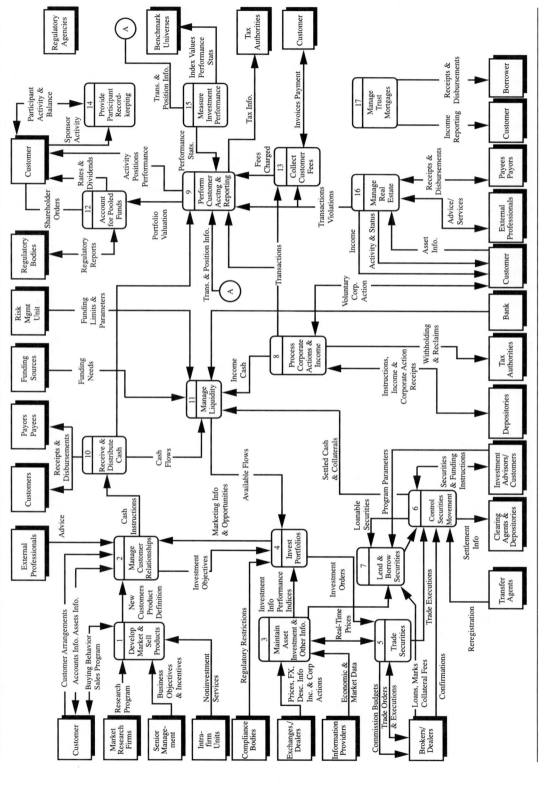

Source: Providian Trust Business Impact Report.

EXHIBIT 5 (continued) Process 2: Managing Customer Relationships

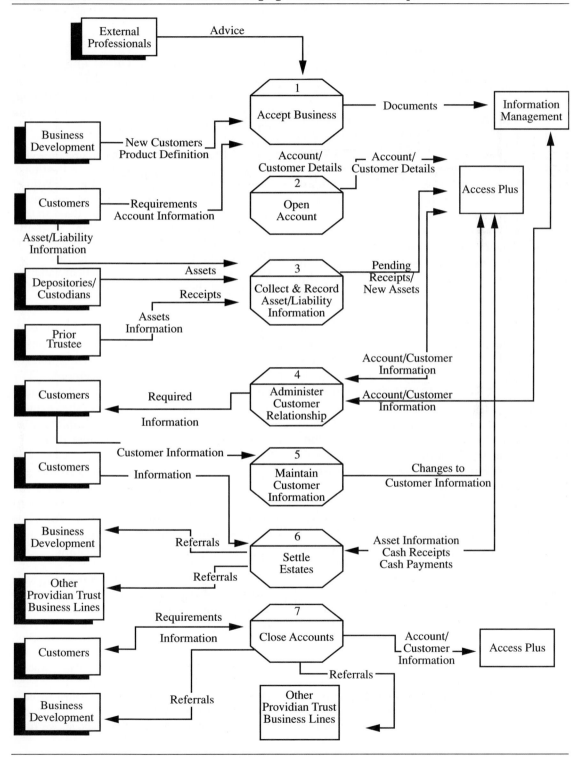

time spent getting user feedback. "There was a problem between the back room and the front room," Brown said. "From the front line perspective, the back room was not listening. The feeling was that the back room knew what the front wanted or needed."

Although the plan seemed to make sense on paper, Benari was beginning to sense a general resistance to change. "We had trust officers with 30 years of experience who had never looked at anything more automated than an adding machine. The process of trying to get people to behave and operate in a different way was almost impossible." Tensions were heightened when Benari's original project manager left Providian Trust for a new position midway through the project, in February, 1995. As confidence in the project faltered, Benari released an updated project plan and announced that the reengineering requirements would be recommended by Trust Operations, but they would have to be approved by the business unit leaders and the Implementation Committee. Brown, James Knowles, and Robert Case—all vice presidents in the Personal Trust Department and all members of the Implementation Committee—sent a largely negative written response to the updated project plan:

> The need for dramatic change is fully recognized both from the point of view of efficiencies and competitive pressures. We support the general concepts contained in the document. It is clear that a great deal of work is still required and that an implementation plan is urgently needed if there is to be a realistic expectation that the current schedule for conversion will be met. The biggest obstacle that needs to be addressed is the resourcing of the various workgroups and, in turn, the ability of the workgroups to deliver within the required time frames. In a general sense, we found that the document seems to view things from a headquarters perspective and it does not always recognize the nature of the existing relationships with our clients.

The vice president of Client and Product Management for Pension and Institutional Trust, David English, also responded negatively to the proposed new operating environment:

> We need much more analysis before we would feel comfortable that the total centralization of backroom functions is appropriate. . . . While I agree with the concept that client accounting and distribution of reports lends itself to centralization, it is imperative that the trust officer or "relationship manager" be in control of the account. Only the trust officer will know the special requirements that a client will have in terms of their preference for receipt of information from us.

In follow-up meetings, project team leaders addressed the concerns of the vice presidents, resulting in each of their signatures on the following written statement: "The meeting produced a consensus that there exist no obstacles to prevent the project team from proceeding with the implementation towards the new trust operating environment." Brown, Knowles, Case, and English all reported directly to LeBlanc.

A few months later, English outlined the impending changes to the trust environment during a staff meeting in Boston. The New England regional office responded with a memo dispatched directly to LeBlanc:

> Some difficulties have crept into the process of implementation: directions and instructions are coming from too many sources. . . . Reactions we are witnessing from employees, although understandable, have created a morale problem and insecurity that may extend itself into other areas. The process leaves us with the impression that the process is not client oriented. There appears to be a lack of consideration of relationships with our client base. As a result of the above, we have

decided to create a regional committee to assist in a more harmonious implementation of Access Plus.

On July 11, the Implementation Committee decided that the concerns of the Boston managers would be addressed through telephone conversations and that it "would not formally respond to the letter."

Software Training

The system license stated that Select One would provide training materials and deliver "one-time training on all systems functions" (see Exhibit 6). Project team members and 60 Operations employees attended Select One's training sessions in March and April 1995, approximately eight months before the first scheduled conversion of accounts. The project plan outlined a "train the trainer" approach—Select One managers would teach the project team how to use Access Plus, and team members would then visit all decentralized departments to deliver instructions.

Trust officers would have to be conversant with computers, Windows and Access Plus's document management functionality in the new operating environment. The steep learning curve was acknowledged as early as November 1994, when the Implementation Committee discussed a document entitled "New Trust Operating Environment: Training and Strategies and Plans." The section "Influencing Factors and Assumptions" included the following two points:

The new trust operating environment will require that virtually all levels of personnel possess the required skills in the use of the new Windows-based workstation technology and production applications.

Providian Trust's network of regional training managers and their training centers across the country, as well as the corporate training departments, are staffed exclusively by retail-banking-experienced training personnel. These centers are, however, equipped with CD-ROM training labs for self-study on personal computer skills and application software.

Project team leaders hired an outside firm to provide training on the Microsoft tool set to trust officers and other front office work groups. In addition, trust officers had access to CD-ROM labs where they could study Microsoft Office, which included Word, Mail, Excel, and PowerPoint. IT support staff, however, were still installing personal computers on the trust officers' desktops in the summer of 1995, making it impossible for trust officers to put their training to use on a daily basis. When trained project team members began visiting the decentralized workgroups in the summer of 1995, they found that many trust officers did not have desktop computers, did not know Windows, and were not prepared to learn the functions of Access Plus. An important aspect of the training—in the document management application that would revise the manner in which trust staff stored, retrieved, viewed, and used documentation ranging from original trust agreements to correspondence to daily vouchers—was never accomplished.

The Human Resources and Conversion Schedule

The board of directors had approved a plan that promised to reduce full time employees by 180. In the summer of 1995 the project team announced that one-quarter of the trust administration staff would lose their jobs as a result of the technology conversion. A wave of stress moved through corporate headquarters.

Job postings for available positions in the new operating environment were made on July 19, with a response date of August 15. Interviewing teams asked applicants three to five standard questions based on

EXHIBIT 6   Access Plus Training Courses

Introduction to Access Plus—1 day

- System overview
- System access
- Activity/Function/Qualifier (AFQs)
- Keyboard usage
- Help features
- Field lookup capabilities
- Screen prints
- Inquiry displays
- Report access

Security Maintenance—2 days

- Minor Security Type
- Security processing classes
- MIS-related code files
- MIS setup and maintenance
- Security setup activities
- Security maintenance activities
- Model securities setup and use
- Use of income processing fields for reconciliation

Advance Security Processing—3 days

- Executed trades
- Exercised and honored options
- Traded FX forward and spot contracts
- Admission of outside source mutual funds
- Repurchase agreements
- Executed short sales

Basic Cash Processing—2 days

- Posting schedule and ad hoc receipts and disbursements
- Check production and other documents for cash items

Basic Income and Corporate Actions—3 days

- Creating, maintaining corporate action events
- Verifying fund availability
- Determining income payment methods
- Processing
- Cash and extraordinary dividends
- Capital gains distributions
- Stock dividends
- Stock splits
- Liquidation
- Fixed and variable rate interest payments
- Maturities
- Rollovers

Income and Corporate Actions Reconciliations—1 day

- Reconciling cash, units from the various corporate actions

Advanced Income and Corporate Actions—3 days

- Called security redemptions
- Security exchanges, mergers
- Securities tendered for purchase
- Rights, warrants
- Stock dividends in a different security
- Spin-offs, split-offs, split-ups
- Loan pool distributions
- Creating FX orders for individual portfolios and linking to income
- Entering standing instructions to create FX orders automatically

Fee Processing—3 days

- Setting up calculation formulas, schedules, events
- Setting up maximum base fees for an account
- Setting up restrictions on portfolio balance
- Maintaining fee share information
- Monitoring scheduled fee processing
- Performing accruals
- Forecasting fees, setting up management reporting
- Processing ad hoc fees and computing/processing memo fees
- Preparing, invoices, collecting receivables, banking fees
- Processing reimbursable expenses
- Relating code files

Events Processing—1 day

- Choosing specific events, establishing processing groups
- Reviewing event characteristics, records; scheduling events
- Batching
- Setting up the server
- Monitoring results

Statement Processing—1 day

- Cataloging new reports, maintaining report packages
- Decision-making for report packages; parameter options
- Setting up events

(continued)

EXHIBIT 6 (continued)   Access Plus Training Courses

Basic Cash Processing—2 days (*cont.*)
- Setting up, managing funds availability (overdrafts, large cash balances)
- Resolving unprocessed items (unpostables)
- Batching, automatic, manual

Advanced Cash Processing—1½ days
- Controlling bank and suspense accounts
- Reconciliations
- Interfaces with SWIFT and EFTS
- Reversals, backdating, reapplication

Security Settlement and Depository Interfaces—4 days
- Contractual and actual settlement processing
- Partial and manual trade settlement
- Reconciling cash and units

Sweep Processing—2 days
- Establishing sweep investment vehicles
- Maintaining sweep securities
- Implementing sweep investment strategies
- Setting up and maintaining participating portfolios
- Realigning portfolios and strategies
- Monitoring sweep processing
- Reconciling cash
- Related code files

Trade Order Entry—2 days
- Taking entering, approving, blocking, relinquishing, executing, linking/buy/ sell orders for:
- Security trades
- Outside mutual funds, GICs
- FX and FX forward and spot contracts

Pricing Interfaces—1 day
- Maintaining manual and automated pricing
- Maintaining price, security, corporate actions, and FX forward pricing events
- Setting up price-related code files
- Setting up security for automatic pricing; corresponding currency and pricing supplier
- Setting up formula pricing and yield curve groups
- Using and interpreting notices
- Troubleshooting techniques; identifying and correcting pricing problems

Real Estate Management—½ day
- Setting up real property assets
- Creating, maintaining tenants, and income-producing units
- Collecting rents
- Selling, distributing, transferring real estate

Tax Processing—4 days
- Setting up tax-related code files
- Setting up security tax information
- Setting up, maintaining account tax information
- Changing base currency cost basis
- Listing assets with unknown tax cost
- Anticipating tax events
- Preparing accounts for final returns
- Performing taxlot accounting
- Previewing tax worksheet preparation, providing worksheets
- Retrieving data generated for tax reporting purposes
- Recording details of filings

Statement Processing—1 day (*cont.*)
- Anticipating, preventing statement out-of-balance conditions; correction transactions on advice from other workgroups
- Producing statements; solving common problems/trouble shooting: transaction reversals, backdates
- Rendering statements

Sponsored Securities Processing— 2 days
- Setting up sponsored funds: mutual, common trust, pooled, STIF; unitized and dollar-allocated master trusts
- Maintaining variable interest rate records
- Calculating earnings
- Processing distribution composition events
- Admitting, redeeming, pricing orders
- Processing systematic purchases, sales
- Valuing funds

Account, Portfolio Code File Maintenance—2 days
- Setting up and maintaining Minor Account Type-related code files
- Setting up and maintaining Minor Portfolio Type-related code files
- Identifying associated account and portfolio relationships

(continued)

663

EXHIBIT 6 (concluded) Access Plus Training Courses

Trade Order Entry—2 days (cont.)
- Repurchase agreements
- Short sales
- Exercising, buying, writing, selling, buying back orders for:
- Options
- Futures

Automated Portfolio Management—2 days
- Setting up APM investment vehicles
- Maintaining APM securities and code files
- Implementing strategies
- Setting up and maintaining participating portfolios
- Realigning portfolios and strategies
- Pricing admission and redemption orders
- Processing and monitoring events
- Reconciling cash, shares

Account, Portfolio, Client Setup/ Maintenance—1 day
- Opening accounts, clients, and associated portfolios
- Setting up events required by their related account, portfolio types/classes
- Maintaining information
- Closing accounts and associated portfolios

Basic Security Processing—1 day
- Processing free receipts, deliveries, including tangible assets—setting up and processing miscellaneous assets, notes, mortgage assets, and liabilities
- Setting up and processing receivables and payables
- Transferring, distributing portfolio positions

Pension Payments—1½ days
- Establishing withholding categories
- Creating pension events
- Processing lump sum or periodic payments
- Processing wage payments
- Processing bulk or individual changes to payments
- Maintaining individual changes to payments
- Maintaining individual recipients
- Generating checks, payments, payables, invoices
- Generating registers
- Establishing audit trails
- Carrying out reconciliation activities

Securities Lending—1½ days
- Setting up related code files
- Establishing and setting up borrower profiles
- Determining the availability of a lendable position
- Opening, closing security loans
- Maintaining inventories by registration and location
- Establishing, deleting collateral positions
- Bulking collateral
- Maintaining borrower records
- Valuing Market-to-Market
- Determining, calculating, charging fees

Help Desk Training
- Participation in all workgroup training courses
- Participation in Events Processing course
- Training on all standards and procedures used to troubleshoot problems, and to interface with Select, including service level standards, and system security

Basic Programming—5 days
- Programming Access Plus reports
- Use format commands
- Using program structure
- Using consolidation commands
- Using computation commands
- Reading Record Definition Language files

predefined skill set requirements for each position. "We went through a two and a half week exercise of 20 minute interviews with all the staff applying for the new positions, just whipping through," explained an interviewer. "They felt that their entire careers came down to a 20 minute interview after they had put in 20 years with the company. It was a very painful experience for them and it certainly affected their pride."

On September 5, 1995, the Implementation Committee reviewed an "Access Plus Project Human Resource Timeline," which showed exactly how many staff would be dismissed as the scheduled conversions of data proceeded (see Exhibit 7).

Scheduled Conversions of Data to the
Access Plus System

Phase I	Personal Trust (headquarters)	November 1, 1995
Phase II	Personal Trust Branches	December 1, 1995
Phase III	Pension and Institutional Trust	January 1, 1996
Phase IV	Kaye Whitney Investment Management	February 1, 1996

The Decision: To Convert or Not to Convert

Walsh realized the serious nature of the conflict regarding the Access Plus implementation when he assumed the position of Providian Trust's CEO. Soon after his arrival, he and chief operating officer Christopher Franks invited the Select One president to their offices and told him that they would like to have an open door policy and that he should feel free to communicate directly with them if he sensed any problems

with the Access Plus implementation. The Select One president indicated that the project was on the right track.

Providian Trust's Audit Services Department did not agree. Over the course of the project implementation, Storey's auditing staff had delivered to LeBlanc and Benari a series of reports warning that the Access Plus system implementation was a high risk project due to the strategic importance of the business line, the significant dollars of assets under administration, and the magnitude of proposed change to the existing operating environment. On July 27, 1995, LeBlanc responded to 13 specific risks detailed in a "Trust Operating Environment Interim Audit Report" (see Exhibit 8). Given the Audit Committee's doubts about Storey, Walsh was more interested in Steinman & Smith's opinions about the Access Plus project. It was unclear whether any of the audit reports ever appeared on Walsh's desk. Walsh dismissed Storey on August 1.

The CEO continued to study the progress reports on the Access Plus project. According to the senior project leaders, everything was under control. The project team had successfully converted $2.5 billion of internal corporate assets and proprietary mutual funds by July 1995. Robert Strong, who was approved as a senior vice president of Corporate Services in February 1995 and subsequently joined the Implementation Committee, somewhat dampened the congratulatory atmosphere, pointing out that because it did not involve any client accounts and the document management system remained untested, the conversion only measured the base functionality of the system. Also, the project team still did not have experience putting live data feeds into the Access Plus system.

The project team answered these concerns by pointing to an upcoming Simulated Work Environment (SWE), which they claimed

EXHIBIT 7   Access Plus Project Human Resource Timeline, 1995–1996

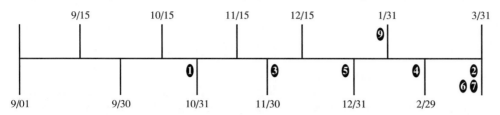

Timeline Notes

1. Personal Trust–New York will convert to Access Plus on the weekend of October 28, 1995.

2. Those Personal Trust–New York staff not selected to a position within the new operating environment will be advised that they will be utilized in term assignments to end 90 days after the last conversion or to March 31, 1996.

3. Personal Trust Branches will convert to Access Plus on the weekend of December 1,1995.

4. Those Personal Trust branch staff not selected to a position within the new operating environment will be advised that they will be utilized in term assignments to end 90 days after the successful conversion of their branch or to February 29, 1996.

5. Pension Branches, including New York, will convert to Access Plus on the weekend of December 30, 1995.

6. Those Pension staff not selected to a position within the new operating environment will be advised that they will be utilized in term assignments to end 90 days after the successful conversion of their branch or to March 31, 1996.

7. Those Trust Operations staff not selected to a position within the new operating environment will be advised that they will be utilized in term assignments to end 90 days after the last conversion to Access Plus or to March 31, 1996.

8. It will be necessary to terminate some employees prior to above dates. This is required as some displaced employees will have a large negative influence on the remaining staff. The target date for this should be by October 15, 1995.

9. Displaced Boston personnel must be let go over time; this spacing should occur 45 days after Personal Trust is converted, or commencing on January 15, 1996.

would test the Access Plus system at a much higher level. The SWE was promoted as a dependable testing methodology that would involve ten teams of trust officers using 500 Access Plus processes starting in October. Had the test actually been carried out as planned, the system would have been tested in New York headquarters, at 20 percent capacity with a few live data feeds. Benari later admitted that the trust officers never actually participated in the SWE, in part because he had no jurisdiction over them. "When the data was made available to me, I wasn't comfortable with it because they hadn't used the system. So what do you think was going to happen when you entered a live environment?"

The Implementation Committee had grown to a total of 20 executives. "Since I was part of a 20 member committee, I thought I had a twentieth of the responsibility for the project," said Benari. Although he

EXHIBIT 8 Risks Outlined by Peter Storey and Audit Services Department, with Management Responses by Michael LeBlanc

Topic	Audit Report Risk Identified	Management Response
1. Identification of risks and control objectives	Without identifying all the critical risks and control objectives upfront, control may not be designed to address these risks and control objectives. This could result in unreliable financial information and impaired client services.	Controls were developed in the business processes. As further simulated work environments are held, controls will be adjusted and fine-tuned, if required. There currently exists over $3 billion in assets on Access Plus, thus controls are being managed each and every day in a production environment. The risks and controls of utilizing the document management system (DMS) will be further documented during the months of July and August and fine-tuned during the minimum one full month of simulated work environment scheduled to commence in October, prior to the headquarters Personal Trust conversion.
2. Segregation of duties and logical security	Segregation of duties may not be fully realized if system access is not adequately restricted. Independent review may not be achieved, requiring compensating controls and processes to be designed. Financial information may be unreliable.	Access prototypes for both the work groups and DMS usage will undergo further review and development during July and August. The access profiles will be tested during the simulated work environment scheduled to run for a minimum of one full month prior to the conversion of the headquarter's Personal Trust accounts. Input will be received prior to and during the SWE from all applicable work group leaders in this process.
3. Access*Plus application (input, processing, and output) controls	Inadequate Access*Plus application controls designed to ensure that the control objectives are achieved effectively and efficiently. This could result in unreliable financial information and impaired client services.	Report packages are in existence today to support the current book of business on Access*Plus. The remaining automated report packages for each work group will be established prior to the simulated work environment in preparation for the headquarters Personal Trust conversion. The responsibility for the review of control reports will be finalized upon the completion of the organizational structure and tested during the SWE.
4. Responsibility and authority	Loss in accountability if responsibility and authority are not clearly defined and established. Financial information may be unreliable and client service may be impaired.	The responsibility of staff and supervisors will be crystallized upon the completion and full staffing of the approved organizational structure for each workgroup. Workgroup leaders will participate in the finalization of workgroup responsibilities for the staff within their units. The responsibilities will be fine-tuned during the simulated work environment, which is scheduled to run for at least one full month prior to the conversion of headquarter's Personal Trust accounts.

EXHIBIT 8 (continued)   Risks Outlined by Peter Storey and Audit Services Department, with Management Responses by Michael LeBlanc

Topic	Audit Report Risk Identified	Management Response
5. Policies and report retention standard	Inadequate policies may result in inconsistent processing. Without a record retention standard and adequate controls over record retention, records may not be maintained to fulfill legal and business requirements.	Policies on fee processing have been received from product management, and the business process updated accordingly. Record retention standards exist today and there is no intention to deviate from these in the immediate future. Upon the development of the new workgroups and applicable staffing, management staff will have the responsibility to review all relevant documentation and adjust/revise the standards in place, in light of the usage of the DMS system.
6. Organizational structure	Work groups may not be structured with clear and distinct responsibilities, resulting in duplication and confusion.	Given that Audit Services did not conduct a formal review of business process 6, project staff were not provided the opportunity to enlighten audit staff on how the trust business trade processing activities operate. The process documentation will be updated to alleviate their concerns.
7. User acceptance testing	The trust operating environment (system and processing) may not function and perform as expected. The network may be unable to support the whole system. Our position may be jeopardized if there is any dispute with the vendor of Access*Plus on the standard software functions since we violate the contract in not testing the standard software.	The base application was tested during the simulated work environment conducted in January and February 1995 by the project team. A further simulated work environment, for a period of one month, prior to the conversion of the headquarter's Personal Trust accounts, is scheduled for October 1995. Code files have been examined through the initial simulated work environment, ongoing customization testing and reviews by the process owners. In addition, Select One is performing a thorough review of our code files at our request. Providian Trust purchased a hardware platform based on our current business volumes and factors in growth projections. In 1996 an additional review will be conducted of the hardware platform in relation to business volumes and growth. Integration testing is performed for all internal/external systems that are linked to Access*Plus. Reviews of security are completed, based on policy. Any weaknesses are identified, and if deemed risky, the appropriate action is undertaken to rectify. Formal testing of the application, operation system, and database management system program change controls is not

EXHIBIT 8 (continued) Risks Outlined by Peter Storey and Audit Services Department, with Management Responses by Michael LeBlanc

Topic	Audit Report Risk Identified	Management Response
7. User acceptance testing (continued)		done. Providian Trust is placing reliance on Select's standard change control procedures that are utilized with other clients, slightly modified for our operating environment.
8. Project deliverables	Delay in completing project deliverables or key tasks may impediment the success of the project. This will result in significant, post-implementation clean-up, inferior system/processing delivered, and adverse impact on client services.	Management has and continues to address resources issues as required. Additional staff have been delegated to the project to support customization and testing activities. Gantt charts are produced, updated and monitored weekly to ensure all activities are being addressed. Critical activities are monitored daily by project management. No implementation will be contemplated if it is deemed that the conversion will cause unnecessary risk to the business. This has been repeatedly stated in the past.
9. Disaster backup recovery and business continuity plan	Potential loss of critical information. Key business and system processing may not be sustained in the event of a disaster or other emergency.	The development, testing, and implementation of a Disaster Backup Recovery and Business Continuity Plan, consistent with the new operating environment, will be scheduled for completion by the end of 1995 and 1996, respectively. A disaster backup test will be conducted to test the setup of the operating environment and the ability to connect users to the system from headquarters. It should be noted that the majority of critical business activities for the trust division are covered by existing continuity plans in existence today. Workgroup management in the new operating environment will be heavily involved in the revision to existing plans.
10. Service level agreement with vendor of Access*Plus	Service may be inadequate to support the system. Providian Trust's interest may be jeopardized if there is any disagreement with Select One on the service to be provided. Our bargaining power may decrease when the system is used in production while violating the Access*Plus contract.	The service agreement with Select One will be finalized. As reported in the weekly Gantt Charts, the agreement is 90 percent complete as of July 21, 1995. It should be noted that Select One is contractually bound to provide the required services. Services and key measurements are identified in the signed contract. The Service Level Agreement merely identifies roles and responsibilities.

EXHIBIT 8 (continued) Risks Outlined by Peter Storey and Audit Services Department, with Management Responses by Michael LeBlanc

Topic	Audit Report Risk Identified	Management Response
11. Phase 1 and 2 implementations	Resources may be used inefficiently, impacting the success and the schedule of future implementation phases. Inadequate control over code file changes may cause unreliable processing.	Project management have reviewed the pros/cons of all implementations to date. A total of over $3 billion in assets have been successfully converted to the new system. Project management does not conduct meetings to identify issues resulting from previous conversions, and future conversions are addressed accordingly. A process has been implemented to deal with production issues on a timely basis as they arise. A simulated work environment, prior to the conversion of the headquarters Personal Trust accounts, will run for a minimum of one month. This will be utilized as the basis for the decision to proceed or not. The codes files are currently undergoing a complete review by Select, and is approximately 80 percent complete.
12. Documentation management system (DMS)—limitation users	Terms of agreement may be violated, resulting in fines and/or adverse publicity. Software cost may increase if a license for additional users is required.	The usage of DMS will be monitored once fully operational. If required, the appropriate license will be obtained. The vendor of the system is aware of our situation and is in agreement with our current licensing arrangement.
13. Training evaluations	Without a structured approach, feedback informally obtained and unsolicited feedback from participants may be lost. This could result in losing the opportunity to improve future training sessions, participants not properly trained, errors, and clean-up efforts.	This is completed.

Source: Trust Operating Environment Interim Audit Report.

and the other executives pondered the possibility, not a single committee member ever walked into Walsh's office to express their fears. "To criticize the freight train that was moving down the path we regarded as an act of corporate disloyalty," explained Strong. "You say to yourself, well, am I here to provide information, ask questions, provide support or am I here to be accountable for the success of this project?"

The SWE was underway but not complete when Steinman & Smith issued their "Access Plus Trust System—Control Documentation Status Report" on October 26. The following is an excerpt from the Steinman & Smith report:

> We note that the project has established a number of criteria which were reviewed by the Implementation Committee in making the implementation decision. In particular, the results of the Simulated Work Environment tests give an accurate indication whether the system can be used to support the Personal Trust business commencing in November 1995. This test provides direct evidence that the system and various key controls, such as reconciliations, can be used effectively to manage Providian Trust's Personal Trust business, first in headquarters and then across the country. Our comments and conclusions which follow relate only to our review of control documentation.
>
> Scope of documentation reviewed: Trust Operating Environment Document, Training Modules, Procedures.
>
> Conclusions: The Trust Operating Environment document and the training modules are mainly complete and they provide users with the ability to use the new system in a knowledgeable and effective fashion. This is a prerequisite for an effective control environment.
>
> The new procedures related to Access Plus which have been provided to date also reinforce directions on how to use the system, but do not focus on control oriented activities. Procedures for a number of areas are still being prepared or enhanced as a result of the Simulated Work Environment test, which is now being completed. An appendix outlines the various procedures which we have requested management to provide prior to conversion to allow us to confirm that control. Each of these items have been communicated to management and we have been assured that, at a minimum, the specific control principles which will be applied will be provided to use before the conversion date. Subject to this documentation containing adequate control information, we have agreed with the October 31 conversion schedule.
>
> While there is other control documentation which should be updated so that it properly reflects the use of Access Plus reports, we believe these activities can wait until after the Personal Trust conversions without any serious risk to the business, given that the recommended senior management monitoring takes place and responds in a timely fashion to any issues which may arise.

Stephen Walsh decided to approve the first scheduled Access Plus conversion. The Personal Trust conversion for all New York accounts took place on November 1, 1995.

Case 5–4

SOUTHWIRE: BEYOND 2000[1]

In Carrollton, Georgia, Roy Richards Senior was a local legend. A plaque in front of the courthouse spoke of his business prominence and his dedication to the community. Richards was the founder and chief executive officer of Southwire, a leading producer of aluminum and copper rod, wire, and cable for the transmission and distribution of electricity. Known as a visionary, a tenacious negotiator and a proponent of an unencumbered free capital market, Richards built Southwire during the rapid-growth post-World War II era. In a tribute to Roy Richards Senior, a writer asked, "How does a newcomer to an old industry revolutionize its way of doing things?" The same question might apply to Roy Richards Junior, who took over the business after his father died in 1985.

Richards knew that variables beyond his control, such as metals prices, fluctuations in interest rates, and government regulations could have an adverse affect on business. The recession of the early 1980s had taken its toll on Southwire according to a 1983 *Industry Week* article that said that the company had been "battered by the recession's effect on housing and autos, industries to which it sells a major portion of its 1,000 aluminum and copper products."[2] Un-

daunted by unpredictable external economic events, Roy Richards Junior was determined to command Southwire's destiny.

In one decade Roy Richards Junior managed to grow annual sales from $500 million in 1985 to $1.9 billion in 1995, an increase he attributed to increasing and streamlining production and total quality management practices. The company's customers included 135 of the major U.S. electric power companies. One-third of the newly constructed buildings in the United States were wired with Southwire products. The company claimed a leading position in the electric wire and cable industry in the United States, with 1995 sales surpassing its domestic competitors (see Exhibit 1). With only a two percent market growth rate in the United States, however, Southwire officers were looking beyond domestic soil to countries that were just beginning to build their infrastructures.

In 1996, Richards was focused on the threat posed by large multinationals that were targeting the same promising territories: Furakawa, based in Tokyo, was vertically integrated in the metals and electric industries and reported $7.6 billion in 1995 sales; England's BICC produced wire for its own $6.6 billion construction business (see Exhibit 2). Roy Richards Junior knew that he would have to lead the 5,000 managers and employees of Southwire through a series of changes to ensure the growth of the company. His financial objective was to more than double shareholder equity by the year 2,000. The shareholders were his family members.

[1]Copyright © 1997 by the President and Fellows of Harvard College.

Harvard Business School case 397-074.

Research associate Melissa Dailey prepared this case under the supervision of Professor F. Warren McFarlan.

[2]Jeffrey Lautenbach, "Southwire's Empire Builder Struggles to Hang On," *Industry Week,* May 2, 1983.

EXHIBIT 1 U.S. Competitors

	Southwire Co.	Alcan Cable Division	Essex Group Inc.*	General Cable Industries[a]	Triangle Wire and Cable Inc.*
Stock ticker symbol	N/A	N/A	D.ENS	N/A	N/A
Stock exchange	N/A	N/A	Other	N/A	N/A
Headquarters location	Carrollton, Georgia	Atlanta, Georgia	Fort Wayne, Indiana	Highland Heights, KY	Lincoln, Rhode Island
Company type	Private	Division of Alcan Aluminum Corp.	Public	Subsidiary of GK Technologies	Private
Primary SIC (Standard Industrial Classification)	3357: Nonferrous wiredrawing and insulating	3355:Aluminum rolling and drawing, NEC	3357: Nonferrous wiredrawing and insulating	3351: rolling, drawing, and extruding of copper	3357: Nonferrous wiredrawing and insulating
Other SICs	3341: Nonferrous metals		3351: Rolling, drawing and extruding of copper 3496: Miscellaneous fabricated wire products	3357: Nonferrous wiredrawing and insulating	
Full company					
Annual sales—net (US$ thousands)	$1,900,000	$120,000	$1,203,590	$853,000	$450,000
Cost of goods sold (US$ thousands)			1,030,511		
Gross profit (US$ thousands)			173,079		
Sales, general and administration (US$ thousands)			93,250		
Net income (US$ thousands)			19,523		
Total assets			744,468		

(continued)

EXHIBIT 1 (concluded) U.S. Competitors

	Southwire Co.	Alcan Cable Division	Essex Group Inc.*	General Cable Industries[a]	Triangle Wire and Cable Inc.*
Wire or cable division					
Annual sales—net (US$ thousands)					
Operating income (US$ thousands)					
Net income (US$ thousands)					
Total assets (US$ thousands)					
Employees	4,531	750	4,102	4,000	1,200
Common shares	N/A	N/A	1	N/A	N/A
Common shares outstanding (thousands)	N/A	N/A	0.1	N/A	N/A
Market value (US$ thousands)	N/A	N/A	N/A	N/A	N/A

*Essex Group Inc. acquired Triangle Wire & Cable Inc. in November 1996. Financial data from company's latest, annual financial performance period. [a]Ultimate parent is Plazahill Ltd. (England).

Source: Compiled from Disclosure, Inc. Worldscope database; Ward's *Directory of Public and Private Companies*, 1996; and Dun & Bradstreet's *Million Dollar Directory of Public and Private Companies*, 1996.

EXHIBIT 2 Non-U.S. Competitors

	Alcatel Cable SA	Alcatel STK ASA	BICC PLC	Furukawa Co. Ltd.	Furukawa Electric	Pirelli SPA
Stock ticker symbol	CALY	STTO	BICC	5715	5801	PIRI
Stock exchange	N/A	Oslo, Norway	London	Tokyo and Osaka	Tokyo and Osaka	Italy, Brussels, France
Headquarters location	France	Oslo, Norway	London, U.K.	Tokyo, Japan	Tokyo, Japan	Milan, Italy
Company type	Public	Public	Public	Public	Public	Public
Primary SIC	3357: Nonferrous wiredrawing and insulating	3357: Nonferrous wiredrawing and insulating	1610: Highway and street construction	3531: Construction machinery	3351: Rolling, drawing, and extruding of copper	3357: Nonferrous wiredrawing and insulating inner tubes
Other SICs	5051: Metals service centers and offices 8711: Engineering services	1623: Water, sewer and utility lines 3669: Communications equipment, NEC 1731: Electrical work 5065: Electronic parts and equipment	1620: Heavy construction, except highway 3350: Nonferrous rolling and drawing	3331: Primary copper 3339: Primary nonferrous metals, NEC 6531: Real estate agents and managers 2860: Industrial organic chemicals	3692: Primary batteries, dry and wet 3674: Semiconductors and related devices	3011: Tires and inner tubes 3069: Fabricated rubber products, NEC 5014: Tires and tubes 5063: Electrical apparatus and equipment
Full company Annual sales—net (US$ thousands)	7,674,560	587,441	6,649,750	1,401,472	6,203,256	7,189,594
Cost of goods sold (US$ thousands)						
Gross profit (US$ thousands)						

(continued)

EXHIBIT 2 (concluded) Non-U.S. Competitors

	Alcatel Cable SA	Alcatel STK ASA	BICC PLC	Furukawa Co. Ltd.	Furukawa Electric	Pirelli SPA
Selling, general, and administration (US$ thousands)						
Operating income (US$ thousands)	474,701	47,058	198,036	58,265	138,518	328,540
Net income (US$ thousands)	288,336	35,764	(214,402)	68,593	58,124	170,110
Total assets (US$ thousands)	7,543,085	399,209	4,026,184	1,893,037	7,673,056	6,810,040
Wire or cable division						
Annual sales—net (US$ thousands)		253,486	2,252,044		3,298,856	3,651,373
Operating income (US$ thousands)		30,431	129,296		49,992	N/A
Net income (US$ thousands)		N/A	N/A		N/A	N/A
Total assets (US$ thousands)		158,585	815,057		2,945,457	N/A
Employees	28,062	2,410	34,088	2,247	9,765	39,123
Common shareholders	N/A	1,178	30,948	17,028	76,845	35,000
Common shares outstanding (thousands)	N/A	8,400	417,720	250,751	656,233	1,557,020
Market value (US$)	N/A	553,402,080	1,992,885,268	1,088,119,805	3,553,816,454	2,764,333,225
Exchange rate	0.19527 US$ per French francs	0.15686 US$ per Norwegian kroner	1.63666 US$ per pounds sterling	0.00882 US$ per Japanese yen	0.00882 US$ per Japanese yen	0.00066 US$ per Italian lire

Note: Financial data from each company's latest annual financial performance.

Source: Compiled from Disclosure Inc. Worldscope database and *Ward Directory of Public and Private Companies.*

Five Lines of Business

Wire and Cable Division

Roy Richards Senior built his business in the South, turning down a job offer from General Electric in Schenectady, New York, a welcome opportunity for a number of his classmates in the Georgia Tech graduating class of 1935. Richards returned to his hometown of Carrollton, located fifty miles west of Atlanta, to work in his father's sawmill. Electricity was a relatively new phenomenon, and his sawmill began preparing poles for utilities. Soon after, at the age of 25, he traveled to Washington, D.C., to bid on an REA (Rural Electrification Administration) contract to string 108 miles of wire in his native county. Despite his youth and inexperience, he won the contract.

In 1942 Richards left his business to serve as an artillery officer in World War II. Upon his return three and a half years later, he discovered that the region's wire manufacturer, Alcoa, could not keep up with demand. So, if Alcoa can't deliver wire, Roy asked his colleagues, why not start our own wire plant? The answer he got was one he had heard many times: it's impossible; it can't be done. His reaction—which came to be a character trademark—let's try."[3] Richards raised the necessary capital from local business people, recruited a former college professor to teach industrial production to local workers, and opened his first plant in 1950. The business grew from 12 employees to 22 employees by the end of the first year. By the end of the second year, Southwire had shipped five million pounds of wire, accrued $560,000 in sales and doubled the plant's size.

The Wire and Cable line of business (LOB), which accounted for 64 percent of the

---

[3]Joseph Cumming, "Roy Richards," Southwire Brochure.

company's 1995 sales, provided electrical wire and cable to the residential and commercial building markets and the utility market. Southwire's products ranged from the wire running along highways, transmitting electricity to homes and businesses, to the smaller wire running behind the walls of homes and businesses. The cable and wire were produced in one of seven plants and distributed through the company's Master Distribution Centers, located throughout the U.S. Contractors and electricians purchased Southwire's products through major electrical distributors such as Graybar, G.E. Supply, and Wesco and through retail outlets such as Home Depot, Lowes, Walmart and Sears. Because people in the construction business tended to buy all of their supplies from one source, Southwire had no plans to retail its products directly. Utility companies generally bought Southwire's products directly, although some smaller utilities or rural electrical co-ops purchased through specialty distributors.

SCR Rod Making Technology

A milestone in the company's history occurred when Roy Richards Senior traveled to Milan, Italy, to meet with an inventor, Illario Properzi. Wire was made by being "drawn" from thick lengths of aluminum or copper called "rod" into the desired diameter of wire. At the time, links of rod were welded together to make continuous rolls, then the rod was stretched into wire, with each weld representing a potential weak spot in the final product. Properzi had developed a continuous casting system to fabricate lead and zinc, and Richards hoped to apply the method to aluminum. After obtaining a contract from Properzi, Richards returned to Georgia, where he and D.B. Cofer, now an executive vice president of Southwire, worked for one year to master the continuous casting system.

In 1953 Southwire became the first company to continuously cast aluminum and in 1963 adapted the system for copper as well. Southwire Continuous Rod, a second line of business, has sold or licensed its continuous casting systems to 58 manufacturers in 24 countries such as China, Russia, and India. Southwire's systems are used to produce over 50 percent of the world's copper rod. As the company pursued its globalization strategy, it would continue to sell its continuous rod casting system to companies that the Wire and Cable line of business might eventually compete with, reasoning that even if Southwire stopped selling the continuous rod casting system, an SCR competitor would step right in and provide the same technology.

Southwire Copper Division
Southwire vertically integrated in the early 1970s, building a secondary copper refinery where copper scrap was melted and recycled into copper rod. Southwire Copper Division sold 60–70 percent of their volume to the Wire and Cable line of business and also sold to other companies such as Packard Electric, which made wire for the automotive industry.

NSA
Southwire was the only electrical wire and cable manufacturer in the United States with its own copper refinery and aluminum smelter. NDS ran an 800-acre plant site located in Hawesville, Kentucky, along the Ohio River. Barges traveled up the river, delivering pure alumnae from the Caribbean and South America to be refined in the primary aluminum reduction plant. While 60–70 percent of the aluminum product was sold to the Wire and Cable LOB, 30–40 percent was sold to other users—primarily automotive parts suppliers for auto makers such as Ford, General Motors, and Toyota— to make aluminum wheels and other parts.

Southwire Specialty Division
Southwire's Specialty Product division managed five plants that produced wire and rod making equipment, machining fabricating systems, and such specialty items as magnetic wire for motors and generators.

Globalization, Diversification, Modernization

Roy Richards Junior called on Southwire's top officers to enter into a period of intense introspection, discussion and strategic planning in early 1995. Vice presidents in Southwire's five LOBs, many of whom had been with the company for over 30 years, directed their senior managers to work in teams with their counterparts from the finance and investment, information technology and human resources divisions. A total of 100 senior managers were involved in the planning process. Richards asked them to determine the best strategy for growing both the domestic and non-U.S. markets. He emphasized the necessity of establishing Southwire as the long term, low cost producer for all strategic product lines, and requested that each division implement a process to do benchmarking of the cost versus the competition every two years. "Most importantly," Richards said, "use IT [information technology] to achieve sustainable and distinctive competitive advantage relative to peers in the industry, and demonstrate how we will use IT to lower cost." With the help of outside consultants, Southwire executives emerged in 1996, after a year of reckoning, with three primary strategic objectives: globalization, diversification, and modernization.

Their aim was to increase the six percent non-U.S. revenue achieved in 1995 to 25 percent by the year 2005. Only two of the company's 17 manufacturing sites were located overseas in 1996. Pointing out that one third of the planet did not have electricity, senior officers worked with their managers to plan manufacturing sites in Asia and Latin America. The shift to an overseas market focus would represent a major cultural readjustment for executives who were comfortable living in a rural area and who prided themselves on the southern roots of their company.

In the area of diversification, Southwire began to add to its product line in North America, developing a new medium-voltage cable for underground use in dense urban areas, for example. Executives also negotiated a research and development contract to work with the U.S. Department of Energy's Oak Ridge National Laboratory in Oak Ridge, Tennessee, to prove the commercial viability of superconducting cable that would deliver electricity at extremely high rates of efficiency.

Southwire had established a strong tradition in technological research and development with nearly 400 patents in 40 countries, covering subjects from metal processing to plastics formulation. Modernization in the "Information Age," however, implied something entirely new. Through the strategic planning process, senior officers came to the realization that Southwire's traditional hierarchical structure could potentially anchor the company, holding it back from growth. The central decision-making structure did not accommodate fast reactions to changing market realities. Furthermore, people at the bottom of the structure were often left out of the decision-making process. In order to realize Southwire's strategic objectives, it was determined that the company would have to transform itself from a centralized, functional business organization to a line of business organization, moving more decision-making authority (including more control over purse strings) from the executive suite to the manufacturing centers. In the proposed management structure, line of business managers would be responsible for profit and loss.

"The future strength and success of Southwire depends upon our ability to improve our processes, technologies, marketing, manufacturing and delivery systems at rates previously unimagined," reported human resources officers in their strategic report, entitled *Southwire 2000*. The report described a new organizational structure for Southwire's future.

> Imagine any Southwire plant of the future where worker output has increased by 80 percent in six years. Absenteeism is a mere two percent. Employee turnover is one percent. If something has to be moved by a fork truck, no one yells that they need a driver because there is no such thing as a driver. Instead, anyone at hand jumps on the fork truck and gets the job done. There are no hourly workers. Everyone is salaried. Everyone is involved in decisions affecting the plant. Everybody participates in such matters as scheduling, solving quality problems, evaluating performance and recommending new equipment . . . in fact, the plant's entire operation, top to bottom, is in the hands of high involvement teams.

"The autocratic style of management had to change," explained Human Resources manager Tommy Gable. "It used to be, 'You do what I tell you to and when you're done, come back and I'll tell you what to do next.' Generals and soldiers. Now we're seeking a high level of involvement from every employee."

IT: The Genetic Code

A November, 1996 issue of *Information Week* entitled, "Technology Spending: The Billion Dollar Club," listed companies such as AT&T, Chase Manhattan, and Prudential that spent over a billion dollars a year on information technology. "How do these CIOs justify such spending to their bosses and shareholders? They have supported and led managers who are already convinced that massive IT investments are crucial to the success, perhaps even the survival, of the enterprise."[4]

Though Southwire was not in the Billion Dollar Club, its senior officers agreed that information technology would provide the genetic code for the company's transformation. Southwire's total IT expenditures, including both annual and capital budgets, increased from $4 million in 1992 to $7.5 million in 1994. In 1996, the vice president responsible for information technology, Lee Hunter, was granted a $19.2 million budget to further implement an information technology architecture that would support Southwire's rapidly changing business envi-

---

[4]Bob Violino, "Technology Spending: The Billion Dollar Club," *Information Week,* November 25, 1996.

ronment (see Exhibit 3). Hunter, who held a degree in electrical engineering from Georgia Tech and an MBA from State University of West Georgia in Carrollton, was a 25-year veteran of Southwire, who had been a chief electrical engineer and had served as Roy Richards Senior's technical assistant from 1982 to 1985, before taking command of information technology in 1987. In 1996, as he directed the company's investments in such major initiatives as a network overhaul, a PC platform upgrade, and the development of a data warehouse. Hunter outlined the following strategic change themes for the 61 IT professionals in his department (see Exhibit 4):

1. *Re-alignment* of the CIS (corporate information systems) organization will be required in order to meet the needs of the newly formed line of business management teams. Additionally, we must add

---

EXHIBIT 3   Information Technology Annual Budget for 1996 ($ millions)

- Corporate Information Service (CIS) Department .... $ 4.1
- E.D.I Department 0.2
- Business Process Re-Design Department 0.7
- Telecommunication Department 2.0
- IT expenditures within the lines of business, separate from CIS expenditures 3.0

    Annual budget subtotal $10.0

Information Technology Project Work

	1996	*1997–2000*
• Networks	$ 2.0	8.0
• PC upgrades	3.5	1.3
• PC software	2.0	1.2
• Telecommunication switches	0.0	1.2
• Integration of voice mail, e-mail, fax, phone mail	0.0	0.5
• Data warehousing	1.2	2.8
• Corporate	0.5	2.5
Capital budget subtotal	$ 9.2	$17.5

EXHIBIT 4 Southwire Company—Corporate Information Services

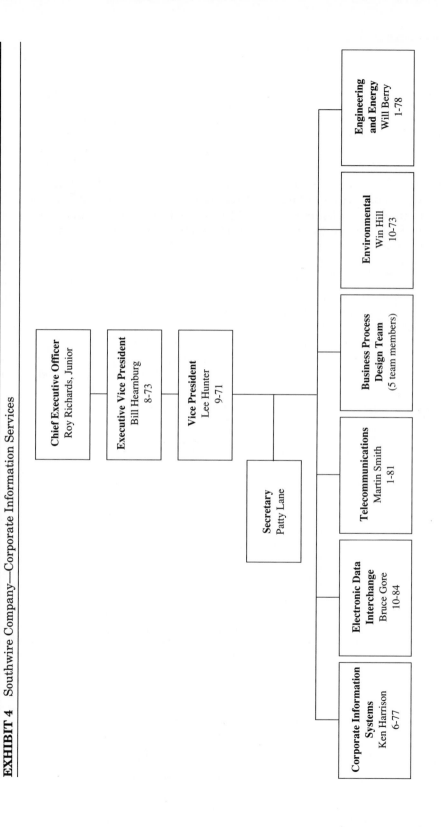

EXHIBIT 4 (continued)   Southwire Company—Corporate Information Services

Vice President Environmental and Technical Support
Lee Hunter
9-71

Secretary
Connie Taylor

Corporate Information Services Director
Ken Harrison
6-77

Applications Development Manager
Denise Crumbley
7-78

Operations/Technical Services End-User Support Manager
Tim Powers
2-85

End-User Support Manager
James Lanier
3-77

Business Analysis
- R. Bowman
- R. Fields
- D. Johnson

Programming Teams

Team Manager
Tom Smith
10-77
- J. Buis
- D. Brown
- R. Johnson
- L. Nook
- J. Reaves
- T. Stamps

Team Manager
Mona Wiggins
6-80
- R. Darivemula
- K. Hannah
- R. Ormond
- M. Swatzell
- S. Wilson

Team Manager
Jim Scott
10-73
- L. Bradley
- R. Kendrick
- D. Mathis
- M. McMahon
- W. M. Smith
- J. Tinker

Team Manager
Tracy Kemp
6-72
- J. Blackston
- E. Cole
- S. Garner
- R. Lamar
- N. Morton
- B. Williams

Operations
- E. Colwell
- C. Davis**
- R. Hartley**
- R. Lane
- A. Langford*
- E. Sanders
- S. Shadrix
- M. Watson**

Technical
- D. Bott
- E. Deitch
- C. Easterwood
- M. J. Smith
- B. Wendel

End-User Support Manager
- D. Cofer
- D. Fuqua
- D. Lanier
- J. Morris
- D. Sloan
- D. West

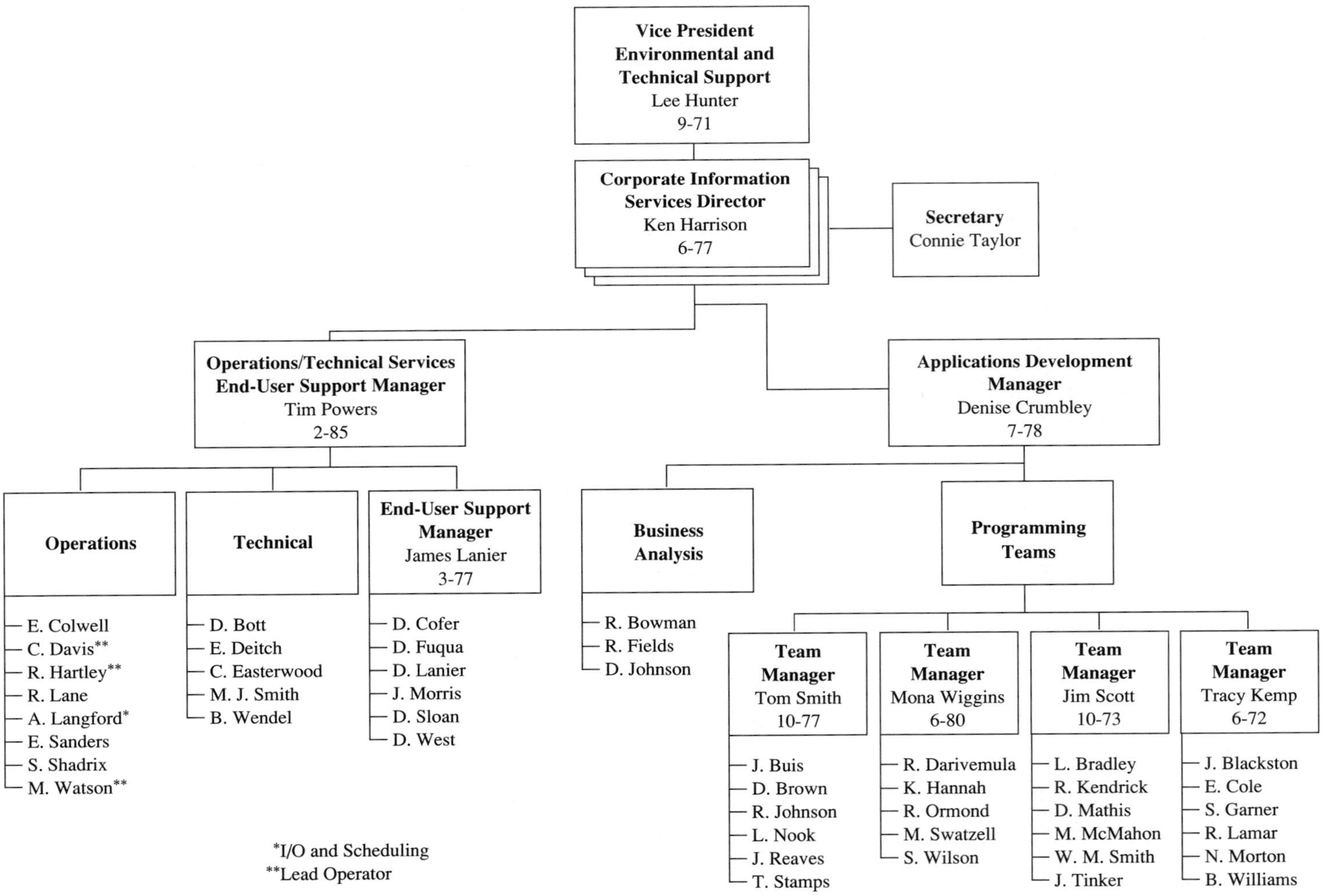

*I/O and Scheduling
**Lead Operator

Note: Employment start dates appear beneath management names.

information technology professionals to each line of business management team. These professionals will work with LOB management in the design of strategic information technology systems that support and respond to their specific business drivers.

2. *Make significant investments* in information technology to enable the lines of business to achieve strategic advantages in their respective marketplaces. Additionally, we must align our information technology architecture with our new business management and information technology support structure.

3. *Achieve the necessary levels of integration* of Southwire's information systems in order to increase organizational productivity, and to facilitate timely access to relevant and accurate information.

4. *Provide comprehensive training* to the end users community (internal customers) in the various business, manufacturing and desktop applications.

5. *Research alternative means for achieving efficiencies and cost reductions* through outsourcing and/or centralization of nonstrategic systems in order to take advantage of potential economies of scale.

IT Architectural Evolution

Southwire's IT architecture was evolving from a centralized, host system to a more distributed and open system (see Exhibit 5). In 1992, Southwire's IT infrastructure consisted of dumb terminals, connected over dedicated phone lines to a mainframe located in corporate headquarters. In the host computing environment a limited number of employees were connected to a mainframe that contained all company information and would perform such functions as financial management and limited inventory control. "The host computing model placed the computer at the center

and connected all terminals and other devices as slaves. Most of these terminals had limited or no intelligence and were therefore totally dependent on the availability of the host computer to perform their intended functionality," explained the authors of *Paradigm Shift: The New Promise of Information Technology.*[5] By 1996, Southwire had implemented a number of customized client-server applications (see Exhibit 6).

In 1996 Southwire was quickly moving to a distributed architecture, with an extensive high bandwidth WAN (wide area network) connecting all of the lines of business and 17 manufacturing plants to Carrollton headquarters. Much of the computing power had shifted outward as the IT department developed a total of 80 LANS (local area networks). Southwire planned to continue increasing bandwidth capacity, staying at least twelve months ahead of anticipated demand. Due to its international expansion in Malaysia, Integral Corporation, part of the specialty products LOB, was quickly moving to set up its connections to the corporate WAN, establishing a Web site and organizing for videoconferencing sessions between its overseas plants and corporate headquarters.

Even as it moved to a more distributed IT architecture, Southwire still needed a mainframe for central processing of corporate data such as marketing, human resources and overall financial data. Southwire's Unisys A15 host mainframe of 1992 was the size of four refrigerators. The company upgraded to a Unisys A18 mainframe in 1995, which was four times smaller yet four times more powerful than the dinosaur they threw out, after moving millions and

---

[5]Don Tapscott and Art Caston, *Paradigm Shift: The New Promise of Information Technology* (NY: McGraw-Hill, 1993), p. 122.

EXHIBIT 5 Southwire IT Architecture

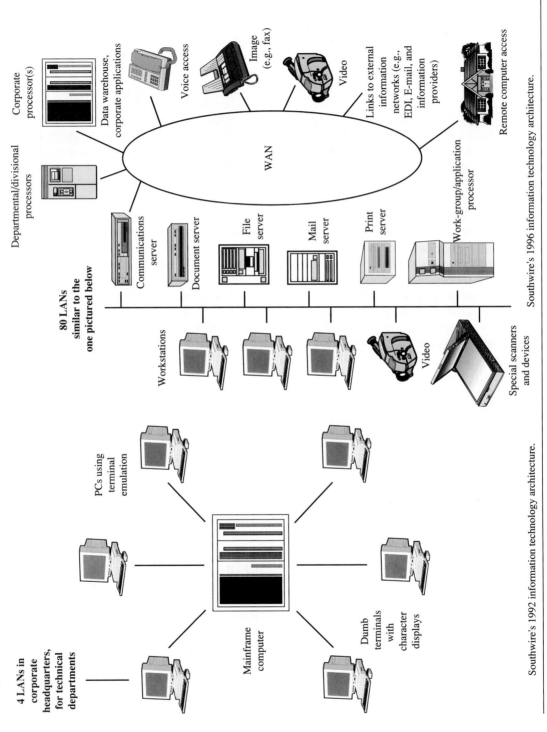

4 LANs in corporate headquarters, for technical departments

PCs using terminal emulation

Mainframe computer

Dumb terminals with character displays

Southwire's 1992 information technology architecture.

80 LANs similar to the one pictured below

Departmental/divisional processors

Corporate processor(s)

Data warehouse, corporate applications

Voice access

Image (e.g., fax)

Video

Links to external information networks (e.g., EDI, E-mail, and information providers)

Remote computer access

WAN

Communications server

Document server

File server

Mail server

Print server

Work-group/application processor

Workstations

Video

Special scanners and devices

Southwire's 1996 information technology architecture.

Source: Adapted from book exhibits. Don Tapscott and Art Caston, *Paradigm Shift: The New Promise of Information Technology* (NY: McGraw-Hill, 1993), pp. 123, 253.

EXHIBIT 5 (continued) Southwire IT Architecture

IT architecture	All company information stored on Unisys A15 mainframe computer. Dumb terminals over dedicated phone lines to mainframe.	Still using Unisys A15 mainframe primarily. Began moving toward client-server architecture.	A networked client-server architecture with a Unisys A18 as host mainframe server LOB servers standardized on Oracle database.
Wide area network (WAN)	No	Small WAN	Extensive MCI public frame relay WAN. T1 lines to plants, 256K lines to distribution centers, 56K lines to all other sites.
Local area networks (LANs)	4 LANs (in technical departments)	20 LANs	80 LANs
Client-server applications	No	2	8
Number of computers on employees' desktops	80 dumb terminals, 400 PCs	1,400 PCs, including 286 Mhz processors and 38630 486 Mhz processors	1,700 new PCs running NT operating system. Compaq Deskpro P133 (Pentium 133 Mhz processors). 24-hour help desk plus training.
Desktop applications	Data entry, word processing, few Lotus spreadsheet applications	85 different word processing spreadsheet, graphic applications	All 1,700 standardized on Microsoft Office, including Word, PowerPoint and Excel.
Number of IT employees	33	40	61
Total budget (annual and capital)	$4 million	$7.5 million	$19.2million

685

EXHIBIT 6   Major IT Applications Running
at Southwire

Accounting general ledger
Order entry
Material resource planning
Shop floor control
Purchasing
Inventory management
Logistic shipping
Accounts payable/accounts receivable
Sales analysis
Insurance claims
HR/payroll
Profit sharing
Plant maintenance schedule system

---

millions of lines of legacy code to the new
mainframe and Oracle databases.

Hunter estimated that the company would
spend a total of one million dollars by the
end of 1997, updating old code for the
numerical transition to the year 2000.
Companies worldwide were busily updating
past programs that used six-digit data fields
to indicate a day, month and year—so that
when the year 2000 arrived, systems would
not automatically assume the year was
1900. *Information Week* estimated that getting software ready for the millennium
would cost as much as $600 billion world-
wide and predicted that only half the companies would be ready.[6]

Southwire defined its network as "the
vehicle for providing access to IT services," a
straightforward definition that camouflaged
the inherent complexity of managing the
system. Network managers were expected to
ensure that any workstation could communicate with any other workstation. They
periodically monitored network response
time and continuously worked to keep the

network running 24 hours a day. A three to
four hour network failure would have major
repercussions throughout the company.
"Compared with mainframe management,
managing distributed networked client/
server enterprises is like trading in a hobby
horse for a bucking bronco," warned *Network
Computing.* "The ride is thrilling—if you can
stay on."[7] In 1996, Southwire's network consisted of 91 Novell servers, 28 Microsoft
Windows NT servers, two Unisys A series
mainframes, one Unix minicomputer, 1,700
PCs and 65 wide area communications links.

Two Days in the Life of a
Warehouse Manager

Southwire's IT architecture was designed
not necessarily to redistribute power, but to
provide a greater sense of power for each
knowledge worker by providing them with
fast, efficient access to information. Information technology would help overcome
the limitations of the hierarchical structure
by opening up a communications network
that would enhance and speed up decision-
making processes. The *Scientific American*
edition *The Computer in the 21st Century*
theorized that corporate information technology systems, such as the one proposed by
Southwire, were enabling a paradoxical
combination of centralization and decentralization. "Because information can be distributed more easily, people lower in the
organization can now become well enough
informed to make more decisions more effectively. At the same time, upper-level managers can more easily review decisions made
at lower levels."[8]

---

[6]Doug Bartholomew, "The Year 2000 Problem: Time's
Running Out," *Information Week,* February 5, 1996,
cover story.

---

[7]Bruce Boardman, "Systems Management: The Next
Corporate IS Frontier," *Network Computing,* November
15, 1996.

[8]Thomas Malone and John Rockart, "Computers,
Networks and the Corporation," *Scientific American,
The Computer in the 21st Century,* special edition, 1995,
p. 145.

Between 1992 and 1996, changes in information technology changed the way business was done at Southwire. The transformation in the way a Wire and Cable Division warehouse manager went about supplying building wire, was one of numerous examples that could have been used to illustrate how information technology improved Southwire's ability to function as a cohesive organization.

1992

1. A sales manager or an assistant would manually enter customer orders using a dumb terminal connected to the corporate mainframe, where all records were stored. If the phone lines were down, the order placement would be postponed.

2. The mainframe received the customer order and would generate a shipment order and send it to the warehouse.

3. The warehouse manager would reference a printed inventory generated by the mainframe every few weeks. The information was only available in summary, rather than in detail. When the warehouse manager wanted to fulfill an order, he knew there were five million pounds of building wire in his warehouse, but he did not know what size or color were available, whether it was stored in a carton or on a reel, or exactly where it was located. He often had to pick up the phone and ask an employee to walk over to the inventory to see what was available.

4. Once inventory was confirmed, the warehouse manager would hand a printed shipping order to an employee who would locate the material, pull it and load it for delivery.

1996

5. The customers often sent their orders in via EDI (electronic data interchange), eliminating the hassle of manually entering orders into the system and eliminating the possibility of data entry errors. Orders not sent via EDI were manually entered.

6. Detailed manufacturing and shipping information was stored in an Oracle database accessible over the local area network. The warehouse manager used his PC to access the inventory data. He knew exactly what product was available and where it was located in the warehouse.

7. Orders were sent electronically to a computer in the warehouse, which passed the information via radio frequency to an employee with a hand-held computer with a scanner. The computer indicated exactly which aisle and bin the product was located in, and the warehouse employee verified the order by laser-scanning a bar code on the product, which might be 15 feet away from where he stood. The product was pulled and loaded onto a truck for delivery.

Telecommunications

Telecommunications manager Martin Smith was interested in finding a way to have a single infrastructure deliver multiple services. Computer-telephone interface (CTI), for example, could provide integrated voice, fax, and e-mail to customers. An advanced system could recognize a caller's phone number, retrieve information about the caller, and display the information to a sales person or customer service representative. As in many other businesses, the widespread business need for videoconferencing, once thought to be the killer application for integrated services, had not quite arrived at Southwire, though usage of the system had increased from 15 total usage hours in 1995 to 20 total usage hours in 1996.

Southwire IT managers recognized the probability that some types of integration would occur via the World Wide Web. Since 1993 Southwire had exchanged business information (such as freight bills, purchase orders and invoices) with over 200 of its largest customers and suppliers via EDI. Experts predicted that the seamless flow of data between computer systems would eventually take place over the Web.

In January 1995, Southwire became the first company in its industry to launch a Web site, featuring a full on-line product catalog and customer support in the form of FAQs (frequently asked questions) and the ability to download technical papers. In November an estimated 800 visitors per week accessed the Southwire Web site; Hunter estimated that about half of those visitors were distributors, retailers and utilities, Southwire's target audience. Smith planned to add search engine capability to the site and an interactive customer help desk using Java-based programs.

Smith launched an Intranet called Wire World in July 1996 in hopes that it would provide a versatile and inexpensive tool for publishing company information on internal job opportunities, health benefits, profit sharing, etc. Richards, who invited all employees to his third quarter review of performance in an auditorium at corporate headquarters in November, demonstrated the Intranet and explained that it would eventually replace all paper and policy manuals in the company. Kiosks with Web access would be set up in plants to service the 3,300 employees who did not have desktop access to computers.

The Data Warehouse and Query Tools

During strategic planning it was determined that every LOB manager should have desktop access to detailed information for business analysis purposes, such as evaluation of vendors, profitability report generation or earnings projections. Applications Development Manager Denise Crumbly estimated that the data warehouse project would cost three to four million dollars and that the ini-

tial version of the warehouse would be tested by a group of 20 (out of 180 total) sales people in December 1996. "Data continues to accumulate and grow, and it won't suddenly all be there on some magical date. We're talking about five to ten years worth of information, and the interface must be easy to use."

The data warehouse pilot was built on a PC platform in December 1995 and was tested by a small group of sales people the following summer. "We knew it was the wrong platform, but we wanted to prove the concept and get information from users on what they wanted," explained Hunter. Though the pilot worked, it took from 15 seconds to half an hour for the system to return answers to queries. "Sales people were not clamoring for the data warehouse because they didn't know what they should be clamoring for," said Crumbly. Southwire evaluated six vendors, including Unisys, Sun, IBM, HP, Digital, and Pyramid, and selected an E6000 Sun with four processors and one GM memory with 100 GM mirrored disk drives.

A major Southwire initiative for 1997— which would depend on the speed and efficiency of the data warehouse—was to improve customer service by enabling representatives to rapidly maneuver through the IT systems, answering any question a customer might have instantaneously, including exactly where their product was in the shipping process, pricing questions, or manufacturing-related questions. "This is a big challenge because we've got to tie together some of the mainframe legacy systems, client-server distributed systems and the data warehouse and give customer service representatives the capability to easily access that system from their PCs," explained Hunter.

The corporate information services group planned to provide training to all PC users in Impromptu and PowerPlay, query tools which would allow users to "mine" and easily analyze warehouse data. In August 1996, Cognos Inc. of Ottawa announced plans to build Web support into PowerPlay and Impromptu, enabling users to use the two tools to create, distribute, and view data-analysis applications over the Web and Intranets.

The PC Platform Project

A February 1995 survey of a cross section of 50 PC users revealed that employees were frustrated with their outdated equipment and the inability of the IT staff to provide support. A total of 66 percent of those surveyed said that their PCs were either unacceptable or did not have sufficient processing power. Furthermore, the machines were running a total of 85 different software programs. "We had one of each application. Trying to support them made our lives miserable. We were spending most of our time putting out fires and not being very successful at it," explained support manager Mike Smith. PC hardware and software expenditures for the Carrollton facility in 1995 totaled $2.1 million, with no help desk or maintenance included in the expenditures. During the strategic planning process, Southwire leaders had agreed that network, hardware and software standardization would be more cost efficient and would enable improved support and training.

In a networked computing environment, how quickly a knowledge worker could accomplish a task often depended on the bandwidth of the network and the speed of the servers on the network. The length of time it would take to accomplish a task using applications on an employee's own computer, however, depended to a large extent on the speed of the computer's processor. In 1996, Southwire donated its 1,400 PCs with 286, 386, and 486 processors to local schools and charities or sold them to

employees. Hunter asked a cross section of employees to evaluate three demo computers, including an IBM, a Hewlett Packard and a Compaq. Based on feedback from the trial run, Southwire decided to purchase 1700 Compaq Deskpro P133 computers. In the line-up of chips, Southwire's new computers had Pentium (586) chips, which processed information at a rate of 133 megahertz, compared with the 30 megahertz maximum processing speed of the 386 chips. Megahertz, a measurement of the speed at which computers process information, was one determinant of how often the hourglass icon appeared and how long it remained on the screen. The faster computers—which also featured 24 MB of memory, a 2 GIG hard drive and a CD-ROM drive—would translate into less waiting time for computer users.

The most important benefit of the PC platform project, from Hunter's perspective, was that standardization would enable seamless communication between employees, eliminating incompatibility problems from office to office or from plant to plant. In addition to hardware, IT managers standardized desktop software, selecting the Windows NT operating system and Microsoft Office 7, which included Word, Excel and PowerPoint. They chose Novel Group Wise for e-mail, expressing their hope that the 5.0 release would provide groupware capability. Computer maintenance and help desk support were outsourced to Unisys; Southwire PC users worldwide could call an 800 number, 24 hours a day, for support. Southwire also outsourced the software application training function, choosing Vanstar to provide five days of required training for each PC.

In November 1996, the PC platform project was complete, with 1,700 computers installed and 1,700 graduates of the five-day training program. "First of all, make sure you've got a commitment from the top of the company to ensure that the transition will take place," Hunter advised other Chief Information Officers about to attempt a major roll-out. "Otherwise, it's very easy for people not to get on board, especially when it will take five days of training to achieve a common base level of knowledge. It also helps to have a strong project management team in place to set a schedule and goals and monitor both weekly."

1997: Business Process Design

Southwire executives were starting to sense that the power of an interactive computer network would shift focus from production processes to customer processes. An *Information Week* analysis argued that emerging communications networks were the impetus behind a new re-engineering trend: "In the 1980s, managers discovered that PCs, local- and wide-area telecommunications networks, and other technologies enabled them to reorganize the work of the corporation far more efficiently and effectively. They could organize work not around functions like sales, marketing and finance, but rather along end-to-end business processes such as order fulfillment, concept to market, and customer acquisition. The technology of the '90s now allows managers to rigorously examine the end-to-end tasks of their end customers. They can use the Internet to transform those tasks and redesign customer processes."[9]

Given the speed of change and the economic imperative to keep existing customers by improving customer processes, Richards deliberated with several of his officers over the potential risks and benefits of implementing a "Business Process Design Team."

After researching similar efforts in other companies, Hunter recommended that the team be put in place to perform three to four projects per year, that the team members have diverse business skills rather than IT backgrounds, and that they serve as "change agents," working with team leaders established in the LOBs.

One of the first business process design efforts approved was a "Supply Chain Integration Project," in the Wire and Cable LOB, which aimed at achieving timely, accurate, paperless information flow in parallel with smooth continual, flexible product flow to customers (see Exhibit 7). "One problem is that all the planning takes place during the last week of the month," Hunter explained. "With supply chain integration, planning will still be done monthly but it will be reviewed on a daily basis as customer requests change. The reality is that if you're running a warehouse, you keep some surplus inventory, some fat in the system. Because the planning process is not that accurate, they keep more inventory than is needed because they don't trust the system. When they do trust the system, they'll be able to operate the plant more efficiently and meet customer needs more accurately."

A similar project called DFT (demand flow technology) had worked for American Standard. "By radically improving production efficiencies in its manufacturing plants, DFT allowed Standard to slash costs by boosting its overall inventory turns," reported *Business Week*. "That's the number of times a company sells its inventory each year; the faster it turns over inventory, the more efficient use it makes of capital, plants and equipment."[10] Southwire hoped to

---

[9]James Champy, "The Rise of the Electronic Community," *Information Week*, 1996.

[10]Joseph Weber, "American Standard Wises Up: Smart Manufacturing Methods Make It a Growth Machine," *Business Week*, November 18, 1996, pp. 73–74.

increase its inventory turns by 25 percent by year-end 2001, while meeting or exceeding customer service expectations.

Conclusion

If Southwire's IT team could provide the capability outlined in their strategic plan, the question of how it would be driven still remained. Not only did Hunter hope that managers in every LOB would embrace the new technologies, he also hoped that their "creative energy would be unleashed" and that they would begin to devise their own ways of using information technology to achieve competitive advantage. "We've got a plan, but we've got a lot of mid-level managers who also have to buy into the use of technology to do their jobs better. That's a real big challenge—getting people who were not immediately involved in the strategic planning process to buy into all this change. Some folks would prefer to ignore it and hope it will go away—passive resistance. A lot of good ideas have bubbled up from some members of the management team. We'd like to see a lot more stuff bubble up."

EXHIBIT 7 What Is Supply Chain Integration?

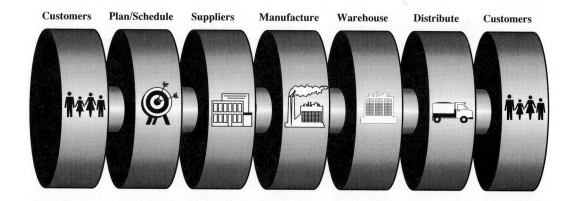

ANNOTATED BIBLIOGRAPHY
GENERAL MANAGEMENT LIBRARY
FOR THE IT MANAGER

Ackoff, Russell L. *Creating the Corporate Future: Plan or Be Planned For.* New York: John Wiley & Sons, 1981. An important book that provides a broad context for IT planning.

Anthony, Robert N. *The Management Control Function.* Boston: Harvard Business School Press, 1988. This book introduces the framework of operational control, management control, and strategic planning and has been a major contributor to thinking about the different areas of IT application and their different management problems.

Argyris, Chris. *On Organizational Learning.* Cambridge, MA: Blackwell Business, 1993. How to achieve organizational effectiveness by managing through improved communication processes.

Badaracco, Joseph L., Jr. *The Knowledge Link.* Boston: Harvard Business School Press, 1991. How firms cooperate to exchange information to capitalize on each other's knowledge.

Barabba, Vincent P., and Gerald Zaltman. *Hearing the Voice of the Market.* Boston: Harvard Business School Press, 1991. How to develop an inquisitive market program that develops competence in utilizing information.

Bartlett, Christopher A., and Sumantra Ghoshal. *Managing across Borders: The Transnational Solution.* Boston: Harvard Business School Press, 1991. A succinct and mind-expanding discussion of the impact, true costs, and strategic value of computer systems and their notable future influence.

Bower, Joseph L. *Managing the Resource Allocation Process: A Study of Corporate Planning and Investment.* Boston: Division of Research, Harvard Business School Classics, 1986. This in-depth analysis of corporate planning and capital budgeting provides critical insights relevant to both the role of steering committees and how IT planning can be done effectively.

Bower, Joseph L.; C. A. Bartlett; H. Unterhoven; and R. E. Walton. *Managing Strategic Processes.* Irwin, 1995. A comprehensive review of the essentials of creating and implementing a global strategy.

Burgleman, Robert A., and Modesto A. Maidique. *Strategic Management of Technology & Innovation, 1992.* An effective lens in establishing an overall view of managing technology for the long run.

Buzzell, Robert D., ed. *Marketing in an Electronic Age.* Boston: Harvard Business School Press, 1985. A series of essays on how information technology will impact the marketing function.

Cash, James I., Jr.; Robert G. Eccles; Nitin Nohria. *Building the Information-Age Organization: Structure, Control, and Information Technologies,* 3rd ed. Harvard University Graduate School of Business Administration, The Irwin Case Book Series in Information Systems Management, July 1993. A case-oriented text that provides an integrated approach to understanding the management implications of the trade-offs between IT systems and the organization, and approaches to exploiting the potential of the technology.

Champy, James, and Michael Hammer. *Reengineering the Corporation.* New York: Harper Collins, 1993. This book discusses the practical barriers and problems to achieving reengineering successes.

Chandler, Alfred D. Jr. *Scale and Scope: The Dynamics of Industrial Capitalism.* Cambridge, MA: The Belknap Press of Harvard University Press, 1990. The synthesis of a lifetime of work in articulating how management, structure, strategy, and industry evolve.

Clark, Kim B., and Takahiro Fujimoto. *Product Development Performance.* Boston: Harvard Business School Press, 1991. A descriptive analysis of European, Japanese, and U.S. automobile manufacturing to demonstrate the salient aspects of quality and timely manufacturing management.

Foulkes, Fred K. *Executive Compensation.* Boston: Harvard Business School Press, 1991. Thirty leading compensation consultants advise on effective programs.

Graham, Pauline. *Mary Parker Follett: Prophet of Management: A Celebration of Writings from the 1920s.* Boston: Harvard Business School Press, 1994. A reprint of a management classic that provides real perspective on the beginning of systematic analysis of the management process.

Hamel, Gary, and C. K. Prahalad. *Competing for the Future.* Boston: Harvard Business School Press, 1994. How to develop core competencies to implement a future oriented strategy.

Heskett, James L. *Managing in the Service Economy.* Boston: Harvard Business School Press, 1986. Practical advice on the issues in managing a service organization. Much of this advice translates directly to the IT resource.

Itami, Hiroyuki, with Thomas W. Roehl. *Mobilizing Invisible Assets.* Cambridge, MA: Harvard University Press, 1987. A description of how the Japanese organization brings experience and analysis to bear in developing and implementing strategy.

Kaplan, Robert S. *Measures for Manufacturing Excellence.* Boston: Harvard Business School Press, 1990. A selection of articles on control systems for manufacturing.

Kimberly Miles and Associates. *The Organizational Life Cycle.* San Francisco: Jossey-Bass, 1981. Reports, findings, and analyses of key issues concerning the creation, transformation, and decline of organizations.

Lawrence, Paul R., and Jay W. Lorsch. *Organization and Environment: Managing Integration and Differentiation.* Boston: Harvard Business School Classics, 1986. This classic presents the underlying thinking of the need for specialized departments and how they should interface with the rest of the organization. It is relevant for all IT organizational decisions.

Lax, David A., and James K. Sebenius. *The Manager as Negotiator: Bargaining for Cooperation and Competitive Gain.* New York: Free Press, 1986. A thoughtful set of insights on the issues and means of negotiation.

McKenney, James L. *Waves of Change: Business Evolution through Information Technology.* Boston: Harvard Business School Press, 1995. This book captures the long-term dynamics of an evolving information architecture as it traces more than 30 years of the history of information technology in four organizations.

Merchant, Kenneth A. *Control in Business Organizations.* Marshfield, MA: Pitman Publishing, 1986. An excellent framework for thinking about contemporary management control issues.

Nohria, Nitin, and Robert G. Eccles. *Network and Organizations: Structure, Form, and Action.* Boston: Harvard Business School Press, 1992. A comprehensive set of 19 papers from a conference on how present theoretical concepts can help influence the functioning of networks to better shape structure and influence actions.

Nolan, Richard L., and David C. Croson. *Creative Destruction: A Six-Step Process for Transforming the Organization.* Boston: Harvard Business School Press, 1995. This book analyzes the very different organization structures that are made possible by new information technology and the problems involved in implementing these structures.

Porter, Michael E., ed. *Competition in Global Industries.* Boston: Harvard Business School Press, 1986. A series of articles relating to competitive issues in the international environment.

Revolution in Real Time: Managing Information Technology in the 1990s, Boston: Harvard Business School Publications, 1991, *The Harvard Business Review Book Series.* A compendium of 17 recent *Harvard Business Review* articles on the art and science of designing, implementing, and managing the evolution of information technology as a competitive means.

Rosenberg, Nathan. *Inside the Black Box: Technology, Economics and History.* Cambridge University Press, 1982. A useful conceptual analysis of technological change as the driver in economic shifts. Frames the issues within the Schumpeterian model to substantiate the shifts and nature of activities in technology that change the competitive basis of industries.

Schein, Edgar H. *Organizational Psychology,* 3rd ed. Englewood Cliffs, NJ: Prentice Hall, 1980 This classic book focuses on how to manage the tension between the individual and the organization.

Simons, Robert. *Levers of Control.* Boston: Harvard Business School Press, 1995. This book provides a refreshing and new way to think about management control.

Smith, H. Jeff. *Managing Privacy Information Technology and Corporate America.* North Carolina: University of North Carolina Press, 1994. This is a very practical book that talks about information technology privacy, current practices, and issues for the future.

Treacy, Michael, and Fred Wiersema. *Disciplines of Market Leaders: Choose Your Customers, Narrow Your Focus, Dominate Your Market.* Reading, MA: Addison-Wesley Publishing Co., 1994. This book presents a view of what needs to be done for firms to be successful in the market.

Utterback, James. *Mastering the Dynamics of Innovation: How Companies Can Seize Opportunities in the Face of Technological Change.* Boston: Harvard Business School Press, 1994. An analysis of the forces to manage in developing new products and processes as a strategic force.

Wheelwright, Steven C., and Kim B. Clark. *Leading Product Development.* New York: Free Press, 1995. A focused view on senior management's role in shaping strategy based on continuous product development as a competitive means. Time from concept to market is the critical success factor.

Yates, Joanne. *Control through Communication: The Rise of System in American Management.* Baltimore, MD: Johns Hopkins University Press, 1993. Traces the evolution of internal communication systems through the late 19th century into the 20th century through a focus on innovative companies such as Du Pont.

IT LIBRARY FOR THE GENERAL MANAGER

Anderla, Georges, and Anthony Dunning. *Computer Strategies: 1990–1999: Technologies, Costs, Markets.* New York: John Wiley & Sons, 1987. A description of the Japanese chip-maker strategy and the economic implications of chip development, and the true "costs" of computing in the 1990s.

Bradley, Stephen P., and Jerry A. Hausman, eds. *Future Competition in Telecommunications.* Boston: Harvard Business School Press, 1989. A symposium of industry suppliers, customers, and regulators discussing the future impacts of deregulation.

Bradley, Stephen P.; Jerry A. Hausman; and Richard L. Nolan. *Globalization, Technology, and Competition: The Fusion of Computers and Telecommunications in the 1990s.* Boston: Harvard Business School Press, 1993. This book is a series of essays on how the new telecommunications technologies change the patterns of global business competition.

Forcht, Karen A. *Computer Security Management.* Danvers, MA: Boyd & Fraser Publishing Company, 1994. This is a practical book that describes the multiple aspects of computer security and the steps to be taken to gain good results.

Keen, Peter G. W. *Every Manager's Guide to Information Technology.* Boston: Harvard Business School Press, 1991. A glossary of key terms and concepts of computer and planning procedures.

Keen, Peter G. W. *Shaping the Future: Business Design through Information Technology.* Boston: Harvard Business School Press, 1991. A succinct and mind-expanding discussion of the impact, true costs, and strategic value of computer systems and their notable future influence.

Leebaert, Derek, ed. *Technology 2001: The Future of Computing and Communications.* Cambridge, MIT Press, 1991. A set of articles by research scientists from every major player in the business (e.g., IBM, DEC, Cray, Apple, etc). A sound view of the future.

Rochester, Jack B., and John Gantz. *The Naked Computer.* New York: William Morrow and Company, Inc., 1983. An interesting and broad compendium of computer lore that has shaped the myths and realities of developing and using computer systems.

Walton, Richard E. *Up and Running: Integrating Information Technology and the Organization.* Boston: Harvard Business School Press, 1989. A thoughtful perspective on how to develop and maintain congruence between the organization and systems in the implementation of an IT-based strategy by a leading organizational scholar/consultant.

Whinston, Patrick H. *Artificial Intelligence,* 3rd ed. Reading, MA: Addison-Wesley, 1992. A comprehensive review of the essentials of artificial intelligence and examples of useful implementations.

Zuboff, Shoshana. *In the Age of the Smart Machine.* New York: Basic Books, 1988. An insightful integration of the dual nature of the influence of computer-based systems on work.

Index